W9-BPM-950

IMPORTANT!

Below is your key code to log in to CoursePort and access the Discovering Computers 2006 Companion Web site.

To create a CoursePort account:

▶ Visit http://login.course.com

▶ Click New User Registration link

▶ Enter the key code found on this card

▶ Follow the onscreen instructions to complete your User Registration

Scratch off to reveal your key code*

Once you have registered, your key code will be invalidated and cannot be reused.

WHAT IS COURSEPORT?

CoursePort provides a central location from which you can access Thomson Course Technology's online learning solutions with convenience and flexibility.

- Gain access to online resources including robust Student Online Companion Web sites.
- Simplify your course work by reducing human error and the need to keep track of multiple passwords.
- Utilize a Universal Gradebook to track and share the work you complete with your instructor.
- Take advantage of CoursePort's tailored services including personalized homepages.

Features of the Discovering Computers 2006 Companion Web site include:

- Fully interactive Web site offers students additional information and unparalleled currency on important topics.
- New DC Track and Field and You're Hired! dynamic games provide students with new and challenging vehicles for learning and reinforcement.
- New Discussion Forum connects students everywhere using Discovering Computers 2006. Enhance your learning experience by posting questions and thoughts about the Chapter Review, Web Research, or Case Studies exercises.
- Discovering Computers 2006 Timeline takes students on an interactive tour of the major computer technology developments during the past 65 years.
- Have fun while learning with the Learn It Online exercises which include online videos, practice tests, learning games, and Web-based activities.

*THIS BOOK CANNOT BE RETURNED or RESOLD IF THE KEY CODE IS MISSING OR EXPOSED.

Discovering Computers

2006

A GATEWAY TO INFORMATION

Web Enhanced — BRIEF

Discovering Computers

2006 A GATEWAY TO INFORMATION

Web Enhanced — BRIEF

Gary B. Shelly
Thomas J. Cashman
Misty E. Vermaat

Contributing Authors
Jeffrey J. Quasney
Susan L. Sebok
Timothy J. Walker
Jeffrey J. Webb

THOMSON

COURSE TECHNOLOGY

COURSE TECHNOLOGY
25 THOMSON PLACE
BOSTON MA 02210

SHELLY
CASHMAN
SERIES.

Australia • Canada • Denmark • Japan • Mexico • New Zealand • Philippines • Puerto Rico • Singapore
South Africa • Spain • United Kingdom • United States

Discovering Computers 2006:
A Gateway to Information, Web Enhanced
Brief

Gary B. Shelly
Thomas J. Cashman
Misty E. Vermaat

Managing Editor:
Alexandra Arnold

Series Consulting Editor:
Jim Quasney

Senior Acquisitions Editor:
Dana Merk

Product Manager:
Reed Cotter

Editorial Assistant:
Selena Coppock

Print Buyer:
Laura Burns

Production Editor:
Aimee Poirier

Researcher:
F. William Vermaat

Copy Editor:
Lyn Markowicz

Proofreader:
Nancy Lamm

Management Services:
Pre-Press Company, Inc.

Interior Designer:
Pre-Press Company, Inc.

Cover Image:
Pre-Press Company, Inc.

Illustrator:
Pre-Press Company, Inc.

Compositor:
Pre-Press Company, Inc.

Indexer:
Nancy Lamm

Printer:
Banta Menasha

COPYRIGHT © 2005 Course Technology, a division of Thomson Learning, Inc. Thomson Learning™ is a trademark used herein under license.

Printed in USA

3 4 5 6 7 8 9 10 BM 08 07 06 05

For more information, contact Course Technology
25 Thomson Place
Boston, Massachusetts 02210

Or find us on the World Wide Web at:
www.course.com

ALL RIGHTS RESERVED. No part of this work covered by the copyright hereon may be reproduced or used in any form or by any means — graphic, electronic, or mechanical, including photocopying, recording, taping, Web distribution, or information storage and retrieval systems — without the written permission of the publisher.

For permission to use material from this text or product, submit a request online at **www.thomsonrights.com**

Any additional questions about permissions can be submitted by e-mail to **thomsonrights@thomson.com**

Course Technology, the Course Technology logo, the Shelly Cashman Series® and **Custom Edition**® are registered trademarks used under license. All other names used herein are for identification purposes only and are trademarks of their respective owners.

Course Technology reserves the right to revise this publication and make changes from time to time in its content without notice.

ISBN 0-619-25544-7

Discovering Computers 2006

A GATEWAY TO INFORMATION

Web Enhanced — BRIEF

Contents

CHAPTER 1

Introduction to Computers..2

A WORLD OF COMPUTERS 4

WHAT IS A COMPUTER?..6
    Data and Information 6
    Information Processing Cycle 6

THE COMPONENTS OF A COMPUTER 7
    Input Devices 7
    Output Devices..8
    System Unit..8
    Storage Devices 8
    Communication Devices..9

ADVANTAGES AND DISADVANTAGES OF
USING COMPTUERS 9

NETWORKS AND THE INTERNET 11
    The Internet...12

COMPUTER SOFTWARE 15
    System Software...15
    Application Software..16
    Installing and Running Programs 17
    Software Development 18

CATEGORIES OF COMPUTERS..18

PERSONAL COMPUTERS 19
    Desktop Computers..20

MOBILE COMPUTERS 20
    Notebook Computers 20
    Mobile Devices 21

MIDRANGE SERVERS 23

MAINFRAMES 23

SUPERCOMPUTERS 23

EMBEDDED COMPUTERS...24

ELEMENTS OF AN INFORMATION SYSTEM 25

EXAMPLES OF COMPUTER USAGE.................................26
    Home User 26
    Small Office/Home User..28

Mobile User...29
Power User 29
Large Business User...30
Putting It All Together...31

COMPUTER APPLICATIONS IN SOCIETY........................32
    Education 32
    Finance...32
    Government 33
    Health Care 34
    Science 34
    Publishing 35
    Travel 36
    Industry..36

CHAPTER SUMMARY 37

HIGH-TECH TALK..38
    Analog versus Digital: Making the Conversion 38

COMPANIES ON THE CUTTING EDGE 39
    Dell 39
    Apple Computer 39

TECHNOLOGY TRAILBLAZERS 39
    Bill Gates 39
    Carly Fiorina 39

CHAPTER REVIEW 40

KEY TERMS 42

CHECKPOINT 43

LEARN IT ONLINE 46

LEARN HOW TO 48

WEB RESEARCH 50

CASE STUDIES 51

Special Feature

TIMELINE 2006 52

CHAPTER 2

The Internet and World Wide Web 66

THE INTERNET 68

HISTORY OF THE INTERNET 69

HOW THE INTERNET WORKS 70
    Connecting to the Internet 70
    Access Providers 71
    How Data Travels the Internet.....................................72
    Internet Addresses 73

THE WORLD WIDE WEB 75
    Browsing the Web 75
    Web Addresses 76
    Navigating Web Pages 77
    Searching for Information on the Web 78
    Types of Web Sites 82
    Evaluating a Web Site 84
    Multimedia on the Web 85
    Web Publishing..89

E-COMMERCE 91

OTHER INTERNET SERVICES...92
    E-Mail...92
    FTP 96
    Newsgroups and Message Boards 96
    Mailing Lists 97
    Chat Rooms..98
    Instant Messaging 98
    Internet Telephony...99

NETIQUETTE 100

CHAPTER SUMMARY 101

HIGH-TECH TALK 102
    A Computer's Internet Protocol (IP) Address 102

COMPANIES ON THE CUTTING EDGE 103
    Google 103
    Yahoo 103

TECHNOLOGY TRAILBLAZERS 103
    Tim Berners-Lee 103
    Meg Whitman...103

CHAPTER REVIEW 104

KEY TERMS 106

CHECKPOINT 107

LEARN IT ONLINE...110

LEARN HOW TO 112

WEB RESEARCH 114

CASE STUDIES 115

Special Feature

MAKING USE OF THE WEB   **116**

CHAPTER 3

Application Software 132

APPLICATION SOFTWARE 134
    The Role of System Software 135
    Working with Application Software 136

BUSINESS SOFTWARE 138
    Word Processing Software 138
    Developing a Document 141
    Spreadsheet Software 142
    Database Software 145
    Presentation Graphics Software.................................146
    Note Taking Software 147
    Personal Information Manager Software 148
    PDA Business Software 148
    Software Suite...148
    Project Management Software 149
    Accounting Software 149
    Enterprise Computing Software 150

GRAPHICS AND MULTIMEDIA SOFTWARE 150
    Computer-Aided Design 150
    Desktop Publishing Software
        (for the Professional) 152
    Paint/Image Editing Software
        (for the Professional) 152
    Video and Audio Editing Software
        (for the Professional) 153
    Multimedia Authoring Software 154
    Web Page Authoring Software....................................154

SOFTWARE FOR HOME, PERSONAL, AND
EDUCATIONAL USE 155
    Software Suite (for Personal Use) 156
    Personal Finance Software 156
    Legal Software 157
    Tax Preparation Software 157
    Desktop Publishing Software
        (for Personal Use)..158
    Paint/Image Editing Software
        (for Personal Use)..158
    Photo Editing Software 159
    Clip Art/Image Gallery..159
    Video and Audio Editing Software
        (for Personal Use)..159
    Home Design/Landscaping Software 160
    Reference and Educational Software 160
    Entertainment Software 160

APPLICATION SOFTWARE FOR COMMUNICATIONS 161

POPULAR STAND-ALONE UTILITY PROGRAMS 162

APPLICATION SOFTWARE ON THE WEB 163
   Application Service Providers 164

LEARNING AIDS AND SUPPORT TOOLS FOR
APPLICATION SOFTWARE 164
   Web-Based Training.......................................166

CHAPTER SUMMARY 167

HIGH-TECH TALK 168
   Computer Viruses: Delivery, Infection,
     and Avoidance 168

COMPANIES ON THE CUTTING EDGE 169
   Adobe Systems 169
   Microsoft 169

TECHNOLOGY TRAILBLAZERS 169
   Dan Bricklin 169
   Masayoshi Son 169

CHAPTER REVIEW 170

KEY TERMS 172

CHECKPOINT 173

LEARN IT ONLINE..176

LEARN HOW TO 178

WEB RESEARCH 180

CASE STUDIES 181

CHAPTER 4

The Components of the System Unit 182

THE SYSTEM UNIT..184
   The Motherboard 186

PROCESSOR 187
   The Control Unit 187
   The Arithmetic Logic Unit 188
   Machine Cycle 188
   Registers 189
   The System Clock..189
   Comparison of Personal Computer
     Processors 190
   Buying a Personal Computer.........................192
   Heat Sinks, Heat Pipes, and Liquid Cooling.............193
   Parallel Processing 194

DATA REPRESENTATION.......................................194

MEMORY 196
   Bytes and Addressable Memory 196
   Memory Sizes 197
   Types of Memory 197
   RAM 201
   Flash Memory...202
   CMOS..203
   Memory Access Times..................................203

EXPANSION SLOTS AND ADAPTER CARDS 204
PC Cards, Flash Memory Cards, and USB
   Flash Drives 205

PORTS AND CONNECTORS 206
   Serial Ports 201
   Parallel Ports..208
   USB Ports...208
   FireWire Ports 209
   Special Purpose Ports 209

BUSES...211
   Expansion Bus 212

BAYS...212

POWER SUPPLY 213

MOBILE COMPUTERS AND DEVICES......................213

PUTTING IT ALL TOGETHER 215

KEEPING YOUR COMPUTER CLEAN.......................216

CHAPTER SUMMARY 217

HIGH-TECH TALK 218
   Random Access Memory (RAM): The Genius
     of Memory..218

COMPANIES ON THE CUTTING EDGE 219
   AMD..219
   Intel 219

TECHNOLOGY TRAILBLAZERS 219
   Jack Kilby 219
   Gordon Moore 219

CHAPTER REVIEW 220

KEY TERMS 222

CHECKPOINT 223

LEARN IT ONLINE..226

LEARN HOW TO 228

WEB RESEARCH 230

CASE STUDIES 231

CHAPTER 5

Input 232

WHAT IS INPUT? 234

WHAT ARE INPUT DEVICES?.................................236

THE KEYBOARD 236
   Keyboard Connections 238
   Keyboard Ergonomics..................................238

POINTING DEVICES 239

MOUSE 239

Mouse Types 239
Using a Mouse 240

OTHER POINTING DEVICES 241
Trackball 241
Touchpad 241
Pointing Stick 242
Light Pen 242
Touch Screen 243
Pen Input 243

VOICE INPUT 245
Audio Input 246

INPUT FOR PDAS, SMART PHONES, AND TABLET PCS..............247
PDAs 247
Smart Phones 248
Tablet PCs 249

DIGITAL CAMERAS..250
Digital Camera Quality 252

VIDEO INPUT..253
PC Video Cameras 253
Web Cams 254
Video Conferencing 254

SCANNERS AND READING DEVICES 255
Optical Scanners 255
Optical Readers 257
Bar Code Readers..258
RFID Readers 259
Magnetic Strip Card Readers 260
MICR Readers..260
Data Collection Devices 261

TERMINALS..261
Point-of-Sale Terminals 261
Automated Teller Machines 262

BIOMETRIC INPUT 262

PUTTING IT ALL TOGETHER 265

INPUT DEVICES FOR PHYSICALLY CHALLENGED USERS..........266

CHAPTER SUMMARY 267

HIGH-TECH TALK 268
Biometrics: Personalized Security 268

COMPANIES ON THE CUTTING EDGE 269
Logitech 269
palmOne 269

TECHNOLOGY TRAILBLAZERS 269
Hideki Komiyama 269
Douglas Engelbart 269

CHAPTER REVIEW 270

KEY TERMS 272

CHECKPOINT..273

LEARN IT ONLINE..276

LEARN HOW TO 278

WEB RESEARCH..280

CASE STUDIES 281

Special Feature

PERSONAL MOBILE DEVICES   282

CHAPTER 6

Output 298

WHAT IS OUTPUT? 300

DISPLAY DEVICES 302

FLAT-PANEL DISPLAYS 302
LCD Monitors and Screens............................302
LCD Technology..304
LCD Quality 304
Graphics Chips, Ports, and LCD Monitors 305
Plasma Monitors 306
Televisions and HDTVs..................................306

CRT MONITORS 307
Quality of a CRT Monitor 308
Graphics Chips and CRT Monitors..................308

PRINTERS 310
Producing Printed Output 311
Nonimpact Printers 312
Ink-Jet Printers 312
Photo Printers 314
Laser Printers 315
Thermal Printers 317
Mobile Printers 317
Label and Postage Printers............................318
Plotters and Large-Format Printers................318
Impact Printers 318

SPEAKERS AND HEADSETS................................320

OTHER OUTPUT DEVICES..................................322
Fax Machines and Fax Modems 322
Multi-Function Peripherals 323
Data Projectors 323
Force-Feedback Joysticks and Wheels 324

PUTTING IT ALL TOGETHER 325

OUTPUT DEVICES FOR PHYSICALLY CHALLENGED USERS 326

CHAPTER SUMMARY 327

HIGH-TECH TALK 328
Sound Cards: Bringing Your Computer
to Life..328

COMPANIES ON THE CUTTING EDGE 329
    Hewlett-Packard...329
    ViewSonic 329

TECHNOLOGY TRAILBLAZERS 329
    Steve Jobs 329
    Donna Dubinsky 329

CHAPTER REVIEW 330

KEY TERMS 332

CHECKPOINT 333

LEARN IT ONLINE 336

LEARN HOW TO 338

WEB RESEARCH 340

CASE STUDIES 341

Special Feature

DIGITAL IMAGING AND VIDEO TECHNOLOGY   **342**

CHAPTER 7

Storage 352

STORAGE 354

MAGNETIC DISKS..357
    Floppy Disks...358
    Zip Disks 359
    Hard Disks 360

OPTICAL DISCS 366
    Care of Optical Discs 368
    Types of Optical Discs 368
    CD-ROMs 369
    CD-Rs and CD-RWs 371
    DVD-ROMs...372
    Recordable and Rewritable DVDs....................373

TAPE 374

PC CARDs...374

MINIATURE MOBILE STORAGE MEDIA 375
    Flash Memory Cards 376
    USB Flash Drives 377
    Smart Cards 378

MICROFILM AND MICROFICHE 379

ENTERPRISE STORAGE 379

PUTTING IT ALL TOGETHER......................................380

CHAPTER SUMMARY 381

HIGH-TECH TALK 382
    Disk Formatting and File Systems 382

COMPANIES ON THE CUTTING EDGE.......................383
    Maxtor 383
    SanDisk Corporation 383

TECHNOLOGY TRAILBLAZERS 383
    Al Shugart 383
    Mark Dean 383

CHAPTER REVIEW 384

KEY TERMS...386

CHECKPOINT 387

LEARN IT ONLINE 390

LEARN HOW TO 392

WEB RESEARCH 394

CASE STUDIES 395

CHAPTER 8

Operating Systems and Utility Programs......................396

SYSTEM SOFTWARE 398

OPERATING SYSTEMS 398

OPERATING SYSTEM FUNCTIONS 400
    Starting a Computer 400
    Providing a User Interface 402
    Managing Programs 403
    Managing Memory 405
    Scheduling Jobs 406
    Configuring Devices 407
    Establishing a Connection 409
    Monitoring Performance....................................409
    Providing File Management and
        Other Utilities 410
    Controlling a Network 410
    Administering Security......................................410

OPERATING SYSTEM UTILITY PROGRAMS 411
    File Manager 412
    Image Viewer 412
    Personal Firewall 413
    Uninstaller 413
    Disk Scanner 414
    Disk Defragmenter..414
    Diagnostic Utility 415
    Screen Saver 415

TYPES OF OPERATING SYSTEMS..............................415

STAND-ALONE OPERATING SYSTEMS.......................416
    DOS 417
    Windows XP 417

Mac OS X 420
UNIX 420
Linux 421

NETWORK OPERATING SYSTEMS 422
NetWare 422
Windows Server 2003 422
UNIX 423
Linux 423
Solaris..423

EMBEDDED OPERATING SYSTEMS 423
Windows CE 423
Windows Mobile 424
Palm OS..424
Embedded Linux 425
Symbian OS..425

STAND-ALONE UTILITY PROGRAMS 425
Antivirus Programs 425
Spyware Removers 426
Internet Filters 426
File Compression 427
File Conversion 427
CD/DVD Burning 428
Personal Computer Maintenance 428

CHAPTER SUMMARY 429

HIGH-TECH TALK 430
Windows XP: A Useful Way to Complete a
Wide Range of Tasks 430

COMPANIES ON THE CUTTING EDGE 431
Red Hat 431
Symbian..431

TECHNOLOGY TRAILBLAZERS 431
Alan Kay 431
Linus Torvalds 431

CHAPTER REVIEW 432

KEY TERMS 434

CHECKPOINT 435

LEARN IT ONLINE..438

LEARN HOW TO 440

WEB RESEARCH..442

CASE STUDIES 443

Special Feature

BUYER'S GUIDE 2006 **444**

APPENDIX A: CODING SCHEMES AND
NUMBER SYSTEMS ....APP 1

APPENDIX B: QUIZ YOURSELF ANSWERS..............................APP 5

APPENDIX C: COMPUTER ACRONYMS....................................APP 13

Preface

The Shelly Cashman Series® offers the finest textbooks in computer education. We are proud of the fact that the previous ten editions of this textbook have been the most widely used in computer education. With each new edition of the book, we have implemented significant improvements based on current computer trends and comments made by instructors and students. *Discovering Computers 2006* continues with the innovation, quality, and reliability you have come to expect from the Shelly Cashman Series.

In *Discovering Computers 2006: A Gateway to Information*, you will find an educationally sound, highly visual, and easy-to-follow pedagogy that presents an in-depth treatment of introductory computer subjects. Students will finish the course with a solid understanding of computers, how to use computers, and how to access information on the World Wide Web.

OBJECTIVES OF THIS TEXTBOOK

Discovering Computers 2006: A Gateway to Information, Brief is intended for use as a stand-alone textbook or in combination with an applications, Internet, or programming textbook in a one-quarter or one-semester introductory computer course. No experience with computers is assumed. The objectives of this book are to:

- Present the most-up-to-date technology in an ever-changing discipline
- Give students an in-depth understanding of why computers are essential components in business and society
- Teach the fundamentals of computers and computer nomenclature, particularly with respect to personal computer hardware and software, the World Wide Web, and enterprise computing
- Present the material in a visually appealing and exciting manner that motivates students to learn
- Assist students in planning a career and getting certified in the computer field
- Provide exercises and lab assignments that allow students to interact with a computer and learn by actually using the computer and the World Wide Web
- Present strategies for purchasing a desktop computer, a notebook computer, a Tablet PC, and a personal mobile device
- Offer alternative learning techniques and reinforcement via the Web
- Offer distance-education providers a textbook with a meaningful and exercise-rich companion Web site

DISTINGUISHING FEATURES

To date, more than six million students have learned about computers using a *Discovering Computers* textbook. With the additional World Wide Web integration and interactivity, streaming up-to-date audio and video, extraordinary step-by-step visual drawings and photographs, unparalleled currency, and the Shelly and Cashman touch, this book will make your computer concepts course exciting and dynamic. Distinguishing features of the Shelly Cashman Series *Discovering Computers* books include:

A Proven Pedagogy

Careful explanations of complex concepts, educationally-sound elements, and reinforcement highlight this proven method of presentation. A pictorial arrangement of the pedagogy can be found beginning on page xvii.

A Visually Appealing Book that Maintains Student Interest

The latest technology, pictures, drawings, and text are combined artfully to produce a visually appealing and easy-to-understand book. Many of the figures include a step-by-step presentation (see page 196), which simplifies the more complex computer concepts. Pictures and drawings reflect the latest trends in computer technology. Finally, the text is set in two columns, which instructors and reviewers say their students prefer. This combination of pictures, step-by-step drawings, and easy-to-read text layout sets a new standard for computer textbook design.

Latest Technologies and Terms

The technologies and terms your students see in this book are those they will encounter when they start using computers. Only the latest application software is shown throughout the book. New topics and terms include embedded computer, handtop computer, smart watch, fixed wireless, satellite modem, static Web page, dynamic Web page, hot spots, blog, moblogs, Internet telephony, Voice over IP, open source software, product activation, dual-core processor, liquid cooling technology, magnetic stripe card reader, magstripe reader, mouse gestures, picture messaging, native resolution, plasma monitor, satellite speakers, Blu-Ray disc, digital photo viewer, Hi-Speed USB, mini disc, pen drive, Serial Advanced Technology Attachment, anti-spam program, embedded Linux, file conversion utility, pop-up ad, pop-up blocker, scripts, spyware, spyware remover, Web filtering software, Windows Server System, and WinFS.

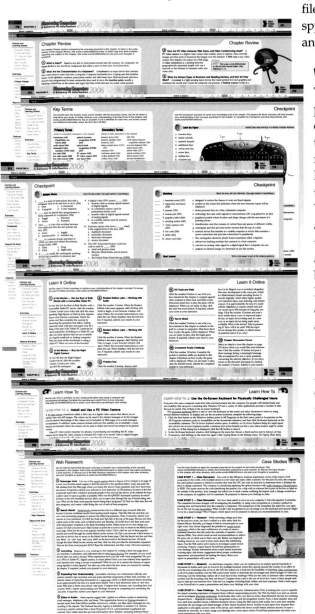

World Wide Web Enhanced

This book uses the World Wide Web as a major supplement. The purpose of integrating the World Wide Web into the book is to (1) offer students additional information and currency on important topics; (2) use its interactive capabilities to offer creative reinforcement and online quizzes; (3) make available alternative learning techniques with Web-based learning games, practice tests, and interactive labs; (4) underscore the relevance of the World Wide Web as a basic information tool that can be used in all facets of society; (5) introduce students to doing research on the Web; and (6) offer instructors the opportunity to organize and administer their traditional campus-based or distance-education-based courses on the Web using WebCT, Blackboard, or MyCourse 2.1. This textbook, however, does not depend on Web access to be used successfully. The Web access adds to the already complete treatment of topics within the book.

Extensive End-of-Chapter Materials

A notable strength of the *Discovering Computers* textbooks is the extensive student activities at the end of each chapter. Well-structured student activities can make the difference between students merely participating in a class and students retaining the information they learn. The activities in the *Discovering Computers 2006* books include: Chapter Review, Key Terms, Checkpoint, Learn It Online, Learn How To, Web Research, and Case Studies. A pictorial presentation of each end-of-chapter activities can be found beginning on page xx.

ORGANIZATION OF THIS TEXTBOOK

Discovering Computers 2006: A Gateway to Information, Brief provides a thorough introduction to computers. The material is divided into eight chapters, five special features, three appendices, and a glossary/index.

Chapter 1 – Introduction to Computers In Chapter 1, students are introduced to basic computer concepts, such as what a computer is, how it works, and what makes it a powerful tool.

Special Feature – Timeline 2006 Milestones in Computer History In this special feature, students learn about the major computer technology developments during the past 65 years.

Chapter 2 – The Internet and World Wide Web In Chapter 2, students learn about the Internet, World Wide Web, browsers, e-mail, FTP, and instant messaging.

Special Feature – Making Use of the Web In this special feature, more than 150 popular up-to-date Web sites are listed and described. Basic searching techniques also are introduced.

Chapter 3 – Application Software In Chapter 3, students are introduced to a variety of business software, graphics and multimedia software, home/personal/educational software, and communications software.

Chapter 4 – The Components of the System Unit In Chapter 4, students are introduced to the components of the system unit; how memory stores data, instructions, and information; and how the system unit executes an instruction.

Chapter 5 – Input Chapter 5 describes the various techniques of input and commonly used input devices.

Special Feature – Personal Mobile Devices In this special feature, students receive a detailed presentation of personal mobile device operating systems, built-in personal mobile device software, personal mobile device application software, and how to obtain and install personal mobile device software. Also included is a personal mobile device buyer's guide.

Chapter 6 – Output Chapter 6 describes the various methods of output and commonly used output devices.

Special Feature – Digital Imaging and Video Technology In this special feature, students are introduced to using a personal computer, digital camera, and video camera to manipulate photographs and video.

Chapter 7 – Storage In Chapter 7, students learn about various storage media and storage devices.

Chapter 8 – Operating Systems and Utility Programs   In Chapter 8, students learn about a variety of stand-alone operating systems, network operating systems, and embedded operating systems.

Special Feature – Buyer's Guide 2006: How to Purchase a Personal Computer   In this special feature, students are introduced to purchasing a desktop computer, notebook computer, and Tablet PC.

Appendix A – Coding Schemes and Number Systems   Appendix A presents the ASCII, EBCDIC, and Unicode coding schemes.

Appendix B – Quiz Yourself Answers   Appendix B provides the answers for the Quiz Yourself questions in the text.

Appendix C – Computer Acronyms   Appendix C summarizes the computer acronyms discussed in the book.

Glossary/Index   The Glossary/Index includes a definition and page references for every key term presented in the book.

SHELLY CASHMAN SERIES INSTRUCTOR RESOURCES

The Shelly Cashman Series is dedicated to providing you with all of the tools you need to make your class a success. Information on all supplementary materials is available through your Course Technology representative or by calling one of the following telephone numbers: Colleges and Universities, 1-800-648-7450; High Schools, 1-800-824-5179; Private Career Colleges, 1-800-347-7707; Canada, 1-800-268-2222; Corporations with IT Training Centers, 1-800-648-7450; and Government Agencies, Health-Care Organizations, and Correctional Facilities, 1-800-477-3692.

Instructor Resources CD-ROM

The Instructor Resources CD-ROM includes both teaching and testing aids. The contents of each item on the Instructor Resources CD-ROM (ISBN 0-619-25483-1) are described below.

Instructors Manual   The Instructor's Manual is made up of Microsoft Word files, which include detailed lesson plans with page number references, lecture notes, classroom activities, discussion topics, and projects to assign.

Syllabus   Sample syllabi, which can be customized easily to a course, are included. The syllabi cover policies, class and lab assignments and exams, and procedural information.

Figure Files   Illustrations for every figure in the textbook are available in electronic form. Use this ancillary to present a slide show in lecture or to print transparencies for use in lecture with an overhead projector. If you have a personal computer and LCD device, this ancillary can be an effective tool for presenting lectures.

Solutions to Exercises   Solutions are included for all end-of-chapter exercises.

Test Bank & Test Engine   The ExamView test bank includes 220 questions for every chapter (50 multiple-choice, 100 true/false, and 70 completion) with page number references, and when appropriate, figure references. Each question also is identified by objective and type of term (primary or secondary). The test bank comes with a copy of the test engine, ExamView, the ultimate tool for your objective-based testing needs.

Printed Test Bank   A Microsoft Word version of the test bank you can print also is included.

Test Out/Final Exam   Use this objective-based test to test students out of your course, or use it as a final examination. A master answer sheet is included.

Pretest/Posttest   Use these carefully prepared tests at the beginning and the end of the semester to measure student progress. A master answer sheet is included.

Data Files for Students   All the files that are required by students to complete the exercises are included. You can distribute the files on the Instructor Resources CD-ROM to your students over a network, or you can have them follow the instructions on the inside back cover of this book to obtain a copy of the Data Disk.

Course Presenter

Course Presenter (ISBN 0-619-25484-X) is a one-click-per-slide presentation system on CD-ROM that provides PowerPoint slides for every subject in each chapter. Use this presentation system to give interesting, well-organized, and knowledge-based lectures. Several up-to-date G4TechTV computer-related video clips are available for optional presentation. Course Presenter provides consistent coverage for multiple lecturers.

Student Edition Labs

Thirty Web-based interactive labs will help your students master hundreds of computer concepts including input and output devices, file management and desktop applications, computer privacy, virus protection, and much more. Featuring up-to-the-minute content, eye-popping graphics, and rich animation, the highly interactive Student Edition Labs offer students an alternative way to learn through dynamic observation, step-by-step practice, and challenging review questions. Access the free Student Edition Labs from the *Discovering Computers 2006* Web site at scsite.com/dc2006 or see the Student Edition Lab exercises on the Learn It Online pages at the end of each chapter.

Online Content

Course Technology offers textbook-based content for Blackboard, WebCT, and MyCourse 2.1.

BlackBoard and WebCT   As the leading provider of IT content for the Blackboard and WebCT platforms, Course Technology delivers rich content that enhances your textbook to give your students a unique learning experience.

MyCoure 2.1   MyCourse 2.1 is Course Technology's powerful online course management and content delivery system. MyCourse 2.1 allows nontechnical users to create, customize, and deliver Web-based courses; post content and assignments; manage student enrollment; administer exams; track results in the online grade book; and more.

SUPPLEMENTS

Two supplements can be used in combination with this textbook.

SAM Computer Concepts

Add the power of assessment and detailed reporting to your Student Edition Lab assignments with SAM Computer Concepts.

SAM (Skills Assessment Manager) Computer Concepts helps you energize your training assignments by allowing students to learn and quiz on important computer skills in an active, hands-on environment. By adding SAM Computer Concepts to your curriculum, you can:

- Reinforce your students' knowledge of key computer concepts with hands-on application exercises.
- Allow your students to "learn by listening," with rich audio in their computer concepts labs.
- Build computer concepts exams from a test bank of more than 50,000 objective-based questions or create your own test questions.
- Schedule your students' computer concepts training and testing assignments with powerful administrative tools.
- Track student exam grades and training progress using more than one dozen student and classroom reports.

Study Guide

This highly popular *Study Guide* (ISBN 0-619-25500-5) includes a variety of activities that help students recall, review, and master introductory computer concepts. The *Study Guide* complements the end-of-chapter material with a guided chapter outline; a self-test consisting of true/false, multiple-choice, short answer, fill-in, and matching questions; an entertaining puzzle; and other challenging exercises.

TO THE STUDENT...Getting the Most Out of Your Book

Welcome to *Discovering Computers 2006: A Gateway to Information, Web Enhanced*. You can save yourself a lot of time and gain a better understanding of the computer concepts presented in this book if you spend a few minutes reviewing this section.

1 Companion Web Site

Use the Companion Web site at scsite.com/dc2006, which includes additional information about important topics and provides unparalleled currency; and make use of online learning games, practice tests, and additional reinforcement. Gain access to this dynamic site with Course Technology's centralized login page, CoursePort.

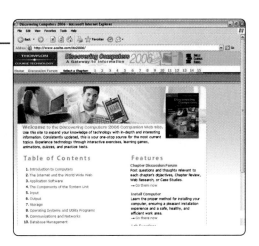

2 Picture Yourself

Picture yourself using the concepts presented in the chapter you are about to read. This section at the beginning of each chapter is intended to help you see how the specific material might apply to your everyday life using computers.

3 Chapter Objectives and Table of Contents

Before you read the chapter, carefully read through the Objectives and Contents so that you know what you should learn from the chapter.

4 Initial Chapter Figure

Carefully study the first figure in each chapter because it will give you an easy-to-follow overview of the major purpose of the chapter.

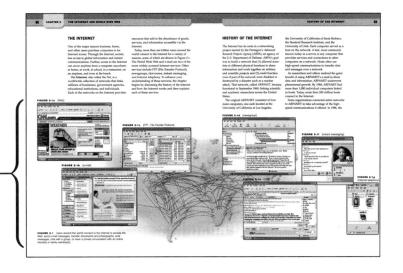

5 Web Link

Obtain current information and a different perspective about key terms and concepts by visiting the Web addresses in the Web Links found in the margins throughout the book.

6 Step Figures

Each chapter includes numerous step figures that present the more complex computer concepts using a step-by-step pedagogy.

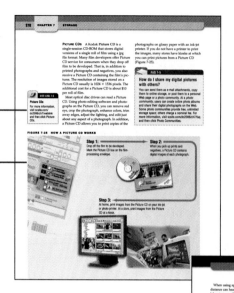

7 At Issue

At Issue boxes provide you with computer-related controversial topics of the day and stimulating questions that offer insight into the general concerns of computers in society.

8 Looking Ahead

The Looking Ahead boxes offer you a glimpse at the latest advances in computer technology that will be available, usually within five years.

9 FAQ

FAQ (frequently asked questions) boxes offer common questions and answers about subjects related to the topic at hand.

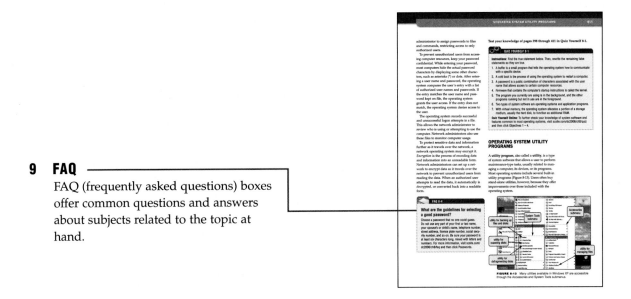

10 Quiz Yourself

Three Quiz Yourself boxes per chapter help ensure that you know the material you just read and are ready to move on in the chapter. Use the answers in Appendix B for a quick check of the answers, and take additional these quizzes on the Web for inter-activity and easy use.

11 Career Corner

Each chapter ends with a Career Corner feature that introduces you to a computer-career opportunity relating to a topic covered in the chapter.

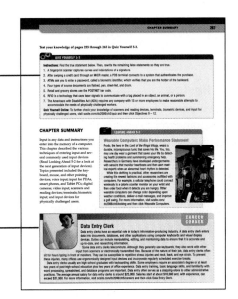

12 High-Tech Talk

If you are technically inclined, you will enjoy the High-Tech Talk article at the end of each chapter. These presentations expand on a topic covered in the chapter and present a more technical discussion.

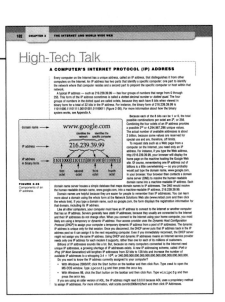

13 Companies on the Cutting Edge

Each chapter includes a profile about two key computer-related companies of which you should be aware, especially if you plan to major in the computer field.

14 Technology Trailblazers

The Technology Trailblazers section in each chapter offers a glimpse into the life and times of the more famous leaders of the computer industry.

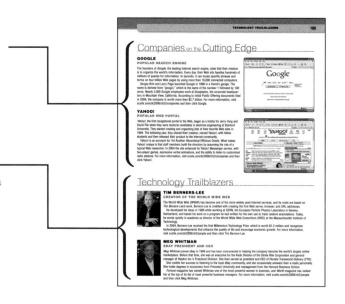

15 Chapter Review

Use the two-page Chapter Review before you take an examination to ensure that you are familiar with the computer concepts presented. This section includes each objective, followed by a one- or two-paragraph summary. Visit a Chapter Review page on the Web, and click the Audio button to listen to the Chapter Review.

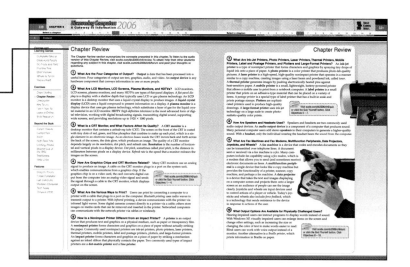

16 Primary and Secondary Key Terms

Before you take a test, use the Key Terms page as a checklist of terms you should know. In the text, primary key terms appear in bold font and secondary key terms appear in italic font. Ask your instructor whether you are responsible for knowing only the primary key terms or all the key terms. Visit a Key Terms page on the Web and click any term for additional information.

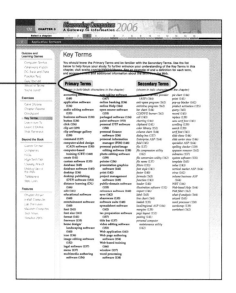

17 Checkpoint

Use these three pages of exercises to reinforce your understanding of the topics presented in the chapter.

18 Learn It Online

If you prefer online reinforcement, then the Learn It Online exercises are for you. The exercises include online videos, practice tests, interactive labs, learning games, and Web-based activities.

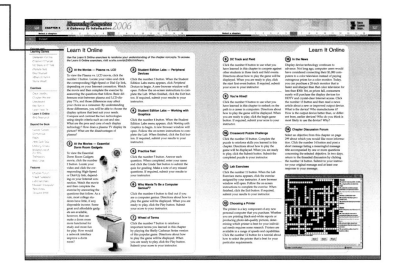

19 Learn How To

Apply what you learn in each chapter to your every day life with the Learn How To exercises. These hands-on activities solidify the concepts presented in the chapter with practical application.

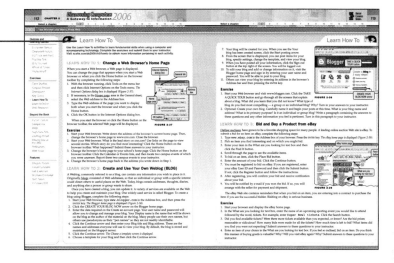

20 Web Research

If you enjoy doing research on the
Web, then you will like the Web
Research exercises. Each exercise in
this section references an element in
the book and suggests you write a
short article or do a class presentation
on your findings.

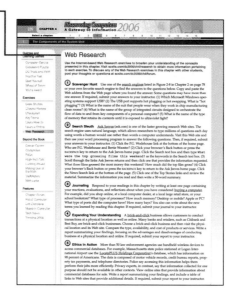

21 Case Studies

Exercise your mind and construct creative
solutions to the thought-provoking case
studies presented in each chapter. The
Case Study exercises are constructed to
discuss in class, research on your own, or
in a team environment.

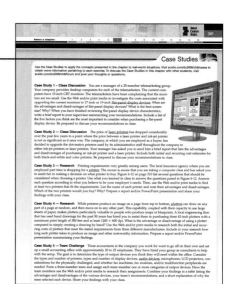

22 Special Features

Five special features following Chapters 1, 2, 5, 6, and 8 encompass topics from the history of computers, to what's hot on the Web, to a buyer's guide, to the latest in new technology.

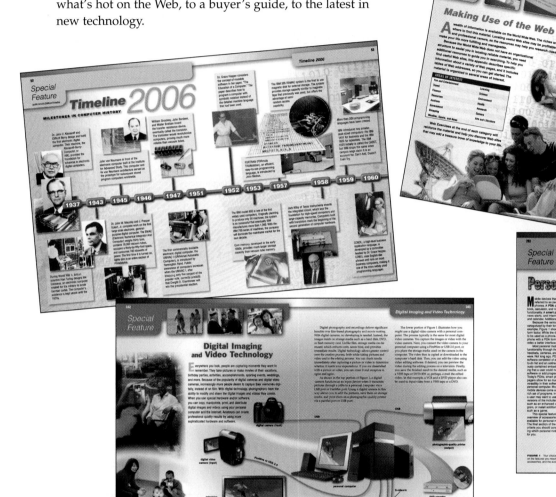

SHELLY CASHMAN SERIES – TRADITIONALLY BOUND TEXTBOOKS

The Shelly Cashman Series presents the following computer subjects in a variety of traditionally bound textbooks. For more information, see your Course Technology representative or call 1-800-648-7450. For Shelly Cashman Series information, visit Shelly Cashman Online at scseries.com

COMPUTERS	
Computers	Discovering Computers 2006: A Gateway to Information, Complete
	Discovering Computers 2006: A Gateway to Information, Introductory
	Discovering Computers 2006: A Gateway to Information, Brief
	Discovering Computers: Fundamentals, Second Edition
	Teachers Discovering Computers: Integrating Technology in the Classroom, Third Edition
	Essential Introduction to Computers, Sixth Edition (40-page)

WINDOWS APPLICATIONS	
Microsoft Office	Microsoft Office 2003: Essential Concepts and Techniques (5 projects)
	Microsoft Office 2003: Brief Concepts and Techniques (9 projects)
	Microsoft Office 2003: Introductory Concepts and Techniques, Second Edition (15 projects)
	Microsoft Office 2003: Advanced Concepts and Techniques (12 projects)
	Microsoft Office 2003: Post Advanced Concepts and Techniques (11 projects)
	Microsoft Office XP: Essential Concepts and Techniques (5 projects)
	Microsoft Office XP: Brief Concepts and Techniques (9 projects)
	Microsoft Office XP: Introductory Concepts and Techniques, Windows XP Edition (15 projects)
	Microsoft Office XP: Introductory Concepts and Techniques, Enhanced Edition (15 projects)
	Microsoft Office XP: Advanced Concepts and Techniques (11 projects)
	Microsoft Office XP: Post Advanced Concepts and Techniques (11 projects)
Integration	Teachers Discovering and Integrating Microsoft Office: Essential Concepts and Techniques, Second Edition
	Integrating Microsoft Office XP Applications and the World Wide Web: Essential Concepts and Techniques
PIM	Microsoft Outlook 2002: Essential Concepts and Techniques • Microsoft Office Outlook 2003: Introductory Concepts and Techniques
Microsoft Works	Microsoft Works 6: Complete Concepts and Techniques[1] • Microsoft Works 2000: Complete Concepts and Techniques[1]
Microsoft Windows	Microsoft Windows XP: Comprehensive Concepts and Techniques[2]
	Microsoft Windows XP: Brief Concepts and Techniques
	Microsoft Windows 2000: Comprehensive Concepts and Techniques[2]
	Microsoft Windows 2000: Brief Concepts and Techniques
	Microsoft Windows 98: Comprehensive Concepts and Techniques[2]
	Microsoft Windows 98: Essential Concepts and Techniques
	Introduction to Microsoft Windows NT Workstation 4
Notebook Organizer	Microsoft Office OneNote 2003: Introductory Concepts and Techniques
Word Processing	Microsoft Office Word 2003: Comprehensive Concepts and Techniques[2] • Microsoft Word 2002: Comprehensive Concepts and Techniques[2]
Spreadsheets	Microsoft Office Excel 2003: Comprehensive Concepts and Techniques[2] • Microsoft Excel 2002: Comprehensive Concepts and Techniques[2]
Database	Microsoft Office Access 2003: Comprehensive Concepts and Techniques[2] • Microsoft Access 2002: Comprehensive Concepts and Techniques[2]
Presentation Graphics	Microsoft Office PowerPoint 2003: Comprehensive Concepts and Techniques[2] • Microsoft PowerPoint 2002: Comprehensive Concepts and Techniques[2]
Desktop Publishing	Microsoft Office Publisher 2003: Comprehensive Concepts and Techniques[2] • Microsoft Publisher 2002: Comprehensive Concepts and Techniques[1]

PROGRAMMING	
Programming	Microsoft Visual Basic .NET: Comprehensive Concepts and Techniques[2] • Microsoft Visual Basic 6: Complete Concepts and Techniques[1] • Java Programming: Comprehensive Concepts and Techniques, Second Edition[2] • Structured COBOL Programming, Second Edition • Understanding and Troubleshooting Your PC • Programming Fundamentals Using Microsoft Visual Basic .NET

INTERNET	
Concepts	Discovering the Internet: Brief Concepts and Techniques • Discovering the Internet: Complete Concepts and Techniques
Browser	Microsoft Internet Explorer 6: Introductory Concepts and Techniques, Windows XP Edition • Microsoft Internet Explorer 5: An Introduction • Netscape Navigator 6: An Introduction
Web Page Creation	Web Design: Introductory Concepts and Techniques • HTML: Comprehensive Concepts and Techniques, Third Edition[2] • Microsoft Office FrontPage 2003: Comprehensive Concepts and Techniques[2] • Microsoft FrontPage 2002: Comprehensive Concepts and Techniques[2] • Microsoft FrontPage 2002: Essential Concepts and Techniques • JavaScript: Complete Concepts and Techniques, Second Edition[1] • Macromedia Dreamweaver MX: Comprehensive Concepts and Techniques[2]

SYSTEMS ANALYSIS	
Systems Analysis	Systems Analysis and Design, Sixth Edition

DATA COMMUNICATIONS	
Data Communications	Business Data Communications: Introductory Concepts and Techniques, Fourth Edition

[1]Also available as an Introductory Edition, which is a shortened version of the complete book, [2]Also available as an Introductory Edition and as a Complete Edition, which are shortened versions of the comprehensive book.

Discovering Computers

2006 A GATEWAY TO INFORMATION

CHAPTER ONE

Introduction to Computers

Picture Yourself in a Computer Class

While waiting for the instructor to begin her first lecture, you hear several classmates announce they will be meeting at the local coffee house to talk about homework and form study groups. Many of them sound nervous and anxious about this Introduction to Computers class. As they talk, you think about your experiences with computers. You had a beginning programming class in high school. You use the Internet regularly to chat with friends. With your digital camera, you take pictures and e-mail them to family members. No study groups for you.

During the lecture, the instructor reads several computer advertisements to the class. The ads use computer terms and acronyms you have never heard, like bus, SDRAM, USB flash drive, TFT, media player, SCSI, HT Technology, Bluetooth, Ethernet, firewall, NIC, and Wi-Fi. Now, *you* get a bit nervous and anxious. When she finishes reading, the instructor tells the class not to worry if some or most of the words in the ads are unfamiliar. "As we work through this course together," she says, "you will learn everything you need to know to buy a computer." While walking out the classroom door, you ask your friend, "What time is everyone meeting at the coffee house? I want to get in one of those study groups."

Read Chapter 1 to become familiar with some of the terms mentioned in the advertisement, discover practical uses of computers, and set a foundation for your further learning throughout this book.

After completing this chapter, you will be able to:

1. Recognize the importance of computer literacy
2. Define the term, computer
3. Identify the components of a computer
4. Discuss the advantages and disadvantages of using computers
5. Recognize the purpose of a network
6. Discuss the uses of the Internet and World Wide Web
7. Distinguish between system software and application software
8. Describe the categories of computers
9. Identify the elements of an information system
10. Describe the various types of computer users
11. Discuss various computer applications in society

CONTENTS

A WORLD OF COMPUTERS

WHAT IS A COMPUTER?
Data and Information
Information Processing Cycle

THE COMPONENTS OF A COMPUTER
Input Devices
Output Devices
System Unit
Storage Devices
Communications Devices

ADVANTAGES AND DISADVANTAGES OF USING COMPUTERS

NETWORKS AND THE INTERNET
The Internet

COMPUTER SOFTWARE
System Software
Application Software
Installing and Running Programs
Software Development

CATEGORIES OF COMPUTERS

PERSONAL COMPUTERS
Desktop Computers

MOBILE COMPUTERS AND MOBILE DEVICES
Notebook Computers
Mobile Devices

MIDRANGE SERVERS

MAINFRAMES

SUPERCOMPUTERS

EMBEDDED COMPUTERS

ELEMENTS OF AN INFORMATION SYSTEM

EXAMPLES OF COMPUTER USAGE
Home User
Small Office/Home Office User
Mobile User
Power User
Large Business User
Putting It All Together

COMPUTER APPLICATIONS IN SOCIETY
Education
Finance
Government
Health Care
Science
Publishing
Travel
Industry

CHAPTER SUMMARY

HIGH-TECH TALK
Analog versus Digital: Making the Conversion

COMPANIES ON THE CUTTING EDGE
Dell
Apple Computer

TECHNOLOGY TRAILBLAZERS
Bill Gates
Carly Fiorina

A WORLD OF COMPUTERS

Computers are everywhere: at work, at school, and at home. Many daily activities either involve the use of or depend on information from a computer. As shown in Figure 1-1, people use all types and sizes of computers for a variety of reasons and in a range of places. Some computers sit on top of a desk or on the floor; others are small enough to carry.

Computers are a primary means of communication for billions of people. People use computers to correspond with businesses, employees with other employees and customers, students with teachers, and family members with friends and other family members. In addition to corresponding via text messages, people use computers to send each other pictures, diagrams, drawings, music, and videos.

Through computers, society has instant access to information from around the globe. Local and national news, weather reports, sports scores, airline schedules, telephone directories, maps and directions, job listings, credit reports, and countless forms of educational material always are accessible. From the computer, you can meet new friends, share photographs and videos, shop, fill prescriptions, file taxes, or take a course.

At home or while on the road, people use computers to manage schedules, balance checkbooks, pay bills, track personal income and expenses, transfer funds, and buy or sell stocks. Banks place automated teller machines (ATMs) all over the world, making it easy for customers to deposit or withdraw funds at anytime. At the grocery store, a computer tracks purchases, calculates the amount of money due, and often

FIGURE 1-1 People use computers in their daily activities.

generates coupons customized to buying patterns. Vehicles include onboard navigation systems that provide directions, call for emergency services, and track the vehicle if it is stolen.

In the workplace, employees use computers to create correspondence such as e-mail messages, memos, and letters; calculate payroll; track inventory; and generate invoices. Some applications such as automotive design and weather forecasting use computers to perform complex mathematical calculations. At school, teachers use computers to assist with classroom instruction. Students complete assignments and do research on computers in lab rooms and at home.

People also spend hours of leisure time on the computer. They play games, listen to music, watch videos and movies, read books and magazines, research genealogy, compose music and videos, retouch photographs, and plan vacations.

As technology continues to advance, computers are becoming more a part of everyday life. Thus, many people believe that computer literacy is vital to success in today's world. **Computer literacy** involves having a knowledge and understanding of computers and their uses.

This book presents the knowledge you need to be computer literate. As you read this first chapter, keep in mind it is an overview. Many of the terms and concepts introduced in this chapter will be discussed in more depth later in the book.

WHAT IS A COMPUTER?

A **computer** is an electronic device, operating under the control of instructions stored in its own memory, that can accept data, process the data according to specified rules, produce results, and store the results for future use.

Data and Information

Computers process data into information. **Data** is a collection of unprocessed items, which can include text, numbers, images, audio, and video. **Information** conveys meaning and is useful to people.

As shown in Figure 1-2, for example, computers process several data items to print information in the form of a payroll check.

FAQ 1-1

Is data a singular or plural word?

The word data is plural for datum. With respect to computers, however, it is accepted and common practice to use the word data in both the singular and plural context. For more information, visit scsite.com/dc2006/ch1/faq and then click Data.

An **FAQ** (frequently asked question) helps you find answers to commonly asked questions. Web sites often post an FAQ section, and each chapter in this book includes FAQ boxes related to topics in the text.

Information Processing Cycle

Computers process data (input) into information (output). A computer often holds data, information, and instructions in storage for future use. *Instructions* are the steps that tell the computer how to perform a particular task. Some people refer to the series of input, process, output, and storage activities as the *information processing cycle*.

Most computers today can communicate with other computers. As a result, communications also has become an essential element of the information processing cycle.

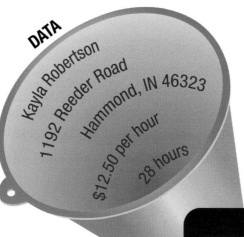

DATA

Kayla Robertson
1192 Reeder Road
Hammond, IN 46323
$12.50 per hour
28 hours

PROCESSES

- Multiplies hourly pay rate by hours to determine gross pay (350.00)
- Organizes data
- Computes payroll taxes (49.00)
- Subtracts payroll taxes from gross pay to determine net pay (301.00)

INFORMATION

FIGURE 1-2   A computer processes data into information. In this simplified example, the employee's name and address, hourly pay rate, and hours worked all represent data. The computer processes the data to produce the payroll check (information).

THE COMPONENTS OF A COMPUTER

A computer contains many electric, electronic, and mechanical components known as **hardware**. These components include input devices, output devices, a system unit, storage devices, and communications devices. Figure 1-3 shows some common computer hardware components.

Input Devices

An **input device** is any hardware component that allows you to enter data and instructions into a computer. Six widely used input devices are the keyboard, mouse, microphone, scanner, digital camera, and PC video camera (Figure 1-3).

A computer keyboard contains keys you press to enter data into the computer. A mouse is a small handheld device. With the mouse, you control movement of a small symbol on the screen, called the pointer, and you make selections from the screen.

A microphone allows a user to speak into the computer to enter data and instructions. A scanner converts printed material (such as text and pictures) into a form the computer can use.

With a digital camera, you take pictures and then transfer the photographed images to the computer or printer instead of storing the images on traditional film. A PC video camera is a digital video camera that allows users to create a movie or take still photographs electronically.

WEB LINK 1-1

Input Devices
For more information, visit scsite.com/dc2006/ch1/weblink and then click Input Devices.

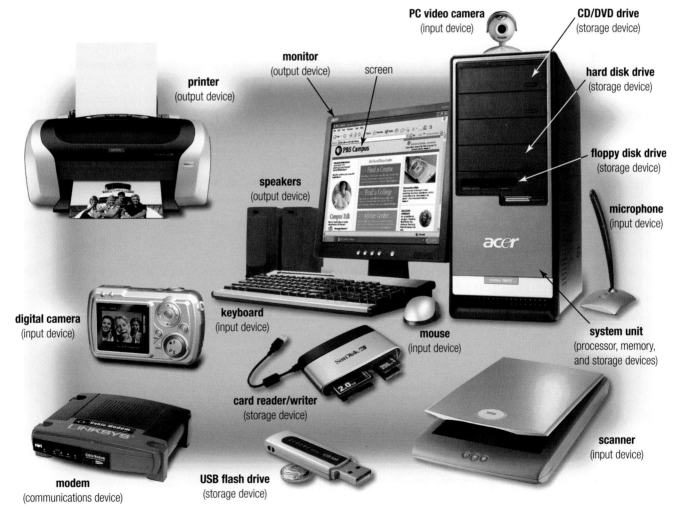

FIGURE 1-3 Common computer hardware components include a keyboard, mouse, microphone, scanner, digital camera, PC video camera, printer, monitor, speakers, system unit, disk drives, USB flash drive, card reader/writer, and modem.

Output Devices

An **output device** is any hardware component that conveys information to one or more people. Three commonly used output devices are a printer, a monitor, and speakers (Figure 1-3 on the previous page).

A printer produces text and graphics on a physical medium such as paper. A monitor displays text, graphics, and videos on a screen. Speakers allow you to hear music, voice, and other audio (sounds).

System Unit

The **system unit** is a case that contains the electronic components of the computer that are used to process data (Figure 1-3). The circuitry of the system unit usually is part of or is connected to a circuit board called the motherboard.

Two main components on the motherboard are the processor and memory. The *processor* is the electronic component that interprets and carries out the basic instructions that operate the computer. *Memory* consists of electronic components that store instructions waiting to be executed and data needed by those instructions. Although some forms of memory are permanent, most memory keeps data and instructions temporarily, which means its contents are erased when the computer is shut off.

FAQ 1-2

What is a CPU?

The processor. Most people in the computer industry use the terms *CPU* (*central processing unit*) and processor to mean the same. For more information, visit scsite.com/dc2006/ch1/faq and then click CPU.

Storage Devices

Storage holds data, instructions, and information for future use. For example, computers can store hundreds or millions of customer names and addresses. Storage holds these items permanently.

A computer keeps data, instructions, and information on **storage media**. Examples of storage media are floppy disks, Zip disks, USB flash drives, hard disks, CDs, DVDs, and memory cards. A **storage device** records (writes) and/or retrieves (reads) items to and from storage media. Drives and readers/writers, which are types of storage devices (Figure 1-3), accept a specific kind of storage media. For example, a CD drive (storage device) accepts a CD (storage media). Storage devices often function as a source of input because they transfer items from storage to memory.

A floppy disk consists of a thin, circular, flexible disk enclosed in a square-shaped plastic shell that is inserted in and removed from a floppy disk drive. A typical floppy disk stores up to about 1.4 million characters. A Zip disk looks similar to a floppy disk but has much greater storage capabilities — up to about 750 million characters. You insert Zip disks in and remove them from Zip drives.

A USB flash drive is a portable storage device that has much more storage capacity than a floppy disk but is small and lightweight enough to be transported on a keychain or in a pocket (Figure 1-3). You plug a USB flash drive in a special, easily accessible opening on the computer.

A hard disk provides much greater storage capacity than a floppy disk, Zip disk, or USB flash drive. The average hard disk can hold more than 80 billion characters. Hard disks are enclosed in an airtight, sealed case. Although some are removable, most are housed inside the system unit (Figure 1-4).

WEB LINK 1-2

Output Devices

For more information, visit scsite.com/dc2006/ch1/weblink and then click Output Devices.

FIGURE 1-4 Hard disks are self-contained devices. The hard disk shown here must be installed in the system unit before it can be used.

A compact disc is a flat, round, portable metal disc with a plastic coating. One type of compact disc is a CD-ROM, which you can access using most CD and DVD drives (Figure 1-5). Another type of compact disc is a DVD-ROM, some of which have enough storage capacity to store two full-length movies. To use a DVD-ROM, you need a DVD drive.

Some portable devices, such as digital cameras, use memory cards as the storage media. You then can transfer the stored items, such as electronic photographs, from the memory card to a computer or printer using a card reader/writer (Figure 1-3 on page 7).

FIGURE 1-5 To use a CD or DVD, you need a CD or DVD drive.

Communications Devices

A **communications device** is a hardware component that enables a computer to send (transmit) and receive data, instructions, and information to and from one or more computers. A widely used communications device is a modem (Figure 1-3).

Communications occur over cables, telephone lines, cellular radio networks, satellites, and other transmission media. Some transmission media, such as satellites and cellular radio networks, are wireless, which means they have no physical lines or wires.

ADVANTAGES AND DISADVANTAGES OF USING COMPUTERS

Society has reaped many benefits from using computers. Both business and home users can make well-informed decisions because they have instant access to information from anywhere in the world. A **user** is anyone who communicates with a computer or utilizes the information it generates. Students, another type of user, have more tools to assist them in the learning process. Read Looking Ahead 1-1 for a look at the next generation of benefits from using computers.

WEB LINK 1-3

Communications Devices

For more information, visit scsite.com/dc2006/ch1/weblink and then click Communications Devices.

LOOKING AHEAD 1-1

Bionic People Benefit from Processor Implants

Computers eventually will become an integral part of the human body. They already are used to help some hearing-impaired people hear by stimulating the nerves within the ear and to help the vision-impaired to see by converting light into electrical impulses.

The next step will involve implanting miniature computers or computer components in the body to help it perform basic functions. A processor, for example, could help release hormones. A brain computer interface may monitor and treat diseases, such as epilepsy and depression, that affect brain activity. A body-scanning machine will evaluate patients' pain when they cannot communicate.

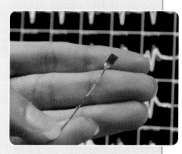

In addition, robotic legs strapped to the body can assist people such as firefighters and soldiers who must bear heavy loads for extended periods of time. For more information, visit scsite.com/dc2006/ch1/looking and then click Processor Implants.

ADVANTAGES OF USING COMPUTERS Benefits of computers are possible because computers have the advantages of speed, reliability, consistency, storage, and communications.

- **Speed**: Computer operations occur through electronic circuits. When data, instructions, and information flow along these circuits, they travel at incredibly fast speeds. Many computers process billions or trillions of operations in a single second. Processing involves computing (adding, subtracting, multiplying, dividing), sorting (e.g., alphabetizing), organizing, formatting, checking spelling and grammar, charting, displaying pictures, recording audio clips, playing music, and showing a movie. For a more technical discussion about how computers process data, read the High-Tech Talk article on page 38.
- **Reliability**: The electronic components in modern computers are dependable and reliable because they rarely break or fail.
- **Consistency**: Given the same input and processes, a computer will produce the same results — consistently. Computers generate error-free results, provided the input is correct and the instructions work. A computing phrase — known as *garbage in, garbage out* — points out that the accuracy of a computer's output depends on the accuracy of the input. For example, if you do not use the flash on a digital camera when indoors, the resulting pictures that are displayed on the computer screen may be unusable because they are too dark.
- **Storage**: A computer can transfer data quickly from storage to memory, process it, and then store it again for future use. Many computers store enormous amounts of data and make this data available for processing anytime it is needed.
- **Communications**: Most computers today can communicate with other computers, often wirelessly. Computers with this capability can share any of the four information processing cycle operations — input, process, output, and storage — with another computer or a user.

DISADVANTAGES OF USING COMPUTERS Some disadvantages of computers relate to the violation of privacy, the impact on the labor force, health risks, and the impact on the environment.

- **Violation of Privacy**: Nearly every life event is stored in a computer somewhere…in medical records, credit reports, tax records, etc. It is crucial that personal and confidential records be protected properly. In many instances, where these records were not properly protected, individuals have found their privacy violated and identities stolen.
- **Impact on Labor Force**: Although computers have improved productivity in many ways and created an entire industry with hundreds of thousands of new jobs, the skills of millions of employees have been replaced by computers. Thus, it is crucial that workers keep their education up-to-date. A separate impact on the labor force is that some companies are outsourcing jobs to foreign countries instead of keeping their homeland labor force employed. Read At Issue 1-1 for a related discussion.

AT ISSUE 1-1

Is Job Outsourcing Inevitable?

To cut costs, some companies are replacing their homeland workers with workers in foreign countries. Many of these displaced workers are computer professionals. In an age of high-speed computer communications, companies believe that computer professionals in countries such as India, China, and Russia can be as effective as, and far less expensive than, their homeland counterparts. Corporate executives claim that outsourcing increases profits, thereby benefiting shareholders and supporting investment in other areas, which in turn creates new jobs. But disgruntled former employees insist that offshore outsourcing hinders technology development, forces customers to deal with workers who have a limited understanding of a country's native language and culture, and endangers national security. In the United States, legislation has been proposed to combat offshore outsourcing, including laws to deny federal funding for companies that outsource, provide tax breaks for companies that do not outsource, or force companies to make their outsourcing practices public, so that consumers can make informed choices. Should companies replace homeland workers with workers in foreign countries? Why or why not? What, if anything, should be done to counter the trend to outsource overseas? Why? Should workers simply accept that, to compete in today's global marketplace, they must develop more flexible skills or be willing to do more for less?

- **Health Risks:** Prolonged or improper computer use can lead to injuries or disorders of the hands, wrists, elbows, eyes, neck, and back. Computer users can protect themselves from these health risks through proper workplace design, good posture while at the computer, and appropriately spaced work breaks.
- **Impact on Environment:** Computer manufacturing processes and computer waste are depleting natural resources and polluting the environment. The amount of resources required to manufacture a personal computer equals that of a mid-sized car. When computers are discarded in landfills, they release toxic materials and potentially dangerous levels of lead, mercury, and flame retardants. Strategies that can help protect the environment include recycling, regulating manufacturing processes, extending the life of computers, and immediately donating replaced computers.

Test your knowledge of pages 4 through 11 in Quiz Yourself 1-1.

 QUIZ YOURSELF 1-1

Instructions: Find the true statement below. Then, rewrite the remaining false statements so they are true.

1. A computer is a motorized device that processes output into input.

2. A storage device records (reads) and/or retrieves (writes) items to and from storage media.

3. An output device is any hardware component that allows you to enter data and instructions into a computer.

4. Computer literacy involves having a knowledge and understanding of computers and their uses.

5. Computers have the disadvantages of fast speeds, high failure rates, producing consistent results, storing small amounts of data, and communicating with others.

6. Three commonly used input devices are a printer, a monitor, and speakers.

Quiz Yourself Online: To further check your knowledge of computer literacy, computers and their components, and the advantages and disadvantages of computers, visit scsite.com/dc2006/ch1/quiz and then click Objectives 1 – 4.

NETWORKS AND THE INTERNET

A **network** is a collection of computers and devices connected together via communications devices and transmission media. When a computer connects to a network, it is **online**.

Networks allow computers to share *resources*, such as hardware, software, data, and information. Sharing resources saves time and money. In many networks, one or more computers act as a server. The *server* controls access to the resources on a network. The other computers on the network, each called a *client* or workstation, request resources from the server (Figure 1-6). The major differences between the server and client computers are that the server ordinarily has more power, more storage space, and expanded communications capabilities.

Many homes and most businesses and schools network their computers and devices. Home networks usually are small, existing within a single structure, and often are wireless. Business and school networks can be small, such as in a room or building, or widespread, connecting computers across a city, country, or the globe. The world's largest computer network is the Internet.

FIGURE 1-6 A server manages the resources on a network, and clients access the resources on the server. This network enables three separate computers to share the same printer, one wirelessly.

The Internet

The **Internet** is a worldwide collection of networks that connects millions of businesses, government agencies, educational institutions, and individuals (Figure 1-7).

More than one billion people around the world use the Internet daily for a variety of reasons, including the following purposes:

- Communicate with and meet other people
- Access a wealth of information, news, and research findings
- Shop for goods and services
- Bank and invest
- Take a class
- Access sources of entertainment and leisure, such as online games, music, videos, books, and magazines

WEB LINK 1-4

The Internet

For more information, visit scsite.com/ dc2006/ch1/weblink and then click Internet.

Figure 1-8 shows examples in each of these areas.

People connect to the Internet to exchange information with others around the world. E-mail allows you to send messages to other users. With instant messaging, you can have a live conversation with another connected user. In a chat room, you can communicate with multiple users at the same time — much like a group discussion.

Businesses, called access providers, offer users and companies access to the Internet free or for a fee. By subscribing to an access provider, you can use your computer and a communications device, such as a modem, to connect to the many services of the Internet.

The Web, short for World Wide Web, is one of the more popular services on the Internet. Think of the Web as a global library of information available to anyone connected to the Internet. The **Web** contains billions of documents called Web pages. A **Web page** can contain text, graphics, audio, and video. The six screens shown in Figure 1-8 are examples of Web pages. Web pages often have built-in connections, or links, to other documents, graphics, other Web pages, or Web sites. A Web site is a collection of related Web pages.

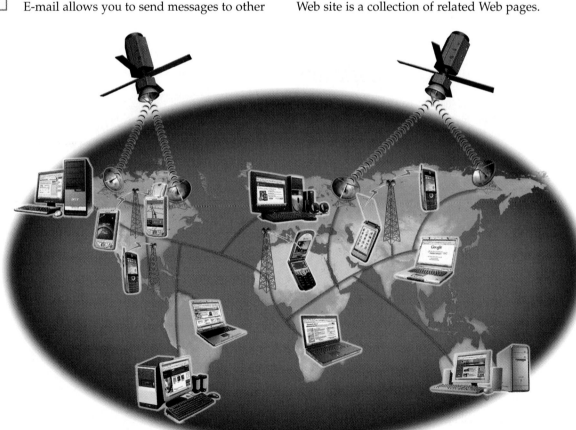

FIGURE 1-7   The Internet is the largest computer network, connecting millions of computers around the world.

FIGURE 1-8b (access information)

FIGURE 1-8a (communicate)

FIGURE 1-8c (shop)

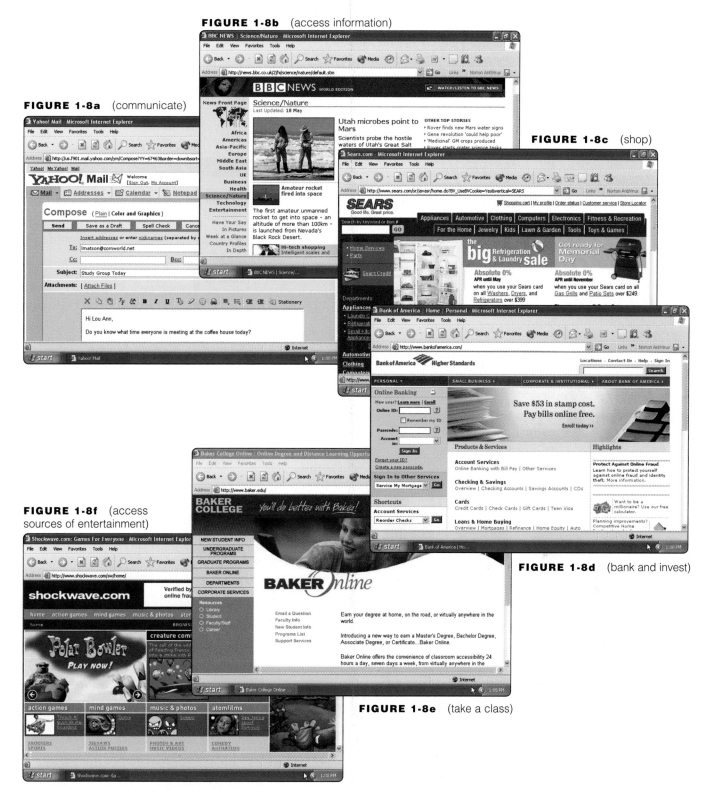

FIGURE 1-8f (access sources of entertainment)

FIGURE 1-8d (bank and invest)

FIGURE 1-8e (take a class)

FIGURE 1-8 Users access the Internet for a variety of reasons: to communicate with others, to access a wealth of information, to shop for goods and services, to bank and invest, to take a class, and for entertainment.

In addition to accessing and using information on the Web, many people use the Web as a means to share personal information, photographs, videos, or artwork with the world. Anyone can create a Web page and then make it available, or *publish* it, on the Internet for others to see (read At Issue 1-2 for a related discussion). A **photo sharing community,** for example, is a Web site that allows users to create an online photo album and store their electronic photographs (Figure 1-9). Some Web sites provide publishing services free.

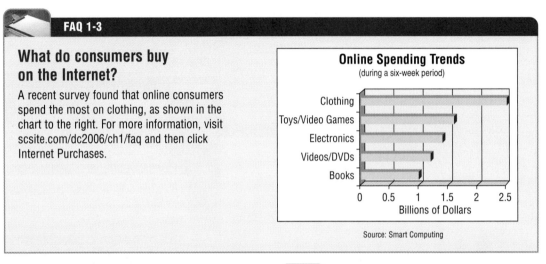

FAQ 1-3

What do consumers buy on the Internet?

A recent survey found that online consumers spend the most on clothing, as shown in the chart to the right. For more information, visit scsite.com/dc2006/ch1/faq and then click Internet Purchases.

Online Spending Trends
(during a six-week period)

Source: Smart Computing

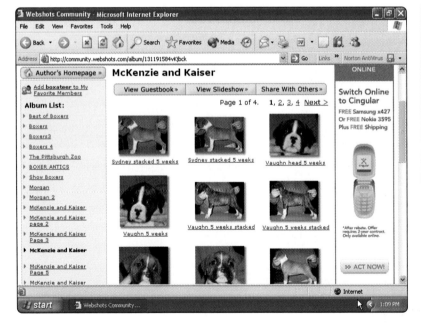

FIGURE 1-9 This proud dog owner posts pictures of her boxers to a photo sharing community.

AT ISSUE 1-2

Is Everything on the Web True?

Recently, a California city council considered banning foam cups when an official-looking Web page revealed that dihydrogen monoxide, which was characterized as a potentially dangerous chemical, was used to produce the cups. The council later was chagrined to discover that the information at the Web site was a hoax. That is, while dihydrogen monoxide is used in making foam cups, it hardly is dangerous — dihydrogen monoxide is the scientific name for water (H_2O). Many people think that anything in print is true, even what they read on the Web. Yet, authors with a wide range of expertise, authority, motives, and biases create Web pages. Web pages can be as accurate as the most scholarly journal, or no truer than the most disreputable supermarket tabloid. The Web makes it easy to obtain information, but Web page readers must make an extra effort to determine the quality of that information. In evaluating a Web page, experts suggest that you consider such factors as the purpose, scope, sponsor, timeliness, presentation, author, and permanence of the page. Ultimately, who is responsible for the accuracy of information on the Web? Why? What factors are most important in evaluating the accuracy of a Web page? Why?

COMPUTER SOFTWARE

Software, also called a **program**, consists of a series of instructions that tells the computer what to do and how to do it.

You interact with a program through its user interface. The user interface controls how you enter data and instructions and how information is displayed on the screen. Software today often has a graphical user interface. With a **graphical user interface** (**GUI** pronounced gooey), you interact with the software using text, graphics, and visual images such as icons (Figure 1-10). An *icon* is a miniature image that represents a program, an instruction, or some other object. You can use the mouse to select icons that perform operations such as starting a program.

The two categories of software are system software and application software. The following sections describe these categories of software.

System Software

System software consists of the programs that control or maintain the operations of the computer and its devices. System software serves as the interface between the user, the application software, and the computer's hardware. Two types of system software are the operating system and utility programs.

OPERATING SYSTEM An *operating system* is a set of programs that coordinates all the activities among computer hardware devices. It provides a means for users to communicate with the computer and other software. Many of today's computers use Windows XP, which is one of Microsoft's operating systems (Figure 1-10).

When a user starts a computer, portions of the operating system load into memory from the computer's hard disk. It remains in memory while the computer is on.

FIGURE 1-10 The graphical user interface of Windows XP.

WEB LINK 1-5

Computer Programs

For more information, visit scsite.com/dc2006/ch1/weblink and then click Computer Programs.

UTILITY PROGRAM A *utility program* allows a user to perform maintenance-type tasks usually related to managing a computer, its devices, or its programs. Most operating systems include several utility programs for managing disk drives, printers, and other devices. You also can buy utility programs that allow you to perform additional computer management functions.

Application Software

Application software consists of programs designed to make users more productive and/or assist them with personal tasks. A widely used type of application software related to communications is a Web browser, which allows users with an Internet connection to access and view Web pages. Other popular application software includes word processing software, spreadsheet software, database software, and presentation graphics software.

Many other types of application software exist that enable users to perform a variety of tasks. These include personal information management, note taking, project management, accounting, computer-aided design, desktop publishing, paint/image editing, audio and video editing, multimedia authoring, Web page authoring, personal finance, legal, tax preparation, home design/landscaping, education, reference, and entertainment (e.g., games or simulations, etc.). As shown in Figure 1-11,

you can purchase application software from a store that sells computer products. Read At Issue 1-3 for a related discussion.

AT ISSUE 1-3

Can Computers Provoke Violence?

Grand Theft Auto is one of today's most popular computer games. In the game, players advance through the mafia by conveying secret packages, following alleged snitches, and planting car bombs. Since its release, shoppers have bought millions of copies of Grand Theft Auto. Purchasers praise the game's vivid graphics, edgy characters, and wide range of allowable behaviors. Some parents and politicians, however, condemn the game's explicit violence and the rewards it gives players for participating in illegal acts. They fear that games like Grand Theft Auto eventually could corrupt players, perhaps leading to antisocial or criminal behavior. Grand Theft Auto is aimed at older gamers who grew up with Mario but now are looking for something more radical. The game is rated M (for Mature, meaning it is suitable for ages 17 and older), but children as young as 12 have purchased and played with it. Even worse, critics fear that the game's popularity may influence future developers of computer games aimed at younger children. What impact, if any, do violent computer games or games that promote unacceptable acts have on individual behavior? Do these games desensitize players to violence or increase aggression? Why or why not? Should restrictions be placed on sales of computer games?

WEB LINK 1-6

Application Software

For more information, visit scsite.com/dc2006/ch1/weblink and then click Application Software.

FIGURE 1-11 Stores that sell computer products have shelves stocked with software for sale.

Installing and Running Programs

The instructions in a program are stored on storage media such as a hard disk or compact disc. When purchasing software from a computer store, you typically receive a box that includes a CD(s) or DVD(s) that contains the program. You also may receive a manual or printed instructions explaining how to install and use the software.

Installing is the process of setting up software to work with the computer, printer, and other hardware components. When you buy a computer, it usually has some software pre-installed on its hard disk. This enables you to use the computer the first time you turn it on. To begin installing additional software from a CD or DVD, insert the program disc in a CD or DVD drive. The computer then copies all or part of the program from the disc to the computer's hard disk.

Once software is installed, you can use, or **run**, it. When you instruct the computer to run an installed program, the computer *loads* it, which means the program is copied from storage to memory. Once in memory, the computer can carry out, or *execute*, the instructions in the program. Figure 1-12 illustrates the steps that occur when a user installs and runs a greeting card program.

FAQ 1-4

Which spelling is correct, disk or disc?

Both are correct, depending on usage. When referring to CD, DVD, and other *optical* (laser) storage, computer professionals typically use the term, disc. The term, disk, normally refers to floppy disks, Zip disks, hard disks, and other nonoptical storage media. For more information, visit scsite.com/dc2006/ch1/faq and then click Disk or Disc.

FIGURE 1-12 INSTALLING AND RUNNING A COMPUTER PROGRAM

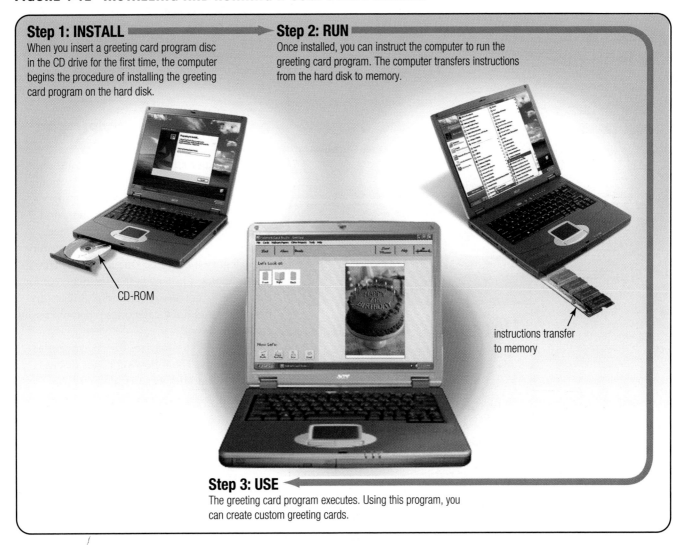

Step 1: INSTALL
When you insert a greeting card program disc in the CD drive for the first time, the computer begins the procedure of installing the greeting card program on the hard disk.

Step 2: RUN
Once installed, you can instruct the computer to run the greeting card program. The computer transfers instructions from the hard disk to memory.

CD-ROM

instructions transfer to memory

Step 3: USE
The greeting card program executes. Using this program, you can create custom greeting cards.

Software Development

A *programmer* is someone who develops software or writes the instructions that direct the computer to process data into information. When writing instructions, a programmer must be sure the program works properly so the computer generates the desired results. Complex programs can require thousands to millions of instructions.

Programmers use a programming language or program development tool to create computer programs. Popular programming languages include C++, C#, Java, JavaScript, and Visual Basic .NET. Figure 1-13 shows some of the instructions a programmer may write to create a Web application.

FIGURE 1-13 The top figure illustrates some of the instructions a programmer writes in JavaScript to create the Web application shown in the bottom figure.

Test your knowledge of pages 11 through 18 in Quiz Yourself 1-2.

QUIZ YOURSELF 1-2

Instructions: Find the true statement below. Then, rewrite the remaining false statements so they are true.

1. A resource is a collection of computers and devices connected together via communications devices and transmission media.

2. Installing is the process of setting up software to work with the computer, printer, and other hardware components.

3. Popular system software includes Web browsers, word processing software, spreadsheet software, database software, and presentation graphics software.

4. The Internet is one of the more popular services on the Web.

5. Two types of application software are the operating system and utility programs.

Quiz Yourself Online: To further check your knowledge of networks, the Internet and Web, and system software versus application software, visit scsite.com/dc2006/ch1/quiz and then click Objectives 5 – 7.

CATEGORIES OF COMPUTERS

Industry experts typically classify computers in six categories: personal computers, mobile computers and mobile devices, midrange servers, mainframes, supercomputers, and embedded computers. A computer's size, speed, processing power, and price determine the category it best fits. Due to rapidly changing technology, however, the distinction among categories is not always clear-cut. Still, many people refer to these categories when discussing computers.

Figure 1-14 summarizes the six categories of computers. The following pages discuss computers and devices that fall in each category.

CATEGORIES OF COMPUTERS

Category	Physical Size	Number of Simultaneously Connected Users	General Price Range
Personal computers (desktop)	Fits on a desk	Usually one (can be more if networked)	Several hundred to several thousand dollars
Mobile computers and mobile devices	Fits on your lap or in your hand	Usually one	Less than a hundred dollars to several thousand dollars
Midrange servers	Small cabinet	Two to thousands	$1,000 to a million dollars
Mainframes	Partial room to a full room of equipment	Hundreds to thousands	$300,000 to several million dollars
Supercomputers	Full room of equipment	Hundreds to thousands	$500,000 to several billion dollars
Embedded computers	Miniature	Usually one	Embedded in the price of the product

FIGURE 1-14 This table summarizes some of the differences among the categories of computers. These should be considered general guidelines only because of rapid changes in technology.

PERSONAL COMPUTERS

A **personal computer** is a computer that can perform all of its input, processing, output, and storage activities by itself. A personal computer contains a processor, memory, and one or more input, output, and storage devices.

Two popular styles of personal computers are the PC (Figure 1-15) and the Apple (Figure 1-16). The term, *PC-compatible,* refers to any personal computer based on the original IBM personal computer design. Companies such as Dell, Gateway, Hewlett-Packard, and Toshiba sell PC-compatible

computers. PC and PC-compatible computers have processors with different architectures than processors in Apple computers. These two types of computers also use different operating systems. PC and PC-compatible computers usually use a Windows operating system. Apple computers use a Macintosh operating system (Mac OS).

Two types of personal computers are desktop computers and notebook computers. The next section discusses desktop personal computers. Notebook computers are discussed in the mobile computers section.

WEB LINK 1-7

Personal Computers
For more information, visit scsite.com/dc2006/ch1/weblink and then click Personal Computers.

FIGURE 1-15 The PC and compatible computers usually use a Windows operating system.

FIGURE 1-16 Apple computers, such as the iMac, use a Macintosh operating system.

FAQ 1-5

How many PCs have been sold worldwide?

One billion PCs were sold during their first 25 years on the market. Experts predict that the next billion PCs will be sold between 2000 and 2008, a mere eight-year period. For more information, visit scsite.com/dc2006/ch1/faq and then click PC Sales.

MOBILE COMPUTERS AND MOBILE DEVICES

A **mobile computer** is a personal computer you can carry from place to place. Similarly, a **mobile device** is a computing device small enough to hold in your hand.

The most popular type of mobile computer is the notebook computer. The following sections discuss the notebook computer and widely used mobile devices.

Desktop Computers

A **desktop computer** is designed so the system unit, input devices, output devices, and any other devices fit entirely on or under a desk or table (Figures 1-15 and 1-16 on the previous page). In many models, the system unit is a tall and narrow *tower*, which can sit on the floor vertically — if desktop space is limited.

Some desktop computers are powerful enough to function as a server on a network. These high-end computers cost much more than the basic desktop computer.

Another expensive, powerful desktop computer is the workstation, which is geared for work that requires intense calculations and graphics capabilities. An architect uses a workstation to design buildings and homes. A graphic artist uses a workstation to create computer-animated special effects for full-length motion pictures and video games.

Notebook Computers

A **notebook computer**, also called a **laptop computer**, is a portable, personal computer designed to fit on your lap. Notebook computers are thin and lightweight, yet they can be as powerful as the average desktop computer. Notebook computers are more expensive than desktop computers with equal capabilities.

On a typical notebook computer, the keyboard is on top of the system unit, and the monitor attaches to the system unit with hinges (Figure 1-17). These computers weigh on average between 2.5 and 9 pounds, which allows users easily to transport the computers from place to place. Most notebook computers can operate on batteries or a power supply or both.

FAQ 1-6

Does the term, workstation, have two meanings?

Yes. In the computer industry, a *workstation* can be a high-powered computer or a client computer on a network. For more information, visit scsite.com/dc2006/ch1/faq and then click Workstation.

WEB LINK 1-8

Notebook Computers

For more information, visit scsite.com/dc2006/ch1/weblink and then click Notebook Computers.

display

CD or DVD drive

hinge

keyboard

FIGURE 1-17 On a typical notebook computer, the keyboard is on top of the system unit, and the display attaches to the system unit with hinges.

TABLET PC Resembling a letter-sized slate, the **Tablet PC** is a special type of notebook computer that allows you to write or draw on the screen using a digital pen (Figure 1-18). With a *digital pen*, users write or draw by pressing the pen on the screen, and issue instructions to the Tablet PC by tapping on the screen. For users who prefer typing instead of handwriting, some Tablet PC designs have an attached keyboard; others allow you to connect a separate keyboard to the device. Tablet PCs also support voice input so users can enter text and issue instructions by speaking into the computer.

Tablet PCs are useful especially for taking notes in lectures, at meetings, conferences, and other forums where the standard notebook computer is not practical. With a cost of about $2,000, some users may find Tablet PCs more appropriate for their needs than traditional notebook computers.

Mobile Devices

Mobile devices, which are small enough to carry in a pocket, usually do not have disk drives. Instead, these devices store programs and data permanently on special memory inside the system unit or on small storage media such as memory cards. You often can connect a mobile device to a personal computer to exchange information between the computer and the mobile device.

Some mobile devices are **Internet-enabled**, meaning they can connect to the Internet wirelessly. With an Internet-enabled device, users can chat, send e-mail and instant messages, and access the Web.

Four popular types of mobile devices are handheld computers, PDAs, smart phones, and smart watches. Some combination mobile devices also are available, for example, a PDA/smart phone.

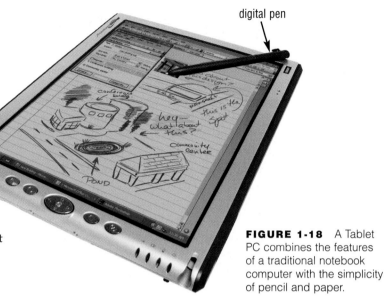

digital pen

FIGURE 1-18 A Tablet PC combines the features of a traditional notebook computer with the simplicity of pencil and paper.

HANDHELD COMPUTER A **handheld computer**, sometimes called a *handtop computer*, is a computer small enough to fit in one hand (Figure 1-19). Because of their reduced size, the screens on handheld computers are small. Many handheld computers communicate wirelessly with other devices or computers and also include a digital pen or stylus for input. Similar to a digital pen, a *stylus* is a small metal or plastic device that looks like a ballpoint pen but uses pressure instead of ink to write, draw, or make selections.

Handheld computers often have specialized keyboards. Many handheld computers are industry-specific and serve the needs of mobile employees, such as meter readers and parcel delivery people, whose jobs require them to move from place to place.

FIGURE 1-19 This handheld computer fits in your hand.

PDA The PDA is one of the more popular lightweight mobile devices in use today. A **PDA** (*personal digital assistant*) provides personal organizer functions such as a calendar, appointment book, address book, calculator, and notepad (Figure 1-20). Most PDAs also offer a variety of other application software such as word processing, spreadsheet, personal finance, and games.

The primary input device of a PDA is a stylus. Some PDAs do have a built-in miniature keyboard. If you prefer to type on a PDA that does not have a keyboard, you can insert the PDA in a special separate keyboard. Some PDAs also support voice input.

Many PDAs are Internet-enabled so users can check e-mail and access the Web. Some also provide telephone capabilities. Because of all the added features, increasingly more people are replacing their pocket-sized appointment books with PDAs.

SMART PHONE Offering the convenience of one-handed operation, a **smart phone** is an Internet-enabled telephone that usually also provides PDA capabilities. In addition to basic telephone capabilities, a smart phone allows you to send and receive e-mail messages and access the Web. Higher-priced models have color screens, play music, and include built-in cameras so you can share photographs or videos with others as soon as you capture the image (Figure 1-21).

As smart phones and PDAs continue a trend of offering similar functions, it is becoming increasingly difficult to differentiate between the two devices. This trend, known as *convergence*, has led manufacturers to refer to PDAs and smart phones simply as *handhelds*. Some factors that affect a consumer's purchasing decision include the device's size, screen size, and capabilities of available software.

FAQ 1-7

Do PDAs have industry-specific applications?

Yes. Restaurant servers use PDAs to record customer orders and transmit them to the kitchen. Doctors use PDAs to access patients' records, view laboratory results, and transmit prescriptions to the pharmacy. Law enforcement officials use PDAs to log license plate numbers, run background checks, and issue tickets. For more information, visit scsite.com/dc2006/ch1/faq and then click PDAs.

FIGURE 1-21 In addition to basic telephone functionality, smart phones allow you to check e-mail, access the Web, and share photos.

stylus

FIGURE 1-20 PDAs provide personal information management functions as well as Internet access and telephone capabilities. Shown here are two different styles of PDAs.

SMART WATCH A **smart watch** is an Internet-enabled watch. In addition to basic timekeeping capabilities, a smart watch automatically adjusts to time zone changes, stores personal messages, reminds you of appointments, and wirelessly accesses news, weather, sports, and stocks (Figure 1-22).

FIGURE 1-22 A smart watch.

MIDRANGE SERVERS

A **midrange server** is more powerful and larger than a workstation computer (Figure 1-23). Midrange servers typically support several hundred and sometimes up to a few thousand connected computers at the same time.

Midrange servers store data and programs. In many cases, one server accesses data on another server. In other cases, people use personal computers or terminals to access programs on a server. A terminal is a device with a monitor, keyboard, and memory.

FIGURE 1-23
A midrange server is more powerful than a workstation, but less powerful than a mainframe.

MAINFRAMES

A **mainframe** is a large, expensive, powerful computer that can handle hundreds or thousands of connected users simultaneously (Figure 1-24). Mainframes store tremendous amounts of data, instructions, and information. Every major corporation uses mainframes for business activities. With mainframes, large businesses are able to bill millions of customers, prepare payroll for thousands of employees, and manage thousands of items in inventory. One study reported that mainframes process more than 83 percent of transactions around the world.

Mainframes also can act as servers in a network environment. Midrange servers and other mainframes can access data and information from a mainframe. People also can access programs on the mainframe using terminals or personal computers.

FIGURE 1-24
Mainframe computers can handle thousands of connected computers and process millions of instructions per second.

SUPERCOMPUTERS

A **supercomputer** is the fastest, most powerful computer — and the most expensive (Figure 1-25). The fastest supercomputers are capable of processing more than 100 trillion instructions in a single second. With weights that exceed 100 tons, these computers can store more than 20,000 times the data and information of an average desktop computer.

Applications requiring complex, sophisticated mathematical calculations use supercomputers. Large-scale simulations and applications in medicine, aerospace, automotive design, online banking, weather forecasting, nuclear energy research, and petroleum exploration use a supercomputer.

FIGURE 1-25 This supercomputer simulates various environmental occurrences such as global climate changes, pollution, and earthquakes.

EMBEDDED COMPUTERS

An **embedded computer** is a special-purpose computer that functions as a component in a larger product. Embedded computers are everywhere — at home, in your car, and at work. The list below identifies a variety of everyday products that contain embedded computers.

- Consumer Electronics: mobile and digital telephones, digital televisions, cameras, video recorders, game consoles, DVD players and recorders, answering machines
- Home Automation Devices and Appliances: thermostats, sprinkling systems, security monitoring systems, microwave ovens, washing machines
- Automobiles: antilock brakes, engine control modules, airbag controller, cruise control
- Process Controllers and Robotics: remote monitoring systems, power monitors, machine controllers, medical devices
- Computer Devices and Office Machines: keyboards, printers, faxes, copiers

Because embedded computers are components in larger products, they usually are small and have limited hardware. These computers perform various functions, depending on the requirements of the product in which they reside. Embedded computers in printers, for example, monitor the amount of paper in the tray, check the ink or toner level, signal if a paper jam has occurred, and so on. Figure 1-26 shows some of the many embedded computers in cars.

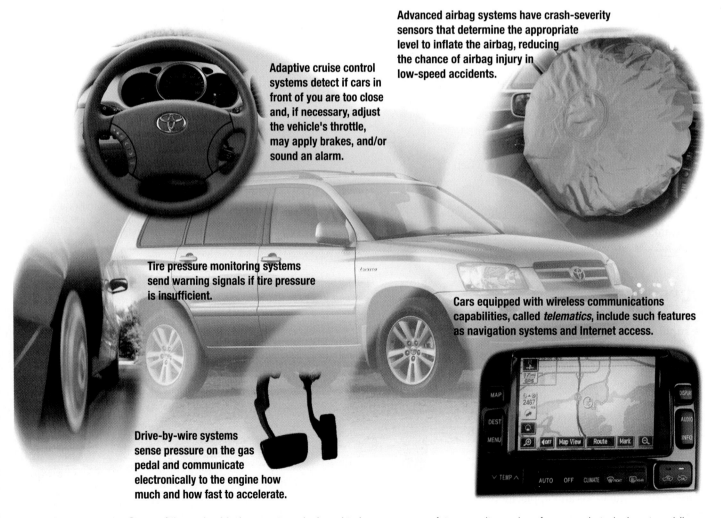

Adaptive cruise control systems detect if cars in front of you are too close and, if necessary, adjust the vehicle's throttle, may apply brakes, and/or sound an alarm.

Advanced airbag systems have crash-severity sensors that determine the appropriate level to inflate the airbag, reducing the chance of airbag injury in low-speed accidents.

Tire pressure monitoring systems send warning signals if tire pressure is insufficient.

Cars equipped with wireless communications capabilities, called *telematics*, include such features as navigation systems and Internet access.

Drive-by-wire systems sense pressure on the gas pedal and communicate electronically to the engine how much and how fast to accelerate.

FIGURE 1-26   Some of the embedded computers designed to improve your safety, security, and performance in today's automobiles.

ELEMENTS OF AN INFORMATION SYSTEM

To be valuable, information must be accurate, organized, timely, accessible, useful, and cost-effective to produce. Generating information from a computer requires the following five elements:

- Hardware
- Software
- Data
- People
- Procedures

Together, these elements (hardware, software, data, people, and procedures) comprise an *information system*. Figure 1-27 shows how each of the elements of an information system in a large business might interact.

The hardware must be reliable and capable of handling the expected workload. The software must be developed carefully and tested thoroughly. The data entered into the computer must be accurate.

Most companies with mid-sized and large computers have an IT (information technology) department. Staff in the IT department should be skilled and up-to-date on the latest technology. IT staff also should train users so they understand how to use the computer properly. Today's users also work closely with IT staff in the development of computer applications that relate to their areas of work.

Finally, all the IT applications should have readily available documented procedures that address operating the computer and using its applications.

FIGURE 1-27   HOW THE ELEMENTS OF AN INFORMATION SYSTEM IN A LARGE BUSINESS MIGHT INTERACT

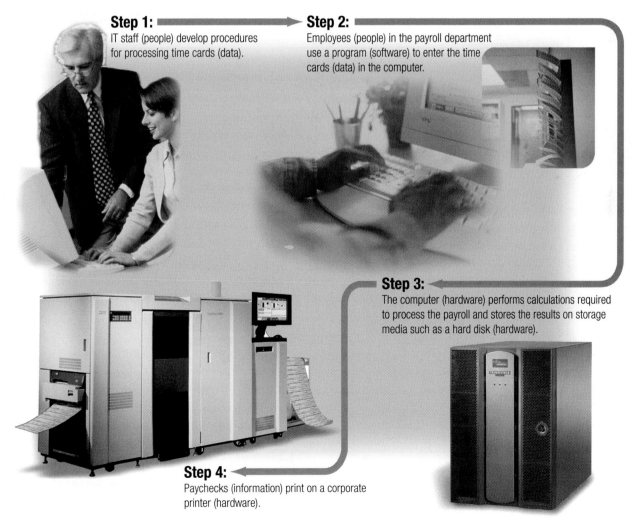

Step 1: IT staff (people) develop procedures for processing time cards (data).

Step 2: Employees (people) in the payroll department use a program (software) to enter the time cards (data) in the computer.

Step 3: The computer (hardware) performs calculations required to process the payroll and stores the results on storage media such as a hard disk (hardware).

Step 4: Paychecks (information) print on a corporate printer (hardware).

WEB LINK 1-9

Women in Technology

For more information, visit scsite.com/dc2006/ch1/weblink and then click Women in Technology.

WEB LINK 1-10

Minorities in Technology

For more information, visit scsite.com/dc2006/ch1/weblink and then click Minorities in Technology.

EXAMPLES OF COMPUTER USAGE

Every day, people around the world rely on different types of computers for a variety of applications. To illustrate the range of uses for computers, this section takes you on a visual and narrative tour of five categories of users:

- Home user
- Small office/home office (SOHO) user
- Mobile user
- Power user
- Large business user

The following paragraphs discuss the types of hardware and software required by each category of user.

Home User

In an increasing number of homes, the computer no longer is a convenience. Instead, it is a basic necessity. Each family member, or **home user**, spends time on the computer for different reasons that include budgeting and personal financial management, Web access, communications, and entertainment (Figure 1-28).

FIGURE 1-28a (personal financial management)

FIGURE 1-28b (Web access)

FIGURE 1-28c (communications)

FIGURE 1-28d (entertainment)

FIGURE 1-28 The home user spends time on a computer for a variety of reasons.

On the Internet, home users access a huge amount of information, take college classes, pay bills, manage investments, shop, listen to the radio, watch movies, read books, play games, file taxes, and make airline reservations. They also communicate with others around the world through e-mail, instant messaging, and chat rooms using personal computers, PDAs, and smart phones. With a digital camera, home users take photographs and then send the electronic images to others (Figure 1-29). Using a PC video camera, which costs less than $100, home users easily have live video calls with friends, family members, and others. Read At Issue 1-4 for a related discussion.

Today's homes typically have one or more desktop computers. Many home users network multiple desktop computers throughout the house, often wirelessly. These small networks allow family members to share an Internet connection and a printer.

To meet their needs, home users have a variety of software. They type letters, homework assignments, and other documents with word processing software. Personal finance software helps the home user with personal finances, investments, and family budgets. Other software assists with preparing taxes, keeping a household inventory, and setting up maintenance schedules.

Reference software, such as encyclopedias, medical dictionaries, or a road atlas, provides valuable information for everyone in the family. With entertainment software, the home user can play games, compose music, research genealogy, or create greeting cards.

Educational software helps adults learn to speak a foreign language and youngsters to read, write, count, and spell.

FAQ 1-8

Can I listen to an audio CD on my computer?

Yes, in most cases. Simply insert the CD in the computer's CD or DVD drive. Within a few seconds, you should hear music from the computer's speakers or in your headset. If no music plays, it is possible you need to run a program that starts the audio CD. For more information, visit scsite.com/dc2006/ch1/faq and then click Audio CDs.

FIGURE 1-29 Home users take and view photographs on a digital camera.

AT ISSUE 1-4

Did You Meet Online?

Once, people met dates through family and friends, work, or community, religious, and recreational activities. These social networks sometimes resulted in a perfect match, but often time constraints, the limited pool of participants, and infrequent meetings made it difficult to find a potential partner. Today, many people are turning to another resource — online dating. Media experts forecast that 40 million people will use online dating services this year, and the market for these services has grown almost 40 percent in the past year. Online dating service members supply information about their interests and personalities and then search the service for people they might like to meet. The services are easy to use, have a large range of participants, allow relationships to develop at a comfortable pace, and usually offer advanced options such as live chat, voice mail, and computer matchmaking. On the other hand, in an online dating service it can be difficult to judge the appearance of members, obtain in-depth profiles, recognize false or exaggerated member claims, and avoid unwanted advertisements. Although introductory memberships often are free, many services require substantial fees for extended benefits. Are online dating services worth it? Why or why not? If you used an online dating service, what would you do to profit from its advantages and avoid its disadvantages?

Small Office/Home Office User

Computers assist small business and home office users in managing their resources effectively. A **small office/home office** (*SOHO*) includes any company with fewer than 50 employees, as well as the self-employed who work from home. Small offices include local law practices, accounting firms, travel agencies, and florists. SOHO users typically have a desktop computer to perform some or all of their duties. Many also have PDAs to manage appointments and contact information.

SOHO users access the Web — often wirelessly — to look up information such as addresses, directions (Figure 1-30a), postal codes, flights, and package shipping rates. Nearly all SOHO users communicate with others through e-mail. Many are entering the *e-commerce* arena and conduct business on the Web. Their Web sites advertise products and services and may provide a means for taking orders. Small business Web sites sometimes use a *Web cam*, which is a video camera that displays its output on a Web page. A Web cam allows SOHO users to show the world a live view of some aspect of their business.

To save money on hardware and software, small offices often network their computers. For example, the small office connects one printer to a network for all employees to share.

SOHO users often have basic business software such as word processing and spreadsheet software to assist with document preparation and finances (Figure 1-30b). They are likely to use other industry-specific types of software. A candy shop, for example, will have software that allows for taking orders and payments, updating inventory, and paying vendors.

FIGURE 1-30a   (Web access)

FIGURE 1-30b   (spreadsheet program)

FIGURE 1-30   People with a home office and employees in small offices typically use a desktop personal computer for some or all of their duties.

Mobile User

Today, businesses and schools are expanding to serve people across the country and around the world. Thus, increasingly more employees and students are **mobile users**, who work on a computer while away from a main office or school (Figure 1-31). Examples of mobile users are sales representatives, real estate agents, insurance agents, meter readers, package delivery people, journalists, consultants, and students.

Mobile users often have a notebook computer, Internet-enabled PDA, or smart phone. With these computers and devices, the mobile user connects to other computers — usually wirelessly — on a network or the Internet. Mobile users can transfer information between their mobile device and another computer, such as one at the main office or school.

The mobile user works with basic business software such as word processing and spreadsheet software. With presentation graphics software, the mobile user can create and deliver presentations to a large audience by connecting a mobile computer or device to a video projector that displays the presentation on a full screen. Many scaled-down programs are available for mobile devices such as PDAs and smart phones.

FIGURE 1-31 Mobile users have notebook computers, Tablet PCs, PDAs, and smart phones so they can work, do homework, send messages, or connect to the Internet while away from a wired connection.

Power User

Another category of user, called a **power user**, requires the capabilities of a workstation or other type of powerful computer (Figure 1-32). Examples of power users include engineers, scientists, architects, desktop publishers, and graphic artists. Power users often work with *multimedia*, combining text, graphics, audio, and video into one application. These users need computers with extremely fast processors because of the nature of their work.

The power user's workstation contains industry-specific software. For example, engineers and architects use software to draft and design floor plans, mechanical assemblies, or vehicles. A desktop publisher uses software to prepare marketing literature such as newsletters, brochures, and annual reports. A geologist uses software to study the earth's surface. This software usually is expensive because of its specialized design.

Power users exist in all types of businesses. Some also work at home. Their computers typically have network connections and Internet access.

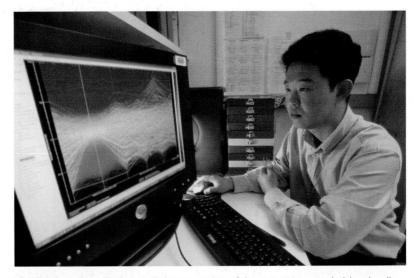

FIGURE 1-32 This scientist uses a powerful computer to study blood cells for diabetes research.

Large Business User

A large business has hundreds or thousands of employees or customers that work in or do business with offices across a region, the country, or the world. Each employee or customer who uses a computer in the large business is a **large business user** (Figure 1-33).

WEB LINK 1-11

Enterprise Computing
For more information, visit scsite.com/ dc2006/ch1/weblink and then click Enterprise Computing.

Many large companies use the words, *enterprise computing*, to refer to the huge network of computers that meets their diverse computing needs. The network facilitates communications among employees at all locations. Users access the network of midrange servers or mainframes through desktop computers, mobile computers, PDAs, and smart phones.

Large businesses use computers and the computer network to process high volumes of transactions in a single day. Although they may differ in size and in the products or services offered, all generally use computers for basic business activities. For example, they bill millions of customers, prepare payroll for thousands of employees, and manage thousands of items in inventory.

Large businesses typically have e-commerce Web sites, allowing customers and vendors to conduct business online. The Web site also showcases products, services, and other company information. Customers, vendors, and other interested parties can access this information on the Web. Once an order is placed, computers update inventory records to reflect goods sold and goods purchased.

The marketing department in the large business uses desktop publishing software to prepare marketing literature. The accounting department uses software for accounts receivable, accounts payable, billing, general ledger, and payroll activities.

The employees in the *information technology (IT) department* keep the computers and the network running. They also determine when and if the company requires new hardware or software.

Large business users work with word processing, spreadsheet, database, and presentation graphics software. They also may use calendar programs to post their schedules on the network. And, they might use PDAs or smart phones to maintain contact information. E-mail and Web browsers enable communications among employees, vendors, and customers.

Some large businesses place kiosks in public locations. A *kiosk* is a freestanding computer, usually with a touch screen (Figure 1-34).

Many employees of large businesses telecommute. **Telecommuting** is a work arrangement in which employees work away from a company's standard workplace and often communicate with the office through the computer. Employees who telecommute have flexible work schedules so they can combine work and personal responsibilities, such as child care.

FIGURE 1-33 A large business can have hundreds or thousands of users in offices across a region, the country, or the world.

FIGURE 1-34 Airline travelers check in using this self-service kiosk.

Putting It All Together

The previous pages discussed the hardware and software requirements for the home user, small office/home office user, mobile user, power user, and large business user. The table in Figure 1-35 summarizes these requirements.

CATEGORIES OF USERS

User	Hardware	Software
HOME 	• Desktop computer • PDA or smart phone • Smart watch	• Business (e.g., word processing) • Personal information manager • Personal finance, online banking, tax preparation • Web browser • E-mail, instant messaging, and chat rooms • Photo editing • Reference (e.g., encyclopedias, medical dictionaries, road atlas) • Entertainment (e.g., games, music composition, greeting cards) • Educational (e.g., tutorials, children's math and reading software)
SMALL OFFICE/ HOME OFFICE 	• Desktop computer • PDA or smart phone • Shared network printer	• Business (e.g., word processing, spreadsheet, database) • Personal information manager • Company specific (e.g., accounting, legal reference) • Network management • Web browser • E-mail
MOBILE 	• Notebook computer equipped with a modem, or a Tablet PC • Video projector • PDA or smart phone	• Business (e.g., word processing, spreadsheet, note taking, presentation graphics) • Personal information manager • Web browser • E-mail
POWER 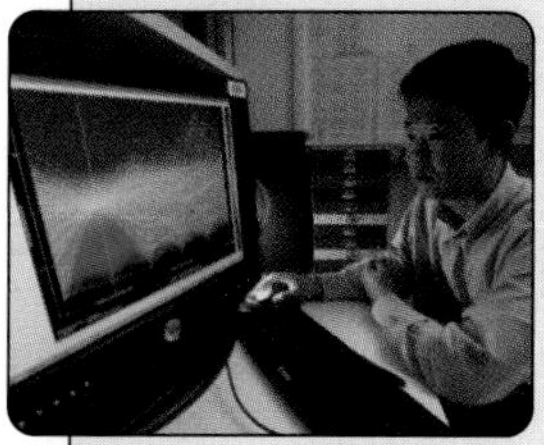	• Workstation or other powerful computer with multimedia capabilities • PDA or smart phone	• Desktop publishing • Multimedia authoring • Computer-aided design • Photo, audio, and video editing • Personal information manager • Web browser • E-mail
LARGE BUSINESS 	• Midrange server or mainframe • Desktop or notebook computer • Industry-specific handheld computer • PDA or smart phone • Kiosk	• Business (e.g., word processing, spreadsheet, database, presentation graphics) • Personal information manager • Accounting • Network management • Web browser • E-mail

FIGURE 1-35 Today, computers are used by millions of people for work tasks, school assignments, and leisure activities. Different computer users require different kinds of hardware and software to meet their needs effectively.

COMPUTER APPLICATIONS IN SOCIETY

The computer has changed society today as much as the industrial revolution changed society in the eighteenth and nineteenth centuries.

People interact directly with computers in fields such as education, finance, government, health care, science, publishing, travel, and industry. In addition, they can reap the benefits from breakthroughs and advances in these fields. The following pages describe how computers have made a difference in people's interactions with these disciplines. Read Looking Ahead 1-2 for a look at the next generation of computer applications in society.

LOOKING AHEAD 1-2

Robots Add the Human Touch

Rosie, the robotic maid from "The Jetsons," delighted millions of television viewers with her household cleaning talents. Today's mobile, intelligent robots likewise perform tasks typically reserved for humans in a $5 billion global market.

Each day, the iRobot Roomba self-propelled vacuum cleans homes, and the da Vinci Surgical System's robotic hands drill through bones and make incisions. Sony's home robot, QRIO, responds to voices and faces, displays emotions, and walks and dances fluidly.

Tomorrow's practical and versatile robots will serve a variety of personal and industrial needs. By 2010, the expected $17 billion market should include products to care for senior citizens, transport people in major cities, and perform hundreds of thousands of mobile utility jobs, such as picking up and delivering items. For more information, visit scsite.com/dc2006/ch1/looking and then click Robots.

Education

Education is the process of acquiring knowledge. In the traditional model, people learn from other people such as parents, teachers, and employers. Many forms of printed material such as books and manuals are used as learning tools. Today, educators also are turning to computers to assist with education (Figure 1-36).

Many schools and companies equip labs and classrooms with computers. Some schools require students to have a notebook computer or PDA, along with textbooks and other supplies. To promote education by computer, many vendors offer substantial student discounts on software.

Sometimes, the delivery of education occurs at one place while the learning occurs at other locations. For example, students can take a class on the Web. Some classes are blended; that is, part of the learning occurs in a classroom and the other part occurs on the Web. More than 70 percent of colleges offer some type of distance learning classes. A few even offer entire degrees online.

FIGURE 1-36 In some schools, students have notebook computers on their desks during classroom lectures.

Finance

Many people and companies use computers to help manage their finances. Some use finance software to balance checkbooks, pay bills, track personal income and expenses, manage investments, and evaluate financial plans. This software usually includes a variety of online services. For example, computer users can track investments and do online banking. With **online banking**, users access account balances, pay bills, and copy monthly transactions from the bank's computer right into their personal computers.

Many financial institutions' Web sites also offer online banking (Figure 1-37). When using a Web site instead of finance software on your computer, all your account information is stored on the bank's computer. The advantage is you can access your financial records from anywhere in the world.

FIGURE 1-37   Many financial institutions' Web sites offer online banking.

Investors often use **online investing** to buy and sell stocks and bonds — without using a broker. With online investing, the transaction fee for each trade usually is much less than when trading through a broker.

Government

A government provides society with direction by making and administering policies. To provide citizens with up-to-date information, most government offices have Web sites. People in the United States access government Web sites to file taxes, apply for permits and licenses, pay parking tickets, buy stamps, report crimes, apply for financial aid, and renew vehicle registrations and driver's licenses.

Employees of government agencies use computers as part of their daily routine. North American 911 call centers use computers to dispatch calls for fire, police, and medical assistance. Military and other agency officials use the U.S. Department of Homeland Security's network of information about domestic security threats to help protect against terrorist attacks. Law enforcement officers have online access to the FBI's National Crime Information Center (NCIC) in police cars that have rugged notebook

computers and fingerprint scanners or through PDAs (Figure 1-38). The NCIC contains more than 52 million missing persons and criminal records, including names, fingerprints, parole/probation records, mug shots, and other information.

FIGURE 1-38   Law enforcement officials have in-vehicle computers and PDAs to access emergency, missing person, and criminal records in computer networks in local, state, and federal agencies.

Health Care

Nearly every area of health care uses computers. Whether you are visiting a family doctor for a regular checkup, having lab work or an outpatient test, or being rushed in for emergency surgery, the medical staff around you will be using computers for various purposes:

- Hospitals and doctors use computers to maintain patient records.
- Computers monitor patients' vital signs in hospital rooms and at home.
- Computers and computerized devices assist doctors, nurses, and technicians with medical tests (Figure 1-39).
- Doctors use the Web and medical software to assist with researching and diagnosing health conditions.
- Doctors use e-mail to correspond with patients.
- Pharmacists use computers to file insurance claims.
- Surgeons implant computerized devices, such as pacemakers, that allow patients to live longer.

- Surgeons use computer-controlled devices to provide them with greater precision during operations, such as for laser eye surgery and robot-assisted heart surgery.

Many Web sites provide up-to-date medical, fitness, nutrition, or exercise information. These Web sites also maintain lists of doctors and dentists to help you find the one that suits your needs. They have chat rooms, so you can talk to others diagnosed with similar conditions. Some Web sites even allow you to order prescriptions online.

An exciting development in health care is telemedicine, which is a form of long-distance health care. Through *telemedicine*, health-care professionals in separate locations conduct live conferences on the computer. For example, a doctor at one location can have a conference with a doctor at another location to discuss a bone X-ray. Live images of each doctor, along with the X-ray, are displayed on each doctor's computer.

Science

All branches of science, from biology to astronomy to meteorology, use computers to assist them with collecting, analyzing, and modeling data. Scientists also use the Internet to communicate with colleagues around the world.

Breakthroughs in surgery, medicine, and treatments often result from scientists' use of computers. Tiny computers now imitate functions of the central nervous system, retina of the eye, and cochlea of the ear. A cochlear implant allows a deaf person to listen. Electrodes implanted in the brain stop tremors associated with Parkinson's disease. Cameras small enough to swallow — sometimes called a camera pill — take pictures inside your body to detect polyps, cancer, and other abnormalities (Figure 1-40).

A *neural network* is a system that attempts to imitate the behavior of the human brain. Scientists create neural networks by connecting thousands of processors together much like the neurons in the brain are connected. The capability of a personal computer to recognize spoken words is a direct result of scientific experimentation with neural networks.

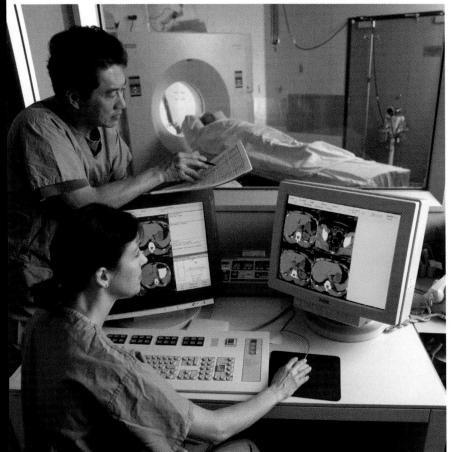

FIGURE 1-39 Doctors, nurses, technicians, and other medical staff use computers while performing tests on patients.

FIGURE 1-40   HOW A CAMERA PILL WORKS

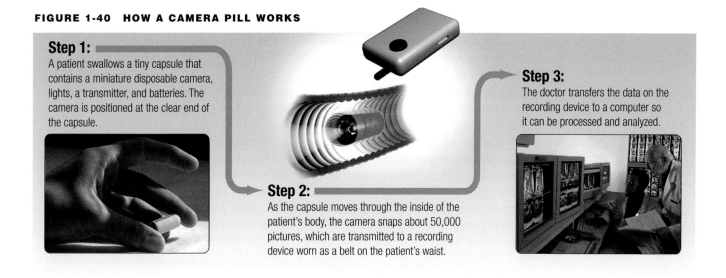

Step 1:
A patient swallows a tiny capsule that contains a miniature disposable camera, lights, a transmitter, and batteries. The camera is positioned at the clear end of the capsule.

Step 2:
As the capsule moves through the inside of the patient's body, the camera snaps about 50,000 pictures, which are transmitted to a recording device worn as a belt on the patient's waist.

Step 3:
The doctor transfers the data on the recording device to a computer so it can be processed and analyzed.

Publishing

Publishing is the process of making works available to the public. These works include books, magazines, newspapers, music, film, and video. Special software assists graphic designers in developing pages that include text, graphics, and photographs; artists in composing and enhancing songs; filmmakers in creating and editing film; and journalists and mobile users in capturing and modifying video clips.

Many publishers make their works available online (Figure 1-41). Some Web sites allow you to copy the work, such as a book or music, to your desktop computer, handheld computer, PDA, or smart phone.

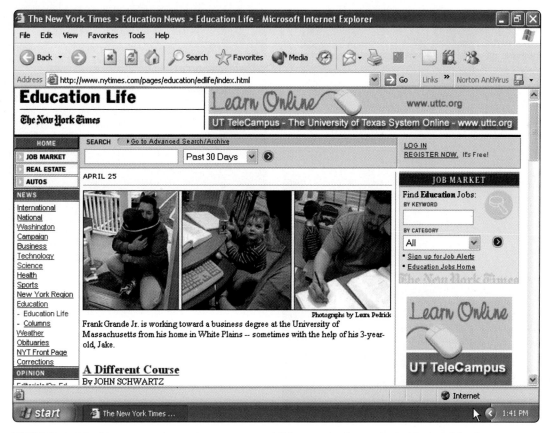

FIGURE 1-41   Many magazine and newspaper publishers make the content of their publications available online.

Travel

Whether traveling by car or airplane, your goal is to arrive safely at your destination. As you make the journey, you may interact with some of the latest technology.

Vehicles manufactured today often include some type of onboard navigation system. Many airlines now provide online access, allowing passengers to connect their mobile computer or device to the Internet (Figure 1-42). Some airlines even provide passengers with Internet-enabled devices during flights.

In preparing for a trip, you may need to reserve a car, hotel, or flight. Many Web sites offer these services to the public. For example, you can order airline tickets on the Web. If you plan to drive somewhere and are unsure of the road to take to your destination, you can print directions and a map from the Web.

Industry

Computer-aided manufacturing (*CAM*) refers to the use of computers to assist with manufacturing processes such as fabrication and assembly. Industries use CAM to reduce product development costs, shorten a product's time to market, and stay ahead of the competition.

Often, robots carry out processes in a CAM environment. CAM is used by a variety of industries, including oil drilling, power generation, food production, and automobile manufacturing. Automobile plants, for example, have an entire line of industrial robots that assemble a car (Figure 1-43).

Special computers on the shop floor record actual labor, material, machine, and computer time used to manufacture a particular product. The computers process this data and automatically update inventory, production, payroll, and accounting records on the company's network.

FAQ 1-9

Do home users book travel on the Web?

Yes, it is estimated that nearly 22 percent ($53 billion) of the travel industry's revenues stem from leisure travel bookings. As shown in the chart, computer users of all ages visit travel agency Web sites. For more information, visit scsite.com/ dc2006/ch1/faq and then click Travel Bookings.

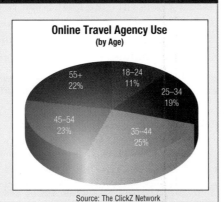

Online Travel Agency Use
(by Age)

55+ 22%
18–24 11%
25–34 19%
45–54 23%
35–44 25%

Source: The ClickZ Network

FIGURE 1-43 Automotive factories use industrial robots to weld car bodies.

FIGURE 1-42 Airlines today offer inflight Internet connections to passengers.

Test your knowledge of pages 18 through 36 in Quiz Yourself 1-3.

QUIZ YOURSELF 1-3

Instructions: Find the true statement below. Then, rewrite the remaining false statements so they are true.

1. A desktop computer is a portable, personal computer designed to fit on your lap.
2. A personal computer contains a processor, memory, and one or more input, output, and storage devices.
3. Each large business user spends time on the computer for different reasons that include budgeting and personal financial management, Web access, communications, and entertainment.
4. A home user requires the capabilities of a workstation or other powerful computer.
5. Mainframes are the fastest, most powerful computers — and the most expensive.
6. The elements of an information system are hardware, e-mail, data, people, and the Internet.
7. With embedded computers, users access account balances, pay bills, and copy monthly transactions from the bank's computer right into their personal computers.

Quiz Yourself Online: To further check your knowledge of categories of computers, information system elements, computer users, and computer applications in society, visit scsite.com/dc2006/ch1/quiz and then click Objectives 8 – 11.

CHAPTER SUMMARY

Chapter 1 introduced you to basic computer concepts such as what a computer is, how it works, and its advantages and disadvantages. You learned about the components of a computer. Next, the chapter discussed networks, the Internet, and computer software. The many different categories of computers, computer users, and computer applications in society also were presented.

This chapter is an overview. Many of the terms and concepts introduced will be discussed further in later chapters. For a history of hardware and software developments, read the Timeline 2006 that follows this chapter.

CAREER CORNER

Personal Computer Salesperson

When you decide to buy or upgrade a personal computer, the most important person with whom you interact probably will be a personal computer salesperson. This individual will be a valuable resource to you in providing the information and expertise you need to select a computer that meets your requirements.

Computer manufacturers and retailers that sell several types of personal computers need competent salespeople. A *personal computer salesperson* must be computer literate and have a specific knowledge of the computers he or she sells. In addition, a successful salesperson has a friendly, outgoing personality that helps customers feel comfortable. Through open-ended questions, the salesperson can determine a customer's needs and level of experience. With this information, the salesperson can choose the best computer for the customer and explain the features of the computer in language the customer will understand.

Most computer salespeople have at least a high school diploma. Before reaching the sales floor, however, salespeople usually complete extensive company training programs. These programs often consist of self-directed, self-paced Web-training classes. Most salespeople also participate in training updates, often on a monthly basis.

Personal computer salespeople generally earn a guaranteed amount plus a commission for each sale. A computer salesperson can earn about $40,000 a year. Top salespeople can be among a company's more highly compensated employees, earning in excess of $70,000. For more information, visit scsite.com/dc2006/ch1/careers and then click Personal Computer Salesperson.

High-Tech Talk

ANALOG VERSUS DIGITAL:
MAKING THE CONVERSION

Data is processed in one of two ways: analog or digital. People generally process *analog* data — that is, continuous wave patterns. The sight and sound of a traveling subway car transmits to your eyes and ears as light and sound waves, or smooth up-and-down patterns (Figure 1-44a). A computer, by contrast, is *digital*, which means computers process data in two discrete states: positive (on, or 1) and non-positive (off, or 0) as shown in Figure 1-44b. The 1 and 0 represent the two digits used by the binary number system. While this system is at the heart of digital computing, binary digital impulses appear as long strings of 1s and 0s.

If sound and light waves are analog and a computer is digital, how does a computer record audio clips, play music, or show a movie? How can a digital computer use an analog telephone line to dial up to access the Internet?

The key lies in analog-to-digital and digital-to-analog conversions. For example, the computer's sound card allows you to record sounds and playback sounds. The sound card performs these conversions to record a digital audio clip of your analog voice. The sound card connects to the microphone, which is an analog input source. The diaphragm in the microphone converts the analog sound waves into an analog electrical signal. This signal flows to the sound card's *analog-to-digital converter (ADC)*, which converts the signal into digital data. The digital data flows to the *digital signal processor (DSP)*, compressing the data to save space. Finally, the compressed data is stored in an audio file format.

To play a recorded sound, the computer reverses the process. The processor retrieves and sends the digital data to the DSP to be decompressed. The DSP sends the decompressed digital data to the sound card's *digital-to-analog converter (DAC)*, which converts the digital data back to an analog voltage for output via a speaker or headset. In other words, a DAC takes that long binary number string of 1s and 0s and turns it into an electronic signal that the sound output devices can decode and use.

Similarly, a video card allows you to record a video or play a movie on a DVD. A camera and microphone capture and send the analog picture and sound signals to a video card. The video card's ADC converts the signals into digital data. The digital data is compressed and saved in a file format such as AVI (audio/video interleave) or MPEG (Moving Picture Experts Group). When playing a movie, the computer decompresses and separates the video and audio data. It then sends the signals to the video card's DAC. The DAC translates the digital data into analog signals and sends them to the monitor and speakers, where they are displayed as your movie.

The modem in a computer also links the analog and digital worlds. When using a dial-up modem, the computer does not transmit digital data directly across analog telephone lines. Instead, the modem converts the computer's digital signals to analog signals (called *modulation*) to be sent over telephone lines. When the analog signal reaches its destination, another modem recreates the original digital signal (*demodulation*). This allows the receiving computer to process the data. The next time you dial up using a modem, pick up the telephone. The loud, screeching noise you hear is the sound of digital data after being converted to analog sound waves. For more information, visit scsite.com/dc2006/ch1/tech and then click Analog versus Digital.

FIGURE 1-44a   (analog signal)

FIGURE 1-44b   (digital signal)

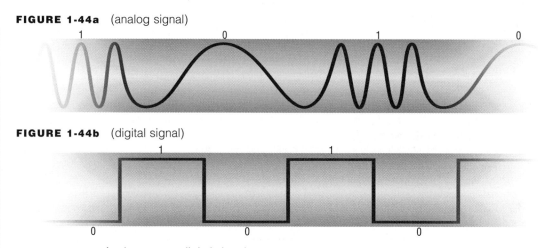

FIGURE 1-44   Analog versus digital signals.

Companies on the Cutting Edge

DELL
COMPUTERS YOUR WAY

As a leading manufacturer of personal computers, *Dell* prides itself on its direct approach to computer sales. Founded by Michael Dell in 1984, the company deals openly with customers, one at a time. This direct approach eliminates retailers that add cost and time to the ordering process.

Dell uses the Internet to enhance the advantages of direct marketing and hosts one of the world's largest volume e-commerce Web sites. Customers can configure and price computers, order systems, and track their orders online.

In response to the U.S. Environmental Protection Agency's estimate that 250 million computers will be discarded from 2002 to 2007, Dell began an aggressive campaign to increase the amount of computer equipment it recycles by 50 percent. For more information, visit scsite.com/dc2006/ch1/companies and then click Dell.

APPLE COMPUTER
INTRODUCING INNOVATIVE TECHNOLOGIES

Millions of computer users in more than 120 countries loyally use *Apple Computer*'s hardware and software with a passion usually reserved for sports teams and musical groups.

Steven Jobs and Stephen Wozniak founded Apple in 1976 when they marketed the Apple I, a circuit board they had developed in Jobs's garage. In 1977, Apple Computer incorporated and introduced the Apple II, the first mass-marketed personal computer. Apple introduced the Macintosh product line in 1984, which featured a graphical user interface.

Under Jobs's direction as CEO, Apple introduced the iMac, the iBook, the Power Mac G5, the iPod digital music player, and Mac OS X. Strong demand for the iPod Mini helped boost the company's earnings. Product sales jumped after Apple introduced its pay-per-download iTunes online music store in 2003. For more information, visit scsite.com/dc2006/ch1/companies and then click Apple Computer.

Technology Trailblazers

BILL GATES
MICROSOFT'S FOUNDER

Bill Gates, the founder and chief software architect of Microsoft Corporation, suggests that college students should learn how to learn by getting the best education they can. Because he is considered by many as the most powerful person in the computing industry, it might be wise to listen to him.

Gates learned to program computers when he was 13. Early in his career, he developed the BASIC programming language for the MITS Altair, one of the first microcomputers. He founded Microsoft in 1975 with Paul Allen, and five years later, they provided the first operating system, called MS-DOS, for the IBM PC. Today, Microsoft's Windows and Office products dominate the software market.

Gates consistently has been placed at the top of *Forbes'* World's Richest People list, with assets of more than $46 billion. For more information, visit scsite.com/dc2006/ch1/people and then click Bill Gates.

CARLY FIORINA
TECHNOLOGY CORPORATE LEADER

Leadership, according to *Carly Fiorina*, involves influencing others and mastering change. As Hewlett-Packard's former chairman and CEO, she worked to return the company to its roots of innovation and invention.

Among the top names in Fortune magazine's list of the world's most powerful corporate women, Fiorina spent nearly 20 years at AT&T and Lucent Technologies, Inc., where she directed Lucent's initial public offering and subsequent spin-off. In 1999, she became CEO of Hewlett-Packard (HP), one of the oldest companies in Silicon Valley. Three years later, she led one of the largest high-tech corporate mergers in history when HP bought rival Compaq Computer.

The New York Stock Exchange named Fiorina to its newly formed board of executives in 2004, and in that year she was appointed as one of eight advisors to the U.S. President on future missions to the moon. For more information, visit scsite.com/dc2006/ch1/people and then click Carly Fiorina.

Quizzes and Learning Games

Computer Genius
Crossword Puzzle
DC Track and Field
Practice Test
Quiz Yourself
Wheel of Terms
You're Hired!

Exercises

Case Studies
▷ Chapter Review
Checkpoint
Key Terms
Learn How To
Learn It Online
Web Research

Beyond the Book

Career Corner
Companies
FAQs
High-Tech Talk
Looking Ahead
Making Use of the Web
Trailblazers
Web Links

Features

Chapter Forum
Install Computer
Lab Exercises
Maintain Computer
Tech News
Timeline 2006

Chapter Review

The Chapter Review section summarizes the concepts presented in this chapter. To listen to the audio version of this Chapter Review, visit scsite.com/dc2006/ch1/review. To obtain help from other students regarding any subject in this chapter, visit scsite.com/dc2006/ch1/forum and post your thoughts or questions.

① Why Is Computer Literacy Important? **Computer literacy** involves having knowledge and understanding of computers and their uses. As computers become more a part of everyday life, many people believe that computer literacy is vital to success.

② What Is a Computer? A **computer** is an electronic device, operating under the control of instructions stored in its own memory, that can accept data, process the data according to specified rules, produce results, and store the results for future use.

③ What Are the Components of a Computer? The electric, electronic, and mechanical components of a computer, or **hardware**, include input devices, output devices, a system unit, storage devices, and communications devices. An **input device** allows you to enter data or instructions into a computer. An **output device** conveys information to one or more people. The **system unit** is a case that contains the electronic components of a computer that are used to process data. A **storage device** records and/or retrieves items to and from **storage media**. A **communications device** enables a computer to send and receive data, instructions, and information to and from one or more computers.

④ What Are the Advantages and Disadvantages of Using Computers? Computers have the advantages of speed, reliability, consistency, storage, and communications. They perform operations at incredibly fast speeds, are dependable and reliable, consistently generate error-free results, can store enormous amounts of data, and can share processing with other computers. Disadvantages of computers relate to the violation of privacy, the impact on the labor force, health risks, and the impact on the environment.

connect Visit scsite.com/dc2006/ch1/quiz or click the Quiz Yourself button. Click Objectives 1 – 4.

⑤ What Is the Purpose of a Network? A **network** is a collection of computers and devices connected together via communications devices and transmission media. Networks allow computers to share *resources*, such as hardware, software, data, and information.

⑥ How Are the Internet and World Wide Web Used? The **Internet** is a worldwide collection of networks that connects millions of businesses, government agencies, educational institutions, and individuals. People use the Internet to communicate with and meet other people, access news and information, shop for goods and services, bank and invest, take classes, and access sources of entertainment and leisure. The **Web**, short for World Wide Web, is a global library of documents containing information that is available to anyone connected to the Internet.

⑦ How Is System Software Different from Application Software? **Software**, also called a **program**, is a series of instructions that tells the computer what to do and how to do it. **System software** consists of the programs that control or maintain the operations of a computer and its devices. Two types of system software are the *operating system*, which coordinates activities among computer hardware devices, and *utility programs*, which perform maintenance-type tasks usually related to a computer, its devices, or its programs. **Application software** consists of programs that perform specific tasks for users. Popular application software includes Web browsers, word processing software, spreadsheet software, database software, and presentation graphics software.

connect Visit scsite.com/dc2006/ch1/quiz or click the Quiz Yourself button. Click Objectives 5 – 7.

Chapter Review

⑧ What Are the Categories of Computers? Industry experts typically classify computers in six categories: personal computers, mobile computers and mobile devices, midrange servers, mainframes, supercomputers, and embedded computers. A **personal computer** is a computer that can perform all of its input, processing, output, and storage activities by itself. A **mobile computer** is a personal computer that you can carry from place to place, and a **mobile device** is a computing device small enough to hold in your hand. A **midrange server** is a more powerful and larger computer that typically supports several hundred and sometimes up to a few thousand connected computers at the same time. A **mainframe** is a large, expensive, powerful computer that can handle hundreds or thousands of connected users simultaneously and can store tremendous amounts of data, instructions, and information. A **supercomputer** is the fastest, most powerful, and most expensive computer and is used for applications requiring complex, sophisticated mathematical calculations. An **embedded computer** is a special-purpose computer that functions as a computer in a larger product.

⑨ What Are the Elements of an Information System? An *information system* combines hardware, software, data, people, and procedures to produce timely and useful information. People in an *information technology (IT) department* develop procedures for processing data. Following these procedures, people use hardware and software to enter the data into a computer. Software processes the data and directs the computer hardware to store changes on storage media and produce information in a desired form.

⑩ What Are the Types of Computer Users? Computer users can be separated into five categories: home users, small office/home office users, mobile users, large business users, and power users. A **home user** is a family member who uses a computer for a variety of reasons, such as budgeting and personal financial management, Web access, communications, and entertainment. A **small office/home office** (*SOHO*) user is a small company or self-employed individual who works from home. SOHO users access the Web to look up information and use basic business software and sometimes industry-specific software. **Mobile users** are employees and students who work on a computer while away from a main office or school. A **power user** uses a workstation or other powerful computer to work with industry-specific software. Power users exist in all types of businesses. A **large business user** works in a company with many employees and uses a computer and computer network to process high volumes of transactions.

⑪ What Computer Applications Are Used in Society? People interact directly with computers in fields such as education, finance, government, health care, science, publishing, travel, and industry. In education, students use computers and software to assist with learning or take distance learning classes. In finance, people use computers for **online banking** and **online investing**. Government offices have Web sites to provide citizens with up-to-date information, and government employees use computers as part of their daily routines. In health care, computers are used to maintain patient records, monitor patients, assist with medical tests and research, correspond with patients, file insurance claims, provide greater precision during operations, and as implants. All branches of science use computers to assist with collecting, analyzing, and modeling data and to communicate with colleagues around the world. Publishers use computers to assist in designing pages and make the content of their works available online. Many vehicles use some type of online navigation system to help people travel more quickly and safely. Industries use **computer-aided manufacturing** (*CAM*) to assist with the manufacturing process.

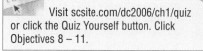

Visit scsite.com/dc2006/ch1/quiz or click the Quiz Yourself button. Click Objectives 8 – 11.

Quizzes and
Learning Games

Computer Genius
Crossword Puzzle
DC Track and Field
Practice Test
Quiz Yourself
Wheel of Terms
You're Hired!

Exercises

Case Studies
Chapter Review
Checkpoint
▶ Key Terms
Learn How To
Learn It Online
Web Research

Beyond the Book

Career Corner
Companies
FAQs
High-Tech Talk
Looking Ahead
Making Use of
the Web
Trailblazers
Web Links

Features

Chapter Forum
Install Computer
Lab Exercises
Maintain Computer
Tech News
Timeline 2006

Key Terms

You should know the Primary Terms and be familiar with the Secondary Terms. Use the list below to help focus your study. To further enhance your understanding of the Key Terms in this chapter, visit scsite.com/dc2006/ch1/terms. See an example of and a definition for each term, and access current and additional information about the term from the Web.

Primary Terms

(shown in bold-black characters in the chapter)

application software (16)
communications device (9)
computer (6)
computer literacy (5)
computer-aided manufacturing (36)
data (6)
desktop computer (20)
embedded computer (24)
FAQ (6)
graphical user interface (GUI) (15)
handheld computer (21)
hardware (7)
home user (26)
information (6)
input device (7)
installing (17)
Internet (12)
Internet-enabled (21)
laptop computer (20)
large business user (30)
mainframe (23)
midrange server (23)
mobile computer (20)
mobile device (20)
mobile users (29)
network (11)
notebook computer (20)
online (11)
online banking (32)
online investing (33)
output device (8)
PDA (22)
personal computer (19)
photo sharing community (14)
power user (29)
program (15)
run (17)
small office/home office (28)
smart phone (22)
smart watch (22)
software (15)
storage device (8)
storage media (8)
supercomputer (23)
system software (15)
system unit (8)
Tablet PC (21)
telecommuting (30)
user (9)
Web (12)
Web page (12)

Secondary Terms

(shown in italic characters in the chapter)

CAM (36)
client (11)
convergence (22)
digital pen (21)
e-commerce (28)
enterprise computing (30)
execute (17)
garbage in, garbage out (10)
handhelds (22)
handtop computer (21)
icon (15)
information processing cycle (6)
information system (25)
information technology (IT) department (30)
instructions (6)
kiosk (30)
loads (17)
memory (8)
multimedia (29)
neural network (34)
operating system (15)
PC-compatible (19)
personal digital assistant (22)
processor (8)
programmer (18)
publish (14)
resources (11)
server (11)
SOHO (28)
stylus (21)
telematics (24)
telemedicine (34)
tower (20)
utility program (16)
Web cam (28)

Checkpoint

Use the Checkpoint exercises to check your knowledge level of the chapter. The Beyond the Book exercises will help broaden your understanding of the concepts presented in this chapter. To complete the Checkpoint exercises interactively, visit scsite.com/dc2006/ch1/check.

 Label the Figure Identify these common computer hardware components.

a. card reader/writer (storage)
b. CD/DVD drive (storage)
c. digital camera (input)
d. floppy disk drive (storage)
e. hard disk drive (storage)
f. keyboard (input)
g. microphone (input)
h. modem (communications)
i. monitor (output)
j. mouse (input)
k. PC video camera (input)
l. printer (output)
m. scanner (input)
n. speaker (output)
o. system unit (processor, memory, storage)
p. USB flash drive (storage)

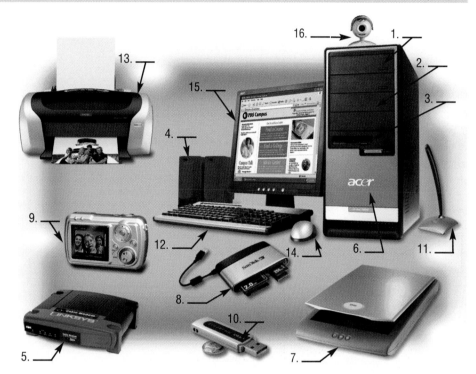

 True/False Mark T for True and F for False. (See page numbers in parentheses.)

_____ 1. Many people believe that computer literacy is vital to success in today's world. (5)

_____ 2. Computers process information into data. (6)

_____ 3. The circuitry of the system unit usually is part of or is connected to a circuit board called the motherboard. (8)

_____ 4. The computing phrase, garbage in, garbage out, points out that the accuracy of a computer's input depends on the accuracy of the output. (10)

_____ 5. When a computer connects to a network, it is offline. (11)

_____ 6. Businesses, called access providers, offer users and companies access to the Internet free or for a fee. (12)

_____ 7. System software serves as the interface between the user, the application software, and the computer's hardware. (15)

_____ 8. Mobile devices usually have disk drives. (21)

_____ 9. To be valuable, information should be accurate, organized, timely, accessible, useful, and cost-effective to produce. (25)

_____ 10. Home users type letters, homework assignments, and other documents with personal finance software. (27)

_____ 11. With online investing, the transaction fee for each trade usually is much more than when trading through a broker. (33)

Quizzes and Learning Games

Computer Genius
Crossword Puzzle
DC Track and Field
Practice Test
Quiz Yourself
Wheel of Terms
You're Hired!

Exercises

Case Studies
Chapter Review
▶ Checkpoint
Key Terms
Learn How To
Learn It Online
Web Research

Beyond the Book

Career Corner
Companies
FAQs
High-Tech Talk
Looking Ahead
Making Use of
the Web
Trailblazers
Web Links

Features

Chapter Forum
Install Computer
Lab Exercises
Maintain Computer
Tech News
Timeline 2006

Checkpoint

 Multiple Choice   Select the best answer. (See page numbers in parentheses.)

1. Computer literacy involves having a knowledge and understanding of _____. (5)
   a. computer programming
   b. computers and their uses
   c. computer repair
   d. all of the above

2. A computer can _____. (6)
   a. accept data
   b. process data according to specified rules
   c. produce and store results
   d. all of the above

3. The series of input, process, output, and storage sometimes is referred to as the _____ cycle. (6)
   a. information processing
   b. computer programming
   c. data entering
   d. Web browsing

4. Commonly used _____ devices are a printer, a monitor, and speakers. (8)
   a. input
   b. storage
   c. output
   d. communications

5. A disadvantage of computers is that _____. (10)
   a. computer operations occur at very slow speeds
   b. the components in computers are undependable
   c. prolonged computer use can lead to injuries
   d. most computers cannot communicate

6. A _____ controls access to the resources on a network. (11)
   a. server
   b. workstation
   c. client
   d. tower

7. _____ can be thought of as a library of information available to anyone connected to the Internet. (12)
   a. The Web
   b. E-mail
   c. Instant messaging
   d. A chat room

8. Popular _____ include(s) Web browsers, word processing software, and spreadsheet software. (16)
   a. system software
   b. operating systems
   c. application software
   d. utility programs

9. Two types of _____ are desktop computers and notebook computers. (19)
   a. embedded computers
   b. supercomputers
   c. midrange servers
   d. personal computers

10. A _____ is a special type of notebook computer that is useful for taking notes in lectures, at meetings, and other forums where the standard notebook computer is not practical. (21)
    a. smart phone
    b. Tablet PC
    c. smart watch
    d. PDA

11. An information system should have readily available documented _____ that address(es) operating the computer and using its applications. (25)
    a. hardware
    b. procedures
    c. software
    d. data

12. Examples of the _____ category of computer users include real estate agents, package delivery people, and meter readers. (29)
    a. mobile user
    b. home user
    c. power user
    d. small office/home office user

13. _____ is a system that attempts to imitate the behavior of the human brain. (34)
    a. Telemedicine
    b. A neural network
    c. E-commerce
    d. A kiosk

14. _____ refers to the use of computers to assist with processes such as fabrication and assembly. (36)
    a. Enterprise computing
    b. Telecommuting
    c. Information processing
    d. Computer-aided manufacturing (CAM)

Checkpoint

Matching

Match the terms with their definitions. (See page numbers in parentheses.)

_____ 1. processor (8)

_____ 2. memory (8)

_____ 3. publish (14)

_____ 4. icon (15)

_____ 5. install (17)

_____ 6. load (17)

_____ 7. execute (17)

_____ 8. stylus (21)

_____ 9. multimedia (29)

_____ 10. kiosk (30)

a. carry out the instructions in a computer program

b. stores instructions waiting to be executed and the data needed

c. set up software to work with a computer and other hardware components

d. collection of computers and devices connected together

e. miniature image that represents a program, an instruction, or some other object

f. combines text, graphics, audio, and video into one application

g. mobile device that can connect to the Internet wirelessly

h. interprets and carries out basic instructions that operate a computer

i. freestanding computer, usually with a touch screen

j. copy a program from storage to memory

k. metal or plastic device that uses pressure to write, draw, or make selections

l. make a Web page available on the Internet for others to see

Short Answer

Write a brief answer to each of the following questions.

1. How is data different from information? _____ What is the information processing cycle? _____

2. How is hardware different from software? _____ What is a programmer? _____

3. What is storage media? _____ What are examples of storage media? _____

4. Why do people use the Web? _____ What can be contained on a Web page? _____

5. What is telecommuting? _____ Why do people telecommute? _____

Beyond the Book

Read the following book elements, learn more about each using the Web, and then write a brief report.

1. At Issue — Is Job Outsourcing Inevitable? (10), Is Everything on the Web True? (14), Can Software Provoke Violence? (16), or Did You Meet Online? (27)

2. Career Corner — Personal Computer Salesperson (37)

3. Companies on the Cutting Edge — Dell or Apple Computer (39)

4. FAQs (6, 8, 14, 17, 20, 20, 22, 27)

5. High-Tech Talk — Analog versus Digital: Making the Conversion (38)

6. Looking Ahead — Bionic People Benefit from Processor Implants (9) or Robots Add the Human Touch (32)

7. Making Use of the Web — Fun and Entertainment (116)

8. Picture Yourself in a Computer Class (2)

9. Technology Trailblazers — Bill Gates or Carly Fiorina (39)

10. Timeline 2006 (52)

11. Web Links (7, 8, 9, 12, 15, 16, 19, 20, 26, 26, 30)

Quizzes and Learning Games

Computer Genius
Crossword Puzzle
DC Track and Field
Practice Test
Quiz Yourself
Wheel of Terms
You're Hired!

Exercises

Case Studies
Chapter Review
Checkpoint
Key Terms
Learn How To
Learn It Online
Web Research

Beyond the Book

Career Corner
Companies
FAQs
High-Tech Talk
Looking Ahead
Making Use of the Web
Trailblazers
Web Links

Features

Chapter Forum
Install Computer
Lab Exercises
Maintain Computer
Tech News
Timeline 2006

Learn It Online

Use the Learn It Online exercises to reinforce your understanding of the chapter concepts. To access the Learn It Online exercises, visit scsite.com/dc2006/ch1/learn.

(1) At the Movies — Walking the PC Pioneer Trail

To view the Walking the PC Pioneer Trail movie, click the number 1 button. Locate your video and click the corresponding High-Speed or Dial-Up link, depending on your Internet connection. Watch the movie and then complete the exercise by answering the question that follows. Many of the pioneers of the technology industry in the United States established their businesses in Silicon Valley. What explanation can you offer for why the founders of these companies all set up shop in this area?

(2) At the Movies — Black Viper's Windows XP Tips

To view the Black Viper's Windows XP Tips movie, click the number 2 button. Locate your video and click the corresponding High-Speed or Dial-Up link, depending on your Internet connection. Watch the movie and then complete the exercise by answering the question that follows. Windows XP is a large and powerful program that often runs many applications that you will never use. These programs require a lot of resources that can be used by other programs. Which of these programs would you turn off to make your computer run more efficiently and faster?

(3) Student Edition Labs — Using Input Devices

Click the number 3 button. When the Student Edition Labs menu appears (screen shown in the figure below), click *Using Input Devices* to begin. A new browser window will open. Follow the on-screen instructions to complete the Lab. When finished, click the Exit button. If required, submit your results to your instructor.

(4) Student Edition Labs — Using Windows

Click the number 4 button. When the Student Edition Labs menu appears, click *Using Windows* to begin. A new browser window will open. Follow the on-screen instructions to complete the Lab. When finished, click the Exit button. If required, submit your results to your instructor.

(5) Practice Test

Click the number 5 button. Answer each question. When completed, enter your name and click the Grade Test button to submit the quiz for grading. Make a note of any missed questions. If required, submit your score to your instructor.

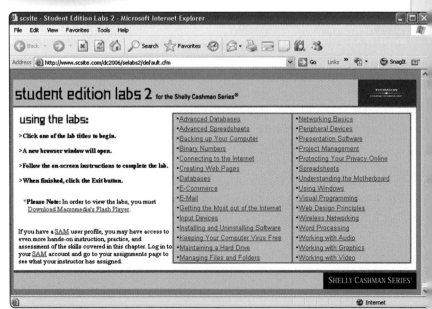

Learn It Online

6 Who Wants To Be a Computer Genius²?

Click the number 6 button to find out if you are a computer genius. Directions about how to play the game will be displayed. When you are ready to play, click the Play button. Submit your score to your instructor.

7 Wheel of Terms

Click the number 7 button to reinforce important terms you learned in this chapter by playing the Shelly Cashman Series version of this popular game. Directions about how to play the game will be displayed. When you are ready to play, click the Play button. Submit your score to your instructor.

8 DC Track and Field

Click the number 8 button to use what you have learned in this chapter to compete against other students in three track and field events. Directions about how to play the game will be displayed. When you are ready to play, click the start first event button. If required, submit your score to your instructor.

9 You're Hired!

Click the number 9 button to use what you have learned in this chapter to embark on the path to a career in computers. Directions about how to play the game will be displayed. When you are ready to play, click the begin game button. If required, submit your score to your instructor.

10 Crossword Puzzle Challenge

Click the number 10 button. Complete the puzzle to reinforce skills you learned in this chapter. Directions about how to play the game will be displayed. When you are ready to play, click the Play button. Submit the completed puzzle to your instructor.

11 Lab Exercises

Click the number 11 button. When the Lab Exercises menu appears, click the exercise assigned by your instructor. A new browser window will open. Follow the on-screen instructions to complete the exercise. When finished, click the Exit button. If required, submit your results to your instructor.

12 Learn the Web

No matter how much computer experience you have, navigating the Web for the first time can be intimidating. How do you get started? Click the number 12 button and click the links to discover how you can find out everything you want to know about the Internet.

13 Chapter Discussion Forum

Select an objective from this chapter on page 3 about which you would like more information. Click the number 13 button and post a short message listing a meaningful message title accompanied by one or more questions concerning the selected objective. In two days, return to the threaded discussion by clicking the number 13 button. Submit to your instructor your original message and at least one response to your message.

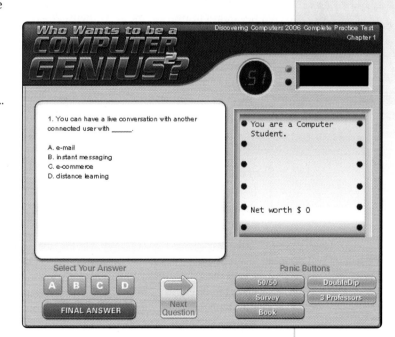

Quizzes and
Learning Games

Computer Genius
Crossword Puzzle
DC Track and Field
Practice Test
Quiz Yourself
Wheel of Terms
You're Hired!

Exercises

Case Studies
Chapter Review
Checkpoint
Key Terms
▶ Learn How To
Learn It Online
Web Research

Beyond the Book

Career Corner
Companies
FAQs
High-Tech Talk
Looking Ahead
Making Use of
the Web
Trailblazers
Web Links

Features

Chapter Forum
Install Computer
Lab Exercises
Maintain Computer
Tech News
Timeline 2006

Learn How To

Use the Learn How To activities to learn fundamental skills when using a computer and accompanying technology. Complete the exercises and submit them to your instructor. Visit scsite.com/dc2006/ch1/howto to obtain more information pertaining to each activity.

LEARN HOW TO 1: Start and Close an Application

An application accomplishes tasks on a computer. You can start any application by using the Start button.

Complete these steps to start the Web browser application called Internet Explorer:

1. Click the Start button (**start**) at the left of the Windows taskbar on the bottom of the screen. _The Start menu is displayed._
2. Point to All Programs on the Start menu. _The All Programs submenu appears (Figure 1-45)._
3. Click the program name, **Internet Explorer**, on the All Programs submenu. _The Internet Explorer browser window opens (Figure 1-46)._

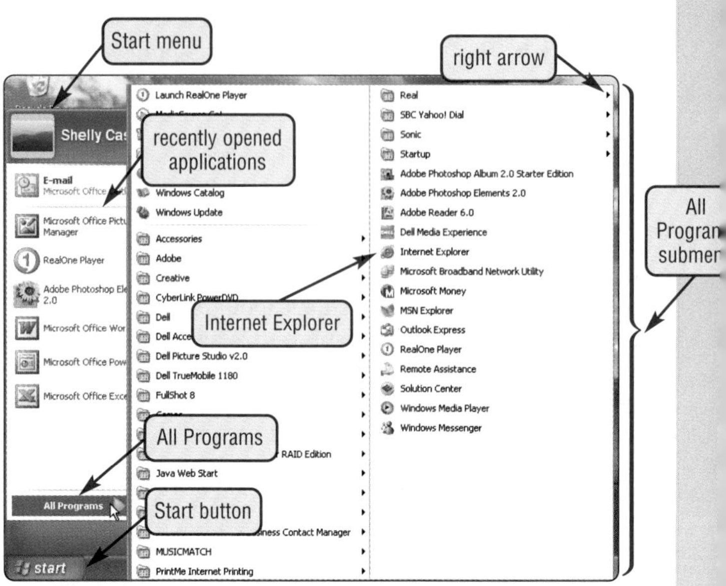

An item on the All Programs submenu might have a small right arrow next to it. When this occurs, point to the item and another submenu will appear. Click the application name on this submenu to start the application. Some application names might appear on the Start menu

FIGURE 1-45

FIGURE 1-46

itself. If so, click any of these names to start the corresponding application.

Below the line on the left side of the Start menu, Windows displays the names of the applications recently opened on the computer. You can start any of these applications by clicking the name of the application.

To close an application, click the Close button (▣) in the upper-right corner of the window. If you have created but not saved a document, Windows will ask if you want to save the document. If you do not want to save it, click the No button in the displayed dialog box. If you want to save it, refer to Learn How To number 1 in Chapter 3 on page 178.

Exercise

1. Using the Start button, start the application named WordPad found on the Accessories submenu of the All Programs submenu. WordPad is a word processing application. Type the following: To start an application, click the application name on the All Programs submenu and then type your name. Click the Print button (🖨) on the toolbar. Submit the printout to your instructor.
2. Close the WordPad application. If you are asked if you want to save changes to the document, click the No button. Start the WordPad application again, type some new text, and then close the WordPad application. When the dialog box is displayed, click the Cancel button. What happened? Now, close the WordPad window without saving the document. Submit your answer to your instructor.

Learn How To

3. Using the Start button, start the e-mail program on the computer. What is the name of the e-mail program? In the program window, what menu names are displayed on the menu bar at the top of the window? Close the e-mail program. Submit your answers to your instructor.

LEARN HOW TO 2: Use the Discovering Computers 2006 Web Site (scsite.com/dc2006)

The Discovering Computers 2006 Web site provides a variety of activities and exercises. To use the site, you first must register and establish a user name and **password**. Perform the following steps to register:
1. Find your key code on the card at the front of this book.
2. Start the Web browser.
3. Type scsite.com/dc2006 in the Address box of the Web browser. Press the ENTER key.
4. When the registration page is displayed, click the New User Registration link.
5. Enter the key code you found in Step 1.
6. Follow the on-screen instructions to complete registration.

When you first type a Web address to display a page from the dc2006 site, you must enter your user name and password to gain access to the site. When you are done using the site, close the browser so no one else can visit the site with your user name and password.

Exercise
1. Start the Web browser on your computer.
2. Type scsite.com/dc2006/ch1/howto in the Address box of the browser and then press the ENTER key.
3. If the registration page is displayed and you have not yet registered, complete the steps above. If you are registered, click Registered User, enter your user name and password, and then click the Submit button.
4. Navigate to the Chapter 1 home page.
5. Visit each of the Exercises Web pages (Chapter Review, Key Terms, Checkpoint, Learn It Online, Learn How To, Web Research, and Case Studies). Use the navigation bar on the left of the screen to display these pages.
6. Click the browser's Close button to close the application.
7. Write a report that describes the use of each of the Exercises pages you visited. Which page do you think will prove the most valuable to you when using the book and the Web site? Why? Which will be the least useful? Why? Submit your report to your instructor.

LEARN HOW TO 3: Find Out About Your Computer

By following these steps, you can find out about your computer:
1. Click the Start button on the Windows XP taskbar.
2. Point to All Programs on the Start menu, point to Accessories on the All Programs submenu, and then point to System Tools on the Accessories submenu.
3. Click **System Information** on the System Tools submenu. Windows displays a system summary in the right side of the window, and an index of categories in the left side of the window (Figure 1-47).

To determine more information about your computer, click any of the plus signs in the left side of the window. Then, click the item about which you want more information.

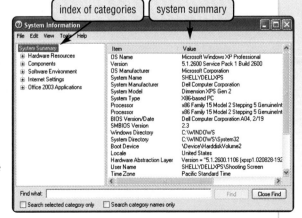

FIGURE 1-47

Exercise
1. Submit the answers to the following questions about your computer:
    a. What type of operating system (OS Name) is in use?
    b. What company manufactured the computer?
    c. How much RAM (physical memory) is on the computer?
    d. How much data can you store on the C: drive?
    e. What is the name of a CD or DVD drive found on the computer?

Quizzes and Learning Games

Computer Genius
Crossword Puzzle
DC Track and Field
Practice Test
Quiz Yourself
Wheel of Terms
You're Hired!

Exercises

Case Studies
Chapter Review
Checkpoint
Key Terms
Learn How To
Learn It Online
▶ Web Research

Beyond the Book

Career Corner
Companies
FAQs
High-Tech Talk
Looking Ahead
Making Use of the Web
Trailblazers
Web Links

Features

Chapter Forum
Install Computer
Lab Exercises
Maintain Computer
Tech News
Timeline 2006

Web Research

Use the Internet-based Web Research exercises to broaden your understanding of the concepts presented in this chapter. Visit scsite.com/dc2006/ch1/research to obtain more information pertaining to each exercise. To discuss any of the Web Research exercises in this chapter with other students, post your thoughts or questions at scsite.com/dc2006/ch1/forum.

① Scavenger Hunt   Use one of the __search engines__ listed in Figure 2-10 in Chapter 2 on page 78 or your own favorite search engine to find the answers to the questions below. Copy and paste the Web address from the Web page where you found the answer. Some questions may have more than one answer. If required, submit your answers to your instructor. (1) What are three accredited online colleges or universities that offer a bachelor's degree in computer information technology? (2) Two National Science Foundation (NSF) programs were established in 1997 to interconnect 50 university and scientific computing sites. What colleges host these two sites? What were the locations of the five original NSF-financed supercomputer centers? (3) Personal finance software helps you balance your checkbook and manage your finances. What is the name of a popular personal finance software program? (4) What is the name of the first spreadsheet program? (5) A programming language developed by the U.S. Department of Defense was named to honor a famous woman mathematician. What is the name of this programming language? Click the Technology link on the left side of the page.

② Search Sleuth   Visit the __Google Web site__ (google.com) and then click the About Google link at the bottom of the page. Using your word processing program, answer the following questions and then, if required, submit your answers to your instructor. (1) Below Our Company, click Corporate Info. Who are the founders of Google? (2) Click the Technology link on the left side of the page. Provide a summary on how Google uses PageRank. (3) Click your browser's Back button or press the BACKSPACE key to return to the About Google page. Below Our Search, click the Google Web Search Features link. What is the purpose of the I'm Feeling Lucky button? What is the purpose of the Similar Pages link? What is Froogle? (4) Click your browser's Back button two times to return to the Google home page. In the Google Search text box, type HTML and click the Google Search button. Approximately how many hits resulted? Do any definitions appear? If so, list the definitions. How much time did it take to complete the search? (5) In the Google Search text box, type HTML Tutorial and click the Search button. Compare this to your earlier search. Are there more or fewer hits? How much time did it take to complete the second search? (6) Click one of the resulting HTML tutorial links and review the tutorial. Write a 50-word summary of the tutorial. Using the information contained within the tutorial, do you think you would be able to create your own Web site?

③ Newsgroups   One of the more popular topics for __newsgroups__ is the Internet. Find three newsgroups, such as those listed in CyberFiber (cyberfiber.com/internet.htm) or Google Groups, that discuss an aspect of the Internet. Read the newsgroup postings and post a reply to one message. Summarize three topics under discussion and your reply to a message.

④ Journaling   Respond to your readings in this chapter by writing at least one page about your reactions, evaluations, and reflections about computer usage in your home. For example, how many appliances in your kitchen have a computer component? Has your __smart phone__ replaced a camera or landline telephone? Have family members reduced their television viewing time with playing online games or surfing the Internet? You also can write about the new terms you learned by reading this chapter. If required, submit your journal to your instructor.

⑤ Ethics in Action   The Internet has increased the ease with which students can plagiarize material for research paper assignments. Teachers are using online services, such as Turnitin.com, to help detect plagiarized papers and to help students understand how to cite sources correctly. Visit the __Turnitin site__ (turnitin.com) and then write a summary of how this service is used. How prevalent is plagiarism on your campus? What action should an instructor take when a student submits a plagiarized paper? If required, submit your summary to your instructor.

Case Studies

Use the Case Studies to apply the concepts presented in the chapter to real-world situations. Visit scsite.com/dc2006/ch1/cases to obtain more information pertaining to each exercise. To discuss the Case Studies in this chapter with other students, visit scsite.com/dc2006/ch1/forum and post your thoughts or questions.

CASE STUDY 1 — Class Discussion   You are a clerical worker for a small property management company. The company manages 30 industrial buildings. Currently, you serve as a receptionist, answer the telephone, file business documents, and perform other clerical tasks. Eventually, however, you would like to be promoted to an administrative position. Your supervisor has just purchased a new computer for the office. She has made it clear that, in order to be promoted, you must become proficient in the use of computers and **computer software**. Review the course offerings at your school. Prepare a list of courses you could take that would help you acquire the knowledge and skills you need to be promoted. Draft a memo to your supervisor detailing the courses you plan to take and explaining why each would be valuable. Be prepared to discuss your findings.

CASE STUDY 2 — Class Discussion   You are a member of your local school district's board of education. Over the past year, the number of computers purchased by the district increased by 85 percent, while the supply of library books declined by almost 10 percent. School officials claim that computers extend learning opportunities and develop the **computer literacy** needed in today's technological world. Yet, some parents are complaining that computer purchases represent frivolous, status-seeking spending. Notebook computers are purchased for teachers, while textbooks and library books are too old, too worn, and too scarce. Use the Web and/or print media to learn how computers are being used in schools. As a school board member, draft a proposal recommending the percentage of the instructional materials budget that should be spent on computers versus the percentage that should be spent on library books and textbooks. Note the factors that influenced your decision. Be prepared to discuss your recommendations.

CASE STUDY 3 — Research   Computers are everywhere. Watching television, driving a car, using a charge card, even ordering fast food all involve computers, not to mention browsing the Web on your personal computer. Your car computer is an **embedded computer** that can be described as special-purpose, because it only accepts specific input and performs limited functions. Your personal computer, on the other hand, is general-purpose, meaning it accepts a wide range of input and can perform a variety of tasks. For one day, make a list of each computer you encounter (be careful not to limit yourself just to the computers you see). How is the computer used? Is the computer special-purpose or general-purpose? Why? How was the task the computer performs accomplished before computers? Write a brief report or use PowerPoint to create a presentation and share your findings.

CASE STUDY 4 — Research   You are an assistant manager at a local computer store. Your manager suspects that for cultural, financial, or societal reasons, certain groups of people are more likely to buy computers than others. To increase the impact of the store's promotions, your manager has asked you to discover if computers are purchased by individuals from a broad spectrum, or if a certain type exists that represents most **computer buyers**. Use the Web and/or print media to learn more about the demographics of computer buyers. What gender are most buyers? In what age range do they fall? What seems to be the typical educational level? What is the approximate average income of a typical buyer? Do buyers tend to share any other characteristics? If you discover any trends, what reasons might be behind the results? Write a brief report or use PowerPoint to create a presentation and share your findings.

CASE STUDY 5 — Team Challenge   People use computers in a variety of fields, including education, finance, government, health care, science, publishing, travel, and industry. Although the way people use computers varies, each use of a computer involves **computer hardware**, computer software, and normally some type of communications capability over networks, such as the Internet. Form a three-member team and choose a field in which you all are interested. Using the Web and/or print media, assign one member of your team to investigate hardware used in the field, another member to investigate software used in the field, and the third member to investigate communications capabilities used in the field. After your investigation, characterize a hypothetical business or organization in the field. Based on your investigation, prepare a report that recommends specific hardware, software, and networking capabilities that would be best for the business or organization; explain your recommendations in the report.

Timeline 2006

MILESTONES IN COMPUTER HISTORY

Dr. John V. Atanasoff and Clifford Berry design and build the first electronic digital computer. Their machine, the Atanasoff-Berry-Computer, or ABC, provides the foundation for advances in electronic digital computers.

John von Neumann in front of the electronic computer built at the Institute for Advanced Study. This computer and its von Neumann architecture served as the prototype for subsequent stored program computers worldwide.

William Shockley, John Bardeen, and Walter Brattain invent the transfer resistance device, eventually called the transistor. The transistor would revolutionize computers, proving much more reliable than vacuum tubes.

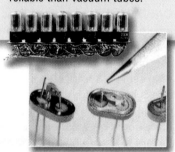

1937 — **1943** — **1945** — **1946** — **1947** — **1951**

Dr. John W. Mauchly and J. Presper Eckert, Jr. complete work on the first large-scale electronic, general-purpose digital computer. The ENIAC (Electronic Numerical Integrator And Computer) weighs 30 tons, contains 18,000 vacuum tubes, occupies a 30-by-50-foot space, and consumes 160 kilowatts of power. The first time it is turned on, lights dim in an entire section of Philadelphia.

The first commercially available electronic digital computer, the UNIVAC I (UNIVersal Automatic Computer), is introduced by Remington Rand. Public awareness of computers increases when the UNIVAC I, after analyzing only five percent of the popular vote, correctly predicts that Dwight D. Eisenhower will win the presidential election.

During World War II, British scientist Alan Turing designs the Colossus, an electronic computer created for the military to break German codes. The computer's existence is kept secret until the 1970s.

Dr. Grace Hopper considers the concept of reusable software in her paper, "The Education of a Computer." The paper describes how to program a computer with symbolic notation instead of the detailed machine language that had been used.

The IBM 305 RAMAC system is the first to use magnetic disk for external storage. The system provides storage capacity similar to magnetic tape that previously was used, but offers the advantage of semi-random access capability.

Fortran (FORmula TRANslation), an efficient, easy-to-use programming language, is introduced by John Backus.

More than 200 programming languages have been created.

IBM introduces two smaller, desk-sized computers: the IBM 1401 for business and the IBM 1620 for scientists. The IBM 1620 initially is called the CADET, but IBM drops the name when campus wags claim it is an acronym for, Can't Add, Doesn't Even Try.

1952   1953   1957   1958   1959   1960

The IBM model 650 is one of the first widely used computers. Originally planning to produce only 50 machines, the system is so successful that eventually IBM manufactures more than 1,000. With the IBM 700 series of machines, the company will dominate the mainframe market for the next decade.

Core memory, developed in the early 1950s, provides much larger storage capacity than vacuum tube memory.

Jack Kilby of Texas Instruments invents the integrated circuit, which lays the foundation for high-speed computers and large-capacity memories. Computers built with transistors mark the beginning of the second generation of computer hardware.

COBOL, a high-level business application language, is developed by a committee headed by Dr. Grace Hopper. COBOL uses English-like phrases and runs on most business computers, making it one of the more widely used programming languages.

Computer Science Corporation becomes the first software company listed on the New York Stock Exchange.

Dr. John Kemeny of Dartmouth leads the development of the BASIC programming language. BASIC will be widely used on personal computers.

IBM

Under pressure from the industry, IBM announces that some of its software will be priced separately from the computer hardware. This unbundling allows software firms to emerge in the industry.

Digital Equipment Corporation (DEC) introduces the first minicomputer, the PDP-8. The machine is used extensively as an interface for time-sharing systems.

In a letter to the editor titled, "GO TO Statements Considered Harmful," Dr. Edsger Dijsktra introduces the concept of structured programming, developing standards for constructing computer programs.

ARPANET

The ARPANET network, a predecessor of the Internet, is established.

1964 — 1965 — 1968 — 1969 — 1970

The number of computers has grown to 18,000. Third-generation computers, with their controlling circuitry stored on chips, are introduced. The IBM System/360 computer is the first family of compatible machines, merging science and business lines.

Alan Shugart at IBM demonstrates the first regular use of an 8-inch floppy (magnetic storage) disk.

Fourth-generation computers, built with chips that use LSI (large-scale integration) arrive. While the chips used in 1965 contained as many as 1,000 circuits, the LSI chip contains as many as 15,000.

IBM introduces the term word processing for the first time with its Magnetic Tape/Selectric Typewriter (MT/ST). The MT/ST was the first reusable storage medium that allowed typed material to be edited without having to retype the document.

MITS, Inc. advertises one of the first microcomputers, the Altair. Named for the destination in an episode of *Star Trek*, the Altair is sold in kits for less than $400. Although initially it has no keyboard, no monitor, no permanent memory, and no software, 4,000 orders are taken within the first three months.

VisiCalc, a spreadsheet program written by Bob Frankston and Dan Bricklin, is introduced. Originally written to run on Apple II computers, VisiCalc will be seen as the most important reason for the acceptance of personal computers in the business world.

The IBM PC is introduced, signaling IBM's entrance into the personal computer marketplace. The IBM PC quickly garners the largest share of the personal computer market and becomes the personal computer of choice in business.

Ethernet, the first local area network (LAN), is developed at Xerox PARC (Palo Alto Research Center) by Robert Metcalf. The LAN allows computers to communicate and share software, data, and peripherals. Initially designed to link minicomputers, Ethernet will be extended to personal computers.

The first public online information services, CompuServe and the Source, are founded.

1971   1975   1976   1979   1980   1981

Dr. Ted Hoff of Intel Corporation develops a microprocessor, or microprogrammable computer chip, the Intel 4004.

IBM offers Microsoft Corporation cofounder, Bill Gates, the opportunity to develop the operating system for the soon-to-be announced IBM personal computer. With the development of MS-DOS, Microsoft achieves tremendous growth and success.

The first computer virus, Elk Cloner, is spread via Apple II floppy disks, which contained the operating system. A short rhyme would appear on the screen when the user pressed Reset after the 50th boot of an infected disk.

Steve Jobs and Steve Wozniak build the first Apple computer. A subsequent version, the Apple II, is an immediate success. Adopted by elementary schools, high schools, and colleges, for many students, the Apple II is their first contact with the world of computers.

Alan Shugart presents the Winchester hard drive, revolutionizing storage for personal computers.

Special Feature

scsite.com/dc2006/ch1/timeline

3,275,000 personal computers are sold, almost 3,000,000 more than in 1981.

Apple introduces the Macintosh computer, which incorporates a unique, easy-to-learn, graphical user interface.

Compaq, Inc. is founded to develop and market IBM-compatible PCs.

Hayes introduces the 300 bps smart modem. The modem is an immediate success.

Hewlett-Packard announces the first LaserJet printer for personal computers.

Microsoft has public stock offering and raises approximately $61 million. Within 20 years, Microsoft's stock is worth nearly $350 billion or 5,735 times the amount raised in the initial public stock offering.

| 1982 | 1983 | 1984 | 1986 | 1988 |

Lotus Development Corporation is founded. Its spreadsheet software, Lotus 1-2-3, which combines spreadsheet, graphics, and database programs in one package, becomes the best-selling program for IBM personal computers.

Instead of choosing a person for its annual award, *TIME* magazine names the computer Machine of the Year for 1982, acknowledging the impact of computers on society.

Microsoft surpasses Lotus Development Corporation to become the world's top software vendor.

While working at CERN, Switzerland, Tim Berners-Lee invents an Internet-based hypermedia enterprise for information sharing. Berners-Lee will call this innovation the World Wide Web.

World Wide Web Consortium releases standards that describe a framework for linking documents on different computers.

Several companies introduce computers using the Pentium processor from Intel. The Pentium chip is the successor to the Intel 486 processor. It contains 3.1 million transistors and is capable of performing 112,000,000 instructions per second.

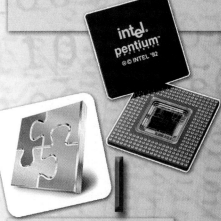

Microsoft releases Microsoft Office 3 Professional, the first version of Microsoft Office.

1989   **1991**   **1992**   **1993**

The Intel 486 becomes the world's first 1,000,000 transistor microprocessor. It crams 1.2 million transistors on a .4" x .6" sliver of silicon and executes 15,000,000 instructions per second — four times as fast as its predecessor, the 80386 chip.

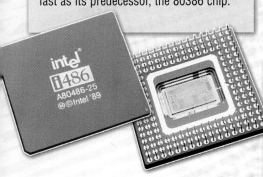

Microsoft releases Windows 3.1, the latest version of its Windows operating system. Windows 3.1 offers improvements such as TrueType fonts, multimedia capability, and object linking and embedding (OLE). In two months, 3,000,000 copies of Windows 3.1 are sold.

The White House launches its Web site, which includes an interactive citizens' handbook and White House history and tours.

Special Feature

U.S. Robotics introduces PalmPilot, a handheld personal organizer. The PalmPilot's user friendliness and low price make it a standout next to more expensive personal digital assistants (PDAs).

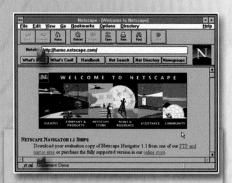

Jim Clark and Marc Andreessen found Netscape and launch Netscape Navigator 1.0, a browser for the World Wide Web.

Sun Microsystems launches Java, an object-oriented programming language that allows users to write one application for a variety of computer platforms. Java becomes one of the hotter Internet technologies.

Microsoft releases Windows NT 4.0, an operating system for client-server networks. Windows NT's management tools and wizards make it easier for developers to build and deploy business applications.

1994   1995   1996

Linus Torvalds creates the Linux kernel, a UNIX-like operating system that he releases free across the Internet for further enhancement by other programmers.

Microsoft releases Windows 95, a major upgrade to its Windows operating system. Windows 95 consists of more than 10,000,000 lines of computer instructions developed by 300 person-years of effort. More than 50,000 individuals and companies test the software before it is released.

Two out of three employees in the United States have access to a personal computer, and one out of every three homes has a personal computer. Fifty million personal computers are sold worldwide and more than 250,000,000 are in use.

Apple and Microsoft sign a joint technology development agreement. Microsoft buys $150,000,000 of Apple stock.

More than 10,000,000 people take up telecommuting, which is the capability of working at home and communicating with an office via computer. Increasingly more firms embrace telecommuting to help increase productivity, reduce absenteeism, and provide greater job satisfaction.

Apple Computer introduces the iMac, the next version of its popular Macintosh computer. The iMac abandons such conventional features as a floppy disk drive but wins customers with its futuristic design, see-through case, and easy setup. Consumer demand outstrips Apple's production capabilities, and some vendors are forced to begin waiting lists.

DVD, the next generation of optical disc storage technology, is introduced. DVD can store computer, audio, and video data in a single format, with the capability of producing near-studio quality. By year's end, 500,000 DVD players are shipped worldwide.

1997

1998

Intel introduces the Pentium II processor with 7.5 million transistors. The new processor, which incorporates MMX technology, processes video, audio, and graphics data more efficiently and supports applications such as movie editing, gaming, and more.

E-commerce, or electronic commerce — the marketing of goods and services over the Internet — booms. Companies such as Dell, E*TRADE, and Amazon.com spur online shopping, allowing buyers to obtain everything from hardware and software to financial and travel services, insurance, automobiles, books, and more.

Microsoft releases Internet Explorer 4.0 and seizes a key place in the Internet arena. This new Web browser is greeted with tremendous customer demand.

Microsoft ships Windows 98, an upgrade to Windows 95. Windows 98 offers improved Internet access, better system performance, and support for a new generation of hardware and software. In six months, more than 10,000,000 copies of Windows 98 are sold worldwide.

Fifty million users are connected to the Internet and World Wide Web.

Special Feature

scsite.com/dc2006/ch1/timeline

Governments and businesses frantically work to make their computers Y2K (Year 2000) compliant, spending more than $500 billion worldwide. Y2K non-compliant computers cannot distinguish whether 01/01/00 refers to 1900 or 2000, and thus may operate using a wrong date. This Y2K bug can affect any application that relies on computer chips, such as ATMs, airplanes, energy companies, and the telephone system. In the end, the Y2K bug turned out not to be a problem.

Shawn Fanning, 19, and his company, Napster, turn the music industry upside down by developing software that allows computer users to swap music files with one another without going through a centralized file server. The Recording Industry of America, on behalf of five media companies, sues Napster for copyright infringement and wins.

U.S. District Judge Thomas Penfield Jackson rules in the antitrust lawsuit brought by the Department of Justice and 19 states that Microsoft used its monopoly power to stifle competition.

1999

2000

Microsoft introduces Office 2000, its premier productivity suite, offering new tools for users to create content and save it directly to a Web site without any file conversion or special steps.

E-commerce achieves mainstream acceptance. Annual e-commerce sales exceed $100 billion, and Internet advertising expenditures reach more than $5 billion.

Open Source Code software, such as the Linux operating system and the Apache Web server created by unpaid volunteers, begin to gain wide acceptance among computer users.

Dot-com companies (Internet based) go out of business at a record pace — nearly one per day — as financial investors withhold funding due to the companies' unprofitability.

Microsoft ships Windows 2000 and Windows Me. Windows 2000 offers improved behind-the-scene security and reliability. Windows Me is designed for home users and lets them edit home movies, share digital photos, index music, and create a home network.

Intel unveils its Pentium 4 chip with clock speeds starting at 1.4 GHz. The Pentium 4 includes 42 million transistors, nearly twice as many contained on its predecessor, the Pentium III.

Microsoft releases major operating system updates with Windows XP for the desktop and servers, and Pocket PC 2002 for handheld computers. Windows XP is significantly more reliable than previous versions, features a 32-bit computing architecture, and offers a new look and feel. Pocket PC 2002 offers the handheld computer user a familiar Windows interface and consistent functionality.

According to the U.S. Department of Commerce, Internet traffic is doubling every 100 days, resulting in an annual growth rate of more than 700 percent. It has taken radio and television 30 years and 15 years, respectively, to reach 60 million people. The Internet has achieved the same audience base in 3 years.

2000

2001

Telemedicine uses satellite technology and videoconferencing to broadcast consultations and to perform distant surgeries. Robots are used for complex and precise tasks. Computer-aided surgery uses virtual reality to assist with training and planning procedures.

Microsoft introduces Office XP, the next version of the world's leading suite of productivity software. Features include speech and handwriting recognition, smart tags, and task panes.

Avid readers enjoy e-books, which are digital texts read on compact computer screens. E-books can hold the equivalent of 10 traditional books containing text and graphics. Readers can search, highlight text, and add notes.

Special Feature

scsite.com/dc2006/ch1/timeline

DVD writers begin to replace CD writers (CD-RW). DVDs can store up to eight times as much data as CDs. Uses include storing home movies, music, photos, and backups. Digital cameras and video editors help the average user develop quality video to store on DVDs.

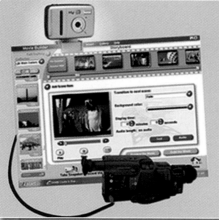

After several years of negligible sales, the Tablet PC is reintroduced as the next-generation mobile PC. The lightweight device, the size of a three-ring notebook, is ideal for people on the go. It runs Windows XP Tablet PC Edition, has wireless capabilities, and features natural input capabilities including pen and speech technologies.

Digital video cameras, DVD writers, easy-to-use video editing software, and improvements in storage capabilities allow the average computer user to create Hollywood-like videos with introductions, conclusions, scenes rearranged, music, and voice-over.

2002

Microsoft launches its .NET strategy, which is a new environment for developing and running software applications featuring ease of development of Web-based services. Users of applications immediately see the benefit of .NET as instant access to data and services in the context of their current task.

Handspring begins shipping the Treo communicator, a handheld computer with cellular telephone, e-mail, text messaging, and wireless Web capabilities.

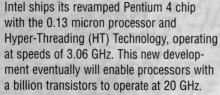

Intel ships its revamped Pentium 4 chip with the 0.13 micron processor and Hyper-Threading (HT) Technology, operating at speeds of 3.06 GHz. This new development eventually will enable processors with a billion transistors to operate at 20 GHz.

U.S. District Judge Colleen Kollar-Kotelly rules against the nine states appealing the antitrust settlement reached between Microsoft and the Justice Department. The nine states were seeking tougher sanctions against the software giant for abusing its monopoly power. Two of the nine states, Massachusetts and West Virginia, plan to appeal the latest ruling to the U.S. District Court of Appeals.

Computer manufacturers and software companies integrate high-end PCs and entertainment devices. The result is PCs with great entertainment functions that let you watch and record TV, burn CDs and DVDs, play games, and more.

IBM puts its weight behind On Demand computing. Its intention is to invest up to $10 billion in hardware and software, and then sell computing time and the use of applications to businesses in a manner similar to an electric utility company.

Wireless computers and devices, such as keyboards, mouse devices, home networks, and public Internet access points become commonplace. Latest operating systems include support for both the Wi-Fi (wireless fidelity) and Bluetooth standards. Wireless capabilities are standard on many PDAs and Tablet PCs.

2003

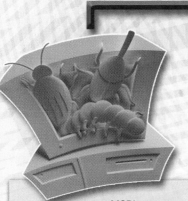

In an attempt to maintain their current business model of selling songs, the Recording Industry Association of American (RIAA) files over 250 lawsuits against individual computer users who offer copyrighted music over peer-to-peer networks.

MSBlast worm and SoBig virus plague Microsoft Windows users. Microsoft Corporation responds by creating the Anti-Virus Reward Program, initially funded with $5 million, to help law enforcement agencies identify and bring to justice those who illegally release damaging worms, viruses and other types of malicious code on the Internet.

Microsoft ships Office 2003, the latest version of its flagship Office suite. New features include a consistent user interface, an overhauled Outlook, increased emphasis on task panes, improved collaboration, enhanced XML functionality, and a new application called OneNote for organizing your notes.

Companies such as RealNetworks, Microsoft, Sony, and Wal-Mart stake out turf in the online music store business started by Apple Computer. In the previous year, Apple's iTunes Music Store Web site sold nearly 20 million songs for 99 cents each.

Flat-panel LCD monitors overtake bulky CRT monitors as the popular choice of computer users. Although flat-panel LCD monitors cost more, they offer several advantages including physical size, weight, true display size, better power consumption, and no radiation emission.

USB Flash Drives, which are small enough to fit on a key chain but can store up to 4 billion characters, become a cost-effective way to transport data and information from one computer to another.

2004

Linux, the open-source operating system, makes major inroads into the server market as a viable alternative to Microsoft Windows, Sun's Solaris, and the UNIX operating systems.

Major retailers begin requiring suppliers to include Radio Frequency Identification (RFID) tags or microchips with antennas, which can be as small as 1/3 of a millimeter across, in the goods they sell. When a transponder receives a certain radio query, it responds by transmitting its unique ID code. Besides carrying out the functions of the bar code, RFIDs may eventually eliminate long checkout lines.

Apple Computer introduces the sleek iMac G5. The new computer's display device contains the system unit.

106 million, or 53 percent, of the 200 million online population in America accesses the Internet via speedy broadband.

Microsoft
Windows^{XP}
Media Center Edition 2005

Spyware
Spam
Phishing
Spim Spit

The Mozilla Foundation, the creators of the free open source Firefox browser, predicts that by the end of 2005, it will have 10 percent of the browser market, primarily at the expense of Microsoft's Internet Explorer (IE) security-plagued browser.

Microsoft unveils Windows XP Media Center Edition 2005. This operating system allows users to access the routine capabilities of a Windows XP-based PC while focusing on delivering media content such as music, digital photography, movies, and television.

Spam, spyware, phishing, spim, and spit take center stage, along with viruses, as major nuisances to the 801 million computer users worldwide. Spam, which accounts for 45 percent of all e-mail, involves the sending of bulk e-mail that is unsolicited and masks its origin. Spyware is a program placed on the computer without the user's knowledge that secretly collects information about the user, often related to Web browsing habits. Phishing is the act of sending an e-mail to a user falsely claiming to be a legitimate enterprise in an attempt to trick the user into surrendering private information that will be used for identity theft. Spim is spam via instant messaging. Spit is spam via Internet telephony.

The OQO handheld computer is a fully-functional Windows XP computer with desktop capabilities. Just 4.9 inches long, 3.4 inches wide, .9 inch thick, and weighing only 14 ounces, the OQO fills the void between the bulk and awkwardness of a notebook computer and the limited capability of a smart phone or PDA.

2005

The smart phone overtakes the PDA as the personal mobile device of choice. A smart phone offers a cellular phone, full personal information management and e-mail functionality, a Web browser, instant message capabilities, and even the ability to listen to music, play video and games, and take pictures with its built-in camera.

To date, Microsoft has sold over 300 million copies of its Windows XP operating system. By early January, Microsoft automatically downloaded to its users' computers over 100 million copies of Service Pack 2 (SP2), its latest update to Windows XP. In addition to a new security center and firewall, SP2 adds a pop-up blocker in Internet Explorer and updated support for Wi-Fi and Bluetooth wireless technologies.

Microsoft introduces Visual Studio 2005. The product includes Visual Basic, Visual C#, Visual J#, Visual C++, and SQL Server. Microsoft also releases a Visual Studio 2005 Express Edition for hobbyists, students, and nonprofessionals.

Microsoft
Visual Studio 2005

CHAPTER TWO

The Internet and World Wide Web

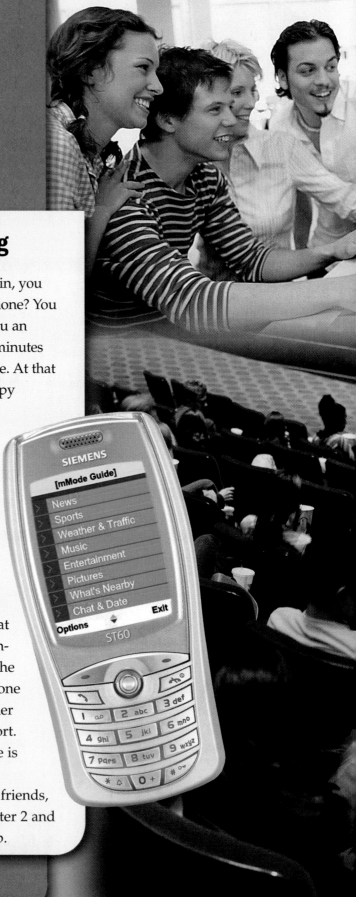

Picture Yourself Instant Messaging

While eating popcorn and waiting for the movie to begin, you hear an alarm. Did you forget to turn off your smart phone? You look at the phone and notice that a friend is sending you an instant message from her home computer. With a few minutes until the lights dim in the theater, you open the message. At that moment, a chorus of your friends' voices singing "Happy Birthday" loudly plays through the phone while the same words appear on the phone's screen. Quickly, you turn off the phone's sound and look around — hoping no one heard. No such luck. Nearly everyone in the theater found it quite amusing.

With the phone's sound turned off, you press some buttons to reply to the instant message, thanking your musical friends for their greeting. Your friend replies that she just bought a PC video camera and wanted to try sending a video instant message over her high-speed Internet line. Everyone gathered at her house to sing and send you the message. After conversing for a few minutes, you punch in C U L8R on the phone and set your online status to Away — so everyone knows you will be unavailable. Then, you press another button to display the Cubs score and the weather report. Next, you decide to check e-mail messages. The movie is starting . . . time to disconnect from the Internet.

To learn how technology allows you access to your friends, sports scores, weather reports, and e-mail, read Chapter 2 and discover features of the Internet and World Wide Web.

After completing this chapter, you will be able to:

1. Discuss the history of the Internet
2. Explain how to access and connect to the Internet
3. Analyze an IP address
4. Identify the components of a Web address
5. Explain the purpose of a Web browser
6. Search for information on the Web
7. Describe the types of Web sites
8. Recognize how Web pages use graphics, animation, audio, video, virtual reality, and plug-ins
9. Identify the steps required for Web publishing
10. Describe the types of e-commerce
11. Explain how e-mail, FTP, newsgroups and message boards, mailing lists, chat rooms, instant messaging, and Internet telephony work
12. Identify the rules of netiquette

CONTENTS

THE INTERNET

HISTORY OF THE INTERNET

HOW THE INTERNET WORKS
Connecting to the Internet
Access Providers
How Data Travels the Internet
Internet Addresses

THE WORLD WIDE WEB
Browsing the Web
Web Addresses
Navigating Web Pages
Searching for Information on the Web
Types of Web Sites
Evaluating a Web Site
Multimedia on the Web
Web Publishing

E-COMMERCE

OTHER INTERNET SERVICES
E-Mail
FTP
Newsgroups and Message Boards
Mailing Lists
Chat Rooms
Instant Messaging
Internet Telephony

NETIQUETTE

CHAPTER SUMMARY

HIGH-TECH TALK
A Computer's Internet Protocol (IP) Address

COMPANIES ON THE CUTTING EDGE
Google
Yahoo!

TECHNOLOGY TRAILBLAZERS
Tim Berners-Lee
Meg Whitman

THE INTERNET

One of the major reasons business, home, and other users purchase computers is for Internet access. Through the Internet, society has access to global information and instant communications. Further, access to the Internet can occur anytime from a computer anywhere: at home, at work, at school, in a restaurant, on an airplane, and even at the beach.

The **Internet**, also called the *Net*, is a worldwide collection of networks that links millions of businesses, government agencies, educational institutions, and individuals. Each of the networks on the Internet provides resources that add to the abundance of goods, services, and information accessible via the Internet.

Today, more than one billion users around the world connect to the Internet for a variety of reasons, some of which are shown in Figure 2-1. The World Wide Web and e-mail are two of the more widely accessed Internet services. Other services include FTP (File Transfer Protocol), newsgroups, chat rooms, instant messaging, and Internet telephony. To enhance your understanding of these services, the chapter begins by discussing the history of the Internet and how the Internet works and then explains each of these services.

FIGURE 2-1a (Web)

FIGURE 2-1c (FTP – File Transfer Protocol)

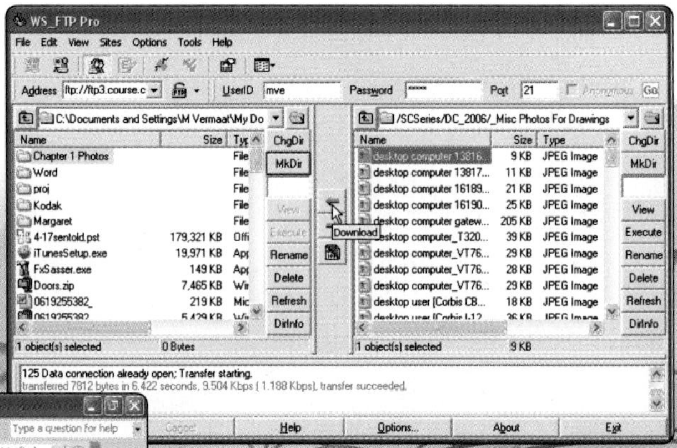

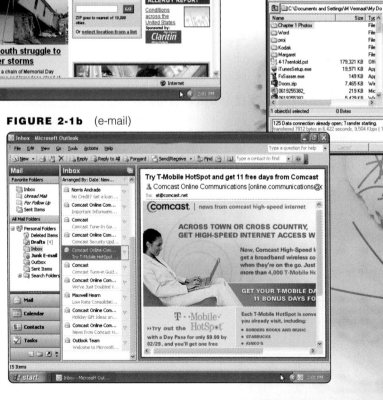

FIGURE 2-1b (e-mail)

FIGURE 2-1 Users around the world connect to the Internet to access the Web, send e-mail messages, transfer documents and photographs, post messages, chat with a group, or have a private conversation with an online friend(s) or family member(s).

HISTORY OF THE INTERNET

The Internet has its roots in a networking project started by the Pentagon's *Advanced Research Projects Agency* (*ARPA*), an agency of the U.S. Department of Defense. ARPA's goal was to build a network that (1) allowed scientists at different physical locations to share information and work together on military and scientific projects and (2) could function even if part of the network were disabled or destroyed by a disaster such as a nuclear attack. That network, called *ARPANET*, became functional in September 1969, linking scientific and academic researchers across the United States.

The original ARPANET consisted of four main computers, one each located at the University of California at Los Angeles, the University of California at Santa Barbara, the Stanford Research Institute, and the University of Utah. Each computer served as a host on the network. A *host*, more commonly known today as a server, is any computer that provides services and connections to other computers on a network. Hosts often use high-speed communications to transfer data and messages over a network.

As researchers and others realized the great benefit of using ARPANET's e-mail to share data and information, ARPANET underwent phenomenal growth. By 1984, ARPANET had more than 1,000 individual computers linked as hosts. Today, more than 200 million hosts connect to the Internet.

Some organizations connected entire networks to ARPANET to take advantage of the high-speed communications it offered. In 1986, the

FIGURE 2-1d (newsgroup)

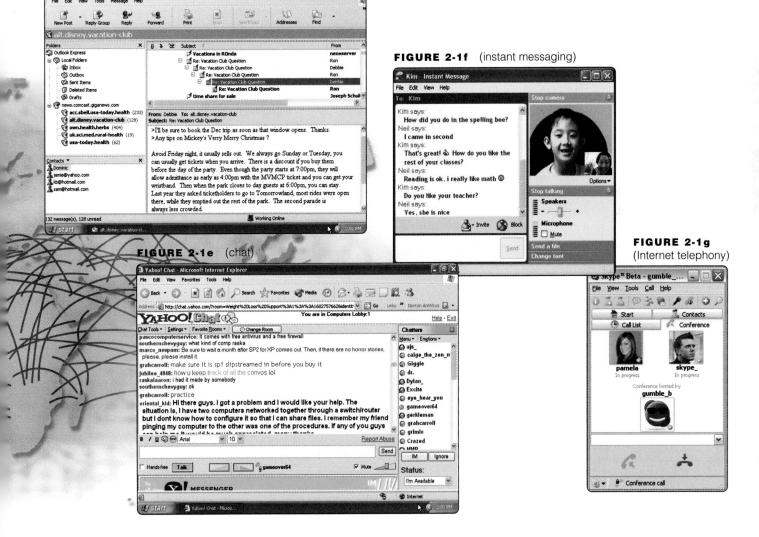

FIGURE 2-1f (instant messaging)

FIGURE 2-1g (Internet telephony)

FIGURE 2-1e (chat)

National Science Foundation (NSF) connected its huge network of five supercomputer centers, called *NSFnet*, to ARPANET. This configuration of complex networks and hosts became known as the Internet.

Until 1995, NSFnet handled the bulk of the communications activity, or **traffic**, on the Internet. In 1995, NSFnet terminated its network on the Internet and resumed its status as a research network.

Today, the Internet consists of many local, regional, national, and international networks. Numerous corporations, commercial firms, and other companies provide networks to handle the Internet traffic. Both public and private organizations own networks on the Internet. These networks, along with telephone companies, cable and satellite companies, and the government, all contribute toward the internal structure of the Internet. Read Looking Ahead 2-1 for a look at the next generation of the Internet.

Even as the Internet grows, it remains a public, cooperative, and independent network. Each organization on the Internet is responsible only for maintaining its own network. No single person, company, institution, or government agency controls or owns the Internet. The *World Wide Web Consortium* (*W3C*), however, oversees research and sets standards and guidelines for many areas of the Internet. The mission of the W3C is to contribute to the growth of the Web. About 350 organizations from around the world are members of the W3C. They advise, define standards, and address other issues.

HOW THE INTERNET WORKS

Data sent over the Internet travels via networks and communications media owned and operated by many companies. The following sections present various ways to connect to these networks on the Internet.

Connecting to the Internet

Employees and students often connect to the Internet through a business or school network. In this case, the computers usually are part of a network that connects to an Internet access provider through a high-speed connection line leased from a telephone company.

Many homes use dial-up access to connect to the Internet. **Dial-up access** takes place when the modem in your computer uses a standard telephone line to connect to the Internet. This type of access is an easy and inexpensive way for users to connect to the Internet. A dial-up connection, however, is slow-speed technology.

Some home and small business users are opting for higher-speed *broadband* Internet connections through DSL, cable television networks, radio signals, or satellite.

- **DSL** (*digital subscriber line*) is a technology that provides high-speed Internet connections using regular copper telephone lines.
- A **cable modem** allows access to high-speed Internet services through the cable television network.
- *Fixed wireless* high-speed Internet connections use an antenna on your house or business to communicate with a tower location via radio signals.
- A *satellite modem* communicates with a satellite dish to provide high-speed Internet connections via satellite.

In most cases, broadband Internet access is always on. That is, it is connected to the Internet the entire time the computer is running. With dial-up access, by contrast, you must establish the connection to the Internet. Usually a modem dials the telephone number to the Internet access provider.

Mobile users access the Internet using a variety of technologies. Most hotels and airports provide dial-up or broadband Internet connections. Wireless Internet access technologies, such as through radio networks, enable mobile users to connect easily to the Internet with notebook computers, Tablet PCs, PDAs, smart

LOOKING AHEAD 2-1

Internet Speeds into the Future

The Internet of the future will be much larger and faster. According to some Internet experts, in the next 20 years, Web surfers will be able to browse more than 250 million Web sites.

This increase in volume will be based, in part, on *Internet2*. This not-for-profit project develops and tests advanced Internet technologies for research, teaching, and learning. Internet2 members include more than 206 universities, 60 companies, and the U.S. government. Their goal is to change the current Internet's inefficiencies, such as relieving bottlenecks.

Recently, Internet2 researchers broke a speed record by sending data from Los Angeles to Geneva, Switzerland, at a speed that is nearly 10,000 times faster than the average home high-speed Internet connection. For more information, visit scsite.com/dc2006/ch2/looking and then click Internet2.

phones, and smart watches while away from a telephone, cable, or other wired connection. Many public locations, such as airports, hotels, schools, shopping malls, and coffee shops, are *hot spots* that provide wireless Internet connections to users with mobile computers or devices.

Access Providers

An **access provider** is a business that provides individuals and companies access to the Internet free or for a fee. The most common fee arrangement for an individual Internet account is a fixed amount, usually about $10 to $25 per month for dial-up, $40 to $55 for DSL and cable, $35 to $70 for fixed wireless, and $60 to $99 for satellite. For this fee, many providers offer unlimited Internet

access. Others specify a set number of access hours per month. With the latter arrangement, the provider charges extra for each hour of connection time that exceeds an allotted number of access hours. To attract more customers, some access providers also offer Web publishing services. Web publishing is discussed later in the chapter.

Users access the Internet through regional or national ISPs, online service providers, and wireless Internet service providers (Figure 2-2).

FAQ 2-1

What does bandwidth have to do with Internet access?

Bandwidth is a measure of how fast data and information travel over transmission media. Thus, higher-speed broadband Internet connections have a higher bandwidth than dial-up connections. For more information, visit scsite.com/dc2006/ch2/faq and then click Bandwidth.

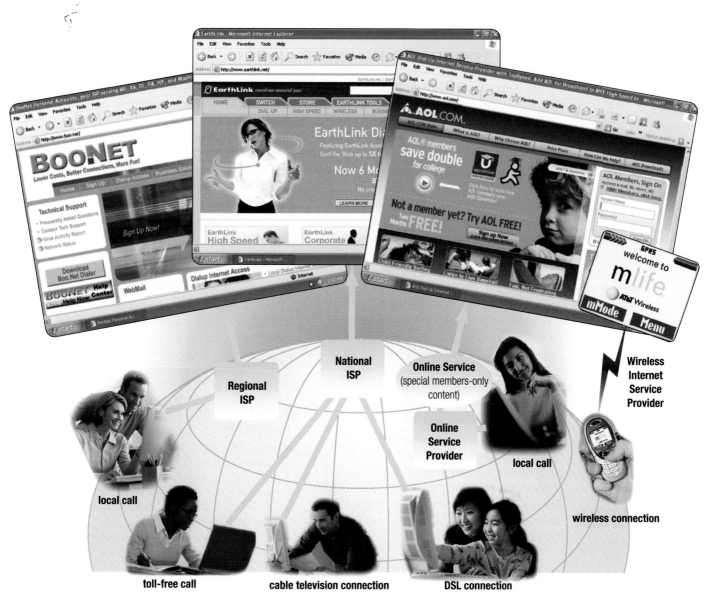

FIGURE 2-2 Common ways to access the Internet are through a regional or national Internet service provider, an online service provider, or a wireless Internet service provider.

An **ISP** (**Internet service provider**) is a regional or national access provider. A *regional ISP* usually provides Internet access to a specific geographic area. A *national ISP* is a business that provides Internet access in cities and towns nationwide. For dial-up access, some national ISPs provide both local and toll-free telephone numbers. Due to their larger size, national ISPs usually offer more services and have a larger technical support staff than regional ISPs. Examples of national ISPs are AT&T Worldnet Service and EarthLink.

In addition to providing Internet access, an **online service provider** (**OSP**) also has many members-only features. These features include special content and services such as news, weather, legal information, financial data, hardware and software guides, games, travel guides, e-mail, photo communities, online calendars, and instant messaging. Some even have their own built-in Web browser. The fees for using an OSP sometimes are slightly higher than fees for an ISP. The two more popular OSPs are AOL (America Online) and MSN (Microsoft Network). AOL differs from many OSPs in that it provides gateway functionality to the Internet, meaning it regulates the Internet services to which members have access.

With dial-up Internet access, the telephone number you dial connects you to an access point on the Internet, called a *point of presence* (*POP*). When selecting an ISP or OSP, ensure it provides at least one local POP telephone number. Otherwise, long-distance telephone charges will apply for the time you connect to the Internet.

A **wireless Internet service provider** (*WISP*) is a company that provides wireless Internet access to computers with wireless modems or access devices or to Internet-enabled mobile computers or devices. Internet-enabled mobile devices include PDAs, smart phones, and smart watches. An antenna on the computer or device typically sends signals through the airwaves to communicate with a wireless Internet service provider. Some examples of wireless Internet service providers include AT&T Wireless, GoAmerica, T-Mobile, and Verizon Wireless.

FAQ 2-2

How many people have broadband Internet access?

According to a recent study, 55 percent of adult Americans access the Internet using high-speed broadband connections at home or at work. Approximately 40 percent of home users have broadband Internet access. The main reason users switch to broadband access is they are frustrated with the slow speeds of dial-up access. For more information, visit scsite.com/dc2006/ch2/faq and then click Broadband.

How Data Travels the Internet

Computers connected to the Internet work together to transfer data and information around the world using servers and clients. On the Internet, your computer is a client that can access data, information, and services on a variety of servers.

The inner structure of the Internet works much like a transportation system. Just as interstate highways connect major cities and carry the bulk of the automotive traffic across the country, several main transmission media carry the heaviest amount of traffic on the Internet. These major carriers of network traffic are known collectively as the *Internet backbone.*

In the United States, the transmission media that make up the Internet backbone exchange data at several different major cities across the country. That is, they transfer data from one network to another until it reaches its final destination (Figure 2-3).

FAQ 2-3

How do I find the right access provider?

The Web provides many comprehensive lists of access providers. These lists often use the terms ISP and OSP interchangeably. One of the more popular lists on the Web is called The List. For more information, visit scsite.com/dc2006/ch2/faq and then click The List.

WEB LINK 2-1

Internet Backbone
For more information, visit scsite.com/dc2006/ch2/weblink and then click Internet Backbone.

FIGURE 2-3   HOW A HOME USER'S DATA MIGHT TRAVEL THE INTERNET USING A CABLE MODEM CONNECTION

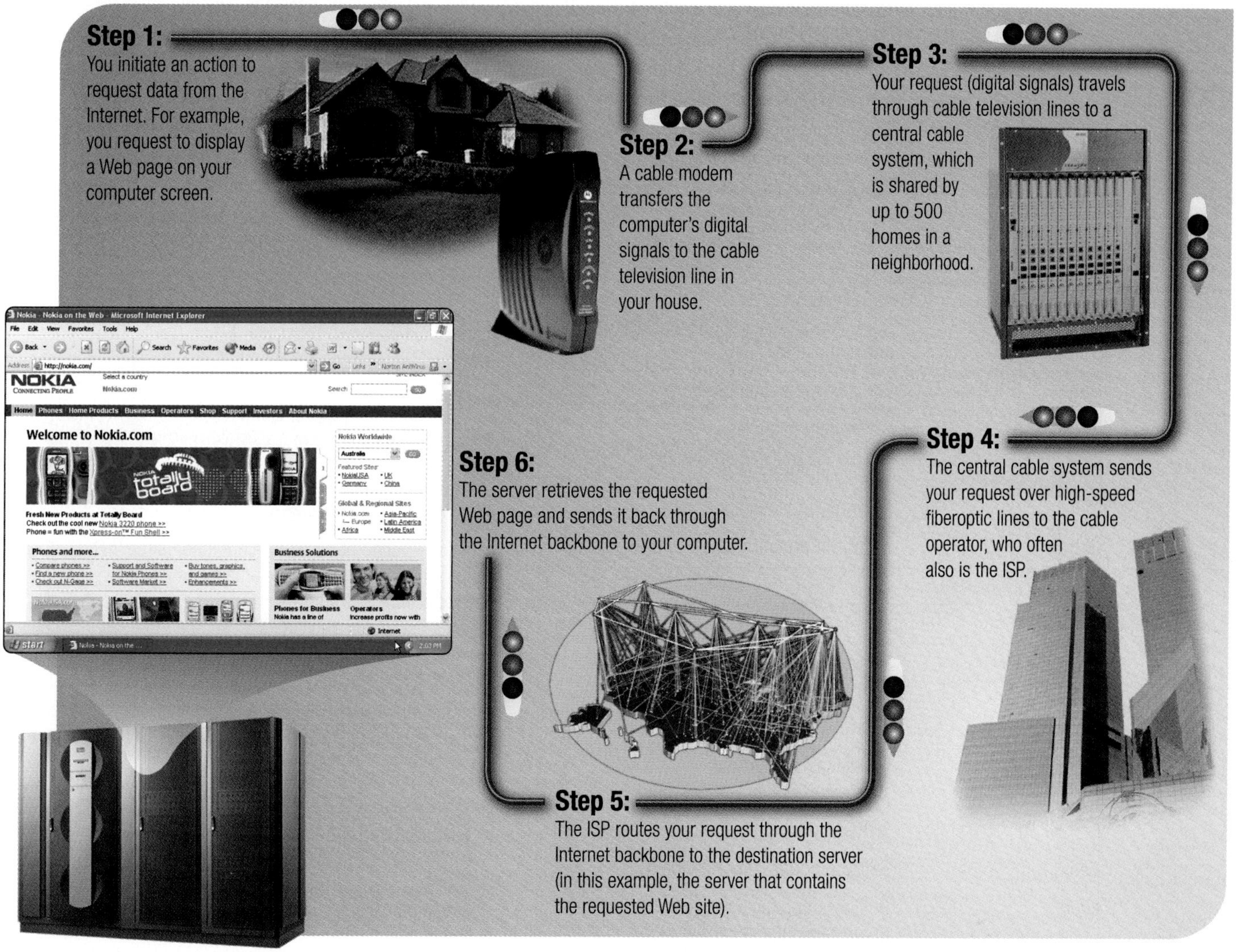

Step 1: You initiate an action to request data from the Internet. For example, you request to display a Web page on your computer screen.

Step 2: A cable modem transfers the computer's digital signals to the cable television line in your house.

Step 3: Your request (digital signals) travels through cable television lines to a central cable system, which is shared by up to 500 homes in a neighborhood.

Step 4: The central cable system sends your request over high-speed fiberoptic lines to the cable operator, who often also is the ISP.

Step 5: The ISP routes your request through the Internet backbone to the destination server (in this example, the server that contains the requested Web site).

Step 6: The server retrieves the requested Web page and sends it back through the Internet backbone to your computer.

Internet Addresses

The Internet relies on an addressing system much like the postal service to send data to a computer at a specific destination. An **IP address**, short for *Internet Protocol address*, is a number that uniquely identifies each computer or device connected to the Internet. The IP address usually consists of four groups of numbers, each separated by a period. The number in each group is between 0 and 255. For example, the numbers 216.239.39.99 are an IP address. In general, the first portion of each IP address identifies the network and the last portion identifies the specific computer.

These all-numeric IP addresses are difficult to remember and use. Thus, the Internet supports the use of a text name that represents one or more IP addresses. A **domain name** is the text version of an IP address. Figure 2-4 shows an IP address and its associated domain name. As with an IP address, the components of a domain name are separated by periods.

In Figure 2-4, the com portion of the domain name is called the top-level domain. Every domain name contains a *top-level domain*, which identifies the type of organization associated with the domain. *Dot-com* is the term sometimes used to describe organizations with a top-level domain of com.

IP address ⟶ 216.239.39.99

Domain name ⟶ www.google.com

top-level domain

FIGURE 2-4   The IP address and domain name for the Google Web site.

The group that assigns and controls top-level domains is the *Internet Corporation for Assigned Names and Numbers (ICANN* pronounced EYE-can). Figure 2-5 lists current top-level domains. For international Web sites outside the United States, the domain name also includes a country code. In this case, the domain name ends with the country code, such as au for Australia or fr for France. For example, www.philips.com.au is the domain name for Philips Australia.

The *domain name system (DNS)* is the method that the Internet uses to store domain names and their corresponding IP addresses. When you specify a domain name, a **DNS server** translates the domain name to its associated IP address so data can be routed to the correct computer. A *DNS server* is an Internet server that usually is associated with an Internet access provider.

For a more technical discussion about Internet addresses, read the High-Tech Talk article on page 102.

TOP-LEVEL DOMAINS

Original Top-Level Domains	Type of Domain
com	Commercial organizations, businesses, and companies
edu	Educational institutions
gov	Goverment agencies
mil	Military organizations
net	Network provider
org	Nonprofit organizations
Newer Top-Level Domains	**Type of Domain**
museum	Accredited museums
biz	Businesses of all sizes
info	Businesses, organizations, or individuals providing general information
name	Individuals or families
pro	Certified professionals such as doctors, lawyers, and accountants
aero	Aviation community members
coop	Business cooperatives such as credit unions and rural electric co-ops
Proposed Top-Level Domains	**Type of Domain**
asia	Businesses that originate in Asian countries
cat	Catalan cultural community
jobs	Employment or human resource businesses
mail	Registries to control spam (Internet junk mail)
mobi	Delivery and management of mobile Internet services
post	Postal service
tel	Internet communications
travel	Travel industry
xxx	Adult content

FIGURE 2-5 With the dramatic growth of the Internet during the last few years, the Internet Corporation for Assigned Names and Numbers (ICANN) recently adopted seven new top-level domains and is evaluating nine additional TLDs.

FAQ 2-4

How does a person or company get a domain name?

For top-level domains of biz, com, info, name, net, and org, you register for a domain name from a *registrar*, which is an organization that maintains the master list of domain names. In addition to determining prices and policies for domain name registration, a registrar may offer additional services such as Web site hosting. For more information, visit scsite.com/dc2006/ch2/faq and then click Registrar.

Test your knowledge of pages 68 through 74 in Quiz Yourself 2-1.

QUIZ YOURSELF 2-1

Instructions: Find the true statement below. Then, rewrite the remaining false statements so they are true.

1. An access provider is a business that provides individuals and companies access to the Internet free or for a fee.

2. A WISP is a number that uniquely identifies each computer or device connected to the Internet.

3. An IP address, such as www.google.com, is the text version of a domain name.

4. Dial-up access takes place when the modem in your computer uses the cable television network to connect to the Internet.

5. The World Wide Web Consortium (W3C) oversees research and owns the Internet.

Quiz Yourself Online: To further check your knowledge of Internet history, accessing and connecting to the Internet, and Internet addresses, visit scsite.com/dc2006/ch2/quiz and then click Objectives 1 – 3.

THE WORLD WIDE WEB

Although many people use the terms World Wide Web and Internet interchangeably, the World Wide Web actually is a newer service of the Internet. While the Internet was developed in the late 1960s, the World Wide Web emerged nearly three decades later — in the early 1990s. Since then, however, it has grown phenomenally to become one of the more widely used services on the Internet.

The **World Wide Web** (*WWW*), or **Web**, consists of a worldwide collection of electronic documents. Each electronic document on the Web is called a **Web page**, which can contain text, graphics, audio (sound), and video. Additionally, Web pages usually have built-in connections to other documents.

Some Web pages are static (fixed); others are dynamic (changing). Visitors to a *static Web page* all see the same content. With a *dynamic Web page*, by contrast, visitors can customize some or all of the viewed content such as desired stock quotes, weather for a region, or ticket availability for flights.

A **Web site** is a collection of related Web pages and associated items, such as documents and pictures, stored on a Web server. A **Web server** is a computer that delivers requested Web pages to your computer. The same Web server can store multiple Web sites. For example, many access providers grant their subscribers free storage space on a Web server for personal or company Web sites.

The following pages discuss how to browse the Web, use a Web address, search for information on the Web, and recognize types of Web sites. Also discussed are multimedia on the Web and Web publishing.

Browsing the Web

A **Web browser**, or **browser**, is application software that allows users to access and view Web pages. To browse the Web, you need a computer that is connected to the Internet and that has a Web browser. The more widely used Web browsers for personal computers are Internet Explorer, Netscape, Mozilla, Opera, and Safari.

With an Internet connection established, you start a Web browser. The browser retrieves and displays a starting Web page, sometimes called the browser's home page. Figure 2-6 shows how a Web browser displays a home page. The initial home page that is displayed

FIGURE 2-6 HOW A WEB BROWSER DISPLAYS A HOME PAGE

Step 1:
Click the Web browser program name to start the Web browser software.

Internet Explorer Web browser name

Step 2:
The Web browser looks up its home page setting, in this case, msn.com.

msn.com

Step 3:
The Web browser communicates with a server maintained by your Internet access provider. The server translates the domain name of the home page to an IP address and then sends the IP address to your computer.

207.68.172.234

Step 4:
The Web browser uses the IP address to contact the Web server associated with the home page and then requests the home page from the server. The Web server sends the home page to the Web browser, which formats the page for display on your screen.

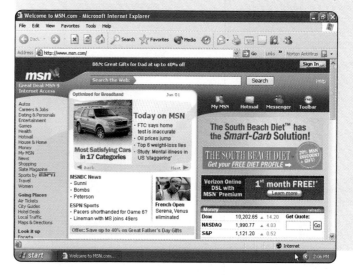

is one selected by your Web browser. You can change your browser's home page at anytime.

The more common usage of the term, **home page**, refers to the first page that a Web site displays. Similar to a book cover or a table of contents for a Web site, the home page provides information about the Web site's purpose and content. Often it provides connections to other documents, Web pages, or Web sites. Many Web sites allow you to personalize the home page so it contains areas of interest to you.

Internet-enabled mobile devices such as PDAs and smart phones use a special type of browser, called a *microbrowser*, which is designed for their small screens and limited computing power. Many Web sites design Web pages specifically for display on a microbrowser (Figure 2-7).

For a computer or mobile device to display a Web page, the page must be downloaded. **Downloading** is the process of a computer receiving information, such as a Web page, from a server on the Internet. While a browser downloads a Web page, it typically displays an animated logo or icon in the top-right corner of the browser window. The animation stops when the download is complete.

Depending on the speed of your Internet connection and the amount of graphics involved, a Web page download can take from a few seconds to several minutes. To speed up the display of Web pages, most Web browsers allow users to turn off the graphics and other multimedia elements.

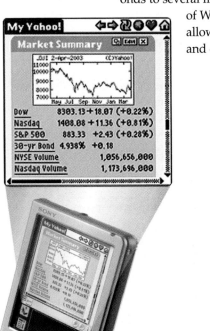

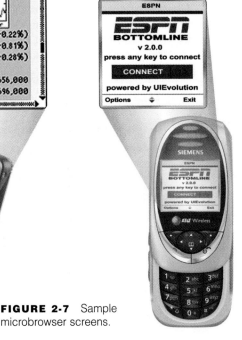

FIGURE 2-7 Sample microbrowser screens.

Web Addresses

A Web page has a unique address, called a **URL** (*Uniform Resource Locator*) or **Web address**. For example, the home page for the San Diego Zoo Web site has http://www.sandiegozoo.org as its Web address. A Web browser retrieves a Web page, such as the zoo's home page, using its Web address.

If you know the Web address of a Web page, you can type it in the Address box at the top of the browser window. For example, if you type the Web address http://www.sandiegozoo.org/wap/condor/home.html in the Address box and then press the ENTER key, the browser downloads and displays a Web page about condors at the San Diego Zoo (Figure 2-8).

As shown in Figure 2-8, a Web address consists of a protocol, domain name, and sometimes the path to a specific Web page or location on a Web page. Many Web page addresses begin with http://. The *http*, which stands for *Hypertext Transfer Protocol*, is a set of rules that defines how pages transfer on the Internet.

To help minimize errors, most current browsers and Web sites do not require the http:// and www portions of the Web address. For example, typing sandiegozoo.org/wap/condor/home.html, instead of the entire address, still accesses the Web site. If you enter an incorrect Web address, a list of similar addresses from which you can select may be displayed in the browser window. Many Web sites also allow users to eliminate the .htm or .html from the Web page name.

When you enter the Web address, sandiegozoo.org/wap/condor/home.html in the Web browser, it sends a request to the Web server that contains the www.sandiegozoo.org Web site. The server then retrieves the Web page named home.html in the wap/condor/ path and delivers it to your browser, which then displays the Web page on the screen.

When you enter a Web address in a browser, you request, or *pull*, information from a Web server. Some Web servers also can *push* content to your computer at regular intervals or whenever updates are made to the site. For example, some Web servers provide the capability of displaying current sporting event scores or weather reports on your computer screen.

For information about useful Web sites and their associated Web addresses, read the Making Use of the Web feature that follows this chapter.

protocol   domain name   path   Web page name

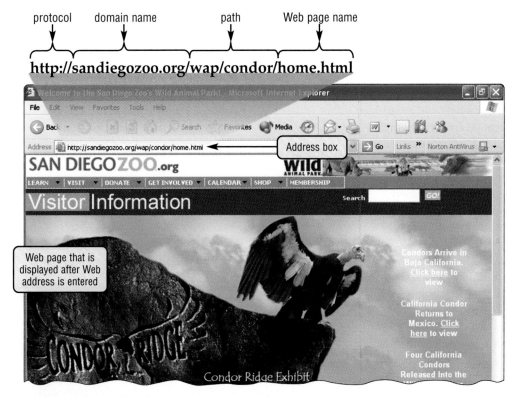

http://sandiegozoo.org/wap/condor/home.html

Address box

Web page that is displayed after Web address is entered

FAQ 2-5

How many Web pages does the average user visit in a month?

More than one thousand. This and other interesting average Web usage statistics are in the table below. For more information, visit scsite.com/dc2006/ch2/faq and then click Web User Statistics.

Web pages visited per month	1,036 pages
Web pages visited per Internet session	34 pages
Time spent surfing per Internet session	51 minutes
Time spent viewing a single Web page	46 seconds
Source: The ClickZ Network	

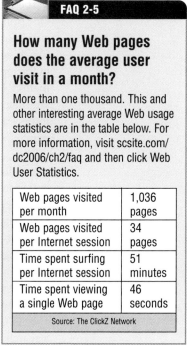

FIGURE 2-8   After entering the Web address http://www.sandiegozoo.org/wap/condor/home.html in the Address box, this Web page at the San Diego Zoo Web site is displayed. Notice the www portion of the domain name does not appear in the Address box after the Web page downloads.

Navigating Web Pages

Most Web pages contain links. A **link**, short for *hyperlink*, is a built-in connection to another related Web page or part of a Web page. Links allow you to obtain information in a nonlinear way. That is, instead of accessing topics in a specified order, you move directly to a topic of interest. Branching from one related topic to another in a nonlinear fashion is what makes links so powerful. Some people use the phrase, **surfing the Web**, to refer to the activity of using links to explore the Web.

On the Web, a link can be text or an image. Text links may be underlined and/or displayed in a color different from other text on the Web page. Pointing to, or positioning the pointer on, a link on the screen typically changes the shape of the pointer to a small hand with a pointing index finger. The Web page shown in Figure 2-9 contains a variety of link types, with the pointer on one of the links.

Each link on a Web page corresponds to another Web address. To activate a link, you *click* it, that is, point to the link and then press the left mouse button. Clicking a link causes the Web page associated with the link to be displayed on the screen. The linked object

might be on the same Web page, a different Web page at the same Web site, or a separate Web page at a different Web site in another city or country. To remind you visually that you have clicked a link, a text link often changes color after you click it.

WEB LINK 2-2

Web Addresses

For more information, visit scsite.com/dc2006/ch2/weblink and then click Web Addresses.

links   link   pointer   links

FIGURE 2-9   This Web page contains various types of links: text that is underlined, text in a different color, and images.

Searching for Information on the Web

The Web is a global resource of information. One primary use of the Web is to search for specific information. The first step in successful searching is to identify the main idea or concept in the topic about which you are seeking information. Determine any synonyms, alternate spellings, or variant word forms for the topic. Then, use a search tool to locate the information.

The two most commonly used search tools are subject directories and search engines. A **subject directory** classifies Web pages in an organized set of categories, such as sports or shopping, and related subcategories. A **search engine** is a program that finds Web sites and Web pages.

Some Web sites offer the functionality of both a subject directory and a search engine. Yahoo! and Google, for example, are widely used search engines that also provide a subject directory. To use Yahoo! or Google, you enter the Web address (yahoo.com or google.com) in the Address box in a browser window. The table in Figure 2-10 lists the

Web addresses of several popular general-purpose subject directories and search engines.

SUBJECT DIRECTORIES A subject directory provides categorized lists of links arranged by subject. Figure 2-11 shows how to use Yahoo!'s

WIDELY USED SEARCH TOOLS

Search Tool	Web Address	Subject Directory	Search Engine
A9.com	a9.com		X
AlltheWeb	alltheweb.com		X
Alta Vista	altavista.com	X	X
AOL Search	search.aol.com		X
AOMI	aomi.com		X
Ask Jeeves	askjeeves.com	X	X
Excite	excite.com	X	X
Gigablast	gigablast.com		X
Google	google.com	X	X
HotBot	hotbot.com		X
LookSmart	looksmart.com	X	X
Lycos	lycos.com	X	X
MSN Search	search.msn.com	X	X
Netscape Search	search.netscape.com	X	X
Open Directory Project	dmoz.org	X	X
Overture	overture.com		X
Teoma	teoma.com		X
WebCrawler	webcrawler.com		X
Yahoo!	yahoo.com	X	X

FIGURE 2-10 Many subject directories and search engines allow searching about any topic on the Web.

FIGURE 2-11 HOW TO USE A SUBJECT DIRECTORY

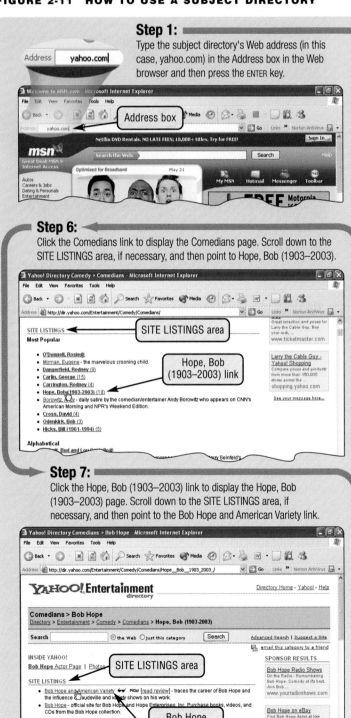

Step 1:
Type the subject directory's Web address (in this case, yahoo.com) in the Address box in the Web browser and then press the ENTER key.

Address box

Step 6:
Click the Comedians link to display the Comedians page. Scroll down to the SITE LISTINGS area, if necessary, and then point to Hope, Bob (1903–2003).

SITE LISTINGS area

Hope, Bob (1903–2003) link

Step 7:
Click the Hope, Bob (1903–2003) link to display the Hope, Bob (1903–2003) page. Scroll down to the SITE LISTINGS area, if necessary, and then point to the Bob Hope and American Variety link.

SITE LISTINGS area

Bob Hope and American Variety link

subject directory to search for information about Bob Hope. As shown in the figure, you locate a particular topic by clicking links through different levels, moving from the general to the specific. Each time you click a category link, the subject directory displays a list of subcategory links, from which you again choose. You continue in this fashion until the search tool displays a list of Web pages about the desired topic.

The major problem with a subject directory is deciding which categories to choose as you work through the menus of links presented.

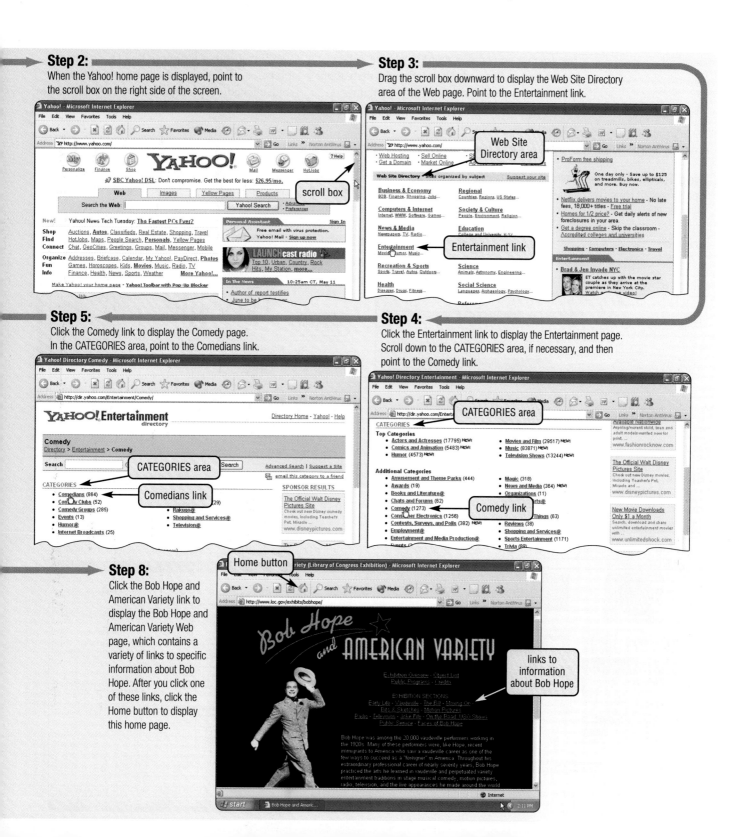

Step 2:
When the Yahoo! home page is displayed, point to the scroll box on the right side of the screen.

Step 3:
Drag the scroll box downward to display the Web Site Directory area of the Web page. Point to the Entertainment link.

Step 5:
Click the Comedy link to display the Comedy page. In the CATEGORIES area, point to the Comedians link.

Step 4:
Click the Entertainment link to display the Entertainment page. Scroll down to the CATEGORIES area, if necessary, and then point to the Comedy link.

Step 8:
Click the Bob Hope and American Variety link to display the Bob Hope and American Variety Web page, which contains a variety of links to specific information about Bob Hope. After you click one of these links, click the Home button to display this home page.

SEARCH ENGINES A search engine is particularly helpful in locating Web pages about certain topics or in locating specific Web pages for which you do not know the exact Web address. Thousands of search engines are available. Some are general and perform searches on any topic; others are restricted to certain subjects, such as finding people, job hunting, or locating real estate.

Instead of clicking through links, search engines require that you enter a word or phrase, called **search text** or *keywords*, that define the item about which you want information. Search engines often respond with results that include thousands of links to Web pages, many of which may have little or no bearing on the information you are seeking. You can eliminate the superfluous pages by carefully crafting a keyword that limits the search.

Figure 2-12 shows how to use the Google search engine to search for the phrase, Bob Hope television career. The results of the search, called *hits*, shown in Step 3 include about 535,000 links to Web pages that reference Bob Hope's television career. Each hit in the list has a link that, when clicked, displays an associated Web site or Web page. Most search engines sequence the

FIGURE 2-12 HOW TO USE A SEARCH ENGINE

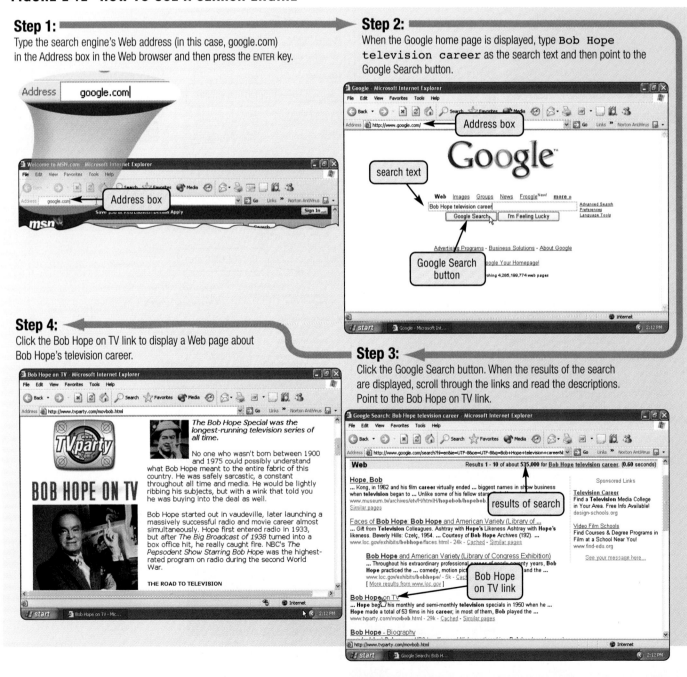

Step 1:
Type the search engine's Web address (in this case, google.com) in the Address box in the Web browser and then press the ENTER key.

Step 2:
When the Google home page is displayed, type **Bob Hope television career** as the search text and then point to the Google Search button.

Step 4:
Click the Bob Hope on TV link to display a Web page about Bob Hope's television career.

Step 3:
Click the Google Search button. When the results of the search are displayed, scroll through the links and read the descriptions. Point to the Bob Hope on TV link.

hits based on how close the words in the search text are to one another in the Web page titles and their descriptions. Thus, the first few links probably contain more relevant information.

If you enter a phrase with spaces between the words in the search text, most search engines display results (hits) that include all of the words, except for common words (e.g., to, the, and). The table in Figure 2-13 lists some common operators you can include in your search text to refine your search. Other techniques you can use to improve your Web searches include the following:

- Use specific nouns and put the most important terms first in the search text.
- List all possible spellings, for example, email, e-mail.
- Before using a search engine, read its Help information.

- If the search is unsuccessful with one search engine, try another.

Many search engines use a program called a *spider* to build and maintain lists of words found on Web sites. When you enter search text, the search engine scans this prebuilt list for hits. The more sophisticated the search engine combined with precise search criteria, the more rapid the response and effective the search.

In addition to searching for Web pages, many search engines allow you to search for images, news articles, and local businesses. Read Looking Ahead 2-2 for a look at the next generation of searching techniques.

FAQ 2-6

Who uses Google to search the Web?

People all around the world use Google to conduct more than 250 million searches per day. Google has been accessed in many languages including English, German, Japanese, Spanish, French, Chinese, and Dutch. For more information, visit scsite.com/dc2006/ch2/faq and then click Google Facts.

SEARCH ENGINE OPERATORS

Operator	Description	Examples	Explanation
Space or +	Use the space or plus operator (+) when you want search results to display hits that include specific words.	art + music art music	Results have both words art and music — in any order.
OR	Use OR operator when you want search results to display hits that include only one word from a list.	dog OR puppy	Results have either the word dog or puppy.
		dog OR puppy OR canine	Results have the word dog or puppy or canine.
-	Use minus operator (-) when you want to exclude a word from your search results.	automobile -convertible	Results include automobile but do not include convertible.
" "	Use quotation marks operator when you want to search for an exact phrase in a certain order.	"19th century literature"	Results include only hits that have the exact phrase, 19th century literature.
*	Use asterisk operator (*) when you want search results to substitute characters in place of the asterisk.	writer*	Results include any word that begins with writer (e.g., writer, writers, writer's).

FIGURE 2-13 Use search engine operators to help refine a search.

LOOKING AHEAD 2-2

3-D Search Engines Get the Picture

Conventional search engines, such as Google, use words to find information. But what happens when a computer user needs to locate a wing nut or camshaft based on a particular shape, not part number or model? The 3-D search engines being developed would help people who work with patterns and contours search for images. These search engines presently are being created to assist designers and engineers at large industrial companies with millions of inventoried parts, but university researchers predict image searches will be common on the Internet within 15 years.

Other search engines of the future will customize the results based on the researcher's background, include a voice interface, and use a thesaurus to keep a query in context. For more information, visit scsite.com/dc2006/ch2/looking and then click Search Engines.

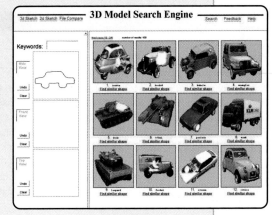

Types of Web Sites

Nine types of Web sites are portal, news, informational, business/marketing, educational, entertainment, advocacy, blog, and personal (Figure 2-14). Many Web sites fall in more than one of these categories. The following pages discuss each of these types of Web sites.

PORTAL   A **portal** is a Web site that offers a variety of Internet services from a single, convenient location (Figure 2-14a). Most portals offer the following free services: search engine and/or subject directory; news; sports and weather; free Web publishing services; reference tools such as yellow pages, stock quotes, and maps; shopping malls and auctions; and e-mail and other forms of online communications. Companies often create their own portals for use by employees, vendors, and customers.

Many portals have Web communities. A **Web community** is a Web site that joins a specific group of people with similar interests or relationships. These communities may offer online photo albums, chat rooms, and other services to facilitate communications among members.

When you connect to the Internet, the first Web page that is displayed often is a portal. Popular portals include AltaVista, AOL, Excite, GO.com, HotBot, LookSmart, Lycos, MSN, NBCi, Netscape, and Yahoo!. You may notice that many of these portals are popular search engines or subject directories. Some also are Internet access providers.

A *wireless portal* is a portal designed for Internet-enabled mobile devices. Wireless portals attempt to provide all information a wireless user might require. These portals offer services geared to the mobile user such as search engines, news, stock quotes, weather, maps, e-mail, calendar, instant messaging, and shopping.

NEWS   A news Web site contains newsworthy material including stories and articles relating to current events, life, money, sports, and the weather (Figure 2-14b). Many magazines and newspapers sponsor Web sites that provide summaries of printed articles, as well as articles not included in the printed versions. Newspapers and television and radio stations are some of the media that maintain news Web sites.

INFORMATIONAL   An informational Web site contains factual information (Figure 2-14c). Many United States government agencies have informational Web sites providing information such as census data, tax codes, and the congressional budget. Other organizations provide information such as public transportation schedules and published research findings.

BUSINESS/MARKETING   A business/marketing Web site contains content that promotes or sells products or services (Figure 2-14d). Nearly every business has a business/marketing Web site. Allstate Insurance Company, Dell Inc., General Motors Corporation, Kraft Foods Inc., and Walt Disney Company all have business/marketing Web sites. Many of these companies also allow you to purchase their products or services online.

EDUCATIONAL   An educational Web site offers exciting, challenging avenues for formal and informal teaching and learning (Figure 2-14e). On the Web, you can learn how airplanes fly or how to cook a meal. For a more structured learning experience, companies provide online training to employees; and colleges offer online classes and degrees (read At Issue 2-1 for a related discussion). Instructors often use the Web to enhance classroom teaching by publishing course materials, grades, and other pertinent class information.

AT ISSUE 2-1

Diplomas Online?

College can be a rewarding experience, both personally and professionally. Some people, however, do not have the opportunity, time, or money needed to attend a traditional college. Many schools address this problem with online classes. Online classes allow students to learn whenever and wherever they can access a course's Web page, often for less cost than traditional tuitions. A student might be able to complete an entire degree program without ever physically attending a class. Many online classes present material using captivating simulations, real-life case studies, and interactive tools. And, online classes seem to work — one research report found that online students learn as well as or better than their classroom-based brethren. Yet, even the best online classes lack some of the most important features of the bricks-and-mortar campus experience, such as casual talks with professors, informal study groups in the dorm, or enthusiastic discussions in the campus coffee shop. What are the most important advantages and disadvantages of online classes? Why? Does a degree earned online have the same value as a traditional degree? Why? Does the answer depend more on the college or on the course of study? Why? What type of student is best, and least, suited for online classes? Why?

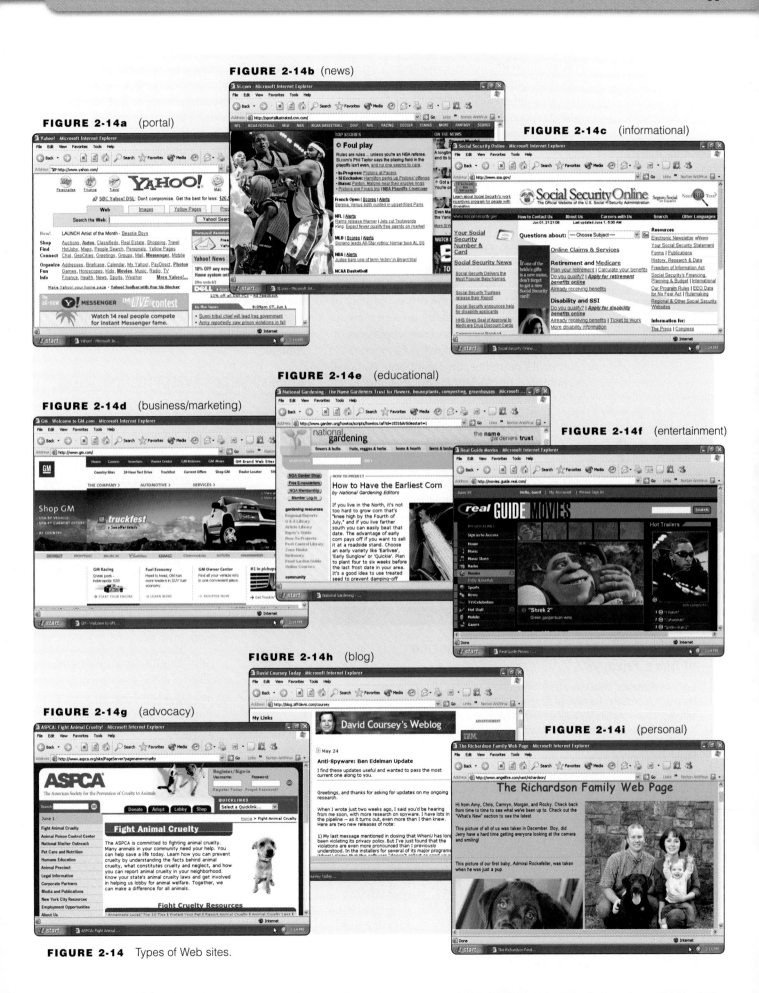

FIGURE 2-14b (news)

FIGURE 2-14a (portal)

FIGURE 2-14c (informational)

FIGURE 2-14e (educational)

FIGURE 2-14d (business/marketing)

FIGURE 2-14f (entertainment)

FIGURE 2-14h (blog)

FIGURE 2-14g (advocacy)

FIGURE 2-14i (personal)

FIGURE 2-14 Types of Web sites.

ENTERTAINMENT   An entertainment Web site offers an interactive and engaging environment (Figure 2-14f on the previous page). Popular entertainment Web sites offer music, videos, sports, games, ongoing Web episodes, sweepstakes, chats, and more. Sophisticated entertainment Web sites often partner with other technologies. For example, you can cast your vote about a topic on a television show.

ADVOCACY   An advocacy Web site contains content that describes a cause, opinion, or idea (Figure 2-14g on the previous page). The purpose of an advocacy Web site is to convince the reader of the validity of the cause, opinion, or idea. These Web sites usually present views of a particular group or association. Sponsors of advocacy Web sites include the Democratic National Committee, the Republican National Committee, the Society for the Prevention of Cruelty to Animals, and the Society to Protect Human Rights.

BLOG   A **blog**, short for *Web log*, is a Web site that uses a regularly updated journal format to reflect the interests, opinions, and personalities of the author and sometimes site visitors (Figure 2-14h on the previous page). Blogs have an informal style that consists of a single individual's ideas (similar to a diary) or a collection of ideas and thoughts among visitors. Read At Issue 2-2 for a related discussion.

PERSONAL   A private individual or family not usually associated with any organization may maintain a personal Web site or just a single Web page (Figure 2-14i on the previous page). People publish personal Web pages for a variety of reasons. Some are job hunting. Others simply want to share life experiences with the world.

Evaluating a Web Site

Do not assume that information presented on the Web is correct or accurate. Any person, company, or organization can publish a Web page on the Internet. No one oversees the content of these Web pages. Figure 2-15 lists guidelines for assessing the value of a Web site or Web page before relying on its content.

GUIDELINES FOR EVALUATING THE VALUE OF A WEB SITE

Evaluation Criteria	Reliable Web Sites
Affiliation	A reputable institution should support the Web site without bias in the information.
Audience	The Web site should be written at an appropriate level.
Authority	The Web site should list the author and the appropriate credentials.
Content	The Web site should be well organized and the links should work.
Currency	The information on the Web page should be current.
Design	The pages at the Web site should download quickly and be visually pleasing and easy to navigate.
Objectivity	The Web site should contain little advertising and be free of preconceptions.

FIGURE 2-15   Criteria for evaluating a Web site's content.

AT ISSUE 2-2

Mobile Web Logs with Photos — an Invasion of One's Privacy?

Camera-equipped smart phones are popular — almost 50 million were sold last year. A growing number of people use these phones to create online photo albums, called mobile Web blogs or *moblogs*, to share their visions of the world with thousands of people. Most moblogs are personal and, like family photo albums, interesting to a limited audience. To capture more exciting pictures, some moblog photographers use their smart phone cameras in private places. As a result, smart phone cameras have been banned from health club locker rooms, movie screenings, and corporate offices. Congress even is considering barring covert cameras from places where people should be able to expect some privacy. But, even in public, moblog paparazzi photograph unaware people at private, or embarrassing, times. The subjects of these moblog pictures often object to living in a fishbowl, where even personal moments can be captured and posted on the Web. Recognizing this, some Web sites that monitor moblogs refuse to show certain photos or encourage photographers to obtain permission from photo subjects. Yet, photographers insist they have the right to post any pictures they take. What, if anything, can be done to protect personal privacy? Should laws be enacted to regulate smart phone photographers, moblogs, or both? Why? Must we accept that, outside of our homes, private moments no longer exist?

Multimedia on the Web

Most Web pages include more than just formatted text and links. The more exciting Web pages use multimedia. **Multimedia** refers to any application that combines text with graphics, animation, audio, video, and/or virtual reality. Multimedia brings a Web page to life, increases the types of information available on the Web, expands the Web's potential uses, and makes the Internet a more entertaining place to explore. Multimedia Web pages often require proper hardware and software and take more time to download because they contain large graphics files and video or audio clips.

The sections that follow discuss how the Web uses graphics, animation, audio, video, and virtual reality.

FAQ 2-7

What is a file?

A *file* is a unit of storage. When you want the computer to store items (e.g., data, information, programs, graphics, audio clips, or video clips), it places them in files on storage media such as a hard disk. File sizes vary depending on items being stored. For example, graphics files usually consume more storage space than data files. For more information, visit scsite.com/dc2006/ch2/faq and then click Files.

GRAPHICS A **graphic**, or *graphical image*, is a digital representation of nontext information such as a drawing, chart, or photograph. Today, many Web pages use colorful graphical designs and images to convey messages (Figure 2-16).

The Web contains countless images about a variety of subjects. You can download many of these images at no cost and use them for non-commercial purposes. Recall that downloading is the process of transferring an object from the Web to your computer. For example, you can insert images into greeting cards, announcements, and other documents.

Of the graphics formats that exist on the Web (Figure 2-17), the two more common are JPEG and GIF formats. *JPEG* (pronounced JAY-peg) is a format that compresses graphics to reduce their file size, which means the file takes up less storage space. Smaller file sizes result in faster downloading of Web pages because small files transmit faster than large files. The

more compressed the file, the smaller the image and the lower the quality. The goal with JPEG graphics is to reach a balance between image quality and file size.

GIF (pronounced jiff) graphics also use compression techniques to reduce file sizes. The GIF format works best for images that have only a few distinct colors. The newer *PNG* (pronounced ping) graphics format improves upon the GIF format, and thus may eventually replace the GIF format.

The BMP and TIFF formats listed in Figure 2-17 may require special viewer software, and they have larger file sizes. Thus, these formats are not used on the Web as frequently as JPEG, GIF, and PNG formats.

FIGURE 2-16 This Web page uses colorful graphical designs and images to convey its messages.

GRAPHICS FORMATS USED ON THE WEB

Abbreviation	Name
BMP	Bit Map
GIF	Graphics Interchange Format
JPEG	Joint Photographic Experts Group
PNG	Portable Network Graphics
TIFF	Tagged Image File Format

FIGURE 2-17 The Web uses graphics file formats for images.

Some Web sites use thumbnails on their pages because graphics can be time-consuming to display. A *thumbnail* is a small version of a larger graphic. You usually can click a thumbnail to display a larger image (Figure 2-18).

FIGURE 2-18 Clicking the thumbnail in the top screen displays a larger image in a separate window.

ANIMATION Many Web pages use **animation**, which is the appearance of motion created by displaying a series of still images in sequence. Animation can make Web pages more visually interesting or draw attention to important information or links. For example, text that animates by scrolling across the screen can serve as a ticker to display stock updates, news, sports scores, weather, or other information. Web-based games often use animation.

Web page developers add animation to Web pages using a variety of techniques. Web page authoring programs, such as Macromedia Flash, enable Web site developers to combine animation and interactivity in Web pages. Developers unfamiliar with Web page authoring programs can create an *animated GIF*, which combines several GIF images in a single GIF file.

AUDIO On the Web, you can listen to audio clips and live audio. **Audio** includes music, speech, or any other sound.

Simple applications on the Web consist of individual audio files available for downloading to a computer. Once downloaded, you can play (listen to) the contents of these files. Some common Web audio file formats are listed in Figure 2-19. Audio files are compressed to reduce their file sizes. For example, the **MP3** format reduces an audio file to about one-tenth its original size, while preserving much of the original quality of the sound.

Some music publishers have Web sites that allow users to download sample tracks free to persuade them to buy the entire CD. Other Web sites allow a user to purchase and download an entire CD of music tracks to the hard disk (Figure 2-20). Keep in mind that it is legal to download copyrighted music only if the song's copyright holder has granted permission for users to download and play the song.

To listen to an audio file on your computer, you need special software called a **player**. Most current operating systems contain a player. Popular players include iTunes, RealOne Player, and Windows Media Player. If your player will not play a particular audio format, you can download the necessary player free from the Web.

Some applications on the Web use streaming audio. **Streaming** is the process of transferring data in a continuous and even flow. Streaming allows users to access and use a file while it is transmitting. For example, *streaming audio* enables you to listen to music as it downloads to your computer. Many radio and television stations use streaming audio to broadcast music, interviews, talk shows, sporting events, music videos, news, live concerts, and other segments.

FAQ 2-8

How long does it take to download a single song from a music Web site?

Depending on the speed of your Internet connection and the size of the file, a single song can take from one to twenty minutes to download. For more information, visit scsite.com/dc2006/ch2/faq and then click Downloading Audio Files.

AUDIO WEB FILE FORMATS

WEB LINK 2-3

Streaming Media
For more information, visit scsite.com/ dc2006/ch2/weblink and then click Streaming Media.

Audio File Format	Description
AA	Audible Audio (commonly used for downloadable e-books)
AAC	Advanced Audio Coding
AIFF	Audio Interchange File Format
ASF	Advanced Streaming (or Systems) Format (part of Windows Media framework)
MP3	Moving Pictures Experts Group Audio Layer 3 (MPEG-3)
WAV	Windows waveform
WMA	Windows Media Audio (part of Windows Media framework)
RA	RealAudio sound file (supported by RealOne Player)
QT	QuickTime audio, video, or 3-D animation (included with Mac OS, also available separately)

FIGURE 2-19 Popular Web audio file formats.

FIGURE 2-20 HOW TO PURCHASE AND DOWNLOAD MUSIC

Step 1:
Display the music Web site on the screen. Search for, select, and pay for the music you want to purchase from the music Web site.

Step 2:
Download the music from the Web site's server to your computer's hard disk.

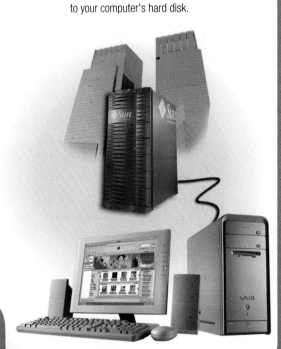

Step 3:
Listen to the music from your computer's hard disk.

VIDEO **Video** consists of full-motion images that are played back at various speeds. Most video also has accompanying audio. Instead of turning on the television, you can use the Internet to watch live and/or prerecorded coverage of your favorite programs (Figure 2-21) or enjoy a live performance of your favorite vocalist.

Simple video applications on the Web consist of individual video files, such as movie or television clips, that you must download completely before you can play them on the computer. Video files often are compressed because they are quite large in size. These clips also are quite short in length, usually less than 10 minutes, because they can take a long time to download. The *Moving Pictures Experts Group (MPEG)* defines a popular video compression standard, a widely used one called *MPEG-4.*

As with streaming audio, *streaming video* allows you to view longer or live video

images as they download to your computer. Widely used standards supported by most Web browsers for transmitting streaming video data on the Internet are AVI (Audio Video Interleaved), QuickTime, Windows Media Format, and RealVideo. Like RealAudio, RealVideo is supported by RealOne Player.

VIRTUAL REALITY **Virtual reality** (**VR**) is the use of computers to simulate a real or imagined environment that appears as a three-dimensional (3-D) space. On the Web, VR involves the display of 3-D images that users explore and manipulate interactively (Figure 2-22).

Using special VR software, a Web developer creates an entire 3-D Web site that contains infinite space and depth, called a *VR world.* A VR world, for example, might show a room with furniture. Users walk through such a VR room by moving an input device forward, backward, or to the side.

Games often use VR. Many practical applications of VR also exist. Science educators create VR models of molecules, organisms, and other structures for students to examine. Companies use VR to showcase products or create advertisements. Architects create VR models of buildings and rooms so clients can see how a completed construction project will look before it is built.

FIGURE 2-21 A video of passengers having fun on a theme park ride.

mouse pointer

FIGURE 2-22 Web site visitors use VR to see the inside of Grand Central Station in New York. As you move the mouse pointer, you see different views inside the station.

PLUG-INS Most Web browsers have the capability of displaying basic multimedia elements on a Web page. Sometimes, a browser might need an additional program, called a plug-in. A **plug-in** is a program that extends the capability of a browser. You can download many plug-ins at no cost from various Web sites (Figure 2-23). Some plug-ins run on all sizes of personal computers and mobile devices. Others have special versions for mobile devices.

Web Publishing

Before the World Wide Web, the means to share opinions and ideas with others easily and inexpensively was limited to the media, classroom, work, or social environments. Generating an advertisement or publication that could reach a massive audience required much expense. Today, businesses and individuals convey information to millions of people by creating their own Web pages. The content of the Web pages ranges from new stories to product information to blogs.

POPULAR PLUG-IN APPLICATIONS

Plug-In Application	Description	Web Address
Acrobat Reader	View, navigate, and print Portable Document Format (PDF) files — documents formatted to look just as they look in print	adobe.com
Flash Player	View dazzling graphics and animation, hear outstanding sound and music, display Web pages across an entire screen	macromedia.com
QuickTime	View animation, music, audio, video, and VR panoramas and objects directly in a Web page	apple.com
RealOne Player	Listen to live and on-demand near-CD-quality audio and newscast-quality video; stream audio and video content for faster viewing; play MP3 files; create music CDs	real.com
Shockwave Player	Experience dynamic interactive multimedia, 3-D graphics, and streaming audio	macromedia.com
Windows Media Player	Listen to live and on-demand audio; play or edit WMA and MP3 files; burn CDs, watch DVD movies	microsoft.com

FIGURE 2-23 Most plug-ins can be downloaded free from the Web.

WEB LINK 2-4

Plug-Ins
For more information, visit scsite.com/dc2006/ch2/weblink and then click Plug-Ins.

Web publishing is the development and maintenance of Web pages. To develop a Web page, you do not have to be a computer programmer. For the small business or home user, Web publishing is fairly easy as long as you have the proper tools. The five major steps to Web publishing are as follows: (1) plan a Web site, (2) analyze and design a Web site, (3) create a Web site, (4) deploy a Web site, and (5) maintain a Web site. Figure 2-24 illustrates these steps with respect to a personal Web site.

FIGURE 2-24   HOW TO PUBLISH YOUR RESUME ON THE WEB

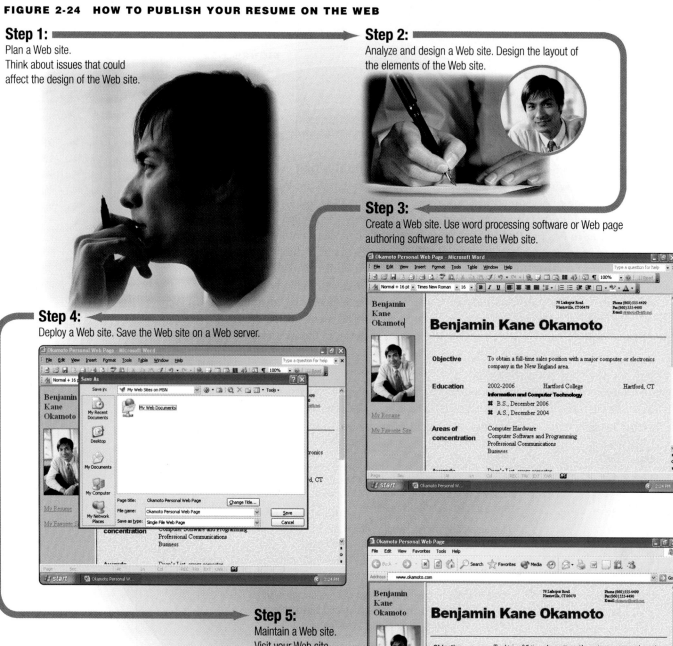

Step 1:
Plan a Web site.
Think about issues that could affect the design of the Web site.

Step 2:
Analyze and design a Web site. Design the layout of the elements of the Web site.

Step 3:
Create a Web site. Use word processing software or Web page authoring software to create the Web site.

Step 4:
Deploy a Web site. Save the Web site on a Web server.

Step 5:
Maintain a Web site. Visit your Web site regularly to be sure it is working and current.

Test your knowledge of pages 75 through 91 in Quiz Yourself 2-2.

QUIZ YOURSELF 2-2

Instructions: Find the true statement below. Then, rewrite the remaining false statements so they are true.

1. A blog is a Web site that uses a regularly updated journal format to reflect the interests, opinions, and personalities of the author and sometimes site visitors.

2. A Web browser classifies Web pages in an organized set of categories, such as sports or shopping, and related subcategories.

3. Audio and video files are downloaded to reduce their file sizes.

4. Popular portals include iTunes, RealOne Player, and Windows Media Player.

5. The more widely used search engines for personal computers are Internet Explorer, Netscape, Mozilla, Opera, and Safari.

6. To develop a Web page, you have to be a computer programmer.

7. To improve your Web searches, use general nouns and put the least important terms first in the search text.

Quiz Yourself Online: To further check your knowledge of Web addresses, Web browsers, searching, types of Web sites, elements of a Web page, and Web publishing, visit scsite.com/dc2006/ch2/quiz and then click Objectives 4 – 9.

E-COMMERCE

E-commerce, short for *electronic commerce*, is a business transaction that occurs over an electronic network such as the Internet. Anyone with access to a computer, an Internet connection, and a means to pay for purchased goods or services can participate in e-commerce (Figure 2-25).

In the past, e-commerce transactions were conducted primarily using desktop computers. Today, many mobile computers and devices, such as PDAs and smart phones, also access the Web wirelessly. Some people use the term *m-commerce* (mobile commerce) to identify e-commerce that takes place using mobile devices.

Popular uses of e-commerce by consumers include shopping, investing, and banking. Users can purchase just about any product or service on the Web. Some examples include flowers, books, computers, prescription drugs, music, movies, cars, airline tickets, and concert tickets. Through online investing, individuals buy and sell stocks or bonds without using a broker.

FIGURE 2-25 E-commerce activities include shopping for goods at an online auction. This user visits an eBay auction for specialty stamps.

Three different types of e-commerce are business-to-consumer, consumer-to-consumer, and business-to-business. *Business-to-consumer (B2C) e-commerce* consists of the sale of goods and services to the general public. For example, Dell has a B2C Web site. Instead of visiting a computer store to purchase a computer, customers can order one that meets their specifications directly from the Dell Web site.

A customer (consumer) visits an online business through an **electronic storefront**, which contains product descriptions, graphics, and a shopping cart. The **shopping cart** allows the customer to collect purchases. When ready to complete the sale, the customer enters personal data and the method of payment, preferably through a secure Internet connection (read At Issue 2-3 for a related discussion).

Instead of purchasing from a business, consumers can purchase from each other. For example, with an **online auction**, users bid on an item being sold by someone else. The highest bidder at the end of the bidding period purchases the item. *Consumer-to-consumer (C2C) e-commerce* occurs when one consumer sells directly to another, such as in an online auction. eBay is one of the more popular online auction Web sites.

WEB LINK 2-5

E-Commerce

For more information, visit scsite.com/ dc2006/ch2/weblink and then click E-Commerce.

AT ISSUE 2-3

To Tax or Not to Tax Internet Sales?

The Supreme Court has ruled that merchants can charge state and local sales taxes only when they have a physical presence, such as a store or office building, where the purchase is made. Because Internet merchants often do not have a physical presence in a buyer's state, online purchases usually are sales tax free. One study predicts that by 2011 online sales will cost state and local governments more than $54 billion in sales tax revenues, forcing them either to raise taxes or cut services. In response, many states have enacted "use" taxes that require residents to report, and pay sales tax on, items purchased online but used at home. Even a use tax, though, does not address other problems. The sales-tax-free status of Internet purchases also may have a negative impact on local businesses that must charge sales tax and on lower-income families who are less likely to buy online. Yet, many feel any tax on e-commerce is unmanageable (forcing vendors to adjust to varying sales tax rates) and unjustified. Should a sales tax be applied to Internet purchases? Why? Is a use tax a viable alternative? Why or why not? How else can the problems of taxing, or not taxing, Internet purchases be addressed?

Most e-commerce, though, actually takes place between businesses, which is called *business-to-business (B2B) e-commerce*. Businesses often provide goods and services to other businesses, such as online advertising, recruiting, credit, sales, market research, technical support, and training. For example, some MasterCard and Visa credit card companies provide corporations with Web-based purchasing, tracking, and transaction downloading capabilities.

FAQ 2-9

How popular is online shopping?

Researchers predict that e-commerce sales will grow at a steady rate of 19 percent per year until at least 2008. At that time, online shopping will account for approximately 10 percent of all retail sales in the United States, or 63 million households. For more information, visit scsite.com/ dc2006/ch2/faq and then click Online Shopping.

OTHER INTERNET SERVICES

The Web is only one of the many services on the Internet. The Web and other Internet services have changed the way we communicate. We can send e-mail messages to the president, have a discussion with experts about the stock market, chat with someone in another country about genealogy, and talk about homework assignments with classmates via instant messages. Many times, these communications take place completely in writing — without the parties ever meeting each other.

At home, work, and school, people use computers and Internet-enabled mobile devices so they always have instant access to e-mail, FTP (File Transfer Protocol), newsgroups and message boards, mailing lists, chat rooms, instant messaging, and Internet telephony. The following pages discuss each of these Internet services.

E-Mail

E-mail (short for *electronic mail*) is the transmission of messages and files via a computer network. E-mail was one of the original services on the Internet, enabling scientists and researchers working on government-sponsored projects to communicate with colleagues at other locations. Today, e-mail is a primary communications method for both personal and business use.

You use an **e-mail program** to create, send, receive, forward, store, print, and delete e-mail messages. Outlook and Outlook Express are two popular e-mail programs. The steps in Figure 2-26 illustrate how to send an e-mail message using Outlook. The message can be simple text or can include an attachment such as a word processing document, a graphic, an audio clip, or a video clip.

FIGURE 2-26   HOW TO SEND AN E-MAIL MESSAGE

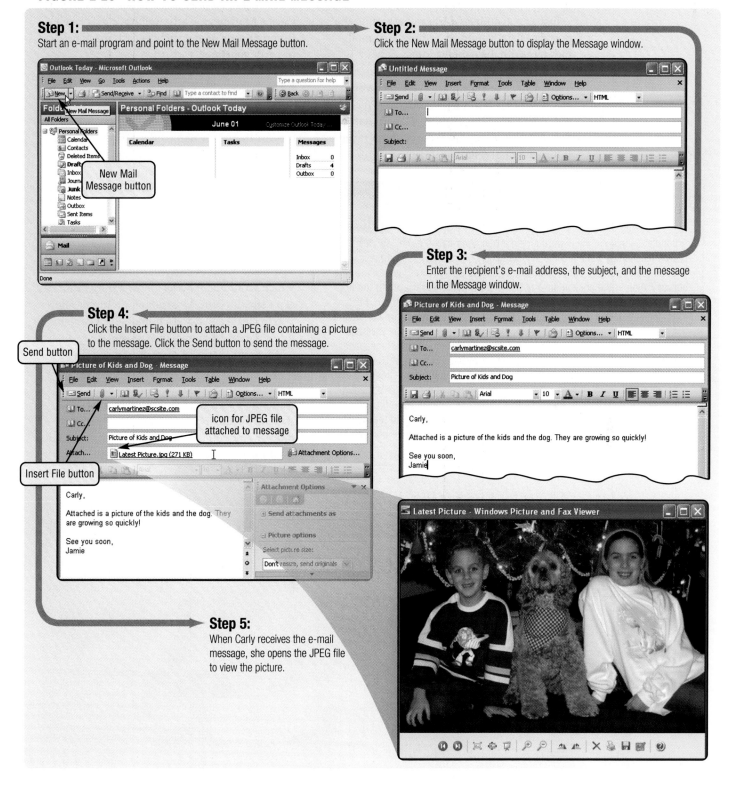

Step 1:
Start an e-mail program and point to the New Mail Message button.

Step 2:
Click the New Mail Message button to display the Message window.

Step 3:
Enter the recipient's e-mail address, the subject, and the message in the Message window.

Step 4:
Click the Insert File button to attach a JPEG file containing a picture to the message. Click the Send button to send the message.

Step 5:
When Carly receives the e-mail message, she opens the JPEG file to view the picture.

Internet access providers typically supply an e-mail program as a standard part of their Internet access services. Some Web sites, such as MSN Hotmail and Yahoo!, provide free e-mail services. To use these Web-based e-mail programs, you connect to the Web site and set up an e-mail account, which typically includes an e-mail address and a password. Read At Issue 2-4 for a related discussion.

Just as you address a letter when using the postal system, you must address an e-mail message with the e-mail address of your intended recipient. Likewise, when someone sends you a message, they must have your e-mail address. An **e-mail address** is a combination of a user name and a domain name that identifies a user so he or she can receive Internet e-mail (Figure 2-27).

A **user name** is a unique combination of characters, such as letters of the alphabet and/or numbers, that identifies a specific user. Your user name must be different from the other user names in the same domain. For example, a user named Carly Martinez whose server has a domain name of scsite.com might want to select CMartinez as her user name. If scsite.com already has a CMartinez (for Carlos Martinez), Carly will have to select a different user name, such as carlymartinez or carly_martinez.

Sometimes, companies decide user names for employees. In many cases, however, users select their own user names, often selecting a nickname or any other combination of characters for their user name. Many users select a combination of their first and last names so others can remember it easily.

In an Internet e-mail address, an @ (pronounced at) symbol separates the user name from the domain name. Your service provider supplies the domain name. Using the example in Figure 2-27, a possible e-mail address for Carly Martinez would be carlymartinez@scsite.com, which would be read as follows: Carly Martinez at s c site dot com. Most e-mail programs allow you to create an **address book**, which contains a list of names and e-mail addresses.

When you send an e-mail message, an outgoing mail server that is operated by your Internet access provider determines how to route the message through the Internet and then sends the message. *SMTP (simple mail transfer protocol)* is a communications protocol used by some outgoing mail servers.

AT ISSUE 2-4

Are Free Web-Based E-Mail Services Worth the Price?

A popular search engine is introducing a free, Web-based e-mail service. The search technology built into the service allows users easily to find messages about a topic. Curious about reactions to a book being read in your literature course? Type in the book's title and see every e-mail message about the book that you have sent or received. But, you probably will see even more. Each message is scanned for key terms, and related advertisements are inserted in the message. So, a message about the book also may contain an advertisement from a book store. Some people feel that scanning personal messages and inserting unwanted advertisements is an invasion of privacy. One security expert also warns that investigators could subpoena the huge depository of messages and search it for evidence in criminal or civil cases. Privacy advocates believe Web-based e-mail services should be banned, even if people want them. Would you use a Web-based e-mail service? Why? Should these services be outlawed? Why or why not? What, if anything, should be done about privacy concerns related to Web-based e-mail services?

carlymartinez@scsite.com

FIGURE 2-27 An e-mail address is a combination of a user name and a domain name.

As you receive e-mail messages, an incoming mail server — also operated by your Internet access provider — holds the messages in your mailbox until you use your e-mail program to retrieve them. *POP3*, the latest version of POP (*Post Office Protocol*), is a communications protocol used by some incoming mail servers. Most e-mail programs have a mail notification alert that informs you via a message or sound when you receive new mail. Figure 2-28 illustrates how an e-mail message may travel from a sender to a receiver.

WEB LINK 2-6

E-Mail
For more information, visit scsite.com/dc2006/ch2/weblink and then click E-Mail.

FAQ 2-10

Can my computer get a virus through e-mail?

Yes. A *virus* is a computer program that can damage files and the operating system. One way that virus authors attempt to spread a virus is by sending virus-infected e-mail attachments. If you receive an e-mail attachment, you should use an antivirus program to verify that it is virus free.

For more information, read the High-Tech Talk article on page 168, the section about viruses and antivirus programs in Chapter 8, and visit scsite.com/dc2006/ch2/faq and then click Viruses.

FIGURE 2-28 HOW AN E-MAIL MESSAGE MAY TRAVEL FROM A SENDER TO A RECEIVER

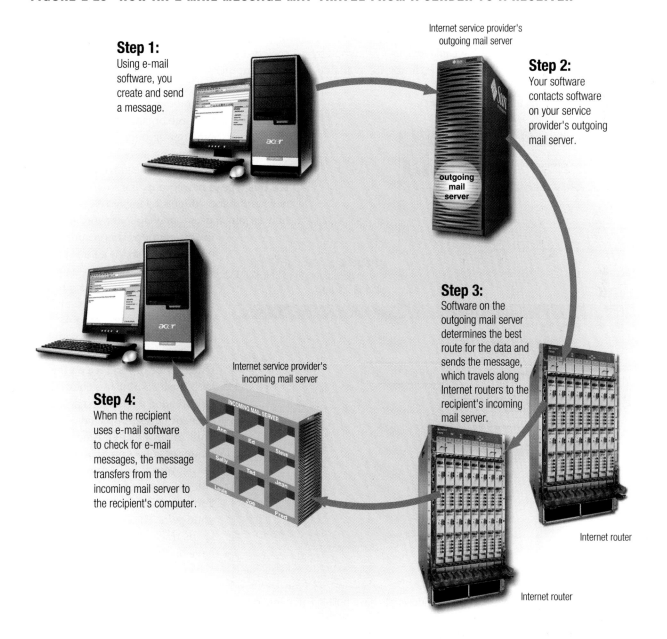

Step 1:
Using e-mail software, you create and send a message.

Internet service provider's outgoing mail server

Step 2:
Your software contacts software on your service provider's outgoing mail server.

outgoing mail server

Step 3:
Software on the outgoing mail server determines the best route for the data and sends the message, which travels along Internet routers to the recipient's incoming mail server.

Internet service provider's incoming mail server

Step 4:
When the recipient uses e-mail software to check for e-mail messages, the message transfers from the incoming mail server to the recipient's computer.

Internet router

Internet router

FTP

FTP (*File Transfer Protocol*) is an Internet standard that permits file uploading and downloading (transferring) with other computers on the Internet. Uploading is the opposite of downloading; that is, **uploading** is the process of transferring documents, graphics, and other objects from your computer to a server on the Internet. Web page authors, for example, often use FTP to upload their Web pages to a Web server.

Many operating systems include FTP capabilities (Figure 2-29). If yours does not, you can download FTP programs from the Web, usually for a small fee.

An *FTP server* is a computer that allows users to upload and/or download files using FTP. An FTP site is a collection of files including text, graphics, audio clips, video clips, and program files that reside on an FTP server. Many FTP sites have *anonymous FTP*, whereby anyone can transfer some, if not all, available files. Some FTP sites restrict file transfers to those who have authorized accounts (user names and passwords) on the FTP server.

Large files on FTP sites often are compressed to reduce storage space and download time. Before you can use a compressed (zipped) file, you must uncompress (unzip) it. Chapter 8 discusses utilities that zip and unzip files.

Newsgroups and Message Boards

A **newsgroup** is an online area in which users have written discussions about a particular subject (Figure 2-30). To participate in a discussion, a user sends a message to the newsgroup, and other users in the newsgroup read and reply to the message. The entire collection of Internet newsgroups is called *Usenet*, which contains tens of thousands of newsgroups about a multitude of topics. Some major topic areas include news, recreation, society, business, science, and computers.

A computer that stores and distributes newsgroup messages is called a *news server*. Many universities, corporations, Internet access providers, and other large organizations have a news server. Some newsgroups require you to enter a user name and password to participate in the discussion. Only authorized members can use this type of newsgroup. For example, a newsgroup for students taking a college course may require a user name and password to access the newsgroup. This ensures that only students in the course participate in the discussion.

To participate in a newsgroup, typically you use a program called a *newsreader*. Outlook Express includes a newsreader. You also can download newsreaders free or for a fee on the Web. Instead of using your own newsreader, some Web sites that sponsor newsgroups have a built-in newsreader. A newsreader enables you to access a newsgroup to read previously entered messages, called *articles*. You can *post*, or add, articles of your own. The newsreader also keeps track of which articles you have and have not read.

Newsgroup members frequently post articles as a reply to another article — either to

WEB LINK 2-7

FTP

For more information, visit scsite.com/dc2006/ch2/weblink and then click FTP.

FIGURE 2-29a (FTP site being added to My Network Places folder)

FIGURE 2-29b (FTP site link is displayed in My Network Places folder)

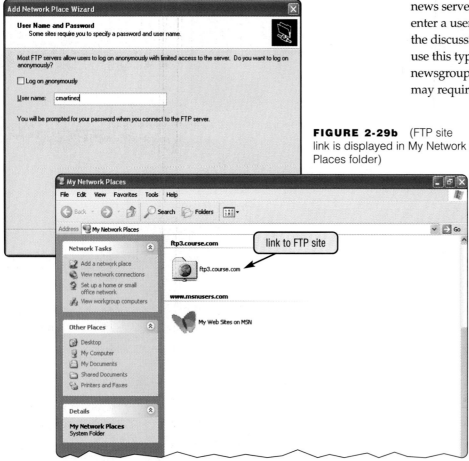

FIGURE 2-29 Many operating systems, such as Windows XP, have built-in FTP capabilities.

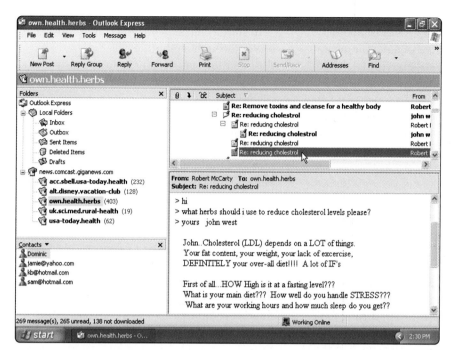

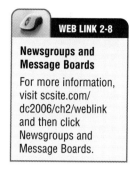

WEB LINK 2-8

Newsgroups and Message Boards

For more information, visit scsite.com/ dc2006/ch2/weblink and then click Newsgroups and Message Boards.

FIGURE 2-30   Users in a newsgroup read and reply to other users' messages.

answer a question or to comment on material in the original article. These replies may cause the author of the original article, or others, to post additional articles related to the original article. A *thread* or *threaded discussion* consists of the original article and all subsequent related replies. A thread can be short-lived or continue for some time, depending on the nature of the topic and the interest of the participants.

Using a newsreader, you can search for newsgroups discussing a particular subject such as a type of musical instrument, brand of sports equipment, or employment opportunities. If you like the discussion in a particular newsgroup, you can *subscribe* to it, which means its location is saved in your newsreader for easy future access.

In some newsgroups, posted articles are sent to a moderator instead of immediately displaying on the newsgroup. The *moderator* reviews the contents of the article and then posts it, if appropriate. With a *moderated newsgroup*, the moderator decides if the article is relevant to the discussion. The moderator may choose to edit or discard inappropriate articles. For this reason, the content of a moderated newsgroup is considered more valuable.

A popular Web-based type of discussion group that does not require a newsreader is a **message board**. Many Web sites use message boards instead of newsgroups because they are easier to use.

Mailing Lists

A **mailing list** is a group of e-mail names and addresses given a single name. When a message is sent to a mailing list, every person on the list receives a copy of the message in his or her mailbox. To add your e-mail name and address to a mailing list, you **subscribe** to it (Figure 2-31). To remove your name, you **unsubscribe** from the mailing list. Some mailing lists are called *LISTSERVs*, named after a popular mailing list program.

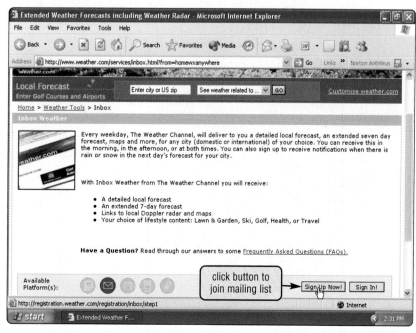

FIGURE 2-31   When you join a mailing list, you and all others on the mailing list receive e-mail messages from the Web site.

WEB LINK 2-9

Mailing Lists

For more information, visit scsite.com/ dc2006/ch2/weblink and then click Mailing Lists.

Thousands of mailing lists exist about a variety of topics in areas of entertainment, business, computers, society, culture, health, recreation, and education. To locate a mailing list dealing with a particular topic, search for the keywords, mailing list or LISTSERV, in a search engine. Many vendors use mailing lists to communicate with their customer base.

Chat Rooms

A **chat** is a real-time typed conversation that takes place on a computer. **Real time** means that you and the people with whom you are conversing are online at the same time. A **chat room** is a location on an Internet server that permits users to chat with each other. Anyone in the chat room can participate in the conversation, which usually is specific to a particular topic.

WEB LINK 2-10

Chat Rooms

For more information, visit scsite.com/ dc2006/ch2/weblink and then click Chat Rooms.

As you type on your keyboard, a line of characters and symbols is displayed on the computer screen. Others connected to the same chat room server also see what you have typed (Figure 2-32). Some chat rooms support voice chats and video chats, in which people hear or see each other as they chat.

To start a chat session, you connect to a chat server through a program called a *chat client*. Today's browsers usually include a chat client. If yours does not, you can download a chat client from the Web.

Once you have installed a chat client, you can create or join a conversation on the chat server to which you are connected. The chat room should indicate the discussion topic. The person who creates a chat room acts as the operator and has responsibility for monitoring the conversation and disconnecting anyone who becomes disruptive. Operator status can be shared or transferred to someone else.

Instant Messaging

Instant messaging (**IM**) is a real-time Internet communications service that notifies you when one or more people are online and then allows you to exchange messages or files or join a private chat room with them. Some IM services support voice and video conversations (Figure 2-33). Many IM services also can alert you to information such as calendar appointments, stock quotes, weather, or sports scores. They also allow you to send pictures or other documents to a recipient. For IM to work, both parties must be online at the same time. Also, the receiver of a message must be willing to accept messages.

People use IM on all types of computers, including desktop computers and mobile computers and devices, such as smart phones. To use IM, you may have to install *instant messenger* software on the computer or device you plan to use. Some operating systems, such as Windows XP, include an instant messenger. No standards currently exist for IM. To ensure successful communications, all individuals on the notification list need to use the same or a compatible instant messenger.

FIGURE 2-32 As you type, the words and symbols you enter are displayed on the computer screens of other people in the same chat room.

FIGURE 2-33 AN EXAMPLE OF INSTANT MESSAGING

WEB LINK 2-11

Instant Messaging
For more information, visit scsite.com/dc2006/ch2/weblink and then click Instant Messaging.

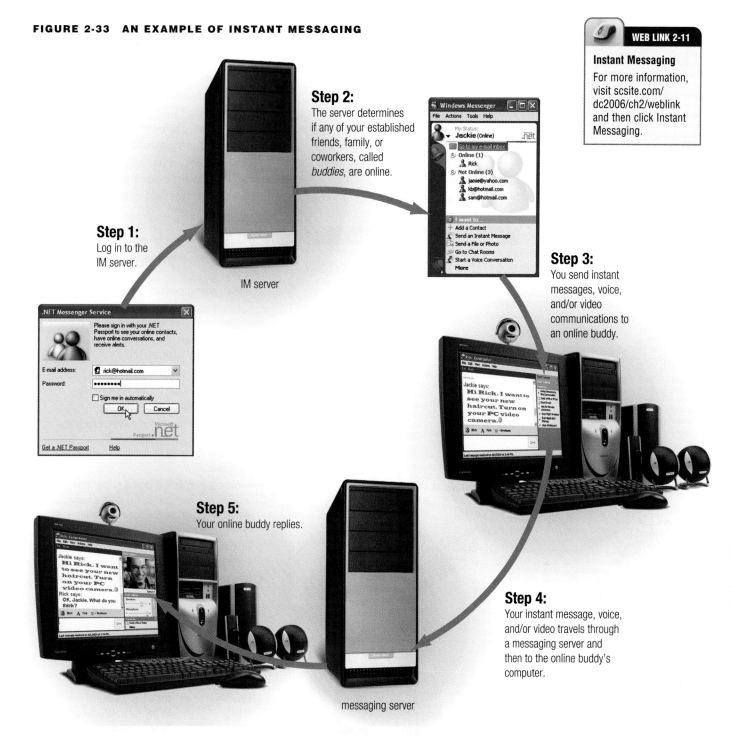

Step 1:
Log in to the IM server.

Step 2:
The server determines if any of your established friends, family, or coworkers, called *buddies*, are online.

IM server

Step 3:
You send instant messages, voice, and/or video communications to an online buddy.

Step 5:
Your online buddy replies.

Step 4:
Your instant message, voice, and/or video travels through a messaging server and then to the online buddy's computer.

messaging server

Internet Telephony

Internet telephony, also called *Voice over IP* (Internet Protocol), enables users to speak to other users over the Internet using their desktop computer, mobile computer, or mobile device. That is, Internet telephony uses the Internet (instead of the public switched telephone network) to connect a calling party to one or more local or long-distance called parties.

To place an Internet telephone call, you need a high-speed Internet connection (e.g., via DSL or cable modem); Internet telephone service; a microphone or telephone, depending on the Internet telephone service; and Internet telephone software or a telephone adapter, depending on the Internet telephone service. Calls to other parties with the same Internet telephone service often are free, while calls that connect to the telephone network typically cost about $15 to $40 per month.

As you speak in a microphone or telephone connected to your computer, the Internet telephone software and the computer's sound card or the telephone adapter convert your spoken words (analog signals) to digital signals and then transmit the digitized audio over the Internet to the called parties. Software and equipment at the receiving end reverse the process so the receiving parties can hear what you have said. Figure 2-34 illustrates a user's equipment configuration for Internet telephony.

FAQ 2-11

How popular is Internet telephony?

One study predicts that by 2007, more than five million people will subscribe to Internet telephony services, which will account for 40 percent of all telephone calls. For more information, visit scsite.com/dc2006/ch2/faq and then click Internet Telephony.

FIGURE 2-34　Equipment configuration for a user making a call via Internet telephony.

NETIQUETTE

Netiquette, which is short for Internet etiquette, is the code of acceptable behaviors users should follow while on the Internet; that is, it is the conduct expected of individuals while online. Netiquette includes rules for all aspects of the Internet, including the World Wide Web, e-mail, FTP, newsgroups and message boards, chat rooms, and instant messaging. Figure 2-35 outlines some of the rules of netiquette.

NETIQUETTE

Golden Rule: Treat others as you would like them to treat you.

1. In e-mail, newsgroups, and chat rooms:
   - Keep messages brief. Use proper grammar, spelling, and punctuation.
   - Be careful when using sarcasm and humor, as it might be misinterpreted.
   - Be polite. Avoid offensive language.
   - Read the message before you send it.
   - Use meaningful subject lines.
   - Avoid sending or posting *flames*, which are abusive or insulting messages. Do not participate in *flame wars*, which are exchanges of flames.
   - Avoid sending spam, which is the Internet's version of junk mail. *Spam* is an unsolicited e-mail message or newsgroup posting sent to many recipients or newsgroups at once.
   - Do not use all capital letters, which is the equivalent of SHOUTING!
   - Use **emoticons** to express emotion. Popular emoticons include

:)	Smile	:\	Undecided
:(	Frown	:o	Surprised
:l	Indifference		

   - Use abbreviations and acronyms for phrases:

BTW	by the way
FYI	for your information
FWIW	for what it's worth
IMHO	in my humble opinion
TTFN	ta ta for now
TYVM	thank you very much

   - Clearly identify a *spoiler*, which is a message that reveals a solution to a game or ending to a movie or program.

2. Read the *FAQ* (frequently asked questions), if one exists. Many newsgroups and Web pages have an FAQ.

3. Do not assume material is accurate or up-to-date. Be forgiving of other's mistakes.

4. Never read someone's private e-mail.

FIGURE 2-35　Some of the rules of netiquette.

Test your knowledge of pages 91 through 100 in Quiz Yourself 2-3.

QUIZ YOURSELF 2-3

Instructions: Find the true statement below. Then, rewrite the remaining false statements so they are true.

1. A chat room is a location on an Internet server that permits users to chat with each other.

2. An e-mail address is a combination of a user name and an e-mail program that identifies a user so he or she can receive Internet e-mail.

3. Business-to-consumer e-commerce occurs when one consumer sells directly to another, such as in an online auction.

4. FTP is an Internet standard that permits file reading and writing with other computers on the Internet.

5. Spam uses the Internet (instead of the public switched telephone network) to connect a calling party to one or more called parties.

6. Netiquette is the code of unacceptable behaviors while on the Internet.

7. On a newsgroup, a subscription consists of the original article and all subsequent related replies.

Quiz Yourself Online: To further check your knowledge of e-commerce, e-mail, FTP, newsgroups and message boards, mailing lists, chat rooms, instant messaging, Internet telephony, and netiquette, visit scsite.com/dc2006/ch2/quiz and then click Objectives 10 – 12.

CHAPTER SUMMARY

This chapter presented the history and structure of the Internet. It discussed the World Wide Web at length, including topics such as browsing, navigating, searching, Web publishing, and e-commerce. It also introduced other services available on the Internet, such as e-mail (read At Issue 2-5 for a related discussion), FTP, news-groups and message boards, chat rooms, instant messaging, and Internet telephony. Finally, the chapter listed rules of netiquette.

AT ISSUE 2-5

E-Mail: Irritant or Liberator?

E-mail is one of the more popular services on the Internet. Worldwide, more than 230 million people send and receive e-mail messages. E-mail makes business managers more productive by allowing them to share information, ideas, and opinions easily. But ironically, this easy sharing also can make managers less productive. Every day, managers wade through rivers of e-mail messages. Some of the messages are important, but many are copies of messages sent to others, notes on minor matters, or observations once shared in brief telephone calls or on walks to the water cooler. Most messages expect a quick reply, so hours can be spent dealing with e-mail. The constant flow of e-mail steals the time and interrupts the concentration needed for every-day work activities. Even worse, as managers become accustomed to the brief, rapid thinking demanded for e-mail, they can become unused to the creative, contemplative, persistent thought processes required for complex projects. Managers use a variety of measures to dam the flood of e-mail, including limiting the amount of time spent on messages, having colleagues telephone when they send important messages, and using filtering software to prioritize messages. What is the best way to deal with e-mail? Why? In terms of productivity, how can a company maximize the advantages of e-mail and minimize the disadvantages?

CAREER CORNER

Web Developer

If you are looking for a job working with the latest Internet technology, then Web developer could be the career for you. A *Web developer* analyzes, designs, develops, implements, and supports Web applications and functionality. Specialized programming skills required include HTML, JavaScript, Java, Perl, C++, and VBScript. Developers also may need multimedia knowledge, including Adobe Photoshop, Macromedia Flash, and Macromedia Director. Developers must be aware of emerging technologies and know how they can be used to enhance a Web presence.

A Web developer must be able to appreciate a client's needs, recognize the technologies involved to meet those needs, and explain those technologies to the client. For example, if the client is a large corporation seeking to set up an online store, a Web developer must understand e-commerce and be able to explain requirements, probable costs, and possible outcomes in a way the client can understand.

Educational requirements vary from company to company and can range from a high school education to a four-year degree. Many companies place heavy emphasis on certifications. Two of the more popular certifications are available through the International Webmasters Association (IWA) and the World Organization of Webmasters (WOW). A wide salary range exists — from $35,000 to $65,000 — depending on educational background and location. For more information, visit scsite.com/dc2006/ch2/careers and then click Web Developer.

High-Tech Talk

A COMPUTER'S INTERNET PROTOCOL (IP) ADDRESS

Every computer on the Internet has a unique address, called an IP address, that distinguishes it from other computers on the Internet. An IP address has two parts that identify a specific computer: one part to identify the network where that computer resides and a second part to pinpoint the specific computer or host within that network.

A typical IP address — such as 216.239.39.99 — has four groups of numbers that range from 0 through 255. This form of the IP address sometimes is called a *dotted decimal number* or *dotted quad*. The four groups of numbers in the dotted quad are called octets, because they each have 8 bits when viewed in binary form for a total of 32 bits in the IP address. For instance, the binary form of 216.239.39.99 is 11011000.11101111.00101001.01100011 (Figure 2-36). For more information about how the binary system works, see Appendix A.

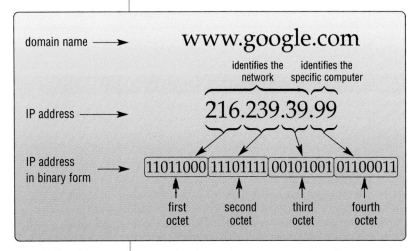

FIGURE 2-36
Components of an IP address.

Because each of the 8 bits can be 1 or 0, the total possible combinations per octet are 2^8, or 256. Combining the four octets of an IP address provides a possible 2^{32} or 4,294,967,296 unique values. The actual number of available addresses is about 3 billion, because some values are reserved for special use and are, therefore, off limits.

To request data such as a Web page from a computer on the Internet, you need only an IP address. For instance, if you type the Web address, http://216.239.39.99, your browser will display the home page on the machine hosting the Google Web site. Of course, remembering one IP address out of billions is a little overwhelming — so you probably would just type the domain name, www.google.com, in your browser. Your browser then contacts a domain name server (DNS) to resolve the human-readable domain name into a machine-readable IP address. Each domain name server houses a simple database that maps domain names to IP addresses. The DNS would resolve the human-readable domain name, www.google.com, into a machine-readable IP address, 216.239.39.99.

Domain names are helpful because they are easier for people to remember than IP addresses. You can learn more about a domain using the whois form at the Network Solutions Web site (www.netsol.com and then click the whois link). If you type a domain name, such as google.com, the form displays the registration information for that domain, including its IP address.

Like all other computers, your computer must have an IP address to connect to the Internet or another computer that has an IP address. Servers generally have *static IP addresses*, because they usually are connected to the Internet and their IP addresses do not change often. When you connect to the Internet using your home computer, you most likely are using a temporary or *dynamic IP address*. Your access provider uses the *Dynamic Host Configuration Protocol (DHCP)* to assign your computer a temporary dynamic IP address from a pool of IP addresses. The dynamic IP address is unique only for that session. Once you disconnect, the DHCP server puts that IP address back in the IP address pool so it can assign it to the next requesting computer. Even if you immediately reconnect, the DHCP server might not assign you the same IP address. Using DHCP and dynamic IP addresses means an Internet service provider needs only one IP address for each modem it supports, rather than one for each of its millions of customers.

Billions of IP addresses sounds like a lot. But, because so many computers connected to the Internet need unique IP addresses, a growing shortage of IP addresses exists. A new IP addressing scheme, called *IPv6* or *IPng (IP Next Generation)* will lengthen IP addresses from 32 bits to 128 bits and increase the number of available IP addresses to a whopping 3.4×10^{38}, or 340,000,000,000,000,000,000,000,000,000,000,000,000.

Do you want to know the IP address currently assigned to your computer?

- With Windows 2000/XP, click the Start button on the taskbar and then click Run. Type `cmd` to open the MS-DOS window. Type `ipconfig` and then press the ENTER key.
- With Windows 98, click the Start button on the taskbar and then click Run. Type `winipcfg` and then press the ENTER key.

If you are using an older version of AOL, the IP address might read 0.0.0.0 because AOL uses a proprietary method to assign IP addresses. For more information, visit scsite.com/dc2006/ch2/tech and then click IP Addresses.

Companies on the Cutting Edge

GOOGLE
POPULAR SEARCH ENGINE

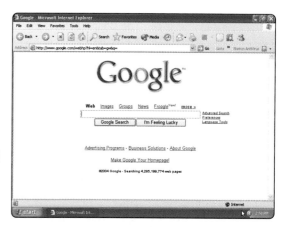

The founders of *Google*, the leading Internet search engine, state that their mission is to organize the world's information. Every day, their Web site handles hundreds of millions of queries for information. In seconds, it can locate specific phrases and terms on four billion Web pages by using more than 10,000 connected computers.

Sergey Brin and Larry Page launched Google in 1998 in a friend's garage. The name is derived from "googol," which is the name of the number 1 followed by 100 zeros. Nearly 2,000 Google employees work at Googleplex, the corporate headquarters in Mountain View, California. According to Initial Public Offering documents filed in 2004, the company is worth more than $2.7 billion. For more information, visit scsite.com/dc2006/ch2/companies and then click Google.

YAHOO!
POPULAR WEB PORTAL

Yahoo!, the first navigational portal to the Web, began as a hobby for Jerry Yang and David Filo when they were doctoral candidates in electrical engineering at Stanford University. They started creating and organizing lists of their favorite Web sites in 1994. The following year, they shared their creation, named Yahoo!, with fellow students and then released their product to the Internet community.

Yahoo! is an acronym for Yet Another Hierarchical Officious Oracle. What makes Yahoo! unique is that staff members build the directory by assuming the role of a typical Web researcher. In 2004 the site enhanced its Yahoo! Messenger service, with two-player games, expressive verbal animations, and the ability to listen to customized radio stations. For more information, visit scsite.com/dc2006/ch2/companies and then click Yahoo!.

Technology Trailblazers

TIM BERNERS-LEE
CREATOR OF THE WORLD WIDE WEB

The World Wide Web (WWW) has become one of the more widely used Internet services, and its roots are based on *Tim Berners-Lee's* work. Berners-Lee is credited with creating the first Web server, browser, and URL addresses.

He developed his ideas in 1989 while working at CERN, the European Particle Physics Laboratory in Geneva, Switzerland, and based his work on a program he had written for his own use to track random associations. Today, he works quietly in academia as director of the World Wide Web Consortium (W3C) at the Massachusetts Institute of Technology.

In 2004, Berners-Lee received the first Millennium Technology Prize, which is worth $1.2 million and recognizes technological developments that enhance the quality of life and encourage economic growth. For more information, visit scsite.com/dc2006/ch2/people and then click Tim Berners-Lee.

MEG WHITMAN
EBAY PRESIDENT AND CEO

Meg Whitman joined eBay in 1998 and has been instrumental in helping the company become the world's largest online marketplace. Before that time, she was an executive for the Keds Division of the Stride Rite Corporation and general manager of Hasbro Inc.'s Preschool Division. She then served as president and CEO of Florists Transworld Delivery (FTD).

She credits her success to listening to the loyal eBay community, and she occasionally answers their e-mails personally. She holds degrees in economics from Princeton University and management from the Harvard Business School.

Fortune magazine has named Whitman one of the most powerful women in business, and *Worth* magazine has ranked her at the top of its list of most powerful business managers. For more information, visit scsite.com/dc2006/ch2/people and then click Meg Whitman.

Quizzes and Learning Games

Computer Genius
Crossword Puzzle
DC Track and Field
Practice Test
Quiz Yourself
Wheel of Terms
You're Hired!

Exercises

Case Studies
Chapter Review
Checkpoint
Key Terms
Learn How To
Learn It Online
Web Research

Beyond the Book

Career Corner
Companies
FAQs
High-Tech Talk
Looking Ahead
Making Use of
the Web
Trailblazers
Web Links

Features

Chapter Forum
Install Computer
Lab Exercises
Maintain Computer
Tech News
Timeline 2006

Chapter Review

The Chapter Review section summarizes the concepts presented in this chapter. To listen to the audio version of this Chapter Review, visit scsite.com/dc2006/ch2/review. To obtain help from other students regarding any subject in this chapter, visit scsite.com/dc2006/ch2/forum and post your thoughts or questions.

(1) What Is the History of the Internet? The **Internet** is a worldwide collection of networks that links millions of businesses, government agencies, educational institutions, and individuals. The Internet has its roots in *ARPANET*, a network started in 1969 to link researchers across the United States. In 1986, the National Science Foundation connected its huge network, called *NSFnet*, to ARPANET, creating a configuration of complex networks and hosts that became known as the Internet.

(2) How Can You Access and Connect to the Internet? Employees and students often connect to the Internet through a business or school network. The networks usually use a high-speed line leased from a telephone company. Many home and small businesses connect to the Internet with **dial-up access**, which uses a modem in the computer and a standard telephone line. Some home and small business users opt for higher-speed *broadband* connections, such as DSL, cable television networks, radio signals, or satellite. **DSL** provides Internet connections using regular copper telephone lines. A **cable modem** allows access to Internet services through the cable television network. *Fixed wireless* connections use an antenna to communicate via radio signals. A *satellite modem* communicates with a satellite dish. An **access provider** is a business that provides access to the Internet free or for a fee. An **ISP** (**Internet service provider**) is a regional or national access provider. An **online service provider** (**OSP**) provides Internet access in addition to members-only features. A **wireless Internet service provider** (*WISP*) provides wireless Internet access to users with wireless modems or Internet-enabled mobile devices.

(3) What Is an IP Address? An **IP address** (*Internet Protocol address*) is a number that uniquely identifies each computer or device connected to the Internet. The Internet relies on IP addresses to send data to computers at specific locations. A **domain name** is the text version of an IP address.

> Visit scsite.com/dc2006/ch2/quiz or click the Quiz Yourself button. Click Objectives 1 – 3.

(4) What Are the Components of a Web Address? The **World Wide Web** (*WWW*), or **Web**, consists of a worldwide collection of electronic documents. Each electronic document is called a **Web page**. A **URL** (*Uniform Resource Locator*), or **Web address**, is a unique address for a Web page. A Web address consists of a protocol, a domain name, and sometimes the path to a specific Web page or location on a Web page.

(5) What Is the Purpose of a Web Browser? A **Web browser**, or **browser**, is application software that allows users to access and view Web pages. When you type a Web address in the Address box of a browser window, a computer called a **Web server** delivers the requested Web page to your computer. Most Web pages contain links. A **link** is a built-in connection that, when clicked, displays a related Web page or part of a Web page.

(6) How Can You Search for Information on the Web? Two commonly used search tools are subject directories and search engines. A **subject directory** classifies Web pages in an organized set of categories. By clicking links, you move through categories to display a list of Web pages about a desired topic. A **search engine** is a program that finds Web sites and Web pages. To use a search engine, you enter a word or phrase, called **search text**, that defines the item about which you want information. The search engine displays a list of *hits*. When clicked, each hit displays an associated Web site or Web page.

Chapter Review

⑦ What Are the Types of Web Sites? A **portal** is a Web site that offers a variety of Internet services from a single location. A news Web site contains newsworthy material. An informational Web site contains factual information. A business/marketing Web site promotes or sells products or services. An educational Web site offers avenues for teaching and learning. An entertainment Web site provides an interactive and engaging environment. An advocacy Web site describes a cause, opinion, or idea. A **blog** is a Web site that uses a regularly updated journal format. A personal Web site is maintained by a private individual or family.

⑧ How Do Web Pages Use Graphics, Animation, Audio, Video, Virtual Reality, and Plug-Ins? Some Web pages use **multimedia**, which combines text with graphics, animation, audio, video, and/or virtual reality. A **graphic** is a digital representation of nontext information such as a drawing or photograph. **Animation** is the appearance of motion created by displaying a series of still images. **Audio** includes music, speech, or any other sound. **Video** consists of full-motion images. **Virtual reality (VR)** is the use of computers to simulate an environment that appears as three-dimensional space. A **plug-in** is a program that extends a browser's capability to display multimedia elements.

⑨ What Are the Steps Required for Web Publishing? **Web publishing** is the development and maintenance of Web pages. The five major steps to Web publishing are: (1) plan a Web site, (2) analyze and design a Web site, (3) create a Web site, (4) deploy a Web site, and (5) maintain a Web site.

connect ► Visit scsite.com/dc2006/ch2/quiz or click the Quiz Yourself button. Click Objectives 4 – 9.

⑩ What Are the Types of E-Commerce? **E-commerce**, short for *electronic commerce*, is a business transaction that occurs over an electronic network such as the Internet. *Business-to-consumer (B2C) e-commerce* consists of the sale of goods and services to the general public. *Consumer-to-consumer (C2C) e-commerce* occurs when one consumer sells directly to another, such as an **online auction**. *Business-to-business (B2B) e-commerce* takes place between businesses that exchange goods and services.

⑪ How Do E-Mail, FTP, Newsgroups and Message Boards, Mailing Lists, Chat Rooms, Instant Messaging, and Internet Telephony Work? **E-mail** (short for *electronic mail*) is the transmission of messages and files via a computer network. **FTP** (*File Transfer Protocol*) is an Internet standard that permits file **uploading** and **downloading** with other computers. A **newsgroup** is an online area in which users have written discussions. A **message board** is a Web-based type of discussion group that is easier to use than a newsgroup. A **mailing list** is a group of e-mail names and addresses given a single name, so that everyone on the list receives a message sent to the list. A **chat room** is a location on an Internet server that permits users to conduct real-time typed conversations. **Instant messaging (IM)** is a real-time Internet communications service that notifies you when one or more people are online. **Internet telephony** enables users to speak over the Internet using a computer or mobile device.

⑫ What Are the Rules of Netiquette? **Netiquette**, which is short for Internet etiquette, is the code of acceptable behaviors users should follow while on the Internet. Netiquette rules include: keep messages short, be polite, avoid sending *flames* or *spam*, use **emoticons** and acronyms, read the *FAQ*, do not assume material is accurate or up-to-date, and never read someone's private e-mail.

connect ► Visit scsite.com/dc2006/ch2/quiz or click the Quiz Yourself button. Click Objectives 10 – 12.

Quizzes and Learning Games

Computer Genius
Crossword Puzzle
DC Track and Field
Practice Test
Quiz Yourself
Wheel of Terms
You're Hired!

Exercises

Case Studies
Chapter Review
Checkpoint
▶ Key Terms
Learn How To
Learn It Online
Web Research

Beyond the Book

Career Corner
Companies
FAQs
High-Tech Talk
Looking Ahead
Making Use of the Web
Trailblazers
Web Links

Features

Chapter Forum
Install Computer
Lab Exercises
Maintain Computer
Tech News
Timeline 2006

Key Terms

You should know the Primary Terms and be familiar with the Secondary Terms. Use the list below to help focus your study. To further enhance your understanding of the Key Terms in this chapter, visit scsite.com/dc2006/ch2/terms. See an example of and a definition for each term, and access current and additional information about the term from the Web.

Primary Terms

(shown in bold-black characters in the chapter)

access provider (71)
address book (94)
animation (86)
audio (86)
blog (84)
browser (75)
cable modem (70)
chat (98)
chat room (98)
dial-up access (70)
DNS server (74)
domain name (73)
downloading (76)
DSL (70)
e-commerce (91)
electronic storefront (92)
e-mail (92)
e-mail address (94)
e-mail program (93)
emoticons (100)
FTP (96)
graphic (85)
home page (76)
instant messaging (IM) (98)
Internet (68)
Internet telephony (99)
IP address (73)
ISP (Internet service provider) (72)
link (77)
mailing list (97)
message board (97)
MP3 (86)
multimedia (85)
netiquette (100)

newsgroup (96)
online auction (92)
online service provider (OSP) (72)
player (86)
plug-in (89)
portal (82)
real time (98)
search engine (78)
search text (80)
shopping cart (92)
streaming (86)
subject directory (78)
subscribe (97)
surfing the Web (77)
traffic (70)
unsubscribe (97)
uploading (96)
URL (76)
user name (94)
video (88)
virtual reality (VR) (88)
Web (75)
Web address (76)
Web browser (75)
Web community (82)
Web page (75)
Web publishing (90)
Web server (75)
Web site (75)
wireless Internet service provider (72)
World Wide Web (75)

Secondary Terms

(shown in italic characters in the chapter)

Advanced Research Projects Agency (ARPA) (69)
animated GIF (86)
anonymous FTP (96)
ARPANET (69)
articles (96)
broadband (70)
business-to-business (B2B) e-commerce (92)
business-to-consumer (B2C) e-commerce (92)
chat client (98)
click (77)
consumer-to-consumer (C2C) e-commerce (92)
digital subscriber line (70)
DNS server (74)
domain name system (DNS) (74)
dot-com (73)
dynamic Web page (75)
electronic commerce (91)
electronic mail (92)
FAQ (100)
File Transfer Protocol (96)
fixed wireless (70)
flame wars (100)
flames (100)
FTP server (96)
GIF (85)
graphical image (85)
hits (80)
host (69)
hot spots (71)
http (76)
hyperlink (77)
Hypertext Transfer Protocol (76)
instant messenger (98)
Internet backbone (72)
Internet Corporation for Assigned Names and Numbers (ICANN) (74)
Internet Protocol address (73)
JPEG (85)
keywords (80)

LISTSERVs (97)
m-commerce (91)
microbrowser (76)
moderated newsgroup (97)
moderator (97)
Moving Pictures Experts Group (MPEG) (88)
MPEG-4 (88)
national ISP (72)
Net (68)
news server (96)
newsreader (96)
NSFnet (70)
PNG (85)
point of presence (POP) (72)
POP3 (95)
post (96)
Post Office Protocol (95)
pull (76)
push (76)
regional ISP (72)
satellite modem (70)
SMTP (simple mail transfer protocol) (94)
spam (100)
spider (81)
spoiler (100)
static Web page (75)
streaming audio (86)
streaming video (88)
subscribe (97)
thread (97)
threaded discussion (97)
thumbnail (86)
top-level domain (73)
Uniform Resource Locator (76)
Usenet (96)
Voice over IP (99)
VR world (88)
Web log (84)
wireless portal (82)
WISP (72)
World Wide Web Consortium (W3C) (70)
WWW (75)

Checkpoint

Use the Checkpoint exercises to check your knowledge level of the chapter. The Beyond the Book exercises will help broaden your understanding of the concepts presented in this chapter. To complete the Checkpoint exercises interactively, visit scsite.com/dc2006/ch2/check.

Label the Figure

Identify the types of Web sites.

a. advocacy

b. blog

c. business/marketing

d. educational

e. entertainment

f. informational

g. news

h. personal

i. portal

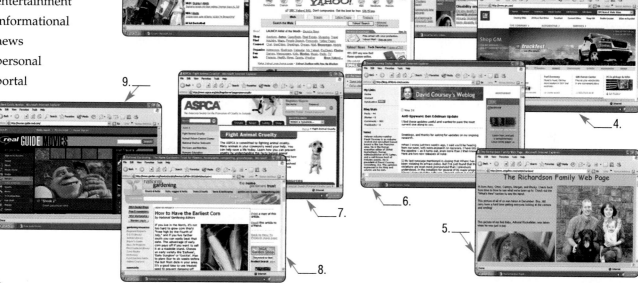

True/False

Mark T for True and F for False. (See page numbers in parentheses.)

_____ 1. A single government agency owns and controls the Internet. (70)

_____ 2. With dial-up Internet access, the telephone number you dial connects you to an access point on the Internet, called a point of presence (POP). (72)

_____ 3. In general, the first portion of each IP address identifies the specific computer and the last portion identifies the network. (73)

_____ 4. Most current browsers and Web sites require the http:// and www portions of a Web address. (76)

_____ 5. Pointing to, or positioning the pointer on, a link on a Web page typically changes the shape of the pointer to a small hand with a pointing index finger. (77)

_____ 6. A major problem with a subject directory is deciding which categories to choose as you work through the menus of links presented. (79)

_____ 7. The purpose of an informational Web site is to convince the reader of the validity of a cause, opinion, or idea. (84)

_____ 8. Developers unfamiliar with Web page authoring programs can create an animated GIF, which combines several GIF images in a single GIF file. (86)

_____ 9. To develop a Web page, you have to be a computer programmer. (90)

_____ 10. An online auction is an example of business-to-consumer (B2C) e-commerce. (92)

_____ 11. Universal standards currently exist for instant messaging (IM). (98)

_____ 12. Using all capital letters in e-mail, newsgroups, and chat rooms is the equivalent of SHOUTING! (100)

Quizzes and Learning Games

Computer Genius
Crossword Puzzle
DC Track and Field
Practice Test
Quiz Yourself
Wheel of Terms
You're Hired!

Exercises

Case Studies
Chapter Review
Checkpoint
Key Terms
Learn How To
Learn It Online
Web Research

Beyond the Book

Career Corner
Companies
FAQ
High-Tech Talk
Looking Ahead
Making Use of the Web
Trailblazers
Web Links

Features

Chapter Forum
Install Computer
Lab Exercises
Maintain Computer
Tech News
Timeline 2006

Checkpoint

 Multiple Choice   Select the best answer. (See page numbers in parentheses.)

1. The Internet has its roots in _____, which was a networking project started by an agency of the U.S. Department of Defense. (69)
   a. ICANN
   b. NSFnet
   c. WISP
   d. ARPANET

2. Many public locations are _____ that provide wireless Internet connections to users with mobile computers or devices. (71)
   a. plug-ins
   b. hot spots
   c. Web logs
   d. chat clients

3. As with an IP address, the components of a domain name are separated by _____. (73)
   a. commas
   b. periods
   c. colons
   d. semicolons

4. Many Web page addresses begin with _____, which stands for a set of rules that defines how pages transfer on the Internet. (76)
   a. http   b. W3C
   c. hits   d. pop

5. Some people use the phrase, _____, to refer to the activity of using links to explore the Web. (77)
   a. surfing the Web
   b. navigating the Net
   c. weaving the Web
   d. bringing in the Net

6. All of the following techniques can be used to improve Web searches except _____. (81)
   a. list all possible spellings
   b. read a search engine's Help information
   c. use general nouns and put the most important terms last
   d. if a search is unsuccessful, try another search engine

7. When you connect to the Internet, the first Web page displayed often is a(n) _____, such as AOL, Lycos, or MSN. (82)
   a. blog
   b. educational Web site
   c. portal
   d. news Web site

8. Some Web sites use _____ on their pages, which are smaller versions of larger graphics. (86)
   a. moderators
   b. threads
   c. players
   d. thumbnails

9. _____ is the process of transferring data in a continuous and even flow, allowing users to access and use a file while it is transmitting. (86)
   a. Streaming
   b. Linking
   c. Surfing
   d. Clicking

10. _____ is not a step in Web publishing. (90)
    a. Planning a Web site
    b. Deploying a Web site
    c. Creating a Web site
    d. Moderating a Web site

11. At a business-to-consumer (B2C) Web site, a _____ allows customers to collect purchases. (92)
    a. news server
    b. chat client
    c. wireless portal
    d. shopping cart

12. In an e-mail address, a _____ is a unique combination of characters that identifies a specific user. (94)
    a. domain name
    b. URL
    c. user name
    d. dot com

13. To add your e-mail name and address to a mailing list, you _____. (97)
    a. upload to it
    b. subscribe to it
    c. download from it
    d. unsubscribe from it

14. Use _____, such as :) for smile and :(for frown, to express emotions in e-mail, newsgroups, and chat rooms. (100)
    a. flames
    b. spam
    c. spoilers
    d. emoticons

Checkpoint

Matching

Match the terms with their definitions. (See page numbers in parentheses.)

_____ 1. traffic (70)

_____ 2. home page (76)

_____ 3. link (77)

_____ 4. spider (81)

_____ 5. Web community (82)

_____ 6. MP3 (86)

_____ 7. player (86)

_____ 8. m-commerce (91)

_____ 9. address book (94)

_____ 10. plug-in

a. software used to listen to an audio file on a computer

b. bulk of communications activity on the Internet

c. joins a specific group of people with similar interests or relationships

d. first page that a Web site displays

e. program that extends the capability of a browser

f. built-in connection to a related Web page or part of a Web page

g. browser designed for the small screens and limited power of PDAs and smart phones

h. term used to identify e-commerce that takes place using mobile devices

i. program used to build and maintain lists of words found on Web sites

j. copy a program from storage to memory

k. format that reduces an audio file to about one-tenth its original size

l. contains a list of names and e-mail addresses

Short Answer

Write a brief answer to each of the following questions.

1. How is a regional ISP different from a national ISP? _____ How is an OSP different from an ISP? _____

2. How is a static Web page different from a dynamic Web page? _____ What is a Web site? _____

3. What three graphics formats are used frequently on the Web? _____ How are they different? _____

4. What is a threaded discussion? _____ What is a moderated newsgroup? _____

5. What are flame wars? _____ How is spam different from a spoiler? ____

Beyond the Book

Read the following book elements, learn more about each using the Web, and then write a brief report.

1. At Issue — Diplomas Online? (82), Mobile Web Logs with Photos — an Invasion of One's Privacy? (84), To Tax or Not to Tax Internet Sales? (92), Are Free Web-Based E-Mail Services Worth the Price? (94), or E-Mail: Irritant or Liberator? (101)

2. Career Corner — Web Developer (101)

3. Companies on the Cutting Edge — Google or Yahoo! (103)

4. FAQs (71, 72, 72, 74, 77, 81, 85, 86, 92, 95, 100)

5. High-Tech Talk — A Computer's Internet Protocol (IP) Address (102)

6. Looking Ahead — Internet Speeds into the Future (70) or 3-D Search Engines Get the Picture (81)

7. Making Use of the Web — Travel (118)

8. Picture Yourself Instant Messaging (66)

9. Technology Trailblazers — Tim Berners-Lee or Meg Whitman (103)

10. Web Links (72, 77, 86, 89, 92, 95, 96, 97, 98, 98, 99)

**Quizzes and
Learning Games**

Computer Genius
Crossword Puzzle
DC Track and Field
Practice Test
Quiz Yourself
Wheel of Terms
You're Hired!

Exercises

Case Studies
Chapter Review
Checkpoint
Key Terms
Learn How To
▶ Learn It Online
Web Research

Beyond the Book

Career Corner
Companies
FAQs
High-Tech Talk
Looking Ahead
Making Use of
the Web
Trailblazers
Web Links

Features

Chapter Forum
Install Computer
Lab Exercises
Maintain Computer
Tech News
Timeline 2006

Learn It Online

**Use the Learn It Online exercises to reinforce your understanding of the chapter concepts.
To access the Learn It Online exercises, visit scsite.com/dc2006/ch2/learn.**

① At the Movies — Google Search Secrets

To view the Google Search Secrets movie, click the number 1 button. Locate your video and click the corresponding High-Speed or Dial-Up link, depending on your Internet connection. Watch the movie and then complete the exercise by answering the question that follows. Using the Internet to gather information can seem daunting. The introduction of powerful search engines has enhanced the Internet research experience. Properly utilizing a search engine can benefit almost any project. How might you go about using Google to search for information for a research paper?

② At the Movies — Instant Message from Anywhere

To view the Instant Message from Anywhere movie, click the number 2 button. Locate your video and click the corresponding High-Speed or Dial-Up link, depending on your Internet connection. Watch the movie, and then complete the exercise by answering the question that follows. Instant messaging (IM) is a fun way to stay in touch with your friends, but until now it has been limited to use on the computer. New technology developments have cut the wires, and now you can take IM on the road. What are some of the limitations of wireless instant messaging?

③ Student Edition Labs — Connecting to the Internet

Click the number 3 button. When the Student Edition Labs menu appears, click *Connecting to the Internet* to begin. A new browser window will open. Follow the on-screen instructions to complete the Lab. When finished, click the Exit button. If required, submit your results to your instructor.

④ Student Edition Labs — Getting the Most out of the Internet

Click the number 4 button. When the Student Edition Labs menu appears, click *Getting the Most out of the Internet* to begin. A new browser window will open. Follow the on-screen instructions to complete the Lab. When finished, click the Exit button. If required, submit your results to your instructor.

⑤ Student Edition Labs — E-mail

Click the number 5 button. When the Student Edition Labs menu appears, click *E-mail* to begin. A new browser window will open. Follow the on-screen instructions to complete the Lab. When finished, click the Exit button. If required, submit your results to your instructor.

⑥ Practice Test

Click the number 6 button. Answer each question. When completed, enter your name and click the Grade Test button to submit the quiz for grading. Make a note of any missed questions. If required, submit your score to your instructor.

⑦ Who Wants To Be a Computer Genius²?

Click the number 7 button to find out if you are a computer genius. Directions about how to play the game will be displayed. When you are ready to play, click the Play button. Submit your score to your instructor.

Learn It Online

8 Wheel of Terms

Click the number 8 button to reinforce important terms you learned in this chapter by playing the Shelly Cashman Series version of this popular game. Directions about how to play the game will be displayed. When you are ready to play, click the Play button. Submit your score to your instructor.

9 DC Track and Field

Click the number 9 button to use what you have learned in this chapter to compete against other students in three track and field events. Directions about how to play the game will be displayed. When you are ready to play, click the start first event button. If required, submit your score to your instructor.

10 You're Hired!

Click the number 10 button to use what you have learned in this chapter to embark on the path to a career in computers. Directions about how to play the game will be displayed. When you are ready to play, click the begin game button. If required, submit your score to your instructor.

11 Crossword Puzzle Challenge

Click the number 11 button. Complete the puzzle to reinforce skills you learned in this chapter. Directions about how to play the game will be displayed. When you are ready to play, click the Play button. Submit the completed puzzle to your instructor.

12 Lab Exercises

Click the number 12 button. When the Lab Exercises menu appears, click the exercise assigned by your instructor. A new browser window will open. Follow the on-screen instructions to complete the exercise. When finished, click the Exit button. If required, submit your results to your instructor.

13 In the News

In her book, *Caught in the Net*, Kimberly S. Young contends that the Internet can be addictive. Young's methodology and conclusions have been questioned by several critics, but Young remains resolute. She points out that at one time, no one admitted to the existence of alcoholism. Click the number 13 button and read a news article about the impact of Internet use on human behavior. What effect did the Internet have? Why? In your opinion, is the Internet's influence positive or negative? Why?

14 Chapter Discussion Forum

Select an objective from this chapter on page 67 about which you would like more information. Click the number 14 button and post a short message listing a meaningful message title accompanied by one or more questions concerning the selected objective. In two days, return to the threaded discussion by clicking the number 14 button. Submit to your instructor your original message and at least one response to your message.

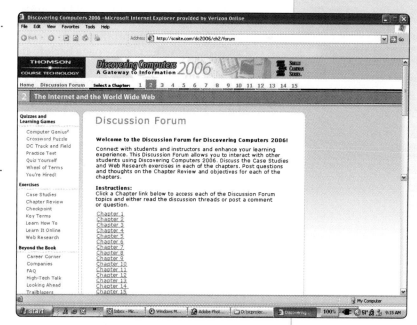

Quizzes and Learning Games

Computer Genius
Crossword Puzzle
DC Track and Field
Practice Test
Quiz Yourself
Wheel of Terms
You're Hired!

Exercises

Case Studies
Chapter Review
Checkpoint
Key Terms
Learn How To
Learn It Online
Web Research

Beyond the Book

Career Corner
Companies
FAQs
High-Tech Talk
Looking Ahead
Making Use of the Web
Trailblazers
Web Links

Features

Chapter Forum
Install Computer
Lab Exercises
Maintain Computer
Tech News
Timeline 2006

Learn How To

Use the Learn How To activities to learn fundamental skills when using a computer and accompanying technology. Complete the exercises and submit them to your instructor. Visit scsite.com/dc2006/ch2/howto to obtain more information pertaining to each activity.

LEARN HOW TO 1: Change a Web Browser's Home Page

When you start a Web browser, a Web page is displayed. You can change the page that appears when you start a Web browser or when you click the Home button on the browser toolbar by completing the following steps:

1. With the browser running, click Tools on the menu bar and then click Internet Options on the Tools menu. *The Internet Options dialog box is displayed (Figure 2-37).*
2. If necessary, in the **Home page** area in the General sheet, select the Web address in the Address box.
3. Type the Web address of the page you want to display both when you start the browser and when you click the Home button.
4. Click the OK button in the Internet Options dialog box.

When you start the browser or click the Home button on the browser toolbar, the selected Web page will be displayed.

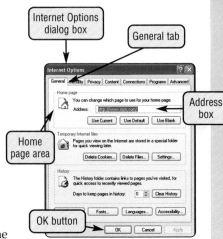

FIGURE 2-37

Exercise

1. Start your Web browser. Write down the address of the browser's current home page. Then, change the browser's home page to www.cnn.com. Close the browser.
2. Start your Web browser. What is the lead story on cnn.com? Use links on the page to view several stories. Which story do you find most interesting? Click the Home button on the browser toolbar. What happened? Submit these answers to your instructor.
3. Change the browser's home page to your school's home page. Click the Home button on the browser toolbar. Click the Calendar or Events link, and then locate two campus events of which you were unaware. Report these two campus events to your instructor.
4. Change the browser's home page back to the address you wrote down in Step 1.

LEARN HOW TO 2: Create and Use Your Own Web Log (Blog)

A Web log, commonly referred to as a blog, can contain any information you wish to place in it. Originally, **blogs** consisted of Web addresses, so that an individual or group with a specific interest could direct others to useful places on the Web. Today, blogs contain addresses, thoughts, diaries, and anything else a person or group wants to share.

Once you have created a blog, you can update it. A variety of services are available on the Web to help you create and maintain your blog. One widely used service is called Blogger. To create a blog using Blogger, complete the following steps:

1. Start your Web browser, type `www.blogger.com` in the Address box, and then press the ENTER key. *The Blogger home page is displayed (Figure 2-38).*
2. Click the CREATE YOUR BLOG NOW arrow on the Blogger home page.
3. Enter the data required on the Create an account page. Your user name and password will allow you to change and manage your blog. Your Display name is the name that will be shown on the blog as the author of the material on the blog. Many people use their own names, but others use pseudonyms as their "pen names" so they are not readily identifiable.
4. Click the Continue arrow and then enter your Blog title and Blog address. These are the names and addresses everyone will use to view your blog. By default, the blog is stored and maintained on the blogspot server.
5. Click the Continue arrow. *The Choose a template screen is displayed.*
6. Choose a template for your blog and then click the Continue arrow.

Learn How To

7. Your blog will be created for you. When you see the Your blog has been created screen, click the Start posting arrow.
8. From the screen that is displayed, you can post items for your blog, specify settings, change the template, and view your blog.
9. When you have posted all your information, click the Sign out button at the top right of the screen. You will be logged out.
10. To edit your blog and add or change information on it, visit the Blogger home page and sign in by entering your user name and password. You will be able to post to your blog.
11. Others can view your blog by entering its address in the browser's Address bar and then pressing the ENTER key.

FIGURE 2-38

Exercise

1. Start your Web browser and visit www.blogger.com. Click the TAKE A QUICK TOUR button and go through all the screens that explain about a blog. What did you learn that you did not know? What type of blog do you find most compelling — a group or an individual blog? Why? Turn in your answers to your instructor.
2. Optional: Create your own blog. Carefully name it and begin your posts at this time. What is your blog name and address? What is its primary purpose? Is it an individual or group blog? Write a paragraph containing the answers to these questions and any other information you feel is pertinent. Turn in this paragraph to your instructor.

LEARN HOW TO 3: Bid and Buy a Product from eBay

Online auctions have grown to be a favorite shopping space for many people. A leading online auction Web site is eBay. To submit a bid for an item on eBay, complete the following steps:

1. Type www.ebay.com in the Address box of your browser. Press the ENTER key. *The eBay home page is displayed (Figure 2-39).*
2. Pick an item you find interesting and on which you might bid.
3. Enter your item in the What are you looking for text box and then click the Find It button.
4. Scroll through the page to see the available items.
5. To bid on an item, click the Place Bid button.
6. Enter the amount of your bid. Click the Continue button.
7. You must be registered to bid on eBay. If you are registered, enter your eBay User ID and Password and then click the Submit button. If not, click the Register button and follow the instructions.
8. After registering, you will confirm your bid and receive notification about your bid.
9. You will be notified by e-mail if you won the bid. If so, you will arrange with the seller for payment and shipment.

FIGURE 2-39

The eBay Web site contains reminders that when you bid on an item, you are entering into a contract to purchase the item if you are the successful bidder. Bidding on eBay is serious business.

Exercise

1. Start your browser and display the eBay home page.
2. In the What are you looking for text box, enter the name of an upcoming sporting event you would like to attend followed by the word, tickets. For example, enter Super Bowl tickets. Click the Search button.
3. Did you find available tickets? Were there more tickets available than you expected, or fewer? Are the bid prices reasonable or ridiculous? How many bids were made for all the tickets? How much time is left to bid? What items did you find you were not expecting? Submit answers to these questions to your instructor.
4. Enter an item of your choice in the What are you looking for text box. If you feel so inclined, bid on an item. Do you think this manner of buying goods is valuable? Why? Will you visit eBay again? Why? Submit answers to these questions to your instructor.

Quizzes and Learning Games

Computer Genius
Crossword Puzzle
DC Track and Field
Practice Test
Quiz Yourself
Wheel of Terms
You're Hired!

Exercises

Case Studies
Chapter Review
Checkpoint
Key Terms
Learn How To
Learn It Online
► Web Research

Beyond the Book

Career Corner
Companies
FAQs
High-Tech Talk
Looking Ahead
Making Use of the Web
Trailblazers
Web Links

Features

Chapter Forum
Install Computer
Lab Exercises
Maintain Computer
Tech News
Timeline 2006

Web Research

Use the Internet-based Web Research exercises to broaden your understanding of the concepts presented in this chapter. Visit scsite.com/dc2006/ch2/research to obtain more information pertaining to each exercise. To discuss any of the Web Research exercises in this chapter with other students, post your thoughts or questions at scsite.com/dc2006/ch2/forum.

(1) Scavenger Hunt Use one of the <u>search engines</u> listed in Figure 2-10 in Chapter 2 on page 78 or your own favorite search engine to find the answers to the questions below. Copy and paste the Web address from the Web page where you found the answer. Some questions may have more than one answer. If required, submit your answers to your instructor. (1) Microsoft Internet Explorer and Netscape Navigator are the two more popular Web browsers. What is the name of the first graphical Web browser? (2) What cable company was established in 1858 to carry instantaneous communications across the ocean that would eventually be used for Internet communications? (3) What American president in 1957 created both the interstate highway system and the Advanced Research Projects Agency (ARPA)? (4) Where is the location of Microsoft's headquarters? (5) How many Web pages is Google currently searching?

(2) Search Sleuth The Internet has provided the opportunity to access encyclopedias online. One of the more comprehensive encyclopedia research sites is **Encyclopedia.com**. Visit this Web site and then use your word processing program to answer the following questions. Then, if required, submit your answers to your instructor. (1) The site's home page provides information about who was born and died and what significant events occurred on this date. What are these facts for today? (2) Type `computer` as the keyword in the Search text box. How many articles discussing computers are found on the Encyclopedia.com Web site? (3) Click your browser's Back button or press the BACKSPACE key to return to the home page. Type `modem` as the keyword in the Search text box. How many articles discussing modems are found on this Web site? (4) In the search results list, click the modem link. What are wireless and a fax modems? (5) Click your browser's Back button or press the BACKSPACE key to return to the home page. Type `Bill Gates` as the keyword in the Search text box and then click the Bill Gates link and read the article. According to this source, why did the Justice Department sue Microsoft in 1997? (6) Click your browser's Back button or press the BACKSPACE key to return to the home page. Click one of the Top Searches links and review the material. Summarize the information you read and then write a 50-word summary.

(3) Newsgroups One of the more popular topics for <u>newsgroups</u> is netiquette. Read the information Borland Software Corporation (info.borland.com/newsgroups/netiquette.html) provides on general newsgroup conduct. Then find three newsgroups, such as those listed in CyberFiber (cyberfiber.com/internet.htm) or Google Groups, that discuss this topic. Read the information and then summarize the advice provided.

(4) Journaling Respond to your readings in this chapter by writing at least one page about your reactions, evaluations, and reflections about the first time you used the **Internet**. For example, to whom did you send your first e-mail message? Have you used chat rooms? Have you bought or sold any items through an online auction Web site? Have you shopped online? Have your instructors required you to access the Internet for class projects? You also can write about the new terms you learned by reading this chapter. If required, submit your journal to your instructor.

(5) Ethics in Action <u>Web cams</u> are video cameras that display their output on a Web page. The feasibility of installing Web cams in 47,000 locations susceptible to terrorist threats, such as nuclear and chemical plants, national airports, and gas storage facilities, is being explored. Citizens would monitor the cameras and report suspicious activity. Critics of this proposal state that the constant surveillance is an invasion of privacy. Visit the USHomeGuard Web site (ushomeguard.org) and then write a summary of the citizen corps' roles in this project. Then locate other Web sites that oppose this plan and summarize their views. If required, submit your summary to your instructor.

Case Studies

Use the Case Studies to apply the concepts presented in the chapter to real-world situations. Visit scsite.com/dc2006/ch2/cases to obtain more information pertaining to each exercise. To discuss the Case Studies in this chapter with other students, visit scsite.com/dc2006/ch2/forum and post your thoughts or questions.

CASE STUDY 1 — Class Discussion   The owner of Deuce Investments, where you are employed part-time as a stock-research analyst, recently attended a one-day continuing education course for small businesses at the local community college. The title of the course was *Ten Reasons Why Your Company Needs the Internet to Compete in Today's Business Environment*. She now feels that the Internet might be useful as an investment-research tool, and she has asked you to investigate the costs associated with making the Internet available for use in the company during business hours. Examine the types of **access providers** available in your community, the monthly cost, and other significant factors that might influence her decision. Draft a memo to the owner summarizing your recommendations. Be prepared to discuss your recommendations in class.

CASE STUDY 2 — Class Discussion   Many retailers, such as Best Buy, Kohl's, and Circuit City, are **brick-and-click businesses**. That is, they allow customers to conduct complete transactions at a physical location as well as online at a Web site. Choose a local brick-and-click business in which you have shopped at the physical location and visit the Web site of the business. Compare the type, availability, and cost (include tax and shipping) of products or services available. Prepare a report that summarizes the advantages and disadvantages of dealing with the physical location versus the Web site of a brick-and-click business. Would you rather shop at the physical location or at the Web site? Why? Does the answer depend on the business, the product, or some other factor? Be prepared to share your findings in class.

CASE STUDY 3 — Research   This chapter lists nine types of Web sites: **portal**, news, informational, business/marketing, educational, entertainment, advocacy, blog, and personal. Use the Internet to find at least one example of each type of Web site. For each Web site, identify the Web address, the multimedia elements used, the purpose of the Web site, and the type of Web site. Explain why you classified each site as you did. Then, keeping in mind the purpose of each Web site, rank the sites in terms of their effectiveness. Write a brief report or use PowerPoint to create a presentation and share your findings with your class.

CASE STUDY 4 — Research   **The Internet** has had a tremendous impact on business. For some businesses, that influence has not been positive. For example, surveys suggest that as a growing number of people order products online, traditional brick-and-mortar businesses are seeing fewer customers. Use the Web and/or print media to learn more about businesses that that have been affected negatively by the Internet. What effect has the Internet had? How can the business compete with the Internet? How has the Internet changed business in positive ways? Write a brief report or use PowerPoint to create a presentation and share your findings with your class.

CASE STUDY 5 — Team Challenge   Recently, Captain Jack Stone, a senior pilot with a major airline, and three of his associates received financial approval to start a new discount airline called Stones Throw. Their plan includes leasing three Boeing 737-200s jetliners and one gate and ticket counter each at LaGuardia airport in New York and LAX airport in Los Angeles. Initially, Stones Throw will offer six daily round-trip flights between New York and Los Angeles. Besides selling tickets at the ticket counter in the airports and through travel agents, they want to develop a compelling Web site that will allow the discount airline to sell seats at declining prices as flight time approaches. Form a three-member team and assist Captain Stone in evaluating current major airline Web sites by listing the advantages and disadvantages of each. Assign each team member the task of evaluating three of the following airlines: American Airlines, AirTran, ATA, Continental, Delta, JetBlue, Southwest, United, and US Airways. Make sure every airline listed is assigned to at least one team member. Have each member print out the **home page** of the airlines they are assigned. In evaluating the Web sites, each team member should pay particular attention to the following areas: (1) design of Web site, (2) ease of use, (3) reservations, (4) online check-in, (5) flight status, (6) award miles, (7) specials, (8) online Help, (9) about the airline, and (10) contact the airline. Meet with your team to share each member's findings and then write a final report or create a PowerPoint presentation that summarizes the team's conclusions and ranks the sites in terms of their effectiveness.

Special Feature

Making Use of the Web

A wealth of information is available on the World Wide Web. The riches are yours if you know where to find this material. Locating useful Web sites may be profitable for your educational and professional careers, as the resources may help you research class assignments and make your life more fulfilling and manageable.

Because the World Wide Web does not have an organizational structure to assist you in locating reliable material, you need additional resources to guide you in searching. To help you find useful Web sites, this Special Feature describes specific information about a variety of Web pages, and it includes tables of Web addresses, so you can get started. The material is organized in several areas of interest.

AREAS OF INTEREST	
Fun and Entertainment	Learning
Travel	Science
Finance	Environment
Resources	Health
Auctions	Research
Government	Careers
Shopping	Arts and Literature
Weather, Sports, and News	

Web Exercises at the end of each category will reinforce the material and help you discover Web sites that may add a treasure trove of knowledge to your life.

Fun and Entertainment
THAT'S ENTERTAINMENT

Rock 'n' Roll on the Web

Consumers place great significance on buying entertainment products for fun and recreation. Nearly 10 percent of the United States's economy is spent on attending concerts and buying DVDs, CDs, reading materials, sporting goods, and toys.

Many Web sites supplement our cravings for fun and entertainment. For example, you can see and hear the musicians inducted into the Rock and Roll Hall of Fame and Museum (Figure 1). If you need an update on your favorite reality-based television program or a preview of an upcoming movie, E! Online and Entertainment Tonight provide the latest features on television and movie stars. The Internet Movie Database contains credits and reviews of more than 400,000 titles.

Watch the surfers riding the waves in Hawaii and romp with pandas at the San Diego Zoo. Web cams, which are video cameras that display their output on Web pages, take armchair travelers across the world for views of natural attractions, historical monuments, colleges, and cities. Many Web sites featuring Web cams are listed in the table in Figure 2.

FUN AND ENTERTAINMENT WEB SITES

Web Cams	URL
AfriCam Virtual Game Reserve	africam.com
Discovery Channel Cams	dsc.discovery.com/cams/cams.html
EarthCam — Webcam Network	earthcam.com
Iowa State Insect Zoo Live Camera	zoocam.ent.iastate.edu
Panda Cam San Diego Zoo	sandiegozoo.org/pandas/pandacam/index.html
The Automated Astrophysical Site-Testing Observatory (AASTO) (South Pole)	www.phys.unsw.edu.au/southpolediaries/webcam.html
Weather and Webcams from OnlineWeather.com and CamVista	onlineweather.com/v4/webcams/index.html
Wild Birds Unlimited Bird FeederCam	wbu.com/feedercam_home.htm
World Surf Cameras	surfrock.com.br/surfcam.htm
WorldLIVE	worldlive.cz/en/webcams

Entertainment	URL
AMG All Music Guide	allmusic.com
E! Online	eonline.com
Entertainment Tonight	etonline.com
Entertainment Weekly's EW.com	ew.com/ew
MSN Entertainment	entertainment.msn.com
Old Time Radio (OTR) — Radio Days: A Soundbite History	otr.com
Rock and Roll Hall of Fame and Museum	rockhall.com
The Internet Movie Database (IMDb)	imdb.com
World Radio Network (WRN)	wrn.org

For more information on fun and entertainment Web sites, visit scsite.com/dc2006/ch2/web.

FIGURE 1 Visitors exploring the Rock and Roll Hall of Fame and Museum Web site will find history, exhibitions, programs, and the names and particulars of the latest inductees.

FIGURE 2 When you visit Web sites offering fun and entertainment resources, you can be both amused and informed.

FUN AND ENTERTAINMENT WEB EXERCISES

1 Visit the WorldLIVE site listed in Figure 2. View two of the Web cams closest to your hometown, and describe the scenes. Then, visit the Discovery Channel Cams Web site and view two of the animal cams in the Featured Cams. What do you observe? Visit another Web site listed in Figure 2 and describe the view. What are the benefits of having Web cams at these locations throughout the world?

2 What are your favorite movies? Use The Internet Movie Database Web site listed in Figure 2 to search for information about two of these films, and write a brief description of the biographies of the major stars and director for each movie. Then, visit one of the entertainment Web sites and describe three of the featured stories. At the Rock and Roll Hall of Fame and Museum Web site, view the information on Elvis and one of your favorite musicians. Write a paragraph describing the information available about these rock stars.

Travel
GET PACKING!

Explore the World without Leaving Home

When you are ready to arrange your next travel adventure or just want to explore destination possibilities, the Internet provides ample resources to set your plans in motion.

To discover exactly where your destination is on this planet, cartography Web sites, including MapQuest (Figure 3), Maps.com, and Rand McNally, allow you to pinpoint your destination. These Web pages generally are divided into geographical areas, such as North America and Europe.

Some good starting places are general travel Web sites such as Expedia Travel, Cheap Tickets, and Travelocity, which is owned by the electronic booking service travel agents use. These all-encompassing Web sites, including those in Figure 4, have tools to help you find the lowest prices and details on flights, car rentals, cruises, and hotels.

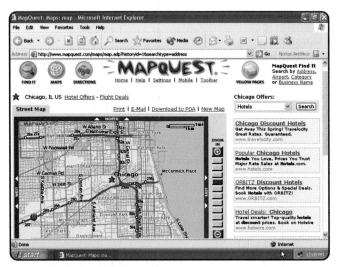

FIGURE 3 MapQuest provides directions, traffic reports, maps, and more.

TRAVEL WEB SITES

General Travel	URL
Cheap Tickets	cheaptickets.com
Expedia.com	expedia.com
Orbitz	orbitz.com
Travelocity.com	travelocity.com
Yahoo! Travel	travel.yahoo.com
Cartography	**URL**
MapQuest	mapquest.com
Maps.com	maps.com
Rand McNally	randmcnally.com
Travel and City Guides	**URL**
All the Largest Cities of the World	greatestcities.com
Frommers.com	frommers.com
U.S.-Parks.com — US National Parks Adventure Travel Guide	us-parks.com

For more information on travel Web sites, visit scsite.com/dc2006/ch2/web.

FIGURE 4 These travel resources Web sites offer travel information to exciting destinations throughout the world.

TRAVEL WEB EXERCISES

1 Visit one of the cartography Web sites listed in Figure 4 and obtain the directions from your campus to one of these destinations: the White House in Washington, D.C.; Elvis's home in Memphis, Tennessee; Walt Disney World in Orlando, Florida; or the Grand Old Opry in Nashville, Tennessee. How many miles is it to your destination? What is the estimated driving time? Then, visit one of the general travel Web sites listed in the table and plan a flight from the nearest major airport to one of the four destinations for the week after finals and a return trip one week later. What is the lowest economy coach fare for this round-trip flight? What airline, flight numbers, and departure and arrival times did you select? Finally, explore car rental rates for a subcompact car for this one-week vacation. What rental agency and rate did you choose?

2 Visit one of the travel and city guides Web sites listed in Figure 4, and choose a destination for a getaway this coming weekend. Write a one-page paper giving details about this location, such as popular hotels and lodging, expected weather, population, local colleges and universities, parks and recreation, ancient and modern history, and tours. Include a map of this place. Why did you select this destination? How would you travel there and back? What is the breakdown of expected costs for this weekend, including travel expenditures, meals, lodging, and tickets to events and activities? What URLs did you use to complete this exercise?

Finance
MONEY MATTERS

Cashing In on Financial Advice

You can manage your money with advice from financial Web sites that offer online banking, tax help, personal finance, and small business and commercial services.

If you do not have a personal banker or a financial planner, consider a Web adviser to guide your investment decisions. The Motley Fool (Figure 5) provides commentary and education on investing strategies, financial news, and taxes.

If you are ready to ride the ups and downs of the NASDAQ and the Dow, an abundance of Web sites listed in Figure 6, including FreeEDGAR and Morningstar.com, can help you pick companies that fit your interests and financial needs.

Claiming to be the fastest, easiest tax publication on the planet, the Internal Revenue Service Web site contains procedures for filing tax appeals and contains IRS forms, publications, and legal regulations.

FINANCE WEB SITES

Advice and Education	URL
Bankrate.com	bankrate.com
LendingTree	lendingtree.com
Loan.com	loan.com
MSN Money	money.msn.com
The Motley Fool	fool.com
Wells Fargo	wellsfargo.com
Yahoo! Finance	finance.yahoo.com
Stock Market	**URL**
E*TRADE Financial	us.etrade.com
Financial Engines	financialengines.com
FreeEDGAR®	www.freeedgar.com
Harris*direct*	harrisdirect.com
Merrill Lynch Direct	mldirect.ml.com
Morningstar.com	www.morningstar.com
The Vanguard Group	vanguard.com
Taxes	**URL**
H&R Block	hrblock.com
Internal Revenue Service	www.irs.gov

For more information on finance Web sites, visit scsite.com/dc2006/ch2/web.

FIGURE 5 The Motley Fool Web site contains strategies and news stories related to personal financing and investing.

FIGURE 6 Financial resources Web sites offer general information, stock market analyses, and tax advice, as well as guidance and money-saving tips.

FINANCE WEB EXERCISES

1. Visit three advice and education Web sites listed in Figure 6 and read their top business world reports. Write a paragraph about each, summarizing these stories. Which stocks or mutual funds do these Web sites predict as being sound investments today? What are the current market indexes for the DJIA (Dow Jones Industrial Average), S&P 500, and NASDAQ, and how do these figures compare with the previous day's numbers?

2. Using two of the stock market Web sites listed in Figure 6, search for information about Microsoft, Adobe Systems, and one other software vendor. Write a paragraph about each of these stocks describing the revenues, net incomes, total assets for the previous year, current stock price per share, highest and lowest prices of each stock during the past year, and other relevant investment information.

Resources
LOOK IT UP

Web Resources Ease Computer Concerns

From dictionaries and encyclopedias to online technical support, the Web is filled with a plethora of resources to answer your computer questions.

Keep up with the latest developments by viewing online dictionaries and encyclopedias that add to their collections of computer and product terms on a regular basis. Shopping for a new computer can be a daunting experience, but many online guides, including PCWorld.com (Figure 7), can help you select the components that best fit your needs and budget.

If you are not confident in your ability to solve a problem alone, turn to online technical support. Web sites, such as those shown in Figure 8, often provide streaming how-to video lessons, tutorials, and real-time chats with experienced technicians. Hardware and software reviews, price comparisons, shareware, technical questions and answers, and breaking technology news are found on comprehensive portals.

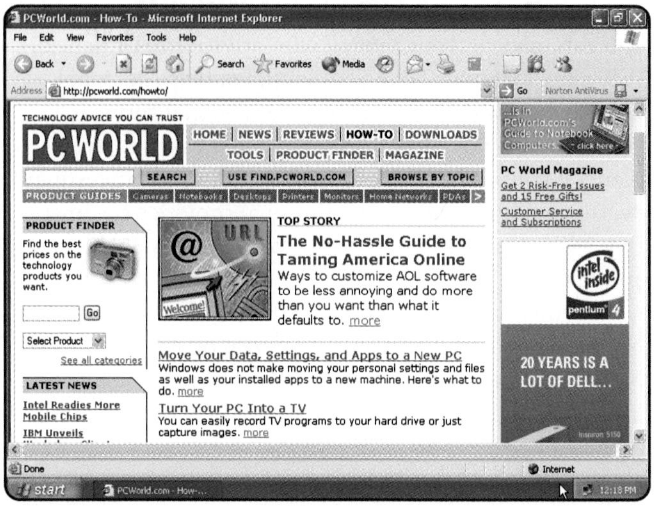

FIGURE 7 Buying and upgrading a computer is simplified with helpful Web sites such as PCWorld.com.

RESOURCES WEB SITES

Dictionaries and Encyclopedias	URL
CDT's Guide to Online Privacy	cdt.org/privacy/guide/terms
ComputerUser High-Tech Dictionary	computeruser.com/resources/dictionary
TechWeb: The Business Technology Network	www.techweb.com/encyclopedia
Webopedia: Online Computer Dictionary for Computer and Internet Terms	webopedia.com
whatis?com	whatis.com

Computer Shopping Guides	URL
A Computer Guide: Reviews on Software and Hardware, Software, Review and More	acomputerguide.com
The CPU Scorecard	cpuscorecard.com
The Online Computer Buying Guide™	grohol.com/computers
Viewz Desktop Computer Buying Guide	viewz.com/shoppingguide/compbuy.shtml
ZDNet	shopper-zdnet.com.com
A Computer Guide: Reviews on Software and Hardware	acomputerguide.com/www/
Online Computer Buying Guide™	grohol.com/computers
Viewz Desktop Computer Buying Guide	viewz.com/shoppingguide/compbuy.shtml
The CPU Scorecard	cpuscorecard.com
ZDNet Shopper	shopper-zdnet.com.com

Upgrading Guides	URL
CNET Shopper.com	shopper.cnet.com
eHow™	ehow.com
Focus on Macs	macs.about.com
PCWorld.com	pcworld.com/howto
Upgrade Source	upgradesource.com

Online Technical Support	URL
Dux Computer Digest	duxcw.com
MSN Tech & Gadgets	computingcentral.msn.com
PC911	pcnineoneone.com
PC Pitstop	pcpitstop.com

Technical and Consumer Information	URL
CNET.com	cnet.com
CompInfo — The Computer Information Center	www.compinfo-center.com
NewsHub	newshub.com/tech
Wired News	wirednews.com
ZDNet	zdnet.com

For more information on resources Web sites, visit scsite.com/dc2006/ch2/web.

FIGURE 8 A variety of Web resources can provide information about buying, repairing, and upgrading computers.

RESOURCES WEB EXERCISES

1 Visit the dictionaries and encyclopedias Web sites listed in Figure 8. Search these resources for five terms. Create a table with two columns: one for the cyberterm and one for the Web definition. Then, create a second table listing five recently added or updated words and their definitions on these Web sites. Next, visit two of the listed computer shopping guides Web sites to choose the components you would buy if you were building a customized desktop computer and notebook computer. Create a table for both computers, listing the computer manufacturer, processor model name or number and manufacturer, clock speed, RAM, cache, number of expansion slots, and number of bays.

2 Visit three upgrading guides Web sites listed in Figure 8. Write a paragraph describing available advice for buying a motherboard. Describe the strengths and weaknesses of these Web sites, focusing on such criteria as clarity of instructions, thoroughness, and ease of navigation. Would you use these Web sites as a resource to troubleshoot computer problems? Then, view two technical and consumer information Web sites listed in the table and write a paragraph about each one, describing the top two news stories of the day.

Auctions
GOING ONCE, GOING TWICE

Rare, Common Items Flood Web Sites

Online auction Web sites can offer unusual items, including *Star Wars* props and memorabilia and a round of golf with Tiger Woods. eBay (Figure 9) is one of thousands of Internet auction Web sites and is the world's largest personal online trading community.

Traditional auction powerhouses, such as Christie's in London and Sotheby's on Manhattan's Upper East Side, are known for their big-ticket items, including a Tyrannosaurus rex fossil that sold for $8.4 million.

If those prices are a bit out of your league, you can turn to a wealth of other auction Web sites, including those listed in Figure 10, to find just the items you need, and maybe some you really do not need, for as little as $1. Categories include antiques and collectibles, automotive, computers, electronics, music, sports, sports cards and memorabilia, and toys.

AUCTION WEB SITES

	URL
Christie's	christies.com
eBay®	ebay.com
Dargate Auction Galleries	dargate.com
musichotbid	musichotbid.com
Penbid.com	penbid.com
Sotheby's	sothebys.com
uBid™	ubid.com
Yahoo! Shopping Auctions	auctions.yahoo.com
For more information on auction Web sites, visit scsite.com/dc2006/ch2/web.	

FIGURE 10 These auction Web sites feature a wide variety of items.

AUCTIONS WEB EXERCISES

1 Visit the Christie's and Sotheby's Web sites and read about the items that have been sold recently. Find two unusual objects and write a paragraph about each one, summarizing your discoveries. What were the opening and final bids on these objects? Then, review two of the upcoming auctions. When are the auctions' dates? What items are available? What are some of the opening bids? What are the advantages and disadvantages of bidding online?

2 Using one of the auction Web sites listed in Figure 10, search for two objects pertaining to your hobbies or interests. For example, if you are a baseball fan, you can search for a complete set of Topps cards. If you are a car buff, search for your dream car. Describe these two items. How many people have bid on these items? Who are the sellers? What are the opening and current bids?

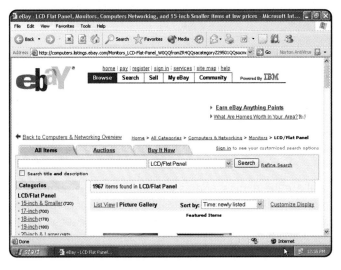

FIGURE 9 eBay is one of the world's more popular auction Web sites.

Government
STAMP OF APPROVAL

Making a Federal Case for Useful Information

When it is time to buy stamps to mail your correspondence, you no longer need to wait in long lines at your local post office. The U.S. Postal Service has authorized several corporations to sell stamps online.

You can recognize U.S. Government Web sites on the Internet by their .gov top-level domain abbreviation. For example, The Library of Congress Web site is lcweb.loc.gov, as shown in Figure 11. Government and military Web sites offer a wide range of information, and some of the more popular sites are listed in Figure 12. The Time Service Department Web site will provide you with the correct time. If you are looking for a federal document, FedWorld lists thousands of documents distributed by the government on its Web site. For access to the names of your congressional representatives, visit the extensive Hieros Gamos Web site.

GOVERNMENT RESOURCES WEB SITES

Postage	URL
Endicia	endicia.com
Pitney Bowes	pb.com
Stamps.com	stamps.com
Government	**URL**
FedWorld	www.fedworld.gov
Hieros Gamos — Law and Legal Research Center	hg.org
NARA — United States National Archives and Records Administration	archives.gov
National Agricultural Library	www.nal.usda.gov
The Library of Congress	lcweb.loc.gov
THOMAS Legislative Information	thomas.loc.gov
Time Service Department	tycho.usno.navy.mil
United States Department of Education	ed.gov
United States Department of the Treasury	www.treas.gov
United States Government Printing Office	www.access.gpo.gov
United States National Library of Medicine	www.nlm.nih.gov
United States Patent and Trademark Office	www.uspto.gov
USAJOBS	www.usajobs.opm.gov
White House	whitehouse.gov

For more information on government Web sites, visit scsite.com/ dc2006/ch2/web.

FIGURE 12 These Web sites offer information about buying U.S.-approved postage online and researching federal agencies.

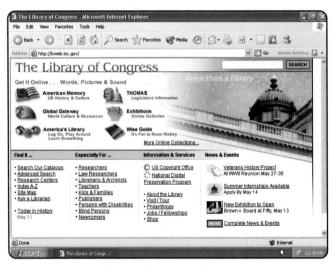

FIGURE 11 The Library of Congress Web site contains more than 119 million items written in 470 languages.

GOVERNMENT WEB EXERCISES

1 View the three postage Web sites listed in Figure 12. Compare and contrast the available services on each one. Consider postage cost, necessary equipment, shipping services, security techniques, and tracking capability. Explain why you would or would not like to use this service.

2 Visit the Hieros Gamos Web site listed in Figure 12. What are the names, addresses, and telephone numbers of your two state senators and your local congressional representative? On what committees do they serve? Who is the chief justice of the Supreme Court, and what has been this justice's opinion on two recently decided cases? Who are the members of the president's cabinet? Then, visit two other Web sites listed in Figure 12. Write a paragraph about each Web site describing its content and features.

Shopping
CYBERMALL MANIA

Let Your Mouse Do Your Shopping

From groceries to clothing to computers, you can buy just about everything you need with just a few clicks of your mouse. Electronic retailers (e-tailers) are cashing in on cybershoppers' purchases. Books, computer software and hardware, and music are the hottest commodities.

Holiday sales account for a large portion of Internet purchases with more than nine million households doing some of their holiday shopping online. During this season, millions of shoppers visit Web sites such as BestBuy.com (Figure 13) daily. Macy's, Bloomingdale's and other e-tailers ship more than 300,000 boxes daily out of warehouses the size of 20 football fields and stocked with five million items.

FIGURE 13 Shopping for popular computer equipment online eliminates waiting in lines in stores.

The two categories of Internet shopping Web sites are those with physical counterparts, such as Eddie Bauer, Wal-Mart, and Tower Records, and those with only a Web presence, such as Amazon.com. Popular Web shopping sites are listed in Figure 14.

SHOPPING WEB SITES

Apparel	URL
Eddie Bauer Since 1920	eddiebauer.com
J.Crew	jcrew.com
Lands' End	landsend.com
Books and Music	**URL**
Amazon.com	amazon.com
Barnes & Noble.com	bn.com
Tower Records	towerrecords.com
Computers and Electronics	**URL**
Crutchfield.com	crutchfield.com
BestBuy.com	bestbuy.com
buy.com	buy.com
Miscellaneous	**URL**
1-800-flowers.com	1800flowers.com
drugstore.com	drugstore.com
Froogle	froogle.com
The Sharper Image	sharperimage.com
Walmart.com	walmart.com

For more information on shopping Web sites, visit scsite.com/dc2006/ch2/web.

FIGURE 14 Making online purchases can help ease the strain of driving to and fighting the crowds in local malls.

SHOPPING WEB EXERCISES

1 Visit two of the three apparel Web sites listed in the table in Figure 14 and select a specific pair of jeans and a shirt from each one. Create a table with these headings: e-tailer, style, fabric, features, price, tax, and shipping fee. Enter details about your selections in the table. Then, visit two of the books and music Web sites and search for a CD you would consider purchasing. Create another table with the names of the Web site, artist, and CD, as well as the price, tax, and shipping fee.

2 Visit two of the computers and electronics and two of the miscellaneous Web sites listed in Figure 14. Write a paragraph describing the features these Web sites offer compared with the same offerings from stores. In another paragraph, describe any disadvantages of shopping at these Web sites instead of actually seeing the merchandise. Then, describe their policies for returning unwanted merchandise and for handling complaints.

Weather, Sports, and News
WHAT'S NEWS?

Weather, Sports, and News Web Sites Score Big Hits

Rain or sun? Hot or cold? Weather is the leading online news item, with at least 10,000 Web sites devoted to this field. The Weather Channel (Figure 15) receives more than 10 million hits each day.

Baseball may be the national pastime, but sports aficionados yearn for everything from auto racing to cricket. The Internet has more than one million pages of multimedia sports news, entertainment, and merchandise.

The Internet has emerged as a major source for news, with one-third of Americans going online at least once a week and 15 percent going online daily for reports of major news events. These viewers, who tend to be under the age of 50 and college graduates, are attracted to the Internet's flashy headline format, immediacy, and in-depth reports. Popular weather, sports, and news Web sites are listed in Figure 16.

WEATHER, SPORTS, AND NEWS WEB SITES

Weather	URL
Infoplease Weather	infoplease.com/weather.html
Intellicast.com	intellicast.com
STORMFAX®	stormfax.com
The Weather Channel	weather.com
WX.com	wx.com

Sports	URL
CBS SportsLine.com	cbs.sportsline.com
ESPN.com	espn.com
NCAAsports.com	ncaasports.com
OFFICIAL WEBSITE OF THE OLYMPIC MOVEMENT	olympic.org
SIRC — A World of Sport Information	sirc.ca
Sporting News Radio	radio.sportingnews.com

News	URL
MSNBC	msnbc.com
NYPOST.COM	nypost.com
onlinenewspapers.com	onlinenewspapers.com
Privacy.org	privacy.org
SiliconValley.com	siliconvalley.com
Starting Page Best News Sites	startingpage.com/html/news.html
USATODAY.com	usatoday.com
washingtonpost.com	washingtonpost.com

For more information on weather, sports, and news Web sites, visit scsite.com/dc2006/ch2/web.

FIGURE 16 Keep informed about the latest weather, sports, and news events with these Web sites.

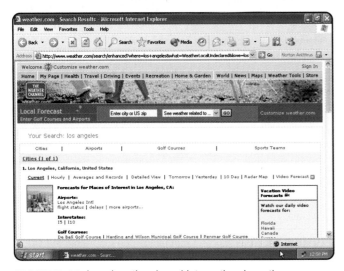

FIGURE 15 Local, national, and international weather conditions and details about breaking weather stories are available on The Weather Channel Web pages.

WEATHER, SPORTS, AND NEWS EXERCISES

1 Visit two of the weather Web sites listed in the table in Figure 16. Do they contain the same local and five-day forecasts for your city? What similarities and differences do they have in coverage of a national weather story? Next, visit two of the sports Web sites in the table and write a paragraph describing the content these Web sites provide concerning your favorite sport.

2 Visit the onlinenewspapers.com and Starting Page Best News Sites Web sites listed in Figure 16 and select two newspapers from each site. Write a paragraph describing the top national news story featured in each of these four Web pages. Then, write another paragraph describing the top international news story displayed at each Web site. In the third paragraph, discuss which of the four Web sites is the most interesting in terms of story selection, photographs, and Web page design.

Learning
YEARN TO LEARN

Discover New Worlds Online

While you may believe your education ends when you finally graduate from college, learning is a lifelong process. For example, enhancing your culinary skills can be a rewarding endeavor. No matter if you are a gourmet chef or a weekend cook, you will be cooking in style with the help of online resources, including those listed in Figure 17.

LEARNING WEB SITES

Cooking	URL
Betty Crocker	bettycrocker.com
recipecenter.com	recipecenter.com
Internet	**URL**
Learn the Net	learnthenet.com
Search Engine Watch	searchenginewatch.com
Wiredguide™	wiredguide.com
Technology and Science	**URL**
HowStuffWorks	howstuffworks.com
ScienceMaster	sciencemaster.com
General Learning	**URL**
Bartleby.com: Great Books Online	bartleby.com
Blue Web'n	www.kn.pacbell.com/ wired/bluewebn
MSN Encarta	encarta.msn.com

For more information on learning Web sites, visit scsite.com/dc2006/ch2/web.

FIGURE 17 The information gleaned from these Web sites can help you learn about many aspects of our existence.

If you would rather sit in front of the computer than stand in front of the stove, you can increase your technological knowledge by visiting several Web sites with tutorials on building your own Web sites, the latest news about the Internet, and resources for visually impaired users.

Have you ever wondered how the Global Positioning System (GPS) works? Take a look at the ScienceMaster site to find details. You might be interested in finding out about how your car's catalytic converter reduces pollution or how the Electoral College functions. Marshall Brain's HowStuffWorks Web site (Figure 18) is filled with articles and animations.

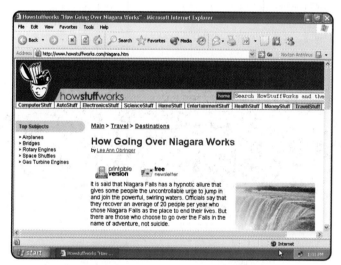

FIGURE 18 The HowStuffWorks Web site provides easy-to-understand information about technology and other facets of our lives.

LEARNING WEB EXERCISES

1. Visit one of the cooking Web sites listed in Figure 17 and find two recipes or cooking tips that you can use when preparing your next meal. Write a paragraph about each one, summarizing your discoveries. What are the advantages and disadvantages of accessing these Web sites on the new Web appliances that might someday be in your kitchen?

2. Using one of the technology and science Web sites and one of the other Web sites listed in Figure 17, search for information about communications and networks. Write a paragraph about your findings. Then, review the material in the general learning Web sites listed in Figure 18, and write a paragraph describing the content on each Web site that is pertinent to your major.

Science

$E = MC^2$

Rocket Science on the Web

For some people, space exploration is a hobby. Building and launching model rockets allow these scientists to participate in exploring the great frontier of space. For others, space exploration is their life. Numerous Web sites, including those in Figure 19, provide in-depth information about the universe.

SCIENCE WEB SITES

Periodicals	URL
Astronomy.com	astronomy.com
Archaeology Magazine	archaeology.org
NewScientist.com	newscientist.com
OceanLink	oceanlink.island.net
Science Magazine	sciencemag.org
SCIENTIFIC AMERICAN.com	sciam.com
Resources	**URL**
National Science Foundation (NSF)	nsf.gov
Science.gov: FirstGov for Science	science.gov
SOFWeb	www.sofweb.vic.edu.au
Science Community	**URL**
American Scientist, The Magazine of Sigma Xi, The Scientific Research Society	amsci.org
Federation of American Scientists	fas.org
NASA	www.nasa.gov
Sigma Xi, The Scientific Research Society	sigmaxi.org

For more information on science Web sites, visit scsite.com/dc2006/ch2/web.

FIGURE 19 Resources available on the Internet offer a wide range of subjects for enthusiasts who want to delve into familiar and unknown territories in the world of science.

The NASA Liftoff Web site contains information about rockets, the space shuttle, the International Space Station, space transportation, and communications. Other science resources explore space-related questions about astronomy, physics, the earth sciences, microgravity, and robotics.

Rockets and space are not the only areas to explore in the world of science. Where can you find the latest pictures taken with the Hubble Space Telescope? Do you know which cities experienced an earthquake today? Have you ever wondered what a 3-D model of the amino acid glutamine looks like? You can find the answer to these questions and many others through the Librarians' Index to the Internet (lii.org) shown in Figure 20.

FIGURE 20 Numerous science resources are organized clearly in the Librarians' Index to the Internet.

SCIENCE WEB EXERCISES

1 Visit the Liftoff to Space Exploration Web site listed in the table in Figure 19. View the links about spacecraft, the universe, or tracking satellites and spacecraft, and then write a summary of your findings.

2 Visit the Librarians' Index to the Internet shown in Figure 20. Click the Science, Computers, & Technology link and then click the Inventions topic. View the Web site for the Greatest Engineering Achievements of the Twentieth Century. Pick two achievements, read their history, and write a paragraph summarizing each of these accomplishments. Then, view two of the science Web sites listed in Figure 19 and write a paragraph about each of these Web sites describing the information each contains.

Environment
THE FATE OF THE ENVIRONMENT

Protecting the Planet's Ecosystem

From the rain forests of Africa to the marine life in the Pacific Ocean, the fragile ecosystem is under extreme stress. Many environmental groups have developed Internet sites, including those listed in Figure 21, in attempts to educate worldwide populations and to increase resource conservation.

ENVIRONMENT WEB SITES

	URL
Central African Regional Program for the Environment (CARPE)	carpe.umd.edu
Earthjustice	www.earthjustice.org
EarthTrends: The Environmental Information Portal	earthtrends.wri.org
Environmental Defense	edf.org
Environmental Sites on the Internet	www.ima.kth.se/im/envsite/envsite.htm
EPA AirData — Access to Air Pollution Data	epa.gov/air/data
Green Solitaire.org	greensolitaire.bizland.com
GreenNet	www.gn.apc.org
The Center for a New American Dream	newdream.org
The Virtual Library of Ecology & Biodiversity	conbio.org/vl
USGS Acid rain data and reports	bqs.usgs.gov/acidrain
UWM Environmental Health, Safety & Risk Management	www.uwm.edu/Dept/EHSRM/EHSLINKS

For more information on environment Web sites, visit scsite.com/dc2006/ch2/web.

FIGURE 21 Environment Web sites provide vast resources for ecological data and action groups.

On an international scale, the Environmental Sites on the Internet Web page developed by the Royal Institute of Technology in Stockholm, Sweden, has been rated as one of the better ecological Web sites. Its comprehensive listing of environmental concerns range from aquatic ecology to wetlands.

The U.S. federal government has a number of Web sites devoted to specific environmental concerns. For example, the U.S. Environmental Protection Agency (EPA) provides pollution data, including ozone levels and air pollutants, for specific areas. Its AirData Web site, shown in Figure 22, displays air pollution emissions and monitoring data from the entire United States and is the world's most extensive collection of air pollution data.

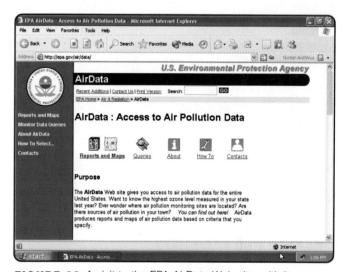

FIGURE 22 A visit to the EPA AirData Web site, with its extensive database, can assist you in checking your community's ozone and air pollutant levels.

ENVIRONMENT WEB EXERCISES

1. The Center for a New American Dream Web site encourages consumers to reduce the amount of junk mail sent to their homes. Using the table in Figure 21, visit the Web site and write a paragraph stating how many trees are leveled each year to provide paper for these mailings, how many garbage trucks are needed to haul this waste, and other statistics. Read the letters that you can use to eliminate your name from bulk mail lists. To whom would you mail these letters? How long does it take to stop these unsolicited letters?

2. Visit the EPA AirData Web site. What is the highest ozone level recorded in your state this past year? Where are the nearest air pollution monitoring Web sites, and what are their levels? Where are the nearest sources of air pollution? Read two reports about two different topics, such as acid rain and air quality, and summarize their findings. Include information on who sponsored the research, who conducted the studies, when the data was collected, and the impact of this pollution on the atmosphere, water, forests, and human health. Whom would you contact for further information regarding the data and studies?

Health
NO PAIN, ALL GAIN

Store Personal Health Records Online

More than 70 million consumers use the Internet yearly to search for health information, so using the Web to store personal medical data is a natural extension of the Internet's capabilities. Internet health services and portals are available online to store your personal health history, including prescriptions, lab test results, doctor visits, allergies, and immunizations. Web sites such as WellMed (Figure 23) are free to consumers.

In minutes, you can register with a health Web site by choosing a user name and password. Then, you create a record to enter your medical history. You also can store data for your emergency contacts, primary care physicians, specialists, blood type, cholesterol levels, blood pressure, and insurance plan. No matter where you are in the world, you and medical personnel can obtain records via the Internet or fax machine. Some popular online health database management systems are shown in Figure 24.

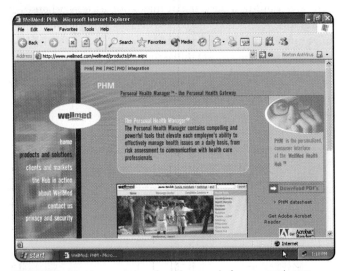

FIGURE 23 You can store health records for you and your family in the WellMed database.

HEALTH WEB SITES

	URL
AboutMyHealth	aboutmyhealth.com
Aetna InteliHealth	intelihealth.com
GlobalMedic	globalmedic.com
PersonalMD	personalmd.com
WebMD®	my.webmd.com/ my_health_record
WellMed	wellmed.com
For more information on health Web sites, visit scsite.com/dc2006/ ch2/web.	

FIGURE 24 These Internet-based health database management systems Web sites allow you to organize your medical information and store it in an online database.

HEALTH WEB EXERCISES

1 Access one of the health Web sites listed in Figure 24. Register yourself or a family member, and then enter the full health history. Create an emergency medical card if the Web site provides the card option. Submit this record and emergency card to your instructor.

2 Visit three of the health Web sites listed in Figure 24. Describe the features of each. Which of the three is the most user-friendly? Why? Describe the privacy policies of these three Web sites. Submit your analysis of these Web sites to your instructor.

Research
SEARCH AND YE SHALL FIND

Info on the Web

A 2004 Web Usability survey conducted by the Nielsen Norman Group found that 88 percent of people log onto a computer and then use a search engine as their first action. Search engines require users to type words and phrases that characterize the information being sought. Yahoo! (Figure 25), Google, and AltaVista are some of the more popular search engines. The key to effective searching on the Web is composing search queries that narrow the search results and place the most relevant Web sites at the top of the results list.

FIGURE 25 The Yahoo! News search results for the phrase, technology, lists more than 83,000 stories.

Subject directories are collections of related Web sites. Yahoo! and LookSmart have two of the more comprehensive subject directories on the Web. Their organized lists often are called trees because a few main categories, such as Entertainment, Computing, Lifestyle, and Work, branch out to more specific subtopics. Popular subject directories and search engines are listed in Figure 26.

RESEARCH WEB SITES

Search Engines	URL
AltaVista	altavista.com
Excite	excite.com
Fast Search & Transfer (FAST)	fastsearch.com
GO.com	go.com
Google	google.com
Northern Light®	northernlight.com
Yahoo!	yahoo.com
Subject Directories	**URL**
About	about.com
Librarians' Index to the Internet	lii.org
LookSmart	looksmart.com
The Internet Public Library	ipl.org
The WWW Virtual Library	vlib.org
Yahoo!	yahoo.com
For more information on research Web sites, visit scsite.com/dc2006/ ch2/web.	

FIGURE 26 Web users can find information by using search engines and subject directories.

RESEARCH WEB EXERCISES

1 Use two of the search engines listed in Figure 26 to find three Web sites that review the latest digital cameras from Sony and Kodak. Make a table listing the search engines, Web site names, and the cameras' model numbers, suggested retail price, megapixels, memory, and features.

2 If money were no object, virtually everyone would have an exquisite car. On the other hand, drivers need a practical vehicle to drive around town daily. Use one of the subject directories listed in Figure 26 to research your dream car and another directory to research your practical car. Write a paragraph about each car describing the particular subject directory tree you used, the manufacturer's suggested retail price (MSRP) of the car, standard and optional equipment, engine size, miles per gallon, and safety features.

Careers
IN SEARCH OF THE PERFECT JOB

Web Helps Career Hunt

While your teachers give you valuable training to prepare you for a career, they rarely teach you how to begin that career. You can broaden your horizons by searching the Internet for career information and job openings.

First, examine some of the job search Web sites. These resources list thousands of openings in hundreds of fields, companies, and locations. For example, the Monster Web site, shown in Figure 27, allows you to choose a broad job area, narrow your search to specific fields within that area, and then search for specific salary ranges, locations, and job functions.

When a company contacts you for an interview, learn as much about it and the industry as possible before the interview. Many of the Web sites listed in Figure 28 include detailed company profiles and links to their corporate Web sites.

CAREER WEB SITES

Job Search	URL
BestJobsUSA.com	ultimatecareerfair.com
CareerBuilder	careerbuilder.com
CareerExchange.com	careerexchange.com
CareerNet	careernet.com
College Grad Job Hunter	collegegrad.com
EmploymentGuide.com	employmentguide.com
HotJobs.com	hotjobs.com
JobBankUSA.com	jobbankusa.com
JobWeb.com	www.jobweb.com
Monster	monster.com
MonsterTRAK	www.jobtrak.com
Spherion	spherion.com
USAJOBS	usajobs.opm.gov
VolunteerMatch	volunteermatch.org

Company/Industry Information	URL
Career ResourceCenter.com	www.resourcecenter.com
Forbes.com	www.forbes.com/2003/03/26/500sland.html
FORTUNE	fortune.com
Hoover's Online	hoovers.com
Occupational Outlook Handbook	stats.bls.gov/oco

For more information on career Web sites, visit scsite.com/dc2006/ch2/web.

FIGURE 28 Career Web sites provide a variety of job openings and information about major companies worldwide.

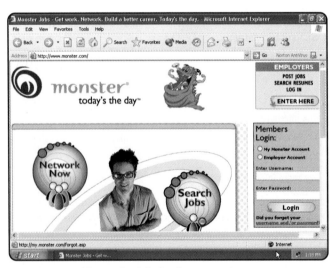

FIGURE 27 Monster's global online network connects companies with career-minded individuals.

CAREERS WEB EXERCISES

1 Use two of the job search Web sites listed in Figure 28 to find three companies with job openings in your field. Make a table listing the Web site name, position available, description, salary, location, desired education, and desired experience.

2 It is a good idea to acquire information before graduation about the industry in which you would like to work. Are you interested in the automotive manufacturing industry, the restaurant service industry, or the financial industry? Use two of the company/industry information Web sites listed in Figure 28 to research a particular career related to your major. Write a paragraph naming the Web sites and the specific information you found, such as the nature of the work, recommended training and qualifications, employment outlook, and earnings. Then, use two other Web sites to profile three companies with positions available in this field. Write a paragraph about each of these companies, describing the headquarters' location, sales and earnings for the previous year, total number of employees, working conditions, perks, and competitors.

Arts and Literature
FIND SOME CULTURE

Get Ready to Read, Paint, and Dance

Brush up your knowledge of Shakespeare, grab a canvas, and put on your dancing shoes. Visual arts and literature Web sites, including those in Figure 29, are about to sweep you off your cyberfeet.

ARTS AND LITERATURE WEB SITES

Arts	URL
Access Place Arts	accessplace.com/arts.htm
Art News — absolutearts.com	absolutearts.com
GalleryGuide.org	galleryguide.org
Louvre Museum	www.louvre.fr
Montreal Museum of Fine Arts	www.mmfa.qc.ca
The Children's Museum of Indianapolis	childrensmuseum.org
The Getty	getty.edu
The New York Times: Arts	nytimes.com/pages/arts/index.html
Virtual Library museums pages (VLmp)	vlmp.museophile.com
Literature	**URL**
Bartleby.com	bartleby.com
Bibliomania	bibliomania.com
Electronic Literature Directory	directory.wordcircuits.com
Fantastic Fiction Bibliographies	fantasticfiction.co.uk
Project Gutenberg	promo.net/pg
shakespeare.com	shakespeare.com
The Modern Library eBook List	randomhouse.com/modernlibrary/ebookslist.html

For more information on arts and literature Web sites, visit scsite.com/dc2006/ch2/web.

FIGURE 29 Discover culture throughout the world by visiting these arts and literature Web sites.

The full text of hundreds of books is available online from the Bibliomania and Project Gutenberg Web sites. Shakespeare.com provides in-depth reviews and news of the world's most famous playwright and his works. The Bartleby.com Web site features biographies, definitions, quotations, dictionaries, and indexes.

When you are ready to absorb more culture, you can turn to various art Web sites. Many museums have images of their collections online. Among them are the Getty Museum in Los Angeles (Figure 30), the Montreal Museum of Fine Arts, and the Louvre Museum in Paris.

Access Place Arts and The New York Times Web sites focus on the arts and humanities and provide fascinating glimpses into the worlds of dance, music, performance, cinema, and other topics pertaining to creative expression.

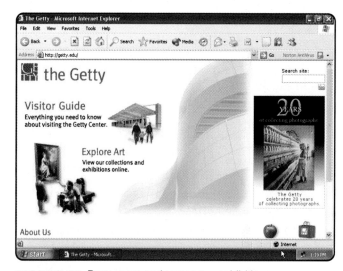

FIGURE 30 Permanent and temporary exhibitions, educational activities, and a bookstore are featured on the Getty Museum Web site.

ARTS AND LITERATURE WEB EXERCISES

1 Visit The Modern Library eBook List Web site listed in Figure 29 and view one book in the 20th CENTURY NOVELS, 19th CENTURY NOVELS, BRITISH LITERATURE, and HISTORY sections. Create a table with columns for the book name, author, cost, online store, local store, and description. Then, read the excerpt from each of the four books and write a paragraph describing which of these four books is the most interesting to you. What are the advantages and disadvantages of reading classic literature electronically?

2 Using the arts Web sites listed in Figure 29, search for three temporary exhibitions in galleries throughout the world. Describe the venues, the artists, and the works. What permanent collections are found in these museums? Some people shop for gifts in the museums' stores. View and describe three items for sale.

CHAPTER THREE

Application Software

Picture Yourself Using Software

As your biology instructor reviews for the upcoming test, you use note taking software and a digital pen to highlight important points in your electronic notes. Then, you circle the animal cell structure diagram and write "Memorize this for test." At the end of class, you start the appointment calendar software in your PDA and record the date of the test.

Later that day, when you open your e-mail program to check messages, you see a message from a friend asking what he missed in biology class. You type a reply to his message, attach a copy of your electronic lecture notes to the message, and then click the Send button.

Time to start composing your philosophy paper about Socrates. You use the research feature of your word processing program to learn about this ancient Greek philosopher and then write the paper — being sure to cite all sources. While writing the paper, your personal finance software alerts you that it is time to download transaction information from the bank's computer to your computer. With this service, your computerized checkbook balance always is up-to-date. Ready for a break, you fire up the flight simulator program and experience the thrill of piloting an airplane.

Read Chapter 3 to learn more about note taking software, PDA application software, e-mail programs, word processing software, personal finance software, and entertainment software, and discover many other types of application software.

OBJECTIVES

After completing this chapter, you will be able to:

1. Identify the categories of application software
2. Explain ways software is distributed
3. Explain how to work with application software
4. Identify the key features of widely used business programs
5. Identify the key features of widely used graphics and multimedia programs
6. Identify the key features of widely used home, personal, and educational programs
7. Identify the types of application software used in communications
8. Describe the function of several stand-alone utility programs
9. Discuss the advantages of using application software on the Web
10. Describe the learning aids available for application software

CONTENTS

APPLICATION SOFTWARE
The Role of System Software
Working with Application Software

BUSINESS SOFTWARE
Word Processing Software
Developing a Document
Spreadsheet Software
Database Software
Presentation Graphics Software
Note Taking Software
Personal Information Manager Software
PDA Business Software
Software Suite
Project Management Software
Accounting Software
Enterprise Computing Software

GRAPHICS AND MULTIMEDIA SOFTWARE
Computer-Aided Design
Desktop Publishing Software (for the Professional)
Paint/Image Editing Software (for the Professional)
Video and Audio Editing Software (for the Professional)
Multimedia Authoring Software
Web Page Authoring Software

SOFTWARE FOR HOME, PERSONAL, AND EDUCATIONAL USE
Software Suite (for Personal Use)
Personal Finance Software
Legal Software

Tax Preparation Software
Desktop Publishing Software (for Personal Use)
Paint/Image Editing Software (for Personal Use)
Photo Editing Software
Clip Art/Image Gallery
Video and Audio Editing Software (for Personal Use)
Home Design/Landscaping Software
Reference and Educational Software
Entertainment Software

APPLICATION SOFTWARE FOR COMMUNICATIONS

POPULAR STAND-ALONE UTILITY PROGRAMS

APPLICATION SOFTWARE ON THE WEB
Application Service Providers

LEARNING AIDS AND SUPPORT TOOLS FOR APPLICATION SOFTWARE
Web-Based Training

CHAPTER SUMMARY

HIGH-TECH TALK
Computer Viruses: Delivery, Infection, and Avoidance

COMPANIES ON THE CUTTING EDGE
Adobe Systems
Microsoft

TECHNOLOGY TRAILBLAZERS
Dan Bricklin
Masayoshi Son

Microsoft® Office
Word

APPLICATION SOFTWARE

With the proper software, a computer is a valuable tool. Software allows users to create letters, memos, reports, and other documents; design Web pages and diagrams; draw and alter images; record and enhance audio and video clips; prepare and file taxes; play single player or multiplayer games; compose e-mail messages and instant messages; and much more. To accomplish these and many other tasks, users work with application software. **Application software** consists of programs designed to make users more productive and/or assist them with personal tasks. Application software has a variety of uses:

1. To make business activities more efficient
2. To assist with graphics and multimedia projects
3. To support home, personal, and educational tasks
4. To facilitate communications

The table in Figure 3-1 categorizes popular types of application software by their general use. Although many types of communications software exist, the ones listed in Figure 3-1 are application software oriented. Utility programs, which are not a category of application software, are widely used to manage and protect computer resources. Successful use of application software generally requires the use of one or more of the utility programs identified in Figure 3-1. These utility programs typically are available stand-alone, that is, as separate programs that are not part of other application software.

As you become familiar with application software, it is likely you will use software from more than one of the categories in Figure 3-1. The four categories are not mutually exclusive. Software listed in one category may be used in other categories. For example, e-mail and Web browser programs, which are categorized as communications software, often are used for business or personal reasons.

Application software is available in a variety of forms: packaged, custom, open source, shareware, freeware, and public domain.

• **Packaged software** is mass-produced, copyrighted retail software that meets the needs of a wide variety of users, not just a single user or company. Word processing and spreadsheet software are examples of packaged software. Packaged software is available in retail stores or on the Web.

CATEGORIES OF APPLICATION SOFTWARE

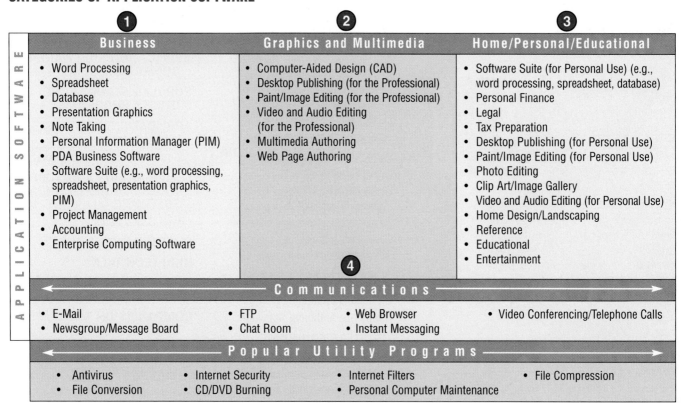

FIGURE 3-1 The four major categories of popular application software are outlined in this table. Communications software often is bundled with other application or system software. Also identified in the table are widely used stand-alone utility programs.

- **Custom software** performs functions specific to a business or industry. Sometimes a company cannot find packaged software that meets its unique requirements. In this case, the company may use programmers to develop tailor-made custom software, which usually costs more than packaged software.
- **Open source software** is software provided for use, modification, and redistribution. This software has no restrictions from the copyright holder regarding modification of the software's internal instructions and redistribution of the software. If redistributed, changes made to the software's internal instructions must be noted and the original copyright notice must remain intact. Open source software usually can be downloaded from the Web at no cost.
- **Shareware** is copyrighted software that is distributed at no cost for a trial period. To use a shareware program beyond that period, you send payment to the program developer. Shareware developers trust users to send payment if software use extends beyond the stated trial period. In some cases, a scaled-down version of the software is distributed free, and payment entitles the user to the fully functional product.
- **Freeware** is copyrighted software provided at no cost by an individual or a company that retains all rights to the software. Thus, programmers typically cannot incorporate freeware in applications they intend to sell. The word, free, in freeware indicates the software has no charge.
- **Public-domain software** has been donated for public use and has no copyright restrictions. Anyone can copy or distribute public-domain software to others at no cost.

Thousands of shareware, freeware, and public-domain programs are available on the Web for users to download. Examples include communications programs, graphics programs, and games. These programs usually have fewer capabilities than retail programs.

After you purchase or download software, you install it. During installation, the program may ask you to register and/or activate the software. Registering the software is optional and usually involves submitting your name and other personal information to the software manufacturer or developer. Registering the

software often entitles you to product support. *Product activation* is a technique that some software manufacturers use to ensure the software is not installed on more computers than legally licensed. Usually, the software does not function or has limited functionality until you activate it via the Internet or telephone. Thus, activation is a required process for programs requesting it.

The Role of System Software

System software serves as the interface between the user, the application software, and the computer's hardware (Figure 3-2). To use application software, such as a word processing program, your computer must be running system software — specifically, an operating system. Three popular personal computer operating systems are Windows XP, Linux, and Mac OS X.

Each time you start a computer, the operating system is *loaded* (copied) from the computer's hard disk into memory. Once the operating system is loaded, it coordinates all the activities of the computer. This includes starting application software and transferring data among input and output devices and memory. While the computer is running, the operating system remains in memory.

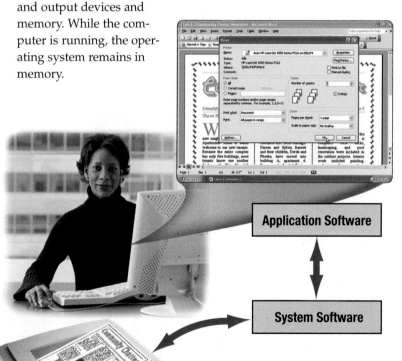

Application Software

System Software

FIGURE 3-2 A user does not communicate directly with the computer hardware. Instead, system software is the interface between the user, the application software, and the hardware. For example, when a user instructs the application software to print, the application software sends the print instruction to the system software, which in turn sends the print instruction to the hardware.

Working with Application Software

To use application software, you must instruct the operating system to start the program. The steps in Figure 3-3 illustrate how to start and interact with the Paint program. The following paragraphs explain the steps in Figure 3-3.

Personal computer operating systems often use the concept of a desktop to make the computer easier to use. The **desktop** is an on-screen work area that has a graphical user interface (Read Looking Ahead 3-1 for a look at the next generation of user interfaces). Step 1 of Figure 3-3 shows icons, a button, and a pointer on the Windows XP desktop. An **icon** is a small image

displayed on the screen that represents a program, a document, or some other object. A **button** is a graphical element that you activate to cause a specific action to take place. One way to activate a button is to click it. To **click** a button on the screen requires moving the pointer to the button and then pressing and releasing a button on the mouse (usually the left mouse button). The **pointer** is a small symbol displayed on the screen that moves as you move the mouse. Common pointer shapes are an I-beam (I), a block arrow ($\mathbb{k}$), and a pointing hand ($\mathbb{m}$).

The Windows XP desktop contains a Start button on the lower-left corner of the taskbar.

FIGURE 3-3 HOW TO START AN APPLICATION

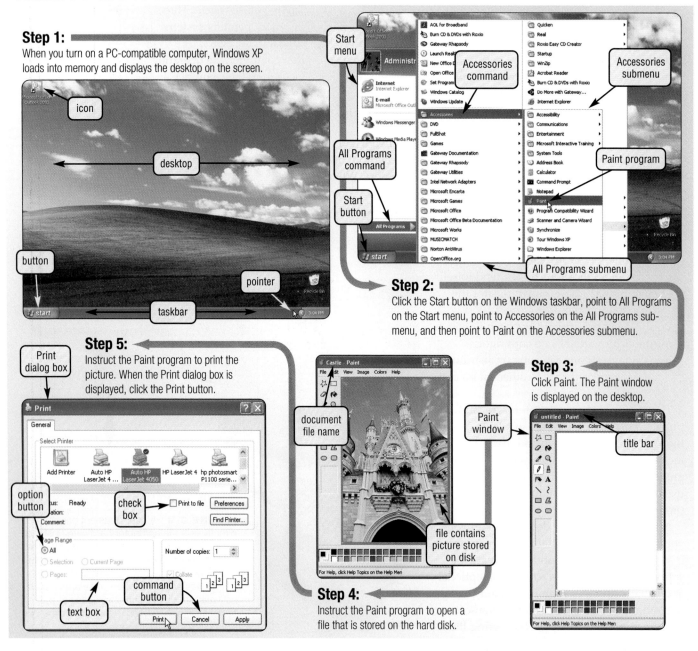

When you click the Start button, the Start menu is displayed on the desktop. A **menu** contains a list of commands from which you make selections. A **command** is an instruction that causes a program to perform a specific action.

The arrowhead symbol at the right edge of some menu commands indicates a submenu of additional commands is available. A *submenu* is a menu that is displayed when you point to a command on a previous menu. As illustrated in Step 2 of Figure 3-3, when you click the Start button and point to the All Programs command on the Start menu, the All Programs submenu is displayed. Pointing to the Accessories command on the All Programs submenu displays the Accessories submenu.

To start a program, you can click its program name on a menu or submenu. This action instructs the operating system to start the application, which means the program's instructions load from a storage medium (such as a hard disk) into memory. For example, when you click Paint on the Accessories submenu, Windows loads the Paint program instructions from the computer's hard disk into memory.

Once loaded into memory, the program is displayed in a window on the desktop (Step 3 of Figure 3-3). A **window** is a rectangular area of the screen that displays data and information. The top of a window has a **title bar**, which is a horizontal space that contains the window's name.

With the program loaded, you can create a new file or open an existing one. A *file* is a named collection of stored data, instructions, or information. A file can contain text, images, audio, and video. To distinguish among various files, each file has a file name. A *file name* is a unique combination of letters of the alphabet, numbers, and other characters that identifies a file. The title bar of the document window usually displays a document's file name. Step 4 of Figure 3-3 shows the contents of the file, Castle, displaying in the Paint window. The file contains an image photographed with a digital camera.

In some cases, when you instruct a program to perform an activity such as printing, the program displays a dialog box. A *dialog box* is a special window that provides information, presents available options, or requests a response. Dialog boxes, such as the one shown in Step 5 of Figure 3-3, often contain option buttons, text boxes, check boxes, and command buttons. Clicking the Print button in the dialog box instructs the computer to print the picture.

FAQ 3-1

Will a document print like it looks on a screen?

Yes, because most application software is *WYSIWYG* (*what you see is what you get*). The software embeds invisible codes around the text and graphics, which instructs the computer how to present the information. For more information, visit scsite.com/dc2006/ch3/faq and then click WYSIWYG.

Test your knowledge of pages 134 through 137 in Quiz Yourself 3-1.

QUIZ YOURSELF 3-1

Instructions: Find the true statement below. Then, rewrite the remaining false statements so they are true.

1. Application software is used to make business activities more efficient; assist with graphics and multimedia projects; support home, personal, and educational tasks; and facilitate communications.
2. Public-domain software is mass-produced, copyrighted retail software that meets the needs of a wide variety of users, not just a single user or company.
3. To use system software, your computer must be running application software.
4. When an application is started, the program's instructions load from memory into a storage medium.

Quiz Yourself Online: To further check your knowledge of application software categories, ways software is distributed, and working with application software, visit scsite.com/dc2006/ch3/quiz and then click Objectives 1 – 3.

LOOKING AHEAD 3-1

User Interfaces of the Future

Most computers today use a graphical user interface. Next-generation user interfaces will be more natural and human-centric, meaning they will enable people to interact with a computer using human-like communication methods. Three developments in this area are gesture recognition, 3-D interfaces, and BrainGate.

With gesture recognition, the computer will detect human motions. Computers with this type of user interface will have the capability of recognizing sign language, reading lips, tracking facial movements, and following eye gazes.

Imagine rotating a window or object to read its flipside, switching from a desktop view to a panoramic view, or tacking sticky notes right on a Web screen. All these scenarios will be possible with the upcoming 3-D user interfaces.

The BrainGate neural interface may help quadriplegic people gain independence with everyday activities, such as maneuvering wheelchairs and typing. The system includes a tiny chip with 100 sensors implanted on the brain and external computers that convert brainwaves into output signals the person can control. For more information, visit scsite.com/dc2006/ch3/looking and then click User Interfaces.

BUSINESS SOFTWARE

Business software is application software that assists people in becoming more effective and efficient while performing their daily business activities. Business software includes programs such as word processing, spreadsheet, database, presentation graphics, note taking, personal information manager software, PDA business software, software suites, project management, accounting, and enterprise computing software. Figure 3-4 lists popular programs for each of these categories.

The following sections discuss the features and functions of business software. Word processing and spreadsheet software have a heavier emphasis because of their predominant use.

Word Processing Software

Word processing software is one of the more widely used types of application software. **Word processing software**, sometimes called a *word processor*, allows users to create and manipulate documents containing mostly text and sometimes graphics (Figure 3-5). Millions of people use word processing software every day to develop documents such as letters, memos, reports, fax cover sheets, mailing labels, newsletters, and Web pages.

Word processing software has many features to make documents look professional and visually appealing. Some of these features include the capability of changing the shape and size of characters, changing the color of characters, and organizing text in newspaper-style columns. When using colors for characters, however, they will print as black or gray unless you have a color printer.

Most word processing software allows users to incorporate many types of graphical images in documents. One popular type of graphical image is clip art. **Clip art** is a collection of

POPULAR BUSINESS PROGRAMS

Application Software	Manufacturer	Program Name
Word Processing	Microsoft	Word
	Sun	StarOffice Writer
	Corel	WordPerfect
Spreadsheet	Microsoft	Excel
	Sun	StarOffice Calc
	Corel	Quattro Pro
Database	Microsoft	Access
	Sun	StarOffice Base
	Corel	Paradox
	Microsoft	Visual FoxPro
	Oracle	Oracle
	MySQL AB	MySQL
Presentation Graphics	Microsoft	PowerPoint
	Sun	StarOffice Impress
	Corel	Presentations
Note Taking	Microsoft	OneNote
	Agilix	GoBinder
	Corel	Grafigo
Personal Information Manager (PIM)	Microsoft	Outlook
	IBM	Lotus Organizer
	Palm	Desktop
PDA Business Software	CNetX	Pocket SlideShow
	Microsoft	Pocket Word
	Microsoft	Pocket Excel
	Microsoft	Pocket Outlook
	PalmOne	VersaMail
	Ultrasoft	Money Pocket Edition

Application Software	Manufacturer	Program Name
Software Suite (for the Professional)	Microsoft	Office
		Office for Mac
	Sun	StarOffice Office Suite
	Corel	WordPerfect Office
	IBM	Lotus SmartSuite
Project Management	Microsoft	Project
	Primavera	SureTrak Project Manager
Accounting	Intuit	QuickBooks
	Peachtree	Complete Accounting
Enterprise Computing Software	PeopleSoft	Enterprise Human Resources
	Best Software	MAS 500 Engineering
	MSC Software	MSC.SimManager Manufacturing
	Oracle	Oracle Manufacturing
	SmartPath	SmartPath MMS Sales
	SAP	mySAP Customer Relationship Management Distribution
	NetSuite	NetERP
	Apropos Technology	Apropos Enterprise Edition

FIGURE 3-4   Popular business software.

drawings, diagrams, maps, and photographs that you can insert in documents. In Figure 3-5, a user inserted a clip art image of a race car in the document. Word processing software usually includes public-domain clip art. You can find additional public-domain and proprietary images on the Web or purchase them on CD or DVD.

All word processing software provides at least some basic capabilities to help users create and modify documents. Defining the size of the paper on which to print and specifying the *margins* — that is, the portion of the page outside the main body of text, including the top, the bottom, and both sides of the paper — are examples of some of these capabilities. If you type text that extends beyond the right page margin, the word processing software automatically positions text at the beginning of the next line. This feature, called *wordwrap*, allows users to type words in a paragraph continually without pressing the ENTER key at the end of each line. When you modify paper size or margins, the word processing software automatically rewraps text so it fits in the adjusted paper size and margins.

As you type more lines of text than can be displayed on the screen, the top portion of the document moves upward, or scrolls, off the screen. *Scrolling* is the process of moving different portions of the document on the screen into view.

A major advantage of using word processing software is that users easily can change what they have written. For example, a user can insert, delete, or rearrange words, sentences, paragraphs, or entire sections. The find, or *search*, feature allows you to locate all occurrences of a certain character, word, or phrase. This feature, in combination with the *replace* feature, allows you to substitute existing characters or words with new ones.

Word processing software includes a *spelling checker*, which reviews the spelling of individual words, sections of a document, or the entire document. The spelling checker compares the words in the document with an electronic dictionary that is part of the word processing software. You can customize the

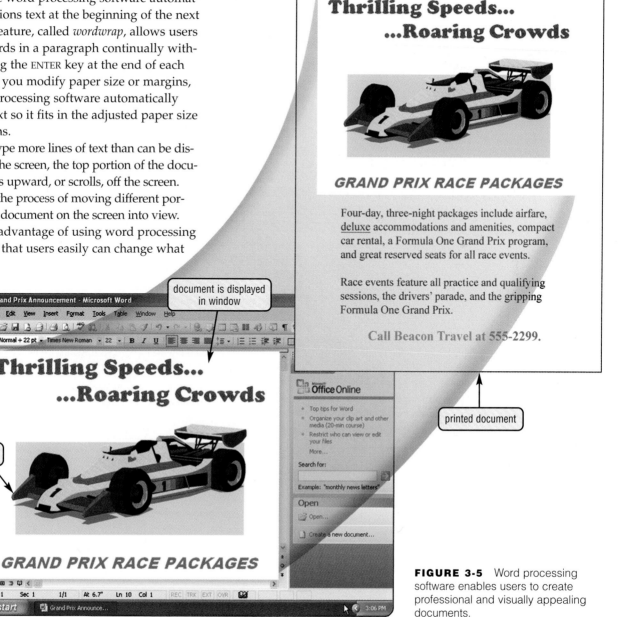

FIGURE 3-5 Word processing software enables users to create professional and visually appealing documents.

WEB LINK 3-1

Word Processing Software

For more information, visit scsite.com/ dc2006/ch3/weblink and then click Word Processing Software.

electronic dictionary by adding words such as companies, streets, cities, and personal names, so the software can check the spelling of those words too.

Another benefit of word processing software is the capability to insert headers and footers in a document. A *header* is text that appears at the top of each page, and a *footer* is text that appears at the bottom of each page. Page numbers, company names, report titles, and dates are examples of items often included in headers and footers.

In addition to these basic capabilities, most current word processing programs provide numerous additional features, which are listed in the table in Figure 3-6.

ADDITIONAL WORD PROCESSING FEATURES

AutoCorrect	As you type words, the AutoCorrect feature corrects common spelling errors. AutoCorrect also corrects capitalization mistakes.
AutoFormat	As you type, the AutoFormat feature automatically applies formatting to the text. For example, it automatically numbers a list or converts a Web address to a hyperlink.
Collaboration	Collaboration includes discussions and online meetings. Discussions allow multiple users to enter comments in a document and read and reply to each other's comments. Through an online meeting, users share documents with others in real time and view changes as they are being made.
Columns	Most word processing software can arrange text in two or more columns to look like a newspaper or magazine. The text from the bottom of one column automatically flows to the top of the next column.
Grammar Checker	The grammar checker proofreads documents for grammar, writing style, sentence structure errors, and reading statistics.
Ink Input	Supports input from a digital pen. Word processing software that supports ink input incorporates user's handwritten text and drawings in a word processing document. Ink input is popular on Tablet PCs.
Macros	A *macro* is a sequence of keystrokes and instructions that a user records and saves. When you want to execute the same series of instructions, execute the macro instead.
Mail Merge	Creates form letters, mailing labels, and envelopes.
Reading Layout	For those users who prefer reading on the screen, reading layout increases the readability and legibility of an on-screen document by hiding unnecessary toolbars, increasing the size of displayed characters, and providing navigation tools.
Research	Some word processing software allows you to search through various forms of online and Internet reference information — based on selected text in a document. Research services available include a thesaurus, English and bilingual dictionaries, encyclopedias, and Web sites that provide information such as stock quotes, news articles, and company profiles.
Smart Tags	*Smart tags* automatically appear on the screen when you perform a certain action. For example, typing an address causes a smart tag to appear. Clicking this smart tag provides options to display a map of the address or driving directions to or from the address.
Tables	Tables organize information into rows and columns. In addition to evenly spaced rows and columns, some word processing programs allow you to draw tables of any size or shape.
Templates	A *template* is a document that contains the formatting necessary for a specific document type. Templates usually exist for memos, fax cover sheets, and letters. In addition to templates provided with the software, users have access to many online templates through the manufacturer's Web site.
Thesaurus	With a thesaurus, a user looks up a synonym (word with the same meaning) for a word in a document.
Tracking Changes	If multiple users work with a document, the word processing software highlights or color-codes changes made by various users.
Voice Recognition	With some word processing programs, users can speak into the computer's microphone and watch the spoken words appear on the screen as they talk. With these programs, users edit and format the document by speaking or spelling an instruction.
Web Page Development	Most word processing software allows users to create, edit, format, and convert documents to be displayed on the World Wide Web.

FIGURE 3-6 Many additional features are included with word processing software.

Developing a Document

With application software, such as word processing, users create, edit, format, save, and print documents. During the process of developing a document, users likely will switch back and forth among all of these activities.

When you **create** a document, you enter text or numbers, insert graphical images, and perform other tasks using an input device such as a keyboard, mouse, microphone, or digital pen. If you are using Microsoft Office Word to design an announcement, for example, you are creating a document.

To **edit** a document means to make changes to its existing content. Common editing tasks include inserting, deleting, cutting, copying, and pasting. Inserting text involves adding text to a document. Deleting text means that you are removing text or other content. Cutting is the process of removing a portion of the document and storing it in a temporary storage location, sometimes called a *clipboard*. A clipboard also contains items that you copy (duplicate) in a document. *Pasting* is the process of transferring an item from a clipboard to a specific location in a document. Read At Issue 3-1 for a related discussion.

When users **format** a document, they change its appearance. Formatting is important because the overall look of a document significantly can affect its ability to communicate clearly. Examples of formatting tasks are changing the font, font size, or font style of text.

A **font** is a name assigned to a specific design of characters. Two basic types of fonts are serif and sans serif. A *serif font* has short decorative lines at the upper and lower ends of the characters. Sans means without. Thus, a *sans serif font* does not have the short decorative lines at the upper and lower ends of the characters. Times New Roman is an example of a serif font. Arial is an example of a sans serif font.

Font size indicates the size of the characters in a particular font. Font size is gauged by a measurement system called points. A single *point* is about 1/72 of an inch in height. The text you are reading in this book is about 10 point. Thus, each character is about 5/36 (10/72) of a inch in height. A *font style* adds emphasis to a font. Bold, italic, and underline are examples of font styles. Figure 3-7 illustrates fonts, font sizes, and font styles.

AT ISSUE 3-1

How Should Schools Deal with Internet Plagiarism?

A high school teacher failed 28 students for plagiarizing, or copying, material from the Internet. When parents complained, the school board passed the students, and the teacher resigned. Plagiarism is not new, but word processing software and the Internet make it easier than ever. With the click of a couple buttons, students can copy parts of Web pages and paste the text into their term papers. Students also can use term paper Web sites to copy complete papers on a variety of topics. According to one study, more than 35 percent of college students had copied material from Internet sources. Students who plagiarize blame peer pressure, classroom competition, the "busy work" nature of some assignments, and the permissive attitude that pervades the Internet. Teachers have several tools to catch plagiarists, including a variety of Web sites that compare suspected papers to papers found on the Internet and produce an originality report highlighting text that may have been copied. Some instructors, however, are reluctant to investigate the integrity of a student's work and possibly ruin an academic career. How should educators deal with plagiarism? Why? Should a school's response to plagiarism depend on such factors as the material copied, the assignment for which it was copied, or the reason it was copied? Why or why not?

FIGURE 3-7 The Times New Roman and Arial fonts are shown in two font sizes and a variety of font styles.

FAQ 3-2

How often should I save a document?

Saving at regular intervals ensures that the majority of your work will not be lost in the event of a power loss or system failure. Many programs have an AutoSave feature that automatically saves open documents at specified time intervals, such as every 10 minutes. For more information, visit scsite.com/dc2006/ch3/faq and then click Saving Documents.

During the process of creating, editing, and formatting a document, the computer holds it in memory. To keep the document for future use requires that you save it. When you **save** a document, the computer transfers the document from memory to a storage medium such as a floppy disk, USB flash drive, hard disk, or CD. Once saved, a document is stored permanently as a file on the storage medium.

When you **print** a document, the computer places the contents of the document on paper or some other medium. One of the benefits of word processing software is the ability to print the same document many times, with each copy looking just like the first. Instead of printing a document and physically distributing it, some users e-mail the document to others on a network such as the Internet.

Spreadsheet Software

Spreadsheet software is another widely used type of application software. **Spreadsheet software** allows users to organize data in rows and columns and perform calculations on the data. These rows and columns collectively are called a *worksheet*. For years, people used paper to organize data and perform calculations by hand. In an electronic worksheet, you organize data in the same manner, and the computer performs the calculations more quickly and accurately (Figure 3-8). Because of spreadsheet software's logical approach to organizing data, many people use this software to organize and present nonfinancial data, as well as financial data.

As with word processing software, most spreadsheet software has basic features to help users create, edit, and format worksheets. Spreadsheet software also incorporates many of the features found in word processing software such as macros, checking spelling, changing fonts and font sizes, adding colors, tracking changes, recognizing voice input, inserting audio and video clips, providing research capabilities, recognizing handwritten text and drawings, and creating Web pages from existing spreadsheet documents.

The following sections describe the features of most spreadsheet programs.

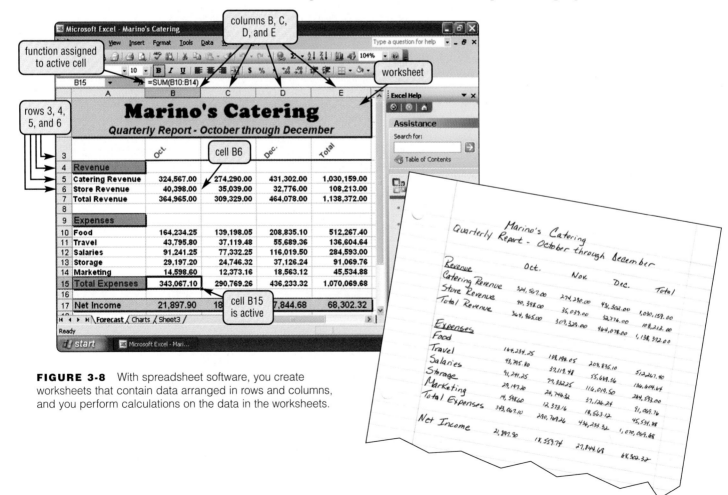

FIGURE 3-8   With spreadsheet software, you create worksheets that contain data arranged in rows and columns, and you perform calculations on the data in the worksheets.

SPREADSHEET ORGANIZATION A spreadsheet file is similar to a notebook with up to 255 related individual worksheets. Data is organized vertically in columns and horizontally in rows on each worksheet (Figure 3-8). Each worksheet typically has 256 columns and 65,536 rows. One or more letters identify each column, and a number identifies each row. The column letters begin with A and end with IV. The row numbers begin with 1 and end with 65,536. Only a small fraction of these columns and rows are displayed on the screen at one time. Scrolling through the worksheet displays different parts of it on the screen.

A *cell* is the intersection of a column and row. Each worksheet has more than 16 million (256 × 65,536) cells in which you can enter data. The spreadsheet software identifies cells by the column and row in which they are located. For example, the intersection of column B and row 6 is referred to as cell B6. As shown in Figure 3-8, cell B6 contains the number, 40,398.00, which represents the store revenue for October.

Cells may contain three types of data: labels, values, and formulas. The text, or *label*, entered in a cell identifies the worksheet data and helps organize the worksheet. Using descriptive labels, such as Total Revenue and Total Expenses, helps make a worksheet more meaningful.

CALCULATIONS Many of the worksheet cells shown in Figure 3-8 contain a number, called a *value*, that can be used in a calculation. Other cells, however, contain formulas that generate values. A *formula* performs calculations on the data in the worksheet and displays the resulting value in a cell, usually the cell containing the formula. When creating a worksheet, you can enter your own formulas.

In many spreadsheet programs, you begin a formula with an equal sign, a plus sign, or a minus sign. Next, you enter the formula, separating cell references (e.g., B10) with operators. Common operators are + for addition, − for subtraction, * for multiplication, and / for division. In Figure 3-8, for example, cell B15 could contain the formula =B10+B11+B12+B13+B14, which would add together (sum) the contents of cells B10, B11, B12, B13, and B14. That is, this formula calculates the total expenses for October. A more efficient way to sum the contents of cells, however, is to use special type of formula, called a function.

A *function* is a predefined formula that performs common calculations such as adding the values in a group of cells or generating a value such as the time or date. For example, instead of using the formula =B10+B11+B12+B13+B14 to calculate the total expenses for October, you could use the SUM function. This function requires you to identify the starting cell and the ending cell in a group to be summed, separating these two cell references with a colon. For example, the function =SUM(B10:B14) instructs the spreadsheet program to add all of the numbers in cells B10 through B14. Figure 3-9 lists functions commonly included in spreadsheet programs.

SPREADSHEET FUNCTIONS

Financial	
FV (rate, number of periods, payment)	Calculates the future value of an investment
NPV (rate, range)	Calculates the net present value of an investment
PMT (rate, number of periods, present value)	Calculates the periodic payment for an annuity
PV (rate, number of periods, payment)	Calculates the present value of an investment
RATE (number of periods, payment, present value)	Calculates the periodic interest rate of an annuity
Date and Time	
DATE	Returns the current date
NOW	Returns the current date and time
TIME	Returns the current time
Mathematical	
ABS (number)	Returns the absolute value of a number
INT (number)	Rounds a number down to the nearest integer
LN (number)	Calculates the natural logarithm of a number
LOG (number, base)	Calculates the logarithm of a number to a specified base
ROUND (number, number of digits)	Rounds a number to a specified number of digits
SQRT (number)	Calculates the square root of a number
SUM (range)	Calculates the total of a range of numbers
Statistical	
AVERAGE (range)	Calculates the average value of a range of numbers
COUNT (range)	Counts how many cells in the range have numeric entries
MAX (range)	Returns the maximum value in a range
MIN (range)	Returns the minimum value in a range
STDEV (range)	Calculates the standard deviation of a range of numbers
Logical	
IF (logical test, value if true, value if false)	Performs a test and returns one value if the result of the test is true and another value if the result is false

FIGURE 3-9 Functions typically found in spreadsheet software.

RECALCULATION One of the more powerful features of spreadsheet software is its capability of recalculating the rest of the worksheet when data in a worksheet changes. When you enter a new value to change data in a cell, any value affected by the change is updated automatically and instantaneously. In Figure 3-8 on page 142, for example, if you change the store revenue for October from 40,398.00 to 45,398.00, the total revenue in cell B7 automatically changes from 364,965.00 to 369,965.00.

Spreadsheet software's capability of recalculating data also makes it a valuable budgeting, forecasting, and decision making tool. Most spreadsheet software includes a *what-if analysis* feature, where you change certain values in a spreadsheet to reveal the effects of those changes.

WEB LINK 3-2

Spreadsheet Software

For more information, visit scsite.com/ dc2006/ch3/weblink and then click Spreadsheet Software.

CHARTING Another standard feature of spreadsheet software is *charting*, which depicts the data in graphical form. A visual representation of data through charts often makes it easier for users to see at a glance the relationship among the numbers.

Three popular chart types are line charts, column charts, and pie charts. Figure 3-10 shows examples of these charts that were plotted from the data in Figure 3-8. A *line chart* shows a trend during a period of time, as indicated by a rising or falling line. For example, a line chart could show the total expenses for the three months. A *column chart*, also called a *bar chart*, displays bars of various lengths to show the relationship of data. The bars can be horizontal, vertical, or stacked on top of one another. For example, a column chart might show the total monthly expenses, with each bar representing a different category of expense. A *pie chart*, which has the shape of a round pie cut into slices, shows the relationship of parts to a whole. For example, you might use a pie chart to show the percentage each expense category contributed to the total expenses.

Charts, as well as any other part of a workbook, can be linked to or embedded in a word processing document.

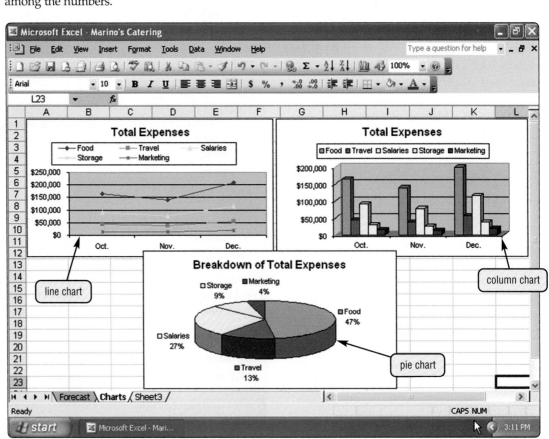

FIGURE 3-10 Three basic types of charts provided with spreadsheet software are line charts, column charts, and pie charts. The charts shown here were created from the data in the worksheet in Figure 3-8.

Database Software

A **database** is a collection of data organized in a manner that allows access, retrieval, and use of that data. In a manual database, you might record data on paper and store it in a filing cabinet. With a computerized database, such as the one shown in Figure 3-11, the computer stores the data in an electronic format on a storage medium such as a hard disk.

Database software is application software that allows users to create, access, and manage a database. Using database software, you can add, change, and delete data in a database; sort and retrieve data from the database; and create forms and reports using the data in the database.

With most popular personal computer database programs, a database consists of a collection of tables, organized in rows and columns. Each row, called a *record*, contains data about a given person, product, object, or event. Each column, called a *field*, contains a specific category of data within a record.

The Store database shown in Figure 3-11 consists of two tables: a Product table and a Supplier table. The Product table contains ten records (rows), each storing data about one item. The product data is grouped into six fields (columns): Product ID, Description, On Hand, Cost, Selling Price, and Supplier Code. The On Hand field, for instance, contains the quantity on hand in inventory. The Product and Supplier tables relate to one another through a common field, Supplier Code.

Users run queries to retrieve data. A *query* is a request for specific data from the database. For example, a query might request products that are low on hand. Database software can take the results of a query and present it in a window on the screen or send it to the printer.

FAQ 3-3

How big is the largest database?

According to a recent survey, the world's largest database holds 29 trillion characters. In the next few years, the size of the largest database is expected to exceed 5 quadrillion characters. For more information, visit scsite.com/dc2006/ch3/faq and then click Enterprise Databases.

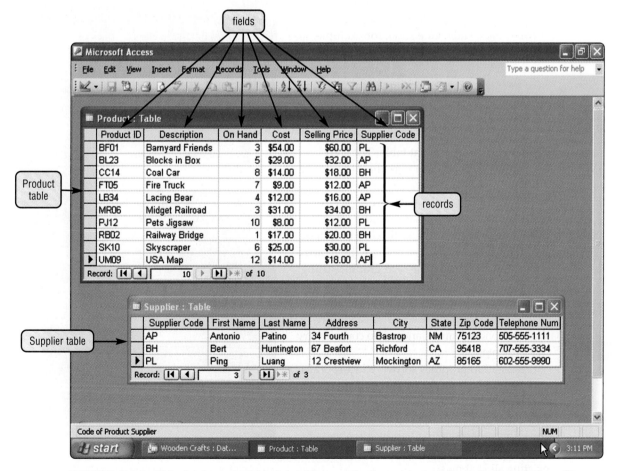

FIGURE 3-11   This database contains two tables: one for the products and one for the suppliers. The Product table has 10 records and 6 fields; the Supplier table has 3 records and 8 fields.

Presentation Graphics Software

Presentation graphics software is application software that allows users to create visual aids for presentations to communicate ideas, messages, and other information to a group. The presentations can be viewed as slides, sometimes called a *slide show*, that are displayed on a large monitor or on a projection screen (Figure 3-12).

Presentation graphics software typically provides a variety of predefined presentation formats that define complementary colors for backgrounds, text, and graphical accents on the slides. This software also provides a variety of layouts for each individual slide such as a title slide, a two-column slide, and a slide with clip art, a picture (Figure 3-13), a chart, a table, or animation. In addition, you can enhance any text, charts, and graphical images on a slide with 3-D and other special effects such as shading, shadows, and textures.

When building a presentation, users can set the slide timing so the presentation automatically displays the next slide after a preset delay. Presentation graphics software allows you to apply special effects to the transition between each slide. One slide, for example, might fade away slowly as the next slide is displayed.

To help organize the presentation, you can view thumbnail versions of all the slides in slide sorter view. *Slide sorter view* presents a screen view similar to how 35mm slides look on a photographer's light table. The slide sorter allows users to arrange the slides in any order.

Presentation graphics software typically includes a clip gallery that provides images, pictures, video clips, and audio clips to enhance multimedia presentations. Users with an artistic ability can create their own graphics using paint/image editing software (discussed later in the chapter) and then *import* (bring in) the graphics into the slide. Users also can insert their own video, music, and audio commentary in a presentation.

Presentation graphics software incorporates some of the features found in word processing software such as checking spelling, formatting, recognizing voice input, providing research capabilities, recognizing handwritten text and drawings, and creating Web pages from existing slide shows.

WEB LINK 3-3

Presentation Graphics Software

For more information, visit scsite.com/dc2006/ch3/weblink and then click Presentation Graphics Software.

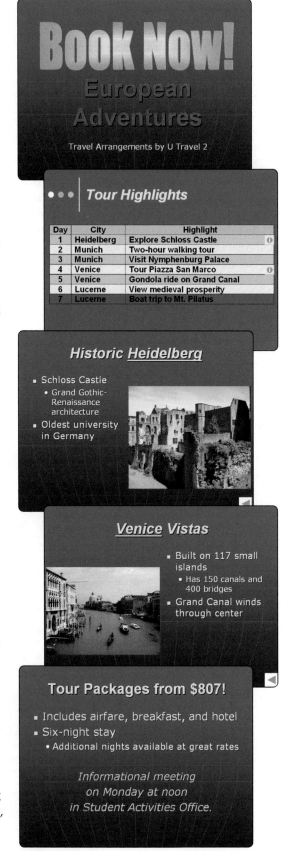

FIGURE 3-12 This presentation created with presentation graphics software consists of five slides.

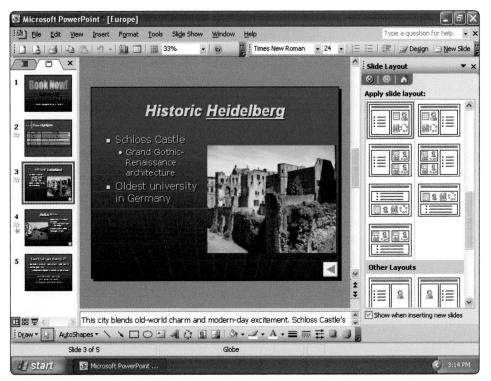

FIGURE 3-13 In presentation graphics software, users can change the design and layout of any slide in a presentation.

Note Taking Software

Note taking software is application software that enables users to enter typed text, handwritten comments, drawings, or sketches anywhere on a page and then save the page as part of a notebook (Figure 3-14). The software can convert handwritten comments to typed text or store the notes in handwritten form. Users also can include audio recordings as part of their notes.

Once the notes are captured (entered and saved), users easily can organize them, reuse them, and share them. This software allows users to search through saved notes for specific text. It even can search through an entire notebook. Users also can flag important notes with color, highlights, and shapes.

On a desktop or notebook computer, users enter notes primarily via the keyboard or microphone. On a Tablet PC, however, the primary input device is a digital pen. Users find note taking software convenient during meetings, class lectures, conferences, in libraries, and other settings that previously required a pencil and tablet of paper for recording thoughts and discussions.

Note taking software incorporates many of the features found in word processing software such as checking spelling, changing fonts and font sizes, adding colors, recognizing voice input, inserting audio and video clips, and providing research capabilities.

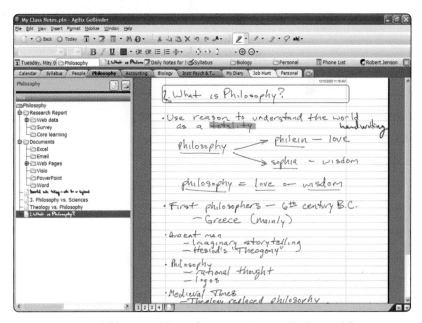

FIGURE 3-14 With note taking software, students and other mobile users can handwrite notes, draw sketches, and type text.

Personal Information Manager Software

A **personal information manager (PIM)** is application software that includes an appointment calendar, address book, notepad, and other features to help users organize personal information. With a PIM, you can take information previously tracked in a weekly or daily calendar, and organize and store it on your computer. The appointment calendar allows you to schedule activities for a particular day and time. With the address book, you can enter and maintain names, addresses, telephone numbers, and e-mail addresses of customers, coworkers, family members, and friends. You can use the notepad to record ideas, reminders, and other important information.

Most PDAs and many smart phones today include, among many other features, PIM functionality. Using a PDA or smart phone, you can synchronize, or coordinate, information so that both the PDA or smart phone and the computer have the latest version of the information. Some PDAs and smart phones synchronize with the computer wirelessly. With others, you connect the PDA or smart phone to the computer with a cable, or you insert the device in a cradle, which has a cable that plugs in the computer (Figure 3-15).

FIGURE 3-15 With most PDAs and smart phones, you can synchronize or transfer information from the device to a desktop computer, so the updated important information always is available.

PDA Business Software

In addition to PIM software, a huge variety of business software is available for PDAs. Although some PDAs have software built in, most have the capability of accessing software on miniature storage media such as memory cards. Business software for PDAs allows users to create documents and worksheets, manage databases and lists, create slide shows, take notes, manage budgets and finances, view and edit photographs, read electronic books, plan travel routes, compose and read e-mail messages, send instant messages, and browse the Web. For additional information about software for PDAs, read the Smart Phones and PDAs feature that follows Chapter 5.

Software Suite

A **software suite** is a collection of individual programs sold as a single package. Business software suites typically include, at a minimum, the following programs: word processing, spreadsheet, e-mail, and presentation graphics. Two of the more widely used software suites are Microsoft Office and Sun StarOffice.

Software suites offer two major advantages: lower cost and ease of use. Buying a collection of programs in a software suite usually costs significantly less than purchasing them individually. Software suites provide ease of use because the programs in a software suite normally use a similar interface and share features such as clip art and spelling checker. For example, once you learn how to print using the software suite's word processing program, you can apply the same skill to the spreadsheet and presentation graphics programs in the software suite.

WEB LINK 3-4

StarOffice

For more information, visit scsite.com/ dc2006/ch3/weblink and then click StarOffice.

FAQ 3-4

What is the difference between Microsoft Office and Microsoft Office System?

Microsoft Office is a suite of core desktop business programs. Office is available in a variety of editions, each of which includes at least Word, Excel, and Outlook. *Microsoft Office System* is a portfolio of programs and services that are tightly integrated yet available for purchase as separate entities. In addition to Microsoft Office, other products in the Microsoft Office System include OneNote, InfoPath, Visio, FrontPage, and Project. For more information, visit scsite.com/dc2006/ch3/faq and then click Microsoft Office System.

Project Management Software

Project management software allows a user to plan, schedule, track, and analyze the events, resources, and costs of a project (Figure 3-16). Project management software helps users manage project variables, allowing them to complete a project on time and within budget. An engineer, for example, might use project management software to manage new product development to schedule product screening, market evaluation, technical product evaluation, and manufacturing processes.

Accounting Software

Accounting software helps companies record and report their financial transactions (Figure 3-17). With accounting software, business users perform accounting activities related to the general ledger, accounts receivable, accounts payable, purchasing, invoicing, and payroll functions. Accounting software also enables users to write and print checks, track checking account activity, and update and reconcile balances on demand.

Newer accounting software supports online credit checks, billing, direct deposit, and payroll services. Some accounting software offers more complex features such as job costing and estimating, time tracking, multiple company reporting, foreign currency reporting, and forecasting the amount of raw materials needed for products. The cost of accounting software for small businesses ranges from less than one hundred to several thousand dollars. Accounting software for large businesses can cost several hundred thousand dollars.

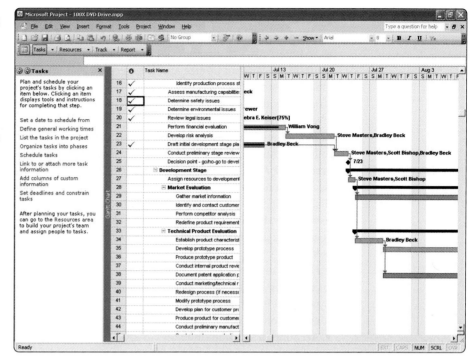

FIGURE 3-16 Project management software allows you to track, control, and manage the events, resources, and costs of a project.

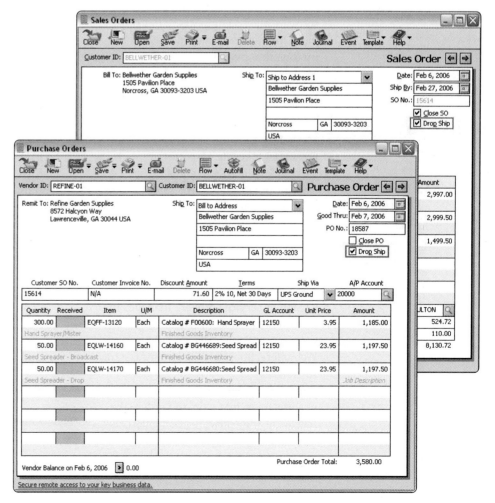

FIGURE 3-17 Accounting software helps companies record and report their financial transactions.

Enterprise Computing Software

A large organization, commonly referred to as an enterprise, requires special computing solutions because of its size and large geographic distribution. A typical enterprise consists of a wide variety of departments, centers, and divisions — collectively known as functional units. Nearly every enterprise has the following functional units: human resources, accounting and finance, engineering or product development, manufacturing, marketing, sales, distribution, customer service, and information technology. Each of these functional units has specialized software requirements, as outlined below.

- Human resources software manages employee information such as benefits, personal information, performance evaluations, training, and vacation time.
- Accounting software manages everyday transactions, such as sales and payments to suppliers. Financial software helps managers budget, forecast, and analyze.
- Engineering or product development software allows engineers to develop plans for new products and test their product designs.
- Manufacturing software assists in the assembly process, as well as in scheduling and managing the inventory of parts and products.
- Marketing software allows marketing personnel to create marketing campaigns and track their effectiveness.
- Sales software enables the sales force to manage contacts, schedule meetings, log customer interactions, manage product information, and take customer orders.
- Distribution software analyzes and tracks inventory and manages product shipping status.
- Customer service software manages the day-to-day interactions with customers, such as telephone calls, e-mail messages, Web interactions, and instant messaging sessions.
- Information technology staff use a variety of software to maintain and secure the hardware and software in an enterprise.

GRAPHICS AND MULTIMEDIA SOFTWARE

In addition to business software, many people work with software designed specifically for their field of work. Power users such as engineers, architects, desktop publishers, and graphic artists often use sophisticated software that allows them to work with graphics and multimedia. This software includes computer-aided design, desktop publishing, paint/image editing, video and audio editing, multimedia authoring, and Web page authoring. Figure 3-18 lists some popular programs in each of these categories. Many of these programs incorporate user-friendly interfaces and/or have scaled-down versions, making it possible for the home and small business users to create documents using these programs. The following sections discuss the features and functions of graphics and multimedia software.

Computer-Aided Design

Computer-aided design (CAD) software is a sophisticated type of application software that assists a professional user in creating engineering, architectural, and scientific designs. For example, engineers create design plans for airplanes and security systems. Architects design building structures and floor plans (Figure 3-19). Scientists design drawings of molecular structures.

CAD software eliminates the laborious manual drafting that design processes can require. Three-dimensional CAD programs allow designers to rotate designs of 3-D objects to view them from any angle. Some CAD software even can generate material lists for building designs.

POPULAR GRAPHICS AND MULTIMEDIA SOFTWARE

Application Software	Manufacturer	Program Name
Computer-Aided Design (CAD)	Autodesk	AutoCAD
	Quality Plans	Chief Architect
	Microsoft	Visio
Desktop Publishing (for the Professional)	Adobe	InDesign
	Corel	Ventura
	Quark	QuarkXPress
Paint/Image Editing (for the Professional)	Adobe	Illustrator
		Photoshop
	Corel	Painter
	Macromedia	FreeHand
Video and Audio Editing (for the Professional)	Adobe	Audition
		Encore DVD
		Premiere Pro
	Cakewalk	SONAR
	Macromedia	SoundEdit
	Sony	ACID Pro
	Ulead	MediaStudio Pro
		DVD Workshop
Multimedia Authoring	SumTotal Systems	ToolBook Instructor
	Macromedia	Authorware
		Director
Web Page Authoring	Adobe	GoLive
	Lotus	FastSite
	Macromedia	Dreamweaver
		Fireworks
		Flash
	Microsoft	FrontPage

FIGURE 3-18 Popular graphics and multimedia programs — for the professional.

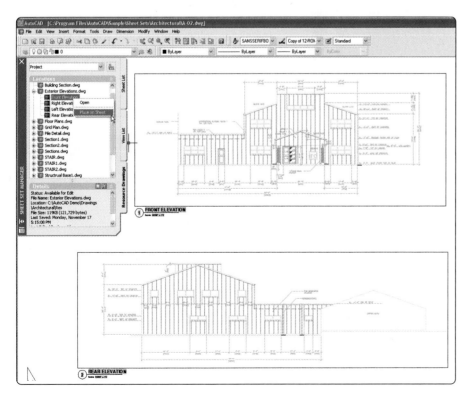

FIGURE 3-19 CAD software is sophisticated software that assists engineers, architects, and scientists in creating designs.

Desktop Publishing Software (for the Professional)

Desktop publishing (DTP) software enables professional designers to create sophisticated documents that contain text, graphics, and many colors. Professional DTP software is ideal for the production of high-quality color documents such as textbooks, corporate newsletters, marketing literature (Figure 3-20), product catalogs, and annual reports. Today's DTP software allows designers to convert a color document into a format for use on the World Wide Web.

Although many word processing programs have some of the capabilities of DTP software, professional designers and graphic artists use DTP software because it supports page layout. *Page layout* is the process of arranging text and graphics in a document on a page-by-page basis. DTP software includes color libraries to assist in color selections for text and graphics. A *color library* is a standard set of colors used by designers and printers to ensure that colors will print exactly as specified. Designers and graphic artists can print finished publications on a color printer, take them to a professional printer, or post them on the Web.

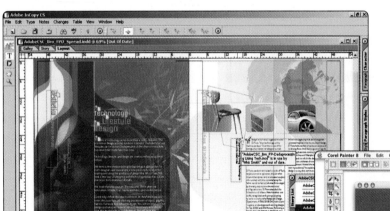

FIGURE 3-20 Professional designers and graphic artists use DTP software to produce sophisticated publications such as marketing literature.

FAQ 3-5

Why am I not able to view some files on the Web that contain company brochures?

In many cases, you need Adobe *Acrobat Reader* software because some companies save documents on the Web, such as brochures, using the Adobe PDF format. To view and print a PDF file, simply download the free Adobe Acrobat Reader software from Adobe's Web site. For more information, visit scsite.com/dc2006/ch3/faq and then click Adobe Acrobat Reader.

Paint/Image Editing Software (for the Professional)

Graphic artists, multimedia professionals, technical illustrators, and desktop publishers use paint software and image editing software to create and modify graphical images such as those used in DTP documents and Web pages. **Paint software**, also called *illustration software*, allows users to draw pictures, shapes, and other graphical images with various on-screen tools such as a pen, brush, eyedropper, and paint bucket. **Image editing software** provides the capabilities of paint software and also includes the capability to enhance and modify existing images and pictures (Figure 3-21). Modifications can include adjusting or enhancing image colors, and adding special effects such as shadows and glows. Read At Issue 3-2 for a related discussion.

FIGURE 3-21 With image editing software, artists can create and modify any type of graphical image.

AT ISSUE 3-2

Altering Digital Photographs — Art or Fraud?

A *Los Angeles Times* photographer combined two digital photographs of the Iraq war, taken minutes apart, to create a single picture that appeared on the newspaper's front page. The photographer merged the photos to improve the composition, but when the source of the picture became known, the newspaper fired the photographer, citing a policy that forbids altering the content of news photos. Many commercial artists, photojournalists, and creators of cartoons, book covers, and billboards use paint and image editing software to alter photographs. With this software, an artist can convert photographs to a digital form that can be colorized, stretched, squeezed, texturized, or otherwise altered. The National Press Photographers Association, however, has expressed reservations about digital altering and endorses the following: "As [photo] journalists we believe the guiding principle of our profession is accuracy; therefore, we believe it is wrong to alter the content of a photograph in any way…that deceives the public." Yet, some insist that the extent to which a photo "deceives the public" is in the eye of the beholder. Is it ethical to alter digital photographs? Why or why not? Does the answer depend on the reason for the alteration, the extent of the alteration, or some other factor? If some alteration is accepted, can photographic integrity still be guaranteed? Why or why not?

Video and Audio Editing Software (for the Professional)

Video editing software (Figure 3-22) allows professionals to modify a segment of a video, called a clip. For example, users can reduce the length of a video clip, reorder a series of clips, or add special effects such as words that move horizontally across the screen.

Video editing software typically includes audio editing capabilities. **Audio editing software** lets users modify audio clips and produce studio-quality soundtracks. Audio editing software usually includes *filters*, which are designed to enhance audio quality. For example, a filter might remove a distracting background noise from the audio clip. Read At Issue 3-3 for a related discussion.

FIGURE 3-22   With video editing software, users modify video images.

AT ISSUE 3-3

What Should Be Done to Prevent Music or Video File Sharing?

It is illegal to use networks to share copyrighted music or video files. Despite this, a number of file-sharing networks exist, and an estimated 60 million Americans use file-sharing software to locate and download copyrighted music and videos without paying. Much of this illegal activity takes place at colleges and universities, where high-speed network connections make file sharing almost instantaneous. To combat illegal file sharing, some schools have turned to new programs that intentionally slow the performance of file-sharing software. The Recording Industry Association of America (RIAA) has gone even further, filing law suits against people suspected of downloading copyrighted music. Individuals found guilty can be liable for fines up to $150,000 for every stolen song. The RIAA maintains that downloading copyrighted music steals from both the recording artist and the recording industry. Yet, many people feel that the response to sharing copyrighted music and video files is excessive. They argue that copying music from the radio to an audio cassette is legal and insist that downloading copyrighted music is no different. Besides, someone who downloads a copyrighted song later may be inspired to purchase an artist's CD or attend a concert. Should it be illegal to share copyrighted music or video files over a network? Why or why not? Are slowing file-sharing software and filing thousand-dollar lawsuits unwarranted reactions to what some people consider a victimless violation? Why?

Multimedia Authoring Software

Multimedia authoring software allows users to combine text, graphics, audio, video, and animation in an interactive application (Figure 3-23). With this software, users control the placement of text and images and the duration of sounds, video, and animation. Once created, multimedia presentations often take the form of interactive computer-based presentations or Web-based presentations designed to facilitate learning, demonstrate product functionality, and elicit direct-user participation. Training centers, educational institutions, and online magazine publishers all use multimedia authoring software to develop interactive applications. These applications may be available on a CD or DVD, over a local area network, or via the Internet.

FAQ 3-6

How do I know which program to buy?

Many companies offer downloadable *trial versions* of their software that allow you to use the software free for a limited time. Try a few. Read computer magazines and Web sites for reviews of various products. For more information, visit scsite.com/dc2006/ch3/faq and then click Trial Versions.

Web Page Authoring Software

Web page authoring software helps users of all skill levels create Web pages that include graphical images, video, audio, animation, and other special effects with interactive content (Figure 3-24). In addition, many Web page authoring programs allow users to organize, manage, and maintain Web sites.

Application software, such as Word and Excel, often includes Web page authoring features. This allows home users to create basic Web pages using application software they already own. For more sophisticated Web pages, users work with Web page authoring software. Many Web page developers also use multimedia authoring software along with, or instead of, Web page authoring software for Web page development.

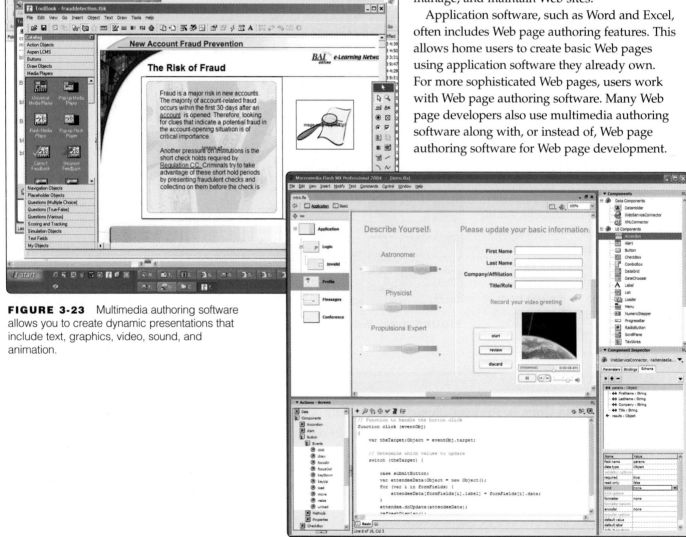

FIGURE 3-23 Multimedia authoring software allows you to create dynamic presentations that include text, graphics, video, sound, and animation.

FIGURE 3-24 With Web page authoring software, users create sophisticated Web pages.

Test your knowledge of pages 138 through 154 in Quiz Yourself 3-2.

QUIZ YOURSELF 3-2

Instructions: Find the true statement below. Then, rewrite the remaining false statements so they are true.

1. Audio editing software typically includes video editing capabilities.
2. Enterprise computing software provides the capabilities of paint software and also includes the capability to modify existing images.
3. Millions of people use spreadsheet software every day to develop documents such as letters, memos, reports, fax cover sheets, mailing labels, newsletters, and Web pages.
4. Professional accounting software is ideal for the production of high-quality color documents such as textbooks, corporate newsletters, marketing literature, product catalogs, and annual reports.
5. Spreadsheet software is application software that allows users to create visual aids for presentations to communicate ideas, messages, and other information to a group.
6. Two of the more widely used CAD programs are Microsoft Office and Sun StarOffice.
7. Web page authoring software helps users of all skill levels create Web pages.

Quiz Yourself Online: To further check your knowledge of types and features of business programs and graphics/multimedia programs, visit scsite.com/dc2006/ch3/quiz and then click Objectives 4 – 5.

SOFTWARE FOR HOME, PERSONAL, AND EDUCATIONAL USE

A large amount of application software is designed specifically for home, personal, and educational use. Most of the programs in this category are relatively inexpensive, often priced less than $100 and sometimes free. Figure 3-25 lists popular programs for many of these categories. The following sections discuss the features and functions of this application software.

POPULAR SOFTWARE PROGRAMS FOR HOME/PERSONAL/EDUCATIONAL USE

Application Software	Manufacturer	Program Name
Software Suite (for Personal Use)	Microsoft	Works
	Sun	OpenOffice.org
Personal Finance	Intuit	Quicken
	Microsoft	Money
Legal	Broderbund	Family Lawyer
	Cosmi	Perfect Attorney
	H&R Block Kiplinger	Home & Business Attorney
		WILLPower
	Nolo	Quicken Legal Business
		Quicken WillMaker
Tax Preparation	2nd Story Software	TaxACT
	H&R Block Kiplinger	TaxCut
	Intuit	Quicken TurboTax
Desktop Publishing (for Personal Use)	Broderbund	The Print Shop PrintMaster
	Microsoft	Publisher
Paint/Image Editing (for Personal Use)	Corel	CorelDRAW
	Jasc	Paint Shop Pro
	Sun	StarOffice Draw
	The GIMP Team (open source software)	The Gimp

Application Software	Manufacturer	Program Name
Photo Editing	Adobe	Photoshop Elements
	Corel	Photobook
	Dell	Image Expert
	Microsoft	Picture It! Photo Picture Manager
	Roxio	PhotoSuite
	Ulead	PhotoImpact Photo Express
Clip Art/Image Gallery	Broderbund	ClickArt
	Nova Development	Art Explosion
Video and Audio Editing (for Personal Use)	Microsoft	Movie Maker
	Pinnacle Systems	Studio Moviebox
	Roxio	VideoWave
	Ulead	VideoStudio
Home Design/ Landscaping	ART	Home Designer Suite
	Broderbund	3D Home Architect Design Suite
	Quality Plans	Home Designer Suite
	ValuSoft	Custom LandDesigner
Reference	American Heritage	Talking Dictionary Classic
	Microsoft	Encarta Streets & Trips
	Rand McNally	StreetFinder TripMaker

FIGURE 3-25   Many popular software programs are available for home, personal, and educational use.

Software Suite (for Personal Use)

A software suite (for personal use) combines application software such as word processing, spreadsheet, database, and other programs in a single, easy-to-use package. Many computer vendors install a software suite for personal use, such as Microsoft Works, on new computers sold to home users.

As mentioned earlier, the programs in a software suite use a similar interface and share some common features. The programs in software suites for personal use typically are available only through the software suite; that is, you cannot purchase them individually. These programs may not have all the capabilities of business application software. For many home users, however, the capabilities of software suites for personal use more than meet their needs.

Personal Finance Software

Personal finance software is a simplified accounting program that helps home users and small office/home office users balance their checkbooks (Figure 3-26), pay bills, track personal income and expenses, set up budgets, manage home inventory, track investments, and evaluate financial plans. Personal finance software helps determine where, and for what purpose, you are spending money so you can manage your finances. Reports can summarize transactions by category (such as dining), by payee (such as the electric company), or by time (such as the last two months). Financial planning features include analyzing home and personal loans, preparing income taxes, and managing retirement savings.

Most of these personal finance programs also offer a variety of online services, which require access to the Internet. For example, users can track investments online, compare insurance rates from leading insurance companies, and bank online. **Online banking** offers access to account balances, provides bill paying services, and allows you to download monthly transactions and statements from the Web directly to your computer.

WEB LINK 3-5

Personal Finance Software

For more information, visit scsite.com/dc2006/ch3/weblink and then click Personal Finance Software.

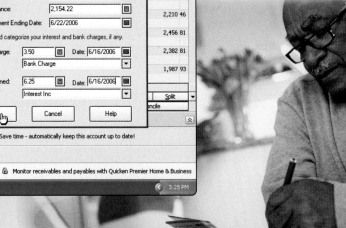

FIGURE 3-26 Personal finance software assists home users with balancing their checkbooks and paying bills.

FAQ 3-7

How many people bank online?

Currently, about 40 million people bank online. By 2010, this number is expected to grow to 50 million. The chart below depicts popular online banking activities. For more information, visit scsite.com/dc2006/ch3/faq and then click Online Banking.

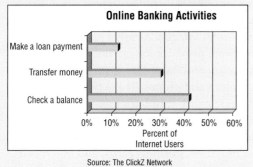

Online Banking Activities

Make a loan payment
Transfer money
Check a balance

0% 10% 20% 30% 40% 50% 60%
Percent of
Internet Users

Source: The ClickZ Network

Legal Software

Legal software assists in the preparation of legal documents and provides legal information to individuals, families, and small businesses (Figure 3-27). Legal software provides standard contracts and documents associated with buying, selling, and renting property; estate planning; marriage and divorce; and preparing a will or living trust. By answering a series of questions or completing a form, the legal software tailors the legal document to specific needs.

Once the legal document is created, you can file the paperwork with the appropriate agency, court, or office; or take the document to your attorney for his or her review and signature. Before using one of these software programs to create a document, you may want to check with your local bar association for its legality.

Tax Preparation Software

Tax preparation software is used to guide individuals, families, or small businesses through the process of filing federal taxes (Figure 3-28). These programs forecast tax liability and offer money-saving tax tips, designed to lower your tax bill. After you answer a series of questions and complete basic forms, the software creates and analyzes your tax forms to search for potential errors and deduction opportunities. Once the forms are complete, you can print any necessary paperwork, and then they are ready for filing.

FAQ 3-8

Can I file my taxes online?

Yes, many taxpayers *e-file*, or use tax software and/or tax preparation Web sites to file federal and state returns electronically. With tax professionals available to answer questions in a chat room or via e-mail, many taxpayers find this service easy-to-use and relatively inexpensive. The IRS hopes that 80 percent of taxpayers will e-file their taxes by 2007. For more information, visit scsite.com/dc2006/ch3/faq and then click E-Filing Taxes.

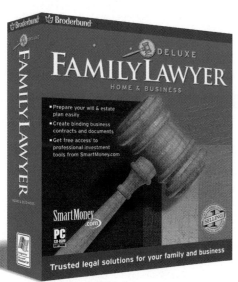

FIGURE 3-27 Legal software provides legal information to individuals, families, and small businesses and assists in record keeping and the preparation of legal documents.

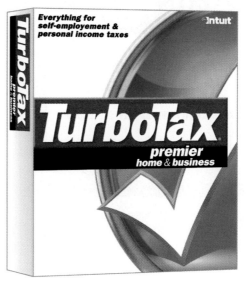

FIGURE 3-28 Tax preparation software guides individuals, families, or small businesses through the process of filing federal taxes.

Desktop Publishing Software (for Personal Use)

Instead of using professional DTP software (as discussed earlier in this chapter), many home and small business users work with simpler, easy-to-understand DTP software designed for smaller-scale desktop publishing projects (Figure 3-29). **Personal DTP software** helps home and small business users create newsletters, brochures, advertisements, post-cards, greeting cards, letterhead, business cards, banners, calendars, logos, and Web pages.

Personal DTP programs provide hundreds of thousands of graphical images. You also can import (bring in) your own digital photographs into the documents. These programs typically guide you through the development of a document by asking a series of questions, offering numerous predefined layouts, and providing standard text you can add to documents. Then, you can print a finished publication on a color printer or post it on the Web.

Many personal DTP programs also include paint/image editing software and photo editing software.

WEB LINK 3-6

Personal DTP Software

For more information, visit scsite.com/ dc2006/ch3/weblink and then click Personal DTP Software.

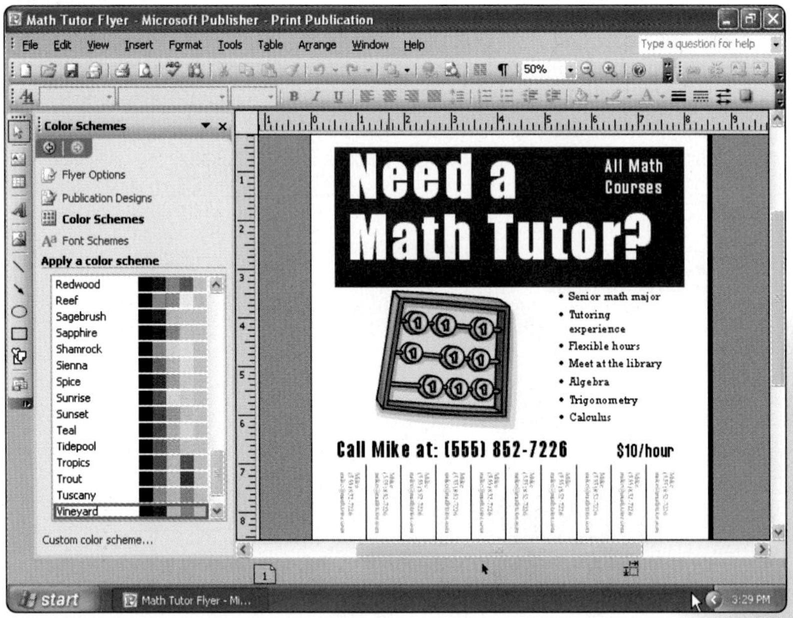

Paint/Image Editing Software (for Personal Use)

Personal paint/image editing software provides an easy-to-use interface, usually with more simplified capabilities than its professional counterpart, including functions tailored to meet the needs of the home and small business user.

As with the professional versions, personal paint software includes various simplified tools that allow you to draw pictures, shapes, and other images. Personal image editing software provides the capabilities of paint software and the ability to modify existing graphics and photos. These products also include many templates to assist you in adding an image to documents such as greeting cards (Figure 3-30), banners, calendars, signs, labels, business cards, and letterhead.

FAQ 3-9

How do pictures get in the computer from a digital camera?

Most digital cameras save pictures on miniature storage media, such as a memory card. By inserting the memory card in a card reader/writer in or attached to the computer, users can access images the same way they access files on a disk drive. With some cameras, pictures also can transfer along a cable that connects the camera to the computer. For more information, visit scsite.com/ dc2006/ch3/faq and then click Digital Imaging.

FIGURE 3-29 With Publisher, home and small business users can create professional looking publications such as this flyer with tear-offs.

FIGURE 3-30 Home users can purchase affordable paint/image editing programs that enable them to include personal pictures and graphics in many different types of documents.

Photo Editing Software

Photo editing software is a popular type of image editing software that allows users to edit digital photographs by removing red-eye, erasing blemishes, restoring aged photos, adding special effects (Figure 3-31), or creating electronic photo albums. When you purchase a digital camera, it usually includes photo editing software. You can print edited photographs on labels, calendars, business cards, and banners; or post them on a Web page. Some photo editing software allows users to send digital photographs to an online print service, which will deliver high-resolution printed images through the postal service. Many online print services have a photo community where users can post photographs on the Web for others to view.

Clip Art/Image Gallery

Application software often includes a **clip art/image gallery**, which is a collection of clip art and photographs. Some applications have links to additional clips available on the Web. You also can purchase clip art/image gallery software that contains hundreds of thousands of images (Figure 3-32).

In addition to clip art, many clip art/image galleries provide fonts, animations, sounds, video clips, and audio clips. You can use the images, fonts, and other items from the clip art/image gallery in all types of documents, including word processing, desktop publishing, spreadsheet, and presentation graphics.

Video and Audio Editing Software (for Personal Use)

Many home users work with easy-to-use video and audio editing software, which is much simpler to use than its professional counterpart, for small-scale movie making projects (Figure 3-33). With these programs, home users can edit home movies, add music or other sounds to the video, and share their movies on the Web. Some operating systems include video editing and audio editing software.

FIGURE 3-31   Photo editing software enables home users to edit digital photographs.

FIGURE 3-32   Clip art/image gallery software contains hundreds of thousands of images.

WEB LINK 3-7

Microsoft Office Clip Art

For more information, visit scsite.com/dc2006/ch3/weblink and then click Microsoft Office Clip Art.

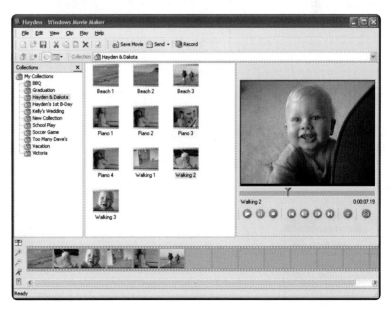

FIGURE 3-33   Operating systems, such as Windows XP, include video and audio editing software so home users can create their own movies.

Home Design/Landscaping Software

Homeowners or potential homeowners can use **home design/landscaping software** to assist them with the design, remodeling, or improvement of a home, deck, or landscape (Figure 3-34). Home design/landscaping software includes hundreds of pre-drawn plans that you can customize to meet your needs. Once designed, many home design/landscaping programs print a materials list outlining costs and quantities for the entire project.

FIGURE 3-34   Home design/landscaping software can help you design or remodel a home, deck, or landscape.

Reference and Educational Software

Reference software provides valuable and thorough information for all individuals (Figure 3-35). Popular reference software includes encyclopedias, dictionaries, health/medical guides, and travel directories.

FIGURE 3-35   This reference software shows text you can read about butterflies and moths and includes a variety of pictures, videos, and links to the Web.

WEB LINK 3-8

Entertainment Software

For more information, visit scsite.com/dc2006/ch3/weblink and then click Entertainment Software.

Educational software is software that teaches a particular skill. Educational software exists for just about any subject, from learning how to type to learning how to cook. Preschool to high school learners use educational software to assist them with subjects such as reading and math or to prepare them for class or college entry exams. Educational software often includes games and other content to make the learning experience more fun.

Many educational programs use a computer-based training approach. **Computer-based training** (**CBT**), also called computer-aided instruction (CAI), is a type of education in which students learn by using and completing exercises with instructional software. CBT typically consists of self-directed, self-paced instruction about a topic. Beginning athletes, for example, use CBT programs to learn the intricacies of baseball, football, soccer, tennis, and golf. The military and airlines use CBT simulations to train pilots to fly in various conditions and environments. Schools use CBT to teach students math, language, and software skills.

Entertainment Software

Entertainment software for personal computers includes interactive games, videos, and other programs designed to support a hobby or provide amusement and enjoyment. For example, you might use entertainment software to play games (Figure 3-36), make a family tree, listen to music, or fly an aircraft.

FIGURE 3-36   Entertainment software can provide hours of recreation.

APPLICATION SOFTWARE FOR COMMUNICATIONS

One of the main reasons people use computers is to communicate and share information with others. Some communications software is considered system software because it works with hardware and transmission media.

Other communications software makes users more productive and/or assists them with personal tasks, and thus, is considered application software. Chapter 2 presented a variety of application software for communications, which are summarized in the table in Figure 3-37. Read At Issue 3-4 for a related discussion.

APPLICATION SOFTWARE FOR COMMUNICATIONS

E-Mail
- Messages and files sent via a network such as the Internet
- Requires an e-mail program
  - Integrated in many software suites and operating systems
  - Available free at portals on the Web
  - Included with paid Internet access service
  - Can be purchased separately from retailers

FTP
- Method of uploading and downloading files with other computers on the Internet
- Download may require an FTP program; upload usually requires an FTP program
  - Integrated in some operating systems
  - Available for download on the Web for a small fee
  - Can be purchased separately from retailers

Web Browser
- Allows users to access and view Web pages on the Internet
- Requires a Web browser program
  - Integrated in some operating systems
  - Available for download on the Web free or for a fee
  - Included with paid Internet access service

Video Conferencing/Telephone Calls
- Meeting/conversation between geographically separated people who use a network such as the Internet to transmit video/audio
- Requires a microphone, speakers, and sometimes a video camera attached to your computer
- Requires video conferencing software

Newsgroup/Message Board
- Online area where users have written discussions
- Newsgroup may require a newsreader program
  - Integrated in some operating systems, e-mail programs, and Web browsers
  - Available for download on the Web, usually at no cost
  - Included with some paid Internet access services
  - Built into some Web sites

Chat Room
- Real-time, online typed conversation
- Requires chat client software
  - Integrated in some operating systems, e-mail programs, and Web browsers
  - Available for download on the Web, usually at no cost
  - Included with some paid Internet access services
  - Built into some Web sites

Instant Messaging
- Real-time exchange of messages, files, audio, and/or video with another online user
- Requires instant messenger software
  - Integrated in some operating systems
  - Available for download on the Web, usually at no cost
  - Included with some paid Internet access services

FIGURE 3-37 A summary of application software for home and business communications.

AT ISSUE 3-4

Should Companies Monitor Employees' E-Mail and Web Browsing?

According to one survey, more than 75 percent of Fortune 500 companies routinely monitor employees' computer use. Employers can use software to see what is on the screen or stored on hard disks, scrutinize e-mail and Web browsing habits, and even supervise keyboard activity. About one company in four has fired an employee based on its discoveries. Companies monitor computer use to improve productivity, increase security, reduce misconduct, and control liability risks. Few laws regulate employee monitoring, and courts have given employers a great deal of leeway in watching work on company-owned computers. In one case, an employee's termination for using her office e-mail system to complain about her boss was upheld, even though the company allowed e-mail use for personal communications. The court decreed that the employee's messages were inappropriate for workplace communications. Many employees believe that monitoring software violates their privacy rights. To reduce employee anxiety about monitoring computer use, one expert suggests that companies publish written policies and accept employee feedback, provide clear descriptions of acceptable and unacceptable behavior, respect employee needs and time, and establish a balance between security and privacy. Should companies monitor how their employees use computers at work? Why or why not? How can a company balance workplace security and productivity with employee privacy? If a company monitors computer use, what guidelines should be followed to maintain worker morale? Why?

POPULAR STAND-ALONE UTILITY PROGRAMS

Utility programs are considered system software because they assist a user with controlling or maintaining the operation of a computer, its devices, or its software. Some utility programs are included with the operating system, and others are available as stand-alone programs.

Stand-alone utility programs typically offer features that provide an environment conducive to successful use of application software. One of the more important utility programs protects a computer against viruses. A computer *virus* is a potentially damaging computer program that affects, or infects, a computer negatively by altering the way the computer works without the user's knowledge or permission. For a technical discussion about viruses, read the High-Tech Talk article on page 168.

Other features of stand-alone utility programs include removing spyware from a computer; filtering e-mail messages, Web content, and advertisements; compressing files; converting files; burning (recording on) a CD or DVD; and maintaining a personal computer. The table in Figure 3-38 briefly describes several stand-alone utility programs. Chapter 8 discusses them in more depth.

FAQ 3-10

How much does a computer virus attack cost a company?

A recent survey found that it typically costs an enterprise about $10,000 to recover from a computer virus attack. When the virus attacks multiple servers, however, the costs can exceed $100,000. For more information, visit scsite.com/dc2006/ch3/faq and then click Computer Virus Attacks.

WEB LINK 3-9

Antivirus Programs

For more information, visit scsite.com/dc2006/ch3/weblink and then click Antivirus Programs.

WIDELY USED STAND-ALONE UTILITY PROGRAMS

Utility Program	Description
Antivirus Program	An *antivirus program* protects a computer against viruses by identifying and removing any computer viruses found in memory, on storage media, or in incoming files.
Spyware Remover	A *spyware remover* detects and deletes spyware on your computer.
Internet Filters	
• Anti-Spam Program	An *anti-spam program* attempts to remove spam (Internet junk mail) before it reaches your e-mail inbox.
• Web Filter	A *Web filter* restricts access to specified Web sites.
• Pop-up Blocker	A *pop-up blocker* stops advertisements from displaying on Web pages and disables pop-up windows.
File Compression	A *file compression utility* shrinks the size of a file(s), so the file takes up less storage space than the original file.
File Conversion	A *file conversion utility* transforms a file from one format to another, eliminating the need to reenter data in a new program.
CD/DVD Burning	A *CD/DVD burner* writes text, graphics, audio, and video files on a recordable or rewritable CD or DVD.
Personal Computer Maintenance	A *personal computer maintenance utility* identifies and fixes operating system problems, detects and repairs disk problems, and includes the capability of improving a computer's performance.

FIGURE 3-38 A summary of widely used stand-alone utility programs.

APPLICATION SOFTWARE ON THE WEB

As discussed earlier in this chapter, users can purchase application software from a software vendor, retail store, or Web-based business. Users typically install purchased application software on a computer before they run it. Installed software has two disadvantages: (1) it requires disk space on your computer, and (2) it can be costly to upgrade as vendors release new versions. As an alternative, some users opt to access Web applications.

A **Web application** is application software that exists on a Web site. Users access Web applications anywhere from any computer or device, as long as it has an Internet connection (read Looking Ahead 3-2 for a look at the next generation of Web access). Web applications usually store users' data and information on their servers. For this reason, users concerned with data security may shy away from this option.

Some Web sites provide free access to the application. For example, one site creates a map and driving directions when a user enters a starting and destination point (Figure 3-39). Other Web sites allow you to use the program free and pay a fee when a certain action occurs. For example, you can prepare your tax return free using TurboTax for the Web, but if you elect to print it or file it electronically, you pay a minimal fee.

LOOKING AHEAD 3-2

Driving Down the Web Highway

Analysts predict you will access the Internet from practically everywhere: home, office, airport, grocery store, and the local coffee shop. Why not from your car?

As it sits in your garage, your car's computer could connect to your home computer and then relay information about fluid levels and the amount of gas in the tank. It could notify you when the oil needs to be changed and when the tires should be rotated. You even could start the car remotely on chilly days by pressing a button on your notebook computer as you eat your breakfast cereal at the kitchen table.

Automobile manufacturers are touting their cyber cars of the future equipped with Internet access. They are planning in-dash screens with continuous information about traffic, weather forecasts, and restaurant guides. Their plans also call for having the Internet access disconnect when the vehicle is in motion so that drivers do not attempt to drive and surf the Web simultaneously. For more information, visit scsite.com/dc2006/ch3/looking and then click Cyber Cars.

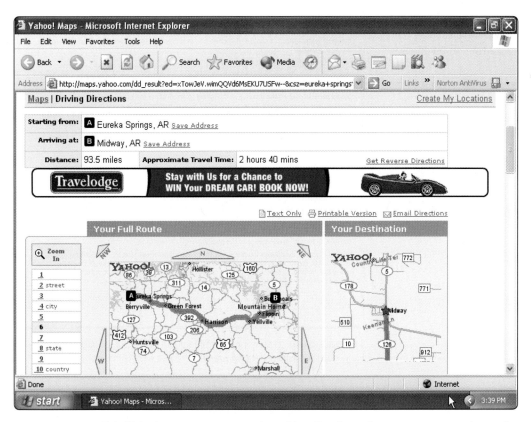

FIGURE 3-39   This Web site creates a map and provides directions when you enter a starting and destination point.

Application Service Providers

Storing and maintaining programs can be a costly investment for businesses. Thus, some have elected to outsource one or more facets of their information technology (IT) needs to an application service provider. An *application service provider* (*ASP*) is a third-party organization that manages and distributes software and services on the Web. That is, instead of installing the software on your computer, you run the programs from the Internet.

The five categories of ASPs are:

1. *Enterprise ASP*: customizes and delivers high-end business applications, such as finance and database
2. *Local/Regional ASP*: offers a variety of software applications to a specific geographic region
3. *Specialist ASP*: delivers applications to meet a specific business need, such as human resources or project management
4. *Vertical Market ASP*: provides applications for a particular industry, such as construction, health care, or retail
5. *Volume Business ASP*: supplies prepackaged applications, such as accounting, to businesses

A variety of payment schemes are available. Some rent use of the application on a monthly basis or charge based on the number of user accesses. Others charge a one-time fee.

LEARNING AIDS AND SUPPORT TOOLS FOR APPLICATION SOFTWARE

Learning how to use application software effectively involves time and practice. To assist in the learning process, many programs provide online Help, Web-based Help, wizards, and templates.

Online Help is the electronic equivalent of a user manual (Figure 3-40a). It usually is integrated in a program. In most programs, a function key or a button on the screen starts the Help feature. When using a program, you can use the Help feature to ask a question or access the Help topics in subject or alphabetical order.

Most online Help also links to Web sites that offer *Web-based Help*, which provides updates and more comprehensive resources to respond to technical issues about software (Figure 3-40b). Some Web sites contain chat rooms, in which a user can talk directly with a technical support

FIGURE 3-40a (online Help)

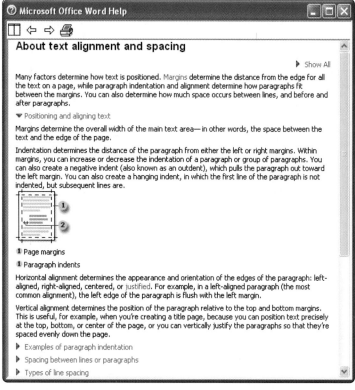

FIGURE 3-40 Many programs include online Help, Web-based Help, and templates. *(continued)*

FIGURE 3-40b (Web-based Help)

FIGURE 3-40c (template)

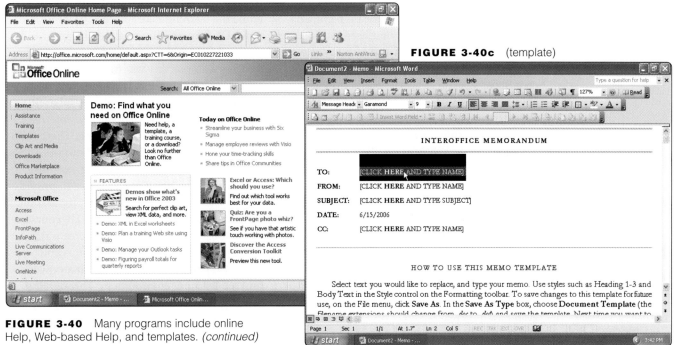

FIGURE 3-40 Many programs include online Help, Web-based Help, and templates. *(continued)*

person or join a conversation with other users who may be able to answer questions or solve problems.

A *wizard* is an automated assistant that helps a user complete a task by asking questions and then automatically performing actions based on the responses. A *template* is a document that contains the formatting necessary for a specific document type (Figure 3-40c). Many software applications include wizards and templates. For example, word processing software uses wizards for creating charts and documents and contains templates for memorandums, meeting agendas, fax cover sheets, flyers, letters, and resumes. Spreadsheet software includes wizards for creating charts and building functions and templates for invoices and purchase orders.

If you want to learn more about a particular program from a printed manual, many books are available to help you learn to use the features of personal computer programs. These books typically are available in bookstores and software stores (Figure 3-41).

Many colleges and schools provide training on several of the applications discussed in this chapter. For more information, contact your local school for a list of class offerings.

FIGURE 3-41
Bookstores often sell trade books to help you learn to use the features of personal computer application software.

Web-Based Training

Web-based training (*WBT*) is a type of CBT (computer-based training) that uses Internet technology and consists of application software on the Web. Similar to CBT, WBT typically consists of self-directed, self-paced instruction about a topic. WBT is popular in business, industry, and schools for teaching new skills or enhancing existing skills of employees, teachers, or students. When using a WBT product, students actively become involved in the learning process instead of remaining passive recipients of information.

Many Web sites offer WBT to the general public (Figure 3-42). Such training covers a wide range of topics, from how to change a flat tire to creating documents in Word. Many of these Web sites are free. Others require registration and payment to take the complete Web-based course.

WBT often is combined with other materials for distance learning courses. **Distance learning** (**DL**) is the delivery of education at one location while the learning takes place at other locations. DL courses provide time, distance, and place advantages for students who live far from a college campus or work full time. These courses enable students to attend class from anywhere in the world and at times that fit their schedules. Many national and international companies offer DL training. These training courses eliminate the costs of airfare, hotels, and meals for centralized training sessions.

WBT companies often specialize in providing instructors with the tools for preparation, distribution, and management of DL courses. These tools enable instructors to create rich, educational Web-based training sites and allow the students to interact with a powerful Web learning environment. Through the training site, students can check their progress, take practice tests, search for topics, send e-mail, and participate in discussions and chats.

WEB LINK 3-10

Web-Based Training

For more information, visit scsite.com/ dc2006/ch3/weblink and then click Web-Based Training.

FIGURE 3-42 At the HowStuffWorks Web-based training site, you can learn how computers, autos, electronics, and many other products work.

Test your knowledge of pages 155 through 166 in Quiz Yourself 3-3.

QUIZ YOURSELF 3-3

Instructions: Find the true statement below. Then, rewrite the remaining false statements so they are true.

1. An anti-spam program protects a computer against viruses by identifying and removing any computer viruses found in memory, on storage media, or in incoming files.
2. Computer-based training is a type of Web-based training that uses Internet technology and consists of application software on the Web.
3. E-mail and Web browsers are examples of communications software that are considered application software.
4. Legal software is a simplified accounting program that helps home users and small office/home office users balance their checkbooks, pay bills, track investments, and evaluate financial plans.
5. Personal DTP software is a popular type of image editing software that allows users to edit digital photographs.

Quiz Yourself Online: To further check your knowledge of types and features of home, personal, educational, and communications programs, stand-alone utility programs, Web applications, and software learning aids, visit scsite.com/dc2006/ch3/quiz and then click Objectives 6 – 10.

CHAPTER SUMMARY

This chapter illustrated how to start and use application software. It then presented an overview of a variety of business software, graphics and multimedia software, home/personal/educational software, and communications software (read At Issue 3-5 for a related discussion).

The chapter also described widely used stand-alone utility programs and identified various Web applications. Finally, learning aids and support tools for application software were presented.

AT ISSUE 3-5

Copying Software — A Computer Crime!

Usually, when you buy software, you legally can make one copy of the software for backup purposes. Despite the law, many people make multiple copies, either to share or to sell. In one survey, more than 50 percent of respondents admitted that they had illegally copied, or would illegally copy, software. Microsoft, a leading software manufacturer, estimates that almost 25 percent of software in the United States has been copied illegally. Among small businesses, the rate may be even higher. The Business Software Alliance, an industry trade association, believes that 40 percent of small U.S. businesses use illegally copied software. Illegally copied software costs the software industry more than $13 billion a year in lost revenues. People and companies copy software illegally for a variety of reasons, insisting that software prices are too high, software manufacturers make enough money, software often is copied for educational or other altruistic purposes, copied software makes people more productive, no restrictions should be placed on the use of software after it is purchased, and everyone copies software. What should be the penalty for copying software? Why? Can you counter the reasons people give for copying software illegally? How? Would you copy software illegally? Why or why not?

CAREER CORNER

Help Desk Specialist

A Help Desk specialist position is an entryway into the information technology (IT) field. A *Help Desk specialist* deals with problems in hardware, software, or communications systems. Job requirements may include the following: solve procedural and software questions both in person and over the telephone, develop and maintain Help Desk operations manuals, and assist in training new Help Desk personnel

Usually, a Help Desk specialist must be knowledgeable about the major programs in use. Entry-level positions primarily involve answering calls from people with questions. Other positions provide additional assistance and assume further responsibilities, often demanding greater knowledge and problem-solving skills that can lead to more advanced IT positions. This job is ideal for people who must work irregular hours, because many companies need support people to work evenings, weekends, or part-time.

Educational requirements are less stringent than they are for other jobs in the computer field. In some cases, a high school diploma is sufficient. Advancement requires a minimum of a two-year degree, while management generally requires a bachelor's degree in IT or a related field. Certification is another way Help Desk specialists can increase their attractiveness in the marketplace. Entry-level salaries range from $27,500 to $56,500 per year. Managers range from $49,000 to $72,500. For more information, visit scsite.com/dc2006/ch3/careers and then click Help Desk Specialist.

High-Tech Talk

COMPUTER VIRUSES:
DELIVERY, INFECTION, AND AVOIDANCE

Sasser. Netsky. Lovgate. Nachi. Like the common cold, virtually countless variations of computer viruses exist. Unlike the biological viruses that cause the common cold, people create computer viruses. To create a virus, an unscrupulous programmer must code and then test the virus code to ensure the virus can replicate itself, conceal itself, monitor for certain events, and then deliver its *payload* — the destructive event or prank the virus was created to deliver. Despite the many variations of viruses, most have two phases to their execution: infection and delivery.

To start the infection phase, the virus must be activated. Today, the most common way viruses spread is by people running infected programs disguised as e-mail attachments. During the infection phase, viruses typically perform three actions:

1. First, a virus replicates by attaching itself to program files. A *macro virus* hides in the macro language of an application, such as Word. A *boot sector virus* targets the master boot record and executes when the computer boots up. A *file virus* attaches itself to program files. The file virus, Win32.Hatred, for example, replicates by first infecting Windows executable files for the Calculator, Notepad, Help, and other programs on the hard disk. The virus then scans the computer to locate .exe files on other drives and stores this information in the system registry. The next time an infected file is run, the virus reads the registry and continues infecting another drive.

2. Viruses also conceal themselves to avoid detection. A *stealth virus* disguises itself by hiding in fake code sections, which it inserts within working code in a file. A *polymorphic virus* actually changes its code as it infects computers. Win32.Hatred uses both concealment techniques. The virus writes itself to the last file section, while modifying the file header to hide the increased file size. It also scrambles and encrypts the virus code as it infects files.

3. Finally, viruses watch for a certain condition or event and activate when that condition or event occurs. The event might be booting up the computer or hitting a date on the system clock. A *logic bomb* activates when it detects a specific condition (say, a name deleted from the employee list). A *time bomb* is a logic bomb that activates on a particular date or time. Win32.Hatred, for instance, unleashes its destruction when the computer clock hits the seventh day of any month. If the triggering condition does not exist, the virus simply replicates.

During the delivery phase, the virus unleashes its payload, which might be a harmless prank that displays a silly message — or it might be destructive, corrupting or deleting data and files. When Win32.Hatred triggers, it displays the author's message and then covers the screen with black dots. The virus also deletes several antivirus files as it infects the system. The most dangerous viruses do not have an obvious payload, instead they quietly modify files. A virus, for example, could randomly change numbers in an inventory program or introduce delays to slow a computer.

STEPS TO VIRUS PROTECTION

1. Install the latest Windows updates.
2. Purchase a good antivirus program.
3. After installing an antivirus program, scan your entire computer to be sure your system is clean.
4. Update your antivirus definitions regularly.
5. Be suspicious of any and all unsolicited e-mail attachments.
6. Stay informed about viruses and virus hoaxes.
7. Install a personal firewall program.
8. Download software only if you are sure the Web site is legitimate.
9. Avoid as best you can visiting unscrupulous Web sites.

FIGURE 3-43 Guidelines to keep your computer virus free.

Other kinds of electronic annoyances exist in addition to viruses. While often called viruses, worms and Trojan horse applications actually are part of a broader category called *malicious-logic programs*.

- A *worm*, such as the CodeRed or Sircam worm, resides in active memory and replicates itself over a network to infect machines, using up the system resources and possibly shutting the system down.

- A *Trojan horse* is a destructive program disguised as a real application, such as a screen saver. When a user runs a seemingly innocent program, a Trojan horse hiding inside can capture information, such as user names and passwords, from your system or open up a backdoor that allows a hacker remotely to control your computer. Unlike viruses, Trojan horses do not replicate themselves.

As with the common cold, every computer user is susceptible to a computer virus. In 1995, the chance that a virus would infect your computer was 1 in 1,000; by 2004, the odds were only 1 in 7. Even with better antivirus software, viruses are tough to avoid, as deceitful programmers craft new electronic maladies to infect your computer. Figure 3-43 lists steps you can follow to protect your computer from a virus infection. For more information, visit scsite.com/dc2006/ch3/tech and then click Computer Viruses.

Companies on the Cutting Edge

ADOBE SYSTEMS
DIGITAL IMAGING LEADER

Practically every image seen on a computer and in print has been shaped by software developed by *Adobe Systems, Inc.* The company, based in San Jose, California, is one of the world's largest application software corporations and is committed to helping people communicate effectively.

Adobe Photoshop and Photoshop Album have set the industry standard for digital imaging and digital video software, while Creative Suite is used for design and publishing. The company's Portable Document Format (PDF) and Adobe Reader are used to share documents among users electronically. More than 600 million copies of the free Adobe Reader have been downloaded.

Fortune magazine named Adobe as the best high-tech company to work for in America in 2004. For more information, visit scsite.com/dc2006/ch3/companies and then click Adobe.

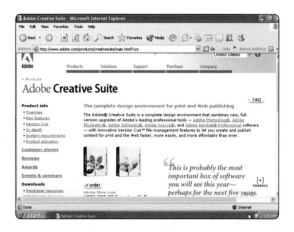

MICROSOFT
REALIZING POTENTIAL WITH BUSINESS SOFTWARE

Microsoft's mission is "to enable people and businesses throughout the world to realize their potential." As the largest software company in the world, *Microsoft* has indeed helped computer users in every field reach their goals.

When Microsoft was incorporated in 1975, the company had three programmers, one product, and revenues of $16,000. Thirty years later, the company employs more than 56,000 people, produces scores of software titles with Office and Windows leading the industry, and has annual revenue of more than $32 billion.

The company's recent efforts have focused on developing the next version of its operating system, which is named Longhorn, and the Smart Personal Objects Technology (SPOT), which brings computing power into everyday objects, such as wristwatches. For more information, visit scsite.com/dc2006/ch3/companies and then click Microsoft.

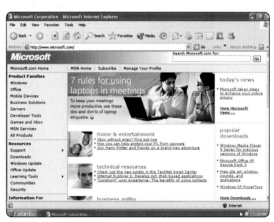

Technology Trailblazers

DAN BRICKLIN
VISICALC DEVELOPER

When *Dan Bricklin* was enrolled at the Harvard Business School in the 1970s, he often used his calculator to determine the effect of changing one value on a balance sheet. He recognized the need to develop a program that would perform a series of calculations automatically when the first number was entered.

He named his creation VisiCalc, short for Visible Calculator. He and a friend formed a company called Software Arts and programmed the VisiCalc prototype using Apple Basic on an Apple II computer. The small program was the first piece of application software that provided a reason for businesses to buy Apple computers. It laid the foundation for the development of other spreadsheets and included many of the features found in today's spreadsheet software.

His current venture is Trellix, which lets people turn everyday documents into Web pages with colors, graphics, and links. For more information, visit scsite.com/dc2006/ch3/people and then click Dan Bricklin.

MASAYOSHI SON
SOFTBANK PRESIDENT AND CEO

Many students carry photographs of family and friends in their wallets and book bags. As a 16-year-old student in the 1970s, *Masayoshi Son* carried a picture of a microchip. He predicted that the microchip was going to change people's lives, and he wanted to be part of that trend.

While majoring in economics at the University of California, Berkeley, he earned his first million dollars by importing arcade games from Japan to the campus, developing new computer games, and selling a patent for a multilingual pocket translator to Sharp Corporation.

At age 23 he founded Softbank, which is Japan's foremost software distributor and publisher and the country's largest broadband Internet service provider. Today, he is one of the world's wealthiest entrepreneurs. For more information, visit scsite.com/dc2006/ch3/people and then click Masayoshi Son.

Quizzes and Learning Games

Computer Genius
Crossword Puzzle
DC Track and Field
Practice Test
Quiz Yourself
Wheel of Terms
You're Hired!

Exercises

Case Studies
Chapter Review
Checkpoint
Key Terms
Learn How To
Learn It Online
Web Research

Beyond the Book

Career Corner
Companies
FAQs
High-Tech Talk
Looking Ahead
Making Use of the Web
Trailblazers
Web Links

Features

Chapter Forum
Install Computer
Lab Exercises
Maintain Computer
Tech News
Timeline 2006

Chapter Review

The Chapter Review section summarizes the concepts presented in this chapter. To listen to the audio version of this Chapter Review, visit scsite.com/dc2006/ch3/review. To obtain help from other students regarding any subject in this chapter, visit scsite.com/dc2006/ch3/forum and post your thoughts or questions.

(1) What Are the Categories of Application Software? **Application software** consists of programs designed to make users more productive and/or assist them with personal tasks. The major categories of application software are business software; graphics and multimedia software; home, personal, and educational software; and communications software.

(2) How Is Software Distributed? Application software is available in a variety of forms. **Packaged software** is mass-produced, copyrighted retail software that meets the needs of a variety of users. **Custom software** performs functions specific to a business or industry. **Open source software** is provided for use, modification, and redistribution. **Shareware** is copyrighted software that is distributed free for a trial period. **Freeware** is copyrighted software provided at no cost by an individual or a company that retains all rights to the software. **Public-domain software** is free software donated for public use and has no copyright restrictions.

(3) How Do You Work with Application Software? Personal computer operating systems often use the concept of a **desktop**, which is an on-screen work area that has a graphical user interface. To start an application in Windows XP, move the **pointer** to the Start **button** in the corner of the desktop and **click** the Start button by pressing and releasing a button on the mouse. Then, click the program name on the Start **menu** or on the *submenu* that displays when you point to a **command**. Once loaded into memory, the program is displayed in a **window** on the desktop.

> *connect* Visit scsite.com/dc2006/ch3/quiz or click the Quiz Yourself button. Click Objectives 1 – 3.

(4) What Are the Key Features of Widely Used Business Programs? **Business software** assists people in becoming more effective and efficient while performing daily business activities. Business software includes the following programs. **Word processing software** allows users to **create** a document by entering text and inserting graphical images, **edit** the document by making changes, and **format** the document by altering its appearance. **Spreadsheet software** allows users to organize data in rows and columns, perform calculations, recalculate when data changes, and chart the data. **Database software** allows users to create a **database**, which is a collection of data organized to allow access, retrieval, and use of that data. **Presentation graphics software** allows users to create a *slide show* that is displayed on a monitor or projection screen. **Note taking software** enables users to enter typed text, handwritten comments, drawings, or sketches on a page and then save the page as part of a notebook. A **personal information manager (PIM)** is software that includes features to help users organize personal information. A **software suite** is a collection of individual programs sold as a single package. **Project management software** allows users to plan, schedule, track, and analyze a project. **Accounting software** helps companies record and report their financial transactions.

(5) What Are the Key Features of Widely Used Graphics and Multimedia Programs? Graphics and multimedia software includes the following programs. **Computer-aided design (CAD) software** assists in creating engineering, architectural, and scientific designs. **Desktop publishing (DTP) software** enables professional designers to create sophisticated documents that contain text, graphics, and colors. **Paint software** lets users draw graphical images with various on-screen tools. **Image editing software** provides the capabilities of paint software and includes the capability to modify existing images. **Video editing software** allows professionals to modify segments of a video.

> *connect* Visit scsite.com/dc2006/ch3/quiz or click the Quiz Yourself button. Click Objectives 4 – 5.

Chapter Review

Audio editing software lets users modify audio clips and produce studio-quality soundtracks. **Multimedia authoring software** allows users to combine text, graphics, audio, video, and animation into an interactive application. **Web page authoring software** helps users create Web pages that include graphical images, video, audio, animation, and other special effects.

(6) What Are the Key Features of Widely Used Home, Personal, and Educational Programs?
Software for home, personal, and educational use includes the following applications. A software suite (for personal use) combines application software such as word processing, spreadsheet, and database into a single package. **Personal finance software** is an accounting program that helps users balance their checkbooks, pay bills, track income and expenses, track investments, and evaluate financial plans. **Legal software** assists in the preparation of legal documents. **Tax preparation software** guides users through filing federal taxes. **Personal DTP software** helps users create newsletters, brochures, advertisements, greeting and business cards, logos, and Web pages. **Personal paint/image editing software** provides an easy-to-use interface with functions tailored to meet the needs of home and small business users. **Photo editing software** is a type of image editing software used to edit digital photographs. Application software often includes a **clip art/image gallery**, which is a collection of clip art and photographs. **Home design/landscaping software** assists with the design, remodeling, or improvement of a home or landscape. **Educational software** teaches a particular skill. **Reference software** provides valuable and thorough information for all individuals. **Entertainment software** includes interactive games, videos, and other programs to support hobbies or provide amusement.

(7) What Are the Types of Application Software Used in Communications? Application software for communications includes e-mail programs to transmit messages via a network; FTP programs to upload and download files on the Internet; Web browsers to access and view Web pages; video conferencing/telephone call software for meetings or conversations on a network; newsreader/message board programs that allow online written discussions; chat room software to have real-time, online typed conversations; and instant messaging software for real-time exchange of messages or files.

(8) What Are the Functions of Stand-Alone Utility Programs? Stand-alone utility programs support the successful use of application software. An *antivirus program* protects a computer against a computer *virus*, which is a potentially damaging computer program. A *spyware remover* detects and deletes spyware. An *anti-spam program* removes spam (Internet junk-mail). A *Web filter* restricts access to specified Web sites. A *pop-up blocker* disables pop-up windows. A *file compression utility* shrinks the size of a file. A *file conversion utility* transforms a file from one format to another. A *CD/DVD burner* writes files to a recordable CD or DVD. A *personal computer maintenance utility* fixes operating system and disk problems.

(9) What Are the Advantages of Using Application Software on the Web? A **Web application** is application software that exists on a Web site. Web applications require less disk space on a computer than installed software and are less costly to upgrade. An *application service provider (ASP)* is a third-party organization that manages and distributes software and services on the Web.

(10) What Learning Aids Are Available for Application Software? To assist in the learning process, many programs offer Help features. **Online Help** is the electronic equivalent of a user manual. Most online Help links to *Web-based help*, which provides updates and more comprehensive resources. A *wizard* is an automated assistant that helps users complete a task by asking questions and then performing actions based on the responses. A *template* is a document that contains the formatting necessary for a specific document type.

Visit scsite.com/dc2006/ch3/quiz or click the Quiz Yourself button. Click Objectives 6 – 10.

Quizzes and Learning Games

Computer Genius
Crossword Puzzle
DC Track and Field
Practice Test
Quiz Yourself
Wheel of Terms
You're Hired!

Exercises

Case Studies
Chapter Review
Checkpoint
▸ Key Terms
Learn How To
Learn It Online
Web Research

Beyond the Book

Career Corner
Companies
FAQs
High-Tech Talk
Looking Ahead
Making Use of
the Web
Trailblazers
Web Links

Features

Chapter Forum
Install Computer
Lab Exercises
Maintain Computer
Tech News
Timeline 2006

Key Terms

You should know the Primary Terms and be familiar with the Secondary Terms. Use the list below to help focus your study. To further enhance your understanding of the Key Terms in this chapter, visit scsite.com/dc2006/ch3/terms. See an example of and a definition for each term, and access current and additional information about the term from the Web.

Primary Terms

(shown in bold-black characters in the chapter)

accounting software (149)
application software (134)
audio editing software (153)
business software (138)
button (136)
click (136)
clip art (139)
clip art/image gallery (159)
command (137)
computer-aided design (CAD) software (150)
computer-based training (CBT) (160)
create (141)
custom software (135)
database (145)
database software (145)
desktop (136)
desktop publishing (DTP) software (152)
distance learning (DL) (166)
edit (141)
educational software (160)
entertainment software (160)
font (141)
font size (141)
format (141)
freeware (135)
home design/ landscaping software (160)
icon (136)
image editing software (152)
legal software (157)
menu (137)
multimedia authoring software (154)

note taking software (147)
online banking (156)
online Help (164)
open source software (135)
packaged software (134)
paint software (152)
personal DTP software (158)
personal finance software (156)
personal information manager (PIM) (148)
personal paint/image editing software (158)
photo editing software (159)
pointer (136)
presentation graphics software (146)
print (142)
project management software (149)
public-domain software (135)
reference software (160)
save (142)
shareware (135)
software suite (148)
spreadsheet software (142)
tax preparation software (157)
title bar (137)
video editing software (153)
Web application (163)
Web page authoring software (154)
Web-based training (166)
window (137)
word processing software (138)

Secondary Terms

(shown in italic characters in the chapter)

application service provider (ASP) (164)
anti-spam program (162)
antivirus program (162)
bar chart (144)
CD/DVD burner (162)
cell (143)
charting (144)
clipboard (141)
color library (152)
column chart (144)
dialog box (137)
Enterprise ASP (164)
field (145)
file (137)
file compression utility (162)
file conversion utility (162)
file name (137)
filters (153)
font style (141)
footer (140)
formula (143)
function (143)
header (140)
illustration software (152)
import (146)
label (143)
line chart (144)
loaded (135)
local/regional ASP (164)
margins (139)
page layout (152)
pasting (141)
personal computer maintenance utility (162)

pie chart (144)
point (141)
pop-up blocker (162)
product activation (135)
query (145)
record (145)
replace (139)
sans serif font (141)
scrolling (139)
search (139)
serif font (141)
slide show (146)
slide sorter view (146)
specialist ASP (164)
spelling checker (139)
spyware remover (162)
submenu (137)
system software (135)
template (165)
value (143)
vertical market ASP (164)
virus (162)
volume business ASP (164)
WBT (166)
Web-based Help (164)
Web filter (162)
what-if analysis (144)
wizard (165)
word processor (138)
wordwrap (139)
worksheet (142)

Checkpoint

Use the Checkpoint exercises to check your knowledge level of the chapter. The Beyond the Book exercises will help broaden your understanding of the concepts presented in this chapter. To complete the Checkpoint exercises interactively, visit scsite.com/dc2006/ch3/check.

Label the Figure

Identify these elements in the Windows XP graphical user interface.

a. Accessories command
b. Accessories submenu
c. All Programs command
d. All Programs submenu
e. Start button
f. Start menu
g. Paint command

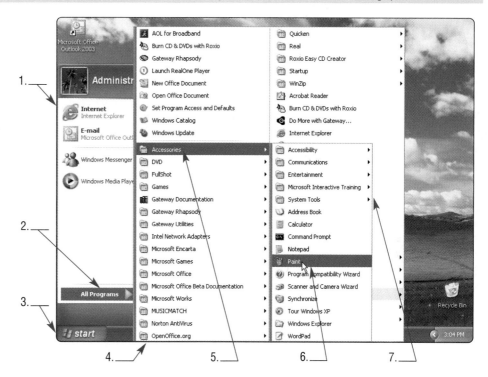

True/False

Mark T for True and F for False. (See page numbers in parentheses.)

_____ 1. The four categories of application software are mutually exclusive. (134)

_____ 2. Programmers typically can incorporate freeware in applications they intend to sell. (135)

_____ 3. To click a button on the screen requires moving the pointer away from the button and then pressing and holding down a button on the mouse (usually the right mouse button). (136)

_____ 4. The wordwrap feature allows users of word processing software to type words in a paragraph continually without pressing the ENTER key. (139)

_____ 5. In many spreadsheet programs, you begin a formula with an equal sign, a plus sign, or a minus sign. (143)

_____ 6. Many graphics and multimedia programs have user-friendly interfaces and scaled-down versions, making it possible for the home and small business user to create documents using these programs. (150)

_____ 7. Most of the programs for home, personal, and educational use are priced at more than $100. (155)

_____ 8. Personal DTP programs never include paint/image editing software or photo editing software. (158)

_____ 9. Some communications software is considered system software because it works with hardware and transmission media. (161)

_____ 10. Utility programs are considered application software because they make users more productive or assist with personal tasks. (162)

_____ 11. Web applications store users' data and information on their servers, so users concerned with data security may shy away from this option. (163)

_____ 12. Few software applications include wizards or templates. (164)

Discovering Computers 2006
A Gateway to Information

Quizzes and Learning Games

Computer Genius
Crossword Puzzle
DC Track and Field
Practice Test
Quiz Yourself
Wheel of Terms
You're Hired!

Exercises

Case Studies
Chapter Review
▶ Checkpoint
Key Terms
Learn How To
Learn It Online
Web Research

Beyond the Book

Career Corner
Companies
FAQs
High-Tech Talk
Looking Ahead
Making Use of the Web
Trailblazers
Web Links

Features

Chapter Forum
Install Computer
Lab Exercises
Maintain Computer
Tech News
Timeline 2006

Checkpoint

 Multiple Choice   Select the best answer. (See page numbers in parentheses.)

1. Presentation graphics software, project management software, accounting software, and enterprise computing software are examples of _____ software. (134)
   a. business
   b. graphics and multimedia
   c. communications
   d. home/personal/educational

2. _____ has no restrictions from the copyright holder regarding modification of the software's internal instructions and redistribution of the software. (135)
   a. Packaged software
   b. Custom software
   c. Open source software
   d. Shareware

3. In a document window, the _____ usually displays a document's file name. (137)
   a. status bar   b. submenu
   c. title bar   d. dialog box

4. In word processing, pasting is the process of _____. (141)
   a. moving different portions of the document on the screen into view
   b. transferring an item from the clipboard to a specific location in a document
   c. locating all occurrences of a certain character, word, or phrase
   d. removing a portion of a document and storing it in a temporary storage location

5. Most spreadsheet software includes a what-if analysis feature, where you _____. (144)
   a. depict the data in a spreadsheet in graphical form
   b. enter labels to identify worksheet data and organize the worksheet
   c. review the spelling of individual words and sections of a worksheet
   d. change values in a spreadsheet to identify the effects of those changes

6. With database software, users can run a _____, which is a request for specific data from the database. (145)
   a. query   b. function
   c. record   d. field

7. Users find _____ software convenient during meetings, class lectures, and other settings that previously required a pencil and paper for recording thoughts and discussions. (147)
   a. word processing   b. database
   c. note taking   d. accounting

8. DTP software supports page layout, which is the process of _____. (152)
   a. creating engineering, architectural, and scientific designs
   b. arranging text and graphics in a document on a page-by-page basis
   c. enhancing and modifying existing images and pictures
   d. standardizing the colors on a page used by designers and printers

9. _____ helps home users determine where, and for what purpose, they are spending money. (156)
   a. Legal software
   b. Personal DTP software
   c. Tax preparation software
   d. Personal finance software

10. Many educational programs use a _____ approach, in which students learn by using and completing exercises with instructional software. (160)
    a. computer-aided design (CAD)
    b. desktop teaching program (DTP)
    c. computer-based training (CBT)
    d. personal information manager (PIM)

11. A(n) _____, which can be used to upload and download files with other computers and on the Internet, is integrated in some operating systems. (161)
    a. FTP program   b. Web browser
    c. e-mail program   d. chat client

12. A(n) _____ is a stand-alone utility program that attempts to remove Internet junk mail before it reaches your e-mail inbox. (162)
    a. anti-spam program b. Web filter
    c. spyware remover   d. antivirus program

13. Vertical market ASP _____. (164)
    a. supplies packaged applications
    b. provides applications for a particular industry
    c. customizes and delivers high-end business applications
    d. offers a variety of software applications to specific regions

14. _____ is the delivery of education at one location while the learning takes place at other locations. (166)
    a. Online Help (OH)
    b. Software wizards (SW)
    c. Online banking (OB)
    d. Distance learning (DL)

Checkpoint

 Matching   Match the terms with their definitions. (See page numbers in parentheses.)

_____ 1. icon (136)
_____ 2. button (136)
_____ 3. menu (137)
_____ 4. clip art (139)
_____ 5. cell (143)
_____ 6. slide sorter view (146)
_____ 7. color library (152)
_____ 8. online banking (156)
_____ 9. volume business ASP (164)
_____ 10. wizard (165)

a. list of commands from which you make a selection
b. small symbol on the screen that moves as you move the mouse
c. intersection of a row and column in a spreadsheet
d. small image that represents a program, document, or some other object
e. offers access to account balances and provides bill paying services
f. automated assistant that helps users complete a task
g. standard set of colors used by designers and printers
h. text that appears at the bottom of every page
i. graphical image activated to cause a specific action to take place
j. screen view similar to how 35mm slides look on a light table
k. provides prepackaged applications, such as accounting, to businesses
l. collection of drawings, diagrams, maps, and photographs that can be inserted

 Short Answer   Write a brief answer to each of the following questions.

1. When using spreadsheet software, what is charting? _____ How are line charts, column charts, and pie charts different? _____
2. What is a software suite? _____ What are the major advantages of using a software suite? _____
3. Why do professional designers use DTP software instead of word processing programs? _____ What is a color library? _____
4. What are disadvantages of installed software? _____ How can you access a Web application? _____
5. In most programs, how do you start the online Help feature? _____ How is a wizard different from a template? _____

Beyond the Book   Read the following book elements, learn more about each using the Web, and then write a brief report.

1. At Issue — How Should Schools Deal with Internet Plagiarism? (141), Altering Digital Photographs — Art or Fraud? (153), What Should Be Done to Prevent Music or Video File Sharing? (153), or Should Companies Monitor Employees' E-Mail and Web Browsing? (161), or Copying Software — A Computer Crime! (167)
2. Career Corner — Help Desk Specialist (167)
3. Companies on the Cutting Edge — Adobe Systems or Microsoft (169)
4. FAQs (137, 142, 145, 148, 152, 154, 157, 158, 162)

5. High-Tech Talk — Computer Viruses: Delivery, Infection, and Avoidance (168)
6. Looking Ahead — User Interfaces of the Future (137) or Driving Down the Web Highway (163)
7. Making Use of the Web — Finance (119)
8. Picture Yourself Using Software (132)
9. Technology Trailblazers — Dan Bricklin or Masayoshi Son (169)
10. Web Links (140, 144, 146, 148, 156, 158, 159, 160, 162, 166)

Quizzes and Learning Games

Computer Genius
Crossword Puzzle
DC Track and Field
Practice Test
Quiz Yourself
Wheel of Terms
You're Hired!

Exercises

Case Studies
Chapter Review
Checkpoint
Key Terms
Learn How To
Learn It Online
Web Research

Beyond the Book

Career Corner
Companies
FAQs
High-Tech Talk
Looking Ahead
Making Use of the Web
Trailblazers
Web Links

Features

Chapter Forum
Install Computer
Lab Exercises
Maintain Computer
Tech News
Timeline 2006

Learn It Online

Use the Learn It Online exercises to reinforce your understanding of the chapter concepts. To access the Learn It Online exercises, visit scsite.com/dc2006/ch3/learn.

(1) At the Movies — Detect Spyware on Your Computer

To view the Detect Spyware on Your Computer movie, click the number 1 button. Locate your video and click the corresponding High-Speed or Dial-Up link, depending on your Internet connection. Watch the movie and then complete the exercise by answering the question that follows. Many of the programs installed on your computer also installed spyware along with the program you loaded. Several different types of spyware exist, two of which are keystroke recorders and advertising spyware. Spyware either collects information and sends it over the Internet to whoever installed it or stores it for later retrieval. Why might you want to detect and delete a keystroke recorder from your computer?

(2) At the Movies — History of Adobe

To view the History of Adobe movie, click the number 2 button. Locate your video and click the corresponding High-Speed or Dial-Up link, depending on your Internet connection. Watch the movie and then complete the exercise by answering the question that follows. At the dawn of the computer age, computers were used mostly by scientists, and printers were large, cumbersome machines. The advent of desktop publishing gave average people access to the power of computing. Users finally were able to publish documents and images easily, and the computer became a tool for creative expression for everyone. Compare how you complete your homework assignments now to how homework was

done in the 1950s. How has desktop publishing changed the way students research and write reports?

(3) Student Edition Labs — Word Processing

Click the number 3 button. When the Student Edition Labs menu appears, click *Word Processing* to begin. A new browser window will open. Follow the on-screen instructions to complete the Lab. When finished, click the Exit button. If required, submit your results to your instructor.

(4) Student Edition Labs — Spreadsheets

Click the number 4 button. When the Student Edition Labs menu appears, click *Spreadsheets* to begin. A new browser window will open. Follow the on-screen instructions to complete the Lab. When finished, click the Exit button. If required, submit your results to your instructor.

(5) Student Edition Labs — Databases

Click the number 5 button. When the Student Edition Labs menu appears, click *Databases* to begin. A new browser window will open. Follow the on-screen instructions to complete the Lab. When finished, click the Exit button. If required, submit your results to your instructor.

(6) Student Edition Labs — Presentation Software

Click the number 6 button. When the Student Edition Labs menu appears, click *Presentation Software* to begin. A new browser window will open. Follow the on-screen instructions to complete the Lab. When finished, click the Exit button. If required, submit your results to your instructor.

(7) Practice Test

Click the number 7 button. Answer each question. When completed, enter your name and click the Grade Test button to submit the

Learn It Online

quiz for grading. Make a note of any missed questions. If required, submit your score to your instructor.

(8) Who Wants To Be a Computer Genius²?

Click the number 8 button to find out if you are a computer genius. Directions about how to play the game will be displayed. When you are ready to play, click the Play button. Submit your score to your instructor.

(9) Wheel of Terms

Click the number 9 button to reinforce important terms you learned in this chapter by playing the Shelly Cashman Series version of this popular game. Directions about how to play the game will be displayed. When you are ready to play, click the Play button. Submit your score to your instructor.

(10) DC Track and Field

Click the number 10 button to use what you have learned in this chapter to compete against other students in three track and field events. Directions about how to play the game will be displayed. When you are ready to play, click the start first event button. If required, submit your score to your instructor.

(11) You're Hired!

Click the number 11 button to use what you have learned in this chapter to embark on the path to a career in computers. Directions about how to play the game will be displayed. When you are ready to play, click the begin game button. If required, submit your score to your instructor.

(12) Crossword Puzzle Challenge

Click the number 12 button. Complete the puzzle to reinforce skills you learned in this chapter. Directions about how to play the game will be displayed. When you are ready to play, click the Play button. Submit the completed puzzle to your instructor.

(13) Lab Exercises

Click the number 13 button. When the Lab Exercises menu appears, click the exercise assigned by your instructor. A new browser window will open. Follow the on-screen instructions to complete the exercise. When finished, click the Exit button. If required, submit your results to your instructor.

(14) In the News

It is a computer user's worst fear — he or she opens an unfamiliar e-mail message or uses a disk of unknown origin and a computer virus is released that damages and/or deletes files. Fortunately, specialized software prevents such things from happening to your computer. Click the number 14 button and read a news article about antivirus programs. Which program does the article recommend? What does it do? Who will benefit from using this software? Why? Where can the software be obtained? Would you be interested in this software? Why or why not?

(15) Chapter Discussion Forum

Select an objective from this chapter on page 133 about which you would like more information. Click the number 15 button and post a short message listing a meaningful message title accompanied by one or more questions concerning the selected objective. In two days, return to the threaded discussion by clicking the number 15 button. Submit to your instructor your original message and at least one response to your message.

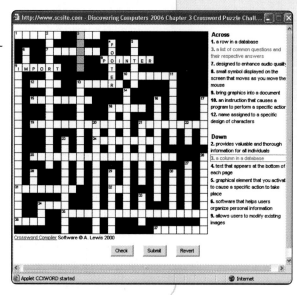

Quizzes and Learning Games

Computer Genius
Crossword Puzzle
DC Track and Field
Practice Test
Quiz Yourself
Wheel of Terms
You're Hired!

Exercises

Case Studies
Chapter Review
Checkpoint
Key Terms
Learn How To
Learn It Online
Web Research

Beyond the Book

Career Corner
Companies
FAQs
High-Tech Talk
Looking Ahead
Making Use of the Web
Trailblazers
Web Links

Features

Chapter Forum
Install Computer
Lab Exercises
Maintain Computer
Tech News
Timeline 2006

 ## Learn How To

Use the Learn How To activities to learn fundamental skills when using a computer and accompanying technology. Complete the exercises and submit them to your instructor. Visit scsite.com/dc2006/ch3/howto to obtain more information pertaining to each activity.

LEARN HOW TO 1: Save a File in Application Software

When you use application software, usually you either will create a new file or modify an existing file. If you turn off your computer or lose electrical power while working on the file, the file will not be retained. In order to retain the file, you must save it.

To save a new file, you must complete several tasks:
1. Initiate an action indicating you want to save the file, such as clicking the Save button.
2. Designate where the file should be stored. This includes identifying both the device (such as drive C) and the folder (such as My Documents).
3. Specify the name of the file.
4. Click the Save button to save the file.

Tasks 2 through 4 normally can be completed using a dialog box such as shown in Figure 3-44.

If you close a program prior to saving a new or modified file, the program will display a dialog box asking if you want to save the file. If you click the Yes button, a modified file will be saved using the same file name in the same location. Saving a new file requires that you complete tasks 2 through 4.

Exercise
1. Start the **WordPad program** from the Accessories submenu on the All Programs submenu.
2. Type Saving a file is the best insurance against losing work.
3. Click the Save button on the WordPad toolbar. What dialog box is displayed? Where will the file be saved? What is the default file name? If you wanted to save the file on the desktop, what would you do? Click the Cancel button in the dialog box. Submit your answers to your instructor.
4. Click the Close button in the WordPad window. What happened? Click the Yes button in the WordPad dialog box. What happened? Place either a floppy disk in drive A or a USB drive in a USB port. Select either the floppy disk or the USB drive as the location for saving the file. Name the file, Chapter 3 How To 1. Save the file. What happened? Submit your answers to your instructor.

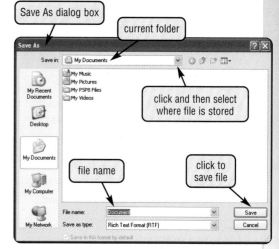

FIGURE 3-44

LEARN HOW TO 2: Install and Uninstall Application Software

When you purchase application software, you must install the software on the computer where you want to run it. The exact installation process varies with each program, but generally you must complete the following steps:
1. Insert the CD-ROM containing the application software into a drive.
2. The opening window will appear. If the CD-ROM contains more than one program, choose the program you want to install. Click the Continue or Next button.
3. Some file extractions will occur and then an Install Wizard will begin. You normally must accomplish the following steps by completing the directions within the wizard:
   a. Accept the terms of the license agreement.
   b. Identify where on your computer the software will be stored. The software usually selects a default location on drive C, and you normally will accept the default location.

Learn How To

c. Select any default options for the software.

d. Click a button to install the software.

4. A Welcome/Help screen often will be displayed. Click a button to finish the installation process.

At some point, you may want to remove software. Most software includes uninstall programming that will remove the program and all its software components. To uninstall a program, complete the following steps:

1. Click the Start button on the Windows taskbar.
2. Click Control Panel on the Start menu.
3. Click or double-click **Add or Remove Programs**. *The Add or Remove Programs window will open (Figure 3-45).*
4. Select the program you wish to remove. *In Figure 3-45, Macromedia Dreamweaver is selected as the program to remove.*
5. Click the Change/Remove button.
6. A dialog box will be displayed informing you that the software is being prepared for uninstall. You then will be informed that the process you are following will remove the program. You will be asked if you want to continue. To uninstall the program, click the Yes button.

The program will be removed from the computer.

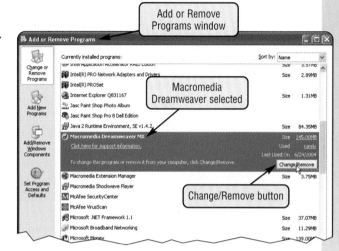

FIGURE 3-45

Exercise

1. Optional: Insert the CD-ROM containing the software you want to install into a drive and follow the instructions for installing the software. **Warning: If you are using a computer other than your own, particularly in a school laboratory, do not perform this exercise unless you have specific permission from your instructor.**
2. Optional: Follow the steps above to uninstall software you want to remove. Be aware that if you uninstall software, the software will not be available for use until you reinstall it. **Warning: If you are using a computer other than your own, particularly in a school laboratory, do not perform this exercise unless you have specific permission from your instructor.**

LEARN HOW TO 3: **Check Application Software Version**

Most application software will be modified from time to time by its developer. Each time the software is changed, it acquires a **new version number** and sometimes an entirely new name. To determine what version of software you have, perform the following steps:

1. Start the application program.
2. Click Help on the menu bar and then click About on the Help menu (the program name often follows the word, About). *The program displays the About window (Figure 3-46).*
3. To close the About window, click the OK button.

Depending on the software, in the About window you also might be able to determine further information.

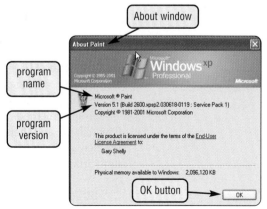

FIGURE 3-46

Exercise

1. Start your Web browser and display the About window for the browser. What is the name of the browser? What version of the browser are you using? What is the product ID? What does the copyright notice say? Submit your answers to your instructor.
2. Start any other application software. Display the About window. What is the name of the program? What is the version number? What information do you find that you did not see in Exercise 1? Which window do you find more useful? Why? Submit your answers to your instructor.

Quizzes and Learning Games

Computer Genius
Crossword Puzzle
DC Track and Field
Practice Test
Quiz Yourself
Wheel of Terms
You're Hired!

Exercises

Case Studies
Chapter Review
Checkpoint
Key Terms
Learn How To
Learn It Online
Web Research

Beyond the Book

Career Corner
Companies
FAQs
High-Tech Talk
Looking Ahead
Making Use of the Web
Trailblazers
Web Links

Features

Chapter Forum
Install Computer
Lab Exercises
Maintain Computer
Tech News
Timeline 2006

Web Research

Use the Internet-based Web Research exercises to broaden your understanding of the concepts presented in this chapter. Visit scsite.com/dc2006/ch3/research to obtain more information pertaining to each exercise. To discuss any of the Web Research exercises in this chapter with other students, post your thoughts or questions at scsite.com/dc2006/ch3/forum.

(1) Scavenger Hunt   Use one of the search engines listed in Figure 2-10 in Chapter 2 on page 78 or your own favorite search engine to find the answers to the questions below. Copy and paste the Web address from the Web page where you found the answer. Some questions may have more than one answer. If required, submit your answers to your instructor. (1) What is the name of the curves Adobe Systems used to define shapes in its PostScript programming language? (2) Microsoft developed what popular entertainment software in 1983 in cooperation with Bruce Artwick of SubLogic? (3) What application software company did Microsoft acquire in 1987 that developed and marketed PowerPoint? (4) What is the name of the first successful spreadsheet program?

(2) Search Sleuth   A virus is a potentially damaging computer program that can harm files and the operating system. The National Institute of Standards and Technology Computer Security Resource Center (csrc.nist.gov/virus/) is one of the more comprehensive Web sites discussing viruses. Visit this Web site and then use your word processing program to answer the following questions. Then, if required, submit your answers to your instructor. (1) The Virus Information page provides general information about viruses and links to various resources that provide more specific details. What two steps does the National Institute recommend to detect and prevent viruses from spreading? (2) Click the Symantec link in the Virus Resources & Other Areas of Interest section. What viruses are the latest threats, and when were they discovered? (3) Click Search at the top of the page and then type "Sasser worm" as the keyword in the Search text box. How many articles discuss the Sasser worm on the Symantec Web site? What three functions does the Sasser Removal Tool perform? (4) Click one of the Latest News links and review the material. Review the information you read and then write a 50-word summary.

(3) Journaling   Respond to your readings in this chapter by writing at least one page about your reactions, evaluations, and reflections about the first time you used word processing software. For example, what word processing software did you use? What was the first document you created? Have your instructors required you to use word processing software for class projects? How did you edit and format your document? Did you back up your file? You also can write about the new terms you learned by reading this chapter. If required, submit your journal to your instructor.

(4) Expanding Your Understanding   Microsoft seeks to help customers use its products by maintaining the Microsoft Help and Support Web site (support.microsoft.com). This Web site has a link to the Knowledge Base, which contains more than 250,000 articles written by Microsoft employees who support the company's products. Also included are software downloads and updates, public newsgroups, methods of getting online or telephone assistance, and the Security Support Center. View this site and then search the Knowledge Base for information on Microsoft Word. Also view the common issues, updates, security issues, and visitors' top links listed on the Web site. Write a report summarizing your findings. If required, submit your report to your instructor.

(5) Ethics in Action   A hacker is someone who tries to access a computer or network illegally. Although the activity sometimes is a harmless prank, it sometimes causes extensive damage. Some hackers say their activities give them a sense of excitement and test their skills. Others say their activities are a form of civil disobedience that allows them to challenge authority and force companies to make their products more secure. View online sites such as Hackers: Outlaws & Angels (tlc.discovery.com/convergence/hackers/hackers.html) that provide information about whether hackers provide some benefit to the Internet society. Write a report summarizing your findings and include a table of links to Web sites that provide additional details. If required, submit your report to your instructor.

Case Studies

Use the Case Studies to apply the concepts presented in the chapter to real-world situations. Visit scsite.com/dc2006/ch3/cases to obtain more information pertaining to each exercise. To discuss the Case Studies in this chapter with other students, visit scsite.com/dc2006/ch3/forum and post your thoughts or questions.

CASE STUDY 1 – Class Discussion   The owner of Mel's Hair Salon for Men and Women has decided to obtain a personal desktop computer for use in his business. In addition to using the computer for writing letters, developing advertising pieces, performing basic accounting, and maintaining lists of customers, the owner would like his employees to use a **digital camera** to take pictures of customers after they have had their hair done and create a file of printed full-color pictures of customers for marketing purposes. The owner has asked you to recommend the type of camera, software, and computer he should buy. Prepare a brief report detailing your findings and recommendations. Be prepared to discuss your recommendations in class.

CASE STUDY 2 – Class Discussion   Your manager at Jane's Discount Furniture Warehouse intends to choose a word processing program that the entire company will use. She prefers to learn about software using trade books — written texts that explain the features of a program and how to use it — rather than using online Help or tutorials. She has asked you to evaluate the **word processing** trade books available in bookstores on the Web. Visit a bookstore Web site and other Web sites that sell books to survey the word processing trade books available for Microsoft Word, StarOffice Writer, DisplayWrite, and WordPerfect. Which word processing program has the most books available? How difficult would it be to learn each program using the trade books at hand? Which trade book do you think is the best? Why? If you were going to purchase software solely on the basis of the related trade books, which program would you buy? Why? Be prepared to discuss your recommendations in class.

CASE STUDY 3 – Research   After attending a seminar on Web applications, the chief financial officer of Eastern Steel, Inc. has asked you to investigate the feasibility of using the Web to collect data from company offices and customers throughout the world. Recall that a **Web application** is application software that exists on a Web site. Users access the Web application through their browser. Use the Web and/or print media to create a brief report describing at least two Web applications and how Eastern Steel could use similar applications effectively. Include in your report a description of each application, a short overview of any online Help, and the Web address for each application. Write a brief report and share your findings with your class.

CASE STUDY 4 – Research   Frank's Custom Design frequently enhances its work with scanned photographs or graphics obtained with **illustration software**. The owner recently read that the Internet is providing a new resource for desktop publishers. Companies such as Corbis, Picture Network International, Muse, and Liaison International are offering archives of artwork and photographs. You have been asked to investigate the feasibility of using this new resource. Information about all four companies can be found on the World Wide Web. Pick two companies that provide digital images and find out more about their product. Prepare a brief report that answers the following questions. What kinds of illustrations are available? How are pictures on a specific subject located? How are the illustrations provided? What fees are involved? Would the cost be different for a high school student creating one paper than for an organization newsletter with a state-wide distribution? Which company do you prefer? Why?

CASE STUDY 5 – Team Challenge   The new superintendent of Lisle Elementary School District 205 has recommended that **educational software** play a major role in the learning process at every grade level. In her presentation to the school board, she claimed that educational software is available for a wide variety of skills and subjects. She also indicated that educational software lets students learn at their own pace, shows infinite patience, and usually offers an entertaining approach. The president of the school board is not so sure. Unlike human instructors, educational software often does not recognize unique problems, fails to address individual goals, and provides limited feedback. Form a three-member team and investigate the use of educational software. Have each member of your team visit a software vendor's Web site, or an educational cooperative's Web site and list the advantages and disadvantages of using educational software. Select a program on the Web or from your school's education department library and use it. Note the subject being taught, the audience to which the software is directed, the approach used, and any special features. Then, meet with your team, discuss your findings, prepare a team report or PowerPoint presentation, and share it with your class.

CHAPTER FOUR

The Components of the System Unit

Picture Yourself Buying a Computer

Your neighbor, who is a computer guru and always has the latest computers and devices, just called to see if you want to buy one of his *old* computers. What he considers old actually still is state of the art. He says it would include the system unit, monitor, speakers, keyboard, and mouse.

He starts rattling off all the features while you frantically make quick notes. The system unit has a 3.0 GHz Pentium 4 processor with HT Technology and 256 KB L2 cache. It has 512 MB of dual channel SDRAM expandable to 2 GB, a 533 MHz bus, and integrated modem and networking capabilities. The back of the system unit has ports for a keyboard, a mouse, a monitor, speakers, a network, and a modem. It also has a serial port, a parallel port, six USB ports (two in front and four in back), and a FireWire port. It is not Bluetooth-enabled, but you can buy a wireless port adapter if you need that capability. He says he will set up the computer for you, clean it for you once a year, and be available for personal support anytime. "Five hundred bucks," he says, "and it's yours." Sold!

After hanging up the telephone, you glance at all your notes. You know he gave you a great deal, but you have no idea what all these terms and numbers mean. To find out, you plan to read Chapter 4 to learn about processor chips, RAM, cache, adapter cards, and ports, and discover the many other components of the system unit.

OBJECTIVES

After completing this chapter, you will be able to:

1. Differentiate among various styles of system units

2. Identify chips, adapter cards, and other components of a motherboard

3. Describe the components of a processor and how they complete a machine cycle

4. Identify characteristics of various personal computer processors on the market today

5. Define a bit and describe how a series of bits represents data

6. Explain how programs transfer in and out of memory

7. Differentiate among the various types of memory

8. Describe the types of expansion slots and adapter cards

9. Explain the differences among a serial port, a parallel port, a USB port, a FireWire port, and other ports

10. Describe how buses contribute to a computer's processing speed

11. Identify components in mobile computers and mobile devices

12. Understand how to clean a system unit

CONTENTS

THE SYSTEM UNIT
The Motherboard

PROCESSOR
The Control Unit
The Arithmetic Logic Unit
Machine Cycle
Registers
The System Clock
Comparison of Personal
  Computer Processors
Buying a Personal Computer
Heat Sinks, Heat Pipes, and
  Liquid Cooling
Parallel Processing

DATA REPRESENTATION

MEMORY
Bytes and Addressable Memory
Memory Sizes
Types of Memory
RAM
Cache
ROM
Flash Memory
CMOS
Memory Access Times

**EXPANSION SLOTS
AND ADAPTER CARDS**
PC Cards, Flash Memory Cards,
  and USB Flash Drives

PORTS AND CONNECTORS
Serial Ports
Parallel Ports
USB Ports
FireWire Ports
Special-Purpose Ports

BUSES
Expansion Bus

BAYS

POWER SUPPLY

**MOBILE COMPUTERS
AND DEVICES**

PUTTING IT ALL TOGETHER

**KEEPING YOUR COMPUTER
CLEAN**

CHAPTER SUMMARY

HIGH-TECH TALK
Random Access Memory (RAM):
  The Genius of Memory

**COMPANIES ON THE
CUTTING EDGE**
AMD
Intel

TECHNOLOGY TRAILBLAZERS
Jack Kilby
Gordon Moore

THE SYSTEM UNIT

Whether you are a home user or a business user, you most likely will make the decision to purchase a new computer or upgrade an existing computer within the next several years. Thus, you should understand the purpose of each component in a computer. As Chapter 1 discussed, a computer includes devices used for input, processing, output, storage, and communications. Many of these components are part of the system unit.

The **system unit** is a case that contains electronic components of the computer used to process data. System units are available in a variety of shapes and sizes. The case of the system unit, sometimes called the *chassis*, is made of metal or plastic and protects the internal electronic components from damage. All computers have a system unit (Figure 4-1).

On desktop personal computers, the electronic components and most storage devices are part of the system unit. Other devices, such as the keyboard, mouse, microphone, monitor, printer, scanner, PC video camera, and speakers, normally occupy space outside the system unit. The trend is toward a smaller form factor, or size and shape, of the desktop personal computer system unit.

FIGURE 4-1   All sizes of computers have a system unit.

On notebook computers, the keyboard and pointing device often occupy the area on the top of the system unit, and the display attaches to the system unit by hinges. The location of the system unit on a Tablet PC varies, depending on the design of the Tablet PC. Some models position the system unit below the keyboard, while others build the system unit behind the display. The system unit on a PDA and smart phone usually consumes the entire device. On these mobile devices, the display often is built into the system unit.

At some point, you might have to open the system unit on a desktop personal computer to replace or install a new electronic component. For this reason, you should be familiar with the electronic components of a system unit. Figure 4-2 identifies some of these components, which include the processor, memory, adapter cards, ports, drive bays, and the power supply.

The processor interprets and carries out the basic instructions that operate a computer. Memory typically holds data waiting to be processed and instructions waiting to be executed. The electronic components and circuitry of the system unit, such as the processor and memory, usually are part of or are connected to a circuit board called the motherboard. Many current motherboards also integrate modem and networking capabilities.

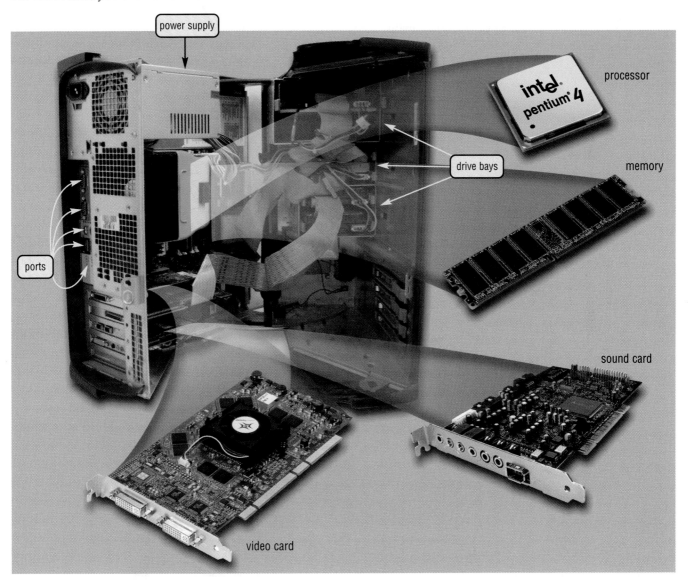

FIGURE 4-2 The system unit on a typical personal computer consists of numerous electronic components, some of which are shown in this figure. The sound card and video card are two types of adapter cards.

Adapter cards are circuit boards that provide connections and functions not built into the motherboard. Two adapter cards found in some desktop personal computers today are a sound card and a video card. Devices outside the system unit often attach to ports on the system unit by a connector on a cable. These devices may include a keyboard, mouse, microphone, monitor, printer, scanner, card reader/writer, digital camera, PC video camera, and speakers. A drive bay holds one or more disk drives. The power supply converts electricity from a power cord plugged in a wall outlet into a form that can be used by the computer.

The Motherboard

The **motherboard**, sometimes called a *system board*, is the main circuit board of the system unit. Many electronic components attach to the motherboard; others are built into it. Figure 4-3 shows a photograph of a current desktop personal computer motherboard and identifies components that attach to it, including adapter cards, a processor chip, and a memory module. Memory chips are installed on memory cards (modules) that fit in a slot on the motherboard.

A computer **chip** is a small piece of semi-conducting material, usually silicon, on which integrated circuits are etched. An *integrated circuit* contains many microscopic pathways capable of carrying electrical current. Each integrated circuit can contain millions of elements such as resistors, capacitors, and transistors. A *transistor*, for example, can act as an electronic switch that opens or closes the circuit for electrical charges. Most chips are no bigger than one-half-inch square. Manufacturers package chips so the chips can be attached to a circuit board, such as a motherboard or an adapter card.

WEB LINK 4-1

Motherboards
For more information, visit scsite.com/ dc2006/ch4/weblink and then click Motherboards.

adapter cards

processor chip in a processor slot

memory module

expansion slots for adapter cards

motherboard

FIGURE 4-3   Many electronic components attach to the motherboard in a desktop personal computer, including a processor chip, memory module, and adapter cards.

PROCESSOR

The **processor**, also called the **central processing unit** (CPU), interprets and carries out the basic instructions that operate a computer. The processor significantly impacts overall computing power and manages most of a computer's operations. On larger computers, such as mainframes and supercomputers, the various functions performed by the processor extend over many separate chips and often multiple circuit boards. On a personal computer, all functions of the processor usually are on a single chip. Some computer and chip manufacturers use the term *microprocessor* to refer to a personal computer processor chip.

Processors contain a control unit and an arithmetic logic unit (ALU). These two components work together to perform processing operations. Figure 4-4 illustrates how other devices connected to the computer communicate with the processor to carry out a task.

The Control Unit

The **control unit** is the component of the processor that directs and coordinates most of the operations in the computer. The control unit has a role much like a traffic cop: it interprets each instruction issued by a program and then initiates the appropriate action to carry out the instruction. Read At Issue 4-1 for a related discussion.

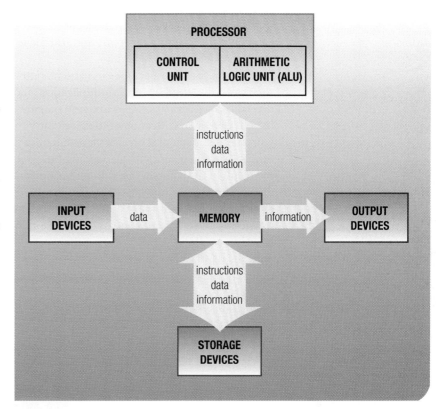

FIGURE 4-4 Most devices connected to the computer communicate with the processor to carry out a task. When a user starts a program, for example, its instructions transfer from a storage device to memory. Data needed by programs enters memory from either an input device or a storage device. The control unit interprets and executes instructions in memory, and the ALU performs calculations on the data in memory. Resulting information is stored in memory, from which it can be sent to an output device or a storage device for future access, as needed.

AT ISSUE 4-1

Can Computers Think?

Ever since a computer defeated world chess champion Gary Kasparov in a chess match, people have wondered, can computers think? As computer processors become more powerful, the question is more hotly debated. People who believe computers can think argue that, if a question was submitted to a person and a computer, it would be impossible to tell the person's response from the computer's response. Therefore, computers can think. Opponents counter this argument by saying that, if a question written in a foreign language was submitted to a person who can read and write the language and a person who cannot read or write the language but has a list of questions and appropriate answers, it might be impossible to tell the response of one person from the other. But, the person who cannot read or write the language really does not understand it, any more than a computer really can think. Besides, computers lack an essential component of human thinking — common sense. Computers can consider millions of chess moves a second, but humans have the common sense to recognize that some moves are not worthy of consideration. Can computers think? Why or why not? If computers cannot think now, might they be able to think in the future? Why?

The Arithmetic Logic Unit

The **arithmetic logic unit** (*ALU*), another component of the processor, performs arithmetic, comparison, and other operations.

Arithmetic operations include basic calculations such as addition, subtraction, multiplication, and division. *Comparison operations* involve comparing one data item with another to determine whether the first item is greater than, equal to, or less than the other item. Depending on the result of the comparison, different actions may occur. For example, to determine if an employee should receive overtime pay, software instructs the ALU to compare the number of hours an employee worked during the week with the regular time hours allowed (e.g., 40 hours). If the hours worked are greater than 40, software instructs the ALU to perform calculations that compute the overtime wage.

Machine Cycle

For every instruction, a processor repeats a set of four basic operations, which comprise a *machine cycle* (Figure 4-5): (1) fetching, (2) decoding, (3) executing, and, if necessary, (4) storing. *Fetching* is the process of obtaining a program instruction or data item from memory. The term *decoding* refers to the process of translating the instruction into signals the computer can execute. *Executing* is the process of carrying out the commands. *Storing*, in this context, means writing the result to memory (not to a storage medium).

In some computers, the processor fetches, decodes, executes, and stores only one instruction at a time. In these computers, the processor waits until an instruction completes all four stages of the machine cycle (fetch, decode, execute, and store) before beginning work on the next instruction.

FIGURE 4-5 THE STEPS IN A MACHINE CYCLE

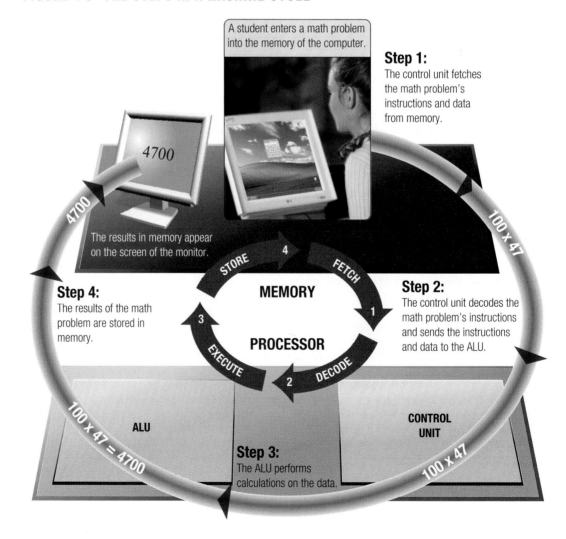

A student enters a math problem into the memory of the computer.

Step 1:
The control unit fetches the math problem's instructions and data from memory.

The results in memory appear on the screen of the monitor.

4700

STORE · 4 · FETCH

MEMORY

PROCESSOR

3 · EXECUTE · DECODE · 2 · 1

Step 4:
The results of the math problem are stored in memory.

Step 2:
The control unit decodes the math problem's instructions and sends the instructions and data to the ALU.

ALU

100 x 47 = 4700

100 x 47

CONTROL UNIT

Step 3:
The ALU performs calculations on the data.

Most of today's personal computers support a concept called pipelining. With *pipelining*, the processor begins fetching a second instruction before it completes the machine cycle for the first instruction. Processors that use pipelining are faster because they do not have to wait for one instruction to complete the machine cycle before fetching the next. Think of a pipeline as an assembly line. By the time the first instruction is in the last stage of the machine cycle, three other instructions could have been fetched and started through the machine cycle (Figure 4-6).

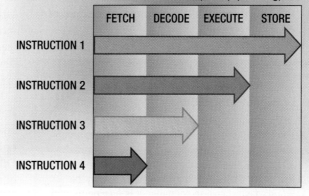

MACHINE CYCLE (without pipelining):

| FETCH | DECODE | EXECUTE | STORE | FETCH | DECODE | EXECUTE | STORE |

INSTRUCTION 1   INSTRUCTION 2

MACHINE CYCLE (with pipelining):

| FETCH | DECODE | EXECUTE | STORE |

INSTRUCTION 1
INSTRUCTION 2
INSTRUCTION 3
INSTRUCTION 4

FIGURE 4-6   Most modern personal computers support pipelining. With pipelining, the processor fetches a second instruction before the first instruction is completed. The result is faster processing.

Registers

A processor contains small, high-speed storage locations, called *registers*, that temporarily hold data and instructions. Registers are part of the processor, not part of memory or a permanent storage device. Processors have many different types of registers, each with a specific storage function. Register functions include storing the location from where an instruction was fetched, storing an instruction while the control unit decodes it, storing data while the ALU computes it, and storing the results of a calculation.

The System Clock

The processor relies on a small quartz crystal circuit called the **system clock** to control the timing of all computer operations. Just as your heart beats at a regular rate to keep your body functioning, the system clock generates regular electronic pulses, or ticks, that set the operating pace of components of the system unit.

Each tick equates to a *clock cycle*. In the past, processors used one or more clock cycles to execute each instruction. Processors today often are *superscalar*, which means they can execute more than one instruction per clock cycle.

The pace of the system clock, called the **clock speed**, is measured by the number of ticks per second. Current personal computer processors have clock speeds in the gigahertz range. Giga is a prefix that stands for billion, and a *hertz* is one cycle per second. Thus, one **gigahertz (GHz)** equals one billion ticks of the system clock per second. A computer that operates at 3.2 GHz has 3.2 billion (giga) clock cycles in one second (hertz).

The system clock is one of the factors that influence a computer's speed. The faster the clock speed, the more instructions the processor can execute per second. The speed of the system clock has no effect on devices such as a printer or disk drive.

FAQ 4-1

Does the system clock also keep track of the current date and time?

No, a separate battery-backed chip, called the *real-time clock*, keeps track of the date and time in a computer. The battery continues to run the real-time clock even when the computer is off. For more information, visit scsite.com/dc2006/ch4/faq and then click Computer Clock.

WEB LINK 4-2

Clock Speed

For more information, visit scsite.com/dc2006/ch4/weblink and then click Clock Speed.

Some computer professionals measure a processor's speed according to the number of *MIPS (millions of instructions per second)* it can process. Current desktop personal computers can process more than 7,000 MIPS. No real standard for measuring MIPS exists, however, because different instructions require varying amounts of processing time. Read Looking Ahead 4-1 for a look at the next generation of processing speeds.

LOOKING AHEAD 4-1

U.S. Plans World's Fastest Computer

Nine of the world's ten fastest computers are located in the United States. The fastest computer is located in Japan, according to the Top500 Project, a group that monitors supercomputers throughout the world.

The U.S. Department of Energy is planning to have the United States regain the record as having the world's fastest civilian computer. It is helping to fund a new supercomputer at a research laboratory in Oak Ridge, Tennessee, with $50 million in federal grants and assistance from Cray Corp., IBM Corp., and Silicon Graphics Inc.

Oak Ridge scientists predict the new computer will be able to perform 50 trillion calculations per second or about 500 trillion (500,000,000,000,000) calculations in the time it takes to blink your eye. The Japanese computer sustains 36 trillion calculations per second. For more information, visit scsite.com/dc2006/ch4/looking and then click Fastest Computer.

Comparison of Personal Computer Processors

The leading processor chip manufacturers for personal computers are Intel, AMD (Advanced Micro Devices), IBM, Motorola, and Transmeta. These manufacturers often identify their processor chips by a model name or model number. Figure 4-7 categorizes the historical development of the personal computer processor and documents the increases in clock speed and number of transistors in chips since 1982. The greater the number of transistors, the more complex and powerful the chip.

With its earlier processors, Intel used a model number to identify the various chips. After learning that processor model numbers could not be trademarked and protected from use by competitors, Intel began identifying its processors with names — thus emerged the series of processors known as the Pentium. Most high-performance PCs use some type of **Pentium** processor. Notebook computers and Tablet PCs use a **Pentium M**

processor. Less expensive, basic PCs use a brand of Intel processor called the **Celeron**. Two more brands, called the **Xeon** and **Itanium** processors, are ideal for workstations and low-end servers.

AMD is the leading manufacturer of *Intel-compatible processors*, which have an internal design similar to Intel processors, perform the same functions, and can be as powerful, but often are less expensive. Transmeta, also a manufacturer of Intel-compatible processors, specializes in processors for mobile computers and devices. Intel and Intel-compatible processors are used in PCs.

In the past, chip manufacturers listed a processor's clock speed in marketing literature and advertisements. Today, however, clock speed is only one factor that impacts processing speed. Other factors include cache and bus speed, each of which is discussed later in this chapter. To help consumers evaluate various processors, manufacturers such as Intel and AMD now use a numbering scheme that more accurately reflects the processing speed of their chips.

Apple computers use an *IBM processor* or a *Motorola processor*, which has a design different from the Intel-style processor. The PowerPC processor has a new architecture that increased the speed of the latest Apple computers.

Processor chips include technologies to improve processing performance. Intel's latest processor chips contain *Hyper-Threading (HT) Technology*, which improves processing power and time by allowing the processor chip to mimic the power of two processors. For even higher levels of performance with lower levels of power consumption, several processor chip manufacturers now offer a *dual-core processor*, which is a chip that has two separate processors. Most processors have built-in instructions to improve the performance of multimedia and 3-D graphics. Processors for notebook computers include technology to integrate wireless capabilities and optimize and extend battery life.

A new type of processor, called *system on a chip*, integrates the functions of a processor, memory, and a video card on a single chip. Lower-priced personal computers, Tablet PCs, networking devices, and consumer electronics such as music players and game consoles sometimes have a system-on-a-chip processor. The goal of system-on-a-chip manufacturers is to create processors that have faster clock speeds, consume less power, are small, and are cost effective.

COMPARISON OF WIDELY USED PERSONAL COMPUTER PROCESSORS

	NAME	DATE INTRODUCED/ UPDATED	MANUFACTURER	CLOCK SPEED	NUMBER OF TRANSISTORS
SERVER PROCESSORS	Xeon MP	2002/2004	Intel	1.4–3 GHz	108–169 million
	Itanium 2	2003/2004	Intel	1.3–1.6 GHz	220–410 million
	Xeon	2001/2003	Intel	1.4–3.6 GHz	42–108 million
	Itanium	2001	Intel	733–800 MHz	25.4–60 million
	Pentium III Xeon	1999/2000	Intel	500–900 MHz	9.5–28 million
	Pentium II Xeon	1998/1999	Intel	400–450 MHz	7.5–27 million
	Opteron	2003	AMD	1.4–2.4 GHz	100 million
	Athlon MP	2002	AMD	1.53–2.25 GHz	54.3 million
DESKTOP PERSONAL COMPUTER PROCESSORS	Pentium 4 with HT Technology	2002/2004	Intel	2.4–3.6 GHz	55–178 million
	Pentium 4	2000/2004	Intel	1.3–3.2 GHz	42–55 million
	Pentium III	1999/2003	Intel	450 MHz–1.4 GHz	9.5–44 million
	Celeron D	2004	Intel	2.4–2.8 GHz	26.2 million
	Celeron	1998/2003	Intel	266 MHz–3.06 GHz	7.5–44 million
	Pentium II	1997/1998	Intel	233–450 MHz	7.5 million
	Pentium with MMX technology	1997	Intel	166–233 MHz	4.5 million
	Pentium Pro	1995/1999	Intel	150–200 MHz	5.5 million
	Pentium	1993/1997	Intel	75–200 MHz	3.3 million
	80486DX	1989/1994	Intel	25–100 MHz	1.6 million
	80386	1985/1990	Intel	16–33 MHz	275,000
	80286	1982	Intel	6–12 MHz	134,000
	Sempron	2004	AMD	1.5–2 GHz	68.5 million
	Athlon 64	2003	AMD	2–2.4 GHz	105.9 million
	Athlon	1999/2002	AMD	500 MHz–1.4 GHz	22–38 million
	Duron	1999/2001	AMD	600 MHz–1.3 GHz	25 million
	AMD–K6 III	1999	AMD	400–450 MHz	21.3 million
	AMD–K6-2	1998	AMD	366–550 MHz	9.3 million
	AMD–K6	1997	AMD	300 MHz	8.8 million
	PowerPC G5	2003/2004	Motorola/IBM	1.4–2.0 GHz	58 million
	PowerPC G4	1999/2004	Motorola/IBM	350 MHz–1.5 GHz	33 million
	PowerPC G3	1997	Motorola/IBM	233 MHz–1.1 GHz	6.35–29 million
	PowerPC G2	1995	Motorola/IBM	75–350 MHz	1.6–5.1 million
	PowerPC G1	1994	Motorola/IBM	60–110 MHz	2.8 million
	68040	1989	Motorola	25–40 MHz	1.2 million
	68030	1987	Motorola	16–50 MHz	270,000
	68020	1984	Motorola	16–33 MHz	190,000
MOBILE PROCESSORS	Celeron M	2004	Intel	900 MHz–1.5 GHz	55 million
	Pentium M	2003/2004	Intel	1–2 GHz	77–140 million
	Mobile Celeron	1999/2003	Intel	266 MHz–2.8 GHz	18.9 million
	Mobile Pentium	1997/2002	Intel	200 MHz–3.2 GHz	55 million
	Mobile Sempron	2004	AMD	1.6–1.8 GHz	37.5 million
	Mobile Athlon	2001/2002	AMD	1.4–2.2 GHz	37.5–105.9 million
	Mobile Duron	2000/2001	AMD	1.3 GHz	25 million
	Efficeon	2003	Transmeta	1–1.2 GHz	79 million
	Crusoe	2000	Transmeta	500 MHz–1 GHz	6.7 million

FIGURE 4-7 A comparison of some of the more widely used processors.

Buying a Personal Computer

If you are ready to buy a new computer, the processor you select should depend on how you plan to use the computer. If you purchase an IBM-compatible PC, you will choose an Intel processor or an Intel-compatible processor (Figure 4-8). Apple Macintosh and Power Macintosh computers have a Motorola or IBM processor. Current Apple processors include the PowerPC G4 and PowerPC G5.

Your intended use also will determine the clock speed you need. A home user surfing the Web, for example, may need only a 2 GHz processor, while an artist working with graphics or applications requiring multimedia capabilities such as full-motion video may require at least a 3 GHz processor. The higher the clock speed, the faster the processor, and the more expensive the computer.

Instead of buying an entirely new computer, you might be able to upgrade your processor to increase the computer's performance. Be certain the processor you buy is compatible with your computer's motherboard; otherwise, you will have to replace the motherboard, too. Replacing a processor is a fairly simple process, whereas replacing a motherboard is much more complicated.

For detailed computer purchasing guidelines, read the Buyer's Guide 2006 feature that follows Chapter 8. Read At Issue 4-2 for a related discussion.

GUIDELINES FOR SELECTING AN INTEL OR INTEL-COMPATIBLE PROCESSOR

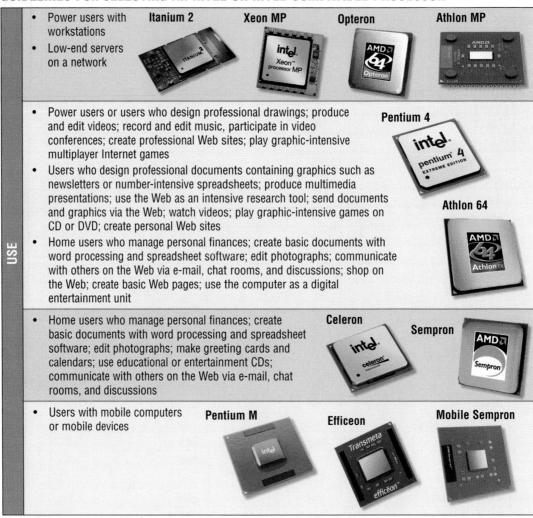

FIGURE 4-8   Determining which processor to obtain when you purchase a computer depends on computer usage.

FAQ 4-2

What is Moore's Law?

Moore's Law is a prediction made by one of the founders of Intel, Gordon Moore, that the number of transistors and resistors placed on computer chips would double every year, with a proportional increase in computing power and decrease in cost. The chart below shows the growth of Intel processors. For more information, read the Technology Trailblazer article on page 219 and visit scsite.com/dc2006/ch4/faq and then click Moore's Law.

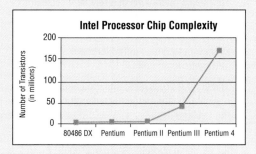

Intel Processor Chip Complexity

AT ISSUE 4-2

Computer Waste and the Environment: Whose Problem Is It?

Experts estimate that about 1 billion computers will be discarded by 2010. As technology advances and prices fall, many people think of computers as disposable items. But, disposing of old system units, monitors, and other computer components is a major problem. Computers contain several toxic elements, including lead, mercury, and barium. Computers thrown into landfills or burned in incinerators can pollute the ground and the air. One solution is to recycle old computers. Computers for Schools refurbishes donated computers and makes them available to schools and students at very low prices, and donors earn tax breaks. Some lawmakers prefer a more aggressive approach, such as setting up a recycling program that would be paid for by adding a $10 fee to a computer's purchase price, or forcing computer makers to be responsible for collecting and recycling their products. Manufacturers already have taken steps. Several have reduced the amount of toxic material in their products, and some have set up their own recycling programs, for which users pay a fee. One manufacturer admits, however, that only seven percent of the computers it has sold have been recycled. What can be done to ensure that computers are disposed of safely? Should government, manufacturers, or users be responsible for safe disposal? Why? How can computer users be motivated to recycle obsolete equipment?

Heat Sinks, Heat Pipes, and Liquid Cooling

Processor chips generate quite a bit of heat, which could cause the chip to burn up. Although the computer's main fan generates airflow, today's processors require additional cooling. A *heat sink* is a small ceramic or metal component with fins on its surface that absorbs and disperses heat produced by electrical components such as a processor (Figure 4-9). Some heat sinks are packaged as part of a processor chip. Others are installed on the top or the side of the chip. Because a heat sink consumes extra space, a smaller device called a *heat pipe* cools processors in notebook computers.

Some computers use liquid cooling technology to reduce the temperature of a processor. *Liquid cooling technology* uses a continuous flow of fluid(s), such as water and glycol, in a process that transfers the heated fluid away from the processor to a radiator-type grill, which cools the liquid, and then returns the cooled fluid to the processor.

FIGURE 4-9   A heat sink, which is attached to the top of a processor, prevents the chip from overheating. The heat sink fan, which attaches to the top of the heat sink, helps distribute air dissipated by the heat sink.

Parallel Processing

Some computers use more than one processor to speed processing times. Known as *parallel processing*, this method uses multiple processors simultaneously to execute a program (Figure 4-10). Parallel processing divides a problem into portions so that multiple processors work on their assigned portion of the problem at the same time. Parallel processing requires special software that recognizes how to divide the problem and then bring the results back together again.

Some personal computers implement parallel processing with dual-core processors or multi-core processors (more than two processors on a single chip). Others have two or more separate processor chips, respectively called dual processor or multiprocessor computers.

Supercomputers use parallel processing for applications such as weather forecasting. Some applications draw on the idle time of home users' personal computers to achieve parallel processing.

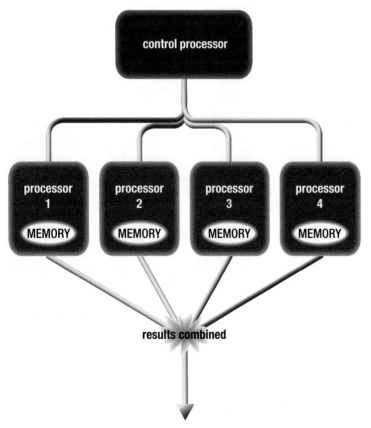

FIGURE 4-10 Parallel processing divides a problem into portions so that multiple processors work on their assigned portion of a problem at the same time. In this illustration, one processor, called the control processor, is managing the operations of four other processors.

Test your knowledge of pages 184 through 194 in Quiz Yourself 4-1.

QUIZ YOURSELF 4-1

Instructions: Find the true statement below. Then, rewrite the remaining false statements so they are true.

1. A computer chip is a small piece of semiconducting material, usually silicon, on which integrated circuits are etched.

2. Four basic operations in a machine cycle are: (1) comparing, (2) decoding, (3) executing, and, if necessary, (4) pipelining.

3. Processors contain a motherboard and an arithmetic logic unit (ALU).

4. The central processing unit, sometimes called a system board, is the main circuit board of the system unit.

5. The leading processor chip manufacturers for personal computers are Microsoft, AMD, IBM, Motorola, and Transmeta.

6. The pace of the system clock, called the clock speed, is measured by the number of ticks per minute.

7. The system unit is a case that contains mechanical components of the computer used to process data.

Quiz Yourself Online: To further check your knowledge of system unit styles, motherboards, processor components and machine cycles, and characteristics of personal computer processors, visit scsite.com/dc2006/ch4/quiz and then click Objectives 1 – 4.

DATA REPRESENTATION

To understand fully the way a computer processes data, you should know how a computer represents data. People communicate through speech by combining words into sentences. Human speech is **analog** because it uses continuous (wave form) signals that vary in strength and quality. Most computers are **digital**. They recognize only two discrete states: on and off. This is because computers are electronic devices powered by electricity, which also has only two states: on and off.

The two digits, 0 and 1, easily can represent these two states (Figure 4-11). The digit 0 represents the electronic state of off (absence of an electronic charge). The digit 1 represents the electronic state of on (presence of an electronic charge).

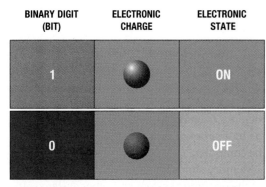

BINARY DIGIT (BIT) | **ELECTRONIC CHARGE** | **ELECTRONIC STATE**

| 1 | | ON |
| 0 | | OFF |

FIGURE 4-11 A computer circuit represents the 0 or the 1 electronically by the presence or absence of an electronic charge.

When people count, they use the digits in the decimal system (0 through 9). The computer, by contrast, uses a binary system because it recognizes only two states. The **binary system** is a number system that has just two unique digits, 0 and 1, called bits. A **bit** (short for *binary digit*) is the smallest unit of data the computer can process. By itself, a bit is not very informative.

When 8 bits are grouped together as a unit, they form a **byte**. A byte provides enough different combinations of 0s and 1s to represent 256 individual characters. These characters include numbers, uppercase and lowercase letters of the alphabet, punctuation marks, and others, such as the letters of the Greek alphabet.

The combinations of 0s and 1s that represent characters are defined by patterns called a coding scheme. In one coding scheme, the number 4 is represented as 00110100, the number 6 as 00110110, and the capital letter E as 01000101 (Figure 4-12). Two popular coding schemes are ASCII and EBCDIC (Figure 4-13). The *American Standard Code for Information Interchange* (*ASCII* pronounced ASK-ee) scheme is the most widely used coding system to represent data. Most personal computers and midrange servers use the ASCII coding scheme. The *Extended Binary Coded Decimal Interchange Code* (*EBCDIC* pronounced EB-see-dik) scheme is used primarily on mainframe computers and high-end servers.

The ASCII and EBCDIC coding schemes are sufficient for English and Western European languages but are not large enough for Asian and other languages that use different alphabets. *Unicode* is a 16-bit coding scheme that has the capacity of representing more than 65,000 characters and symbols. The Unicode coding scheme is capable of representing almost all the world's current written languages, as well as classic and historical languages. To allow for expansion, Unicode reserves 30,000 codes for future use and 6,000 codes for private use. Unicode is implemented in several operating systems, including Windows XP, Mac OS X, and Linux. Unicode-enabled programming languages and software products include Java, XML, Microsoft Office, and Oracle.

Appendix A at the back of this book discusses the ASCII, EBCDIC, and Unicode schemes in more depth, along with the parity bit and number systems.

Coding schemes such as ASCII make it possible for humans to interact with a digital computer that processes only bits. When you press a key on a keyboard, a chip

8-BIT BYTE FOR THE NUMBER 4

| 0 | 0 | 1 | 1 | 0 | 1 | 0 | 0 |

8-BIT BYTE FOR THE NUMBER 6

| 0 | 0 | 1 | 1 | 0 | 1 | 1 | 0 |

8-BIT BYTE FOR THE LETTER E

| 0 | 1 | 0 | 0 | 0 | 1 | 0 | 1 |

FIGURE 4-12 Eight bits grouped together as a unit are called a byte. A byte represents a single character in the computer.

ASCII	SYMBOL	EBCDIC
00110000	0	11110000
00110001	1	11110001
00110010	2	11110010
00110011	3	11110011
00110100	4	11110100
00110101	5	11110101
00110110	6	11110110
00110111	7	11110111
00111000	8	11111000
00111001	9	11111001
01000001	A	11000001
01000010	B	11000010
01000011	C	11000011
01000100	D	11000100
01000101	E	11000101
01000110	F	11000110
01000111	G	11000111
01001000	H	11001000
01001001	I	11001001
01001010	J	11010001
01001011	K	11010010
01001100	L	11010011
01001101	M	11010100
01001110	N	11010101
01001111	O	11010110
01010000	P	11010111
01010001	Q	11011000
01010010	R	11011001
01010011	S	11100010
01010100	T	11100011
01010101	U	11100100
01010110	V	11100101
01010111	W	11100110
01011000	X	11100111
01011001	Y	11101000
01011010	Z	11101001
00100001	!	01011010
00100010	"	01111111
00100011	#	01111011
00100100	$	01011011
00100101	%	01101100
00100110	&	01010000
00101000	(	01001101
00101001	)	01011101
00101010	*	01011100
00101011	+	01001110

FIGURE 4-13 Two popular coding schemes are ASCII and EBCDIC.

in the keyboard converts the key's electronic signal into a special code that is sent to the system unit. Then, the system unit converts the code into a binary form the computer can process and stores it in memory. Every character is converted to its corresponding byte. The computer then processes the data as bytes, which actually is a series of on/off electrical states. When processing is finished, software converts the byte into a human-recognizable number, letter of the alphabet, or special character that is displayed on a screen or is printed (Figure 4-14). All of these conversions take place so quickly that you do not realize they are occurring.

Standards, such as those defined by ASCII, EBCDIC, and Unicode, also make it possible for components in computers to communicate with each other successfully. By following these and other standards, manufacturers can produce a component and be assured that it will operate correctly in a computer.

MEMORY

Memory consists of electronic components that store instructions waiting to be executed by the processor, data needed by those instructions, and the results of processed data (information). Memory usually consists of one or more chips on the motherboard or some other circuit board in the computer.

Memory stores three basic categories of items: (1) the operating system and other system software that control or maintain the computer and its devices; (2) application programs that carry out a specific task such as word processing; and (3) the data being processed by the application programs and resulting information. This role of memory to store both data and programs is known as the *stored program concept*.

Bytes and Addressable Memory

A byte (character) is the basic storage unit in memory. When application program instructions and data are transferred to memory from storage devices, the instructions and data exist as bytes. Each byte resides temporarily in a location in memory that has an *address*. An address simply is a unique number that identifies the location of a byte in memory. The illustration in Figure 4-15 shows how seats in a concert hall are similar to addresses in memory: (1) a seat, which is identified by a unique seat number, holds one person at a time, and a location in memory, which is identified by a unique address, holds a single byte; and (2) both a seat, identified by a seat number, and a byte, identified by an address, can be empty. To access data or instructions in memory, the computer references the addresses that contain bytes of data.

FIGURE 4-14   HOW A LETTER IS CONVERTED TO BINARY FORM AND BACK

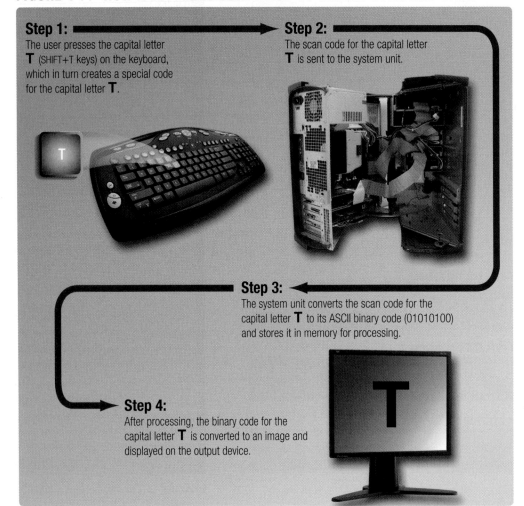

Step 1:
The user presses the capital letter **T** (SHIFT+T keys) on the keyboard, which in turn creates a special code for the capital letter **T**.

Step 2:
The scan code for the capital letter **T** is sent to the system unit.

Step 3:
The system unit converts the scan code for the capital letter **T** to its ASCII binary code (01010100) and stores it in memory for processing.

Step 4:
After processing, the binary code for the capital letter **T** is converted to an image and displayed on the output device.

FIGURE 4-15 Seats in a concert hall are similar to addresses in memory: a seat holds one person at a time, and a location in memory holds a single byte; and both a seat and a byte can be empty.

Memory Sizes

Manufacturers state the size of memory chips and storage devices in terms of the number of bytes the chip or device has available for storage (Figure 4-16). Recall that storage devices hold data, instructions, and information for future use, while most memory holds these items temporarily. A **kilobyte** (**KB** or **K**) is equal to exactly 1,024 bytes. To simplify memory and storage definitions, computer users often round a kilobyte down to 1,000 bytes. For example, if a memory chip can store 100 KB, it can hold approximately 100,000 bytes (characters). A **megabyte** (**MB**) is equal to approximately 1 million bytes. A **gigabyte** (**GB**) equals approximately 1 billion bytes. A **terabyte** (**TB**) is equal to approximately 1 trillion bytes.

Types of Memory

The system unit contains two types of memory: volatile and nonvolatile. When the computer's power is turned off, *volatile memory* loses its contents. *Nonvolatile memory*, by contrast, does not lose its contents when power is removed from the computer. Thus, volatile memory is temporary and nonvolatile memory is permanent. RAM is the most common type of volatile memory. Examples of nonvolatile memory include ROM, flash memory, and CMOS. The following sections discuss these types of memory. Read At Issue 4-3 for a related discussion.

AT ISSUE 4-3

Ready for RFID?

Move over bar codes, make way for RFID. *RFID* (*radio frequency identification*) uses a tiny computer memory chip that is mounted on a tag attached to a product or sewn into an article of clothing. An RFID reader reads identifying information on the memory chip via radio waves. Unlike bar codes, RFID does not require line-of-sight transmission and can identify unique items, not just a category. For merchants, RFID can help to locate items in a warehouse, identify items that need to be replenished, and track items that have been removed from store shelves. For consumers, RFID can supply detailed product information, reduce costs associated with inventory management, and someday let buyers bypass check-out lines and take purchases directly from the store, with the item's cost charged to their card. Privacy advocates worry, however, that RFID could obliterate a buyer's anonymity. They fear that with an RFID reader, any individual or organization could track a purchaser's movements and make that information available to marketers or government agencies. To protect privacy, privacy advocates insist that merchants should be forced to disable RFID transmitters as soon as buyers leave a store. Would you be comfortable purchasing a product using RFID? Why or why not? Should buyers be allowed to request that RFID transmitters be disabled after they make a purchase, or should merchants be required to render transmitters inoperative when the product leaves the store? Why?

MEMORY AND STORAGE SIZES

Term	Abbreviation	Approximate Number of Bytes	Exact Amount of Bytes	Approximate Number of Pages of Text
Kilobyte	KB or K	1 thousand	1,024	1/2
Megabyte	MB	1 million	1,048,576	500
Gigabyte	GB	1 billion	1,073,741,824	500,000
Terabyte	TB	1 trillion	1,099,511,627,776	500,000,000

FIGURE 4-16 Terms commonly used to define memory and storage sizes.

RAM

Users typically are referring to RAM when discussing computer memory. **RAM** (*random access memory*), also called *main memory*, consists of memory chips that can be read from and written to by the processor and other devices. When you turn on power to a computer, certain operating system files (such as the files that determine how the Windows XP desktop appears) load into RAM from a storage device such as a hard disk. These files remain in RAM as long as the computer has continuous power. As additional programs and data are requested, they also load into RAM from storage.

The processor interprets and executes a program's instructions while the program is in RAM. During this time, the contents of RAM may change (Figure 4-17). RAM can accommodate multiple programs simultaneously.

Most RAM is volatile, which means it loses its contents when the power is removed from the computer. For this reason, you must save any data, instructions, and information you

FIGURE 4-17   HOW PROGRAM INSTRUCTIONS TRANSFER IN AND OUT OF RAM

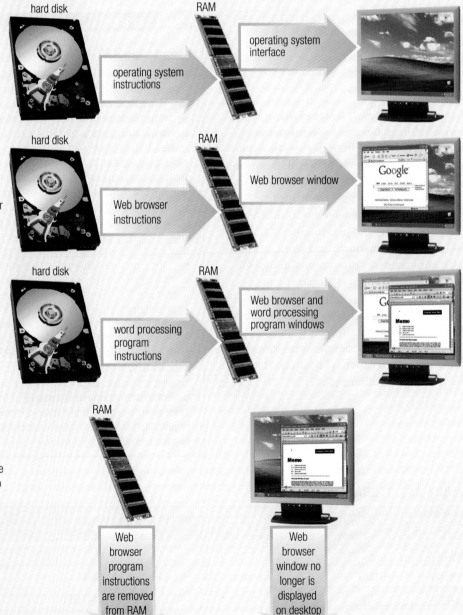

Step 1:
When you start the computer, certain operating system files are loaded into RAM from the hard disk. The operating system displays the user interface on the screen.

Step 2:
When you start a Web browser, the program's instructions are loaded into RAM from the hard disk. The Web browser and certain operating system instructions are in RAM. The Web browser window is displayed on the screen.

Step 3:
When you start a word processing program, the program's instructions are loaded into RAM from the hard disk. The word processing program, along with the Web browser and certain operating system instructions, are in RAM. The word processing program window is displayed on the screen.

Step 4:
When you quit a program, such as the Web browser, its program instructions are removed from RAM. The Web browser no longer is displayed on the screen.

may need in the future. Saving is the process of copying data, instructions, and information from RAM to a storage device such as a hard disk.

Three basic types of RAM chips exist: dynamic RAM, static RAM, and magnetoresistive RAM.

- *Dynamic RAM* (*DRAM* pronounced DEE-ram) chips must be re-energized constantly or they lose their contents. Many variations of DRAM chips exist, most of which are faster than the basic DRAM. *Synchronous DRAM* (*SDRAM*) chips are much faster than DRAM chips because they are synchronized to the system clock. *Double Data Rate SDRAM* (*DDR SDRAM*) chips are even faster than SDRAM chips because they transfer data twice for each clock cycle, instead of just once, and DDR 2 is even faster than DDR. Dual channel SDRAM is faster than single channel SDRAM because it delivers twice the amount of data to the processor. *Rambus DRAM* (*RDRAM*) is yet another type of DRAM that is much faster than SDRAM because it uses pipelining techniques. Most personal computers today use some form of SDRAM chips or RDRAM chips.

- *Static RAM* (*SRAM* pronounced ESS-ram) chips are faster and more reliable than any variation of DRAM chips. These chips do not have to be re-energized as often as DRAM chips, thus, the term static. SRAM chips, however, are much more expensive than DRAM chips. Special applications such as cache use SRAM chips. A later section in this chapter discusses cache.

- A newer type of RAM, called *magnetoresistive RAM* (*MRAM* pronounced EM-ram), stores data using magnetic charges instead of electrical charges. Manufacturers claim that MRAM has greater storage capacity, consumes less power, and has faster access times than electronic RAM. Also, MRAM retains its contents after power is removed from the computer, which could prevent loss of data for users. As the cost of MRAM declines, experts predict MRAM could replace both DRAM and SRAM.

RAM chips usually reside on a **memory module**, which is a small circuit board. **Memory slots** on the motherboard hold memory modules (Figure 4-18). Three types of memory modules are SIMMs, DIMMs, and RIMMs. A *SIMM* (*single inline memory module*) has pins on opposite sides of the circuit board that connect together to form a single set of contacts. With a *DIMM* (*dual inline memory module*), by contrast, the pins on opposite sides of the circuit board do not connect and thus form two sets of contacts. SIMMs and DIMMs typically hold SDRAM chips. A *RIMM* (*Rambus inline memory module*) houses RDRAM chips. For a more technical discussion about RAM, read the High-Tech Talk article on page 218 at the end of this chapter.

WEB LINK 4-3

RAM
For more information, visit scsite.com/ dc2006/ch4/weblink and then click RAM.

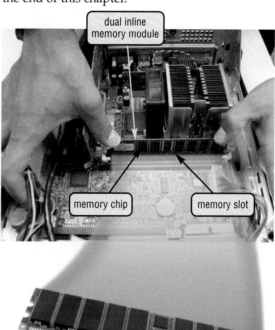

dual inline memory module

memory chip   memory slot

FIGURE 4-18 This photo shows a memory module being inserted in a motherboard.

RAM CONFIGURATIONS The amount of RAM necessary in a computer often depends on the types of software you plan to use. A computer executes programs that are in RAM. Think of RAM as the workspace on the top of your desk. Just as the top of your desk needs a certain amount of space to hold papers, a computer needs a certain amount of memory to store programs, data, and information. The more RAM a computer has, the faster the computer will respond.

A software package typically indicates the minimum amount of RAM it requires. If you want the application to perform optimally, usually you need more than the minimum specifications on the software package. Some programs, such as operating systems, also have specified maximums.

Generally, home users running Windows XP and using basic application software such as word processing should have at least 256 MB of RAM. Most business users who work with accounting, financial, or spreadsheet programs, voice recognition, and programs requiring multimedia capabilities should have a minimum of 512 MB of RAM. Users creating professional Web sites or using graphics-intensive applications will want at least 2 GB of RAM.

Figure 4-19a lists guidelines for the amount of RAM for various types of users. Figure 4-19b shows advertisements that match to each user requirement. Advertisements normally list the type of processor, the clock speed of the processor, and the amount of RAM in the computer. The amount of RAM in computers purchased today ranges from 256 MB to 16 GB. In an advertisement, manufacturers specify the maximum amount of RAM a computer can hold, for example, 512 GB expandable to 2 GB. Read At Issue 4-4 for a related discussion.

FAQ 4-3

Can I add more RAM to my computer?

Check your computer documentation to see how much RAM you can add. RAM modules are relatively inexpensive and usually include easy-to-follow installation instructions. Be sure to purchase RAM compatible with your brand and model of computer. For more information, visit scsite.com/dc2006/ch4/faq and then click Upgrading RAM.

AT ISSUE 4-4

Do Lower Computer Prices Mean Less Value?

Today, you can buy a personal computer for less than $1,000 that can do more than one sold at nearly twice its cost three years ago. Some manufacturers even are offering basic computers for less than $500. Part of the plunge in prices is lower-cost components, but another factor is a growing demand for cheaper machines. One computer maker estimates that it sells almost 3,500 sub-$500 computers a month. Many of the new buyers are from families earning less than $40,000, far below the $50,000 average that once characterized typical computer buyers. These consumers are looking for inexpensive computers that are adequate for the most popular tasks, such as word processing, spreadsheets, and Internet access. They feel that spending higher prices for faster processors, more memory, 3-D graphics cards, higher-quality sound cards, more hard disk space, and other extras is an unnecessary, frivolous expense. As one industry analyst asks, "Why buy a Porsche when you are going to drive only 55 miles per hour?" How might a greater availability of lower costing personal computers change the way people, schools, and businesses buy and use them? With respect to computers, does a higher price always mean greater usefulness? Why or why not? Who might be satisfied with less than the latest and greatest computer technology? Why?

FIGURE 4-19a   (RAM guidelines)

RAM	256 MB to 1 GB	512 MB to 2 GB	2 GB and up
Use	Home and business users managing personal finances; using standard application software such as word processing; using educational or entertainment CD-ROMs; communicating with others on the Web	Users requiring more advanced multimedia capabilities; running number-intensive accounting, financial, or spreadsheet programs; using voice recognition; working with videos, music, and digital imaging; creating Web sites; participating in video conferences; playing Internet games	Power users creating professional Web sites; running sophisticated CAD, 3-D design, or other graphics-intensive software

FIGURE 4-19b   (computers for sale)

Model	A220	P240	A240	P300	X300	A225
Processor	2.20 GHz Athlon XP processor	2.40 GHz Celeron processor	2.40 GHz Athlon 64 processor	3.0 GHz Pentium 4 processor	3.0 GHz Xeon MP processor	2.25 GHz Opteron processor
Memory	256 MB SDRAM	512 MB SDRAM	512 MB SDRAM	1 GB SDRAM	2 GB RDRAM	4 GB SDRAM

FIGURE 4-19   Determining how much RAM you need depends on the applications you intend to run on your computer. Advertisements for computers normally list the type of processor, the speed of the processor, and the amount of RAM installed.

Cache

Most of today's computers improve processing times with **cache** (pronounced cash). Two types of cache are memory cache and disk cache. This chapter discusses memory cache. Chapter 7 discusses disk cache.

Memory cache helps speed the processes of the computer because it stores frequently used instructions and data. Most personal computers today have two types of memory cache: L1 cache and L2 cache. Some also have L3 cache.

- *L1 cache* is built directly in the processor chip. L1 cache usually has a very small capacity, ranging from 8 KB to 128 KB. The more common sizes for personal computers are 8 KB or 16 KB.
- *L2 cache* is slightly slower than L1 cache but has a much larger capacity, ranging from 64 KB to 16 MB. When discussing cache, most users are referring to L2 cache. Current processors include *advanced transfer cache* (*ATC*), a type of L2 cache built directly on the processor chip. Processors that use ATC perform at much faster rates than those that do not use it.

Personal computers today typically have from 512 KB to 2 MB of advanced transfer cache. Servers and workstations have from 2 MB to 6 MB of advanced transfer cache.

- *L3 cache* is a cache on the motherboard that is separate from the processor chip. L3 cache exists only on computers that use L2 advanced transfer cache. Personal computers often have up to 2 MB of L3 cache; servers and workstations have from 2 MB to 6 MB of L3 cache.

Cache speeds up processing time because it stores frequently used instructions and data. When the processor needs an instruction or data, it searches memory in this order: L1 cache, then L2 cache, then L3 cache (if it exists), then RAM — with a greater delay in processing for each level of memory it must search (Figure 4-20). If the instruction or data is not found in memory, then it must search a slower speed storage medium such as a hard disk, CD, or DVD.

ROM

Read-only memory (**ROM** pronounced rahm) refers to memory chips storing permanent data and instructions. The data on most ROM chips cannot be modified — hence, the name read-only. ROM is nonvolatile, which means its contents are not lost when power is removed from the computer. In addition to computers, many devices contain ROM chips. For example, ROM chips in printers contain data for fonts.

WEB LINK 4-4

Cache

For more information, visit scsite.com/dc2006/ch4/weblink and then click Cache.

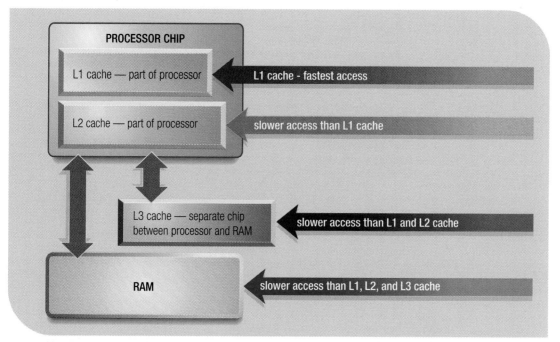

PROCESSOR CHIP

L1 cache — part of processor ← L1 cache - fastest access

L2 cache — part of processor ← slower access than L1 cache

L3 cache — separate chip between processor and RAM ← slower access than L1 and L2 cache

RAM ← slower access than L1, L2, and L3 cache

FIGURE 4-20 Cache helps speed processing times when the processor requests data, instructions, or information.

Manufacturers of ROM chips often record data, instructions, or information on the chips when they manufacture the chips. These ROM chips, called **firmware**, contain permanently written data, instructions, or information.

A *PROM* (*programmable read-only memory*) *chip* is a blank ROM chip on which a programmer can write permanently. Programmers use *microcode* instructions to program a PROM chip. Once a programmer writes the microcode on the PROM chip, it functions like a regular ROM chip and cannot be erased or changed.

A variation of the PROM chip, called an *EEPROM* (*electrically erasable programmable read-only memory*) *chip*, allows a programmer to erase the microcode with an electric signal.

Flash Memory

Flash memory is a type of nonvolatile memory that can be erased electronically and rewritten, similar to EEPROM. Most computers use flash memory to hold their startup instructions because it allows the computer easily to update its contents. For example, when the computer changes from standard time to daylight savings time, the contents of a flash memory chip (and the real-time clock chip) change to reflect the new time.

Flash memory chips also store data and programs on many mobile computers and devices, such as PDAs, smart phones, printers, digital cameras, automotive devices, music players, digital voice recorders, and pagers. When you enter names and addresses in a PDA or smart phone, a flash memory chip stores the data. Some MP3 players store music on flash memory chips (Figure 4-21); others store music on tiny hard disks or flash memory cards. A later section in this chapter discusses flash memory cards, which contain flash memory on a removable device instead of a chip.

WEB LINK 4-5

Flash Memory

For more information, visit scsite.com/ dc2006/ch4/weblink and then click Flash Memory.

FAQ 4-4

How much music can I store on an MP3 player?

MP3 players that store music on flash memory chips can hold up to 8 or 9 hours of music, which is about 120 songs in the WMA format or 60 songs in the MP3 format. MP3 players with tiny hard disks have a much greater storage capacity — from 1,000 to 10,000 songs. For more information, visit scsite.com/ dc2006/ch4/faq and then click MP3 Players.

FIGURE 4-21 HOW AN MP3 MUSIC PLAYER MIGHT STORE MUSIC ON FLASH MEMORY

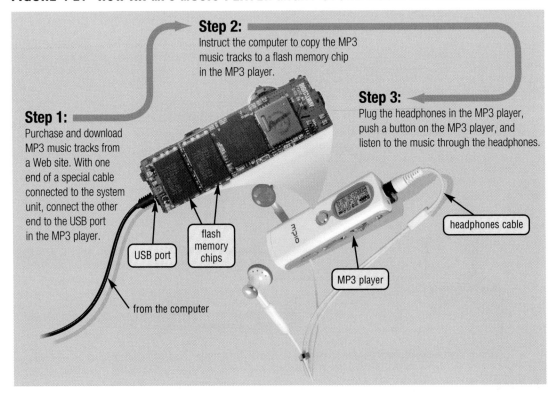

Step 1: Purchase and download MP3 music tracks from a Web site. With one end of a special cable connected to the system unit, connect the other end to the USB port in the MP3 player.

Step 2: Instruct the computer to copy the MP3 music tracks to a flash memory chip in the MP3 player.

Step 3: Plug the headphones in the MP3 player, push a button on the MP3 player, and listen to the music through the headphones.

USB port

flash memory chips

from the computer

MP3 player

headphones cable

CMOS

Some RAM chips, flash memory chips, and other types of memory chips use **complementary metal-oxide semiconductor** (**CMOS** pronounced SEE-moss) technology because it provides high speeds and consumes little power. CMOS technology uses battery power to retain information even when the power to the computer is off. Battery-backed CMOS memory chips, for example, can keep the calendar, date, and time current even when the computer is off. The flash memory chips that store a computer's startup information often use CMOS technology.

FAQ 4-5

What should I do if my computer's date and time are wrong?

First, try resetting the date and time. To do this in Windows XP, double-click the time at the right edge of the taskbar. If the computer continues to lose time or display an incorrect date, you may need to replace the CMOS battery on the motherboard that powers the system clock. For more information, visit scsite.com/dc2006/ch4/faq and then click CMOS Battery.

Memory Access Times

Access time is the amount of time it takes the processor to read data, instructions, and information from memory. A computer's access time directly affects how fast the computer processes data. Accessing data in memory can be more than 200,000 times faster than accessing data on a hard disk because of the mechanical motion of the hard disk.

Today's manufacturers use a variety of terminology to state access times (Figure 4-22). Some use fractions of a second, which for memory occurs in nanoseconds. A **nanosecond** (abbreviated *ns*) is one billionth of a second. A nanosecond is extremely fast (Figure 4-23). In fact, electricity travels about one foot in a nanosecond.

Other manufacturers state access times in MHz; for example, 133 MHz SDRAM. If a manufacturer states access time in megahertz, you can convert it to nanoseconds by dividing the megahertz number into 1 billion ns. For example, 133 MHz equals approximately 7.5 ns (1,000,000,000/133,000,000).

The access time (speed) of memory contributes to the overall performance of the computer. Standard SDRAM chips can have access times up to 133 MHz (about 7.5 ns), and access times of the DDR SDRAM chips reach 533 MHz (about 1.9 ns). The higher the megahertz, the faster the access time; conversely, the lower the nanoseconds, the faster the access time. The faster RDRAM chips can have access times up to 1600 MHz (about 0.625 ns). ROM access times range from 25 to 250 ns.

While access times of memory greatly affect overall computer performance, manufacturers and retailers usually list a computer's memory in terms of its size, not its access time. Thus, an advertisement might describe a computer as having 512 MB of SDRAM upgradeable to 2 GB.

ACCESS TIME TERMINOLOGY

Term	Abbreviation	Speed
Millisecond	ms	One-thousandth of a second
Microsecond	μs	One-millionth of a second
Nanosecond	ns	One-billionth of a second
Picosecond	ps	One-trillionth of a second

FIGURE 4-22 Access times are measured in fractions of a second. This table lists the terms used to define access times.

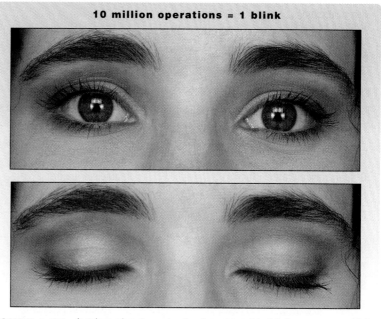

10 million operations = 1 blink

FIGURE 4-23 It takes about one-tenth of a second to blink your eye, which is the equivalent of 100 million nanoseconds. In the time it takes to blink your eye, a computer can perform some operations 10 million times.

Test your knowledge of pages 194 through 203 in Quiz Yourself 4-2.

QUIZ YOURSELF 4-2

Instructions: Find the true statement below. Then, rewrite the remaining false statements so they are true.

1. A computer's memory access time directly affects how fast the computer processes data.

2. A gigabyte (GB) equals approximately 1 trillion bytes.

3. Memory cache helps speed the processes of the computer because it stores seldom used instructions and data.

4. Most computers are analog, which means they recognize only two discrete states: on and off.

5. Most RAM retains its contents when the power is removed from the computer.

6. Read-only memory (ROM) refers to memory chips storing temporary data and instructions.

Quiz Yourself Online: To further check your knowledge of bits, bytes, data representation, and types of memory, visit scsite.com/dc2006/ch4/quiz and then click Objectives 5 – 7.

EXPANSION SLOTS AND ADAPTER CARDS

An **expansion slot** is a socket on the motherboard that can hold an adapter card. An **adapter card**, sometimes called an *expansion card*, is a circuit board that enhances functions of a component of the system unit and/or provides connections to peripherals. A **peripheral** is a device that connects to the system unit and is controlled by the processor in the computer. Examples of peripherals are modems, disk drives, printers, scanners, and keyboards.

Figure 4-24 lists currently used types of adapter cards. Sometimes, all functionality is built in the adapter card. With others, a cable connects the adapter card to a peripheral, such as a scanner, outside the system unit. Figure 4-25 shows an adapter card being inserted in an expansion slot on a personal computer motherboard.

Some motherboards include all necessary capabilities and do not require adapter cards. Other motherboards may require adapter cards to provide capabilities such as sound and video. A **sound card** enhances the sound-generating capabilities of a personal computer by allowing sound to be input through a microphone and output through external speakers or headset. A **video card**, also called a *graphics card*, converts computer output into a video signal that travels through a cable to the monitor, which displays an image on the screen.

WEB LINK 4-6

Adapter Cards

For more information, visit scsite.com/dc2006/ch4/weblink and then click Adapter Cards.

TYPES OF ADAPTER CARDS

Adapter Card	Purpose
Disk controller	Connects disk drives
FireWire	Connects to FireWire devices
Graphics accelerator	Increases the speed at which graphics are displayed
MIDI	Connects musical instruments
Modem	Connects other computers through telephone or cable television lines
Network	Connects other computers and peripherals
PC-to-TV converter	Connects a television
Sound	Connects speakers or a microphone
TV tuner	Allows viewing of television channels on the monitor
USB 2.0	Connects to USB 2.0 devices
Video	Connects a monitor
Video capture	Connects a camcorder

FIGURE 4-24   Currently used adapter cards and their functions.

FIGURE 4-25   An adapter card being inserted in an expansion slot on the motherboard of a personal computer.

In the past, installing a card was not easy and required you to set switches and other elements on the motherboard. Many of today's computers support **Plug and Play**, which means the computer automatically can configure adapter cards and other peripherals as you install them. Having Plug and Play support means you can plug in a device, turn on the computer, and then immediately begin using the device.

PC Cards, Flash Memory Cards, and USB Flash Drives

Notebook and other mobile computers have at least one **PC Card slot**, which is a special type of expansion slot that holds a PC Card. A **PC Card** is a thin, credit card-sized device that adds memory, storage, sound, fax/modem, network, and other capabilities to mobile computers (Figure 4-26). Because of their small size and versatility, some consumer electronics products such as digital cameras use PC Cards.

All PC Cards conform to standards developed by the *Personal Computer Memory Card International Association* (these cards originally were called *PCMCIA cards*). These standards help to ensure the interchangeability of PC Cards among mobile computers. Although some PC cards contain tiny hard disks, many PC Cards are a type of flash memory card.

A **flash memory card** is a removable flash memory device that allows users to transfer data and information conveniently from mobile devices to their desktop computers (Figure 4-27). Many mobile and consumer devices, such as PDAs, smart phones, digital cameras, and digital music players, use these memory cards. Some printers and computers have built-in card readers/writers or slots that read flash memory cards. In addition, you can purchase an external card reader/writer that attaches to any computer. Flash memory cards are available in a variety of shapes and sizes. The type of flash memory card you have will determine the type of card reader/writer you need. Storage capacities of flash memory cards range from 64 MB to 5 GB.

Another widely used type of removable flash memory is the USB flash drive (Figure 4-27). A *USB flash drive* is a flash memory storage device that plugs in a USB port on a computer or portable device. (The next section discusses USB ports.) Storage capacities of USB flash drives range from 64 MB to 1 GB.

Unlike adapter cards that require you to open the system unit and install the card on the motherboard, you can change a removable flash memory device without having to open the system unit or restart the computer. This feature, called *hot plugging*, allows you to insert and remove the removable flash memory and other devices while the computer is running.

WEB LINK 4-7

Removable Flash Memory Devices

For more information, visit scsite.com/dc2006/ch4/weblink and then click Removable Flash Memory Devices.

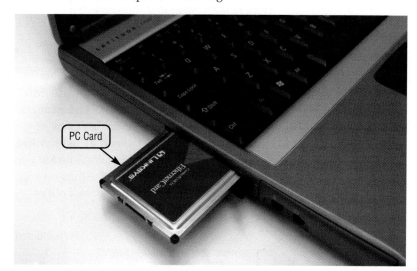

FIGURE 4-26 A PC card slides in a PC Card slot on a notebook computer.

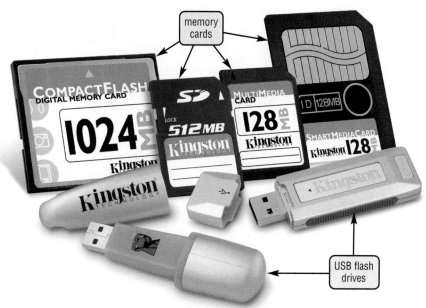

FIGURE 4-27 Removable flash memory devices are available in a range of sizes.

PORTS AND CONNECTORS

A **port** is the point at which a peripheral attaches to a system unit so the peripheral can send data to or receive information from the computer. An external device, such as a keyboard, monitor, printer, mouse, and microphone, often attaches by a cable to a port on the system unit. Instead of port, the term **jack** sometimes is used to identify audio and video ports. The back of the system unit contains many ports; some newer personal computers also have ports on the front of the system unit (Figure 4-28).

Ports have different types of connectors. A **connector** joins a cable to a peripheral. One end of a cable attaches to the connector on the system unit, and the other end of the cable attaches to a connector on the peripheral. Most connectors are available in one of two genders: male or female. *Male connectors* have one or more exposed pins, like the end of an electrical cord you plug in the wall. *Female connectors* have matching holes to accept the pins on a male connector, like an electrical wall outlet.

Sometimes, attaching a new peripheral to the computer is not possible because the connector on the system unit is the same gender as the connector on the cable. In this case, purchasing a gender changer solves this problem. A *gender changer* is a device that enables you to join two connectors that are both female or both male.

Manufacturers often identify the cables by their connector types to assist you with purchasing a cable to connect a computer to a peripheral. Figure 4-29 shows the different types of connectors on a system unit. Some system units include these connectors when you buy the computer. You add other connectors by inserting adapter cards on the motherboard. Certain adapter cards have ports that allow you to attach a peripheral to the adapter card.

Most desktop personal computers have at least one serial port, one parallel port, several USB ports, and a FireWire port. The next section discusses these and other ports.

WEB LINK 4-8

Ports and Connectors

For more information, visit scsite.com/dc2006/ch4/weblink and then click Ports and Connectors.

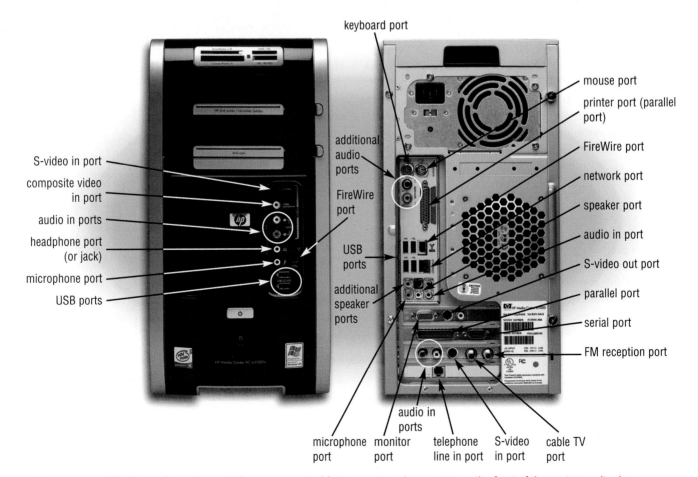

FIGURE 4-28   The back of a system unit has many ports. Most computers have ports on the front of the system unit, also.

CONNECTOR TYPES

Connector Type	Picture	Connector Type	Picture
Audio in		Mouse	
Cable TV		Network	
Composite video in		Printer	
FireWire		Serial	
FM reception		Speaker	
Headphone		S-video in	
Keyboard		S-video out	
Microphone		Telephone line in	
Monitor		USB	

FIGURE 4-29 Examples of different types of connectors on a system unit.

Serial Ports

A **serial port** is a type of interface that connects a device to the system unit by transmitting data one bit at a time (Figure 4-30). Serial ports usually connect devices that do not require fast data transmission rates, such as a mouse, keyboard, or modem. The *COM port* (short for communications port) on the system unit is one type of serial port.

Some modems that connect the system unit to a telephone line use a serial port because the telephone line expects the data in a specific frequency. Serial ports conform to either the RS-232 or RS-422 standard, which specifies the number of pins used on the port's connector.

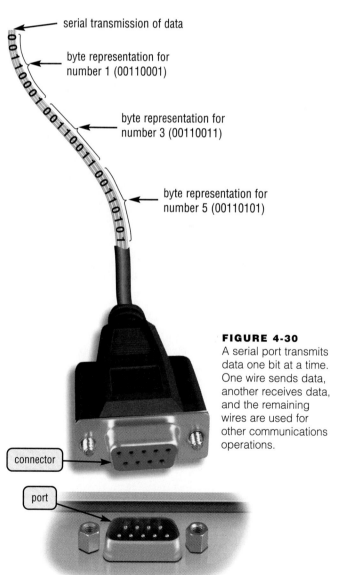

serial transmission of data

byte representation for number 1 (00110001)

byte representation for number 3 (00110011)

byte representation for number 5 (00110101)

connector

port

FIGURE 4-30
A serial port transmits data one bit at a time. One wire sends data, another receives data, and the remaining wires are used for other communications operations.

Parallel Ports

Unlike a serial port, a **parallel port** is an interface that connects devices by transferring more than one bit at a time (Figure 4-31). Originally, parallel ports were developed as an alternative to the slower speed serial ports.

Many printers connect to the system unit using a parallel port. This parallel port can transfer eight bits of data (one byte) simultaneously through eight separate lines in a single cable.

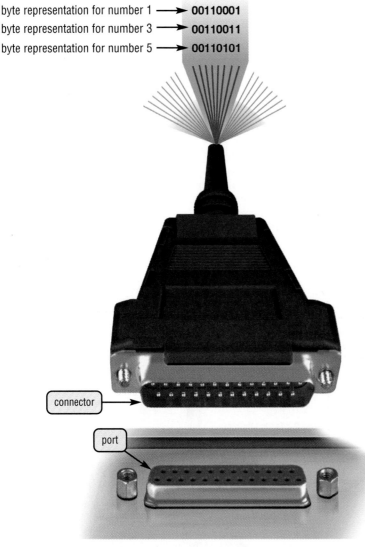

byte representation for number 1 ⟶ 00110001
byte representation for number 3 ⟶ 00110011
byte representation for number 5 ⟶ 00110101

connector

port

FIGURE 4-31 A parallel port is capable of transmitting more than one bit at a time. The port shown in this figure has eight wires that transmit data; the remaining wires are used for other communications operations.

USB Ports

A **USB port**, short for *universal serial bus port*, can connect up to 127 different peripherals together with a single connector type. Devices that connect to a USB port include the following: mouse, printer, digital camera, scanner, speakers, MP3 music player, CD, DVD, and removable hard disk. Personal computers typically have six to eight USB ports either on the front or back of the system unit (Figure 4-28 on page 206). The latest version of USB, called *USB 2.0*, is a more advanced and faster USB, with speeds 40 times higher than that of its predecessor.

To attach multiple peripherals using a single USB port, you can daisy chain the devices together outside the system unit. *Daisy chain* means the first USB device connects to the USB port on the computer, the second USB device connects to the first USB device, the third USB device connects to the second USB device, and so on. An alternative to daisy chaining is to use a USB hub. A **USB hub** is a device that plugs in a USB port on the system unit and contains multiple USB ports in which you plug cables from USB devices.

USB also supports hot plugging and Plug and Play, which means you can attach peripherals while the computer is running. With serial and parallel port connections, by contrast, you often must restart the computer after attaching the peripheral.

Some newer peripherals may attach only to a USB port. Others attach to either a serial or parallel port, as well as a USB port.

FAQ 4-6

Can older USB devices plug in a USB 2.0 port?

Yes. USB 2.0 is *backward compatible*, which means that it supports older USB devices as well as new USB 2.0 devices. Keep in mind, though, that older USB devices do not run any faster in a USB 2.0 port. For more information, visit scsite.com/dc2006/ch4/faq and then click USB 2.0.

FireWire Ports

Previously called an *IEEE 1394 port*, a **FireWire port** is similar to a USB port in that it can connect multiple types of devices that require faster data transmission speeds, such as digital video cameras, digital VCRs, color printers, scanners, digital cameras, and DVD drives, to a single connector. A FireWire port allows you to connect up to 63 devices together. The FireWire port supports Plug and Play.

Some newer peripherals may attach only to a FireWire port. Having standard ports and connectors, such as FireWire and USB, greatly simplify the process of attaching devices to a personal computer. For newer computers that do not have a parallel port, users plug the device in a USB or FireWire port — as specified by the device's manufacturer. In general, FireWire has replaced parallel and SCSI ports, which are discussed in the next section. USB ports have replaced mouse, keyboard, serial, audio, and parallel ports. Figure 4-32 shows how FireWire and USB ports are replacing other ports completely.

Special-Purpose Ports

Four special-purpose ports are MIDI, SCSI, IrDA, and Bluetooth. These ports are not included in typical computers. For a computer to have these ports, you must customize the computer purchase order. The following sections discuss MIDI, SCSI, IrDA, and Bluetooth ports.

MIDI PORT A special type of serial port that connects the system unit to a musical instrument, such as an electronic keyboard, is called a **MIDI port**. Short for *Musical Instrument Digital Interface*, MIDI (pronounced MID-dee) is the electronic music industry's standard that defines how devices, such as sound cards and synthesizers, represent sounds electronically. A *synthesizer*, which can be a peripheral or a chip, creates sound from digital instructions.

A system unit with a MIDI port has the capability of recording sounds that have been created by a synthesizer and then processing the sounds (the data) to create new sounds. Nearly every sound card supports the MIDI standard, so you can play and manipulate on one computer sounds that originally were created on another computer.

TRADITIONAL PORTS

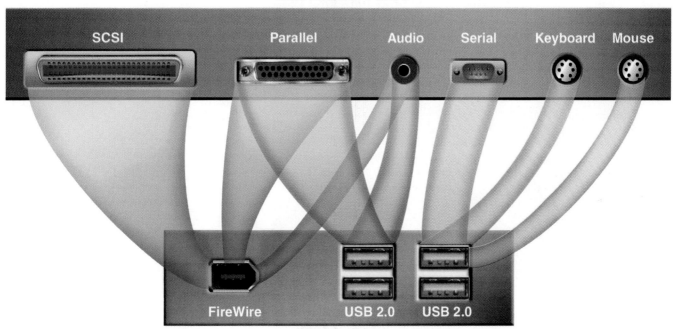

NEW PORTS

FIGURE 4-32 USB and FireWire ports are replacing traditional ports completely.

SCSI PORT   A special high-speed parallel port, called a **SCSI port**, allows you to attach SCSI (pronounced skuzzy) peripherals such as disk drives and printers. Depending on the type of *SCSI*, which stands for *small computer system interface*, you can daisy chain up to either 7 or 15 devices together. Some computers include a SCSI port. Others have a slot that supports a SCSI card.

IrDA PORT   Some devices can transmit data via infrared light waves. For these wireless devices to transmit signals to a computer, both the computer and the device must have an **IrDA port** (Figure 4-33). These ports conform to standards developed by the *IrDA* (*Infrared Data Association*).

To ensure nothing obstructs the path of the infrared light wave, you must align the IrDA port on the device with the IrDA port on the computer, similarly to the way you operate a television remote control. Devices that use IrDA ports include a PDA, smart phone, keyboard, mouse, printer, and pager. Several of these devices use a high-speed IrDA port, sometimes called a *fast infrared port*.

BLUETOOTH PORT   An alternative to IrDA, **Bluetooth** technology uses radio waves to transmit data between two devices (Figure 4-34). Unlike IrDA, the Bluetooth devices do not have to be aligned with each other. Many computers, peripherals, PDAs, smart phones, cars, and other consumer electronics are Bluetooth-enabled, which means they contain a small chip that allows them to communicate with other Bluetooth-enabled computers and devices. The latest version of Bluetooth, called Bluetooth 2.0, supports higher connection speeds and is backward compatible with its predecessors.

If you have a computer that is not Bluetooth enabled, you can purchase a Bluetooth wireless port adapter that will convert an existing USB port or serial port into a Bluetooth port. Also available are Bluetooth PC Cards for notebook computers and Bluetooth cards for PDAs and smart phones.

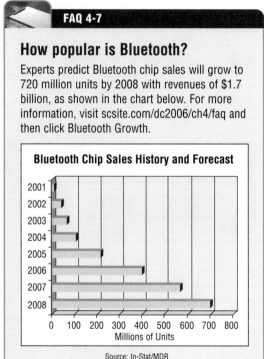

FAQ 4-7

How popular is Bluetooth?

Experts predict Bluetooth chip sales will grow to 720 million units by 2008 with revenues of $1.7 billion, as shown in the chart below. For more information, visit scsite.com/dc2006/ch4/faq and then click Bluetooth Growth.

Bluetooth Chip Sales History and Forecast

Source: In-Stat/MDR

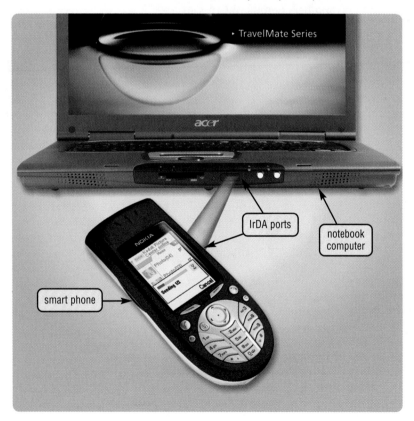

FIGURE 4-33   Many devices communicate wirelessly with desktop or notebook computers through IrDA ports.

FIGURE 4-34 This smart phone wirelessly communicates with a Bluetooth-enabled notebook computer.

BUSES

As explained earlier in this chapter, a computer processes and stores data as a series of electronic bits. These bits transfer internally within the circuitry of the computer along electrical channels. Each channel, called a **bus**, allows the various devices both inside and attached to the system unit to communicate with each other. Just as vehicles travel on a highway to move from one destination to another, bits travel on a bus (Figure 4-35).

Buses transfer bits from input devices to memory, from memory to the processor, from the processor to memory, and from memory to output or storage devices. Buses consist of two parts: a data bus and an address bus. The *data bus* transfers actual data and the *address bus* transfers information about where the data should reside in memory.

The size of a bus, called the *bus width*, determines the number of bits that the computer can transmit at one time. For example, a 32-bit bus can transmit 32 bits (4 bytes) at a time. On a 64-bit bus, bits transmit from one location to another 64 bits (8 bytes) at a time. The larger the number of bits handled by the bus, the faster the computer transfers data. Using the highway analogy again, assume that one lane on a highway can carry one bit. A 32-bit bus is like a 32-lane highway. A 64-bit bus is like a 64-lane highway.

If a number in memory occupies 8 bytes, or 64 bits, the computer must transmit it in two separate steps when using a 32-bit bus: once for the first 32 bits and once for the second 32 bits. Using a 64-bit bus, the computer can transmit the number in a single step, transferring all 64 bits at once. The wider the bus, the fewer number of transfer steps required and the faster the transfer of data. Most personal computers today use a 64-bit bus.

In conjunction with the bus width, many computer professionals refer to a computer's word size. **Word size** is the number of bits the processor can interpret and execute at a given time. That is, a 64-bit processor can manipulate 64 bits at a time. Computers with a larger word size can process more data in the same amount of time than computers with a smaller word size. In most computers, the word size is the same as the bus width.

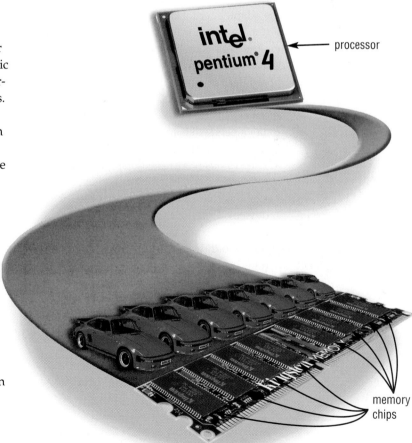

FIGURE 4-35 Just as vehicles travel on a highway, bits travel on a bus. Buses transfer bits from input devices to memory, from memory to the processor, from the processor to memory, and from memory to output or storage devices.

Every bus also has a clock speed. Just like the processor, manufacturers state the clock speed for a bus in hertz. Recall that one megahertz (MHz) is equal to one million ticks per second. Most of today's processors have a bus clock speed of 400, 533, or 800 MHz. The higher the bus clock speed, the faster the transmission of data, which results in applications running faster.

A computer has two basic types of buses: a system bus and an expansion bus. A *system bus* is part of the motherboard and connects the processor to main memory. An *expansion bus* allows the processor to communicate with peripherals. When computer professionals use the term bus by itself, they usually are referring to the system bus.

WEB LINK 4-9

Buses

For more information, visit scsite.com/ dc2006/ch4/weblink and then click Buses.

Expansion Bus

Some peripherals outside the system unit connect to a port on an adapter card, which is inserted in an expansion slot on the motherboard. This expansion slot connects to the expansion bus, which allows the processor to communicate with the peripheral attached to the adapter card. Data transmitted to memory or the processor travels from the expansion slot via the expansion bus and the system bus.

The types of expansion buses on a motherboard determine the types of cards you can add to the computer. Thus, you should understand these expansion buses commonly found in today's personal computers: PCI bus, AGP bus, USB, FireWire bus, and PC Card bus.

- The *PCI bus* (*Peripheral Component Interconnect bus*) is a high-speed expansion bus that connects higher speed devices. Types of cards you can insert in a PCI bus expansion slot include video cards, sound cards, SCSI cards, and high-speed network cards.
- The *Accelerated Graphics Port* (*AGP*) is a bus designed by Intel to improve the speed with which 3-D graphics and video transmit. With an AGP video card in an AGP bus slot, the AGP bus provides a faster, dedicated interface between the video card and memory. Newer processors support AGP technology.
- The USB (*universal serial bus*) and *FireWire bus* are buses that eliminate the need to install cards in expansion slots. In a computer with a USB, for example, USB devices connect to each other

outside the system unit, and then a single cable attaches to the USB port. The USB port then connects to the USB, which connects to the PCI bus on the motherboard. The FireWire bus works in a similar fashion. With these buses, expansion slots are available for devices not compatible with USB or FireWire.

- The expansion bus for a PC Card is the *PC Card bus*. With a PC Card inserted in a PC Card slot, data travels on the PC Card bus to the PCI bus.

BAYS

After you purchase a computer, you may want to install an additional storage device, such as a disk drive, in the system unit. A **bay** is an opening inside the system unit in which you can install additional equipment. A bay is different from a slot, which is used for the installation of adapter cards. Rectangular openings, called **drive bays**, typically hold disk drives.

Two types of drive bays exist: external and internal. An *external drive bay* allows a user to access the drive from outside the system unit (Figure 4-36). Floppy disk drives, CD drives, DVD drives, Zip drives, and tape drives are examples of devices installed in external drive bays. An *internal drive bay* is concealed entirely within the system unit. Hard disk drives are installed in internal bays.

CD drive

DVD drive

floppy disk drive

FIGURE 4-36 External drive bays usually are located beside or on top of one another.

POWER SUPPLY

Many personal computers plug in standard wall outlets, which supply an alternating current (AC) of 115 to 120 volts. This type of power is unsuitable for use with a computer, which requires a direct current (DC) ranging from 5 to 12 volts. The **power supply** is the component of the system unit that converts the wall outlet AC power into DC power. Different motherboards and computers require different wattages on the power supply. If a power supply is not providing the necessary power, the computer will not function properly.

Near the power supply is a fan that keeps the power supply and other components of the system unit cool. This fan dissipates heat generated by the processor and other components of the system unit. Many newer computers have additional fans near certain components in the system unit such as the processor, hard disk, and ports.

Some external peripherals such as an external modem, speakers, or a tape drive have an **AC adapter**, which is an external power supply. One end of the AC adapter plugs in the wall outlet and the other end attaches to the peripheral. The AC adapter converts the AC power into DC power that the peripheral requires.

FAQ 4-8

How many fans are in a system unit?

Most systems units have at least three fans: one in the power supply, one on the case, and one on the processor heat sink. Some computers allow you to turn off noisy fans until they are needed. You also can purchase utility programs that slow or stop the fan until the temperature reaches a certain level. For more information, visit scsite.com/dc2006/ch4/faq and then click Computer Fan.

MOBILE COMPUTERS AND DEVICES

As businesses and schools expand to serve people across the country and around the world, increasingly more people need to use a computer while traveling to and from a main office or school to conduct business, communicate, or do homework. As Chapter 1 discussed, users with such mobile computing needs — known as mobile users — often have a mobile computer, such as a notebook computer or Tablet PC, or a mobile device such as a smart phone or PDA (Figure 4-37).

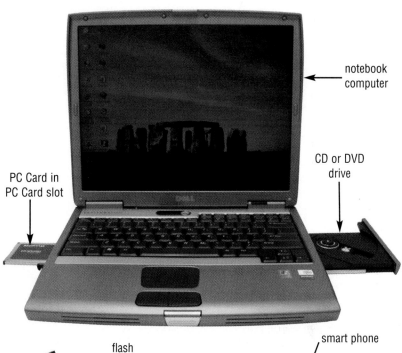

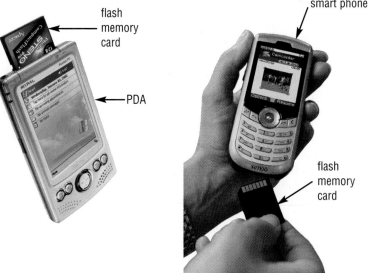

FIGURE 4-37 Users with mobile computing needs often have a notebook computer, PDA, and/or smart phone.

Weighing on average between 2.5 and 8 pounds, notebook computers can run either using batteries or using a standard power supply. Smaller PDAs and smart phones run strictly on batteries. Like their desktop counterparts, mobile computers and devices have a motherboard that contains electronic components that process data. Read At Issue 4-5 for a related discussion.

A notebook computer usually is more expensive than a desktop computer with the same capabilities because it is more costly to miniaturize the components. The typical notebook computer often has video, serial, parallel,

modem, network, FireWire, USB, headphones, and microphone ports (Figure 4-38).

Two basic designs of Tablet PC are available: slate and convertible. With the slate Tablet PC (shown in Figure 4-1 on page 184), all the hardware is behind the display — much like a PDA. Users can attach a removable keyboard to the slate Tablet PC. The display on the convertible Tablet PC, which is attached to a keyboard, can be rotated 180 degrees and folded down over the keyboard. Thus, the convertible Tablet PC can be repositioned to look like either a notebook computer or a slate Tablet PC. Tablet PCs usually include several slots and ports (Figure 4-39).

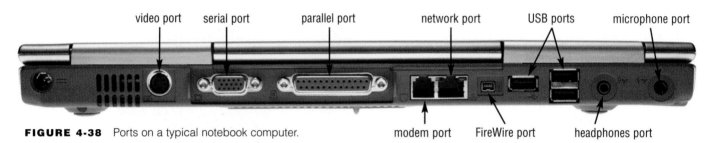

FIGURE 4-38 Ports on a typical notebook computer.

AT ISSUE 4-5

Should Smart Shoes Be Banned from Competitive Events?

Titanium golf clubs. Graphite tennis rackets. Aluminum baseball bats. Advances in technology have impacted many sports. Now, Adidas is changing the sport of running with the introduction of a computerized running shoe. The lightweight, battery-powered shoe, sometimes called a "smart shoe," contains a sensor and a 20 MHz microprocessor. Every second, the sensor sends thousands of readings to the tiny mobile computer, which uses a motorized screw and cable system to adjust the heel cushion based on the conditions and the runner's style. The goal is to ensure ideal cushioning for the runner and the situation. The smart shoe is innovative, but is it fair? To maintain competitive balance, the governing bodies of golf and tennis place restrictions on the composition of equipment. Some racers would like similar limitations placed on running shoes. At a cost of about $250, the smart shoe could provide an unfair advantage to wealthier runners. The advantage would be evident at high school, college, and amateur races, where not all competitors could afford the shoe. Should smart shoes be banned from races? Why or why not? Baseball banned aluminum bats at the professional level; should smart shoes be banned at the high school, college, and amateur levels, where they would be most apt to upset competitive balance? Why?

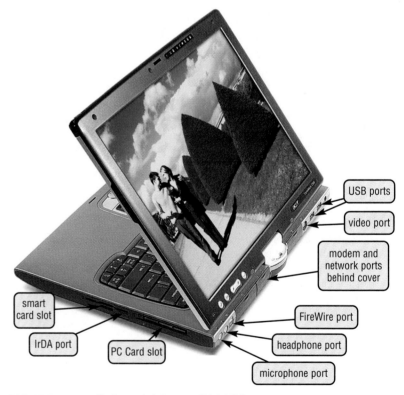

FIGURE 4-39 Ports and slots on a Tablet PC.

PDAs and smart phones are quite affordable, usually priced at a few hundred dollars or less. These mobile devices often have an IrDA port or are Bluetooth enabled so users can communicate wirelessly with other computers or devices such as a printer. Read Looking Ahead 4-2 for a look at the next generation of mobile computer.

LOOKING AHEAD 4-2

DNA Computer Works to Fight Cancer

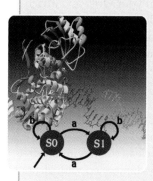

One of the newest computers is so tiny that one trillion of them can fit inside a drop of water. The hardware of this biological invention is composed of enzymes that manipulate DNA, and the software is composed of actual DNA.

The concept for this computer had been proposed in 1936, but the actual computer was developed at the Weizmann Institute in Israel in 2001. Today, researchers at the Weizmann Institute are developing applications that process biological information. Their most current success is being able to program the computer to diagnose and treat cancer.

The researchers are hopeful they will be able to have the medical computer function inside a human cell. For more information, visit scsite.com/dc2006/ch4/looking and then click DNA Computer.

PUTTING IT ALL TOGETHER

When you purchase a computer, it is important to understand how the components of the system unit work. Many components of the system unit influence the speed and power of a computer. These include the type of processor, the clock speed of the processor, the amount of RAM, bus width, and the clock speed of the bus. The configuration you require depends on your intended use.

The table in Figure 4-40 lists the suggested minimum processor, clock speed, and RAM requirements based on the needs of various types of computer users.

SUGGESTED MINIMUM CONFIGURATIONS BY USER

User	Processor, Clock Speed, and RAM
HOME 	Celeron (3 GHz or higher) or Sempron (2 GHz or higher) or Pentium 4 (2.8 GHz or higher) or Sempron (2 GHz or higher) Minimum RAM: 256 MB
SMALL OFFICE/ HOME OFFICE 	Pentium 4 (3 GHz or higher) or Athlon 64 (2.4 GHz or higher) Minimum RAM: 512 MB
MOBILE 	Celeron M (1.5 GHz or higher) or Pentium M (2 GHz or higher) or Mobile Sempron (1.8 GHz or higher) Minimum RAM: 512 MB
POWER 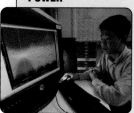	Itanium 2 (1.6 GHz or higher) or Opteron (2.4 GHz or higher) or Xeon MP (3 GHz or higher) or Athlon MP (2.25 GHz or higher) Minimum RAM: 2 GB
LARGE BUSINESS 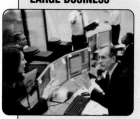	Pentium 4 (3.4 GHz or higher) or Athlon 64 (2.4 GHz or higher) Minimum RAM: 1 GB

FIGURE 4-40 Suggested processor, clock speed, and RAM configurations by user.

KEEPING YOUR COMPUTER CLEAN

Over time, the system unit collects dust — even in a clean environment. Built up dust can block airflow in the computer, which can cause it to overheat, corrode, or even stop working. By cleaning your computer once or twice a year, you can help extend its life. This preventive maintenance task requires a few basic products (Figure 4-41):

- can of compressed air — removes dust and lint from difficult-to-reach areas
- lint-free antistatic wipes and swabs
- bottle of rubbing alcohol
- small computer vacuum (or small attachments on your house vacuum)
- antistatic wristband — to avoid damaging internal components with static electricity
- small screwdriver (may be required to open the case or remove adapter cards)

Before cleaning the computer, turn it off, unplug it from the electrical outlet, and unplug all cables from the ports. Blow away any dust from all openings on the computer case, such as drives, slots, and ports. Vacuum the power supply fan on the back of the computer case to remove any dust that has accumulated on it. Next, release short blasts of compressed air on the power supply fan. Then, use an antistatic wipe to clean the exterior of the case.

If you need assistance opening the computer case, refer to the instructions that came with the computer. Once the case is open, put the antistatic wristband on your wrist and attach its clip to the case of the computer. Use the antistatic wipes to clean dust and grime inside the walls of the computer case. Vacuum as much dust as possible from the interior of the case, including the wires, chips, adapter cards, and fan blades. Next, release short blasts of compressed air in areas the vacuum cannot reach. If the motherboard and adapter cards still look dirty, gently clean them with lint-free wipes or swabs lightly dampened with alcohol.

When finished, be sure all adapter cards are tightly in their expansion slots. Then close the case, plug in all cables, and attach the power cord. Write down the date you cleaned the computer so you have a record for your next cleaning.

If you do not feel comfortable cleaning the system unit yourself, have a local computer company clean it for you.

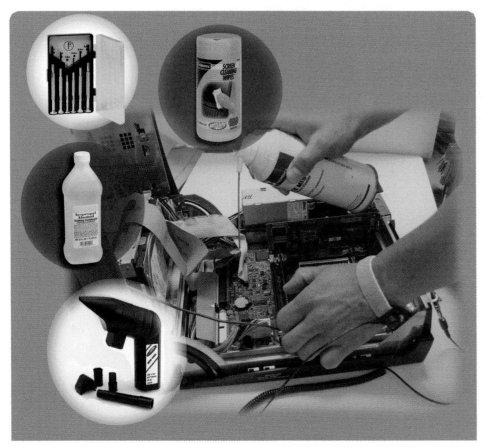

FIGURE 4-41 With a few products, this computer user keeps his computer clean.

FAQ 4-9

How do I clean components in the system unit?

Never pour or spray any form of liquid on the motherboard — or on any hardware. Always apply the liquid to a cloth or swab, and then use the cloth or swab to clean the hardware. If you can squeeze liquid out of the cloth or swab, then it is too moist. For more information, visit scsite.com/dc2006/ch4/faq and then click PC Hygiene.

Test your knowledge of pages 204 through 216 in Quiz Yourself 4-3.

QUIZ YOURSELF 4-3

Instructions: Find the true statement below. Then, rewrite the remaining false statements so they are true.

1. A bus is the point at which a peripheral attaches to a system unit so the peripheral can send data to or receive information from the computer.

2. An AC adapter is a socket on the motherboard that can hold an adapter card.

3. Near the power supply is a heater that keeps components of the system unit warm.

4. Serial ports can connect up to 127 different peripherals together with a single connector type.

5. The higher the bus clock speed, the slower the transmission of data.

6. When cleaning the inside of the system unit, wear an antistatic wristband to avoid damaging internal components with static electricity.

Quiz Yourself Online: To further check your knowledge of expansion slots, adapter cards, ports, buses, components of mobile computers and devices, and cleaning a computer, visit scsite.com/dc2006/ch4/quiz and then click Objectives 8 – 12.

CHAPTER SUMMARY

Chapter 4 presented the components of the system unit; described how memory stores data, instructions, and information; and discussed the sequence of operations that occur when a computer executes an instruction. The chapter included a comparison of various personal computer processors on the market today. It also discussed how to clean a system unit.

CAREER CORNER

Computer Engineer

A *computer engineer* designs and develops the electronic components found in computers and peripheral devices. They also can work as researchers, theorists, and inventors. Companies may hire computer engineers for permanent positions or as consultants, with jobs that extend from a few months to a few years, depending on the project. Engineers in research and development often work on projects that will not be released to the general public for two years.

Responsibilities vary from company to company. All computer engineering work, however, demands problem-solving skills and the ability to create and use new technologies. The ability to handle multiple tasks and concentrate on detail is a key component. Assignments often are taken on as part of a team. Therefore, computer engineers must be able to communicate clearly with both computer personnel and computer users, who may have little technical knowledge.

Before taking in-depth computer engineering design and development classes, students usually take mathematics, physics, and basic engineering. Computer engineering degrees include B.S., M.S., and Ph.D. Because computer engineers employed in private industry often advance into managerial positions, many computer engineering graduates obtain a master's degree in business administration (M.B.A.). Most computer engineers earn between $56,000 and $92,000 annually, depending on their experience and employer, but salaries can exceed $115,000. For more information, visit scsite.com/dc2006/ch4/careers and then click Computer Engineer.

High-Tech Talk

RANDOM ACCESS MEMORY (RAM): THE GENIUS OF MEMORY

Inside your computer, RAM takes the form of separate microchip modules that plug in slots on the computer's motherboard. These slots connect through a line (bus) or set of electrical paths to the computer's processor. Before you turn on a computer, its RAM is a blank slate. As you start and use your computer, the operating system files, applications, and any data currently being used by the processor are written to and stored in RAM so the processor can access them quickly.

How is this data written to and stored in RAM? In the most common form of RAM, dynamic random access memory (DRAM), *transistors* (in this case, acting as switches) and a *capacitor* (as a data storage element) create a *memory cell*, which represents a single bit of data.

Memory cells are etched onto a silicon wafer in a series of columns (bitlines) and rows (wordlines), known as an *array*. The intersection of a column and row constitutes the *address* of the memory cell (Figure 4-42). Each memory cell has a unique address that can be found by counting across columns and then counting down by row. The address of a character consists of a series of memory cell addresses put together.

To write data to RAM, the processor sends the memory controller the address of a memory cell in which to store data. The *memory controller* organizes the request and sends the column and row address in an electrical charge along the appropriate address lines, which are very thin electrical lines etched into the RAM chip. This causes the transistors along those address lines to close.

These transistors act as a switch to control the flow of electrical current in an either closed or open circuit. While the transistors are closed, the software sends bursts of electricity along selected data lines. When the electrical charge traveling down the data line reaches an address line where a transistor is closed, the charge flows through the closed transistor and charges the capacitor.

A capacitor works as electronic storage that holds an electrical charge. Each charged capacitor along the address line represents a 1 bit. An uncharged capacitor represents a 0 bit. The combination of 1s and 0s from eight data lines forms a single byte of data.

The capacitors used in dynamic RAM, however, lose their electrical charge. The processor or memory controller continuously has to recharge all of the capacitors holding a charge (a 1 bit) before the capacitor discharges. During this *refresh operation*, which happens automatically thousands of times per second, the memory controller reads memory and then immediately rewrites it. This refresh operation is what gives dynamic RAM its name. Dynamic RAM has to be refreshed continually, or it loses the charges that represent bits of data. A specialized circuit called a counter tracks the refresh sequence to ensure that all of the rows are refreshed.

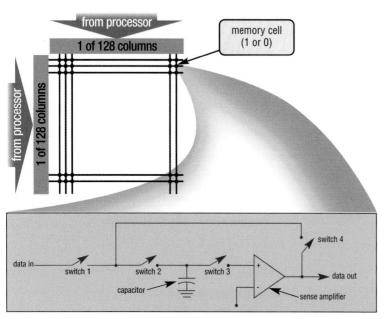

FIGURE 4-42   An illustration of one type of DRAM. When writing data, switches 1 and 2 in the circuit are closed and switches 3 and 4 are open. When reading data, switches 2, 3, and 4 in the circuit are closed and switch 1 is open. Most DRAM chips actually have arrays of memory cells (upper-left corner of figure) that are 16 rows deep.

The process of reading data from RAM uses a similar, but reverse, series of steps. When the processor gets the next instruction it is to perform, the instruction may contain the address of a memory cell from which to read data. This address is sent to the memory controller. To locate the memory cell, the memory controller sends the column and row address in an electrical charge down the appropriate address lines.

This electrical charge causes the transistors along the address line to close. At every point along the address line where a capacitor is holding a charge, the capacitor discharges through the circuit created by the closed transistors, sending electrical charges along the data lines.

A specialized circuit called a *sense amplifier* determines and amplifies the level of charge in the capacitor. A capacitor charge over a certain voltage level represents the binary value 1; a capacitor charge below that level represents a 0. The sensed and amplified value is sent back down the address line to the processor.

As long as a computer is running, data continuously is being written to and read from RAM. As soon as you shut down a computer, RAM loses its data. The next time you turn on a computer, operating system files and other data are again loaded into RAM and the read/write process starts all over. For more information, visit scsite.com/dc2006/ch4/tech and then click Memory.

Companies on the Cutting Edge

AMD
PC PROCESSOR SUPPLIER

Customer needs influence the integrated circuits *Advanced Micro Devices* (*AMD*) develops for the computing, communications, and consumer electronics industries. AMD calls this philosophy "customer-centric innovation."

As a global supplier of PC processors, AMD engineers its technologies at its Submicron Development Center (SDC) in Sunnyvale, California. The technologies are put into production at manufacturing facilities in the United States, Europe, Asia, and Japan.

Among the company's most recent products are the AMD Athlon 64 processor for desktop and personal computers and the AMD Opteron processor for servers and workstations. The company also is working with personal computer manufacturers to develop media-center computers based on its Athlon 64 chips for playing and distributing music and video throughout a home. For more information, visit scsite.com/dc2006/ch4/companies and then click AMD.

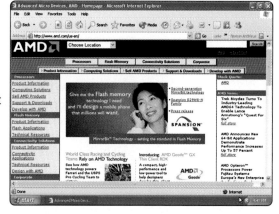

INTEL
CHIP MAKER DOMINATES THE COMPUTER MARKET

When Gordon Moore and Robert Noyce started Intel in 1968, their goal was to replace magnetic core memory with semiconductor memory. Noyce and Moore, together with Andy Grove, refined the process of placing thousands of tiny electronic devices on a silicon chip. In 1971, the company introduced the Intel 4004, the first single-chip microprocessor.

When IBM chose the Intel 8008 chip for its new personal computer in 1980, Intel chips became standard for all IBM-compatible personal computers. Today, Intel's microprocessors are the building blocks in countless personal computers, servers, networks, and communications devices. In 2003, Intel developed its Centrino mobile technology, which integrates wireless capabilities in notebook computers and Tablet PCs. For more information, visit scsite.com/dc2006/ch4/companies and then click Intel.

Technology Trailblazers

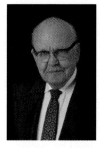

JACK KILBY
INTEGRATED CIRCUIT INVENTOR

Jack Kilby holds more than 60 patents, but one has changed the world. His integrated circuit, or microchip, invention made microprocessors possible.

Kilby started his work with miniature electrical components at Centralab, where he developed transistors for hearing aids. He then took a research position with Texas Instruments and developed a working model of the first integrated circuit, which was patented in 1959. Kilby applied this invention to various industrial, military, and commercial applications, including the first pocket calculator, called the Pocketronic.

Kilby is retired from Texas Instruments and works as a consultant and teacher. He was awarded the Nobel Prize in physics in 2000 for his invention of the integrated circuit, an invention he believes will continue to change the world. For more information, visit scsite.com/dc2006/ch4/people and then click Jack Kilby.

GORDON MOORE
INTEL COFOUNDER

More than 40 years ago, *Gordon Moore* predicted that the number of transistors and resistors placed on computer chips would double every year, with a proportional increase in computing power and decrease in cost. This bold forecast, now known as Moore's Law, proved amazingly accurate for 10 years. Then, Moore revised the estimate to doubling every two years.

Convinced of the future of silicon chips, Moore founded Intel in 1968. Moore's lifelong interest in technology was kindled at an early age when he experimented with a neighbor's chemistry set. Even then, he displayed the passion for practical outcomes that has typified his work as a scientist and engineer.

Moore says that the semiconductor industry's progress will far surpass that of nearly all other industries. For more information, visit scsite.com/dc2006/ch4/people and then click Gordon Moore.

Quizzes and Learning Games

Computer Genius
Crossword Puzzle
DC Track and Field
Practice Test
Quiz Yourself
Wheel of Terms
You're Hired!

Exercises

Case Studies
▷ Chapter Review
Checkpoint
Key Terms
Learn How To
Learn It Online
Web Research

Beyond the Book

Career Corner
Companies
FAQs
High-Tech Talk
Looking Ahead
Making Use of the Web
Trailblazers
Web Links

Features

Chapter Forum
Install Computer
Lab Exercises
Maintain Computer
Tech News
Timeline 2006

Chapter Review

The Chapter Review section summarizes the concepts presented in this chapter. To listen to the audio version of this Chapter Review, visit scsite.com/dc2006/ch4/review. To obtain help from other students regarding any subject in this chapter, visit scsite.com/dc2006/ch4/forum and post your thoughts or questions.

① How Are Various Styles of System Units Different?   The **system unit** is a case that contains electronic components of the computer used to process data. On desktop personal computers, most storage devices also are part of the system unit. On notebook computers, the keyboard and pointing device often occupy the area on top of the system unit, and the display attaches to the system unit by hinges. On mobile devices, the display often is built into the system unit.

② What Are Chips, Adapter Cards, and Other Components of the Motherboard?   The **motherboard** is the main circuit board of the system unit. The motherboard contains many electronic components including a processor chip, memory chips, expansion slots, and adapter cards. A **chip** is a small piece of semiconducting material, usually silicon, on which integrated circuits are etched. Expansion slots hold adapter cards that provide connections and functions not built into the motherboard.

③ What Are the Components of a Processor, and How Do They Complete a Machine Cycle?   The **processor** interprets and carries out the basic instructions that operate a computer. Processors contain a **control unit** that directs and coordinates most of the operations in the computer and an **arithmetic logic unit** (*ALU*) that performs arithmetic, comparison, and other operations. The *machine cycle* is a set of four basic operations — *fetching, decoding, executing,* and *storing* — that the processor repeats for every instruction. The control unit fetches program instructions and data from memory and decodes the instructions into commands the computer can execute.

④ What Are the Characteristics of Various Personal Computer Processors?   Intel produces the **Pentium** processor for high-performance PCs, the **Celeron** processor for basic PCs, and the **Xeon** and **Itanium** processors for workstations and low-end servers. AMD manufactures *Intel-compatible processors,* which have an internal design similar to Intel processors. Motorola produces the *Motorola processor,* with a design different from the Intel-style processor, for Apple computers. Some devices have a *system on a chip* processor that integrates the functions of a processor, memory, and a video card on a single chip.

> connect
> Visit scsite.com/dc2006/ch4/quiz or click the Quiz Yourself button. Click Objectives 1 – 4.

⑤ What Is a Bit, and How Does a Series of Bits Represent Data?   Most computers are **digital** and recognize only two discrete states: off and on. To represent these states, computers use the **binary system**, which is a number system that has just two unique digits — 0 (for off) and 1 (for on) — called bits. A **bit** is the smallest unit of data a computer can process. Grouped together as a unit, 8 bits form a **byte**, which provides enough different combinations of 0s and 1s to represent 256 individual characters. The combinations are defined by patterns, called coding schemes, such as *ASCII, EBCDIC,* and *Unicode.*

⑥ How Do Programs Transfer In and Out of Memory?   When an application program starts, the program's instructions load into memory from the hard disk. The program and operating system instructions are in memory, and the program's window is displayed on the screen. When you quit the program, the program instructions are removed from memory, and the program no longer is displayed on the screen.

Chapter Review

(7) What Are the Various Types of Memory? The system unit contains volatile and nonvolatile memory. *Volatile memory* loses its contents when the computer's power is turned off. *Nonvolatile memory* does not lose its contents when the computer's power is turned off. RAM is the most common type of volatile memory. ROM, flash memory, and CMOS are examples of nonvolatile memory. **RAM** consists of memory chips that can be read from and written to by the processor and other devices. **ROM** refers to memory chips storing permanent data and instructions that usually cannot be modified. **Flash memory** can be erased electronically and rewritten. **CMOS** technology uses battery power to retain information even when the power to the computer is turned off.

Visit scsite.com/dc2006/ch4/quiz or click the Quiz Yourself button. Click Objectives 5 – 7.

(8) What Are the Types of Expansion Slots and Adapter Cards? An **expansion slot** is a socket on the motherboard that can hold an adapter card. An **adapter card** is a circuit board that enhances functions of a component of the system unit and/or provides a connection to a **peripheral** such as a modem, disk drive, printer, scanner, or keyboard. Several types of adapter cards exist. A **sound card** enhances the sound-generating capabilities of a personal computer. A **video card** converts computer output into a video signal that displays an image on the screen. Many computers today support **Plug and Play**, which enables the computer to configure adapter cards and peripherals automatically.

(9) How Are a Serial Port, a Parallel Port, a USB Port, a FireWire port, and Other Ports Different? A **port** is the point at which a peripheral attaches to a system unit so it can send data to or receive information from the computer. A **serial port**, which transmits data one bit at a time, usually connects devices that do not require fast data transmission, such as a mouse, keyboard, or modem. A **parallel port**, which transfers more than one bit at a time, often connects a printer to the system unit. A **USB port** can connect up to 127 different peripherals together with a single connector type. A **FireWire port** can connect multiple types of devices that require faster data transmission speeds. Four special-purpose ports are MIDI, SCSI, IrDA, and Bluetooth. A **MIDI port** connects the system unit to a musical instrument. A **SCSI port** attaches the system unit to SCSI peripherals, such as disk drives. An **IrDA port** and **Bluetooth** technology allow wireless devices to transmit signals to a computer via infrared light waves or radio waves.

(10) How Do Buses Contribute to a Computer's Processing Speed? A **bus** is an electrical channel along which bits transfer within the circuitry of a computer, allowing devices both inside and attached to the system unit to communicate. The size of a bus, called the *bus width*, determines the number of bits that the computer can transmit at one time. The larger the bus width, the faster the computer transfers data.

(11) What Are the Components in Mobile Computers and Mobile Devices? In addition to the motherboard, processor, memory, sound card, PC Card slot, and **drive bay**, a mobile computer's system unit also houses devices such as the keyboard, pointing device, speakers, and display. The system unit for a typical notebook computer often has video, serial, parallel, modem, network, FireWire, USB, headphone, and microphone ports. Tablet PCs usually include several slots and ports. PDAs often have an IrDA port or are Bluetooth enabled so users can communicate wirelessly.

(12) How Do You Clean a System Unit? Before cleaning a system unit, turn off the computer and unplug it from the wall. Use a small vacuum and a can of compressed air to remove external dust. After opening the case, wear an antistatic wristband and vacuum the interior. Wipe away dust and grime using lint-free antistatic wipes and rubbing alcohol.

Visit scsite.com/dc2006/ch4/quiz or click the Quiz Yourself button. Click Objectives 8 – 12.

Quizzes and Learning Games

Computer Genius
Crossword Puzzle
DC Track and Field
Practice Test
Quiz Yourself
Wheel of Terms
You're Hired!

Exercises

Case Studies
Chapter Review
Checkpoint
▶ Key Terms
Learn How To
Learn It Online
Web Research

Beyond the Book

Career Corner
Companies
FAQs
High-Tech Talk
Looking Ahead
Making Use of the Web
Trailblazers
Web Links

Features

Chapter Forum
Install Computer
Lab Exercises
Maintain Computer
Tech News
Timeline 2006

Key Terms

You should know the Primary Terms and be familiar with the Secondary Terms. Use the list below to help focus your study. To further enhance your understanding of the Key Terms in this chapter, visit scsite.com/dc2006/ch4/terms. See an example of and a definition for each term, and access current and additional information about the term from the Web.

Primary Terms

(shown in bold-black characters in the chapter)

AC adapter (213)
access time (203)
adapter card (204)
analog (194)
arithmetic logic unit (188)
bay (212)
binary system (195)
bit (195)
Bluetooth (210)
bus (211)
byte (195)
cache (201)
Celeron (190)
central processing unit (CPU) (187)
chip (186)
clock speed (189)
complementary metal-oxide semiconductor (CMOS) (203)
connector (206)
control unit (187)
digital (194)
drive bays (212)
expansion slot (204)
FireWire port (209)
firmware (202)
flash memory (202)
flash memory card (205)
gigabyte (GB) (197)
gigahertz (GHz) (189)
IrDA port (210)
Itanium (190)
jack (206)

kilobyte (KB or K) (197)
megabyte (MB) (197)
memory (196)
memory cache (201)
memory module (199)
memory slots (199)
MIDI port (209)
motherboard (186)
nanosecond (203)
parallel port (207)
PC Card (205)
PC Card slot (205)
Pentium (190)
Pentium M (190)
peripheral (204)
Plug and Play (205)
port (206)
power supply (213)
processor (187)
RAM (198)
read-only memory (ROM) (201)
SCSI port (210)
serial port (207)
sound card (204)
system clock (189)
system unit (184)
terabyte (TB) (197)
USB hub (208)
USB port (207)
video card (204)
word size (211)
Xeon (190)

Secondary Terms

(shown in italic characters in the chapter)

Accelerated Graphics Port (AGP) (212)
address (196)
address bus (211)
advanced transfer cache (ATC) (201)
ALU (188)
American Standard Code for Information Interchange (ASCII) (195)
arithmetic operations (188)
binary digit (195)
bus width (211)
chassis (184)
clock cycle (189)
COM port (207)
comparison operations (188)
daisy chain (208)
data bus (211)
decoding (188)
DIMM (dual inline memory module) (199)
Double Data Rate SDRAM (DDR SDRAM) (199)
dual-core processor (190)
dynamic RAM (DRAM) (199)
EEPROM (electrically erasable programmable read-only memory) chip (202)
executing (188)
expansion bus (212)
expansion card (204)
Extended Binary Coded Decimal Interchange Code (EBCDIC) (195)
external drive bay (212)
fast infrared port (210)
female connectors (206)
fetching (188)
FireWire bus (212)
gender changer (206)
graphics card (204)
heat pipe (193)
heat sink (193)
hertz (189)
hot plugging (205)
Hyper-Threading (HT) Technology (190)
IBM processor (190)
IEEE 1394 port (209)
integrated circuit (186)
Intel-compatible processors (190)
internal drive bay (212)
IrDA (Infrared Data Association) (210)

L1 cache (201)
L2 cache (201)
L3 cache (201)
liquid cooling technology (193)
machine cycle (188)
magnetoresistive RAM (MRAM) (199)
main memory (198)
male connectors (206)
microcode (202)
microprocessor (187)
MIPS (millions of instructions per second) (190)
Motorola processor (190)
Musical Instrument Digital Interface (209)
nonvolatile memory (197)
ns (203)
parallel processing (194)
PC Card bus (212)
PCI bus (Peripheral Component Interconnect bus) (212)
Personal Computer Memory Card International Association (PCMCIA) cards (205)
pipelining (189)
PROM (programmable read-only memory) chip (202)
Rambus DRAM (RDRAM) (199)
random access memory (198)
registers (189)
RIMM (Rambus inline memory module) (199)
SCSI (small computer system interface) (210)
SIMM (single inline memory module) (199)
static RAM (SRAM) (199)
stored program concept (196)
storing (188)
superscalar (189)
synchronous DRAM (SDRAM) (199)
synthesizer (209)
system board (186)
system bus (212)
system on a chip (190)
transistor (186)
Unicode (195)
universal serial bus (212)
universal serial bus port (208)
USB 2.0 (208)
USB flash drive (205)
volatile memory (197)

Checkpoint

Use the Checkpoint exercises to check your knowledge level of the chapter. The Beyond the Book exercises will help broaden your understanding of the concepts presented in this chapter. To complete the Checkpoint exercises interactively, visit scsite.com/dc2006/ch4/check.

Label the Figure

Identify these components.

a. processor chip in a processor slot
b. motherboard
c. memory module
d. expansion slots
e. adapter cards

True/False

Mark T for True and F for False. (See page numbers in parentheses.)

_____ 1. On notebook computers, the keyboard and pointing device attach to the system unit by hinges. (185)

_____ 2. The processor interprets and carries out the basic instructions that operate a computer. (185)

_____ 3. The greater the number of transistors, the more complex and powerful the processor chip. (190)

_____ 4. A Pentium M processor typically is used for workstations and low-end servers. (192)

_____ 5. Replacing a motherboard is a fairly simple process, whereas replacing a processor is much more complicated. (192)

_____ 6. Computers can use only one processor at a time. (194)

_____ 7. A byte is the smallest unit of data the computer can process. (195)

_____ 8. Coding schemes make it possible for humans to interact with a digital computer that processes only bits. (195)

_____ 9. Magnetoresistive RAM stores data using magnetic charges instead of electrical charges. (199)

_____ 10. Two types of cache are memory cache and disk cache. (201)

_____ 11. Serial ports usually connect devices that require fast data transmission rates. (207)

_____ 12. Serial ports transfer more than one bit at a time. (207)

Quizzes and Learning Games

Computer Genius
Crossword Puzzle
DC Track and Field
Practice Test
Quiz Yourself
Wheel of Terms
You're Hired!

Exercises

Case Studies
Chapter Review
Checkpoint
Key Terms
Learn How To
Learn It Online
Web Research

Beyond the Book

Career Corner
Companies
FAQs
High-Tech Talk
Looking Ahead
Making Use of the Web
Trailblazers
Web Links

Features

Chapter Forum
Install Computer
Lab Exercises
Maintain Computer
Tech News
Timeline 2006

Checkpoint

 Multiple Choice   Select the best answer. (See page numbers in parentheses.)

1. On _____, the display often is built into the system unit. (185)
   a. desktop personal computers
   b. notebook computers
   c. mobile devices
   d. all of the above

2. The processor also is called the _____. (187)
   a. chip
   b. adapter card
   c. motherboard
   d. central processing unit (CPU)

3. Processors contain _____. (187)
   a. a chip and an adapter
   b. a motherboard and a port
   c. a control unit and an arithmetic logic unit
   d. adapter cards

4. _____ is the process of obtaining a program instruction or data item from memory. (188)
   a. Fetching   b. Decoding
   c. Executing   d. Storing

5. A processor contains small, high-speed storage locations, called _____, that temporarily hold data and instructions. (189)
   a. flash drives   b. registers
   c. jacks   d. heat sinks

6. Processors that can execute more than one instruction per clock cycle are said to be _____. (189)
   a. superscalar
   b. dual-core processors
   c. system on a chip
   d. flash drives

7. _____ is a 16-bit coding scheme that is capable of representing more than 65,000 characters and symbols, enough for almost all the world's current written languages. (195)
   a. Unicode   b. ASCII
   c. Microcode   d. EBCDIC

8. Memory stores _____. (196)
   a. the operating system and other system software
   b. application programs that carry out specific tasks
   c. the data being processed by the application program
   d. all of the above

9. A _____ of memory is equal to exactly 1,024 bytes, but often is rounded down to 1,000 bytes. (197)
   a. kilobyte (KB or K)
   b. megabyte (MB)
   c. gigabyte (GB)
   d. terabyte (TB)

10. A _____ is a type of memory module with pins on opposite sides of the circuit board that do not connect, and thus form two sets of contacts. (199)
    a. RIMM (Rambus inline memory module)
    b. DIMM (dual inline memory module)
    c. ROMM (Rambus online memory module)
    d. SIMM (single inline memory module)

11. Many of today's computers support _____, which means the computer automatically can configure adapter cards and other peripherals as you install them. (205)
    a. Pack and Go
    b. Park and Ride
    c. Pick and Choose
    d. Plug and Play

12. Personal computers typically have six to eight _____ either on the front or back of the system unit. (208)
    a. MIDI ports
    b. serial ports
    c. USB ports
    d. parallel ports

13. Word size is the _____. (211)
    a. pace of the system clock
    b. size of the bus
    c. amount of time it takes the processor to read instructions from memory
    d. number of bits the processor can interpret and execute at a given time.

14. _____ usually are installed in internal bays. (212)
    a. Floppy disk drives
    b. DVD drives
    c. Zip drives
    d. Hard disk drives

Checkpoint

Matching

Match the terms with their definitions. (See page numbers in parentheses.)

_____ 1. motherboard (186)

_____ 2. chip (186)

_____ 3. ALU (188)

_____ 4. byte (195)

_____ 5. memory (196)

_____ 6. RAM (198)

_____ 7. flash memory (202)

_____ 8. expansion slot (204)

_____ 9. PC Card (205)

_____ 10. FireWire port (209)

a. electronic components that store instructions, data, and results of processed data

b. eight bits formed together as a unit

c. thin, credit card-sized device that adds memory, storage, sound, fax/modem, network, and other capabilities to mobile computers

d. memory chips that can be read from and written to by the processor and other devices

e. performs arithmetic, comparison, and other operations

f. amount of time it takes the processor to read data, instructions, and information from memory

g. socket on the motherboard that can hold an adapter card

h. connects multiple types of devices that require faster data transmission speeds

i. main circuit board of the system unit

j. number of bits the processor can interpret and execute at a given time

k. nonvolatile memory that can be erased electronically and rewritten

l. small piece of semiconducting material on which integrated circuits are etched

Short Answer

Write a brief answer to each of the following questions.

1. What are the two parts of a processor? _____ What does each do? _____

2. What are the four basic operations in a machine cycle? _____ What is pipelining, and how does it affect processing speed? _____

3. What is the system clock? _____ How does clock speed affect a computer's speed? _____

4. What is a system on a chip? _____ What types of devices typically have them? _____

5. What is the difference between volatile and nonvolatile memory? _____ How does dynamic RAM differ from RAM? _____

Beyond the Book

Read the following book elements, learn more about each using the Web, and then write a brief report.

1. At Issue — Can Computers Think? (187), Computer Waste and the Environment: Whose Problem Is It? (193), Ready for RFID? (197), Do Lower Computer Prices Mean Less Value? (200), or Should Smart Shoes Be Banned from Competitive Events? (214)

2. Career Corner — Computer Engineer (217)

3. Companies on the Cutting Edge — AMD or Intel (219)

4. FAQs (189, 193, 200, 202, 203, 208, 210, 213, 216)

5. High-Tech Talk — Random Access Memory (RAM): The Genius of Memory (218)

6. Looking Ahead — U.S. Plans World's Fastest Computer (190) or DNA Computer Works to Fight Cancer (215)

7. Making Use of the Web — Resources (xx)

8. Picture Yourself Buying a Computer (182)

9. Technology Trailblazers — Jack Kilby or Gordon Moore (219)

10. Web Links (186, 189, 199, 201, 202, 204, 205, 206, 212)

Quizzes and Learning Games

Computer Genius
Crossword Puzzle
DC Track and Field
Practice Test
Quiz Yourself
Wheel of Terms
You're Hired!

Exercises

Case Studies
Chapter Review
Checkpoint
Key Terms
Learn How To
▷ Learn It Online
Web Research

Beyond the Book

Career Corner
Companies
FAQs
High-Tech Talk
Looking Ahead
Making Use of the Web
Trailblazers
Web Links

Features

Chapter Forum
Install Computer
Lab Exercises
Maintain Computer
Tech News
Timeline 2006

Learn It Online

Use the Learn It Online exercises to reinforce your understanding of the chapter concepts. To access the Learn It Online exercises, visit scsite.com/dc2006/ch4/learn.

1 At the Movies — Computing Clusters

To view the Computing Clusters movie, click the number 1 button. Locate your video and click the corresponding High-Speed or Dial-Up link, depending on your Internet connection. Watch the movie and then complete the exercise by answering the questions below. Many graphics and animation programs have heavy data loads. When using a processing cluster, these difficult, memory-intensive tasks can be divided over several different computers linked through a network. Using multiple computers to perform a big job means it gets done faster. What types of tasks are best accomplished by a cluster? How would you handle a large, time-consuming project?

2 At the Movies — USB Basics

To view the USB Basics movie, click the number 2 button. Locate your video and click the corresponding High-Speed or Dial-Up link, depending on your Internet connection. Watch the movie and then complete the exercise by answering the questions below. A universal serial bus (USB) is a peripheral bus standard developed by Intel which allows you to connect external equipment such as digital cameras and MP3 players to your computer. The USB enables the external equipment to communicate with your computer and share information and power. How can you tell if your USB port is working? What are some ways you can troubleshoot your USB ports?

3 Student Edition Labs — Understanding the Motherboard

Click the number 3 button. When the Student Edition Labs menu appears, click *Understanding the Motherboard* to begin. A new browser window will open. Follow the on-screen instructions to complete the Lab. When finished, click the Exit button. If required, submit your results to your instructor.

4 Student Edition Labs — Binary Numbers

Click the number 4 button. When the Student Edition Labs menu appears, click *Binary Numbers* to begin. A new browser window will open. Follow the on-screen instructions to complete the Lab. When finished, click the Exit button. If required, submit your results to your instructor.

5 Practice Test

Click the number 5 button. Answer each question. When completed, enter your name and click the Grade Test button to submit the quiz for grading. Make a note of any missed questions. If required, submit your score to your instructor.

6 Who Wants To Be a Computer Genius[2]?

Click the number 6 button to find out if you are a computer genius. Directions about how to play the game will be displayed. When you are ready to play, click the Play button. Submit your score to your instructor.

7 Wheel of Terms

Click the number 7 button to reinforce important terms you learned in this chapter by playing the Shelly Cashman Series version of this popular game. Directions about how to play the game will be displayed. When you are ready to play, click the Play button. Submit your score to your instructor.

Learn It Online

⑧ DC Track and Field

Click the number 8 button to use what you have learned in this chapter to compete against other students in three track and field events. Directions about how to play the game will be displayed. When you are ready to play, click the start first event button. If required, submit your score to your instructor.

⑨ You're Hired!

Click the number 9 button to use what you have learned in this chapter to embark on the path to a career in computers. Directions about how to play the game will be displayed. When you are ready to play, click the begin game button. If required, submit your score to your instructor.

⑩ Crossword Puzzle Challenge

Click the number 10 button. Complete the puzzle to reinforce skills you learned in this chapter. Directions about how to play the game will be displayed. When you are ready to play, click the Play button. Submit the completed puzzle to your instructor.

⑪ Lab Exercises

Click the number 11 button. When the Lab Exercises menu appears, click the exercise assigned by your instructor. A new browser window will open. Follow the on-screen instructions to complete the exercise. When finished, click the Exit button. If required, submit your results to your instructor.

⑫ In the News

In February 2006, the forerunner of the modern computer will have its 60th anniversary. By today's standards for electronic computers, the ENIAC (Electronic Numerical Integrator And Computer) was a grotesque monster. With 30 separate units, plus a power supply and forced-air cooling, it weighed more than 30 tons. Its 19,000 vacuum tubes, 1,500 relays, and hundreds of thousands of resistors, capacitors, and inductors consumed almost 200 kilowatts of electrical power. The ENIAC performed fewer than 1,000 calculations per minute; today, personal computers can process more than 300 million instructions per second. The rapid development of computing power and capabilities is astonishing, and the rate of that development is accelerating. Click the number 12 button and read a news article about the introduction of a new or improved computer component. What is the component? Who is introducing it? Will the component change the way people use computers? If so, how?

⑬ Chapter Discussion Forum

Select an objective from this chapter on page 183 about which you would like more information. Click the number 13 button, and post a short message listing a meaningful message title accompanied by one or more questions concerning the selected objective. In two days, return to the threaded discussion by clicking the number 13 button. Submit to your instructor your original message and at least one response to your message.

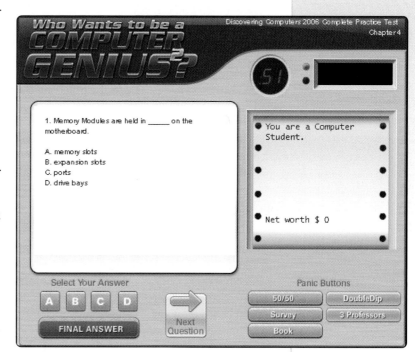

Quizzes and Learning Games

Computer Genius
Crossword Puzzle
DC Track and Field
Practice Test
Quiz Yourself
Wheel of Terms
You're Hired!

Exercises

Case Studies
Chapter Review
Checkpoint
Key Terms
Learn How To
Learn It Online
Web Research

Beyond the Book

Career Corner
Companies
FAQs
High-Tech Talk
Looking Ahead
Making Use of the Web
Trailblazers
Web Links

Features

Chapter Forum
Install Computer
Lab Exercises
Maintain Computer
Tech News
Timeline 2006

 Learn How To

Use the Learn How To activities to learn fundamental skills when using a computer and accompanying technology. Complete the exercises and submit them to your instructor. Visit scsite.com/dc2006/ch4/howto to obtain more information pertaining to each activity.

LEARN HOW TO 1: Purchase and Install Memory in a Computer

One of the less expensive and more effective ways to speed up a computer, make it capable of processing more programs at the same time, and enable it to handle graphics, gaming, and other high-level programs is to increase the amount of memory. The process of increasing memory is accomplished in two phases — purchasing the memory and installing the memory. To purchase memory for a computer, complete the following steps:

1. Determine the amount of memory currently in the computer. For a method to do this, see Learn How To number 3 in Chapter 1.
2. Determine the maximum amount of memory your computer can contain. This value can change for different computers, based primarily on the number of slots on the motherboard available for memory and the size of the **memory modules** you can place in each slot. On most computers, different size memory modules can be inserted in slots. A computer, therefore, might allow a 128 MB, 256 MB, or 512 MB memory module to be inserted in each slot. To determine the maximum memory for a computer, multiply the number of memory slots on the computer by the maximum size memory module that can be inserted in each slot.

    For example, if a computer contains four memory slots and is able to accept memory modules of 128 MB, 256 MB, or 512 MB in each of its memory slots, the maximum amount of memory the computer can contain is 2 GB (4 x 512 MB).

    You can find the number of slots and the allowable sizes of each memory module by contacting the computer manufacturer, looking in the computer's documentation, or contacting sellers of memory such as Kingston (www.kingston.com) or Crucial (www.crucial.com) on the Web. These sellers have documentation for most computers, and even programs you can download to run on your computer that will specify how much memory your computer currently has and how much you can add.

3. Determine how much memory you want to add, which will be somewhere between the current memory and the maximum memory allowed on the computer.
4. Determine the current configuration of memory on the computer. For example, if a computer with four memory slots contains 512 MB of memory, it could be using one memory module of 512 MB in a single slot and the other three slots would be empty; two memory modules of 256 MB each in two slots with two slots empty; one memory module of 256 MB and two memory modules of 128 MB each in three slots with one slot empty; or four memory modules of 128 MB each in four slots with no slots empty. You may be required to look inside the system unit to make this determination. The current memory configuration on a computer will determine what new memory modules you should buy to increase the memory to the amount determined in Step 3.

    You also should be aware that a few computers require memory to be installed in matching pairs. This means a computer with four slots could obtain 512 MB of memory with two memory modules of 256 MB in two slots, or four memory modules of 128 MB in four slots.

5. Determine the number of available memory slots on your computer and the number and size memory modules you must buy to fulfill your requirement. Several scenarios can occur (in the following examples, assume you can install memory one module at a time).
    a. Scenario 1: The computer has one or more open slots. In this case, you might be able to purchase a memory module that matches the amount of memory increase you desire. For example, if you want to increase memory by 256 MB, you should purchase a 256 MB memory module for insertion in the open slot. Generally, you should buy the maximum size module you can for an open slot. So, if you find two empty slots and wish to increase memory by 256 MB, it is smarter to buy one 256 MB module and leave one empty slot rather than buy two 128 MB memory modules and use both slots. This allows you to increase memory again without removing currently used modules.

Learn How To

    b. Scenario 2: The computer has no open slots. For example, a computer containing 512 MB of memory could have four slots each containing 128 MB memory modules. If you want to increase the memory on the computer to 1 GB, you will have to remove some of the 128 MB memory modules and replace them with the new memory modules you purchase. In this example, you want to increase the memory by 512 MB. You would have several options: (1) You could replace all four 128 MB memory modules with 256 MB memory modules; (2) You could replace all four 128 MB memory modules with two 512 MB memory modules; (3) You could replace one 128 MB memory module with a 512 MB memory module, and replace a second 128 MB module with a 256 MB memory module. Each of these options results in a total memory of 1 GB. The best option will depend on the price of memory and whether you anticipate increasing the memory size at a later time. The least expensive option probably would be number 3.

    c. Scenario 3: Many combinations can occur. You may have to perform calculations to decide the combination of modules that will work for the number of slots on the computer and the desired additional memory.

6. Determine the type of memory to buy for the computer. Computer memory has many types and configurations, and it is critical that you buy the kind of memory for which the computer was designed. It is preferable to buy the same type of memory that currently is found in the computer. That is, if the memory is DDR SDRAM with a certain clock speed, then that is the type of additional memory you should place in the computer. The documentation for the computer should specify the memory type. In addition, the Web sites cited above, and others as well, will present a list of memory modules that will work with your computer. Enough emphasis cannot be placed on the fact that the memory you buy must be compatible with the type of memory usable on your computer. Because there are so many types and configurations, you must be especially diligent to ensure you purchase the proper memory for your computer.

7. Once you have determined the type and size of memory to purchase, buy it from a reputable dealer. Buying poor or mismatched memory is a major reason for a computer's erratic performance and is a difficult problem to troubleshoot.

After purchasing the memory, you must install it on your computer. Complete the following steps to install memory:

1. Unplug the computer, and remove all electrical cords and device cables from the ports on the computer. Open the case of the system unit. You may want to consult the computer's documentation to determine the exact procedure.

2. Ground yourself so you do not generate static electricity that can cause memory or other components within the system unit to be damaged. To do this, wear an antistatic wristband you can purchase inexpensively in a computer or electronics store; or, before you touch any component within the system unit, touch an unpainted metal surface. If you are not wearing an antistatic wristband, periodically touch an unpainted metal surface to dissipate any static electricity.

3. Within the system unit, find the memory slots on the motherboard. The easiest way to do this is look for memory modules that are similar to those you purchased. The memory slots often are located near the processor. If you cannot find the slots, consult the documentation. A diagram often is available to help you spot the memory slots.

4. Insert the memory module in the next empty slot. Orient the memory module in the slot to match the modules currently installed. A notch or notches on the memory module will ensure you do not install the module backwards. If your memory module is a DIMM, insert the module straight down into grooves on the clips and then apply gentle pressure. If your memory is SIMM, insert the module at a 45 degree angle and then rotate it to a vertical position until the module snaps into place.

5. If you must remove one or more memory modules before inserting the new memory, carefully release the clips before lifting the memory module out of the memory slot.

6. Plug in the machine and replace all the device cables without replacing the cover.

7. Start the computer. In most cases, the new memory will be recognized and the computer will run normally. If an error message appears, determine the cause of the error.

8. Replace the computer cover.

Exercise

1. Assume you have a computer that contains 256 MB of memory. It contains four memory slots. Each slot can contain 128 MB or 256 MB memory modules. Two of the slots contain 128 MB memory modules. What memory chip(s) would you buy to increase the memory on the computer to 512 MB? What is the maximum memory on the computer? Submit your answers to your instructor.

2. Assume you have a computer that contains 1 GB of memory. It contains four memory slots. Each slot can contain 128 MB, 256 MB, 512 MB, or 1 GB memory modules. Currently, each slot contains a 256 MB memory module. What combinations of memory modules will satisfy your memory upgrade to 2 GB? Visit a Web site to determine which of these combinations is the least expensive. Submit your answers and recommendations to your instructor.

Quizzes and Learning Games

Computer Genius
Crossword Puzzle
DC Track and Field
Practice Test
Quiz Yourself
Wheel of Terms
You're Hired!

Exercises

Case Studies
Chapter Review
Checkpoint
Key Terms
Learn How To
Learn It Online
Web Research

Beyond the Book

Career Corner
Companies
FAQs
High-Tech Talk
Looking Ahead
Making Use of the Web
Trailblazers
Web Links

Features

Chapter Forum
Install Computer
Lab Exercises
Maintain Computer
Tech News
Timeline 2006

Web Research

Use the Internet-based Web Research exercises to broaden your understanding of the concepts presented in this chapter. Visit scsite.com/dc2006/ch4/research to obtain more information pertaining to each exercise. To discuss any of the Web Research exercises in this chapter with other students, post your thoughts or questions at scsite.com/dc2006/ch4/forum.

(1) Scavenger Hunt   Use one of the **search engines** listed in Figure 2-8 in Chapter 2 on page 78 or your own favorite search engine to find the answers to the questions below. Copy and paste the Web address from the Web page where you found the answer. Some questions may have more than one answer. If required, submit your answers to your instructor. (1) Which Microsoft Windows operating systems support USB? (2) The USB port supports hot plugging or hot swapping. What is "hot plugging"? (3) What is the name of the suit that people wear when they work in chip manufacturing clean rooms? (4) What is the name of the group of integrated circuits designed to orchestrate the flow of data to and from key components of a personal computer? (5) What is the name of the type of memory that retains its contents until it is exposed to ultraviolet light?

(2) Search Sleuth   **Ask Jeeves** (ask.com) is one of the faster growing research Web sites. The search engine uses natural language, which allows researchers to type millions of questions each day using words a human would use rather than words a computer understands. Visit this Web site and then use your word processing program to answer the following questions. Then, if required, submit your answers to your instructor. (1) Click the P.G. Wodehouse link at the bottom of the home page. Who are P.G. Wodehouse and Bertie Wooster? (2) Click your browser's Back button or press the BACKSPACE key to return to the Ask Jeeves home page. Click the Search text box and then type `What were the top grossing films this weekend?` as the keywords in the Search text box. (3) Scroll through the links Ask Jeeves returns and then click one that provides the information requested. What three films grossed the most money this weekend? How much did the top film gross? (4) Click your browser's Back button or press the BACKSPACE key to return to the Ask Jeeves home page. Click the News Search link at the bottom of the page. (5) Click one of the Top Stories links and review the material. Summarize the information you read and then write a 50-word summary.

(3) Journaling   Respond to your readings in this chapter by writing at least one page containing your reactions, evaluations, and reflections about when you have considered **buying a computer**. For example, did you shop online, at a local computer dealer, at a local large retail store, or your school bookstore? What type of processor? How much memory? Desktop or mobile? Apple or PC? What type of ports did the computer have? How many bays? You also can write about the new terms you learned by reading this chapter. If required, submit your journal to your instructor.

(4) Expanding Your Understanding   A **brick-and-click** business allows customers to conduct transactions at a physical location as well as online. Many banks and retailers, such as Citibank and Best Buy, are brick-and-click businesses. Choose a brick-and-click business and then visit the physical location and its Web site. Compare the type, availability, and cost of products or services. Write a report summarizing your findings, focusing on the advantages and disadvantages of conducting business at a physical location and online. If required, submit your report to your instructor.

(5) Ethics in Action   More than 50 law enforcement agencies use handheld wireless devices to access commercial databases. For example, Massachusetts state police stationed at Logan International Airport use the **LocatePLUS Holdings Corporation**'s database, which has information on 98 percent of Americans. The data is composed of motor vehicle records, credit bureau reports, property tax payments, and telephone directories. Police say accessing this information helps them perform their jobs more efficiently. Privacy experts, in contrast, say that information collected for one purpose should not be available in other contexts. View online sites that provide information about commercial databases for sale. Write a report summarizing your findings, and include a table of links to Web sites that provide additional details. If required, submit your report to your instructor.

Case Studies

Use the Case Studies to apply the concepts presented in the chapter to real-world situations. Visit scite.com/dc2006/ch4/cases to obtain more information pertaining to each exercise. To discuss the Case Studies in this chapter with other students, visit scite.com/dc2006/ch4/forum and post your thoughts or questions.

CASE STUDY 1 — Class Discussion   You are the office manager at SportsGraphics, a company that designs and produces apparel for local school and recreational sports teams. The company has 25 nonnetworked computers that are used by various departments for common business applications. The computers are four years old, and you would like to replace them. The director of information technology agrees, but he has reservations. He has asked you to complete a study on the cost of new computers, comparing the major features found on **system units** at three different price levels: less than $800; $800 to $1,500; and greater than $1,500. Prepare a brief summary report on the major features of system units at the various price levels. Include recommendations on which system units would meet the company's needs most economically. Be prepared to discuss your recommendations in class.

CASE STUDY 2 — Class Discussion   On Demand Computing, Inc. has decided to upgrade several hundred PCs used in their offices nationwide. The Information Technology Department has recommended that the company again purchase PCs for approximately $1,200 each. The system units would include Pentium 4 processors with speeds of 3.0 GHz with 512 MB of RAM. From her days in college, the CFO has preferred Apple computers and currently uses an **Apple iMac** at home. She has hired you as a consultant to determine if the company would be better off purchasing iMacs in the same price range and with similar capabilities. Use the Web and/or print media to select a comparable iMac. Which one starts faster? Which one opens files faster? Which one loads Web pages faster? Is the iMac in the same price range as the PC? List any other advantages and disadvantages of each. Prepare a brief summary report and be prepared to discuss your findings in class.

CASE STUDY 3 — Research   Your family has decided to purchase a computer for use at home. Because you are enrolled in a computer course, you have been asked to make recommendations. Your instructor has pushed the premise "software drives hardware." List the application programs you and your family members plan to use. Visit the Web sites of the manufacturers of each application program, and note the capabilities required of the system unit (type of processor, amount of **RAM**, and so on). On the basis of your findings, what are the minimum system requirements you and your family would require in a personal computer? What system requirements would be sufficient to provide a "cushion" so that you could be sure the system also could run other, or new, application packages? Write a brief report and share your findings with your class.

CASE STUDY 4 — Research   Many system unit manufacturers provide a toll-free telephone number that customers can call with technical problems or questions. If the **service technician** determines a difficulty is a hardware problem that the customer can fix, the technician might ask the customer to open the system unit and make some adjustments. For this reason, every computer user can benefit by being familiar with the inside of the system unit. If you own a personal computer or have access to a personal computer, unplug the power supply and take the cover off the system unit. Be careful not to touch any of the system unit components. Make a sketch of the system unit and try to identify each part. By referring to the computer's *User Guide*, list some of the computer's specifications (clock speed, memory size, and so on). Compare your sketch and list with a classmate who has done this exercise with a different computer. How are the computers similar? How are they different?

CASE STUDY 5 — Team Challenge   The chief financial officer of SkateJam, Inc. has asked her Information Technology Department to look into replacing the company's desktop computers with **notebook computers**. The director of information technology has hired your team as consultants to examine the advantages and disadvantages of notebook computers. Form a three-member team and assign each team member one of the following companies — Dell, HP, and Apple. Have each member of your team use the Web and/or print media to find a notebook computer and a desktop computer with comparable middle-of-the-road system units sold by the company assigned to them. What is the price of each computer? How are the processors and RAM similar? How are they different? Meet with the members of your team to discuss results of your investigations. Is the notebook computer the better buy? If so, why? Write a summary report or use PowerPoint to create a group presentation and share your findings with the class.

CHAPTER FIVE

Input

Picture Yourself Going Digital

Your daughter claims you have been stuck in the last decade — still connected by cords, still writing appointments in a daily planner, still using the house telephone as your main method of communication, and still visiting photo labs to process 35 mm film. To get up to speed with digital technology, you have been using gift cards that you have received for birthdays and other occasions to purchase new devices for your computer.

First, you bought a wireless keyboard and mouse, which the sales clerk explained communicates via radio waves. More importantly to you, these two devices give you the freedom to work without the clutter of cords. You now can position the keyboard and mouse anywhere on your desk and not worry about whether the cord is long enough.

You then bought a smart phone that has PDA capabilities. First, you learned how to enter contact information and appointments and how to use the digital pen. Next, you learned how to send picture messages and post them to a Web site. You plan to send or post regular photo updates to keep friends and family up-to-date of all your activities.

Most recently, you purchased a digital camera. You have become quite adept at transferring the digital images to your computer, editing them with your photo editing software, printing the images in a variety of sizes, and, of course, e-mailing the pictures.

To learn more about keyboards, mouse devices, input for PDAs and smart phones, and digital cameras, read Chapter 5 and discover features of many other types of input devices.

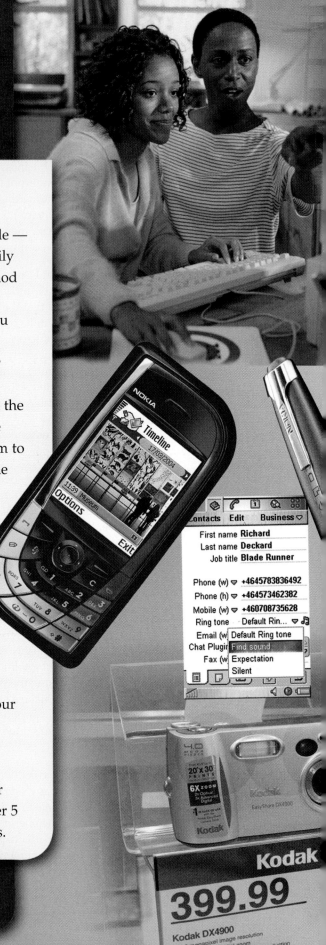

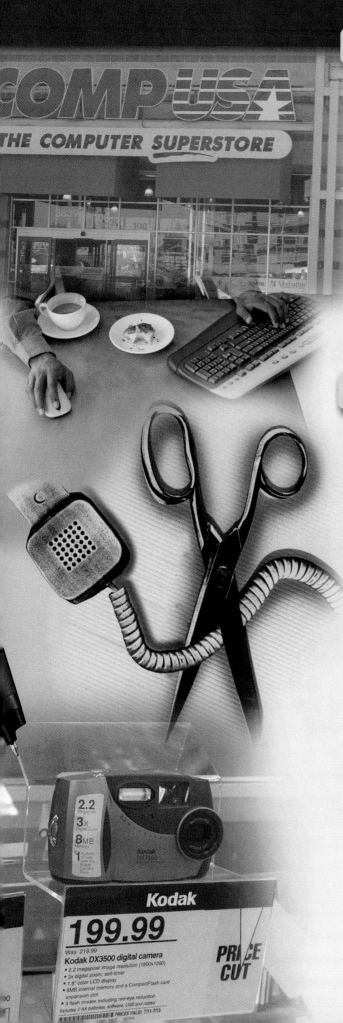

Kodak

199.99

Was 219.99
Kodak DX3500 digital camera
• 2.2 megapixel image resolution (1800x1200)
• 3x digital zoom; self-timer
• 1.8" color LCD display
• 8MB internal memory and a CompactFlash card
• expansion slot
• 3 flash modes including red-eye reduction
• Includes 2 AA batteries, software, USB and cables

PRICES VALID: 7/11-7/13

PRICE CUT

OBJECTIVES

After completing this chapter, you will be able to:

1. Define input
2. List the characteristics of a keyboard
3. Describe different mouse types and how they work
4. Summarize how various pointing devices work
5. Explain how voice recognition works
6. Describe various input devices for PDAs, smart phones, and Tablet PCs
7. Explain how a digital camera works
8. Describe the uses of PC video cameras, Web cams, and video conferencing
9. Discuss various scanners and reading devices and how they work
10. Explain the types of terminals
11. Summarize the various biometric devices
12. Identify alternative input devices for physically challenged users

CONTENTS

WHAT IS INPUT?

WHAT ARE INPUT DEVICES?

THE KEYBOARD
Keyboard Connections
Keyboard Ergonomics

POINTING DEVICES

MOUSE
Mouse Types
Using a Mouse

OTHER POINTING DEVICES
Trackball
Touchpad
Pointing Stick
Joystick and Wheel
Light Pen
Touch Screen
Pen Input

VOICE INPUT
Audio Input

INPUT FOR PDAs, SMART PHONES, AND TABLET PCs
PDAs
Smart Phones
Tablet PCs

DIGITAL CAMERAS
Digital Camera Quality

VIDEO INPUT
PC Video Cameras
Web Cams
Video Conferencing

SCANNERS AND READING DEVICES
Optical Scanners
Optical Readers
Bar Code Readers
RFID Readers
Magnetic Stripe Card Readers
MICR Readers
Data Collection Devices

TERMINALS
Point-of-Sale Terminals
Automated Teller Machines

BIOMETRIC INPUT

PUTTING IT ALL TOGETHER

INPUT DEVICES FOR PHYSICALLY CHALLENGED USERS

CHAPTER SUMMARY

HIGH-TECH TALK
Biometrics: Personalized Security

COMPANIES ON THE CUTTING EDGE
Logitech
palmOne

TECHNOLOGY TRAILBLAZERS
Hideki Komiyama
Douglas Engelbart

WHAT IS INPUT?

Input is any data and instructions entered into the memory of a computer. As shown in Figure 5-1, people have a variety of options for entering data or instructions into a computer.

Input to a computer consists of either data or instructions. As discussed in Chapter 1, *data* is a collection of unprocessed text, numbers, images, audio, and video. Once data is in memory, the computer interprets and executes instructions to process the data into information. Instructions entered into the computer can be in the form of programs, commands, and user responses.

• A *program* is a series of instructions that tells a computer what to do and how to do it. When a programmer writes a program, he or she enters the program into the computer by using a keyboard, mouse, or other input device. The programmer then stores the program in a file that a user can execute

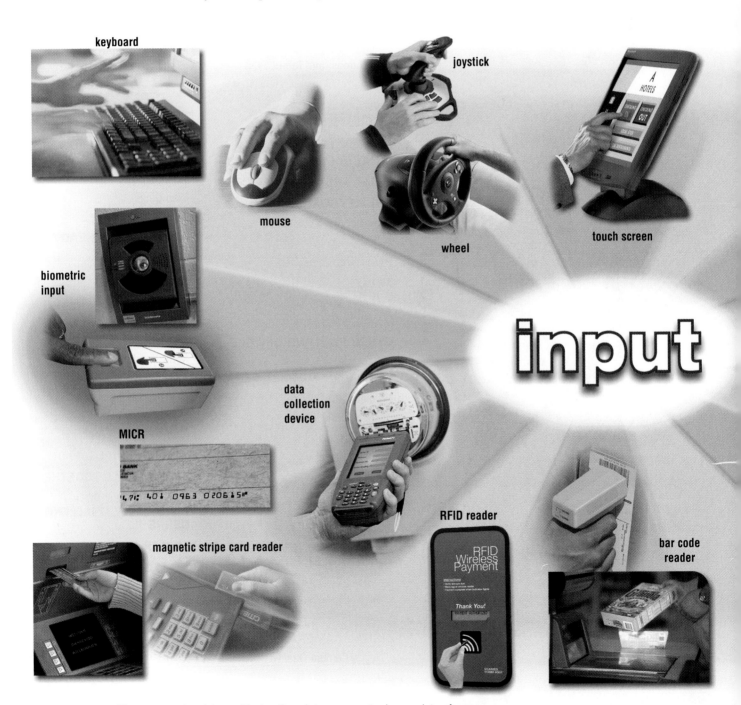

FIGURE 5-1 Users can enter data and instructions into a computer in a variety of ways.

(run). When a user runs a program, the computer loads the program from a storage medium into memory. Thus, a program is entered into a computer's memory.

- Programs respond to commands that a user issues. A *command* is an instruction that causes a program to perform a specific action. Users issue commands by typing or pressing keys on the keyboard, clicking a mouse button, speaking into a microphone, or touching an area on a screen.

- A *user response* is an instruction a user issues by replying to a question displayed by a program. A response to the question instructs the program to perform certain actions. Assume the program asks the question, Is the time card correct? If you answer Yes, the program processes the time card. If you answer No, the program gives you the opportunity to modify the time card entries.

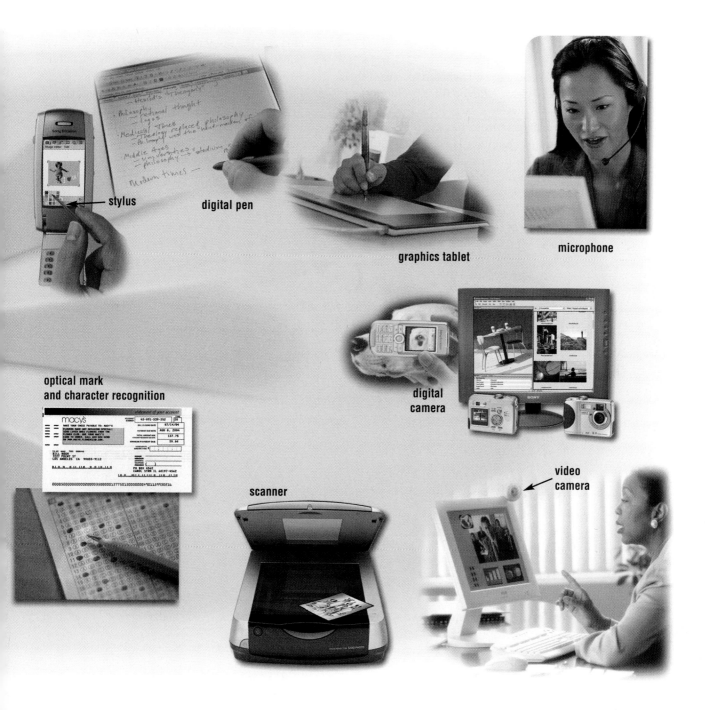

stylus

digital pen

graphics tablet

microphone

optical mark and character recognition

digital camera

video camera

scanner

WHAT ARE INPUT DEVICES?

An **input device** is any hardware component that allows users to enter data and instructions (programs, commands, and user responses) into a computer. Depending on the application and your particular requirements, the input device selected may vary. The following pages discuss a variety of input devices.

Storage devices, such as disk drives, serve as both input and output devices. Chapter 7 discusses storage devices.

THE KEYBOARD

Many people use a keyboard as one of their input devices. A **keyboard** is an input device that contains keys users press to enter data and instructions into a computer (Figure 5-2).

Desktop computer keyboards typically have from 101 to 105 keys. Keyboards for smaller computers such as notebook computers contain fewer keys. All computer keyboards have a typing area that includes the letters of the alphabet, numbers, punctuation marks, and other basic keys. Many desktop computer keyboards also have a numeric keypad on the right side of the keyboard. A keyboard also contains other keys that allow users to enter data and instructions into the computer. Read At Issue 5-1 for a related discussion.

Most of today's desktop computer keyboards are enhanced keyboards. An *enhanced keyboard* has twelve function keys along the top; it also has two CTRL keys, two ALT keys, and a set of arrow and additional keys between the typing area and the numeric keypad (Figure 5-2). *Function keys,* which are labeled with the letter F followed by a number, are special keys programmed to issue commands to a computer. The command associated with a function key may vary, depending on the program with which you are interacting. For example, the F3 key may issue one command to an operating system and an entirely different

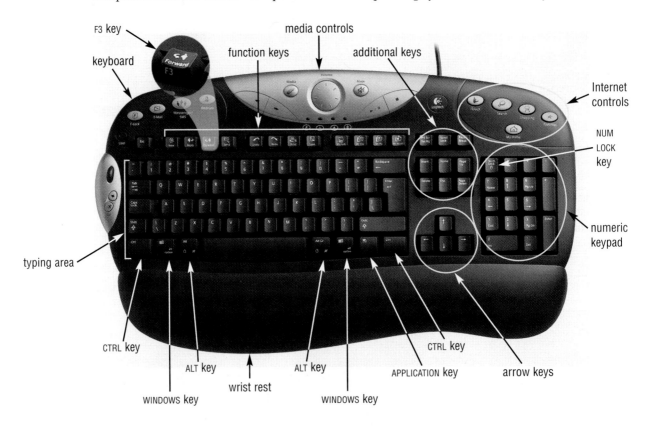

FIGURE 5-2 On a desktop computer keyboard, you type using keys in the typing area and on the numeric keypad.

AT ISSUE 5-1

Keyboard Monitoring — Privacy Risk?

Are you nervous about your employees' work on company computers? Are you curious about your spouse's long e-mail messages to a mutual friend? Are you concerned about your teenager's conversations in Internet chat rooms? Keyboard monitoring software can dispel your doubts. When installed on a computer, *keyboard monitoring software* records every keystroke in a hidden file, which later can be accessed by supplying the correct password. With keyboard monitoring software, you can see everything that was typed on the computer keyboard, including documents, e-mail, and other messages. In an office, keyboard monitoring software can be used to measure employee productivity by counting the number of keystrokes per hour. Some programs also store a record of software used, Web sites visited, user logons, and periodic screen shots. The software can run completely undetected. With keyboard monitoring software, you can catch a disgruntled employee preparing a resume on company time, discover that your spouse is e-mailing gardening tips, or recognize that your teenager has made a potentially dangerous contact in a chat room. Many maintain, however, that keyboard monitoring software is an invasion of privacy. Should keyboard monitoring software ever be used? If so, when? Some marketers of keyboard monitoring software recommend computer users be informed that the software is installed. Is this a good idea? Why or why not?

command to a word processing program. To issue commands, users often can press a function key in combination with other special keys (SHIFT, CTRL, ALT, and others).

Nearly all keyboards have toggle keys. A *toggle key* is a key that switches between two states each time a user presses the key. When you press the NUM LOCK key, for example, it locks the numeric keypad so you can use the keypad to type numbers. When you press the NUM LOCK key again, the numeric keypad unlocks so the same keys can serve to move the insertion point. Many keyboards have status lights that light up when you activate a toggle key.

Keyboards also often have a WINDOWS key(s) and an APPLICATION key. When pressed, the WINDOWS key displays the Start menu, and the APPLICATION key displays an item's shortcut menu.

Keyboards also contain keys that allow you to position the insertion point, also known as a *cursor* in some programs. The **insertion point** is a symbol on the screen, usually a blinking vertical bar, that indicates where the next character you type will be displayed (Figure 5-3). Users can move the insertion point left, right, up, or down by pressing the arrow keys and other keys on the keyboard.

Newer keyboards include media control buttons that allow you to access the computer's CD/DVD drive and adjust speaker volume, and Internet control buttons that allow you to open an e-mail program, start a Web browser, and search the Internet. Some keyboards also have USB ports so a user can plug a USB device directly in the keyboard instead of in the system unit.

FAQ 5-1

What is the rationale for the arrangement of keys in the typing area?

The keys originally were arranged to reduce the frequency of key jams on old mechanical typewriters. Called a *QWERTY keyboard*, the first letters on the top alphabetic line spell QWERTY. A *Dvorak keyboard*, by contrast, places frequently typed letters in the middle of the typing area. Despite the Dvorak keyboard's logical design, most people and computers use a QWERTY keyboard. For more information, visit scsite.com/dc2006/ch5/faq and then click Keyboards.

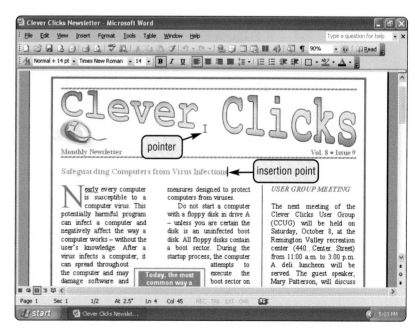

FIGURE 5-3 In most programs, such as Word, the insertion point is a blinking vertical bar. You use the keyboard or other input device to move the insertion point. The pointer, another symbol that is displayed on the screen, is controlled using a pointing device such as a mouse.

Keyboard Connections

Desktop computer keyboards often attach via a cable to a serial port, a keyboard port, or a USB port on the system unit. Some keyboards, however, do not use wires at all. A *wireless keyboard*, or *cordless keyboard*, is a battery-powered device that transmits data using wireless technology, such as radio waves or infrared light waves. Wireless keyboards often communicate with a receiver attached to a port on the system unit. The port type varies depending on the type of wireless technology. For example, a Bluetooth-enabled keyboard communicates via radio waves with a Bluetooth receiver plugged in a serial, parallel, or USB port (Figure 5-4).

On notebook computers and some handheld computers, PDAs, and smart phones, the keyboard is built in the top of the system unit. To fit in these mobile computers and devices, the keyboards usually are smaller and have fewer keys. A typical notebook computer keyboard usually has only about 85 keys. To provide all of the functionality of a desktop computer keyboard, manufacturers design many of the keys to serve two or three purposes.

Keyboard Ergonomics

Regardless of size, many keyboards have a rectangular shape with the keys aligned in straight, horizontal rows. Users who spend a lot of time typing on these keyboards sometimes experience repetitive strain injuries (RSI) of their wrists and hands. For this reason, some manufacturers offer ergonomic keyboards. An *ergonomic keyboard* has a design that reduces the chance of wrist and hand injuries. Even keyboards that are not ergonomically designed attempt to offer a user more comfort by including a wrist rest or palm rest (Figure 5-2 on page 236).

The goal of **ergonomics** is to incorporate comfort, efficiency, and safety in the design of the workplace. Employees can be injured or develop disorders of the muscles, nerves, tendons, ligaments, and joints from working in an area that is not ergonomically designed.

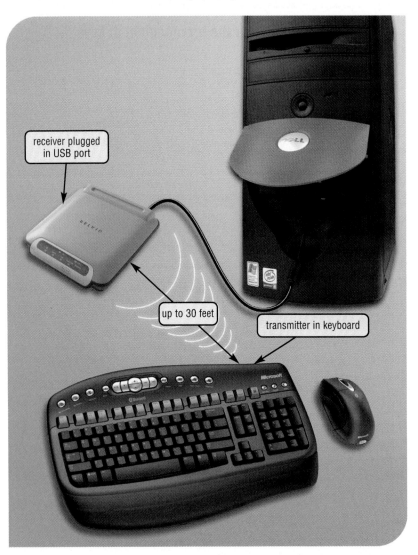

receiver plugged in USB port

up to 30 feet

transmitter in keyboard

FIGURE 5-4   Some personal computers have built-in Bluetooth technology. On computers that are not Bluetooth-enabled, you plug a Bluetooth receiver in a USB port or serial port on the system unit. A transmitter inside the keyboard communicates with the receiver, which should be within 30 feet from each other.

FAQ 5-2

What can I do to reduce chances of experiencing repetitive strain injuries?

Do not rest your wrist on the edge of a desk; use a wrist rest. Keep your forearm and wrist level so your wrist does not bend. Do hand exercises every 15 minutes. Keep your shoulders, arms, hands, and wrists relaxed while you work. Maintain good posture. Keep feet flat on the floor, with one foot slightly in front of the other. For more information, visit scsite.com/dc2006/ch5/faq and then click Repetitive Strain Injuries.

POINTING DEVICES

A **pointing device** is an input device that allows a user to control a pointer on the screen. In a graphical user interface, a **pointer** is a small symbol on the screen (Figure 5-3 on page 237) whose location and shape change as a user moves a pointing device. A pointing device can be used to move the insertion point; select text, graphics, and other objects; and click buttons, icons, links, and menu commands. The following sections discuss the mouse and other pointing devices.

MOUSE

A **mouse** is a pointing device that fits under the palm of your hand comfortably. The mouse is the most widely used pointing device on desktop computers.

With a mouse, users control the movement of the pointer, often called a *mouse pointer* in this case. As you move a mouse, the pointer on the screen also moves. Generally, you use the mouse to move the pointer on the screen to an object such as a button, a menu, an icon, a link, or text. Then, you press a mouse button to perform a certain action associated with that object. The top and sides of a mouse have one to four buttons; some also have a small wheel. The bottom of a mouse is flat and contains a mechanism that detects movement of the mouse.

Mouse Types

A *mechanical mouse* has a rubber or metal ball on its underside (Figure 5-5). When the ball rolls in a certain direction, electronic circuits in the mouse translate the movement of the mouse into signals the computer can process. You should place a mechanical mouse on a mouse pad. A **mouse pad** is a rectangular rubber or foam pad that provides better traction than the top of a desk. The mouse pad also protects the ball in the mouse from a build-up of dust and dirt, which could cause it to malfunction.

An optical mouse, by contrast, has no moving mechanical parts inside. Instead, an *optical mouse* uses devices that emit and sense light to detect the mouse's movement. Some use optical sensors, others use a laser (Figure 5-6). You can place an optical mouse on nearly all types of surfaces, eliminating the need for a mouse pad. An optical mouse is more precise than a

mechanical mouse and does not require cleaning as does a mechanical mouse, but it also is more expensive.

A mouse connects to a computer in several ways. Many types connect with a cable that attaches to a serial port, mouse port, or USB port on the system unit. A *wireless mouse*, or *cordless mouse*, is a battery-powered device that transmits data using wireless technology, such as radio waves or infrared light waves. The technology used for a wireless mouse is similar to that of a wireless keyboard discussed earlier. Some users prefer a wireless mouse because it frees up desk space and eliminates the clutter of a cord.

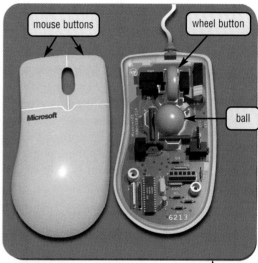

FIGURE 5-5 A mechanical mouse contains a small ball.

FIGURE 5-6a (optical mouse that uses optical sensor)

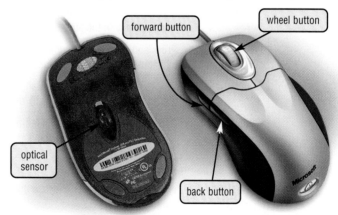

FIGURE 5-6b (optical mouse that uses laser)

FIGURE 5-6 An optical mouse uses an optical sensor or a laser. Many also include buttons you push with your thumb that enable forward and backward navigation through Web pages.

Using a Mouse

Windows users work with a mouse that has at least two buttons. For a right-handed user, the left button usually is the primary mouse button, and the right mouse button is the secondary mouse button. Left-handed people, however, can reverse the function of these buttons.

Operations you can perform with the mouse include point, click, right-click, double-click, triple-click, drag, right-drag, rotate wheel, press wheel button, and tilt wheel. The table in Figure 5-7 explains how to perform these mouse operations. Some programs also use keys in combination with the mouse to perform certain actions. The function of the mouse buttons and the wheel varies depending on the program. Read At Issue 5-2 for a related discussion.

Some programs support *mouse gestures*, where the user performs certain operations by holding a mouse button while moving the

mouse in a particular pattern. For example, moving the mouse down and to the left may close all open windows. Mouse gestures minimize the amount of time users spend navigating through menus or toolbars because users can perform these tasks by simply moving (gesturing) the mouse.

WEB LINK 5-1

Mouse

For more information, visit scsite.com/dc2006/ch5/weblink and then click Mouse.

FAQ 5-3

How do I use a wheel on a mouse?

Roll it forward or backward to scroll up or down. Tilt it to the right or left to scroll horizontally. Hold down the CTRL key while rolling the wheel to make the text on the screen bigger or smaller. These scrolling and zooming functions work with most software and also on the Web. For more information, visit scsite.com/dc2006/ch5/faq and then click Using a Mouse.

MOUSE OPERATIONS

Operation	Mouse Action	Example
Point	Move the mouse across a flat surface until the pointer on the desktop is positioned on the item of choice.	Position the pointer on the screen.
Click	Press and release the primary mouse button, which usually is the left mouse button.	Select or deselect items on the screen or start a program or program feature.
Right-click	Press and release the secondary mouse button, which usually is the right mouse button.	Display a shortcut menu.
Double-click	Quickly press and release the left mouse button twice without moving the mouse.	Start a program or program feature.
Triple-click	Quickly press and release the left mouse button three times without moving the mouse.	Select a paragraph.
Drag	Point to an item, hold down the left mouse button, move the item to the desired location on the screen, and then release the left mouse button.	Move an object from one location to another or draw pictures.
Right-drag	Point to an item, hold down the right mouse button, move the item to the desired location on the screen, and then release the right mouse button.	Display a shortcut menu after moving an object from one location to another.
Rotate wheel	Roll the wheel forward or backward.	Scroll vertically.
Press wheel button	Press the wheel button while moving the mouse on the desktop.	Scroll continuously.
Tilt wheel	Press the wheel toward the right or left.	Scroll horizontally.

FIGURE 5-7 The more common mouse operations.

AT ISSUE 5-2

Should the Government Set Computer Use Standards?

When you consider the causes of workplace injuries, you might not put clicking a mouse in the same category with lifting a bag of concrete, but perhaps you should. According to the chairman of a National Academy of Sciences panel that investigated workplace injuries, every year one million Americans lose workdays because of repetitive strain injuries. Repetitive strain injuries are caused when muscle groups perform the same actions over and over again. Once, repetitive strain injuries were common among factory workers who performed the same tasks on an assembly line for hours a day. Today, these injuries, which often result from prolonged use of a computer mouse and keyboard, are the largest job-related injury and illness problem in the United States. OSHA proposed standards whereby employers would have to establish programs to prevent workplace injuries with respect to computer use. Yet, congress rejected the standards, accepting the argument that the cost to employers would be prohibitive and unfair, because no proof exists that the injuries are caused exclusively by office work. Should the government establish laws regarding computer use? Why or why not? Who is responsible for this type of workplace injury? Why?

OTHER POINTING DEVICES

The mouse is the most widely used pointing device today. Some users, however, work with other pointing devices. These include the trackball, touchpad, pointing stick, joystick, wheel, light pen, touch screen, stylus, and pens. The following sections discuss each of these pointing devices.

Trackball

Similar to a mechanical mouse that has a ball on the bottom, a **trackball** is a stationary pointing device with a ball on its top or side (Figure 5-8). The ball in most trackballs is about the size of a Ping-Pong ball.

To move the pointer using a trackball, you rotate the ball with your thumb, fingers, or the palm of your hand. In addition to the ball, a trackball usually has one or more buttons that work just like mouse buttons.

A trackball requires frequent cleaning because it picks up oils from fingers and dust from the environment. For users who have limited desk space, however, a trackball is a good alternative to a mouse because the device is stationary.

Touchpad

A **touchpad** is a small, flat, rectangular pointing device that is sensitive to pressure and motion (Figure 5-9). To move the pointer using a touchpad, slide your fingertip across the surface of the pad. Some touchpads have one or more buttons around the edge of the pad that work like mouse buttons. On most touchpads, you also can tap the pad's surface to imitate mouse operations such as clicking. Touchpads are found most often on notebook computers.

WEB LINK 5-2

Touchpad
For more information, visit scsite.com/dc2006/ch5/weblink and then click Touchpad.

FIGURE 5-8 You rotate the ball on a trackball to move the pointer on the screen.

touchpad

FIGURE 5-9 Most notebook computers have a touchpad that allows users to control the movement of the pointer.

Pointing Stick

A **pointing stick** is a pressure-sensitive pointing device shaped like a pencil eraser that is positioned between keys on a keyboard (Figure 5-10). To move the pointer using a pointing stick, you push the pointing stick with a finger. The pointer on the screen moves in the direction you push the pointing stick. By pressing buttons below the keyboard, users can click and perform other mouse-type operations with a pointing stick.

A pointing stick does not require any additional desk space. In addition, it does not require cleaning like a mechanical mouse or trackball. IBM developed the pointing stick for its notebook computers.

WEB LINK 5-3

Pointing Stick

For more information, visit scsite.com/dc2006/ch5/weblink and then click Pointing Stick.

pointing stick

FIGURE 5-10
Some notebook computers include a pointing stick to allow a user to control the movement of the pointer.

Joystick and Wheel

Users running game software or flight and driving simulation software often use a joystick or wheel as a pointing device (Figure 5-11). A **joystick** is a vertical lever mounted on a base.

You move the lever in different directions to control the actions of the simulated vehicle or player. The lever usually includes buttons called triggers that you press to activate certain events. Some joysticks also have additional buttons you set to perform other actions.

A **wheel** is a steering-wheel-type input device. Users turn the wheel to simulate driving a car, truck, or other vehicle. Most wheels also include foot pedals for acceleration and braking actions. A joystick and wheel typically attach via a cable to a USB port.

Light Pen

A **light pen** is a handheld input device that can detect the presence of light. Some light pens require a specially designed monitor, while others work with a standard monitor (Figure 5-12). To select objects on the screen, a user presses the light pen against the surface of the screen or points the light pen at the screen and then presses a button on the pen.

Light pens also are ideal for areas where employees' hands might contain food, dirt, grease, or other chemicals that could damage the computer. Health-care professionals, such as doctors, use light pens because they can slide a protective sleeve over the pen — keeping their fingers free of contaminants.

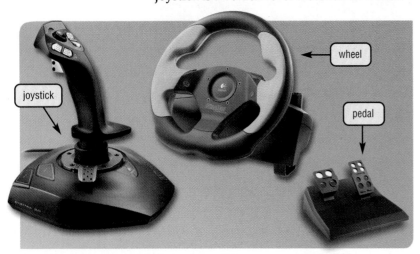

joystick

wheel

pedal

FIGURE 5-11   Joysticks and wheels help a user control the actions of players and vehicles in game and simulation software.

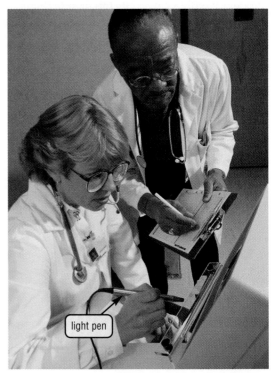

light pen

FIGURE 5-12   To use a light pen, you press the pen against the screen or press a button on the pen while pointing the pen toward an object on the screen.

Touch Screen

A **touch screen** is a touch-sensitive display device. Users can interact with these devices by touching areas of the screen. Because touch screens require a lot of arm movements, you do not enter large amounts of data using a touch screen. Instead, you touch words, pictures, numbers, letters, or locations identified on the screen.

Kiosks, which are freestanding computers, often have touch screens (Figure 5-13). Travelers use kiosks in airports to print tickets ordered online and in hotels for easy check in and check out. Museum kiosks give visitors information. To allow easy access of your bank account from a car, many ATM machines have touch screens.

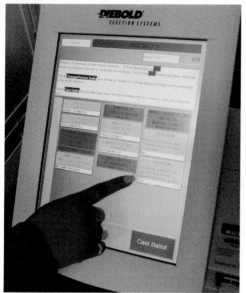

FIGURE 5-13 A voter uses a kiosk touch screen to cast ballots in an election.

Pen Input

Mobile users often enter data and instructions with a pen-type device. With **pen input**, users write, draw, and tap on a flat surface to enter input. The surface may be a monitor, a screen, or a special type of paper. Two devices used for pen input are the stylus and digital pen. A **stylus** is a small metal or plastic device that looks like a tiny ink pen but uses

pressure instead of ink (Figure 5-14). A **digital pen**, which is slightly larger than a stylus, is available in two forms: some are pressure-sensitive; others have built-in digital cameras.

Some mobile computers and nearly all mobile devices have touch screens. Instead of using a finger to enter data and instructions, most of these devices include a pressure-sensitive digital pen or stylus. You write, draw, or make selections on the computer screen by touching the screen with the pen or stylus. For example, Tablet PCs use a pressure-sensitive digital pen (Figure 5-15) and PDAs use a stylus. Pressure-sensitive digital pens, often simply called pens, typically provide more functionality than a stylus, featuring electronic erasers and programmable buttons.

Computers and mobile devices often use *handwriting recognition software* that translates the handwritten letters and symbols into characters that the computer or device can process.

stylus

FIGURE 5-14 PDAs and smart phones use a stylus.

WEB LINK 5-4

Touch Screen

For more information, visit scsite.com/dc2006/ch5/weblink and then click Touch Screen.

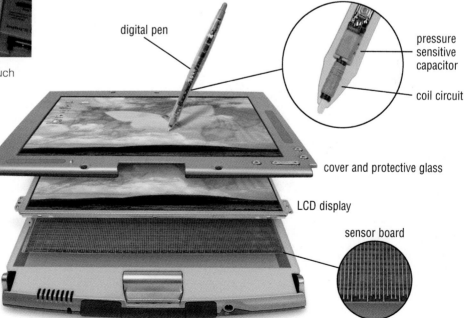

digital pen

pressure sensitive capacitor

coil circuit

cover and protective glass

LCD display

sensor board

FIGURE 5-15 Tablet PCs use a pressure-sensitive digital pen.

If you want to use pen input on a computer that does not have a touch screen, you can attach a graphics tablet to the computer. A **graphics tablet** is a flat, rectangular, electronic, plastic board. Architects, mapmakers, designers, artists, and home users create drawings and sketches by using a pressure-sensitive pen or a cursor on a graphics tablet (Figure 5-16). A *cursor* looks similar to a mouse, except it has a window with cross hairs, so the user can see through to the tablet. Each location on the graphics tablet corresponds to a specific location on the screen. When drawing on the tablet with a pen or cursor, the tablet detects and converts the movements into digital signals that are sent in the computer. Large-scale applications sometimes refer to the graphics tablet as a *digitizer*.

Digital pens that have built-in digital cameras work differently from pressure-sensitive digital pens. These pens look much like a ballpoint pen and typically do not contain any additional buttons. In addition to the tiny digital camera, these pens contain a processor, memory, and an ink cartridge. As you write or draw on special digital paper with the pen, it captures every handwritten mark by taking more than 100 pictures per second and then stores the images in the pen's memory. You transfer the images from the pen to a computer (Figure 5-17) or mobile device, such as a smart phone. Some pens have a cradle for transferring images; others communicate wirelessly using Bluetooth.

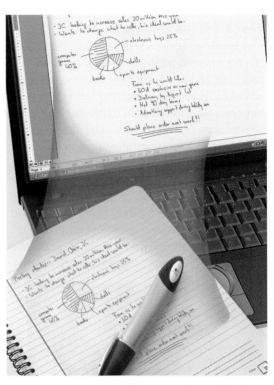

FIGURE 5-17 Some digital pens have built-in digital cameras that store handwritten marks and allow you to transfer your handwriting to a computer.

Test your knowledge of pages 234 through 244 in Quiz Yourself 5-1.

WEB LINK 5-5

Pen Input

For more information, visit scsite.com/dc2006/ch5/weblink and then click Pen Input.

QUIZ YOURSELF 5-1

Instructions: Find the true statement below. Then, rewrite the remaining false statements so they are true.

1. A keyboard is an output device that contains keys users press to enter data in a computer.

2. A light pen is a flat, rectangular, electronic, plastic board.

3. A trackball is a small, flat, rectangular pointing device commonly found on notebook computers.

4. Input is any data or instructions entered into the memory of a computer.

5. Operations you can perform with a wheel include point, click, right-click, double-click, triple-click, drag, right-drag, rotate wheel, press wheel button, and tilt wheel.

6. PDAs use a pressure-sensitive digital pen, and Tablet PCs use a stylus.

Quiz Yourself Online: To further check your knowledge of input techniques, the keyboard, the mouse, and other pointing devices, visit scsite.com/dc2006/ch5/quiz and then click Objectives 1 – 4.

FIGURE 5-16a (artist using a pen)

FIGURE 5-16b (civil engineer using a cursor)

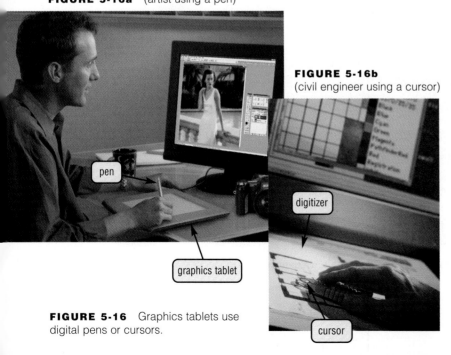

pen

digitizer

graphics tablet

cursor

FIGURE 5-16 Graphics tablets use digital pens or cursors.

VOICE INPUT

As an alternative to using a keyboard to enter data and instructions, some users talk to their computers and watch the spoken words appear on the screen as they talk. **Voice input** is the process of entering input by speaking into a microphone. The microphone may be a stand-alone peripheral that sits on top of a desk, or built in the computer or device, or in a headset. Some external microphones have a cable that attaches to a port on the sound card on the computer. Others communicate using wireless technology such as Bluetooth.

Voice recognition, also called *speech recognition*, is the computer's capability of distinguishing spoken words. Popular voice recognition programs include IBM ViaVoice and Dragon NaturallySpeaking. Many programs, such as Microsoft Office, support voice recognition. Figure 5-18 illustrates how Word recognizes dictated words and voice commands.

FIGURE 5-18   HOW TO DICTATE WORDS AND COMMANDS

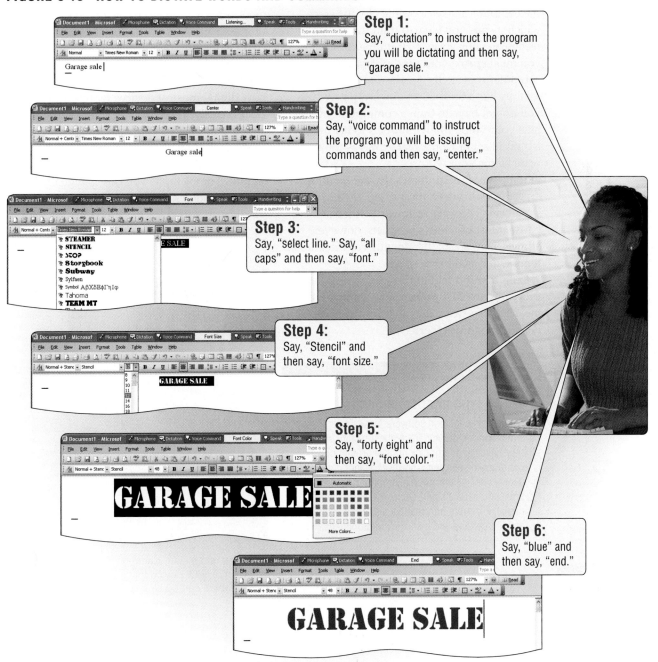

Step 1:
Say, "dictation" to instruct the program you will be dictating and then say, "garage sale."

Step 2:
Say, "voice command" to instruct the program you will be issuing commands and then say, "center."

Step 3:
Say, "select line." Say, "all caps" and then say, "font."

Step 4:
Say, "Stencil" and then say, "font size."

Step 5:
Say, "forty eight" and then say, "font color."

Step 6:
Say, "blue" and then say, "end."

Voice recognition programs recognize a vocabulary of preprogrammed words. The vocabulary of voice recognition programs can range from two words to millions of words. The automated telephone system at your bank may ask you to answer questions by speaking the words Yes or No into the telephone. A voice recognition program on your computer, by contrast, may recognize up to two million words.

Most voice recognition programs are a combination of speaker dependent and speaker independent. With *speaker-dependent software*, the computer makes a profile of your voice, which means you have to train the computer to recognize your voice. To train the computer, you must speak words and phrases into the computer repeatedly. *Speaker-independent software* has a built-in set of word patterns so you do not have to train a computer to recognize your voice. Many products today include a built-in set of words that grows as the software learns your words.

Some voice recognition software requires *discrete speech*, which means you have to speak slowly and separate each word with a short pause. Most of today's products, however, allow you to speak in a flowing conversational tone, called *continuous speech*.

Keep in mind that the best voice recognition programs are 90 to 95 percent accurate, which means the software may interpret as many as one in ten words incorrectly.

Audio Input

Voice input is part of a larger category of input called audio input. **Audio input** is the process of entering any sound into the computer such as speech, music, and sound effects. To enter high-quality sound into a personal computer, the computer must have a sound card. Users enter sound into a computer via devices such as microphones, tape players, CD/DVD players, or radios, each of which plugs in a port on the sound card.

Some users also enter music and other sound effects into a computer using external MIDI devices such as an electronic piano keyboard (Figure 5-19). As discussed in the previous chapter, in addition to being a port, *MIDI* (*musical instrument digital interface*) is the electronic music industry's standard that defines how digital musical devices represent sounds electronically. These devices connect to the sound card on a computer. Software that conforms to the MIDI standard allows users to compose and edit music and many other sounds. For example, you can change the speed, add notes, or rearrange the score to produce an entirely new sound.

FAQ 5-4

Which type of microphone is best?

For voice recognition software, headsets that have a microphone provide the highest quality because they typically do not pick up background noises. For group discussions, however, where multiple people will use the same microphone at the same time, you need a stand-alone or built-in microphone. For more information, visit scsite.com/dc2006/ch5/faq and then click Microphones.

FIGURE 5-19 An electronic piano keyboard is an external MIDI device that allows users to record music, which can be stored in the computer.

WEB LINK 5-6

Voice Input

For more information, visit scsite.com/dc2006/ch5/weblink and then click Voice Input.

INPUT FOR PDAs, SMART PHONES, AND TABLET PCs

Mobile devices, such as the PDA and smart phone, and mobile computers, such as the Tablet PC, offer convenience for the mobile user. A variety of alternatives for entering data and instructions is available for these devices and computers.

PDAs

A user enters data and instructions into a PDA in many ways (Figure 5-20). PDAs ship with a basic stylus, which is the primary input device. Users often purchase a more elaborate stylus that has a ballpoint pen at one end and a stylus at the other. With the stylus, you enter data in two ways: using an on-screen keyboard or using handwriting recognition software that

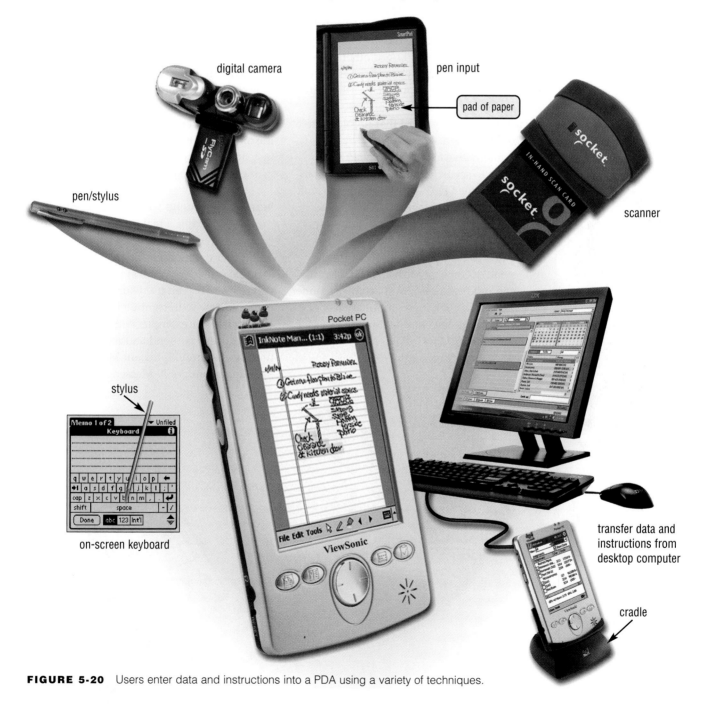

FIGURE 5-20   Users enter data and instructions into a PDA using a variety of techniques.

is built in the PDA. For example, drawing a straight vertical line in a downward motion displays the number 1 on the PDA. With a specialized pen and data reader, you can transfer notes as you write them on a pad of paper.

For users who prefer typing to handwriting, some PDAs have a built-in mini keyboard. Other users type on a desktop computer or notebook computer keyboard and transfer the data to the PDA. Some users prefer to enter data into a PDA using a portable keyboard. A *portable keyboard* is a full-sized keyboard you conveniently use with a PDA or other mobile device. Some portable keyboards physically attach to and remove from a PDA; others are wireless. Figure 5-21 shows a pocket-sized portable wireless keyboard that unfolds into a full-sized keyboard.

As an alternative to typing, some PDAs allow users to speak data and instructions into the device. Some PDAs also have cameras built in so you can take photographs and view them on a PDA. On other models, you simply attach a digital camera directly to the PDA. You also can use a PDA to scan small documents, such as business cards and product labels, by attaching a scanner to the PDA. For more information about PDAs, read the Personal Mobile Devices feature that follows this chapter.

Smart Phones

Voice is the traditional method of input for smart phones. That is, a user speaks into the phone. Today, however, text messaging, instant messaging, and picture messaging have become popular methods of entering data and instructions into a smart phone.

TEXT MESSAGING Instead of calling someone's smart phone or cellular telephone, users can enter and send typed messages using *text messaging*. To send a text message, you type a short message, typically less than 160 characters, to another smart phone by pressing buttons on the telephone's keypad. As with chat rooms and instant messaging, text messaging uses abbreviations and emoticons to minimize the amount of typing required. For example, instead of typing the text, I am surprised, a user can type the emoticon, :-O.

INSTANT MESSAGING Recall that instant messaging (IM) is a real-time communications service that allows you to exchange messages with other online users. Some wireless Internet services providers (WISPs) partner with IM services so you can use your smart phone to communicate with computer users of the same IM service. For example, with AT&T Wireless service, users can send and receive instant messages with AOL Instant Messenger, Yahoo! Messenger, and MSN Messenger.

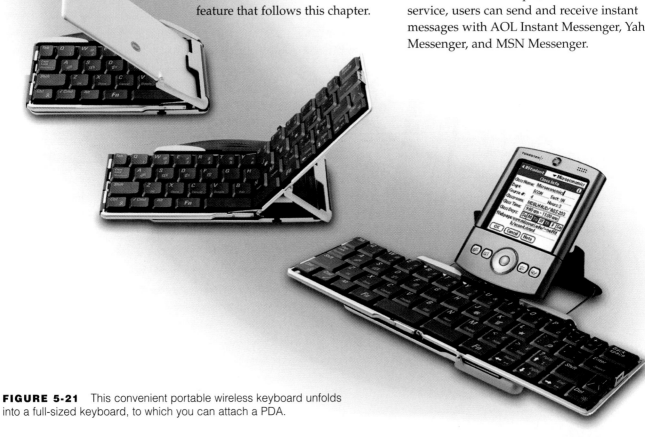

FIGURE 5-21 This convenient portable wireless keyboard unfolds into a full-sized keyboard, to which you can attach a PDA.

PICTURE MESSAGING With *picture messaging*, users can send graphics, pictures, video clips, and sound files, as well as short text messages to another smart phone with a compatible picture messaging service. Many smart phones today have a built-in or attachable camera so users easily can take pictures and videos and even incorporate short voice recordings in their picture messages (Figure 5-22).

As an alternative to text messaging, some users write a message with a digital pen, transfer the message from the pen to the smart phone, and then use picture messaging to send the handwritten message. Read At Issue 5-3 for a related discussion.

Most smart phones include PDA capabilities. Thus, input devices used with PDAs typically also are available for smart phones.

AT ISSUE 5-3

Should Driving While Using Smart Phones Be Illegal?

Smart phone sales are soaring. In addition to providing a cellular telephone's capability to communicate wirelessly, smart phones allow users to send and receive text messages, instant messages, picture messages, and e-mail, and to access and view Web pages. For drivers, however, smart phones may be a liability. Estimates vary widely, but news accounts link up to 8,000 fatalities on U.S. highways to cell phone use. Because of their additional capabilities, some experts believe smart phones pose an even greater risk. Many countries have placed bans or restrictions on the use of mobile phones while driving. In the United States, several states have considered or enacted similar legislation. New York, for example, permits vehicle operators to use only hands-free mobile phones. Yet, some studies report that just talking on a portable phone can cause enough driver inattention to trigger an accident. Supporters of a mobile phone ban cite a British study that found drivers talking on cell phones had reaction times 50 percent slower than when not talking on a phone, and 30 percent slower than drivers who were intoxicated. Opponents of a ban note, however, that other driver activities, like tuning a radio or having a conversation, can be equally distracting. Should the use of cell phones and/or smart phones be banned while driving? Why? What other measures, if any, could be taken to prevent drivers from endangering themselves and others while using cell phones or smart phones?

FIGURE 5-22 Many smart phones include a digital camera so users can send pictures and videos to others.

Tablet PCs

The primary input device for a Tablet PC is a pressure-sensitive digital pen, which allows users to write on the device's screen. A Tablet PC's handwriting recognition software works similarly to that of a PDA. The computer converts the handwriting into characters it can process.

Both the slate and convertible designs of Tablet PC provide a means for keyboard input for those users who prefer typing to handwriting. You can attach a removable keyboard to the slate Tablet PC. The convertible Tablet PC has an attached keyboard that can be rotated 180 degrees so the computer resembles a notebook computer.

To access peripherals at their home or office, users can slide their Tablet PC in a docking station. A *docking station*, which is an external device that attaches to a mobile computer or device, contains a power connection and provides connections to peripherals. In the docking station, Tablet PC users can work with a full-sized keyboard, mouse, CD/DVD drives, and other desktop peripherals (Figure 5-23). The design of docking stations varies, depending on the type of mobile computer or the device to which they are attached.

FAQ 5-5

Can a mobile computer or device get a virus?

Yes. Mobile computers and devices can get a virus from a downloaded Web page. A virus can transfer from a desktop computer to a mobile device when users connect the two to synchronize data. Viruses also can transmit via wireless data transfer when two wireless devices communicate with one another, such as when receiving a text or picture message. For more information, visit scsite.com/dc2006/ch5/faq and then click Viruses and Mobile Devices.

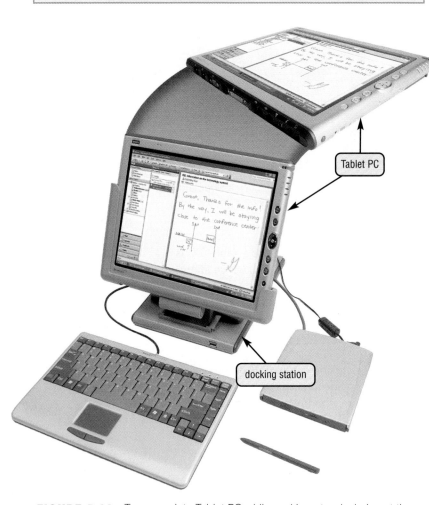

Tablet PC

docking station

FIGURE 5-23 To use a slate Tablet PC while working at a desk, insert the Tablet PC in a docking station. Devices such as a keyboard and CD drive can be plugged in the docking station.

DIGITAL CAMERAS

A **digital camera** allows users to take pictures and store the photographed images digitally, instead of on traditional film (Figure 5-24). While many digital cameras look like a traditional camera, some models attach to or are built in PDAs and smart phones. Mobile users such as real estate agents, insurance agents, general contractors, and photojournalists use digital cameras so they immediately can view photographed images on the camera. Home and business users have digital cameras to save the expense of film developing, duplication, and postage.

Some digital cameras use internal flash memory to store images. Others store images on mobile storage media, such as a flash memory card, memory stick, and mini-disc. Chapter 7 discusses these and other storage media in depth. Generally, higher-capacity storage devices can hold more pictures.

Digital cameras typically allow users to review, and sometimes edit, images while they are in the camera. Some digital cameras can connect to or communicate wirelessly with a printer or television, allowing users to print or view images directly from the camera.

FIGURE 5-24 With a digital camera, users can view photographed images immediately through a small screen on the camera to see if the picture is worth keeping.

Often users prefer to *download*, or transfer a copy of, the images from the digital camera to the computer's hard disk. With some digital cameras, images download through a cable that connects between the digital camera (or the camera's docking station) and a USB port or a FireWire port on the system unit. For cameras that store images on miniature mobile storage media, simply insert the media in a reading/writing device that communicates wirelessly or attaches to a port on the system unit. Copying images from the miniature media to the computer's hard disk is just like copying files from any other disk drive. Some cameras store images on a mini CD/DVD. In this case, insert the disc in the computer's disc drive and then copy the pictures to the computer's hard disk (or you can view the contents of the disc by inserting it in a CD or DVD player).

When you copy images to the hard disk in a computer, the images are available for editing with photo editing software, printing, faxing, sending via e-mail, including in another document, or posting to a Web site or photo community for everyone to see. Many users add pictures to greeting cards, a computerized photo album, a family newsletter, certificates, and awards.

The three basic types of digital cameras are studio cameras, field cameras, and point-and-shoot cameras. The most expensive and highest quality of the three is a *studio camera*, which is a stationary camera used for professional studio work. Often used by photojournalists, a *field camera* is a portable camera that has many lenses and other attachments. As with the studio camera, a field camera can be quite expensive. A *point-and-shoot camera* is much more affordable and lightweight and provides acceptable quality photographic images for the home or small business user. Figure 5-25 illustrates how one make of point-and-shoot digital camera works.

A point-and-shoot camera often features flash, zoom, automatic focus, and special effects. Some allow users to record short audio narrations for photographed images. Others even record short video clips in addition to still images. Point-and-shoot digital cameras often have a built-in TV out port, allowing users to

FAQ 5-6

Are professional photographers switching to digital cameras?

Yes. A recent study found that nearly 80 percent of professional photographers use digital cameras. The biggest obstacle to switching is the expensive initial cost of the digital equipment (cameras, printers, storage, etc.). For more information, visit scsite.com/dc2006/ch5/faq and then click Professional Digital Photography.

FIGURE 5-25 HOW A DIGITAL CAMERA MIGHT WORK

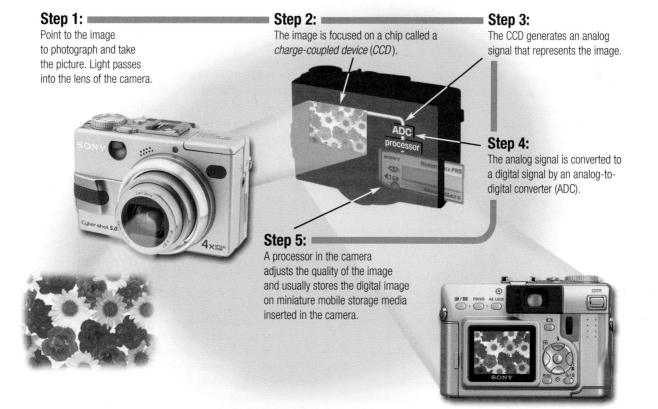

Step 1:
Point to the image to photograph and take the picture. Light passes into the lens of the camera.

Step 2:
The image is focused on a chip called a *charge-coupled device* (*CCD*).

Step 3:
The CCD generates an analog signal that represents the image.

Step 4:
The analog signal is converted to a digital signal by an analog-to-digital converter (ADC).

Step 5:
A processor in the camera adjusts the quality of the image and usually stores the digital image on miniature mobile storage media inserted in the camera.

display photographed images or play recorded video clips directly on a television.

For additional information about digital cameras, read the Digital Imaging and Video Technology feature that follows Chapter 6.

Digital Camera Quality

One factor that affects the quality of a digital camera is its resolution. **Resolution** is the number of horizontal and vertical pixels in a display device. A *pixel* (short for picture element) is the smallest element in an electronic image (Figure 5-26). The greater the number of pixels the camera uses to capture an image, the better the quality of the image. Thus, the higher the resolution, the better the image quality, but the more expensive the camera.

Digital camera resolutions range from approximately 1 million to more than 8 million pixels (*MP*). A camera with a 5.1-megapixel (5,100,000 pixels) resolution will provide a better quality than one with a 3.2-megapixel resolution. As a general rule, a 1-megapixel camera is fine for pictures sent via e-mail or posted on the Web. For good quality printed photographs, users should have a 2-megapixel camera for 4 × 6 inch photographs, a 3-megapixel camera for 8 × 10 photographs, and 5-megapixel or greater camera for larger size prints.

Manufacturers often use pixels per inch to represent a digital camera's resolution. *Pixels per inch (ppi)* is the number of pixels in one inch of screen display. For example, a 2304 ×

1728 (pronounced 2304 by 1728) ppi camera has 2,304 pixels per vertical inch and 1,728 pixels per horizontal inch. Multiplying these two numbers together gives an approximate total number of megapixels. For example, 2304 times 1728 equals approximately 4 million, or 4 megapixels. If just one number is stated, such as 1600 ppi, then both the vertical and horizontal numbers are the same.

Many digital cameras provide a means to adjust the ppi to the desired resolution. With a lower ppi, you can capture and store more images in the camera. For example, a camera set at 800 × 600 ppi might capture and store 61 images, if it has sufficient storage capacity. The number of images may reduce to 24 on the same camera set at 1600 × 1200 ppi, because each image consumes more storage space.

The actual photographed resolution is known as the *optical resolution*. Some manufacturers state *enhanced resolution*, instead of, or in addition to, optical resolution. Optical resolution is different from enhanced resolution. The enhanced resolution usually is higher because it uses a special formula to add pixels between those generated by the optical resolution. Be aware that some manufacturers compute a digital camera's megapixels from the enhanced resolution, instead of optical resolution.

Another measure of a digital camera's quality is the number of bits it stores in a pixel. Each pixel consists of one or more bits of data. The more bits used to represent a pixel, the more colors and shades of gray that can be represented. One bit per pixel is enough for simple one-color images. For multiple colors and shades of gray, each pixel requires more than one bit of data. A point-and-shoot camera should be at least 24 bit.

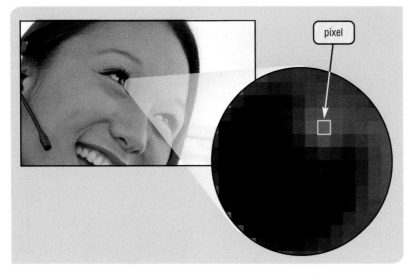

FIGURE 5-26   A pixel is a single point in an electronic image.

FAQ 5-7

What is dpi?

Some advertisements incorrectly use dpi to mean the same as ppi. The acronym *dpi*, which stands for *dots per inch*, is a measure of a print resolution. For screen resolution, the proper measurement term is ppi (pixels per inch). For more information, visit scsite.com/dc2006/ch5/faq and then click Resolution.

VIDEO INPUT

Video input is the process of capturing full-motion images and storing them on a computer's storage medium such as a hard disk or DVD.

Some video devices record video using analog signals. Computers, by contrast, use digital signals. To enter video from an analog device into a personal computer, the analog signal must be converted to a digital signal. To do this, plug a video camera, VCR, or other analog video device in a video capture port on the system unit. One type of adapter card that has a video capture port is a *video capture card*, which converts an analog video signal into a digital signal that a computer can process. Most new computers are not equipped with a video capture card because not all users have the need for this type of adapter card.

A **digital video (DV) camera**, by contrast, records video as digital signals instead of analog signals. Many DV cameras can capture still frames, as well as motion. To transfer recorded images to a hard disk or CD or DVD, users connect DV cameras directly to a USB port or a FireWire port on the system unit. Thus, the computer does not need a video capture card. Simply connect the video device to the computer and begin transferring images. After saving the video on a storage medium, such as a hard disk or DVD, you can play it or edit it using video editing software on a computer (Figure 5-27).

PC Video Cameras

A **PC video camera**, or **PC camera**, is a type of digital video camera that enables a home or small business user to capture video and still images, send e-mail messages with video attachments, add live images to instant messages, broadcast live images over the Internet, and make video telephone calls. During a *video telephone call*, both parties see each other as they communicate over the Internet (Figure 5-28). The cost of PC video cameras usually is less than $100.

Attached to the computer's USB port or FireWire port, a PC video camera usually sits on top of the monitor. For more flexibility, some PC video cameras are portable. That is, you can detach them from the base and use them as a stand-alone digital camera.

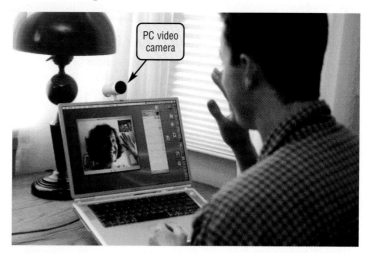

PC video camera

FIGURE 5-28 Using a PC video camera, home users can see each other as they communicate over the Internet.

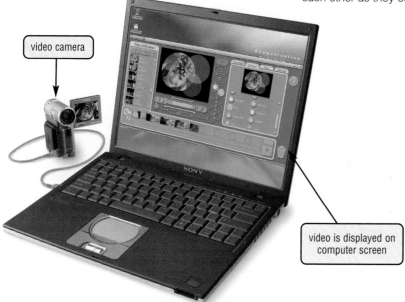

video camera

video is displayed on computer screen

FIGURE 5-27 Home users can transfer videos to their computers and then use video editing software to edit the video.

WEB LINK 5-7

PC Video Cameras

For more information, visit scsite.com/ dc2006/ch5/weblink and then click PC Video Cameras.

Web Cams

A **Web cam** is any video camera that displays its output on a Web page. A Web cam attracts Web site visitors by showing images that change regularly. Home or small business users might use Web cams to show a work in progress, weather and traffic information, employees at work, photographs of a vacation, and countless other images. Read At Issue 5-4 for a related discussion.

Some Web sites have live Web cams that display still pictures and update the displayed image at a specified time or time intervals, such as 15 seconds. Another type of Web cam, called a *streaming cam*, has the illusion of moving images because it sends a continual stream of still images.

AT ISSUE 5-4

Should Cameras Be Able to Monitor Your Every Move?

Imagine if while driving to school you could use your cell phone or an Internet-enabled device to find out which campus parking lot had the most spaces available. Far-fetched? Maybe not. IrisNet (Internet-scale Resource-Intensive Sensor Network Services), a project under development by Intel and Carnegie Mellon University, someday may be able to give you just this sort of information. IrisNet's goal is to provide current information about the outside world. IrisNet relies on a sensor network made up of Internet-connected personal computers equipped with sensing devices such as Web cams. Project planners envision a worldwide sensor network storing real-time and historical data from thousands, or even millions, of widely distributed sensors. IrisNet would provide the software infrastructure for the network, allowing users to query the collected data. Users could ask what the weather conditions are in a distant city, when a child arrived safely at school, or where spaces are available in campus parking lots. IrisNet raises, however, certain privacy concerns. Should every action captured by one of IrisNet's sensors be available to anyone who creates a query? Should queries be prioritized or even rejected? Why or why not? Can IrisNet's potential benefits be balanced with its possible pitfalls? How?

Video Conferencing

A **video conference** is a meeting between two or more geographically separated people who use a network or the Internet to transmit audio and video data (Figure 5-29). To participate in a video conference, you need video conferencing software along with a microphone, speakers, and a video camera attached to a computer.

As you speak, members of the meeting hear your voice on their speakers. Any image in front of the video camera, such as a person's face, appears in a window on each participant's screen. A *whiteboard* is another window on the screen that displays notes and drawings simultaneously on all participants' screens. This window provides multiple users with an area on which they can write or draw.

As the costs of video conferencing hardware and software decrease, increasingly more business meetings, corporate training, and educational classes will be conducted as video conferences.

FAQ 5-8

How popular is video conferencing?

A recent survey found that 40 percent of computer users participate in video conferences with desktop equipment. Annual expenditures exceed $7.7 billion on voice and video conferencing equipment. For more information, visit scsite.com/dc2006/ch5/faq and then click Video Conferencing.

FIGURE 5-29 To save on travel expenses, many large businesses are turning to video conferencing.

Test your knowledge of pages 245 through 254 in Quiz Yourself 5-2.

QUIZ YOURSELF 5-2

Instructions: Find the true statement below. Then, rewrite the remaining false statements so they are true.

1. A digital camera allows users to take pictures and store the photographed images digitally, instead of on traditional film.

2. DV cameras record video as analog signals.

3. Instant messaging is the computer's capability of distinguishing spoken words.

4. Many smart phones today have a built-in or attachable camera so users easily can send text messages.

5. The lower the resolution of a digital camera, the better the image quality, but the more expensive the camera.

Quiz Yourself Online: To further check your knowledge of voice input; input for PDAs, smart phones, and Tablet PCs; digital cameras; and video input, visit scsite.com/dc2006/ch5/quiz and then click Objectives 5 – 8.

SCANNERS AND READING DEVICES

Some input devices save users time by eliminating manual data entry. With these devices, users do not type, speak, or write into the computer. Instead, these devices capture data from a *source document*, which is the original form of the data. Examples of source documents include time cards, order forms, invoices, paychecks, advertisements, brochures, photographs, inventory tags, or any other document that contains data to be processed.

Devices that can capture data directly from a source document include optical scanners, optical readers, bar code readers, RFID readers, magnetic stripe card readers, and magnetic-ink character recognition readers. The following pages discuss each of these devices.

Optical Scanners

An *optical scanner*, usually called a **scanner**, is a light-sensing input device that reads printed text and graphics and then translates the results into a form the computer can process. Four types of scanners are flatbed, pen, sheet-fed, and drum (Figure 5-30).

TYPES OF SCANNERS

Scanner	Method of Scanning and Use	Scannable Items
Flatbed	• Similar to a copy machine • Scanning mechanism passes under the item to be scanned, which is placed on a glass surface	• Single-sheet documents • Bound material • Photographs • Some models include trays for slides, transparencies, and negatives
Pen or Handheld 	• Move pen over text to be scanned, then transfer data to computer • Ideal for mobile users, students, and researchers • Some connect to a PDA or smart phone	• Any printed text
Sheet-fed 	• Item to be scanned is pulled into a stationary scanning mechanism • Smaller than a flatbed scanner • A model designed specifically for photographs is called a *photo scanner*	• Single-sheet documents • Photographs • Slides (with an adapter) • Negatives
Drum 	• Item to be scanned rotates around stationary scanning mechanism • Very expensive • Used in publishing industry	• Single-sheet documents • Photographs • Slides • Negatives

FIGURE 5-30 This table describes the various types of scanners.

A **flatbed scanner** works in a manner similar to a copy machine except it creates a file of the document in memory instead of a paper copy (Figure 5-31). Once you scan a document or picture, you can display the scanned object on the screen, store it on a storage medium, print it, fax it, attach it to an e-mail message, include it in another document, or post it to a Web site or photo community for everyone to see.

As with a digital camera, the quality of a scanner is measured by the number of bits it stores in a pixel and the number of pixels per inch, or resolution. The higher each number, the better the quality, but the more expensive the scanner. Most of today's affordable color desktop scanners for the home or small business range from 30 to 48 bits and have an optical resolution ranging from 600 to 4800 ppi. Commercial scanners designed for power users range from 4800 to 14,000 ppi.

Many scanners include *OCR (optical character recognition) software*, which can read and convert text documents into electronic files. OCR software is useful if you need to modify a document but do not have the original word processing file. For example, if you scan a business report with a flatbed scanner and do not use OCR software, you cannot edit the report because the scanner saves the report as an image. This is because the scanner does not differentiate between text and graphics. OCR software, however, would convert the scanned image into a text file that you could edit, for example, with a word processing program. Current OCR software has a high success rate and usually can identify more than 99 percent of scanned material.

Businesses often use scanners for *image processing*, which consists of capturing, storing, analyzing, displaying, printing, and manipulating images. Image processing allows users to convert paper documents such as reports, memos, and procedure manuals into electronic images. Users distribute and publish these electronic documents on networks and the Internet.

Business users typically store and index electronic documents with an image processing system. An *image processing system* is similar to an electronic filing cabinet that provides access to exact reproductions of the original documents. Local governments, for example, use image processing systems to store property deeds and titles to provide the public and professionals, such as lawyers and loan officers, quick access to electronic documents.

WEB LINK 5-8

Scanners

For more information, visit scsite.com/dc2006/ch5/weblink and then click Scanners.

FAQ 5-9

How can I improve the quality of scanned documents?

Place a blank sheet of paper behind translucent papers, newspapers, and other see-through types of paper. If the original image is crooked, draw a line on the back at the bottom of the image. Use that mark to align the original on the scanner. Use photo editing software to fix imperfections in images. For more information, visit scsite.com/dc2006/ch5/faq and then click Scanning.

FIGURE 5-31 HOW A FLATBED SCANNER WORKS

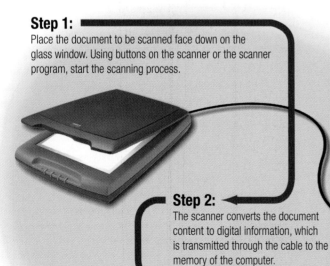

Step 1: Place the document to be scanned face down on the glass window. Using buttons on the scanner or the scanner program, start the scanning process.

Step 2: The scanner converts the document content to digital information, which is transmitted through the cable to the memory of the computer.

Step 3: Once in the memory of the computer, users can display the image, print it, e-mail it, include it in a document, or place it on a Web page.

Optical Readers

An *optical reader* is a device that uses a light source to read characters, marks, and codes and then converts them into digital data that a computer can process. Two technologies used by optical readers are optical character recognition and optical mark recognition.

OPTICAL CHARACTER RECOGNITION Optical **character recognition** (OCR) is a technology that involves reading typewritten, computer-printed, or hand-printed characters from ordinary documents and translating the images into a form that the computer can process. Most **OCR devices** include a small optical scanner for reading characters and sophisticated software to analyze what is read.

OCR devices range from large machines that can read thousands of documents per minute to handheld wands that read one document at a time. OCR devices read printed characters in an OCR font. A widely used OCR font is called OCR-A (Figure 5-32). During the scan of a document, an OCR device determines the shapes of characters by detecting patterns of light and dark. OCR software then compares these shapes with predefined shapes stored in memory and converts the shapes into characters the computer can process.

```
ABCDEFGHIJKLM
NOPQRSTUVWXYZ
1234567890
- = █ ; ' ⌐ . /
```

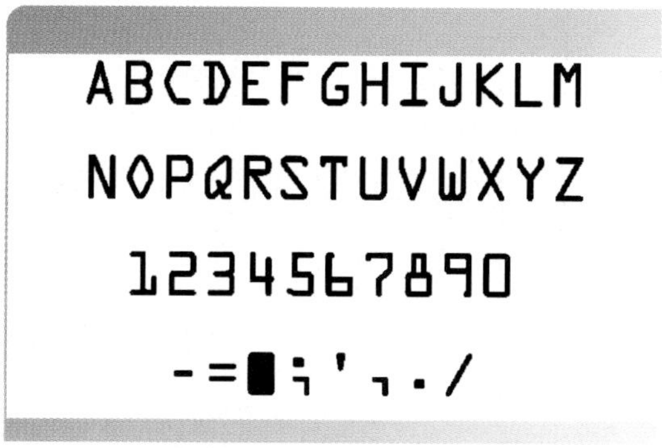

FIGURE 5-32   A portion of the characters in the OCR-A font. Notice how characters such as the number 0 and the letter O are shaped differently so the reading device easily can distinguish between them.

Many companies use OCR characters on turnaround documents. A **turnaround document** is a document that you return (turn around) to the company that creates and sends it. For example, when consumers receive a bill, they often tear off a portion of the bill and send it back to the company with their payment (Figure 5-33). The portion of the bill they return usually has their payment amount, account number, and other information printed in OCR characters.

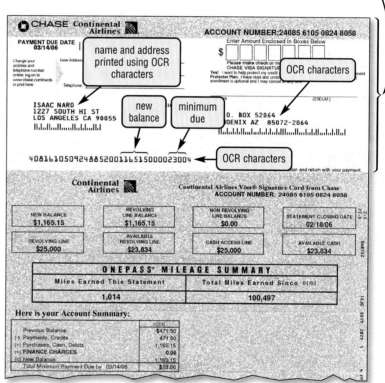

FIGURE 5-33   OCR characters frequently are used with turnaround documents. With this bill, you tear off the top portion and return it with a payment.

OPTICAL MARK RECOGNITION Optical **mark recognition** (OMR) is a technology that reads hand-drawn marks such as small circles or rectangles. A person places these marks on a form, such as a test, survey, or questionnaire answer sheet. With a test, the OMR device first scans the answer key sheet to record correct answers based on patterns of light. The OMR device then scans the remaining documents and matches their patterns of light against the answer key sheet.

Bar Code Readers

A **bar code reader**, also called a **bar code scanner**, is an optical reader that uses laser beams to read bar codes by using light patterns that pass through the bar code lines (Figure 5-34). A **bar code** is an identification code that consists of a set of vertical lines and spaces of different widths. The bar code represents data that identifies the manufacturer and the item.

Manufacturers print a bar code either on a product's package or on a label that is affixed to a product. A variety of products such as groceries, books, clothing, vehicles, mail, and packages have bar codes. Each industry uses its own type of bar code. The United States Postal Service (USPS) uses a POSTNET bar code. Retail and grocery stores use the *UPC* (*Universal Product Code*) bar code (Figure 5-35). Read At Issue 5-5 for a related discussion.

FIGURE 5-34 A bar code reader uses laser beams to read bar codes on products such as groceries and books.

AT ISSUE 5-5

Scanner Errors at the Checkout Counter?

Have you ever taken an item to a store's check-out and discovered that the price displayed when the item's bar code was scanned was different from the price shown on a shelf tag, sign, or advertisement? If you have, you are not alone. A government survey found that eight percent of the time, an item's scanned price is different from the price presented elsewhere. When an item is scanned at a store's checkout counter, a computer finds the item's price in the store's database. Store owners claim that discrepancies between the scanned price and a listed price are the result of human error — either failure to update the store's price database or incorrect shelf tags, signs, or advertisements. Yet, some consumer advocates claim that the discrepancy is intentional. They accuse stores of *scanner fraud*, insisting that some stores advertise one price and then charge another, hoping buyers will not recognize the difference. Even if consumers identify a pricing error, they may not bring the mistake to the store's attention, especially if the discrepancy is detected after the item is purchased or if the amount at issue is small. Who do you think is responsible for differences between scanned prices and posted costs? Why? Should stores be responsible for pricing errors? Why or why not?

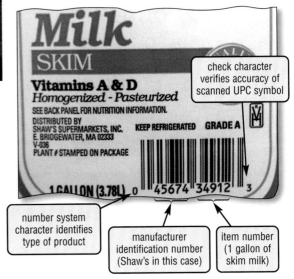

check character verifies accuracy of scanned UPC symbol

number system character identifies type of product

manufacturer identification number (Shaw's in this case)

item number (1 gallon of skim milk)

FIGURE 5-35 This UPC identifies a carton of skim milk.

RFID Readers

RFID (*radio frequency identification*) is a technology that uses radio signals to communicate with a tag placed in or attached to an object, an animal, or a person. RFID tags, which contain a memory chip and an antenna, are available in many shapes and sizes and sometimes are embedded in glass, labels, or cards. Some RFID tags are as small as a grain of sand; others are the size of a luggage tag. An **RFID reader** reads information on the tag via radio waves. RFID readers can be handheld devices or mounted in a stationary object such as a doorway.

Many retailers see RFID as an alternative to bar code identification because it does not require direct contact or line-of-site transmission. Each product in a store would contain a tag that identifies the product (Figure 5-36). As consumers remove products from the store shelves and walk through a checkout area, an RFID reader reads the tag(s) and communicates with a computer that calculates the amount due, eliminating the need for checking out each item.

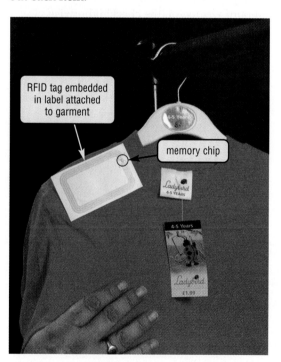

RFID tag embedded in label attached to garment

memory chip

FIGURE 5-36 RFID readers read information stored on an RFID tag and then communicate this information to computers, which instantaneously compute payments and update inventory records. In this example, the RFID tag is embedded in a label attached to the garment.

Other uses of RFID include tracking times of runners in a marathon; tracking location of soldiers, employee wardrobes, and airline baggage; checking lift tickets of skiers; gauging pressure and temperature of tires on a vehicle; checking out library books; and tracking payment as vehicles pass through booths on tollway systems. Read Looking Ahead 5-1 for a look at the next generation of tracking devices.

FAQ 5-10

Do all RFID tags look alike?

No. Depending on the application, the shape and size of an RFID tag varies. RFID tags are embedded in glass, plastic, cards, buttons, key rings, and paper labels. For more information, visit scsite.com/dc2006/ch5/faq and then click RFID Tags.

LOOKING AHEAD 5-1

Smart Dust Monitors the Environment

If you are too hot at work while your office mate is too cold, smart dust may one day solve the problem. Researchers at the University of California at Berkeley are testing tiny airborne devices called smart dust or dust motes, which combine sensors and communication components. Eventually the smart dust will be the size of a grain of sand.

Many uses for the ubiquitous smart dust are planned. The sensors could measure the temperature and humidity in various areas of a room and then send readings to a central computer that can regulate the air flow. In the warehouse, they could help track packages by sensing and transmitting product locations. In the battlefield, they could sense vehicle and missile movement. For more information, visit scsite.com/dc2006/ch5/looking and then click Smart Dust.

Magnetic Stripe Card Readers

A **magnetic stripe card reader**, often called a *magstripe reader*, reads the magnetic stripe on the back of credit cards, entertainment cards, bank cards, and other similar cards. The stripe, which is divided in three horizontal tracks, contains information identifying you and the card issuer (Figure 5-37). Some information stored in the stripe includes your name, account number, the card's expiration date, and a country code.

When a consumer swipes a credit card through the magstripe reader, it reads the information stored on the magnetic stripe on the card. If the magstripe reader rejects your card, it is possible that the magnetic stripe on the card is scratched, dirty, or erased. Exposure to a magnet or magnetic field can erase the contents of a card's magnetic stripe.

In many cases, a magstripe reader is part of a point-of-sale terminal. The function of point-of-sale terminals is discussed later in this chapter.

MICR Readers

MICR (*magnetic-ink character recognition*) devices read text printed with magnetized ink. An **MICR reader** converts MICR characters into a form the computer can process. The banking industry almost exclusively uses MICR for check processing. Each check in your checkbook has precoded MICR characters beginning at the lower-left edge (Figure 5-38). The MICR characters represent the bank number, the customer account number, and the check number. These numbers may appear in a different order than the ones shown in the sample in Figure 5-38.

When a bank receives a check for payment, it uses an MICR inscriber to print the amount of the check in MICR characters in the lower-right corner. The check then is sorted or routed to the customer's bank, along with thousands of others. Each check is inserted in an MICR reader, which sends the check information — including the amount of the check — to a computer for processing. When you balance your checkbook, verify that the amount printed in the lower-right corner is the same as the amount written on the check; otherwise, your statement will not balance.

The banking industry has established an international standard not only for bank numbers, but also for the font of the MICR characters. This standardization makes it possible for people to write checks in other countries.

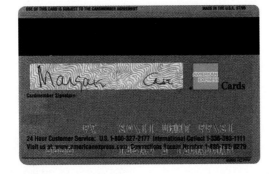

FIGURE 5-37 A magnetic stripe card reader reads information encoded on the stripe on the back of your credit card.

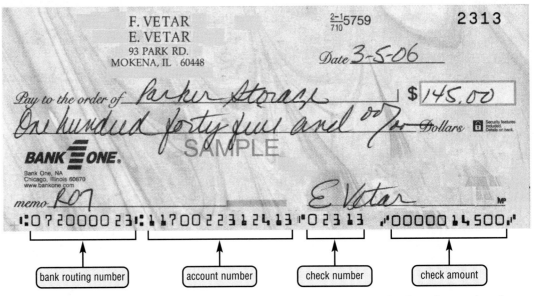

FIGURE 5-38 The MICR characters preprinted on the check represent the bank routing number, the customer account number, and the check number. The amount of the check in the lower-right corner is added after the check is cashed.

Data Collection Devices

Instead of reading or scanning data from a source document, a *data collection device* obtains data directly at the location where the transaction or event takes place. For example, employees use bar code readers, PDAs, handheld computers, or other mobile devices to collect data wirelessly (Figure 5-39). These types of data collection devices are used in restaurants, factories, warehouses, the outdoors, or other locations where heat, humidity, and cleanliness are not easy to control.

Data collection devices and many mobile computers and devices have the capability of wirelessly transmitting data over a network or the Internet. Increasingly more users today send data wirelessly to central office computers using these devices.

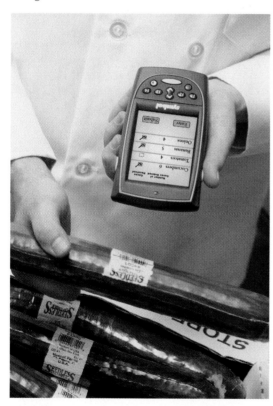

FIGURE 5-39 A chef uses this rugged handheld computer, which includes a bar code reader, that wirelessly transmits information about the scanned produce to the restaurant's inventory system.

TERMINALS

A *terminal* consists of a keyboard, a monitor, a video card, and memory. Often, these components are housed in a single unit.

Terminals fall into three basic categories: dumb terminals, smart terminals, and special-purpose terminals. A *dumb terminal* has no processing power; thus, it cannot function as an independent device. Users enter data and instructions in a dumb terminal and then transmit the data to a host computer over a network. The host computer processes the input and then, if necessary, sends information (output) back to the dumb terminal. The host computer usually is a midrange server or mainframe. A *smart terminal* has a processor, giving it the capability of performing some functions independent of the host computer. In recent years, personal computers have replaced most smart terminals.

Special-purpose terminals perform specific tasks and contain features uniquely designed for use in a particular industry. Two widely used special-purpose terminals are point-of-sale (POS) terminals and automated teller machines.

Point-of-Sale Terminals

The location in a retail or grocery store where a consumer pays for goods or services is the *point of sale (POS)*. Most retail stores use a **POS terminal** to record purchases, process credit or debit cards, and update inventory.

In a grocery store, the POS terminal is a combination of an electronic cash register, bar code reader, and printer. When the checkout clerk scans the bar code on the food product, the computer uses the manufacturer and item numbers to look up the price of the item and the complete product name in a database. Then, the price of the item in the database shows on the display device, the name of the item and its price print on a receipt, and the item being sold is recorded so the inventory can be updated. Thus, the output from a POS terminal serves as input to other computers to maintain sales records, update inventory, verify credit, and perform other activities associated with the sales transactions that are critical to running the business. Some POS terminals are Web-enabled, which allows updates to inventory at geographically separate locations.

Many POS terminals handle credit card or debit card payments and thus also include a magstripe reader. After swiping your card through the reader, the POS terminal connects to a system that authenticates the purchase. Once the transaction is approved, the terminal prints a receipt for the customer.

A self-service POS terminal allows consumers to perform all checkout-related activities (Figure 5-40). That is, they scan the items, bag the items, and pay for the items themselves. Consumers with small orders find the new self-service POS terminals convenient because these terminals often eliminate the hassle of waiting in long lines.

which verifies that you are the holder of the bankcard. When your transaction is complete, the ATM prints a receipt for your records.

FIGURE 5-41 An ATM is a self-service banking terminal that allows customers to access their bank accounts.

FIGURE 5-40 Some grocery stores offer self-serve checkouts, where the consumers themselves use the POS terminals to scan purchases, scan their store saver card and coupons, and then pay for the goods. This POS terminal prints a receipt for the customer.

Automated Teller Machines

An **automated teller machine (ATM)** is a self-service banking machine that connects to a host computer through a network (Figure 5-41). Banks place ATMs in convenient locations, including grocery stores, convenience stores, retail outlets, shopping malls, and gas stations, so customers conveniently can access their bank accounts.

Using an ATM, people withdraw cash, deposit money, transfer funds, or inquire about an account balance. Some ATMs have a touch screen; others have special buttons or keypads for entering input. To access a bank account, you insert a plastic bankcard in the ATM's magstripe reader. The ATM asks you to enter a password, called a *personal identification number (PIN)*,

BIOMETRIC INPUT

Biometrics is the technology of authenticating a person's identity by verifying a personal characteristic. Biometric devices grant users access to programs, systems, or rooms by analyzing some biometric identifier. A *biometric identifier* is a physiological (related to physical or chemical activities in the body) or behavioral characteristic. Examples include fingerprints, hand geometry, facial features, voice, signatures, and eye patterns.

A *biometric device* translates a personal characteristic (the input) into a digital code that is compared with a digital code stored in the computer. If the digital code in the computer does not match the personal characteristic's code, the computer denies access to the individual.

The most widely used biometric device today is a fingerprint scanner. A **fingerprint scanner** captures curves and indentations of a fingerprint. With the cost of fingerprint scanners less than $100, home and small business users install fingerprint scanners to authenticate users before they can access a personal computer. Instead of lunch money, grade schools use fingerprint scanners to identify students in the cafeteria and adjust account balances for each lunch purchased (Figure 5-42).

External fingerprint scanners usually plug into a parallel or USB port. To save on desk space, some newer keyboards and notebook computers have a fingerprint scanner built into them. For a technical discussion about fingerprint scanners, read the High-Tech Talk article on page 268.

A *face recognition system* captures a live face image and compares it with a stored image to determine if the person is a legitimate user. Some buildings use face recognition systems to secure access to rooms. Law enforcement, surveillance systems, and airports use face recognition to protect the public. Some notebook computers use this security technique to safeguard a computer. The computer will not start unless the user is legitimate. These programs are becoming more sophisticated and can recognize people with or without glasses, makeup, or jewelry, and with new hairstyles.

Biometric devices measure the shape and size of a person's hand using a *hand geometry system* (Figure 5-43). Because their cost is more than $1,000, larger companies use these systems as time and attendance devices or as security devices. Colleges use hand geometry systems to verify students' identities. Day-care centers and hospital nurseries use them to verify parents who pick up their children.

A *voice verification system* compares a person's live speech with their stored voice pattern. Larger organizations sometimes use voice verification systems as time and attendance devices. Many companies also use this technology for access to sensitive files and networks. Some financial services use voice verification systems to secure telephone banking transactions. These systems use speaker-dependent voice recognition software. That is, users train the computer to recognize their inflection patterns.

A *signature verification system* recognizes the shape of your handwritten signature, as well as measures the pressure exerted and the motion used to write the signature. Signature verification systems use a specialized pen and tablet.

FIGURE 5-42 This elementary school student pays for lunch by placing his finger on a fingerprint scanner.

FIGURE 5-43 A hand geometry system verifies this student's identity before he is allowed access to the school library.

WEB LINK 5-9

Biometric Input

For more information, visit scsite.com/ dc2006/ch5/weblink and then click Biometric Input.

High security areas use iris recognition systems. The camera in an *iris recognition system* uses iris recognition technology to read patterns in the iris of the eye (Figure 5-44). These patterns are as unique as a fingerprint. Iris recognition systems are quite expensive and are used by government security organizations, the military, and financial institutions that deal with highly sensitive data.

Sometimes, fingerprint, iris, and other biometric data are stored on a smart card. A **smart card**, which is comparable in size to a credit card or ATM card, stores the personal data on a thin microprocessor embedded in the card (Figure 5-45). Smart cards add an extra layer of protection. For example, when a user places a smart card through a smart card reader, the computer compares a fingerprint stored on the card with the one read by the fingerprint scanner. Some credit cards are smart cards; that is, the microprocessor contains the card holder's information instead of a magnetic stripe.

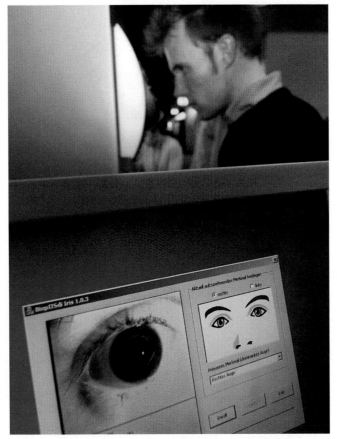

FIGURE 5-44 An iris recognition system.

FAQ 5-11

How popular is biometrics technology?

One study estimates that revenue from biometric solutions has and will continue to grow by about 35 percent annually for the next several years, as shown in the chart below. For more information, visit scsite.com/dc2006/ch5/faq and then click Biometrics.

Revenues from Biometric Solutions

Year	(in millions of dollars)

Source: International Biometric Group

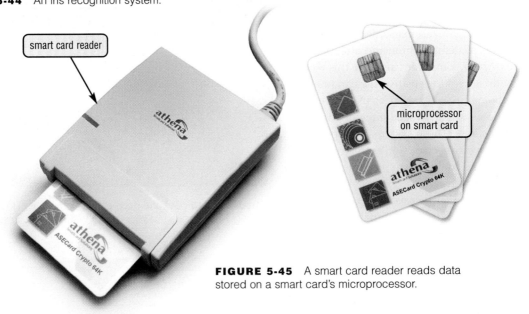

smart card reader

microprocessor on smart card

FIGURE 5-45 A smart card reader reads data stored on a smart card's microprocessor.

PUTTING IT ALL TOGETHER

When you purchase a computer, you should have an understanding of the input devices included with the computer, as well as those you may need that are not included. Many factors influence the type of input devices you may use: the type of input desired, the hardware and software in use, and the desired cost. The type of input devices you require depends on your intended use. Figure 5-46 outlines several suggested input devices for specific computer users.

SUGGESTED INPUT DEVICES BY USER

User	Input Device
HOME 	• Enhanced keyboard or ergonomic keyboard • Mouse • Stylus for PDA or smart phone • Joystick or wheel • 30-bit 600 x 1200 ppi color scanner • 2-megapixel digital camera • Headset that includes a microphone • PC video camera
SMALL OFFICE/ HOME OFFICE 	• Enhanced keyboard or ergonomic keyboard • Mouse • Stylus and portable keyboard for PDA or smart phone, or digital pen for Tablet PC • 36-bit 600 x 1200 ppi color scanner • 2-megapixel digital camera • Headset that includes a microphone • PC video camera
MOBILE 	• Wireless mouse for notebook computer • Trackball, touchpad, or pointing stick on notebook computer • Stylus and portable keyboard for PDA or smart phone, or digital pen for Tablet PC • 2- or 3-megapixel digital camera • Headset that includes a microphone • Fingerprint scanner for notebook computer
POWER 	• Enhanced keyboard or ergonomic keyboard • Mouse • Stylus and portable keyboard for PDA or smart phone • Pen for graphics tablet • 48-bit 1200 x 1200 ppi color scanner • 5- or 6-megapixel digital camera • Headset that includes a microphone • PC video camera
LARGE BUSINESS 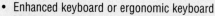	• Enhanced keyboard or ergonomic keyboard • Mouse • Stylus and portable keyboard for PDA or smart phone, or digital pen for Tablet PC • Touch screen • Light pen • 42-bit 1200 x 1200 ppi color scanner • OCR/OMR readers, bar code readers, MICR reader, or data collection devices • Microphone • Video camera for video conferences • Fingerprint scanner or other biometric device

FIGURE 5-46 This table recommends suggested input devices.

INPUT DEVICES FOR PHYSICALLY CHALLENGED USERS

The ever-increasing presence of computers in everyone's lives has generated an awareness of the need to address computing requirements for those who have or may develop physical limitations. The **Americans with Disabilities Act (ADA)** requires any company with 15 or more employees to make reasonable attempts to accommodate the needs of physically challenged workers.

Besides voice recognition, which is ideal for blind or visually impaired users, several other input devices are available. A *keyguard* is a metal or plastic plate placed over the keyboard that allows users to rest their hands on the keyboard without accidentally pressing any keys (Figure 5-47). A keyguard also guides a finger or pointing device so a user presses only one key at a time.

Keyboards with larger keys also are available. Still another option is the *on-screen keyboard*, in which a graphic of a standard keyboard is displayed on the user's screen (Figure 5-48).

Various pointing devices are available for users with motor disabilities. Small trackballs that the user controls with a thumb or one finger can be attached to a table, mounted to a wheelchair, or held in the user's hand. Another option for people with limited hand movement is a *head-mounted pointer* to control the pointer or insertion point (Figure 5-49). To simulate the functions of a mouse button, a user works with switches that control the pointer. The switch might be a hand pad, a foot pedal, a receptor that detects facial motions, or a pneumatic instrument controlled by puffs of air.

Two exciting developments in this area are gesture recognition and computerized implant devices. Both in the prototype stage, they attempt to provide users with a natural computer interface.

With *gesture recognition*, the computer will detect human motions. Computers with gesture recognition capability have the potential to recognize sign language, read lips, track facial movements, or follow eye gazes. For paralyzed or speech impaired individuals, a doctor will implant a computerized device into the brain. This device will contain a transmitter. As the user thinks thoughts, the transmitter will send signals to the computer.

FIGURE 5-47   A keyguard.

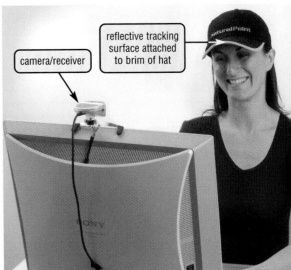

reflective tracking surface attached to brim of hat

camera/receiver

FIGURE 5-49   A camera/receiver mounted on the monitor tracks the position of the head-mounted pointer, which is reflective material that this user is wearing on the brim of her hat. As the user moves her head, the pointer on the screen also moves.

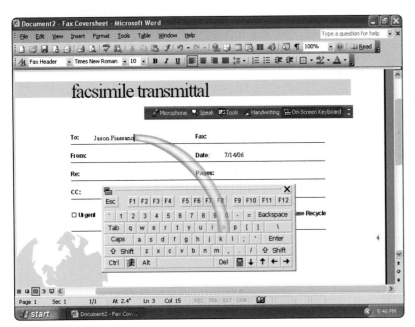

FIGURE 5-48   As you click letters on the on-screen keyboard, they appear in the document at the location of the insertion point.

Test your knowledge of pages 255 through 266 in Quiz Yourself 5-3.

QUIZ YOURSELF 5-3

Instructions: Find the true statement below. Then, rewrite the remaining false statements so they are true.

1. A fingerprint scanner captures curves and indentations of a signature.
2. After swiping a credit card through an MICR reader, a POS terminal connects to a system that authenticates the purchase.
3. ATMs ask you to enter a password, called a biometric identifier, which verifies that you are the holder of the bankcard.
4. Four types of source documents are flatbed, pen, sheet-fed, and drum.
5. Retail and grocery stores use the POSTNET bar code.
6. RFID is a technology that uses laser signals to communicate with a tag placed in an object, an animal, or a person.
7. The Americans with Disabilities Act (ADA) requires any company with 15 or more employees to make reasonable attempts to accommodate the needs of physically challenged workers.

Quiz Yourself Online: To further check your knowledge of scanners and reading devices, terminals, biometric devices, and input for physically challenged users, visit scsite.com/dc2006/ch5/quiz and then click Objectives 9 – 12.

CHAPTER SUMMARY

Input is any data and instructions you enter into the memory of a computer. This chapter described the various techniques of entering input and several commonly used input devices (Read Looking Ahead 5-2 for a look at the next generation of input devices). Topics presented included the keyboard, mouse, and other pointing devices; voice input; input for PDAs, smart phones, and Tablet PCs; digital cameras; video input; scanners and reading devices; terminals; biometric input; and input devices for physically challenged users.

LOOKING AHEAD 5-2

Wearable Computers Make Performance Statement

Frodo, the hero in the *Lord of the Rings* trilogy, wears a durable, inconspicuous tunic that saves his life. You, too, may one day wear a garment that saves your life by detecting health problems and summoning emergency help. Researchers in Germany have developed undergarments with sensors that monitor heartbeats and then alert medical experts when an abnormal heart rhythm is detected.

While this clothing is practical, other researchers are creating the newest fashions and accessories outfitted with computers. For example, a cellular telephone could connect wirelessly to a calorie counter monitor on your wrist and then order food when it detects you are hungry. Other wearable computers can change color depending upon weather conditions, deliver e-mail messages, and improve a golf swing. For more information, visit scsite.com/dc2006/ch5/looking and then click Wearable Computers.

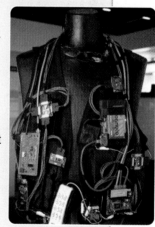

CAREER CORNER

Data Entry Clerk

Data entry clerks have an essential role in today's information-producing industry. A *data entry clerk* enters data into documents, databases, and other applications using computer keyboards and visual display devices. Duties can include manipulating, editing, and maintaining data to ensure that it is accurate and up-to-date, and researching information.

Some data entry clerks telecommute. Although they generally use keyboards, they also work with other input from scanners or electronically transmitted files. Because of the nature of their job, data entry clerks often sit for hours typing in front of monitors. They can be susceptible to repetitive stress injuries and neck, back, and eye strain. To prevent these injuries, many offices use ergonomically designed input devices and incorporate regularly scheduled exercise breaks.

Data entry clerks usually are high school graduates with keyboarding skills. Some employers require an associate's degree or at least two years of post-high-school education plus two years of office experience. Data entry training, basic language skills, and familiarity with word processing, spreadsheet, and database programs are important. Data entry often serves as a stepping-stone to other administrative positions. The average annual salary for data entry clerks is around $23,000. Salaries start at about $18,000 and, with experience, can exceed $31,000. For more information, visit scsite.com/dc2006/ch5/careers and then click Data Entry Clerk.

High-Tech Talk

BIOMETRICS: PERSONALIZED SECURITY

Biometric authentication is based on the measurement of an individual's unique physiological and behavioral characteristics. The most common measurements, described earlier in this chapter, such as fingerprints, hand geometry, facial features, and eye patterns are physiological biometrics. Some of the more novel measurements, such as body odor, brain wave patterns, DNA, ear shape, sweat pores, and vein patterns also fall into the category of physiological biometrics. Voice scan and signature scan are examples of behavioral biometrics.

Any biometric technology process involves two basic steps — enrollment and matching. To illustrate these steps, this High-Tech Talk uses the most common biometric technology, finger-scan technology.

ENROLLMENT   Enrollment is the process in which a user presents the fingerprint data to be stored in a template for future use, as shown in the top of Figure 5-50. This initial template is called the *enrollment template*. Creating the enrollment template involves four basic steps: (1) acquire fingerprint, (2) extract fingerprint feature, (3) create enrollment template, and (4) store enrollment template. The enrollment template usually is created only after the user has submitted several samples of the same fingerprint. Most fingerprint images will have false details, usually caused by cuts, scars, or even dirt, which must be filtered out.

The first step, acquire fingerprint, presents a major challenge to finger-scan technology. The quality of a fingerprint may vary substantially from person to person and even finger to finger. The two main methods of acquiring images are optical and silicon. With optical technology, a camera is used to register the fingerprint image against a plastic or glass platen (scanner). Silicon technology uses a silicon chip as a platen, which usually produces a higher quality fingerprint image than optical devices.

The second step, extract fingerprint feature, involves thinning the ridges of the raw image to a minuscule size and then converting the characteristics to binary format. Fingerprints are comprised of ridges and valleys that have unique patterns, such as arches, loops, and swirls. Irregularities and discontinuities in these ridges and valleys are known as *minutiae*. Minutiae are the distinctive characteristics upon which most finger-scan technology is based. The fingerprint-feature extraction process used is highly sophisticated, patented, and a closely-held vendor secret.

In the third step, the binary format is used to create the enrollment template. The fourth and final step involves storing the template on a storage device, such as a hard disk or smart card for future use when the same person attempts to be authenticated.

MATCHING   Matching is the process of comparing a match template to an enrollment template. A *match template* is created when the user attempts to gain access through a fingerprint scanner. Most computer and network systems are set up so that the person also must claim an identity, such as a user name, along with the fingerprint. In this case, the match template is compared directly to the enrollment template for that user name. Other systems, such as those used for criminal investigations, will search the entire enrollment template database for a match.

The match template is created in the same fashion as the enrollment template described earlier. Rather than storing the match template on disk, however, it is compared to the user's stored enrollment template, as shown in the bottom of Figure 5-50. The result of the matching process is a score. The score is compared against a threshold. The threshold is a predefined number that can be adjusted depending on the desired level of security.

The scoring process leads to the decision process. The decision process will produce one of three actions: (1) the threshold has been exceeded, thereby resulting in a match; (2) the threshold has not been met, thereby resulting in a nonmatch; or (3) the data may have been insufficient, resulting in the system requesting a new sample from the user to begin a new comparison.

Finger-scan technology is likely to continue to grow as the centerpiece of the biometric industry. For more information, visit scsite.com/dc2006/ch5/tech and then click Biometrics.

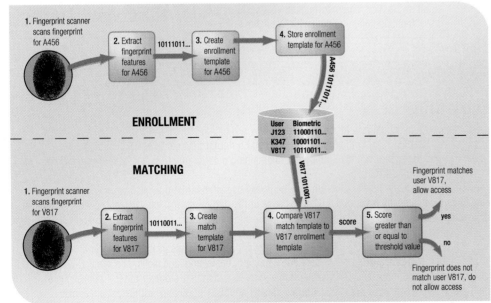

FIGURE 5-50 The two steps in biometric technology.

Companies on the Cutting Edge

LOGITECH
PERSONAL INTERFACE PRODUCTS LEADER

The average Internet user has more than 40 inches of cords on his desktop, according to a *Logitech* survey. This company is working to reduce desktop clutter with a variety of cordless peripherals, including mouse devices, keyboards, mobile headsets, and game controllers.

A market leader, Logitech has sold more than 45 million wireless devices. It also designs, manufactures, and markets corded devices. The company's retail sales account for more than 80 percent of its revenue.

Two engineering students from Stanford University, Italian-born Pierluigi Zappacosta and Swiss-born Daniel Borel, launched Logitech in 1981. Today, the corporation is the world's largest manufacturer of the mouse, having sold more than 500 million since the company's founding. For more information, visit scsite.com/dc2006/ch5/companies and then click Logitech.

palmOne
HANDHELD COMPUTING DEVICES MANUFACTURER

The PalmPilot holds the distinction of being the most rapidly adopted new computing product ever manufactured. More than two million units of this PDA were sold since Palm Computing introduced the product in 1996.

Palm Computing was founded in 1992 and became a subsidiary of 3Com Corp. in 1997. In 2000, the Palm subsidiary became an independent, publicly traded company. In 2003, shareholders voted to spin off PalmSource, Inc., maker of the Palm operating system, as an independent company and acquire Handspring, Inc. The combined company is known as *palmOne, Inc.*

The palmOne product family includes the Zire and Tungsten handheld devices and the Treo smart phones. For more information, visit scsite.com/dc2006/ch5/companies and then click palmOne.

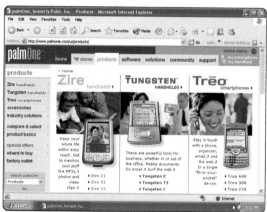

Technology Trailblazers

HIDEKI KOMIYAMA
SONY ELECTRONICS PRESIDENT AND CEO

Sony introduced its first U.S. product more than 30 years ago much to the credit of *Hideki Komiyama*. The Trinitron color television was the start of Sony's dominance in the consumer electronics field.

Under Komiyama's leadership, Sony has introduced a music download service and engineered new products, including liquid crystal display televisions and DVD recorders. Popular consumer electronics products include the VAIO personal computer and the Mavica and Cyber-shot digital cameras. Komiyama's goal is to make new consumer products extremely user friendly. He believes that the consumer electronics industry gradually will shift from audio and video technologies to information technology.

Komiyama was promoted to president and CEO in 2003. He joined Sony in 1967, and his other executive-level positions in the United States have included senior vice president of consumer video products and president of the Consumer Television Company. For more information, visit scsite.com/dc2006/ch5/people and then click Hideki Komiyama.

DOUGLAS ENGELBART
CREATOR OF THE MOUSE

The phrase "point and click" might not be part of every computer user's vocabulary if *Douglas Engelbart* had not pursued his engineering dreams. In 1964, he developed the first prototype computer mouse with the goal of making it easier to move a cursor around a computer screen.

Ten years later, engineers at Xerox refined Engelbart's prototype and showed the redesigned product to Apple's Steve Jobs, who applied the concept to his graphical Macintosh computer. The mouse was mass produced in the mid-1980s, and today it is the most widely used pointing device.

Engelbart currently serves as director of the Bootstrap Institute, a company he founded with his daughter to form strategic alliances and consequently improve corporations' performances. For more information, visit scsite.com/dc2006/ch5/people and then click Douglas Engelbart.

Quizzes and Learning Games

Computer Genius
Crossword Puzzle
DC Track and Field
Practice Test
Quiz Yourself
Wheel of Terms
You're Hired!

Exercises

Case Studies
▸ Chapter Review
Checkpoint
Key Terms
Learn How To
Learn It Online
Web Research

Beyond the Book

Career Corner
Companies
FAQs
High-Tech Talk
Looking Ahead
Making Use of
the Web
Trailblazers
Web Links

Features

Chapter Forum
Install Computer
Lab Exercises
Maintain Computer
Tech News
Timeline 2006

Chapter Review

The Chapter Review section summarizes the concepts presented in this chapter. To listen to the audio version of this Chapter Review, visit scsite.com/dc2006/ch5/review. To obtain help from other students regarding any subject in this chapter, visit scsite.com/dc2006/ch5/forum and post your thoughts or questions.

① What Is Input?   Input is any *data* or instructions entered into the memory of a computer. An **input device** is any hardware component that allows users to enter data and instructions.

② What Are the Characteristics of a Keyboard?   A **keyboard** is an input device that contains keys users press to enter data into a computer. Computer keyboards have a typing area that includes letters of the alphabet, numbers, punctuation marks, and other basic keys. Most keyboards also have *function keys* programmed to issue commands; keys used to move the **insertion point**, usually a blinking vertical bar, on the screen; and *toggle keys* that switch between two states when pressed.

③ What Are Different Mouse Types, and How Do They Work?   A **pointing device** is an input device that allows users to control a small graphical symbol, called a **pointer**, on the computer screen. A **mouse** is a pointing device that fits under the palm of your hand. As you move a mouse, the pointer on the screen also moves. A *mechanical mouse* translates the movement of a ball on its underside into signals the computer can process. An *optical mouse* uses devices that emit and sense light to detect the mouse's movement. A *cordless mouse* transmits data using wireless technology.

④ How Do Pointing Devices Work?   A **trackball** is a stationary pointing device with a ball that you rotate to move the pointer. A **touchpad** is a flat, pressure-sensitive device that you slide your finger across to move the pointer. A **pointing stick** is a device positioned on the keyboard that you push to move the pointer. A **joystick** is a vertical lever that you move to control a simulated vehicle or player. A **wheel** is a steering-wheel-type device that you turn to simulate driving a vehicle. A **light pen** is a light-sensitive device that you press against or point at the screen to select objects. A **touch screen** is a touch-sensitive display device that you interact with by touching areas of the screen. A **stylus** and a **digital pen** use pressure to write or draw.

> *connect*
> Visit scsite.com/dc2006/ch5/quiz or click the Quiz Yourself button. Click Objectives 1 – 4.

⑤ How Does Voice Recognition Work?   **Voice recognition** is the computer's capability of distinguishing spoken words. Voice recognition programs recognize a vocabulary of preprogrammed words. Most voice recognition programs are a combination of *speaker-dependent software*, which makes a profile of your voice, and *speaker-independent software*, which has a built-in set of word patterns.

⑥ What Are Input Devices for PDAs, Smart Phones, and Tablet PCs?   A primary input device for a PDA is a basic stylus. Some PDAs have a built-in keyboard or support voice input. You can attach a full-sized *portable keyboard* to a PDA. Voice is the traditional input method for smart phones. Users can send typed messages using *text messaging*. Some smart phones can use IM to communicate over the Internet, and many have a camera so that users can use *picture messaging*. The primary input device for a Tablet PC is a digital pen, with which you can write on the device's screen. If you slide a Tablet PC into a *docking station*, you can use a full-sized keyboard and mouse.

⑦ How Does a Digital Camera Work?   A **digital camera** allows users to take pictures and store the photographed images digitally. When you take a picture, light passes into the camera lens, which focuses the image on a *charge-coupled device (CCD)*. The CCD generates an analog signal that represents the image. An analog-to-digital converter (ADC) converts the analog signal to a digital signal. A processor in the camera stores the digital image on the camera's storage media. The image is downloaded to a computer's hard disk via cable or copied from the camera's storage media.

Chapter Review

8 **How Are PC Video Cameras, Web Cams, and Video Conferencing Used?** A **PC video camera** is a digital video camera that enables users to capture video and still images and then send or broadcast the images over the Internet. A **Web cam** is any video camera that displays its output on a Web page. A **video conference** is a meeting between geographically separated people who use a network or the Internet to transmit audio and video data.

> **connect**
> Visit scsite.com/dc2006/ch5/quiz or click the Quiz Yourself button. Click Objectives 5 – 8.

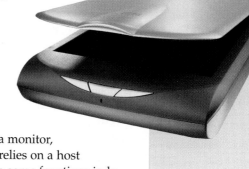

9 **What Are Various Types of Scanners and Reading Devices, and How Do They Work?** A **scanner** is a light-sensing input device that reads printed text and graphics and translates the results into a form the computer can process. A **flatbed scanner** works in a manner similar to a copy machine except it creates a file of the document. An optical reader uses a light source to read characters, marks, and codes and converts them into digital data. **Optical character recognition (OCR)** reads characters from ordinary documents. **Optical mark recognition (OMR)** reads hand-drawn marks such as small circles. A **bar code reader** is an optical reader that uses laser beams to read a **bar code**, or identification code. **RFID** (*radio frequency identification*) uses radio signals to communicate with an embedded tag. **MICR** (*magnetic-ink character recognition*) reads text printed with magnetized ink.

10 **What Are Types of Terminals?** A *terminal* consists of a keyboard, a monitor, a video card, and memory. A *dumb terminal* has no processing power and relies on a host computer for processing. A *smart terminal* has a processor and can perform some functions independent of the host computer. POS terminals and ATMs are special-purpose terminals. A **POS (point-of-sale) terminal** records purchases, processes credit or debit cards, and updates inventory. An **automated teller machine (ATM)** is a self-service banking machine that connects to a host computer. To access a bank account, you insert a bankcard into the ATM's card reader and enter a *personal identification number (PIN)*.

11 **What Are Various Biometric Devices?** A *biometric device* translates a personal characteristic into digital code that is compared with a digital code stored in the computer to identify an individual. A **fingerprint scanner** captures curves and indentations of a fingerprint. A *face recognition system* captures a live face image. A *hand geometry system* measures the shape and size of a hand. A *voice verification system* compares live speech with a stored voice pattern. A *signature verification system* recognizes the shape of a signature. An *iris recognition system* reads patterns in the iris of the eye.

12 **What Are Alternative Input Devices for Physically Challenged Users?** Voice recognition is ideal for visually impaired users. A *keyguard* is a plate placed over the keyboard that allows users with limited hand mobility to rest their hands and press only one key at a time. Keyboards with larger keys or an *on-screen keyboard* displayed on a user's screen also are available. A small trackball or a *head-mounted pointer* helps users with limited hand movement to control the pointer. Two developments in the prototype stage are *gesture recognition* and computerized implant devices.

> **connect**
> Visit scsite.com/dc2006/ch5/quiz or click the Quiz Yourself button. Click Objectives 9 – 12.

Quizzes and Learning Games

Computer Genius
Crossword Puzzle
DC Track and Field
Practice Test
Quiz Yourself
Wheel of Terms
You're Hired!

Exercises

Case Studies
Chapter Review
Checkpoint
▶ Key Terms
Learn How To
Learn It Online
Web Research

Beyond the Book

Career Corner
Companies
FAQs
High-Tech Talk
Looking Ahead
Making Use of the Web
Trailblazers
Web Links

Features

Chapter Forum
Install Computer
Lab Exercises
Maintain Computer
Tech News
Timeline 2006

Key Terms

You should know the Primary Terms and be familiar with the Secondary Terms. Use the list below to help focus your study. To further enhance your understanding of the Key Terms in this chapter, visit scsite.com/dc2006/ch5/terms. See an example of and a definition for each term, and access current and additional information about the term from the Web.

Primary Terms

(shown in bold-black characters in the chapter)

Americans with Disabilities Act (ADA) (266)
audio input (246)
automated teller machine (ATM) (262)
bar code (258)
bar code reader (258)
bar code scanner (258)
digital camera (250)
digital pen (243)
digital video (DV) camera (253)
ergonomics (238)
fingerprint scanner (262)
flatbed scanner (256)
graphics tablet (244)
input (234)
input device (236)
insertion point (237)
joystick (242)
keyboard (236)
light pen (242)
magnetic stripe card reader (260)
MICR (260)
MICR reader (260)
mouse (239)
mouse pad (239)
OCR devices (257)

optical character recognition (OCR) (257)
optical mark recognition (OMR) (257)
PC camera (253)
PC video camera (253)
pen input (243)
pointer (239)
pointing device (239)
pointing stick (241)
POS terminal (261)
resolution (252)
RFID (259)
RFID reader (259)
scanner (255)
smart card (264)
stylus (243)
touch screen (242)
touchpad (241)
trackball (241)
turnaround document (257)
video conference (254)
video input (253)
voice input (245)
voice recognition (245)
Web cam (254)
wheel (242)

Secondary Terms

(shown in italic characters in the chapter)

biometric device (262)
biometric identifier (262)
biometrics (262)
charge-coupled device (CCD) (251)
command (235)
continuous speech (246)
cordless keyboard (238)
cordless mouse (239)
cursor (application program) (237)
cursor (graphics tablet) (244)
data (234)
data collection device (261)
digitizer (244)
discrete speech (246)
docking station (249)
download (251)
dumb terminal (261)
enhanced keyboard (237)
enhanced resolution (252)
ergonomic keyboard (238)
face recognition system (263)
field camera (251)
function keys (236)
gesture recognition (266)
hand geometry system (263)
handwriting recognition software (243)
head-mounted pointer (266)
image processing (256)
image processing system (256)
iris recognition system (264)
keyguard (266)
magnetic-ink character recognition (260)
magstripe reader (260)
mechanical mouse (239)
MIDI (musical instrument digital interface) (246)
mouse gestures (240)
mouse pointer (239)

MP (252)
OCR (optical character recognition) software (256)
on-screen keyboard (266)
optical mouse (239)
optical reader (257)
optical resolution (252)
optical scanner (255)
personal identification number (PIN) (262)
picture messaging (249)
pixel (252)
pixels per inch (ppi) (252)
point-and-shoot camera (251)
point of sale (POS) (261)
portable keyboard (248)
program (234)
radio frequency identification (259)
signature verification system (263)
smart terminal (261)
source document (255)
speaker-dependent software (246)
speaker-independent software (246)
speech recognition (245)
streaming cam (254)
studio camera (251)
terminal (261)
text messaging (248)
toggle key (237)
UPC (Universal Product Code) (258)
user response (235)
video capture card (253)
video telephone call (253)
voice verification system (263)
whiteboard (254)
wireless keyboard (238)
wireless mouse (239)

Checkpoint

Use the Checkpoint exercises to check your knowledge level of the chapter. The Beyond the Book exercises will help broaden your understanding of the concepts presented in this chapter. To complete the Checkpoint exercises interactively, visit scsite.com/dc2006/ch5/check.

Label the Figure   Identify these areas and keys on a desktop computer keyboard.

a. function keys

b. media controls

c. numeric keypad

d. additional keys

e. APPLICATION key

f. arrow keys

g. typing area

h. WINDOWS key

True/False   Mark T for True and F for False. (See page numbers in parentheses.)

_____ 1. Once data is in memory, the computer interprets and executes instructions to process the data into information. (234)

_____ 2. An input device is any hardware component that allows users to enter data and instructions into a computer. (236)

_____ 3. The command associated with a function key will remain the same from program to program. (236)

_____ 4. An optical mouse has a rubber or metal ball on its underside. (239)

_____ 5. The trackball is the most widely used pointing device today. (241)

_____ 6. A pointing stick requires special cleaning, just like a mechanical mouse or trackball. (241)

_____ 7. Pressure-sensitive digital pens typically provide more functionality than a stylus. (243)

_____ 8. A stylus is the primary input device for a PDA. (247)

_____ 9. The primary input device for a Tablet PC is a pressure-sensitive digital pen. (249)

_____ 10. Digital cameras typically allow users to review, and sometimes edit, images while they are in the camera. (250)

_____ 11. A scanner is a light-sensing input device that reads printed text and graphics and then translates the results into a form the computer can process. (255)

_____ 12. Many companies use optical mark recognition (OMR) to read hand-printed characters on turnaround documents. (257)

Quizzes and Learning Games

Computer Genius
Crossword Puzzle
DC Track and Field
Practice Test
Quiz Yourself
Wheel of Terms
You're Hired!

Exercises

Case Studies
Chapter Review
Checkpoint
Key Terms
Learn How To
Learn It Online
Web Research

Beyond the Book

Career Corner
Companies
FAQs
High-Tech Talk
Looking Ahead
Making Use of the Web
Trailblazers
Web Links

Features

Chapter Forum
Install Computer
Lab Exercises
Maintain Computer
Tech News
Timeline 2006

Checkpoint

 Multiple Choice   Select the best answer. (See page numbers in parentheses.)

1. _____ is a series of instructions that tells a computer what to do and how to do it. (234)
   a. Data
   b. A program
   c. A command
   d. A user response

2. _____ keys are special keys programmed to issue commands to a computer. (236)
   a. Toggle
   b. Arrow
   c. Function
   d. Numeric

3. A(n) _____ is a key that switches between two states each time the user presses the key. (237)
   a. arrow
   b. insertion point
   c. toggle
   d. function key

4. _____ is a common mouse operation in which you press and release the primary mouse button. (240)
   a. Point
   b. Click
   c. Drag
   d. Right-click

5. A _____ is a small, flat, rectangular pointing device that is sensitive to pressure and motion. (241)
   a. stylus
   b. pointing stick
   c. trackball
   d. touchpad

6. Architects, mapmakers, designers, artists, and home users create drawings and sketches on a _____. (244)
   a. trackball
   b. touch screen
   c. graphics tablet
   d. touchpad

7. A portable keyboard _____. (248)
   a. is an infrared image of a keyboard projected on a flat surface
   b. is built into the top of a handheld computer
   c. has a design that reduces the chance of wrist and hand injuries
   d. is a full-sized keyboard you use with a PDA or other mobile device

8. The most expensive and highest quality digital camera is a _____, which is a stationary camera used for professional work. (251)
   a. PC camera
   b. point-and-shoot camera
   c. studio camera
   d. field camera

9. A digital video (DV) camera _____. (253)
   a. records video as analog signals instead of digital signals
   b. is a stationary camera used for professional studio work
   c. records video as digital signals instead of analog signals
   d. is a mobile camera used for amateur studio work

10. Scanners capture data from a _____, which is the original form of the data. (255)
    a. duplicate document
    b. secondary document
    c. derivative document
    d. source document

11. The UPC (Universal Product Code) bar code is used by _____. (258)
    a. retail and grocery stores
    b. libraries, blood banks, and air parcel carriers
    c. the United States Postal Service (USPS)
    d. nonretail applications such as game tickets

12. Point-of-sale terminals and automated teller machines are types of _____ that perform specific tasks and contain features uniquely designed for use in a particular industry. (261)
    a. smart terminals
    b. dumb terminals
    c. general-purpose terminals
    d. special-purpose terminals

13. The most widely used biometric device is the _____. (262)
    a. face recognition system
    b. fingerprint scanner
    c. hand geometry system
    d. iris recognition system

14. A(n) _____ is a metal or plastic plate that allows users to rest their hands on the keyboard without accidentally pressing any keys. (266)
    a. on-screen keyboard
    b. keyguard
    c. head-mounted pointer
    d. computerized implant

Checkpoint

Matching

Match the terms with their definitions. (See page numbers in parentheses.)

_____ 1. insertion point (237)

_____ 2. ergonomic keyboard (238)

_____ 3. pointer (239)

_____ 4. mouse pad (239)

_____ 5. graphics tablet (244)

_____ 6. docking station (249)

_____ 7. video capture card (253)

_____ 8. bar code (258)

_____ 9. RFID (259)

_____ 10. smart card (264)

a. designed to reduce the chance of wrist and hand injuries

b. symbol on the screen that indicates where the next character typed will be displayed

c. stores personal data on a thin, embedded computer

d. technology that uses radio signals to communicate with a tag placed in an item

e. graphical symbol whose location and shape change with the movement of a pointing device

f. identification code that consists of vertical lines and spaces of different widths

g. rectangular pad that provides better traction than the top of a desk

h. external device that attaches to a mobile computer or device that contains a power connection and provides connections to peripherals

i. flat, rectangular, electronic plastic board sometimes called a digitizer

j. self-service banking machine that connects to a host computer

k. converts an analog video signal to a digital signal that a computer can use

l. projects an infrared image of a keyboard on any flat surface

Short Answer

Write a brief answer to each of the following questions.

1. How does voice recognition work? _____ How is discrete speech different from continuous speech? _____

2. What is a video capture card? _____ Why is a video capture card not needed with a digital video (DV) camera? _____

3. What is OCR (optical character recognition) software? _____ What is an image processing system? _____

4. What is a bar code reader? _____ Define RFID, and list some of its uses. _____

5. What is the Americans with Disabilities Act (ADA)? _____ How might gesture recognition and computerized implant devices help physically challenged users in the future? _____

Beyond the Book

Read the following book elements, learn more about each using the Web, and then write a brief report.

1. At Issue — Keyboard Monitoring — Privacy Risk? (237), Should the Government Set Computer Use Standards? (240), Should Driving While Using Smart Phones Be Illegal? (249), Should Cameras Be Able to Monitor Your Every Move? (254), or Scanner Errors at the Checkout Counter? (258)

2. Career Corner — Data Entry Clerk (267)

3. Companies on the Cutting Edge — Logitech or palmOne (269)

4. FAQs (237, 238, 240, 246, 250, 251, 252, 254, 256, 259, 264)

5. High-Tech Talk — Biometrics: Personalized Security (268)

6. Looking Ahead — Smart Dust Monitors the Environment (259) or Wearable Computers Make Performance Statement (267)

7. Making Use of the Web — Auctions (121)

8. Picture Yourself Going Digital (232)

9. Technology Trailblazers — Hideki Komiyama and Douglas Engelbart (269)

10. Web Links (240, 241, 242, 244, 246, 253, 256, 264)

Quizzes and Learning Games

Computer Genius
Crossword Puzzle
DC Track and Field
Practice Test
Quiz Yourself
Wheel of Terms
You're Hired!

Exercises

Case Studies
Chapter Review
Checkpoint
Key Terms
Learn How To
Learn It Online
Web Research

Beyond the Book

Career Corner
Companies
FAQs
High-Tech Talk
Looking Ahead
Making Use of the Web
Trailblazers
Web Links

Features

Chapter Forum
Install Computer
Lab Exercises
Maintain Computer
Tech News
Timeline 2006

Learn It Online

Use the Learn It Online exercises to reinforce your understanding of the chapter concepts. To access the Learn It Online exercises, visit scsite.com/dc2006/ch5/learn.

(1) At the Movies — Get the Best of Both Worlds with a Convertible Tablet PC

To view the Get the Best of Both Worlds with a Convertible Tablet PC movie, click the number 1 button. Locate your video and click the corresponding High-Speed or Dial-Up link, depending on your Internet connection. Watch the movie, and then complete the exercise by answering the questions that follow. Taking classroom notes with pen and paper may be a thing of the past if the Tablet PC continues its rise in popularity. Switching to a Tablet PC can offer you some options that are not available on a regular notebook or desktop computer. What are some of the drawbacks to using a Tablet PC? What are some of the benefits?

(2) At the Movies — Buy the Right Digital Camera

To view the Buy the Right Digital Camera movie, click the number 2 button. Locate your video and click the corresponding High-Speed or Dial-Up link, depending on your Internet connection. Watch the movie and then complete the exercise by answering the questions that follow. A single digital camera that is perfect for every user simply does not exist. When making the decision about which model to purchase, you must consider how and where you will use the camera and what results you will expect. If you wanted to purchase a digital camera, what options would be important to you? Which options would not be important to you? How important would portability be? What about picture quality?

(3) Student Edition Labs — Working with Audio

Click the number 3 button. When the Student Edition Labs menu appears, click *Working with Audio* to begin. A new browser window will open. Follow the on-screen instructions to complete the Lab. When finished, click the Exit button. If required, submit your results to your instructor.

(4) Student Edition Labs — Working with Video

Click the number 4 button. When the Student Edition Labs menu appears, click *Working with Video* to begin. A new browser window will open. Follow the on-screen instructions to complete the Lab. When finished, click the Exit button. If required, submit your results to your instructor.

(5) Practice Test

Click the number 5 button. Answer each question. When completed, enter your name and click the Grade Test button to submit the quiz for grading. Make a note of any missed questions. If required, submit your results to your instructor.

(6) Who Wants To Be a Computer Genius^2?

Click the number 6 button to find out if you are a computer genius. Directions about how to play the game will be displayed. When you are ready to play, click the Play button. Submit your score to your instructor.

(7) Wheel of Terms

Click the number 7 button to reinforce important terms you learned in this chapter by playing the Shelly Cashman Series version of this popular game. Directions about how to play the game will be displayed. When you are ready to play, click the Play button. Submit your score to your instructor.

Learn It Online

 8 DC Track and Field

Click the number 8 button to use what you have learned in this chapter to compete against other students in three track and field events. Directions about how to play the game will be displayed. When you are ready to play, click the start first event button. If required, submit your score to your instructor.

 9 You're Hired!

Click the number 9 button to use what you have learned in this chapter to embark on the path to a career in computers. Directions about how to play the game will be displayed. When you are ready to play, click the begin game button. If required, submit your score to your instructor.

10 Crossword Puzzle Challenge

Click the number 10 button. Complete the puzzle to reinforce skills you learned in this chapter. Directions about how to play the game will be displayed. When you are ready to play, click the Submit button. Submit the completed puzzle to your instructor.

11 Lab Exercises

Click the number 11 button. When the Lab Exercises menu appears, click the exercise assigned by your instructor. A new browser window will open. Follow the on-screen instructions to complete the exercise. When finished, click the Exit button. If required, submit your results to your instructor.

 12 In the News

Many people spend a great deal of time jotting notes on scratch pads, napkins, or self-stick notes. This may be fine for the occasional thought; however, in a situation where you would rather concentrate on the substance of the ideas being expressed, you may need a more sophisticated method for taking notes. Tape recorders have long been the mainstay for recording lectures, interviews, or one's thoughts, but they are restricted by the fact that the tapes last only so long before they

have to be flipped over or switched altogether. One new development is the voice pen, which is a flash-memory-based recording device. It records digitally, which offers higher quality over standard tapes, easy indexing, and instant erasure. It is approximately the size of a small cellular telephone or remote control unit and can record up to 500 minutes on long play settings. Click the number 12 button and read a news article about a new or improved input device, an input device being used in a new way, or an input device being made more available. What is the device? Who is promoting it? How will it be used? Will the input device change the number, or effectiveness, of potential users? If so, why?

13 Chapter Discussion Forum

Select an objective from this chapter on page 233 about which you would like more information. Click the number 13 button and post a short message listing a meaningful message title accompanied by one or more questions concerning the selected objective. In two days, return to the threaded discussion by clicking the number 13 button. Submit to your instructor your original message and at least one response to your message.

Quizzes and Learning Games

Computer Genius
Crossword Puzzle
DC Track and Field
Practice Test
Quiz Yourself
Wheel of Terms
You're Hired!

Exercises

Case Studies
Chapter Review
Checkpoint
Key Terms
▶ Learn How To
Learn It Online
Web Research

Beyond the Book

Career Corner
Companies
FAQs
High-Tech Talk
Looking Ahead
Making Use of the Web
Trailblazers
Web Links

Features

Chapter Forum
Install Computer
Lab Exercises
Maintain Computer
Tech News
Timeline 2006

 Learn How To

Use the Learn How To activities to learn fundamental skills when using a computer and accompanying technology. Complete the exercises and submit them to your instructor. Visit scsite.com/dc2006/ch5/howto to obtain more information pertaining to each activity.

LEARN HOW TO 1: Install and Use a PC Video Camera

A **PC video camera**, sometimes called a Web cam, is a digital video camera that allows you to capture video and still images. The videos can be used in live instant messages or for live images over the Internet. Recordings of the videos can be included on Web pages or in e-mail messages as attachments. In addition, some cameras include software that enables you to establish a visual security environment where the camera can be used to detect and record movement in its general vicinity.

Using a PC video camera requires two phases: 1) purchasing and installing the PC video camera, and 2) using the video camera to transmit live video or to record video or digital images.

To purchase and install a PC video camera, complete the following steps:

1. Determine how you want to use the video camera in order to decide the quality of camera you require and the camera software you need. PC video cameras range in price from about $25 to more than $125, and vary in picture quality, features, and accompanying software. If you are not sure of all features and prices, search the Web to determine the best camera for your use.

2. After making your purchase, you will find that most cameras are accompanied by a CD-ROM containing the software that enables the camera to communicate and work with the computer. Often, the instructions with the device will specify that you should place the CD-ROM in a CD or DVD drive and follow the on-screen instructions to install the software on the computer.

3. After the software is installed, you likely will be told to connect the camera to the computer. You do so by connecting the USB cable first to the camera and then to a USB port on your computer. When the camera is connected, you will be able to start the camera software from either the All Programs submenu or the Windows taskbar.

Once you have started the camera software, you will be able to use the camera for any of the tasks you require. Each camera and its accompanying software will allow you to create a video, use instant messaging to send live video to your IM contacts, and other uses as well. In addition, you often will be able to control the quality of your video output by modifying brightness, contrast, and clarity. With many cameras, you will be able to zoom in and out, and, from your keyboard, enter commands to move the camera lens left, right, up, and down.

On some cameras, you even can use a feature called face tracking, where the camera will remain focused on your face even when you move. This feature allows you to be more natural and not be concerned with always making sure you are placed exactly right for the camera.

As you can see, once you have purchased and installed a PC video camera, you will open an entirely new world of communication right from your computer.

Exercise

1. Assume you have decided to purchase a PC video camera to use for instant messaging. Search the Web to find the highest rated cameras available for purchase that can be used for your purposes. What is the most expensive camera you found? The least expensive? What features distinguish the two? Based on your use of the camera for instant messaging, what camera would you choose to buy? Why? Submit your answers to your instructor.

2. Optional: Purchase a PC video camera or borrow one from a friend. Install the camera software on a computer. Warning: If you are using a computer that is not your own, complete this exercise only with the owner's permission. Connect the camera to the computer. Practice with the camera and the accompanying software. What features does the software provide? Which feature do you find the most compelling? What features could you do without? Record a video of yourself answering these questions. Submit the video to your instructor.

Learn How To

LEARN HOW TO 2: Use the On-Screen Keyboard for Physically Challenged Users

Everyone who uses a computer must enter data and instructions into the computer. For people with limited hand and arm mobility, this can prove a daunting task. Windows XP and a variety of other applications provide a number of aids that can be useful. One of these is the on-screen keyboard.

The __on-screen keyboard__ allows a user to view the keyboard on the screen and select characters to enter by using several different methods. To display and use the on-screen keyboard, complete the following steps:

1. Click the Start button on the Windows taskbar, point to All Programs on the Start menu, point to Accessories on the All Programs submenu, point to Accessibility on the Accessories submenu, and then click On-Screen Keyboard on the Accessibility submenu. *The On-Screen Keyboard window opens. In addition, an On-Screen Keyboard dialog box might appear that indicates the on-screen keyboard provides a minimum level of functionality and that a more robust product might be needed for daily use.* If this dialog box is displayed, click the OK button to close it.
2. In the On-Screen Keyboard window, click Settings on the menu bar. Ensure a check mark is next to Always on Top.
3. If necessary, click Settings on the menu bar again. Click Typing Mode on the Settings menu. *The Typing Mode dialog box is displayed (Figure 5-51).*
4. Ensure the Click to select button is selected and then click the OK button in the Typing Mode dialog box.
5. Start your Web browser and click the Address bar.
6. Using the on-screen keyboard, enter the characters www.cnn.com and then click the ent key.
7. When the cnn.com Web page appears, click the enter symbol box in the Stock/Fund Quotes section of the page. Using the on-screen keyboard, enter ibm and then click the ent key.
8. After finding the stock price for IBM, close the browser window.
9. Start the WordPad program (see Learn How To number 1 on page 48).
10. In the On-Screen Keyboard window, click Settings on menu bar and then click Typing Mode on the Settings menu.
11. Ensure the Hover to select button is selected in the Typing Mode dialog box. Click the Minimum time to hover box arrow and select 1.00 seconds in the list. Click the OK button.
12. Click in the WordPad window to position the insertion point.
13. You can cause a character to be entered in the WordPad window by placing the mouse pointer over the desired key (hovering) for one second. Type the following using the on-screen keyboard: Accessibility tools are vital for computer users.
14. Close the WordPad window and then close the On-Screen Keyboard window.

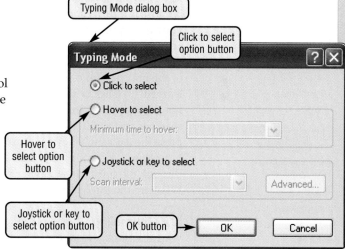

FIGURE 5-51

You have seen how one of the Accessibility tools within Windows XP functions. You are encouraged to explore all of the tools and discover how these tools can be useful to those people for whom they were designed.

Exercise

1. Start WordPad and then display the on-screen keyboard. In the On-Screen Keyboard window, click Settings on the menu bar and then click Typing Mode. In the Typing Mode dialog box, select Joystick or key to select. Click the Advanced button. Ensure the Keyboard key box contains a checkmark and then click Space in the list. Click the OK buttons to close the dialog boxes. Then, on the Keyboard menu, select Block Layout. Click in the WordPad window and then press the SPACEBAR. What happened? Keep pressing the SPACEBAR until you cause a character to be entered in the WordPad window. Use the bksp key on the on-screen keyboard to backspace and erase the character, and then use the on-screen keyboard to type On-Screen Keyboard usage in the WordPad window. When you are done, close the WordPad window and the On-Screen Keyboard window. Which means of using the on-screen keyboard (click a key, hover, or the SPACEBAR) did you find easiest to use? Why? Why would a physically challenged person prefer one method over another? Prepare your answers using the on-screen keyboard and then submit your answers to your instructor.

Quizzes and Learning Games

Computer Genius
Crossword Puzzle
DC Track and Field
Practice Test
Quiz Yourself
Wheel of Terms
You're Hired!

Exercises

Case Studies
Chapter Review
Checkpoint
Key Terms
Learn How To
Learn It Online
Web Research

Beyond the Book

Career Corner
Companies
FAQs
High-Tech Talk
Looking Ahead
Making Use of the Web
Trailblazers
Web Links

Features

Chapter Forum
Install Computer
Lab Exercises
Maintain Computer
Tech News
Timeline 2006

Web Research

Use the Internet-based Web Research exercises to broaden your understanding of the concepts presented in this chapter. Visit scsite.com/dc2006/ch5/research to obtain more information pertaining to each exercise. To discuss any of the Web Research exercises in this chapter with other students, post your thoughts or questions at scsite.com/dc2006/ch5/forum.

① Scavenger Hunt Use one of the search engines listed in Figure 2-10 in Chapter 2 on page 78 or your own favorite search engine to find the answers to the questions below. Copy and paste the Web address from the Web page where you found the answer. Some questions may have more than one answer. If required, submit your answers to your instructor. (1) The primary inventor of the first commercial typewriter wanted to persuade people to buy and use the device, so he ordered the keys to allow users to type as quickly as possible. Who was the QWERTY keyboard's primary inventor? (2) Many of the new handheld devices allow you to input data through the use of handwriting software. What are the three more popular handwriting/input programs? (3) Find two Web sites that sell these programs, and create a table listing the cost of each of these programs.

② Search Sleuth MetaCrawler (metacrawler.com) is a different type of search Web site because it returns combined results from leading search engines. Visit this Web site and then use your word processing program to answer the following questions. Then, if required, submit your answers to your instructor. (1) Click the Tools and Tips link at the top of the page. Browse and then explore some of the tools, such as MiniCrawler and MetaSpy. (2) Scroll down and then read some of the information contained in the Basic Searching section. Makes notes of two new things you learned. (3) Click your browser's Back button or press the BACKSPACE key to return to the MetaCrawler home page. What are the six most popular searches today? Click a link for one of these popular searches and scroll through the results MetaCrawler returns. (4) Click your browser's Back button or press the BACKSPACE key to return to the MetaCrawler home page. Click the Search text box and then type `What is the top selling SUV?` as the keywords in the Search text box. (5) Scroll through the links MetaCrawler returns and then click one that provides the information requested. What are the three most popular SUVs? Read the information and then write a 50-word summary.

③ Journaling Respond to your readings in this chapter by writing at least one page about your reactions, evaluations, and reflections about using input devices. For example, do you recall the first time you used a mouse? What experiences have you had with voice recognition? Do you own a PDA or Tablet PC, digital camera, or smart phone? Have you ever suffered from repetitive strain injuries from using a mouse or keyboard? What do you do to reduce the chances of experiencing repetitive strain injuries? You also can write about the new terms you learned by reading this chapter. If required, submit your journal to your instructor.

④ Expanding Your Understanding Journalists, attorneys, law enforcement officials, and students consider tape recorders and notepads essential components of their daily activities. An alternate means of capturing information is a voice pen, which is a flash-memory-based recording device approximately the size of a small smart phone. Visit a local electronics store or view electronics Web sites to learn more about voice pens. Compare their features, cost, recording time, and warranty. Write a report summarizing your findings, focusing on comparing and contrasting the voice pens. If required, submit your report to your instructor.

⑤ Ethics in Action Some reports suggest that a global surveillance system is monitoring e-mail messages, telephone calls, and faxes. This organization known as Echelon attempts to intercept more than three billion satellite, microwave, cellular, and fiber-optic messages per day, according to the reports. The National Security Agency is forbidden to monitor U.S. citizens, but privacy experts contend that at least 90 percent of U.S. communication is gathered and reviewed. View online sites that provide information about Echelon, including Echelon Watch (www.echelonwatch.org). Write a report summarizing your findings, and include a table of links to Web sites that provide additional details. If required, submit your report to your instructor.

Case Studies

Use the Case Studies to apply the concepts presented in the chapter to real-world situations. Visit scsite.com/dc2006/ch5/cases to obtain more information pertaining to each exercise. To discuss the Case Studies in this chapter with other students, visit scsite.com/dc2006/ch5/forum and post your thoughts or questions.

CASE STUDY 1 — Class Discussion   You work in the Efficiency Analysis department of one of the largest retail companies in the world, with multiple stores in every state and many other countries. For the past 25 years, the company has used optical scanners at checkout counters that read the UPC bar code on products to determine from a database the price to charge customers. The company is considering replacing the optical scanners with **radio frequency identification**, or RFID. The reader receives the code identifying the product via a chip with an antenna that is part of the box or label on the outside of the product. Your manager has asked you to draft a memo outlining the impact such a change would have on the company, its suppliers, and its customers. Be prepared to discuss your findings in class.

CASE STUDY 2 — Class Discussion   You have been asked to serve on your company's Voice Recognition Committee. The committee has been charged with investigating the feasibility of using voice recognition as a primary method for entering data and instructions into the company's computers. The chairperson of the committee has asked for your opinion on the use of **voice recognition**. When would voice recognition be an advantage over the keyboard and mouse? Might it ever be a disadvantage? Why? Prepare a brief report and be prepared to discuss your recommendations in class.

CASE STUDY 3 — Research   While attending college part-time for the past two years, you have worked as a data entry clerk for Salmon Mirror. Recently, you began to feel an unusual pain in your right wrist. Your doctor diagnosed the problem as **carpal tunnel syndrome**, which is the most well-known of a series of musculoskeletal disorders that fall under the umbrella of repetitive strain injuries (RSIs). Your doctor made several recommendations to relieve the pain, one of which was to find a new job. Before you begin job hunting, however, you want to learn more about this debilitating injury. Use the Web and/or print media to investigate carpal tunnel syndrome. Prepare a report and/or PowerPoint presentation on your findings. Include information about carpal tunnel syndrome warning signs, risk factors, suggestions about proper workstation ergonomics, and procedures for healing the injury. Share your report or presentation with your class.

CASE STUDY 4 — Research   An electronics company where you are employed as an analyst spends hundreds of thousands of dollars each year on travel to the multiple locations where they operate around the country. In an effort to curb the ever-increasing costs of travel, the CFO has asked you to look into the feasibility of adopting **video conferencing** at all of its major locations. Use the Web and/or print media to determine the advantages and disadvantages of video conferencing. Can the technology replace all or most face-to-face meetings? What are the costs of common video conferencing systems and the recurring costs their use incurs? Compare those costs to the cost of travel for a team of three people making six trips per year between New York and Los Angeles, including hotel, airline, and food expenses. Write a brief report or use PowerPoint to create a presentation and share your findings with your class.

CASE STUDY 5 — Team Challenge   The Transportation Security Administration (TSA) is looking into ways to expedite the airport screening experience of frequent flyers without compromising security. The TSA has hired your team as consultants to investigate **biometric technology**. In particular, they want your team to review three biometric devices for screening frequent flyers — fingerprint scanner, face recognition system, and iris recognition system. Form a three-member team and have each team member choose a different biometric device. Using the Web and/or print media, have each team member determine the advantages and disadvantages of their chosen biometric device. Include in each report how frequent flyer applicants would apply, accuracy rates of the device, and whether the device would indeed enhance security or open a loophole for terrorists. As a team, merge your findings into a team report and/or PowerPoint presentation and share your recommendations with your class.

Special Feature

Personal Mobile Devices

Mobile devices that usually can fit in your pocket, such as PDAs, smart phones, and smart pagers, are referred to as personal mobile devices (Figure 1). Page 22 in Chapter 1 discusses PDAs and smart phones. A **PDA** provides personal organizer functions, such as calendar, appointment book, address book, calculator, and notepad. A **smart phone** is an Internet-enabled telephone that usually provides PDA functionality. A **smart pager** is a wireless mobile device that provides data services, such as e-mail alerts, news alerts, and Internet access. Smart pagers usually provide PDA functionality, such as an address book and calendar. Additionally, some smart pagers include telephone capabilities.

Because the various types of personal mobile devices often offer similar capabilities, they typically are categorized by their form factor. A device's **form factor** refers to its size, shape, and configuration. For example, Figure 1 shows a smart phone that has a PDA form factor and a smart phone that has a phone form factor. While the device with the phone form factor may include PDA functionality, its main purpose is to be used as a phone. Its smaller size may make using it as a PDA more cumbersome than the smart phone with a PDA form factor. The PDA form factor, while larger, provides a better interface for accessing the PDA functionality.

Most personal mobile devices allow you to enhance their functionality through the use of accessories — such as headsets, cameras, and memory cards — and software. Not long ago, PDA (personal digital assistant) software consisted of a few programs, such as a to-do list and an address book. PDAs previously contained embedded software, meaning that a user could not change the software or add programs to the PDA. Today's PDAs, smart phones, and smart pagers allow for as much choice and versatility in their software as a typical personal computer. Most personal mobile devices come equipped with a rich set of programs. In some cases, a user may want to use enhanced versions of the included software, such as an enhanced calculator program, or install additional software, such as a game.

This special feature provides an overview of accessories and software available for personal mobile devices. The final section of the feature lists the criteria you should consider when deciding which personal mobile device is right for you.

PDA

smart pager

smart phone with PDA form factor

smart phone with phone form factor

FIGURE 1 Your choice of a personal mobile device depends on the features you require, the desired form factor, the available accessories, and the available software for the device.

PERSONAL MOBILE DEVICE OPERATING SYSTEMS

As with personal computers, personal mobile devices run an operating system. A personal mobile device runs software made only for the operating system of the device. Personal mobile devices can be categorized by the operating system that each runs. Figure 2 lists the common personal mobile device operating systems, the manufacturer, and a brief description of the operating system.

PERSONAL MOBILE DEVICE OPERATING SYSTEMS

Operating System	Manufacturer	Device Types	Description
Palm OS (versions 5 and later)	PalmSource	PDA Smart phone	The latest version of the operating system for Palm OS-based PDAs supports faster processors, multimedia, and more memory.
Palm OS (earlier versions)	PalmSource	PDA Smart phone	Several PDA manufacturers continue to use earlier versions of the Palm OS operating system because of the simplicity and lower power requirements, resulting in longer usage between recharges.
Windows Mobile for Pocket PC	Microsoft	PDA	The Windows Mobile operating system tightly integrates with Microsoft's Windows operating systems and includes scaled-down versions of many of Microsoft's popular programs, including Word, Outlook, Excel, and MSN Messenger.
Windows Mobile for Pocket PC Phone Edition	Microsoft	Smart phone with PDA form factor	The Pocket PC Phone Edition includes enhancements for the Windows Mobile operating system geared for phone use, such as enhancing the contact manager with the ability to dial a telephone number. This edition includes all of the Windows Mobile PDA functionality.
Windows Mobile for Smartphone	Microsoft	Smart phone with phone form factor	The Smartphone edition of the Windows Mobile operating system is designed for smaller screens and devices with less functionality than a typical PDA.
Blackberry	Research in Motion (RIM)	Smart pager Smart phone with PDA form factor	The Blackberry operating system runs on devices supplied by RIM. The devices include enhanced messaging and e-mail features when compared to smart phones.
Symbian OS	Symbian	Smart phone	Symbian OS is a popular PDA operating system commonly used on cellular telephones. Symbian OS is more popular in Europe and with business users.
Embedded Linux	Open source	PDA Smart phone	Some PDAs use a scaled down version of the free Linux operating system.

FIGURE 2 Personal mobile device capabilities depend on the operating system that they run.

ACCESSORIES FOR PERSONAL MOBILE DEVICE SOFTWARE

Most personal mobile devices have the capability to take advantage of add-on accessories. For example, using an external keyboard with a device greatly enhances the ability to enter data or notes quickly. Figure 3 lists the more common accessories available for a personal mobile device.

ACCESSORIES FOR PERSONAL MOBILE DEVICES

Accessory	Description
Keyboard	External keyboards provide much faster input when taking notes as opposed to using a small, built-in keyboard on a device. Keyboards may be wireless or attached to the device using a special cable.
Memory card	Memory cards provide additional storage space for a device. Some memory cards may include hardware enhancements such as wireless capability, a camera, or Bluetooth capability. Some cards come with preinstalled software or vast amount of data, such as a dictionary, on them.
Car kit	Car kits allow you to integrate a device with your car by providing mounting and/or hands-free operation of a device.
Chargers	Special chargers allow you to recharge a device's battery almost anywhere, such as an airplane, hotel, or foreign country. Some chargers provide emergency battery backup in case the device's batteries start running low when no electrical outlet is nearby.
Camera	Add-on cameras provide picture and video taking capability to devices with no such built-in functionality.
Case	Most mobile devices can be placed in a case or holster for protection while the device is not in use. Some devices include built-in flip screens to protect the device. You may want a case that fits comfortably in your shirt pocket, or one that includes a belt clip. A good case protects the device when it is dropped from a height of 3 or 4 feet.
Headset/earphones	Headsets allow you to wear a combined earpiece and microphone while keeping the device in your hand, pocket, or next to you. Some headsets use Bluetooth to communicate wirelessly with the device. Earphones are used when you want to listen to sound on your device, such as when listening to music or an e-book, or when watching a video.
GPS receiver	A GPS receiver contains an antenna, radio receiver, and processor and receives signals from GPS satellites to determine a location and/or speed. GPS receivers turn a personal mobile device into a complete GPS unit. The receivers typically include software that you must install on the device.

FIGURE 3   Some accessories for personal mobile devices are common to most devices, while others are specialized.

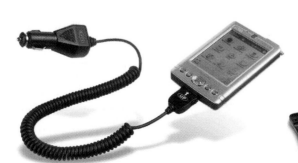

BUILT-IN PERSONAL MOBILE DEVICE SOFTWARE

Most personal mobile devices include several programs that provide basic functionality, such as an **address book** and **date book**. Figure 4 lists the types of software that usually are preinstalled on a personal mobile device.

BUILT-IN PERSONAL MOBILE DEVICE SOFTWARE

Application	Description
Address book and contacts	Maintains a list of acquaintances, including names, addresses, telephone numbers, e-mail addresses, and notes.
To-do list	Maintains a list of tasks. Tasks can be categorized and assigned a priority.
Calculator	Offers functionality of standard desktop calculators.
Datebook and calendar	Maintains appointments and important dates, such as birthdays and holidays. A user also sets audio or visual alarms to trigger when an appointment time arrives.
Memos and notepad	Keeps track of notes.
Launcher	The interface that allows a user to execute, or launch, programs, shown on the PDA screen in Figure 4.
Dialer	Smart phones typically include dialer software that assists you in using the telephone capabilities of a device. Some dialer software is integrated into the operating system so that you use dialing capabilities in other applications. For example, you can select a telephone number in the word processing program and request that the number be dialed.

FIGURE 4   Personal mobile devices typically contain this preinstalled software.

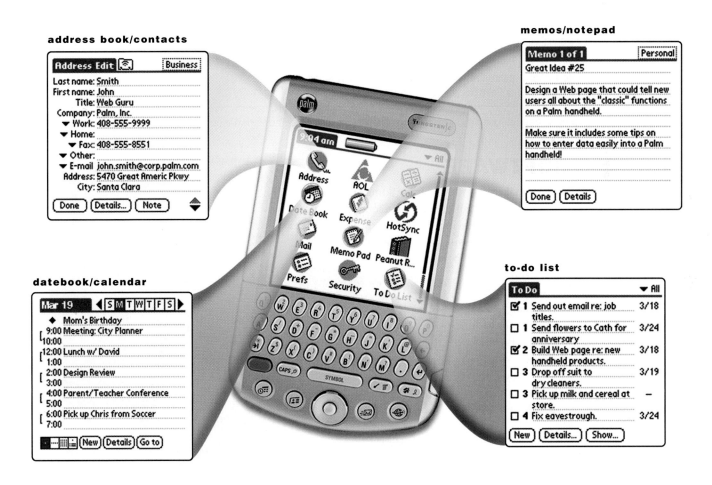

SYNCHRONIZATION SOFTWARE

Most personal mobile devices allow a user to share data and information between his or her personal computer and the device. The software that enables the sharing is called **synchronization software**. A personal mobile device may synchronize, or sync (pronounced sink), with a personal computer or a server on a network. Corporations often standardize their synchronization software so that employees share data across the corporate network, and so the data is backed up properly on a server. Figure 5 lists popular synchronization software for personal mobile devices.

SYNCHRONIZATION SOFTWARE FOR PERSONAL MOBILE DEVICES

Application	Description	Samples
Built-in	Most devices include software that the user loads on a personal computer that allows the computer to communicate with the device and share data and information.	• The Palm OS includes HotSync software • Pocket PC PDAs include ActiveSync software • Blackberry devices use the Blackberry Desktop Software
Synching many sources	Some device users have data and information stored in many places. For example, users may want to have their address books on the Web, on their personal computers, on their cellular telephones, and on their PDAs. Special synchronization software allows users to keep all of the address books up-to-date.	• Starfish TrueSync • PocketMirror • XTNDConnect Server
SyncML	**SyncML** is a standard that is being adopted by many companies that create personal mobile devices. SyncML allows for common information stored on a device to be shared among many devices, such as cellular telephones, other personal mobile devices, and personal computers.	• IBM WebSphere Everyplace Access • Pumatech Intellisync • Starfish TrueSync • fusionOne MightyPhone • Symbian based devices use SyncML
iSync	Apple's iSync software allows a user to keep a calendar and contact information synchronized up to the minute between a smart phone, an Apple iPod, a Palm OS device, or multiple Macs.	• Apple iSync

FIGURE 5   Personal mobile devices use synchronization software to share data and information with a personal computer or server.

BUSINESS SOFTWARE

Most programs used on a personal mobile device have some counterpart program on a desktop computer. For example, both a personal computer and a PDA or smart phone may include a word processing program. Many business programs have counterparts on personal mobile devices. The personal mobile device versions of these programs generally have fewer features and options. For example, a word processing program on a PDA may not have a spelling checker, and a spreadsheet program may not include all of the built-in calculations of its desktop computer counterpart. A smart phone with a phone form factor may allow you only to view documents, rather than edit documents. Figure 6 lists business software for personal mobile devices.

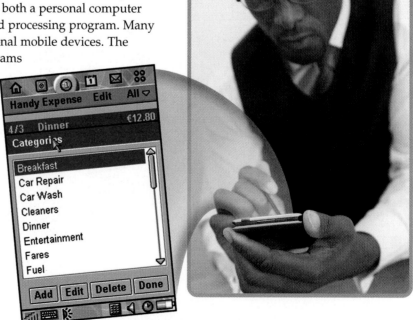

BUSINESS SOFTWARE FOR PERSONAL MOBILE DEVICES

Application	Description	Samples
Word processing	Allows for simple creation, editing, and viewing of documents.	• Documents To Go • WordSmith • PocketWord
Spreadsheet	Allows a user to create, edit, and view worksheets on a personal mobile device.	• Pocket Excel • TinySheet • Quickoffice • SmartSheet
Readers	Allows read-only (view only) access to word processing documents, spreadsheets, or databases that a user downloads to a personal mobile device from a personal computer. Readers are useful for taking large documents on the road to read them without the ability to modify them. Some readers allow the user to view all of these types of documents, while others are targeted to specific desktop program counterparts, such as presentation viewers or word processing document viewers.	• Pocket SlideShow • TealDoc • iSilo • Microsoft Reader
Database and list management	Allows creation, editing, and viewing of databases or lists. List management is a popular use of personal mobile devices. Some examples of lists that are handy to store on a device include shopping lists, to-do lists, exercise logs, and automobile maintenance logs.	• HanDBase • thinkDB • SmartList To Go • JFile • ListPro • Mobile Data Viewer
Financial	Financial software includes programs to manage a bank account, track expenses during a trip, manage a budget, or track an investment portfolio. Many personal computer financial programs include personal mobile device companion software that keeps the information on a device synchronized with the financial information on a personal computer or the Web.	• Microsoft Money for Pocket PC • Pocket Quicken • BankBook • Ultrasoft Money • Handy Expense

FIGURE 6   Business software provides scaled-down versions of common desktop programs.

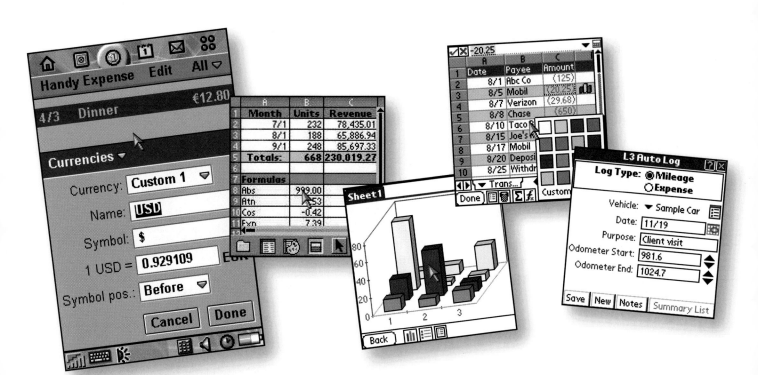

SOFTWARE FOR WIRELESS DEVICES

Most of the software used to interact with the Internet using a personal computer has a counterpart on wireless mobile devices. Some devices come equipped with e-mail software or a Web browser. Often, special servers allow the device to communicate securely with corporate databases or Web sites. For personal mobile devices that do not include wireless Internet connectivity, a special modem connects the device to the Internet. Often, a device without built-in wireless capability can be connected to a mobile phone that can connect the device to the Internet. Web content and e-mail also synchronize to the device from a personal computer, and the information may be browsed offline while using the device. Figure 7 provides a list of popular communications software for personal mobile devices.

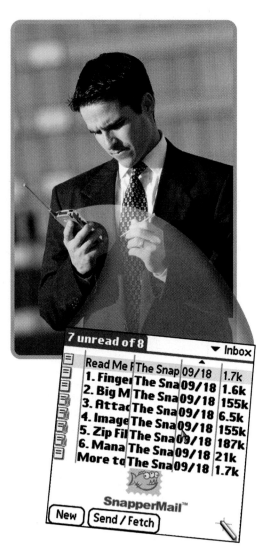

COMMUNICATIONS SOFTWARE FOR PERSONAL MOBILE DEVICES

Application	Description	Samples
E-mail	Used for composing and reading e-mail.	• Pocket Outlook • riteMail • Mail+ • SnapperMail
Web browsers	Allows Web browsing. Some browsers use an **intermediate server** to make the pages smaller by stripping out images or making images smaller. Others attempt to display the full Web page on the personal mobile device.	• Pocket Internet Explorer • Blazer • AvantGo • Opera browser
Clipping	**Web clippings** are programs that gather and display only the critical elements, or clips, of a Web page.	• Travelocity.com • The Weather Channel • Moviefone.com
Instant messaging	Instant messaging programs usually allow the user to use the same instant messaging ID as that used on a personal computer.	• MSN Messenger • AIM for Palm OS • Agile Messenger

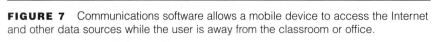

FIGURE 7 Communications software allows a mobile device to access the Internet and other data sources while the user is away from the classroom or office.

CORPORATE/GOVERNMENT SOFTWARE

Large organizations, such as corporations and government agencies, take advantage of personal mobile devices' capability of keeping current information in the hands of their personnel. The organization's central employee telephone book is kept up-to-date and synchronized to each employee's device on a regular basis. Executives synchronize key corporate information. Traveling sales personnel and field technicians synchronize appointments, e-mail, notes about contact with customers, product lists, and sales information. Corporate/government software for personal mobile devices is listed in Figure 8.

CORPORATE/GOVERNMENT SOFTWARE FOR PERSONAL MOBILE DEVICES

Application	Description	Samples
Executive	Executives keep up-to-date corporate information on their personal mobile devices. Executives may keep current sales information, financial information, and inventory information available to make informed decisions.	• mySAP.com • Siebel 7 Mobile Solutions
Sales	Sales people working out of the office are perhaps the largest group of personal mobile device users. The devices are useful for keeping product information handy, keeping scheduled appointments, and maintaining customer information.	• Siebel 7 Mobile Sales • Salesforce.com • ActionNames
Field technicians and mobile workers	Field technicians visit customer locations to troubleshoot problems. Personal mobile devices help technicians keep track of customer information, maintain up-to-date information on replacement parts, and log troubleshooting information.	• UPS and FedEx use specialized devices and software for their drivers to track package pickups and drop offs.
Military and law enforcement	The military and law enforcement agencies deploy personal mobile devices to manage the special needs of the military and law enforcement.	• Most software of this nature is custom made for the needs of particular agencies. Such programs help track cases or serve as legal references.
Connecting and synchronizing with corporate data sources	Several solutions exist for synchronizing corporate data with personal mobile devices. Special software keeps track of user permissions and makes certain that the right people get the data they require on a day-to-day basis.	• Pumatech Intellisync • Starfish TrueSync Server • MessageWireless
Large organization management issues	In organizations with thousands of personal mobile device users, the support of those devices becomes tedious, especially when users install unsupported software on the devices that may interfere with the corporate software and data for which the device was intended. Server software may detect these conflicts when the user synchronizes with the corporate server and deletes or reports the offending software.	• Much of the software of this nature is custom built for each enterprise, as needs and infrastructure of each organization are different.

FIGURE 8 Large organizations utilize special software to keep their employees synchronized.

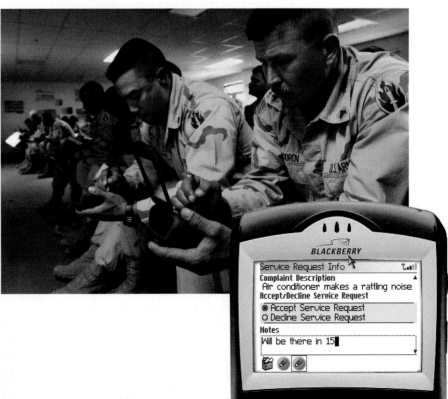

MEDICAL SOFTWARE

One of the largest communities to adopt personal mobile device software in significant numbers is the medical community. Physicians and other medical workers routinely use specialized software to track patient charts, check information on drugs, and browse electronic versions of large reference books. The end result is a savings in time and money, and an increase in the level of care for the patient. Figure 9 lists some popular medical software for personal mobile devices.

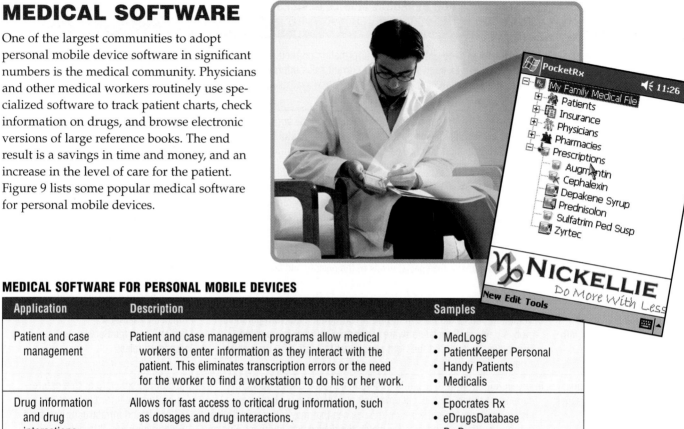

MEDICAL SOFTWARE FOR PERSONAL MOBILE DEVICES

Application	Description	Samples
Patient and case management	Patient and case management programs allow medical workers to enter information as they interact with the patient. This eliminates transcription errors or the need for the worker to find a workstation to do his or her work.	• MedLogs • PatientKeeper Personal • Handy Patients • Medicalis
Drug information and drug interactions	Allows for fast access to critical drug information, such as dosages and drug interactions.	• Epocrates Rx • eDrugsDatabase • Dr Drugs
Reference books	Medical workers often rely on a large collection of references to do their jobs. Electronic versions of many popular references, such as the *Physicians' Desk Reference*, are available in electronic format and are kept up-to-date easily through regular downloads.	• PDRDrugs • eDrugs Database • DiagnosisPro for Pocket PC • MedRules
Prescriptions	With electronic prescribing, physicians write prescriptions electronically. Physicians print legible prescriptions and hand the prescriptions to the patient. If the personal mobile device is connected to the Internet or hospital network, the physician checks the patient's medication or medical history.	• iScribe • PocketRx • Medicalis
Medical calculations	Medical workers often make quick calculations for medication dosages or patient status. Programs assist many of these calculations and target the worker's specialty.	• MedMath • MedCalc • Medical MathPad

FIGURE 9 The medical community quickly has become one of the larger users of specialized PDA software.

SCIENTIFIC SOFTWARE

The mobility of personal mobile devices makes them valuable tools for scientific use. Researchers use these devices to gather and record data in the field and later download the data to a personal computer or server. Scientists also use specialized software targeted to their specific field, such as astronomy or meteorology, as a replacement for bulky reference manuals or observation notes (Figure 10).

SCIENTIFIC SOFTWARE FOR PERSONAL MOBILE DEVICES

Application	Description	Samples
Data gathering	Scientists can enter observations quickly into a personal mobile device. These programs often are used in the field for gathering research statistics.	• iCollect
Calculations and conversions	Users can perform specialized calculations or data conversions. Many fields of science, such as astronomy, require special calculations that are useful to have available on a personal mobile device.	• ME Tools • CoolCalc for the Pocket PC • Convert It! • APCalc Converter
Reference	Scientists can look up information quickly, rather than using cumbersome manuals or textbooks.	• ChemRef Basic • PTE (Periodic Table of the Elements) • Gene • ABC's of Science
Astronomy	Observers can follow the stars. With the large number of amateur astronomers in the world, programs specific to astronomy are some of the more popular scientific titles.	• Pocket Universe • Planetarium • Star Pilot • Pocket Stars
Weather	Meteorologists' specific needs are addressed because these programs allow quick calculations or data gathering in a changing environment. Some programs are linked to add-on hardware that measure temperature, humidity, and other meteorological data.	• Weather Manager • WorldMate • Weather Calculator for Palm OS • Weather.com

FIGURE 10   Scientific programs help scientists manage complex information.

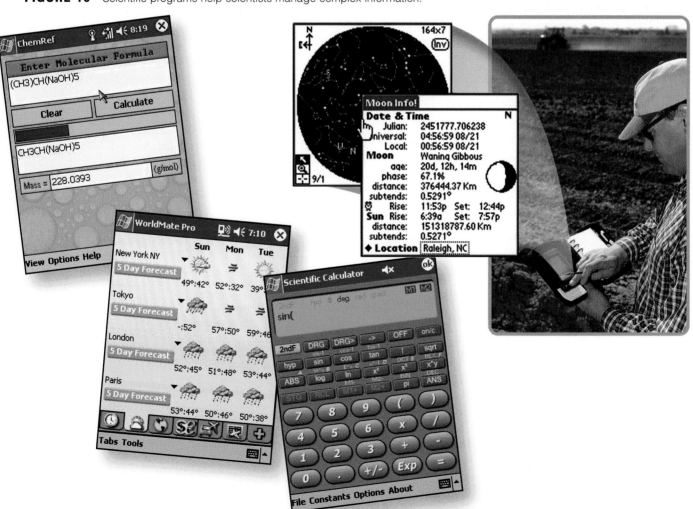

TRAVEL SOFTWARE

The portable nature of personal mobile devices makes them ideal for the business or leisure traveler. Even a night on the town can be enhanced by a list of popular hot spots. The user keeps his or her itinerary handy along with maps and directions while traveling to new places. A GPS-enabled mobile device tracks a user's route and keeps the user on course. Wireless connectivity allows the user to book flights and hotels from the back of a taxi cab. Figure 11 lists travel software for personal mobile devices.

TRAVEL SOFTWARE FOR PERSONAL MOBILE DEVICES

Application	Description	Samples
Itinerary consolidation	Manages travel itineraries, including flights, hotels, and car rentals. The software may keep track of travel preferences and make suggestions about travel and accommodations when planning a new trip.	• Traveler (Pocket PC edition) • Time Traveler • Travel Pal
Mapping	Mapping software may download maps from the Web or a personal computer. Or, the software may include maps. The software may suggest travel routes from point to point, or simply serve as a reference.	• Vindigo for Palm OS or Pocket PC • Pocket Streets • HandMap
City guides	City guides are one of the more popular personal mobile device programs. The user installs city guides for specific cities or an entire country. Guides include restaurant listings and ratings, hotels, directions, popular attractions, and local customs.	• Weissmann City Profiles • Vindigo for Palm OS or Pocket PC • WorldMate • Frommer's Port@ble Guide • iFodor's
Hotel and flight	Users can view current hotel and flight information while planning a trip. Some of these programs require the device to connect to the Internet. Others occasionally allow downloading the information to a device from a personal computer. Some programs link to booking systems on the Internet, so the user makes reservations directly from a personal mobile device.	• OAG Club • SkyGuide
GPS	Usually requires additional GPS hardware connected to the device. Some software includes mapping data or only displays and saves GPS information, such as location and speed.	• GPS Port@ble Navigator — Travelers Edition • GPS Wireless Navigation System • GPS Atlas

FIGURE 11 Travel software acts as a personal concierge for the business or leisure traveler.

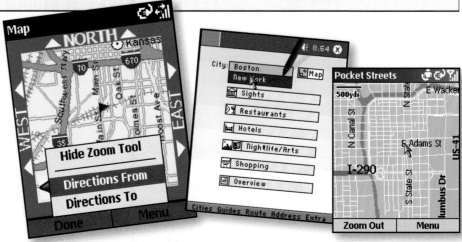

EDUCATIONAL SOFTWARE

With so much to organize, students and instructors greatly benefit from mobile software geared for educational uses (Figure 12). Students load textbook chapters or entire textbooks onto expansion cards and use special software to read the books and highlight key material. Instructors distribute electronic versions of the class syllabus, automatically updating each student's calendar on the students' devices. Some schools even acquire PDAs for the entire student body and require their use in the classroom.

EDUCATIONAL SOFTWARE FOR PERSONAL MOBILE DEVICES

Application	Description	Samples
E-books and references	E-books are electronic versions of books. E-books are specially formatted files that may be viewed using Reader software, as noted in Figure 6 on page 287. Many e-books are available at no cost, and many authors and publishing companies make e-books available to those who have purchased a hard copy of a particular book.	• TomeRaider • PocketLingo Pro • Formulas for Palm OS • Speed Reader Plus • The collected works of William Shakespeare for Microsoft Reader • eWord for Blackberry • Mobipocket Reader Pro for Symbian OS
Class schedules and course management	Helps instructors and students manage their respective schedules. The information may include syllabus details distributed in electronic format by an instructor. The software also may link to a central data repository of a school. The software helps track grading, assignments, to-do lists, instructor office hours, and notes.	• 4.0Student by Handmark course management • Pocket ClassPro for Pocket PC • MyClasses
Roster	Manages grading, rosters, attendance, and contact information for students.	• Teachers PET • Head Start • Teach File
Review	Includes programs for quizzing students and reviewing coursework. Students often train the application to help them review troublesome material.	• Math Classic • Mental Arithmetic • Quizzler

FIGURE 12 Educational software benefits both students and instructors.

MULTIMEDIA SOFTWARE

Most personal mobile devices include the capability of viewing images, and some are powerful enough to view short video clips. Some devices also double as audio players, allowing the user to take his or her favorite music anywhere. Devices that are more recent contain, or allow the user to attach, a camera or recording device to capture video or audio and then download the captured media to a personal computer. Some image viewers allow the user to use a personal mobile device as an electronic picture frame while the device rests in its cradle on the user's desk. Popular multimedia software for personal mobile devices is listed in Figure 13.

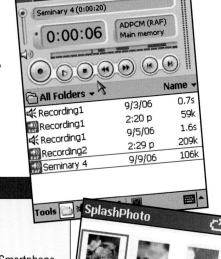

MULTIMEDIA SOFTWARE FOR PERSONAL MOBILE DEVICES

Application	Description	Samples
Picture viewer	Allows a user to view images uploaded to a personal mobile device using software on a personal computer or camera. Some viewers have a slide show mode that rotates through a list of images automatically.	• SplashPhoto • PocketPhoto • Palbum Picture Viewer • Resco Photo Viewer for Smartphone • FireViewer
Video player	Allows the user to watch video clips on a personal mobile device.	• Windows Media Player for Pocket PC • PocketTV for Pocket PC • ActiveSky Media Player
Audio player	Permits a user to listen to his or her favorite music or record and playback voice recordings for meetings or personal audio notes. Some devices are equipped with additional hardware such as microphones, headphones, or audio controls to enhance the audio experience.	• AudioPlus • Windows Media Player for Pocket PC • Replay Radio

FIGURE 13 Multimedia software gives personal mobile device users the ability to view images, watch video, and listen to audio.

ENTERTAINMENT SOFTWARE

While on the train ride to work or waiting at the airport, a personal mobile device user can enjoy his or her favorite games. The infrared port or wireless connectivity of a device allows a user to play some games against other players. Most devices include buttons to control games. Figure 14 lists popular entertainment software for personal mobile devices.

ENTERTAINMENT SOFTWARE FOR PERSONAL MOBILE DEVICES

Application	Description	Samples
Strategy	Includes classic board games such as chess, backgammon, and Monopoly.	• PocketChess • ChessGenius • Handmark Monopoly • SimCity
Card	Includes casino games, solitaire games, and other card games.	• AcidSolitaire • BlackJack++ • Pocket Cribbage
Action	Games that require quick reflexes, including many arcade-style games.	• Tomb Raider • Bejeweled • Breakfast • Vexed for Symbian
Puzzle	Thought-provoking puzzles to pass time and sharpen the mind, such as crossword puzzles, mazes, and word games.	• Handmark SCRABBLE • Crossword • ChessPuzzles

FIGURE 14 Entertainment software allows a user to relax with a personal mobile device and enjoy his or her favorite games.

OBTAINING AND INSTALLING PERSONAL MOBILE DEVICE SOFTWARE

Software often is available at computer or electronics stores. A significant number of programs are available as shareware, freeware, or trial editions at various Web sites. Most of the software listed in the previous figures is accessible on the Web sites listed in Figure 15. Because software for personal mobile devices usually is smaller than the personal computer counterparts, downloading the software from the Web to your personal computer and then uploading it to your device often is the best alternative when you want to try something new. Software downloaded from the Web to a personal computer requires that the software be installed using the device's synchronization software. Additionally, some personal computer application software includes accompanying mobile device software that corresponds with the personal computer software. Wireless devices, such as smart phones and smart pagers, may allow you to download new software over the wireless connection.

Software for personal mobile devices sold in a retail location often is supplied on a CD-ROM. The CD-ROM first installs the software on a personal computer. The device's synchronization software then is used to load the software onto the device while the device is connected to the personal computer. Depending on the type of software installed, this process may be automatic. Some software is packaged as an add-on card that the user inserts into the device's expansion slot. Some Web sites allow the user to browse a software catalog from a wireless device's Web browser and download the software directly to the device. When synchronizing a personal mobile device on a corporate network, some companies automatically install software to the employees' devices with no interaction required from the employee.

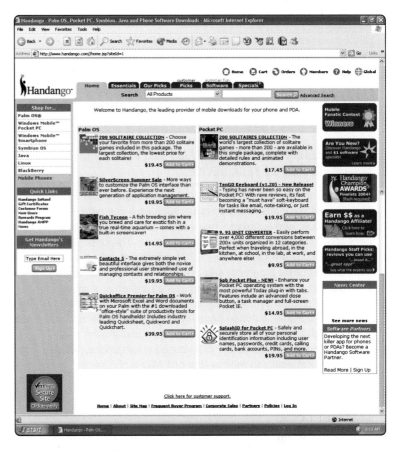

WHERE TO OBTAIN PERSONAL MOBILE DEVICE SOFTWARE

Application	Description	Samples
Web sites	Software publishers make their products available at their Web sites. Several Web sites also exist specifically to distribute mobile device software. Tens of thousands of titles are available, and most can be downloaded on a trial basis.	www.palmgear.com www.handandgo.com www.pdamd.com www.tucows.com
Retail	Many popular software titles can be purchased at electronic and computer stores. The most popular titles at these locations include productivity and entertainment software.	www.bestbuy.com www.compusa.com
Develop in-house	Many corporations develop their own personal mobile device software to use internally to meet specific needs. These programs usually tap into existing corporate databases of product and customer information. The companies that produce mobile device operating systems often make the development tools for such software available at no cost or a minimal cost.	www.palmsource.com www.microsoft.com/mobile/developer http://www.blackberry.net/developers/index.shtml http://www.symbian.com/developer/index.html

For an updated list of where to obtain PDA software, visit scsite.com/dc2006/ch5/pda.

FIGURE 15 Personal mobile device software is available from a number of sources.

HOW TO PURCHASE A PERSONAL MOBILE DEVICE

Whether you choose a PDA, smart phone, or smart pager depends on where, when, and how you will use the device. If you need to stay organized when you are on the go, then a PDA may be the right choice. PDAs typically are categorized by the operating system they run (Figure 2 on page 283). If you need to stay organized and in touch when on the go, then a smart phone or smart pager may be the right choice. Just as with PDAs, smart phones, and smart pagers are categorized by the operating system they run. The six primary operating systems for these devices are the Palm OS, Windows Mobile for Pocket PC, Windows Mobile for Smartphone, Symbian OS, Blackberry, and Embedded Linux.

This section lists guidelines you should consider when purchasing a PDA, smart phone, or smart pager. You also should visit the Web sites listed in Figure 16 to gather more information about the type of personal mobile device that best suits your computing needs.

 DETERMINE THE PROGRAMS YOU PLAN TO RUN ON YOUR DEVICE.

All PDAs and most smart phones and smart pagers can handle basic organizer-type software such as a calendar, address book, and notepad. The availability of other software depends on the operating system you choose. The depth and breadth of software for the Palm OS is significant, with more than 20,000 basic programs and over 600 wireless programs. Devices that run Windows-based operating systems, such as Windows Mobile or Windows Smartphone, may have fewer programs available, but the operating system and application software are similar to those with which you are familiar, such as Word and Excel. Some Symbian-based smart phones also include the capability to read and/or edit Microsoft Office documents.

 CONSIDER HOW MUCH YOU WANT TO PAY.

The price of a personal mobile device can range from $100 to $800, depending on its capabilities. Some Palm OS devices are at the lower end of the cost spectrum, and Windows-based devices often are at the higher end. For the latest prices, capabilities, and accessories, visit the Web sites listed in Figure 16.

 DETERMINE WHETHER YOU NEED WIRELESS ACCESS TO THE INTERNET AND E-MAIL OR MOBILE TELEPHONE CAPABILITIES WITH YOUR DEVICE.

Smart pagers give you access to e-mail and other data and Internet services. Smart phones typically include these features, but also include the ability to make and receive phone calls on cellular networks. Some PDAs and smart phones include wireless networking capability to allow you to connect to the Internet wirelessly. These wireless features and services allow personal mobile device users to access real-time information from anywhere to help make decisions while on the go.

 FOR WIRELESS DEVICES, DETERMINE HOW AND WHERE YOU WILL USE THE SERVICE.

When purchasing a wireless device, you must subscribe to a wireless service. Determine if the wireless network (carrier) you choose has service in the area where you plan to use the device. Some networks have high-speed data networks only in certain areas, such as large cities or business districts. Also, a few carriers allow you to use your device in other countries.

When purchasing a smart phone, determine if you plan to use the device more as a phone, PDA, or wireless data device. Some smart phones, such as those based on the Pocket PC Phone edition or the Palm OS, are geared more for use as a PDA and have a PDA form factor. Other smart phones, such as those based on Microsoft Smartphone or Symbian operating systems, mainly are phone devices that include robust PDA functionality. RIM Blackberry-based smart phones include robust data features that are oriented to accessing e-mail and wireless data services.

 MAKE SURE YOUR DEVICE HAS ENOUGH MEMORY.

Memory (RAM) is not a major issue with low-end devices with monochrome displays and basic organizer functions. Memory is a major issue, however, for high-end devices that have color displays and wireless features. Without enough memory, the performance level of your device will drop dramatically. If you plan to purchase a high-end device running the Palm OS operating system, the device should have at least 16 MB of RAM. If you plan to purchase a high-end device running the Windows Mobile operating system, the PDA should have at least 48 MB of RAM.

PRACTICE WITH THE TOUCH SCREEN, HANDWRITING RECOGNITION, AND BUILT-IN KEYBOARD BEFORE DECIDING ON A MODEL.

To enter data into a PDA or smart phone, you use a pen-like stylus to handwrite on the screen or a keyboard. The keyboard either slides out or is mounted on the front of the device. With handwriting recognition, the device translates the handwriting into a computerized font. You also can use the stylus as a pointing device to select items on the screen and enter data by tapping on an on-screen keyboard. By practicing data entry before buying a device, you can learn if one device may be easier for you to use than another. You also can buy third-party software to improve a device's handwriting recognition.

DECIDE WHETHER YOU WANT A COLOR DISPLAY.

Pocket PC devices usually come with a color display that supports as many as 65,536 colors. Palm OS devices also have a color display, but the less expensive models display in 4 to 16 shades of gray. Symbian- and Blackberry-based devices also have the option for color displays. Having a color display does result in greater on-screen detail, but it also requires more memory and uses more power. Resolution also influences the quality of the display.

COMPARE BATTERY LIFE.

Any mobile device is good only if it has the power required to run. For example, Palm OS devices with monochrome screens typically have a much longer battery life than Pocket PC devices with color screens. The use of wireless networking will shorten battery time considerably. To help alleviate this problem, most devices have incorporated rechargeable batteries that can be recharged by placing the device in a cradle or connecting it to a charger.

SERIOUSLY CONSIDER THE IMPORTANCE OF ERGONOMICS.

Will you put the device in your pocket, a carrying case, or wear it on your belt? How does it feel in your hand? Will you use it indoors or outdoors? Many screens are unreadable outdoors. Do you need extra ruggedness, such as would be required in construction, in a plant, or in a warehouse?

CHECK OUT THE ACCESSORIES.

Determine which accessories you want for your personal mobile device. Accessories include carrying cases, portable mini- and full-sized keyboards, removable storage, modems, synchronization cradles and cables, car chargers, wireless communications, global positioning system modules, digital camera modules, expansion cards, dashboard mounts, replacement styli, hands-free headsets, and more.

DECIDE WHETHER YOU WANT ADDITIONAL FUNCTIONALITY.

In general, off-the-shelf Microsoft operating system-based devices have broader functionality than devices with other operating systems. For example, voice-recording capability, e-book players, MP3 players, and video players are standard on most Pocket PC devices. If you are leaning towards a Palm OS device and want these additional functions, you may need to purchase additional software or expansion modules to add them later. Determine whether your employer permits devices with cameras on the premises, and if not, do not consider devices with cameras.

DETERMINE WHETHER SYNCHRONIZATION OF DATA WITH OTHER DEVICES OR PERSONAL COMPUTERS IS IMPORTANT.

Most devices come with a cradle that connects to the USB or serial port on your computer so you can synchronize data on your device with your desktop or notebook computer. Increasingly more devices are Bluetooth and/or wireless networking enabled, which gives them the capability of synchronizing wirelessly. Many devices today also have an infrared port that allows you to synchronize data with any device that has a similar infrared port, including desktop and notebook computers or other personal mobile devices.

Web Site	Web Address
Hewlett-Packard	hp.com
CNET Shopper	shopper.cnet.com
palmOne	palmone.com
Microsoft	windowsmobile.com pocketpc.com microsoft.com/smartphone
PDA Buyers Guide	pdabuyersguide.com
Research in Motion	rim.com
Danger	danger.com
Symbian	symbian.com
Wireless Developer Network	wirelessdevnet.com
Sharp	myzaurus.com
For an updated list of reviews and information about personal mobile devices and their Web addresses, visit scsite.com/dc2006/ch5/pda.	

FIGURE 16 Web site reviews and information about personal mobile devices.

CHAPTER SIX

Output

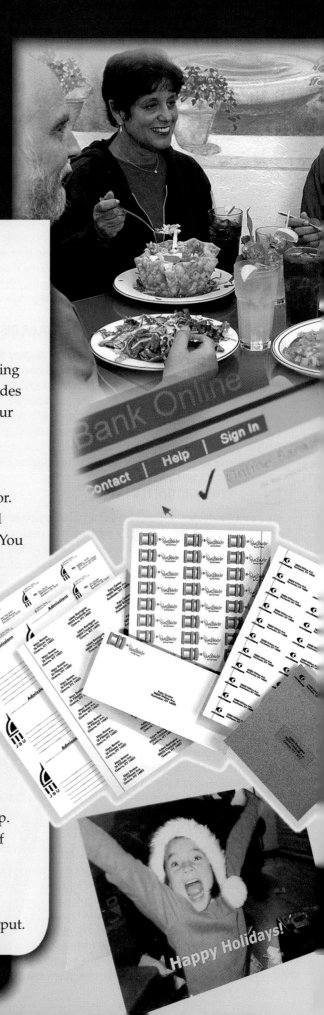

Picture Yourself Saving Money Using a Computer

While eating lunch with some friends, your conversation centers around rising prices and the cost of hotels, postage stamps, greeting cards, gasoline, and services such as banking and film developing. After the discussion, each of you decides to take measures to reduce some of these costs by using your computers.

Instead of paying for personal checks and postage, you decide to use online banking to pay your bills and balance your statements while viewing them on a computer monitor. For those items that still must be mailed through the postal service, you will print the postage stamps on your printer. You also will print addresses directly on the envelopes or print mailing labels. You soon discover that not only do you save on costs but also the amount of time it takes to complete these activities. No more time spent driving to the post office!

With greeting card software, you will design your own greeting cards on the computer screen, personalizing them with pictures and special notes, and then print them in color on card stock paper. You also will make personalized T-shirts as gifts by printing pictures on T-shirt transfer paper and then ironing the transfer on a plain T-shirt.

The next time photo paper is on sale, you plan to stock up. With the photo paper in the printer, you will print copies of your digital pictures in a variety of sizes — wallet, 4 × 6, 5 × 7, and 8 × 10.

Read Chapter 6 to learn about various types of monitors, printers, and paper and to discover many other forms of output.

OBJECTIVES

After completing this chapter, you will be able to:

1. Describe the four categories of output

2. Summarize the characteristics of LCD monitors, LCD screens, plasma monitors, and HDTVs

3. Describe the characteristics of a CRT monitor and factors that affect its quality

4. Explain the relationship between graphics chips and monitors

5. Describe various ways to print

6. Differentiate between a nonimpact printer and an impact printer

7. Summarize the characteristics of ink-jet printers, photo printers, laser printers, thermal printers, mobile printers, label and postage printers, and plotters and large-format printers

8. Describe the uses of speakers and headsets

9. Identify the output characteristics of fax machines and fax modems, multifunction peripherals, data projectors, joysticks, and wheels

10. Identify output options for physically challenged users

CONTENTS

WHAT IS OUTPUT?

DISPLAY DEVICES

FLAT-PANEL DISPLAYS
LCD Monitors and Screens
LCD Technology
LCD Quality
Graphics Chips, Ports, and LCD Monitors
Plasma Monitors
Televisions and HDTVs

CRT MONITORS
Quality of a CRT Monitor
Graphics Chips and CRT Monitors

PRINTERS
Producing Printed Output
Nonimpact Printers
Ink-Jet Printers
Photo Printers
Laser Printers
Thermal Printers
Mobile Printers
Label and Postage Printers
Plotters and Large-Format Printers
Impact Printers

SPEAKERS AND HEADSETS

OTHER OUTPUT DEVICES
Fax Machines and Fax Modems
Multifunction Peripherals
Data Projectors
Force-Feedback Joysticks and Wheels

PUTTING IT ALL TOGETHER

OUTPUT DEVICES FOR PHYSICALLY CHALLENGED USERS

CHAPTER SUMMARY

HIGH-TECH TALK
Sound Cards: Bringing Your Computer to Life

COMPANIES ON THE CUTTING EDGE
Hewlett-Packard
ViewSonic

TECHNOLOGY TRAILBLAZERS
Steve Jobs
Donna Dubinsky

WHAT IS OUTPUT?

Output is data that has been processed into a useful form. That is, computers process data (input) into information (output). A computer generates several types of output, depending on the hardware and software being used and the requirements of the user.

Users view output on a screen, print it, or hear it through speakers or headsets. Monitors, notebook computers, Tablet PCs, PDAs, and smart phones have screens that allow users to view documents, Web sites, e-mail messages, and other types of output. Some printers produce black-and-white documents, and others produce brilliant colors, enabling users to print color documents, photographs, and transparencies. Through the computer's speakers or a headset, users listen to sounds, music, and voice messages.

While working with a computer, a user encounters four basic categories of output: text, graphics, audio, and video (Figure 6-1). Very often, a single form of output, such as a Web page, includes more than one of these categories.

- Text — Examples of text-based output are memos, letters, announcements, press releases, reports, advertisements, newsletters, envelopes, mailing labels, and e-mail messages. On the Web, users view and print many other types of text-based output. These include newspapers, magazines, books, play or television show transcripts, stock quotes, famous speeches, and historical lectures.

- Graphics — Output often includes graphics to enhance its visual appeal and convey information. Business letters have logos. Reports include charts. Newsletters use drawings, clip art, and photographs. Users print high-quality photographs taken with a

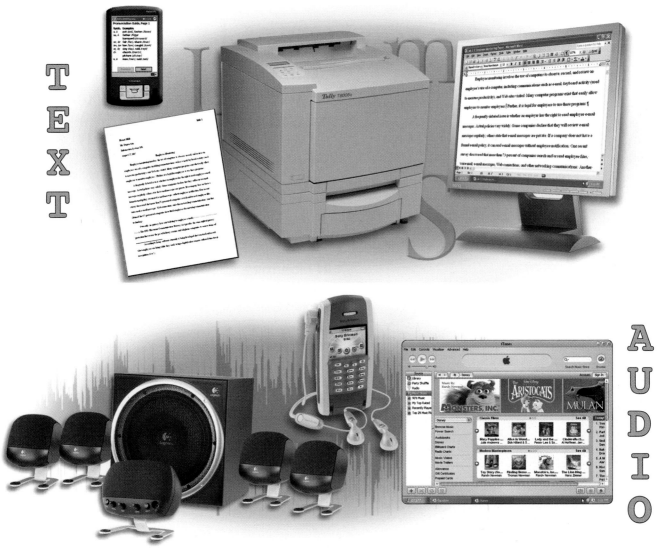

FIGURE 6-1 Four categories of output are text, graphics, audio, and video.

digital camera, eliminating the need for film or film developers. Many Web sites use animated graphics, such as blinking icons, scrolling messages, or simulations.

- Audio — Users insert their favorite music CD in a CD or DVD drive and listen to the music while working on the computer. Software such as games, encyclopedias, and simulations often have musical accompaniments for entertainment and audio clips, such as narrations and speeches, to enhance understanding. On the Web, users tune into radio and television stations and listen to audio clips or live broadcasts of interviews, talk shows, sporting events, news, music, and concerts. They also use the Internet to conduct real-time conversations with friends, coworkers, or family members, just as if they were speaking on the telephone.
- Video — As with audio, software and Web sites often include video clips to enhance

understanding. Users watch a live or prerecorded news report, view a movie, see a doctor perform a life-saving surgery, observe a hurricane in action, or enjoy a live performance of their favorite musician or musical group on the computer.

Attaching a video camera to the computer allows users to watch home movies on the computer. They also can attach a television's antenna or cable to the computer and watch a television program on the computer screen.

An **output device** is any type of hardware component that conveys information to one or more people. Commonly used output devices include display devices, printers, speakers and headsets, fax machines and fax modems, multifunction peripherals, data projectors, and force-feedback joysticks and wheels. This chapter discusses each of these output devices.

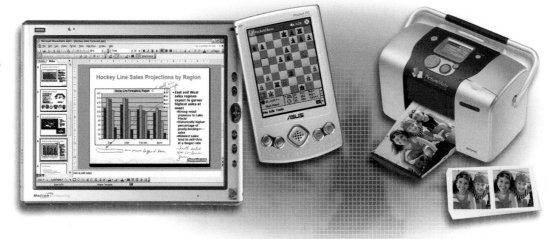

DISPLAY DEVICES

A **display device**, or simply *display*, is an output device that visually conveys text, graphics, and video information. Information on a display device, sometimes called *soft copy*, exists electronically and appears for a temporary period.

Display devices consist of a screen and the components that produce the information on the screen. Desktop computers typically use a monitor as their display device. A **monitor** is a display device that is packaged as a separate peripheral. Most monitors have a tilt-and-swivel base that allows users to adjust the angle of the screen to minimize neck strain and reduce glare from overhead lighting. Monitor controls permit users to adjust the brightness, contrast, positioning, height, and width of images.

Most mobile computers and devices integrate the display and other components into the same physical case. For example, the display on a notebook computer attaches with hinges. Some PDA and smart phone displays also attach with a hinge to the device; with others, the display is built into the PDA or smart phone case.

Most display devices show text, graphics, and video information in color. Some, however, are monochrome. *Monochrome* means the information appears in one color (such as white, amber, green, black, blue, or gray) on a different color background (such as black or grayish-white). Some PDAs and other mobile devices use monochrome displays to save battery power.

Two types of display devices are flat-panel displays and CRT monitors. The following sections discuss each of these display devices.

FAQ 6-1

What can I do to ease eyestrain while using my computer?

Blink your eyes every five seconds. Adjust the room lighting. Use larger fonts or zoom a display. Take an eye break every 30 minutes: look into the distance and focus on an object for 20 to 30 seconds, roll your eyes in a complete circle, and then close your eyes for at least 30 seconds. If you wear glasses, ask your doctor about computer glasses. For more information, visit scsite.com/dc2006/ch6/faq and then click Eye Strain.

FLAT-PANEL DISPLAYS

A *flat-panel display* is a lightweight display device with a shallow depth and flat screen that typically uses LCD (liquid crystal display) or gas plasma technology. Types of flat-panel displays include LCD monitors, LCD screens, plasma monitors, and many HDTVs.

LCD Monitors and Screens

An **LCD monitor**, also called a *flat panel monitor*, is a desktop monitor that uses a liquid crystal display to produce images (Figure 6-2). These monitors produce sharp, flicker-free images.

LCD monitors have a small *footprint*; that is, they do not take up much desk space. For additional space savings, some LCD monitors are wall mountable. LCD monitors are available in a variety of sizes, with the more common being 15, 17, 18, 19, 20, 21, and 23 inches — some are 30 or 40 inches. You measure a monitor the same way you measure a television, that is, diagonally from one corner to the other.

Determining what size monitor to purchase depends on your intended use. A large monitor allows you to view more information on the screen at once, but usually is more expensive. You may want to invest in a 19-inch monitor if you use multiple applications at one time or do a lot of research on the Web. Users working with intense graphics applications, such as desktop publishing and engineering, typically have larger monitors.

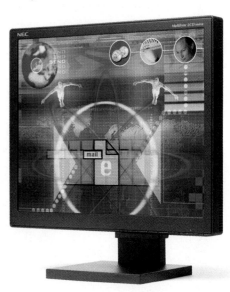

FIGURE 6-2   An LCD monitor is thin and lightweight.

For an even wider screen area, some users position two or more monitors side by side or stacked (Figure 6-3). For example, one monitor can show the left side of a document, game, graphic design, or other item, with the other monitor showing the right side. This arrangement also is convenient if you want to run multiple applications simultaneously. Users of side-by-side or stacked monitors include music editors, video editors, network administrators, gamers, researchers, Web developers, graphic designers, and engineers.

Mobile computers, such as notebook computers and Tablet PCs, and mobile devices, such as PDAs and smart phones, often have built-in LCD screens (Figure 6-4). Notebook computer screens are available in a variety of sizes, with the more common being 14.1, 15.4, and 17.1 inches. Tablet PC screens range from 10.4 inches to 15 inches. PDA screens average 3.5 inches. On smart phones, screen sizes range from 2.5 to 3.5 inches.

FIGURE 6-3 Users sometimes have multiple LCD monitors stacked or side by side to increase their viewing area.

FAQ 6-2

Can I read a book on a PDA or smart phone screen?

Yes, you can download an electronic book, called an *e-book*, to a mobile device or computer. To read an e-book, your mobile device or computer requires a reader program such as *Microsoft Reader* or *Adobe Reader*. Both of these programs can be downloaded free on the Web. For more information, visit scsite.com/dc2006/ch6/faq and then click E-Books.

notebook computer

Tablet PC

PDA

smart phone

FIGURE 6-4 Notebook computers and Tablet PCs have color LCD screens. Many PDAs and smart phones also have color displays.

LCD Technology

A **liquid crystal display (LCD)** uses a liquid compound to present information on a display device. Computer LCDs typically contain fluorescent tubes that emit light waves toward the liquid-crystal cells, which are sandwiched between two sheets of material. When an electrical charge passes through the cells, the cells twist. This twisting causes some light waves to be blocked and allows others to pass through, creating images on the display.

LCD monitors and LCD screens produce color using either passive-matrix or active-matrix technology. An *active-matrix display*, also known as a *TFT (thin-film transistor) display*, uses a separate transistor to apply charges to each liquid crystal cell and thus displays high-quality color that is viewable from all angles. A newer type of TFT technology, called *organic LED (OLED)*, uses organic molecules that produce an even brighter, easier-to-read display than standard TFT displays. OLEDs are less expensive to produce, consume less power, and can be fabricated on flexible surfaces. Read Looking Ahead 6-1 for a look at the next generation of OLEDs.

A *passive-matrix display* uses fewer transistors, requires less power, and is less expensive than an active-matrix display. The color on a passive-matrix display often is not as bright as an active-matrix display. Users view images on a passive-matrix display best when working directly in front of it.

WEB LINK 6-1

LCD Technology

For more information, visit scsite.com/dc2006/ch6/weblink and then click LCD Technology.

LOOKING AHEAD 6-1

Flexible Screens Lock and Roll

Your newspaper arrives each morning at your front door rolled up and secured with a rubber band or in a plastic bag. Your computer monitor soon may arrive rolled up so you can transport it easily in your book bag or luggage.

Flexible screens are being developed to curve against your car's dashboard and bend around corners. Unlike today's flat-panel displays manufactured from rigid, weighty glass, the flexible screens are made from pliable organic light-emitting diodes (OLEDs). These screens are based on layers of carbon that are sealed perfectly to prevent any exposure to moisture or air. They could be mass produced using a low-cost, high-efficiency method.

The OLED technology also could be used for televisions, cellular telephones, and PDAs. For more information, visit scsite.com/dc2006/ch6/looking and then click Flexible Screens.

LCD Quality

The quality of an LCD monitor or LCD screen depends primarily on its resolution, response time, brightness, and pixel pitch.

- As mentioned in Chapter 5, **resolution** is the number of horizontal and vertical pixels in a display device. For example, a monitor that has a 1600 × 1200 resolution displays up to 1600 pixels per horizontal row and 1200 pixels per vertical row, for a total of 1,920,000 pixels to create a screen image. Recall that a *pixel* (short for picture element) is a single point in an electronic image. A higher resolution uses a greater number of pixels and thus provides a smoother, sharper, and clearer image. As you increase the resolution, however, some items on the screen appear smaller, such as menu bars, toolbars, and rulers (Figure 6-5).

  With LCD monitors and screens, resolution generally is proportional to the size of the device. That is, the resolution increases for larger monitors and screens. For example, a 17-inch LCD monitor typically has a resolution of 1280 × 1024, while a 20-inch LCD monitor has a resolution of 1600 × 1200. LCDs are geared for a specific resolution, called the *native resolution*. When set at other resolutions, the quality may not be as good as the native resolution.

- *Response time* of an LCD monitor or screen is the time in milliseconds (ms) that it takes to turn a pixel on or off. LCD monitors' and screens' response times range from 16 to 25 ms. The lower the number, the faster the response time.

- Brightness of an LCD monitor or LCD screen is measured in nits. A *nit* is a unit of visible light intensity equal to one candela (formerly called candlepower) per square meter. The *candela* is the standard unit of luminous intensity. LCD monitors and screens today range from 200 to 350 nits. The higher the nits, the brighter the images.

- *Pixel pitch*, sometimes called *dot pitch*, is the distance in millimeters between pixels on a display device. Text created with a smaller dot pitch is easier to read. Advertisements normally specify a monitor's pixel pitch or dot pitch. Average pixel pitch on LCD monitors and screens should be .28 mm or lower. The lower the number, the sharper the image.

FIGURE 6-5a (screen resolution at 800 × 600)

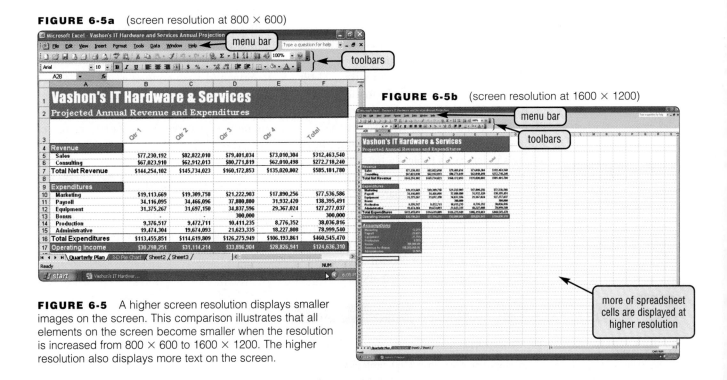

FIGURE 6-5b (screen resolution at 1600 × 1200)

FIGURE 6-5 A higher screen resolution displays smaller images on the screen. This comparison illustrates that all elements on the screen become smaller when the resolution is increased from 800 × 600 to 1600 × 1200. The higher resolution also displays more text on the screen.

Graphics Chips, Ports, and LCD Monitors

A cable on a monitor plugs in a port on the system unit, which enables communications from a graphics chip. This chip, called the *graphics processing unit*, controls the manipulation and display of graphics on a display device. The graphics processing unit either is integrated on the motherboard or resides on a video card in a slot in the motherboard. Video cards usually contain a fan or heat sink to keep this and other chips from overheating.

LCD monitors use a digital signal to produce a picture. To display the highest quality images, an LCD monitor should plug in a *DVI* (*Digital Video Interface*) *port*, which enables digital signals to transmit directly to the LCD monitor. Current models of system units either have an integrated DVI chip or contain a video card that has a DVI port. They usually also have a standard monitor port and an *S-video port*, allowing users to connect external devices such as a television, DVD player, or video recorder, to the computer (Figure 6-6).

Over the years, several video standards have been developed to define the resolution, number of colors, and other display properties.

Current video standards include *SVGA* (Super Video Graphics Array), which has a resolution of 800 × 600; *XGA* (eXtended Graphics Array), a resolution of 1024 × 768; *SXGA* (Super XGA), a resolution of 1280 × 1024; and *UGA* (Ultra XGA), a resolution of 1600 × 1200. Many display devices have resolutions beyond UGA, such as 2048 × 1536. Some display devices support all of these standards; others support only a subset of them. For a display device to show images as defined by a video standard, both the display device and graphics processing unit must support the same video standard.

FIGURE 6-6 Ports on current video cards.

The number of colors a graphics processing unit displays is determined by bit depth. The *bit depth*, also called *color depth*, is the number of bits used to store information about each pixel. For example, a video card with a 24-bit depth uses 24 bits to store information about each pixel. Thus, this video card can display 2^{24} or 16.7 million colors. The greater the number of bits, the better the resulting image. Today's video cards typically have a 24-bit depth or a 32-bit depth.

A video card or motherboard, in the case of integrated video, must have enough video memory to generate the resolution and number of colors you want to display. This memory, which often is 128 MB or 256 MB on current video cards, stores information about each pixel.

WEB LINK 6-2

Video Memory

For more information, visit scsite.com/dc2006/ch6/weblink and then click Video Memory.

FAQ 6-3

How much do video cards cost?

Although video cards for the home user cost less than $100, professional artists and designers use video cards that can cost up to $1,500. These cards have more than 384 MB of memory and support resolutions of 2048 × 1536. For more information, visit scsite.com/dc2006/ch6/faq and then click Video Cards.

Plasma Monitors

Large business or power users sometimes have plasma monitors, which often measure more than 60 inches wide (Figure 6-7). A **plasma monitor** is a display device that uses gas plasma

FIGURE 6-7 Large plasma monitors can measure more than 60 inches wide.

technology, which sandwiches a layer of gas between two glass plates. When voltage is applied, the gas releases ultraviolet (UV) light. This UV light causes the pixels on the screen to glow and form an image.

Plasma monitors offer larger screen sizes and higher display quality than LCD monitors but are more expensive. These monitors also can hang directly on a wall.

FAQ 6-4

What is the largest monitor to date?

The Sydney Olympics had a monitor wall that contained more than 400 screens, measuring about 150 feet wide and 7½ feet tall. For more information, visit scsite.com/dc2006/ch6/faq and then click Monitor Wall.

Televisions and HDTVs

Home users sometimes use their television as a display device (Figure 6-8). Connecting a computer to an analog television requires a converter that translates the digital signal from the computer into an analog signal that the television can display. The best analog televisions have a resolution of only 520 × 400 pixels. Thus, users are turning to *digital television* (*DTV*) for crisper, higher-quality output.

Digital television signals provide two major advantages over analog signals. First, digital signals produce a higher-quality picture. Second, many programs can be broadcast on a single digital channel, whereas only one program can be broadcast on an analog channel. By 2006, all broadcast stations must be transmitting digital signals, as mandated by the FCC.

HDTV (*high-definition television*) is the most advanced form of digital television, working with digital broadcast signals, transmitting digital sound, supporting wide screens, and providing resolutions up to 1920 × 1080 pixels. With HDTV, the broadcast signals are digitized when they are sent via over-the-air (OTA) broadcasts from local television networks, satellite, or cable. To receive the HDTV signals via OTA broadcasts, you need a VHF/UHF antenna; via satellite, you need an HDTV-compatible satellite receiver/tuner; and via cable, you need an HDTV-compatible cable box.

As HDTV becomes more affordable, home users may begin to use it as their computer's display device. HDTV also is ideal for presenting material to a large group. HDTV technology makes the use of interactive TV more widespread because HDTV works directly with interactive TV.

Interactive TV is a two-way communications technology in which users interact with television programming. Although interactive TV can be set up to work with analog televisions, it has much higher levels of performance when used with digital televisions. Uses of interactive TV include selecting a movie from a central library of movies, voting or responding to network questionnaires, banking and shopping, playing games, pausing or recording live television programs, and video conferencing.

FAQ 6-5

Can I watch digital television broadcasts on my analog television?

Yes, if you buy a device that converts the digital signal to an analog signal. The image on your analog television, however, will not have HDTV resolution. For more information, visit scsite.com/dc2006/ch6/faq and then click HDTV.

FIGURE 6-8   This user tests HDTV as a display device. Notice how much bigger the screen area is compared to the notebook computer.

CRT MONITORS

A **CRT monitor** is a desktop monitor that contains a cathode-ray tube (Figure 6-9). A *cathode-ray tube* (*CRT*) is a large, sealed glass tube. The front of the tube is the screen. Tiny dots of phosphor material coat the screen on a CRT. Each dot consists of a red, a green, and a blue phosphor. The three dots combine to make up each pixel. Inside the CRT, an electron beam moves back and forth across the back of the screen. This causes the dots on the front of the screen to glow, which produces an image on the screen.

CRT monitors have a much larger footprint than do LCD monitors; that is, they take up more desk space. CRT monitors for desktop computers are available in various sizes, with the more common being 15, 17, 19, 21, and 22 inches. In addition to monitor size, advertisements also list a CRT monitor's viewable size. The *viewable size* is the diagonal measurement of the actual viewing area provided by the screen in the CRT monitor. A 21-inch monitor, for example, may have a viewable size of 20 inches.

In the past, CRT monitor screens were curved slightly. Today's models have flat screens. A flat screen reduces glare, reflection, and distortion of images. With a flat screen, users do not notice as much eyestrain and fatigue.

A CRT monitor costs less than an LCD monitor, but it also generates more heat and uses more power than an LCD monitor. To help reduce the amount of electricity used by monitors and other computer components, the United States Department of Energy (DOE) and the United States Environmental Protection Agency (EPA) developed the **ENERGY STAR program**. This program encourages manufacturers to create energy-efficient devices that require little power when they are not in use. Monitors and devices that meet ENERGY STAR guidelines display an ENERGY STAR label.

FIGURE 6-9   The core of a CRT monitor is a cathode-ray tube.

CRT monitors produce a small amount of electromagnetic radiation. *Electromagnetic radiation (EMR)* is a magnetic field that travels at the speed of light. Excessive amounts of EMR can pose a health risk. To be safe, all high-quality CRT monitors comply with MPR II standards. *MPR II* is a set of standards that defines acceptable levels of EMR for a monitor. To protect yourself even further, sit at arm's length from the CRT monitor because EMR travels only a short distance. In addition, EMR is greatest on the sides and back of the CRT monitor.

FAQ 6-6

Is a flat display the same as a flat-panel display?

No. A *flat display* refers to a CRT monitor that has a flat screen. A flat-panel display, by contrast, has a shallow depth and uses LCD, gas plasma, or some technology other than CRT. For more information, visit scsite.com/dc2006/ch6/faq and then click Flat-Panel Displays.

Quality of a CRT Monitor

The quality of a CRT monitor depends largely on its resolution, dot pitch, and refresh rate.
- Most CRT monitors support a variety of screen resolutions. Standard CRT monitors today usually display up to a maximum of 1800 × 1440 pixels, with 1280 × 1024 often the norm. High-end CRT monitors (for the power user) can display 2048 × 1536 pixels or more. The display resolution you choose is a matter of preference. Larger monitors typically look best at a higher resolution, and smaller monitors look best at a lower resolution.
- As with LCD monitors, text created with a smaller dot pitch, or pixel pitch, is easier to read. To minimize eye fatigue, use a CRT monitor with a dot pitch of .27 millimeters or lower.
- Electron beams inside a CRT monitor "draw" an image on the entire screen many times per second so the phosphor dots, and therefore the image, do not fade. The number of times the image is drawn per second is called the *refresh rate*, or *scan rate*. A CRT monitor's refresh rate, which is expressed in hertz (Hz), should be fast enough to maintain a constant,

WEB LINK 6-3

CRT Monitors

For more information, visit scsite.com/ dc2006/ch6/weblink and then click CRT Monitors.

flicker-free image. A slower refresh rate causes the image to fade and then flicker as it is redrawn. This flicker can lead to eye fatigue and cause headaches for some users.

A high-quality CRT monitor will provide a vertical refresh rate of at least 68 Hz. This means the image on the screen redraws itself vertically 68 times in a second.

Graphics Chips and CRT Monitors

Many CRT monitors use an analog signal to produce an image. As with an LCD monitor, a cable on the CRT monitor plugs in a port on the system unit, which enables communications from a graphics chip. If the graphics chip resides on a video card, for example, the video card converts digital output from the computer into an analog video signal and sends the signal through the cable to the monitor, which displays output on the screen (Figure 6-10).

As with LCD monitors, the greater the video card's bit depth, the better the resulting image. Both the video card and the monitor must support the video standard to generate the desired resolution and number of colors, and the video card must have enough memory to generate the resolution and number of colors you want to display.

FAQ 6-7

What type of video content do users view on display devices?

Music videos and newscasts are the most widely viewed video content on display devices, as shown in the chart below. For more information, visit scsite.com/dc2006/ch6/faq and then click Video Output Content.

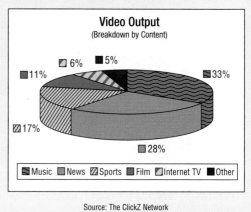

Video Output
(Breakdown by Content)

- Music 33%
- News 28%
- Sports 17%
- Film 11%
- Internet TV 6%
- Other 5%

Source: The ClickZ Network

FIGURE 6-10 HOW VIDEO TRAVELS FROM THE PROCESSOR TO A CRT MONITOR VIA A VIDEO CARD

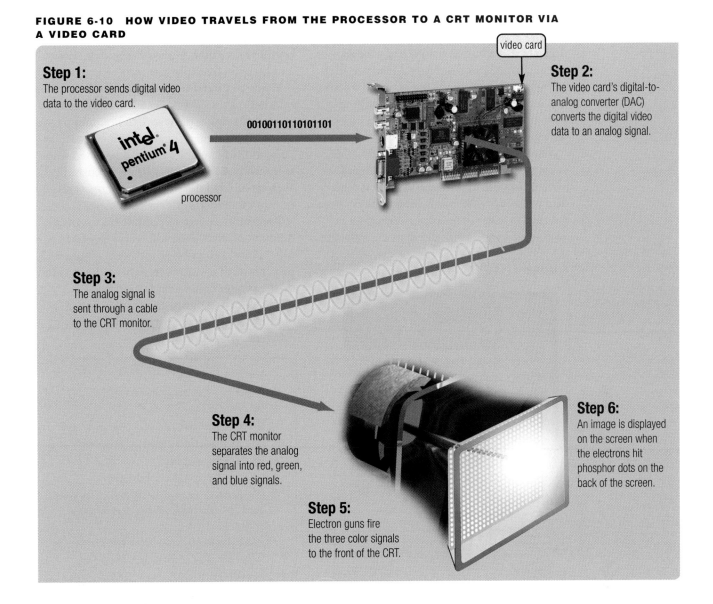

Step 1:
The processor sends digital video data to the video card.

00100110110101101

processor

video card

Step 2:
The video card's digital-to-analog converter (DAC) converts the digital video data to an analog signal.

Step 3:
The analog signal is sent through a cable to the CRT monitor.

Step 4:
The CRT monitor separates the analog signal into red, green, and blue signals.

Step 5:
Electron guns fire the three color signals to the front of the CRT.

Step 6:
An image is displayed on the screen when the electrons hit phosphor dots on the back of the screen.

Test your knowledge of pages 300 through 309 in Quiz Yourself 6-1.

 QUIZ YOURSELF 6-1

Instructions: Find the true statement below. Then, rewrite the remaining false statements so they are true.

1. A lower resolution uses a greater number of pixels and thus provides a smoother image.

2. An output device is any type of software component that conveys information to one or more people.

3. Documents often include text to enhance their visual appeal and convey information.

4. LCD monitors have a larger footprint than CRT monitors.

5. Types of CRTs include LCD monitors, LCD screens, plasma monitors, and many HDTVs.

6. You measure a monitor diagonally from one corner to the other.

Quiz Yourself Online: To further check your knowledge of output, flat-panel displays, and CRT monitors, visit scsite.com/dc2006/ch6/quiz and then click Objectives 1 – 4.

PRINTERS

A **printer** is an output device that produces text and graphics on a physical medium such as paper or transparency film. Printed information, called *hard copy*, exists physically and is a more permanent form of output than that presented on a display device (soft copy).

A hard copy, also called a *printout*, is either in portrait or landscape orientation (Figure 6-11). A printout in *portrait orientation* is taller than it is wide, with information printed across the shorter width of the paper. A printout in *landscape orientation* is wider than it is tall, with information printed across the widest part of the paper. Letters, reports, and books typically use portrait orientation. Spreadsheets, slide shows, and graphics often use landscape orientation.

Home computer users might print less than a hundred pages a week. Small business computer users might print several hundred pages a day. Users of mainframe computers, such as large utility companies that send printed statements to hundreds of thousands of customers each month, require printers that are capable of printing thousands of pages per hour.

To meet this range of printing needs, many different printers exist with varying speeds, capabilities, and printing methods. Figure 6-12 presents a list of questions to help you decide on the printer best suited to your needs.

The following pages discuss various ways of producing printed output, as well as many different types of printers.

FIGURE 6-11a (portrait orientation)

FIGURE 6-11b (landscape orientation)

Fitness Progress Chart for Men

Instructions: Replace the sample data in the first five (white) columns, and in the Height boxes to the right. The last four (yellow) columns will be calculated for you using formulas. Then, see your progress by looking at the Measurements, Weight and BMI, and Weight and Body Fat Charts on the other worksheets. For more information on formulas or using data in charts, see Excel Help.

| | | | | | | | | Height (feet) | 6 |
| | | | | | | | | Height (inches) | 3/8 |

Date	Weight (pounds)	Chest (inches)	Waist (inches)	Hips (inches)	Estimated Lean Body Weight	Estimated Body Fat Weight	Estimated Body Fat Percentage	Estimated Body Mass Index (BMI)
10-Jun	200	42	36	34	161 3/7	38 4/7	19 2/7	26.84
17-Jun	200	42	36	34	161 3/7	38 4/7	19 2/7	26.84
24-Jun	199	42	35.5	33.6	162 2/5	36 3/5	18 2/5	26.71
1-Jul	199	42	35	33	164 1/2	34 1/2	17 1/3	26.71
8-Jul	198	42.5	35	33	163 2/5	34 3/5	17 1/2	26.57
15-Jul	197	42.5	35	33	162 1/3	34 2/3	17 3/5	26.44
22-Jul	197	42.5	35	33	162 1/3	34 2/3	17 3/5	26.44
29-Jul	196	42.5	34.5	33	163 1/3	32 2/3	16 2/3	26.30
5-Aug	196	42.5	34.5	33	163 1/3	32 2/3	16 2/3	26.30
12-Aug	195	42.5	34.5	33	162 1/4	32 3/4	16 4/5	26.17
19-Aug	193	42.5	34.5	33	160	33	17	25.90
26-Aug	191	42.5	34.5	33	158	33	17 1/3	25.63
2-Sep	190	42.5	34.5	33	156 5/6	33 1/6	17 1/2	25.50
9-Sep	190	43	34.5	33	156 5/6	33 1/6	17 1/2	25.50
16-Sep	190	43	34.5	33	156 5/6	33 1/6	17 1/2	25.50
23-Sep	189	43	34	32	157 4/5	31 1/5	16 1/2	25.37
30-Sep	189	43	34	32	157 4/5	31 1/5	16 1/2	25.37
7-Oct	190	43	34	33	158 8/9	31 1/9	16 3/8	25.50
14-Oct	192	43	34	33	161	31	16 1/9	25.77
21-Oct	191	43	34	32	160	31	16 1/4	25.63
28-Oct	191	43	34	32	160	31	16 1/4	25.63
4-Nov	192	43	34	33	161	31	16 1/9	25.77
11-Nov	192	43	34	33	161	31	16 1/9	25.77
18-Nov	193	43	34	33	162 1/7	30 6/7	16	25.90
25-Nov	193	43	34	33	162 1/7	30 6/7	16	25.90
2-Dec	192	43	34	33	161	31	16 1/9	25.77
9-Dec	193	43	34	33	162 1/7	30 6/7	16	25.90

FIGURE 6-11 Portrait orientation is taller than it is wide. Landscape orientation is wider than it is tall.

1. What is my budget?
2. How fast must my printer print?
3. Do I need a color printer?
4. What is the cost per page for printing?
5. Do I need multiple copies of documents?
6. Will I print graphics?
7. Do I want to print photographs?
8. Do I want to print directly from a memory card or other type of miniature storage media?
9. What types of paper does the printer use?
10. What sizes of paper does the printer accept?
11. Do I want to print on both sides of the paper?
12. How much paper can the printer tray hold?
13. Will the printer work with my computer and software?
14. How much do supplies such as ink and paper cost?
15. Can the printer print on envelopes and transparencies?
16. How many envelopes can the printer print at a time?
17. How much do I print now, and how much will I be printing in a year or two?
18. Will the printer be connected to a network?
19. Do I want wireless printing capability?

FIGURE 6-12 Questions to ask when purchasing a printer.

Producing Printed Output

Until a few years ago, printing a document required connecting a computer to a printer with a cable via the USB or parallel port on the computer. Although many users today continue to print using this method, a variety of printing options are available, as shown in Figure 6-13.

Today, wireless printing technology makes the task of printing from a notebook computer, Tablet PC, PDA, or smart phone much easier. As discussed in Chapter 4, two wireless technologies for printing are Bluetooth and infrared. With *Bluetooth printing*, a device transmits output to a printer via radio waves. The computer and devices do not have to be aligned with each other; rather, they need to be within an approximate 30-foot range. With *infrared printing*, a printer communicates with a device using infrared light waves. To print from a smart phone, for example, a user lines up the IrDA port on the smart phone with the IrDA port on the printer.

Users can print images taken with a digital camera without downloading the images to the computer using a variety of techniques. Some cameras connect directly to a printer via a cable. Others store images on media cards that can be removed and inserted in the printer. Some printers have a docking station, into which the user inserts the camera to print pictures stored in the camera.

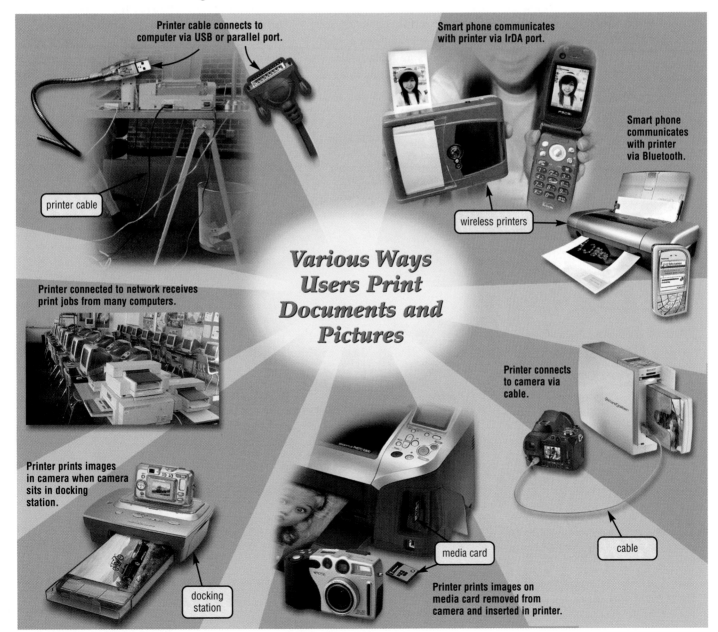

Printer cable connects to computer via USB or parallel port.

printer cable

Smart phone communicates with printer via IrDA port.

Smart phone communicates with printer via Bluetooth.

wireless printers

Printer connected to network receives print jobs from many computers.

Various Ways Users Print Documents and Pictures

Printer connects to camera via cable.

Printer prints images in camera when camera sits in docking station.

docking station

media card

cable

Printer prints images on media card removed from camera and inserted in printer.

FIGURE 6-13 Users print documents and pictures using a variety of printing methods.

Finally, many home and business users print to a central printer on a network. Their computer may communicate with the network printer via cables or wirelessly.

FAQ 6-8

Where did the name Bluetooth originate?

Harald Blatand was king of Denmark circa 950. This king, whose last name they say roughly translates to blue tooth, was able to unite Denmark and Norway despite their differences. When Ericsson, Intel, IBM, Nokia, and Toshiba collectively were able to develop this wireless communications standard, they named it Bluetooth — after the Danish leader. For more information, visit scsite.com/dc2006/ch6/faq and then click Bluetooth.

Nonimpact Printers

A **nonimpact printer** forms characters and graphics on a piece of paper without actually striking the paper. Some spray ink, while others use heat or pressure to create images.

Commonly used nonimpact printers are ink-jet printers, photo printers, laser printers, thermal printers, mobile printers, label and postage printers, plotters, and large-format printers.

Ink-Jet Printers

An **ink-jet printer** is a type of nonimpact printer that forms characters and graphics by spraying tiny drops of liquid ink onto a piece of paper. Ink-jet printers have become a popular type of color printer for use in the home. A reasonable quality ink-jet printer costs less than $100.

Ink-jet printers produce text and graphics in both black-and-white and color on a variety of paper types (Figure 6-14). These printers normally use individual sheets of paper stored in one or two removable or stationary trays. Ink-jet printers accept papers in many sizes, ranging from 3×5 inches to $8^{1}/_{2} \times 14$ inches. Available paper types include plain paper, ink-jet paper, photo paper, glossy paper, and banner paper. Most ink-jet

FIGURE 6-14   Ink-jet printers are a popular type of color printer used in the home.

printers can print photographic-quality images on any of these types of paper.

Ink-jet printers also print on other materials such as envelopes, labels, index cards, greeting card paper (card stock), transparencies, and iron-on T-shirt transfers. Many ink-jet printers include software for creating greeting cards, banners, business cards, letterheads, and transparencies.

As with many other input and output devices, one factor that determines the quality of an ink-jet printer is its resolution. Printer resolution is measured by the number of *dots per inch* (*dpi*) a printer can print. With an ink-jet printer, a dot is a drop of ink. A higher dpi means the drops of ink are smaller. Most ink-jet printers can print from 600 to 4800 dpi.

As shown in Figure 6-15, the higher the dpi, the better the print quality. The difference in quality becomes noticeable when the size of the printed image increases. That is, a wallet-sized image printed at 600 dpi may look similar in quality to one printed at 1200 dpi. When you increase the size of the image, to 8 × 10 for example, the printout of the 600 dpi resolution

may look grainier than the one printed using a 1200 dpi resolution.

The speed of an ink-jet printer is measured by the number of pages per minute (ppm) it can print. Most ink-jet printers print from 3 to 26 ppm. Graphics and colors print at a slower rate. For example, an ink-jet printer may print 20 ppm for black text and only 15 ppm for color and/ or graphics.

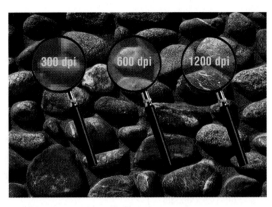

FIGURE 6-15 You will notice a higher quality output with printers that can print at a higher dpi.

The print head mechanism in an ink-jet printer contains ink-filled print cartridges. Each cartridge has fifty to several hundred small ink holes, or nozzles. The steps in Figure 6-16 illustrate how a drop of ink appears on a page. The ink propels through any combination of the nozzles to form a character or image on the paper.

FIGURE 6-16 HOW AN INK-JET PRINTER WORKS

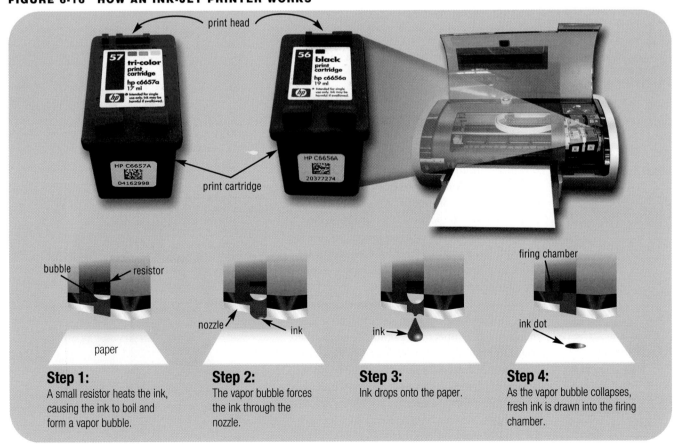

Step 1:
A small resistor heats the ink, causing the ink to boil and form a vapor bubble.

Step 2:
The vapor bubble forces the ink through the nozzle.

Step 3:
Ink drops onto the paper.

Step 4:
As the vapor bubble collapses, fresh ink is drawn into the firing chamber.

When the print cartridge runs out of ink, you simply replace the cartridge. Most ink-jet printers have at least two print cartridges: one containing black ink and the other(s) containing colors. Cartridges with black ink cost $15 to $30 each. Color ink cartridge prices range from $20 to $35 each. The number of pages a single cartridge can print varies by manufacturer and the type of documents you print. For example, black ink cartridges typically print from 200 to 800 pages, and color ink cartridges from 125 to 450 pages. Read At Issue 6-1 for a related discussion.

WEB LINK 6-4

Ink-Jet Printers

For more information, visit scsite.com/ dc2006/ch6/weblink and then click Ink-Jet Printers.

AT ISSUE 6-1

Ink-Jet Ink Wars?

In 1903, King Camp Gillette introduced an innovative product — a safety razor with disposable blades. Gillette accompanied his product with an even more innovative idea — sell the razor, which was purchased once, at or below cost, and rely on sales of the razor blades, which were purchased repeatedly, for profit. The idea made Gillette a millionaire. Manufacturers of ink-jet printers use a similar approach. The printers are inexpensive, often less than $200. The ink cartridges the printers use, however, can cost from $30 to $50 each time they are replaced. To avoid the high cost of cartridges, some people use ink refill kits. These kits, which are far less expensive than a new cartridge, typically include several vials of ink and a syringe-like tool used to inject the ink into existing ink cartridges. To counter the kits, some printer manufacturers have inserted special chips that keep a cartridge from being refilled and, some claim, shut down a cartridge before it really is out of ink. Ink refill kits cost much less than a new cartridge, but the kits can be messy, contain low-quality ink, and even damage a print head if used improperly. Should manufacturers be allowed to prevent people from refilling ink cartridges? Why? Would you use an ink refill kit? Why or why not?

Photo Printers

A **photo printer** is a color printer that produces photo-lab-quality pictures (Figure 6-17). Some photo printers print just one or two sizes of images, for example, 3 × 5 inches and 4 × 6 inches. Others print up to letter size, legal size, or even larger. Some even print panoramic photographs. Generally, the more sizes the printer prints, the more expensive the printer.

Many photo printers use ink-jet technology. With models that can print letter-sized documents, users connect the photo printer to their computer and use it for all their printing needs. For a few hundred dollars, this type of photo printer is ideal for the home or small business user. Other photo printer technologies are discussed later in the chapter. Read At Issue 6-2 for a related discussion.

WEB LINK 6-5

Photo Printers

For more information, visit scsite.com/ dc2006/ch6/weblink and then click Photo Printers.

prints only 4 × 6 size

prints 4 × 6, 5 × 7, 8 × 10, 8½ × 11, and panoramic sizes

prints 4 × 6, 5 × 7, 8 × 10, 8½ × 11, 11 × 14, 13 × 19, and panoramic sizes

FIGURE 6-17   Photo printers print in a range of sizes.

AT ISSUE 6-2

Who Is Responsible for Stopping Counterfeiting?

Some college students found a solution to their money problems: they made their own. With a scanner, personal computer, and color printer, they produced bogus bills and passed more than $1,000 in counterfeit currency before they were caught. As printer quality continues to improve, it is estimated that more than $1 million in fraudulent funds is produced every week. Police have arrested counterfeiters ranging from high school students to senior citizens. As one federal agent points out, counterfeiting has gone from a high-skill, low-tech job to a high-tech, low-skill job. While counterfeiters used to specialize in higher-domination bills ($20, $50, and $100), today phony $10, $5, and even $1 bills are circulated. Spotting fake money is not that difficult, but most people never look that closely. Counterfeiting does not stop with money. With templates for diplomas, degrees, transcripts, social security cards, driver's licenses, birth certificates, deeds, certified checks, and green cards available on the Web, almost any document can be produced. Should the manufacturers of high-quality printers take responsibility for this problem? Why or why not? What, if anything, could printer manufacturers do? It is illegal to pass counterfeit currency knowingly. Should it be illegal to offer templates knowingly online that could be used to produce counterfeit documents? Can you offer any other possible solutions?

Many photo printers have a built-in card slot so the printer can print digital photographs directly from a media card. Simply remove the media card from the digital camera and insert it in the printer's card slot. Then, push buttons on the printer to select the desired photo, specify the number of copies, and indicate the size of the printed image. Some photo printers have built-in LCD color screens, allowing users to view and enhance the pictures before printing them.

FAQ 6-9

What type of paper is available for a photo printer?

Many photo papers are available in various surface finishes, brightness, and weights. Surface finishes include high gloss, soft gloss, satin, or matte. The higher the brightness rating, the more brilliant the whiteness. The greater the paper weight, which is measured in pounds, the thicker the paper. In the United States, the weight of paper is stated in pounds per 500 sheets of 17" × 22" paper, each sheet of which equals four letter-sized sheets. For more information, visit scsite.com/dc2006/ch6/faq and then click Photo Paper.

Laser Printers

A **laser printer** is a high-speed, high-quality nonimpact printer (Figure 6-18). Laser printers are available in both black-and-white and color models. A laser printer for personal computers ordinarily uses individual $8\frac{1}{2}$ × 11-inch sheets of paper stored in one or more removable trays that slide in the printer case. Some laser printers have built-in trays that accommodate different sizes of paper, while others require separate trays for letter- and legal-sized paper. Most laser printers have a manual feed slot where you can insert individual sheets and envelopes. You also can print transparencies on a laser printer.

Laser printers print text and graphics in high-quality resolutions, usually 1200 dpi for black-and-white printers and up to 2400 dpi for color printers. While laser printers usually cost more than ink-jet printers, they also are much faster. A laser printer for the home and small office user typically prints black-and-white text at speeds of 15 to 50 ppm. Color laser printers print 4 to 24 ppm. Laser printers for large business users print more than 150 ppm.

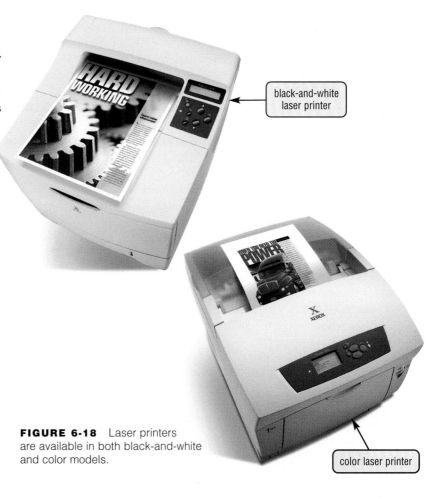

black-and-white laser printer

color laser printer

FIGURE 6-18 Laser printers are available in both black-and-white and color models.

Depending on the quality, speed, and type of laser printer, the cost ranges from a few hundred to several thousand dollars for the home and small office user, and several hundred thousand dollars for the large business user. Color laser printers are slightly higher priced than otherwise equivalent black-and-white laser printers.

When printing a document, laser printers process and store the entire page before they actually print it. For this reason, laser printers sometimes are called page printers. Storing a page before printing requires that the laser printer has a certain amount of memory in the device.

Depending on the amount of graphics you intend to print, a laser printer for the home or small business user can have up to 416 MB of memory and a 20 GB hard disk. To print a full-page 1200-dpi picture, for instance, you might need 32 MB of memory in the printer. If the printer does not have enough memory to print the picture, either it will print as much of the picture as its memory will allow, or it will display an error message and not print any of the picture.

Laser printers use software that enables them to interpret a *page description language* (*PDL*), which tells the printer how to lay out the contents of a printed page. When you purchase a laser printer, it comes with at least one of two common page description languages: PCL or PostScript. Developed by Hewlett-Packard, a leading printer manufacturer, *PCL* (*Printer Control Language*) is a standard printer language

that supports the fonts and layout used in standard office documents. Professionals in the desktop publishing and graphic art fields commonly use *PostScript* because it is designed for complex documents with intense graphics and colors.

Operating in a manner similar to a copy machine, a laser printer creates images using a laser beam and powdered ink, called *toner*. The laser beam produces an image on a special drum inside the printer. The light of the laser alters the electrical charge on the drum wherever it hits. When this occurs, the toner sticks to the drum and then transfers to the paper through a combination of pressure and heat (Figure 6-19).

When the toner runs out, you replace the toner cartridge. Toner cartridge prices range from $50 to $100 for about 5,000 printed pages.

WEB LINK 6-6

Laser Printers

For more information, visit scsite.com/dc2006/ch6/weblink and then click Laser Printers.

FAQ 6-10

How do I dispose of toner cartridges?

Do not throw them in the garbage. The housing contains iron, metal, and aluminum that is not biodegradable. The ink toner inside the cartridges contains toxic chemicals that pollute water and soil if discarded in dumps. Instead, recycle empty toner cartridges. Contact your printer manufacturer to see if it has a recycling program. For more information, visit scsite.com/dc2006/ch6/faq and then click Recycling Toner Cartridges.

FIGURE 6-19 HOW A BLACK-AND-WHITE LASER PRINTER WORKS

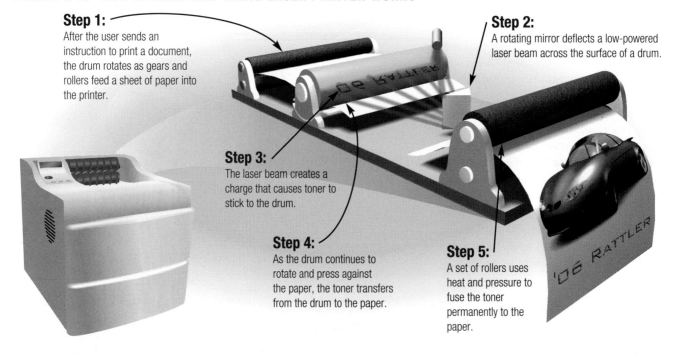

Step 1:
After the user sends an instruction to print a document, the drum rotates as gears and rollers feed a sheet of paper into the printer.

Step 2:
A rotating mirror deflects a low-powered laser beam across the surface of a drum.

Step 3:
The laser beam creates a charge that causes toner to stick to the drum.

Step 4:
As the drum continues to rotate and press against the paper, the toner transfers from the drum to the paper.

Step 5:
A set of rollers uses heat and pressure to fuse the toner permanently to the paper.

Thermal Printers

A **thermal printer** generates images by pushing electrically heated pins against heat-sensitive paper. Basic thermal printers are inexpensive, but the print quality is low and the images tend to fade over time. Self-service gas pumps often print gas receipts using a built-in lower-quality thermal printer.

Two special types of thermal printers have high print quality. A *thermal wax-transfer printer* generates rich, nonsmearing images by using heat to melt colored wax onto heat-sensitive paper. Thermal wax-transfer printers are more expensive than ink-jet printers, but less expensive than many color laser printers.

A *dye-sublimation printer*, sometimes called a *digital photo printer*, uses heat to transfer colored dye to specially coated paper. Most dye-sublimation printers create images that are of photographic quality (Figure 6-20). Professional applications requiring high image quality, such as photography studios, medical labs, and security identification systems, use dye-sublimation printers. These high-end printers cost thousands of dollars and print images in a wide range of sizes. Most dye-sublimation printers for the home or small business user, by contrast, typically print images in only one or two sizes and are much slower than their professional counterparts. These lower-end dye-sublimation printers are comparable in cost to a photo printer based on ink-jet technology. Some are small enough for the mobile user to carry the printer in a briefcase.

Mobile Printers

A **mobile printer** is a small, lightweight, battery-powered printer that allows a mobile user to print from a notebook computer, Tablet PC, PDA, or smart phone while traveling (Figure 6-21). Barely wider than the paper on which they print, mobile printers fit easily in a briefcase alongside a notebook computer.

Mobile printers mainly use ink-jet, thermal, thermal wax-transfer, or dye-sublimation technology. Many of these printers connect to a parallel port or USB port. Others have a built-in wireless port through which they communicate with the computer wirelessly.

FIGURE 6-20a (dye-sublimation printer for the professional)

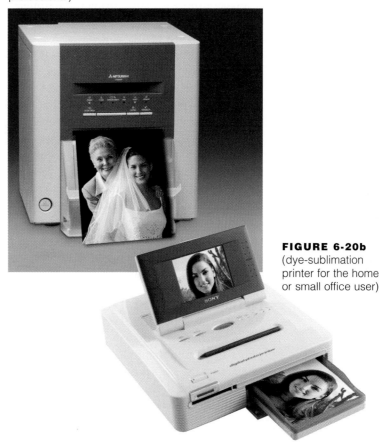

FIGURE 6-20b (dye-sublimation printer for the home or small office user)

FIGURE 6-20 The printers shown in this figure use dye-sublimation technology to create photographic-quality output.

FIGURE 6-21 A mobile printer is a compact printer that allows the mobile user to print from a notebook computer or mobile device.

Label and Postage Printers

A **label printer** is a small printer that prints on an adhesive-type material (Figure 6-22) that can be placed on a variety of items such as envelopes, packages, floppy disks, CDs, DVDs, audio-cassettes, photographs, file folders, and toys. Most label printers also print bar codes. Label printers typically use thermal technology.

A *postage printer* is a special type of label printer that has a built-in digital scale and prints postage stamps. Postage printers allow users to buy and print digital postage, called *Internet postage*, right from their computer. That is, you purchase an amount of postage from an authorized postal service Web site. As you need a stamp, you print it on the postage printer. Each time a postage stamp prints, your postage account is updated.

FIGURE 6-22
A label printer.

Plotters and Large-Format Printers

Plotters are sophisticated printers used to produce high-quality drawings such as blueprints, maps, and circuit diagrams. These printers are used in specialized fields such as engineering and drafting and usually are very costly. Current plotters use a row of charged wires (called styli) to draw an electrostatic pattern on specially coated paper and then fuse toner to the pattern. The printed image consists of a series of very small dots, which provides high-quality output.

Using ink-jet printer technology, but on a much larger scale, a **large-format printer** creates photo-realistic-quality color prints. Graphic artists use these high-cost, high-performance printers for signs, posters, and other professional quality displays (Figure 6-23).

Plotters and large-format printers can accommodate paper with widths up to 60 inches because blueprints, maps, signs, posters and other such drawings and displays can be quite large. Some plotters and large-format printers use individual sheets of paper, while others take large rolls.

Impact Printers

An **impact printer** forms characters and graphics on a piece of paper by striking a mechanism against an inked ribbon that physically contacts the paper. Impact printers characteristically are noisy because of this striking activity. These printers commonly produce *near letter quality (NLQ)* output, which is print quality slightly less clear than what is acceptable for business letters. Companies may use impact printers for routine jobs such as printing mailing labels, envelopes, and invoices. Impact printers also are ideal for printing multipart forms because they easily print through many layers of paper. Factories and retail counters use impact printers because these printers withstand dusty environments, vibrations, and extreme temperatures.

Two commonly used types of impact printers are dot-matrix printers and line printers.

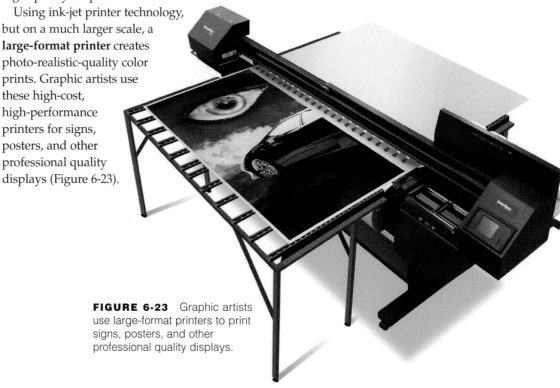

FIGURE 6-23 Graphic artists use large-format printers to print signs, posters, and other professional quality displays.

DOT-MATRIX PRINTERS A **dot-matrix printer** is an impact printer that produces printed images when tiny wire pins on a print head mechanism strike an inked ribbon (Figure 6-24). When the ribbon presses against the paper, it creates dots that form characters and graphics.

Most dot-matrix printers use *continuous-form paper*, in which thousands of sheets of paper are connected together end to end. The pages have holes along the sides to help feed the paper through the printer.

The print head mechanism on a dot-matrix printer contains 9 to 24 pins, depending on the manufacturer and the printer model. A higher number of pins means the printer prints more dots per character, which results in higher print quality.

The speed of a dot-matrix printer is measured by the number of characters per second (cps) it can print. The speed of most dot-matrix printers ranges from 400 to 1100 characters per second (cps), depending on the desired print quality.

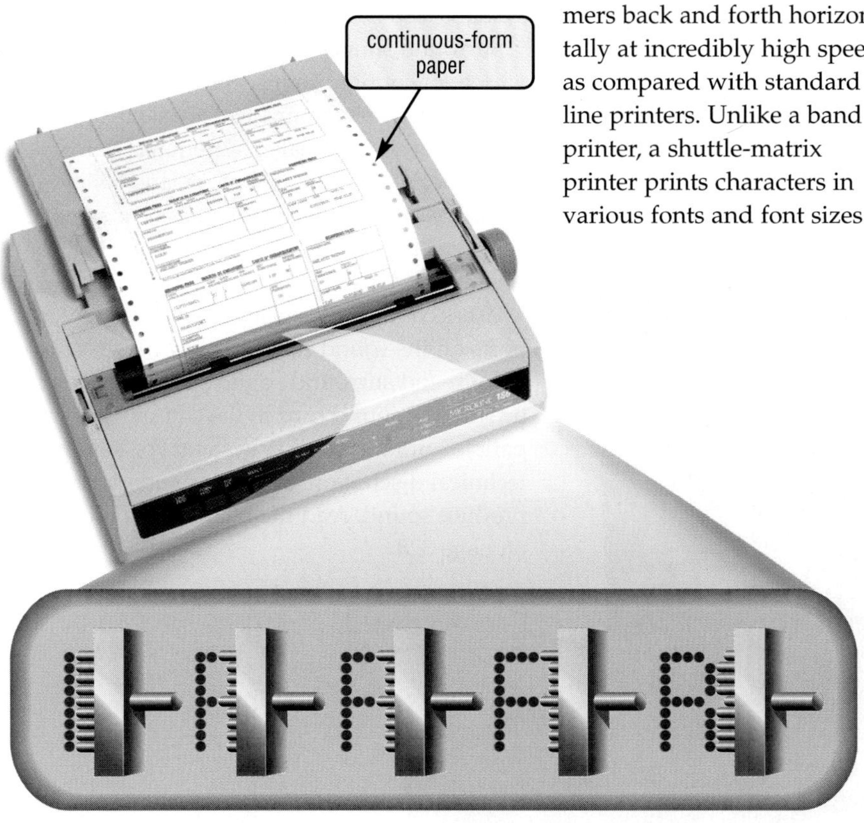

LINE PRINTERS A **line printer** is a high-speed impact printer that prints an entire line at a time (Figure 6-25). The speed of a line printer is measured by the number of lines per minute (lpm) it can print. Some line printers print as many as 3,000 lpm. Mainframes, midrange servers, or networked applications, such as manufacturing, distribution, or shipping, often use line printers. These printers typically use 11-by-17-inch continuous-form paper.

Two popular types of line printers used for high-volume output are band and shuttle-matrix. A *band printer* prints fully formed characters when hammers strike a horizontal, rotating band that contains shapes of numbers, letters of the alphabet, and other characters. A *shuttle-matrix printer* functions more like a dot-matrix printer. The difference is the shuttle-matrix printer moves a series of print hammers back and forth horizontally at incredibly high speeds, as compared with standard line printers. Unlike a band printer, a shuttle-matrix printer prints characters in various fonts and font sizes.

FIGURE 6-25 A line printer is a high-speed printer often connected to a mainframe, midrange server, or network.

continuous-form paper

FIGURE 6-24 A dot-matrix printer produces printed images when tiny pins strike an inked ribbon.

Test your knowledge of pages 310 through 319 in Quiz Yourself 6-2.

QUIZ YOURSELF 6-2

Instructions: Find the true statement below. Then, rewrite the remaining false statements so they are true.

1. A laser printer generates images by pushing electrically heated pins against heat-sensitive paper.
2. A photo printer creates images using a laser beam and powdered ink, called toner.
3. An ink-jet printer is a type of impact printer that forms characters and graphics by spraying tiny drops of liquid nitrogen onto a piece of paper.
4. Printed information is called soft copy.
5. Two commonly used types of impact printers are ink-jet printers and line printers.
6. With Bluetooth printing, a device transmits output to a printer via radio waves.

Quiz Yourself Online: To further check your knowledge of ways to print and various type of printers, visit scsite.com/dc2006/ch6/quiz and then click Objectives 5 – 7.

SPEAKERS AND HEADSETS

An **audio output device** is a component of a computer that produces music, speech, or other sounds, such as beeps. Two commonly used audio output devices are speakers and headsets.

Most personal computers have a small internal speaker that usually emits only low-quality sound. Thus, many personal computer users add surround sound **speakers** to their computers to generate a higher-quality sound for playing games, interacting with multimedia presentations, listening to music CDs, and viewing DVDs (Figure 6-26).

Most surround sound computer speaker systems include one or two center speakers and two or more *satellite speakers* that are positioned so sound emits from all directions. Speakers typically have tone and volume controls, allowing users to adjust settings. To boost the low bass sounds, surround sound speaker systems also include a *subwoofer*.

Surround sound systems are available in a variety of configurations. For example, a 2.1 speaker system contains two speakers and a subwoofer. A 5.1 speaker system has four satellite speakers, a center speaker, and a subwoofer. A 6.1 speaker system has four satellite speakers, a front center speaker, a rear center speaker, and a subwoofer.

Users connect the speakers and subwoofer to ports on the sound card. To take full advantage of high-end surround sound speaker systems, be sure the sound card in the computer is compatible with the speaker system. For a more technical discussion about how sound cards produce sound, read the High-Tech Talk article on page 328.

FIGURE 6-26 Most personal computer users add high-quality surround sound speaker systems to their computers.

When using speakers, anyone in listening distance can hear the output. In a computer laboratory or other crowded environment, speakers might not be practical. Instead, users can plug a headset in a port on the sound card, in a speaker, or on the front of the system unit. With the **headset**, only the individual wearing the headset hears the sound from the computer (Figure 6-27). Read At Issue 6-3 for a related discussion.

Electronically produced voice output is growing in popularity. **Voice output** occurs when you hear a person's voice or when the computer talks to you through the speakers on the computer. In some software applications, the computer can speak the contents of a document through voice output. On the Web, you can listen to (or download and then listen to) interviews, talk shows, sporting events, news, recorded music, and live concerts from many radio and television stations. Some Web sites dedicate themselves to providing voice output, where you can hear songs, quotes, historical lectures, speeches, and books (Figure 6-28).

WEB LINK 6-7

Speakers and Headsets

For more information, visit scsite.com/dc2006/ch6/weblink and then click Speakers and Headsets.

FIGURE 6-27 In a crowded environment where speakers are not practical, users wear headsets to hear audio output.

FIGURE 6-28 Users can listen to book contents from the Web. Shown here is a sample audio broadcast of the book titled *Around the World In Eighty Days*. For users desiring to hear the entire book, they can purchase and download the entire audio file.

AT ISSUE 6-3

Wearable Web Devices: Help or Hindrance?

In addition to the time, a new watch from Microsoft can deliver news headlines, sports notes, local weather, and stock prices. The service uses portions of the FM radio band and can import several types of information, including calendar items and personal messages sent through MSN Messenger. Microsoft's watch may be only the tip of the iceberg. A Hewlett-Packard executive predicts that someday the boundary between people and the Internet may disappear. The reason for its dissolution is a concept called *Internet wearables*, which consist of portable, wireless output devices that people can wear to access the Internet. On the surface, these devices may appear as innocuous as eyeglasses or a hearing aid. But, when a wearer speaks into a tiny microphone attached to the device, information from a remote computer or a Web site is seen on a lens of the eyeglasses or heard through a speaker in the hearing aid. Advocates say products like Microsoft's new watch and Internet wearables will make people more efficient by providing immediate material to those who need it. Critics argue, however, that people could become over-dependent on, or easily distracted by, the devices. Will Internet wearables help people be more productive? Why or why not? When would Internet wearables be a good idea? When would they not be a good idea? Why?

Very often, voice output works with voice input. For example, when you call an airline to check the status of gates, terminals, and arrival times, your voice interacts with a computer-generated voice output. Another example is *Internet telephony*, which allows users to speak to other users over the Internet using their desktop computer, mobile computer, or mobile device.

Sophisticated programs enable the computer to converse with you. Talk into the microphone and say, "I'd like today's weather report." The computer replies, "For which city?" You reply, "Chicago." The computer says, "Sunny and 80 degrees."

OTHER OUTPUT DEVICES

In addition to display devices, printers, and speakers, many other output devices are available for specific uses and applications. These devices include fax machines and fax modems, multifunction peripherals, data projectors, and force-feedback joysticks and wheels.

WEB LINK 6-8

Fax Modems

For more information, visit scsite.com/dc2006/ch6/weblink and then click Fax Modems.

Fax Machines and Fax Modems

A **fax machine** is a device that codes and encodes documents so they can be transmitted over telephone lines. The documents can contain text, drawings, or photographs, or can be handwritten. The term *fax* refers to a document that you send or receive via a fax machine.

A stand-alone fax machine scans an original document, converts the image into digitized data, and transmits the digitized image (Figure 6-29). A fax machine at the receiving end reads the incoming data, converts the digitized data back into an image, and prints or stores a copy of the original image.

Many computers include fax capability by using a fax modem. A *fax modem* is a modem that also allows you to send (and sometimes receive) electronic documents as faxes (Figure 6-30). A fax modem transmits computer-prepared documents, such as a word processing letter, or documents that have been digitized with a scanner or digital camera. A fax modem transmits these faxes to a fax machine or to another fax modem.

FIGURE 6-29 A stand-alone fax machine.

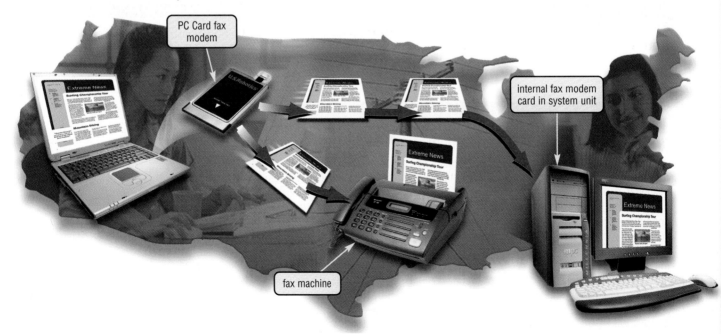

PC Card fax modem

internal fax modem card in system unit

fax machine

FIGURE 6-30 A fax modem allows users to send (and sometimes receive) electronic documents as faxes to a fax machine or another computer.

When a computer (instead of a fax machine) receives a fax, users can view the fax on the screen, saving the time and expense of printing it. If necessary, you also can print the fax. The quality of a viewed or printed fax is less than that of a word processing document because the fax actually is an image. Optical character recognition (OCR) software, which was discussed in Chapter 5, enables you to convert the image to text and then edit it.

A fax modem can be an external device that plugs in a port on the system unit, an internal adapter card inserted in an expansion slot on the motherboard, a chip integrated on the motherboard, or a PC Card that inserts in a PC Card slot.

Multifunction Peripherals

A **multifunction peripheral** is a single device that looks like a copy machine but provides the functionality of a printer, scanner, copy machine, and perhaps a fax machine (Figure 6-31). The features of these devices, which sometimes are called *all-in-one devices*, vary. For example, some use color ink-jet printer technology, while others include a black-and-white laser printer.

Small offices and home office (SOHO) users have multifunction peripherals because these devices require less space than having a separate printer, scanner, copy machine, and fax machine. Another advantage of these devices is they are significantly less expensive than if you purchase each device separately. If the device breaks down, however, you lose all four functions, which is the primary disadvantage.

Data Projectors

A **data projector** is a device that takes the text and images displaying on a computer screen and projects them on a larger screen so an audience can see the image clearly (Figure 6-32). For example, many classrooms use data projectors so all students easily can see an instructor's presentation on the screen.

Some data projectors are large devices that attach to a ceiling or wall in an auditorium. Others are small portable devices. Two types of smaller, lower-cost units are LCD projectors and DLP projectors.

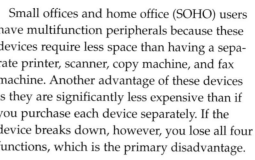

WEB LINK 6-9

Multifunction Peripherals

For more information, visit scsite.com/ dc2006/ch6/weblink and then click Multifunction Peripherals.

FIGURE 6-31 This multifunction peripheral is a color printer, scanner, copy machine, and fax machine all-in-one device.

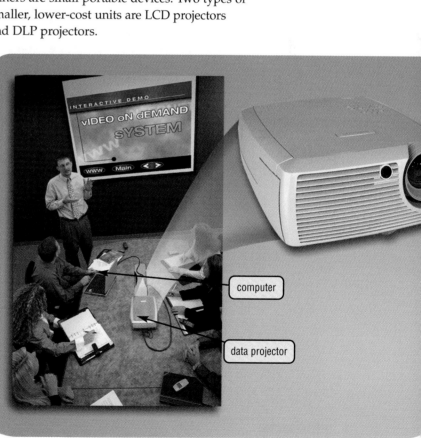

computer

data projector

FIGURE 6-32 A data projector projects an image from a computer screen on a larger screen so an audience easily can see the image.

An *LCD projector*, which uses liquid crystal display technology, attaches directly to a computer, and uses its own light source to display the information shown on the computer screen. Because LCD projectors tend to produce lower-quality images, users often prefer DLP projectors for their sharper, brighter images.

A *digital light processing* (*DLP*) *projector* uses tiny mirrors to reflect light, which produces crisp, bright, colorful images that remain in focus and can be seen clearly even in a well-lit room. Read Looking Ahead 6-2 for a look at the next generation of digital cinema projectors.

Force-Feedback Joysticks and Wheels

As discussed in Chapter 5, joysticks and wheels are input devices for computer simulations and games used to control actions of a player or movements of a vehicle. Today's joysticks and wheels also include *force feedback*, which is a technology that sends resistance to the device in response to actions of the user (Figure 6-33). For example, as you use the simulation software to drive from a smooth road onto a gravel alley, the steering wheel trembles or vibrates, making the driving experience as realistic as possible. In addition to games, these devices are used in practical training applications such as in the military and aviation.

LOOKING AHEAD 6-2

Digital Cinema Just the Right Picture

Computers have influenced the motion picture business by modifying how movies are produced, distributed, and exhibited. Digital technology is expected to replace film by 2007, and the new

technology's superior sound and visual clarity have been heralded as the greatest innovations since talkies replaced silent movies 80 years ago.

The seven larger Hollywood movie studios have cleared the final hurdle in the digital cinema process: agreeing on a compression scheme to deliver the movies to theaters. Called *JPG 2000*, this image coding system will allow the studios to distribute the movies without having to make thousands of prints, thus saving millions of dollars annually.

With the compression standard in place, manufacturers now can intensify their efforts to develop digital cinema projectors. For more information, visit scsite.com/dc2006/ch6/looking and then click Digital Cinema.

WEB LINK 6-10

Force Feedback Devices

For more information, visit scsite.com/ dc2006/ch6/weblink and then click Force Feedback Devices.

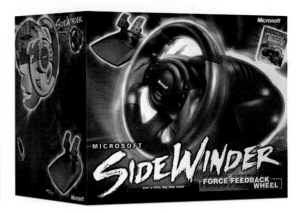

FIGURE 6-33 Joysticks, wheels, and other gaming devices often provide force feedback, giving the user a realistic experience.

PUTTING IT ALL TOGETHER

Many factors influence the type of output devices you should use: the type of output desired, the hardware and software in use, and the anticipated cost. Figure 6-34 outlines several suggested monitors, printers, and other output devices for various types of computer users.

SUGGESTED OUTPUT DEVICES BY USER

User	Monitor	Printer	Other
HOME 	• 17- or 19-inch LCD monitor	• Ink-jet color printer; or • Photo printer	• Speakers • Headset • Force-feedback joystick and wheel
SMALL OFFICE/ HOME OFFICE 	• 19- or 21-inch LCD monitor • Color LCD screen on Tablet PC, PDA, or smart phone	• Multifunction peripheral; or • Ink-jet color printer; or • Laser printer • Label printer • Postage printer	• Fax machine • Speakers
MOBILE 	• 15.7-inch LCD screen on notebook computer • Color LCD screen on Tablet PC, PDA, or smart phone	• Mobile color printer • Ink-jet color printer; or • Laser printer for in-office use • Photo printer	• Fax modem • Headset • DLP data projector
POWER 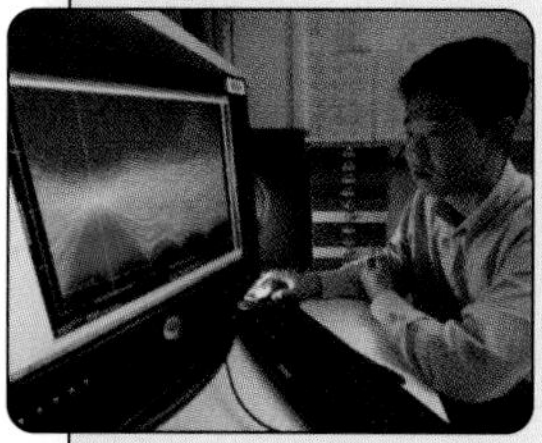	• 23-inch LCD monitor	• Laser printer • Plotter or large-format printer; or • Photo printer; or • Dye-sublimation printer	• Fax machine or fax modem • Speakers • Headset
LARGE BUSINESS 	• 19- or 21-inch LCD monitor • Color LCD screen on Tablet PC, PDA, or smart phone	• High-speed laser printer • Laser printer, color • Line printer (for large reports from a mainframe) • Label printer	• Fax machine or fax modem • Speakers • Headset • DLP data projector

FIGURE 6-34 This table recommends suggested output devices for various types of users.

OUTPUT DEVICES FOR PHYSICALLY CHALLENGED USERS

As Chapter 5 discussed, the growing presence of computers has generated an awareness of the need to address computing requirements for those with physical limitations. Read At Issue 6-4 for a related discussion.

For users with mobility, hearing, or vision disabilities, many different types of output devices are available. Hearing-impaired users, for example, can instruct programs to display words instead of sounds. With the Windows XP operating system, users also can set options to make programs easier to use. The Magnifier command, for example, enlarges text and other items in a window on the screen (Figure 6-35).

Visually impaired users can change Windows XP settings, such as increasing the size or changing the color of the text to make the words easier to read. Instead of using a monitor, blind users can work with voice output. That is, the computer reads the information that is displayed on the screen. Another alternative is a *Braille printer*, which prints information on paper in Braille (Figure 6-36).

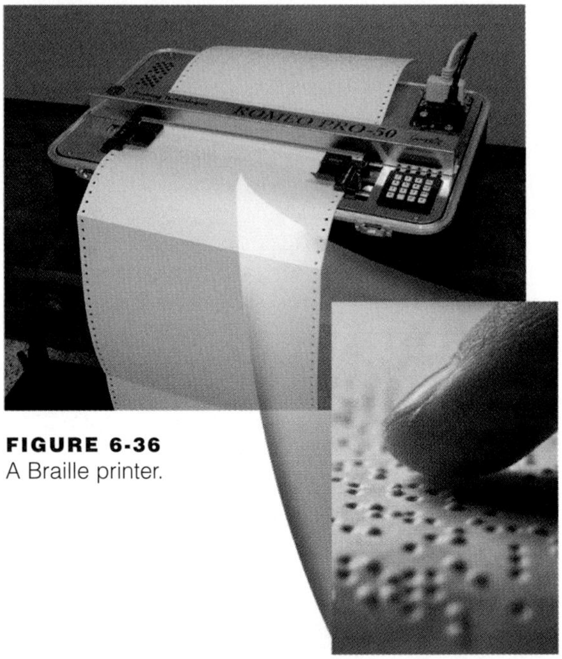

FIGURE 6-36
A Braille printer.

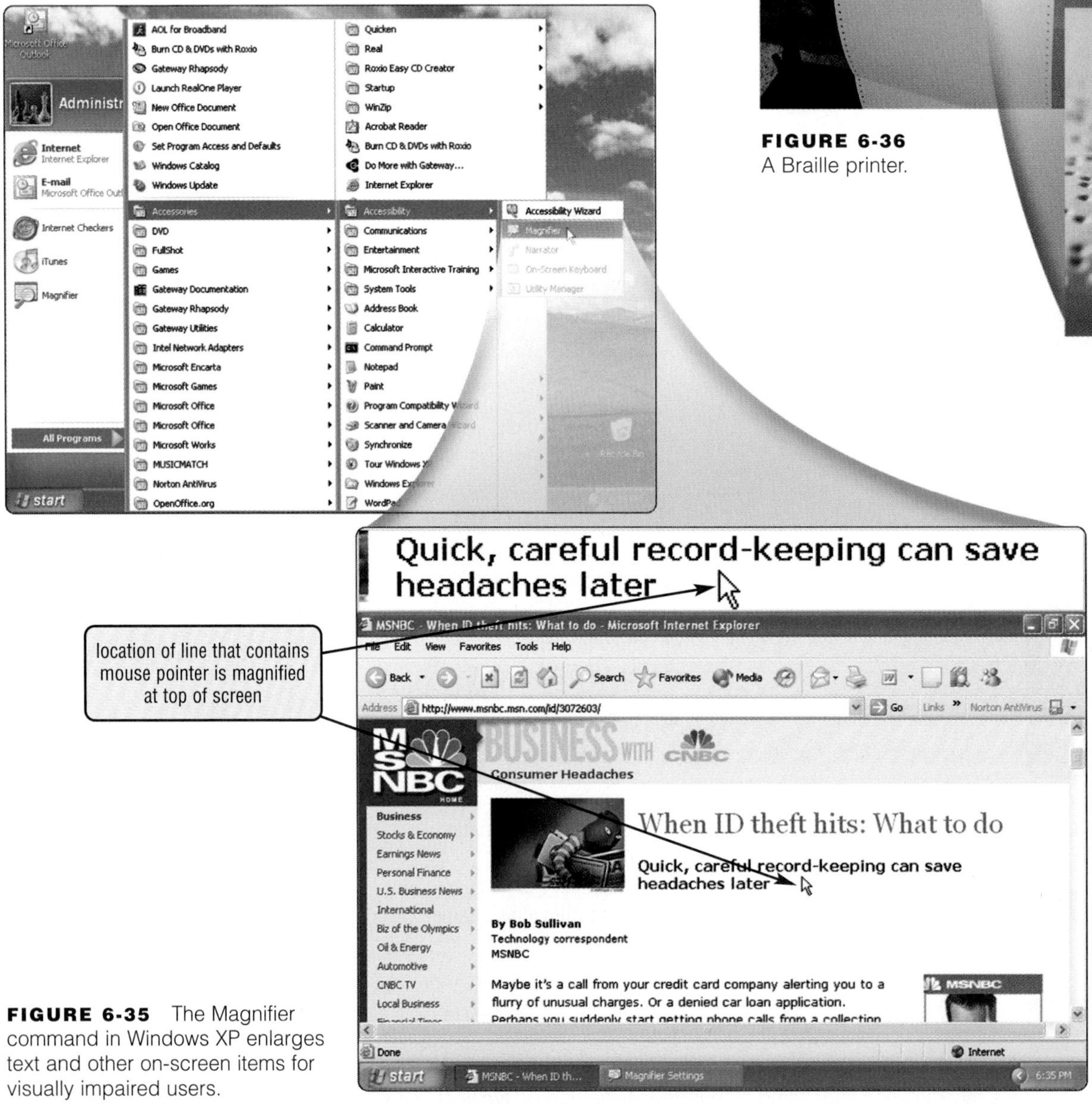

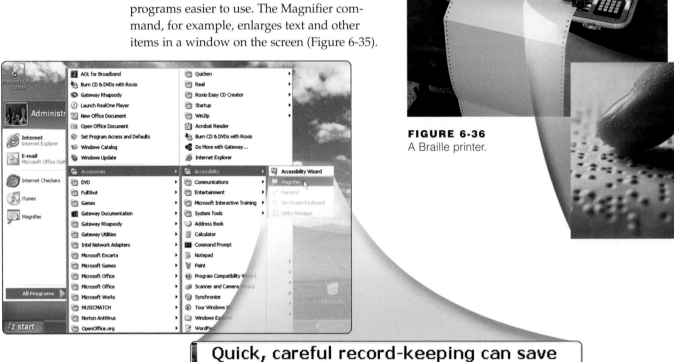

FIGURE 6-35 The Magnifier command in Windows XP enlarges text and other on-screen items for visually impaired users.

location of line that contains mouse pointer is magnified at top of screen

AT ISSUE 6-4

Should Web Sites Geared for Physically Challenged People Be Held Accountable for Accessibility Levels?

The World Wide Web Consortium (W3C) has published accessibility guidelines for Web sites. The guidelines specify measures that Web site designers can take to increase accessibility for physically challenged users. Among its guidelines, the W3C urges Web site designers to provide equivalent text for audio or visual content, include features that allow elements to be activated and understood using a variety of input and output devices, and make the user interface follow principles of accessible design. A recent report found that most Web sites do not meet all of the W3C guidelines. This failure is disappointing, because many physically challenged users could benefit from the Web's capability to bring products and services into the home. Ironically, a survey discovered that more than 50 percent of the Web sites run by disability organizations also fail to meet the W3C guidelines. Critics contend that these Web sites neglect the needs of their users and fail to lead by example. Web site apologists contend, however, that many sponsoring organizations lack the funding necessary to comply with the guidelines. Should all Web sites meet the W3C accessibility guidelines? Why or why not? Do Web sites run by disability organizations have a moral obligation to meet the guidelines? Why? What can be done to encourage sponsors to make their Web sites more accessible?

Test your knowledge of pages 320 through 327 in Quiz Yourself 6-3.

QUIZ YOURSELF 6-3

Instructions: Find the true statement below. Then, rewrite the remaining false statements so they are true.

1. A digital light processing (DLP) projector uses tiny lightbulbs to reflect light.
2. A stand-alone fax machine scans an original document, converts the image into digitized data, and transmits the digitized image.
3. Many personal computer users add surround sound printer systems to their computers to generate a higher-quality sound.
4. Multifunction peripherals require more space than having a separate printer, scanner, copy machine, and fax machine.
5. Some joysticks and wheels include real-time action, which is a technology that sends resistance to the device in response to actions of the user.

Quiz Yourself Online: To further check your knowledge of speakers and headsets, other output devices, and output for physically challenged users, visit scsite.com/dc2006/ch6/quiz and then click Objectives 8 – 10.

CHAPTER SUMMARY

Computers process and organize data (input) into information (output). This chapter described the various methods of output and several commonly used output devices. Output devices presented were flat-panel displays, CRT monitors, printers, speakers and headsets, fax machines and fax modems, multifunction peripherals, data projectors, and force-feedback joysticks and wheels.

CAREER CORNER

Graphic Designer/Illustrator

Graphic designers and *graphic illustrators* are artists, but many do not create original works. Instead, they portray visually the ideas of their clients. Illustrators create pictures for books and other publications and sometimes for commercial products, such as greeting cards. They work in fields such as fashion, technology, medicine, animation, or even cartoons. Illustrators often prepare their images on a computer. Designers combine practical skills with artistic talent to convert abstract concepts into designs for products and advertisements. Many use computer-aided design (CAD) tools to create, visualize, and modify designs. Designer careers usually are specialized in particular areas, such as:

- Graphic designers — book covers, stationery, and CD covers
- Commercial and industrial designers — products and equipment
- Costume and theater designers — costumes and settings for theater and television
- Interior designers — layout, decor, and furnishings of homes and buildings
- Merchandise displayers — commercial displays
- Fashion designers — clothing, shoes, and other fashion accessories

Certificate, two-year, four-year, and masters-level educational programs are available within design areas. About 30 percent of graphic illustrators/designers choose to freelance, while others work with advertising agencies, publishing companies, design studios, or specialized departments within large companies. Salaries range from $25,000 to $80,000-plus, based on experience and educational background. For more information, visit scsite.com/dc2006/ch6/careers and then click Graphic Designer/Illustrator.

High-Tech Talk

SOUND CARDS: BRINGING YOUR COMPUTER TO LIFE

Speakers, headsets, and other audio output devices rely on sound cards or integrated sound card functionality to produce sounds such as music, voice, beeps, and chimes. Sound cards contain the chips and circuitry to record and play back a wide range of sounds using analog-to-digital conversion and digital-to-analog conversion, as described in the Chapter 1 High-Tech Talk on page 38.

To record a sound, the sound card must be connected to an input device, such as a microphone or audio CD player. The input device sends the sound to the sound card as an analog signal. The analog signal flows to the sound card's analog-to-digital-converter (ADC). The ADC converts the signal into digital (binary) data of 1s and 0s by sampling the signal at set intervals.

The analog sound is a continuous waveform, with a range of frequencies and volumes. To represent the waveform in a recording, the computer would have to store the waveform's value at every instant in time. Because this is not possible, the sound is recorded using a sampling process. *Sampling* involves breaking up the waveform into set intervals and representing all values during that interval with a single value.

Several factors in the sampling process — sampling rate, audio resolution, and mono or stereo recording — affect the quality of the recorded sound during playback.

- *Sampling rate*, also called sampling frequency, refers to the number of times per second the sound is recorded. The more frequently a sound is recorded, the smaller the intervals and the better the quality. The sampling frequency used for audio CDs, for example, is 44,100 times per second, which is expressed in hertz (Hz) as 44,100 Hz. Cassette-tape-quality multimedia files use a sampling rate of 22,050 Hz; and basic Windows sounds use a sampling rate of 11,025 Hz.

- *Audio resolution* — defined as a bit rate such as 8-bit, 16-bit, or 24-bit — refers to the number of bytes used to represent the sound at any one interval. A sound card using 8-bit resolution, for example, represents a sound with any 1 of 256 values (2^8). A 16-bit sound card uses any 1 of 65,536 values (2^{16}) for each interval. Using a higher resolution provides a finer measurement scale, which results in a more accurate representation of the value of each sample and better sound quality. With 8-bit resolution, the sound quality is like that of an AM radio; 16-bit resolution gives CD-quality sound, and a 24-bit resolution is used for high-quality digital audio editing.

- Mono or stereo recording refers to the number of channels used during recording. *Mono* means that the same sound emits from both the left and right speaker during playback; *stereo* means that two separate channels exist in the recording: one each for the left and right speakers. Most sound cards support stereo recording for better playback.

After the ADC converts the analog sound through sampling, the digital data flows to the digital signal processor (DSP) on the sound card. The DSP then requests instructions from the sound card's memory chip on how to process the digital data. Typically, the DSP then compresses the digital data to save space. Finally, the DSP sends the compressed data to the computer's main processor, which stores the data in .WAV, .MP3, or other audio file format.

To play a recorded sound, such as a WAV, an MP3, or a CD track, the main processor retrieves the sound file from a hard disk, CD, or other storage device (Figure 6-37). The processor then sends the digital data to the DSP, which decompresses the data and looks to the memory chip to determine how to recreate the sound.

The DSP then sends the digital signals to the sound card's digital-to-analog converter (DAC), which converts the sound in digital format back to an analog electrical voltage. An output device, such as a speaker, uses an amplifier to strengthen the electrical voltage. This causes the speaker's cone to vibrate, recreating the sound.

All of this happens in an instant. The next time your computer beeps or chirps, consider the complex process required to make that simple sound. Then, insert your favorite CD and hear your computer come to life with the sweet music provided courtesy of the sound card. For more information, visit scsite.com/dc2006/ch6/tech and then click Sound Cards.

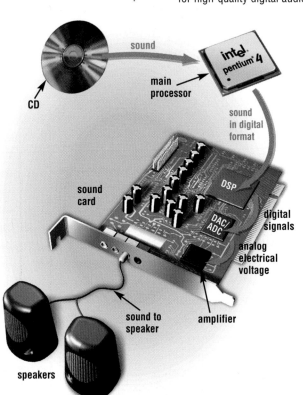

FIGURE 6-37
The path of sound from media to speakers.

Companies on the Cutting Edge

HEWLETT-PACKARD
TECHNOLOGY FOR BUSINESS AND LIFE

If you have printed a document recently, chances are the printer manufacturer was *Hewlett-Packard (HP)*. Market analysts estimate that 60 percent of printers sold today bear the HP logo, and HP says it ships one million printers each week.

HP is noted for a range of high-quality printers, disk storage systems, UNIX and Windows servers, and notebook, desktop, and handheld computers. In 2002, HP enlarged its presence in the computer market with a $25 billion buyout of Compaq Computer Corporation.

William Hewlett and David Packard started the company in a one-car garage in 1939 with the goal of manufacturing test and measurement equipment. HP has been developing personal information devices, including calculators and computers, for the past 30 years. For more information, visit scsite.com/dc2006/ch6/companies and then click Hewlett-Packard.

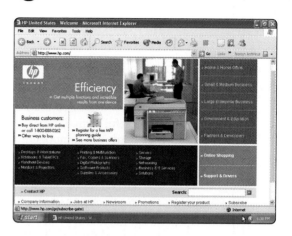

VIEWSONIC
VISUAL TECHNOLOGY LEADER

We live in a "display-centric world" according to industry leaders at *ViewSonic*. Our computer displays, whether viewed on a PDA, a desktop monitor, or a flat-panel screen, influence how we access and control the informative and entertaining output.

ViewSonic's products focus on visual technology, including CRT and LCD monitors, data projectors, plasma screens, and high-definition television. The company also designs mobile products, such as Tablet PCs and wireless monitors.

President and CEO James Chu founded ViewSonic in 1987 with the goal of increasing workers' productivity while creating an ergonomically comfortable work-space. He developed the company's logo consisting of three colorful Gouldian finches to represent outstanding quality and value, radiant color, and crisp resolution. For more information, visit scsite.com/dc2006/ch6/companies and then click ViewSonic.

Technology Trailblazers

STEVE JOBS
APPLE COMPUTER AND PIXAR COFOUNDER

Steve Jobs has an uncompromising drive for perfection. He helped build the first desktop personal computer, cofounded Apple Computer Corporation, marketed a revolutionary operating system, and became a millionaire all before his 35th birthday.

He also is known as being a brilliant motivator and having the ability to bring out the best performance from his employees. They explain that Jobs's "reality-distortion field" allows him to make seemingly unreasonable ideas appear reasonable. The Macintosh computer incorporated one of these ideas: a graphical interface controlled by a mouse.

Under Jobs's supervision, Pixar's award-winning animation studios have created some of the most beloved animated films, such as *Toy Story*, *Toy Story 2*, *A Bug's Life*, *Monsters, Inc.*, and *Finding Nemo*. For more information, visit scsite.com/dc2006/ch6/people and then click Steve Jobs.

DONNA DUBINSKY
palmOne DIRECTOR

PDAs are ubiquitous, partly due to the efforts of *Donna Dubinsky*. In the mid-1990s, she sensed that people wanted to own an electronic version of their paper appointment books. She and Jeff Hawkins introduced the original Palm Pilot prototype made of mahogany and cardboard at Palm Computing in 1996. Sales of more than two million units made the Palm Pilot the most rapidly adopted new computing product ever manufactured.

Dubinsky and Hawkins left Palm in 1998 to cofound Handspring, where they introduced several successful products, including the Treo smart phone. In 2003, Handspring merged with the Palm hardware group to create palmOne.

Dubinsky currently serves as a director of palmOne and of Intuit Corporation. For more information, visit scsite.com/dc2006/ch6/people and then click Donna Dubinsky.

Quizzes and Learning Games

Computer Genius
Crossword Puzzle
DC Track and Field
Practice Test
Quiz Yourself
Wheel of Terms
You're Hired!

Exercises

Case Studies
Chapter Review
Checkpoint
Key Terms
Learn How To
Learn It Online
Web Research

Beyond the Book

Career Corner
Companies
FAQs
High-Tech Talk
Looking Ahead
Making Use of the Web
Trailblazers
Web Links

Features

Chapter Forum
Install Computer
Lab Exercises
Maintain Computer
Tech News
Timeline 2006

Chapter Review

The Chapter Review section summarizes the concepts presented in this chapter. To listen to the audio version of this Chapter Review, visit scsite.com/dc2006/ch6/review. To obtain help from other students regarding any subject in this chapter, visit scsite.com/dc2006/ch6/forum and post your thoughts or questions.

① What Are the Four Categories of Output?   **Output** is data that has been processed into a useful form. Four categories of output are text, graphics, audio, and video. An **output device** is any hardware component that conveys information to one or more people.

② What Are LCD Monitors, LCD Screens, Plasma Monitors, and HDTVs?   LCD monitors, LCD screens, plasma monitors, and many HDTVs are types of flat-panel displays. A *flat-panel display* is a display with a shallow depth that typically uses LCD or gas plasma technology. An **LCD** monitor is a desktop monitor that uses a liquid crystal display to produce images. A **liquid crystal display (LCD)** uses a liquid compound to present information on a display. A **plasma monitor** is a display device that uses gas plasma technology, which substitutes a layer of gas for the liquid crystal material in an LCD monitor. **HDTV** *(high-definition television)* is the most advanced form of digital television, working with digital broadcasting signals, transmitting digital sound, supporting wide screens, and providing resolutions up to 1920 × 1080 pixels.

③ What Is a CRT Monitor, and What Factors Affect Its Quality?   A **CRT monitor** is a desktop monitor that contains a *cathode-ray tube (CRT)*. The screen on the front of the CRT is coated with tiny dots of red, green, and blue phosphor that combine to make up each *pixel*, which is a single element in an electronic image. As an electron beam inside the CRT moves back and forth across the back of the screen, the dots glow, which produces an image. The quality of a CRT monitor depends largely on its resolution, dot pitch, and refresh rate. **Resolution** is the number of horizontal and vertical pixels in a display device. *Dot pitch*, sometimes called *pixel pitch*, is the distance in millimeters between pixels on a display device. *Refresh rate* is the speed that a monitor redraws the images on the screen.

④ How Are Graphics Chips and CRT Monitors Related?   Many CRT monitors use an analog signal to produce an image. A cable on the CRT monitor plugs in a port on the system unit, which enables communications from a graphics chip. If the graphics chip is on a video card, the card converts digital output from the computer into an analog video signal and sends the signal through a cable to the CRT monitor, which displays output on the screen.

> connect
> Visit scsite.com/dc2006/ch6/quiz or click the Quiz Yourself button. Click Objectives 1 – 4.

⑤ What Are the Various Ways to Print?   Users can print by connecting a computer to a printer with a cable that plugs in a port on the computer. *Bluetooth printing* uses radio waves to transmit output to a printer. With *infrared* printing, a device communicates with the printer via infrared light waves. Some digital cameras connect directly to a printer via a cable; others store images on media cards that can be removed and inserted in the printer. Networked computers can communicate with the network printer via cables or wirelessly.

⑥ How Is a Nonimpact Printer Different from an Impact Printer?   A **printer** is an output device that produces text and graphics on a physical medium, such as paper or transparency film. A **nonimpact printer** forms characters and graphics on a piece of paper without actually striking the paper. Commonly used nonimpact printers are ink-jet printers, photo printers, laser printers, thermal printers, mobile printers, label and postage printers, plotters, and large-format printers. An **impact printer** forms characters and graphics on a piece of paper by striking a mechanism against an inked ribbon that physically contacts the paper. Two commonly used types of impact printers are a **dot-matrix printer** and a **line printer**.

Chapter Review

(7) **What Are Ink-Jet Printers, Photo Printers, Laser Printers, Thermal Printers, Mobile Printers, Label and Postage Printers, and Plotters and Large-Format Printers?** An **ink-jet printer** is a type of nonimpact printer that forms characters and graphics by spraying tiny drops of liquid ink onto a piece of paper. A **photo printer** is a color printer that produces photo-lab-quality pictures. A **laser printer** is a high-speed, high-quality nonimpact printer that operates in a manner similar to a copy machine, creating images using a laser beam and powdered ink, called *toner*. A **thermal printer** generates images by pushing electronically heated pins against heat-sensitive paper. A **mobile printer** is a small, lightweight, battery-powered printer that allows a mobile user to print from a notebook computer. A **label printer** is a small printer that prints on an adhesive-type material that can be placed on a variety of items. A *postage printer* is a special type of label printer that has a built-in scale and prints postage stamps. **Plotters** are sophisticated printers used to produce high-quality drawings. A **large-format printer** uses ink-jet technology on a large scale to create photo-realistic-quality color prints.

> **connect**
> Visit scsite.com/dc2006/ch6/quiz or click the Quiz Yourself button. Click Objectives 5 – 7.

(8) **How Are Speakers and Headsets Used?** Speakers and headsets are two commonly used audio output devices. An **audio output device** is a component of a computer that produces sound. Many personal computer users add stereo **speakers** to their computers to generate a higher-quality sound. With a **headset**, only the individual wearing the headset hears the sound from the computer.

(9) **What Are Fax Machines and Fax Modems, Multifunction Peripherals, Data Projectors, Joysticks, and Wheels?** A **fax machine** is a device that codes and encodes documents so they can be transmitted over telephone lines. A document sent or received via a fax machine is a *fax*. Many computers include fax capability using a *fax modem,* which is a modem that allows you to send (and sometimes receive) electronic documents as faxes. A **multifunction peripheral** is a single device that looks like a copy machine but provides the functionality of a printer, scanner, copy machine, and perhaps a fax machine. A **data projector** is a device that takes the text and images displaying on a computer screen and projects them onto a larger screen so an audience of people can see the image clearly. Joysticks and wheels are input devices used to control actions of a player or vehicle. Today's joysticks and wheels also include *force feedback*, which is a technology that sends resistance to the device in response to actions of the user.

(10) **What Output Options Are Available for Physically Challenged Users?** Hearing-impaired users can instruct programs to display words instead of sound. With Windows XP, visually impaired users can enlarge items on the screen and change other settings, such as increasing the size or changing the color of text to make words easier to read. Blind users can work with voice output instead of a monitor. Another alternative is a *Braille printer*, which prints information in Braille on paper.

> **connect**
> Visit scsite.com/dc2006/ch6/quiz or click the Quiz Yourself button. Click Objectives 8 – 10.

Quizzes and
Learning Games

Computer Genius
Crossword Puzzle
DC Track and Field
Practice Test
Quiz Yourself
Wheel of Terms
You're Hired!

Exercises

Case Studies
Chapter Review
Checkpoint
Key Terms
Learn How To
Learn It Online
Web Research

Beyond the Book

Career Corner
Companies
FAQs
High-Tech Talk
Looking Ahead
Making Use of
the Web
Trailblazers
Web Links

Features

Chapter Forum
Install Computer
Lab Exercises
Maintain Computer
Tech News
Timeline 2006

Key Terms

You should know the Primary Terms and be familiar with the Secondary Terms. Use the list below to help focus your study. To further enhance your understanding of the Key Terms in this chapter, visit scsite.com/dc2006/ch6/terms. See an example of and a definition for each term, and access current and additional information about the term from the Web.

Primary Terms

(shown in bold-black characters in the chapter)

audio output device (320)
CRT monitor (307)
data projector (323)
display device (302)
dot-matrix printer (319)
ENERGY STAR program (307)
fax machine (322)
HDTV (306)
headset (321)
impact printer (318)
ink-jet printer (312)
label printer (318)
large-format printer (318)
laser printer (315)
LCD monitor (302)
line printer (319)
liquid crystal display (LCD) (304)
mobile printer (317)
monitor (302)
multifunction peripheral (323)
nonimpact printer (312)
output (300)
output device (301)
photo printer (314)
plasma monitor (306)
plotters (318)
printer (310)
resolution (304)
speakers (320)
thermal printer (317)
voice output (321)

Secondary Terms

(shown in italic characters in the chapter)

active-matrix display (304)
all-in-one devices (323)
band printer (319)
bit depth (306)
Bluetooth printing (311)
Braille printer (326)
candela (304)
cathode-ray tube (CRT) (307)
color depth (306)
continuous-form paper (319)
digital light processing (DLP) projector (324)
digital photo printer (317)
digital television (DTV) (306)
display (302)
dot pitch (304)
dots per inch (dpi) (313)
DVI (Digital Video Interface) port (305)
dye-sublimation printer (317)
electromagnetic radiation (EMR) (308)
fax (322)
fax modem (322)
flat-panel monitor (302)
flat-panel display (302)
footprint (302)
force feedback (324)
graphics processing unit (305)
hard copy (310)
high-definition television (306)
infrared printing (311)
interactive TV (307)
Internet postage (318)

Internet telephony (322)
landscape orientation (310)
LCD projector (324)
monochrome (302)
MPR II (308)
native resolution (304)
near letter quality (NLQ) (318)
nit (304)
organic LED (OLED) (304)
page description language (PDL) (316)
passive-matrix display (304)
PCL (Printer Control Language) (316)
pixel (304)
pixel pitch (304)
portrait orientation (310)
postage printer (318)
PostScript (316)
printout (310)
refresh rate (308)
response time (304)
satellite speakers (320)
scan rate (308)
shuttle-matrix printer (319)
soft copy (302)
subwoofer (320)
S-video port (305)
SVGA (305)
SXGA (305)
TFT (thin-film transistor) display (304)
thermal wax-transfer printer (317)
toner (316)
UGA (305)
viewable size (307)
XGA (305)

Checkpoint

Use the Checkpoint exercises to check your knowledge level of the chapter. The Beyond the Book exercises will help broaden your understanding of the concepts presented in this chapter. To complete the Checkpoint exercises interactively, visit scsite.com/dc2006/ch6/check.

Label the Figure

Identify the ports on this video card.

a. DVI port
b. standard monitor port
c. S-video port

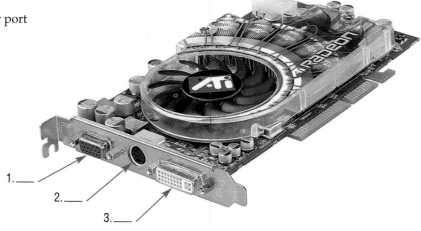

1.____
2.____
3.____

True/False

Mark T for True and F for False. (See page numbers in parentheses.)

_____ 1. A computer generates several types of output, depending on the hardware and software being used and the requirements of the user. (300)

_____ 2. Information on a display device sometimes is called hard copy. (302)

_____ 3. Most mobile computers and devices integrate the display and other components into the same physical case. (302)

_____ 4. A flat-panel display is a display device with a shallow depth that uses CRT technology. (302)

_____ 5. A pixel is a unit of visible light intensity equal to one candela per square meter. (304)

_____ 6. LCD monitors use an analog signal to produce a picture. (305)

_____ 7. Plasma monitors offer larger screen sizes and higher display quality than LCD monitors. (306)

_____ 8. A printout in portrait orientation is wider than it is tall. (310)

_____ 9. With Bluetooth printing, a device transmits output to a printer via radio waves. (311)

_____ 10. A photo printer is a color printer that produces photo-lab-quality pictures. (314)

_____ 11. Operating in a manner similar to a copy machine, a thermal printer creates images using a laser beam and powdered ink, called toner. (316)

_____ 12. A multifunction peripheral is a single device that looks like a copy machine but provides the functionality of a printer, scanner, copy machine, and perhaps a fax machine. (323)

Quizzes and Learning Games

Computer Genius
Crossword Puzzle
DC Track and Field
Practice Test
Quiz Yourself
Wheel of Terms
You're Hired!

Exercises

Case Studies
Chapter Review
▶ Checkpoint
Key Terms
Learn How To
Learn It Online
Web Research

Beyond the Book

Career Corner
Companies
FAQs
High-Tech Talk
Looking Ahead
Making Use of the Web
Trailblazers
Web Links

Features

Chapter Forum
Install Computer
Lab Exercises
Maintain Computer
Tech News
Timeline 2006

Checkpoint

 Multiple Choice   Select the best answer. (See page numbers in parentheses.)

1. Examples of text-based documents are _____. (300)
   a. drawings, clip art, and photographs
   b. letters, reports, and mailing labels
   c. music, narrations, and speeches
   d. home movies and live performances

2. A passive-matrix display _____ an active matrix display. (304)
   a. uses more transistors than
   b. requires more power than
   c. often is not as bright as
   d. is more expensive than

3. An LCD monitor's _____ is the time in milliseconds that it takes to turn a pixel on or off. (304)
   a. candela
   b. pixel pitch
   c. response time
   d. dot pitch

4. The number of colors a graphics processing unit displays is determined by _____. (306)
   a. candela
   b. pixel pitch
   c. dot pitch
   d. bit depth

5. For a display device to show images as defined by a video standard, both the display device and the graphics processing unit must _____. (305)
   a. be the same size
   b. contain a heat sink or fan
   c. use an analog signal
   d. support the same video standard

6. Plasma monitors offer larger screens _____. (306)
   a. but lower display quality than LCD monitors and are less expensive
   b. but lower display quality than LCD monitors and are more expensive
   c. and higher display quality than LCD monitors but are less expensive
   d. and higher display quality than LCD monitors but are more expensive

7. The viewable size of a monitor is the _____ measurement of the actual viewing area provided by the screen in the monitor. (307)
   a. horizontal
   b. vertical
   c. diagonal
   d. three-dimensional

8. Printer resolution is measured by the number of _____ a printer can print. (313)
   a. pages per minute (ppm)
   b. dots per inch (dpi)
   c. lines per minute (lpm)
   d. pixels per inch (ppi)

9. Laser printers usually cost _____. (315)
   a. more than ink-jet printers and are faster
   b. less than ink-jet printers and are faster
   c. more than ink-jet printers and are slower
   d. less than ink-jet printers and are slower

10. The speed of a(n) _____ is measured by the number of characters per second (cps) it can print. (319)
    a. dot-matrix printer
    b. laser printer
    c. ink-jet printer
    d. thermal printer

11. _____ allows users to speak to other users over the Web using their desktop computer, mobile computer, or mobile device. (322)
    a. A plotter
    b. A fax modem
    c. Force feedback
    d. Internet telephony

12. When a computer receives a fax, _____ software enables the user to convert the image to text and then edit it. (323)
    a. optical character recognition (OCR)
    b. magnetic-ink character recognition (MICR)
    c. optical mark recognition (OMR)
    d. bar code recognition (BCR)

13. The disadvantage of multifunction peripherals is that _____. (323)
    a. they require more space than having separate devices
    b. they are significantly more expensive than purchasing each device separately
    c. if the multifunction peripheral breaks down, all functions are lost
    d. all of the above

14. The _____ command in Windows XP enlarges text and other on-screen items for visually impaired users. (326)
    a. Magnifier
    b. On-Screen Keyboard
    c. Narrator
    d. Utility Manager

Checkpoint

Matching

Match the terms with their definitions. (See page numbers in parentheses.)

_____ 1. soft copy (302)

_____ 2. monochrome (302)

_____ 3. pixel pitch (304)

_____ 4. nit (304)

_____ 5. graphics processing unit (305)

_____ 6. electromagnetic radiation (EMR) (308)

_____ 7. hard copy (310)

_____ 8. near letter quality (NLQ) (318)

_____ 9. LCD projector (324)

_____ 10. DLP projector (324)

a. uses many shades of gray from white to black to enhance the quality of graphics

b. printed information that exists physically and is a more permanent form of output

c. distance in millimeters between pixels on a display device

d. changes the brightness and contrast of pixels surrounding each letter

e. graphics chip that controls the manipulation and display of graphics on a display device

f. unit of visible light intensity equal to one candela

g. uses tiny mirrors to reflect light, which produces crisp, bright, colorful images

h. information on a display device that exists electronically and appears for a temporary period

i. magnetic field that travels at the speed of light

j. print quality slightly less clear than what is acceptable for business letters

k. information appears in one color on a different background color

l. attaches directly to a computer and uses its own light source to display information

Short Answer

Write a brief answer to each of the following questions.

1. What factors determine a CRT monitor's quality? _____ What is the ENERGY STAR program? _____

2. What determines the quality of an LCD monitor or LCD screen? _____ What are the differences between active-matrix and passive-matrix displays? _____

3. What advantages do digital television signals provide over analog signals? _____ What is interactive TV? _____

4. How is portrait orientation different from landscape orientation? _____ What is continuous-form paper? _____

5. What is a page description language? _____ How is PCL different from PostScript? _____

Beyond the Book

Read the following book elements, learn more about each using the Web, and then write a brief report.

1. At Issue — Ink-Jet Ink Wars? (314), Who Is Responsible for Stopping Counterfeiting? (315), Wearable Web Devices: Help or Hindrance? (321), or Should Web Sites Geared for Physically Challenged People Be Held Accountable for Accessibility Levels? (327)

2. Career Corner — Graphic Designer/Illustrator (327)

3. Companies on the Cutting Edge — Hewlett-Packard (329) or ViewSonic (329)

4. FAQs (302, 303, 306, 306, 307, 308, 308, 312, 315, 316)

5. High-Tech Talk — Sound Cards: Bringing Your Computer to Life (328)

6. Looking Ahead — Flexible Screens Lock and Roll (304), or Digital Cinema Just the Right Picture (324)

7. Making Use of the Web — Government (122)

8. Picture Yourself Saving Money Using a Computer (298)

9. Technology Trailblazers — Steve Jobs (329) or Donna Dubinsky (329)

10. Web Links (304, 306, 308, 314, 315, 316, 321, 322, 323, 324)

Quizzes and Learning Games

Computer Genius
Crossword Puzzle
DC Track and Field
Practice Test
Quiz Yourself
Wheel of Terms
You're Hired!

Exercises

Case Studies
Chapter Review
Checkpoint
Key Terms
Learn How To
Learn It Online
Web Research

Beyond the Book

Career Corner
Companies
FAQs
High-Tech Talk
Looking Ahead
Making Use of the Web
Trailblazers
Web Links

Features

Chapter Forum
Install Computer
Lab Exercises
Maintain Computer
Tech News
Timeline 2006

Learn It Online

Use the Learn It Online exercises to reinforce your understanding of the chapter concepts. To access the Learn It Online exercises, visit scsite.com/dc2006/ch6/learn.

 At the Movies — Plasma vs. LCD

To view the Plasma vs. LCD movie, click the number 1 button. Locate your video and click the corresponding High-Speed or Dial-Up link, depending on your Internet connection. Watch the movie and then complete the exercise by answering the questions that follow. Basic differences exist between plasma and LCD-display TVs, and those differences may affect your choice as a consumer. By understanding those differences, you will be able to choose the display options that best suit your needs. Compare and contrast the two technologies using simple criteria such as cost and size. What are the pros and cons of each display technology? How does a plasma TV display its picture? What are the disadvantages of plasma?

 At the Movies — Essential Dorm Room Gadgets

To view the Essential Dorm Room Gadgets movie, click the number 2 button. Locate your video and click the corresponding High-Speed or Dial-Up link, depending on your Internet connection. Watch the movie and then complete the exercise by answering the questions that follow. As a rule, most college students have little, if any, disposable income. Some great and affordable gadgets are available, however, that can make a dorm room more functional for study and more fun for play. How would a network interface improve a dorm room?

 Student Edition Labs — Peripheral Devices

Click the number 3 button. When the Student Edition Labs menu appears, click *Peripheral Devices* to begin. A new browser window will open. Follow the on-screen instructions to complete the Lab. When finished, click the Exit button. If required, submit your results to your instructor.

 Student Edition Labs — Working with Graphics

Click the number 4 button. When the Student Edition Labs menu appears, click *Working with Graphics* to begin. A new browser window will open. Follow the on-screen instructions to complete the Lab. When finished, click the Exit button. If required, submit your results to your instructor.

 Practice Test

Click the number 5 button. Answer each question. When completed, enter your name and click the Grade Test button to submit the quiz for grading. Make a note of any missed questions. If required, submit your results to your instructor.

 Who Wants To Be a Computer Genius²?

Click the number 6 button to find out if you are a computer genius. Directions about how to play the game will be displayed. When you are ready to play, click the Play button. Submit your score to your instructor.

⑦ Wheel of Terms

Click the number 7 button to reinforce important terms you learned in this chapter by playing the Shelly Cashman Series version of this popular game. Directions about how to play the game will be displayed. When you are ready to play, click the Play button. Submit your score to your instructor.

Learn It Online

⑧ DC Track and Field

Click the number 8 button to use what you have learned in this chapter to compete against other students in three track and field events. Directions about how to play the game will be displayed. When you are ready to play, click the start first event button. If required, submit your score to your instructor.

⑨ You're Hired!

Click the number 9 button to use what you have learned in this chapter to embark on the path to a career in computers. Directions about how to play the game will be displayed. When you are ready to play, click the begin game button. If required, submit your score to your instructor.

⑩ Crossword Puzzle Challenge

Click the number 10 button. Complete the puzzle to reinforce skills you learned in this chapter. Directions about how to play the game will be displayed. When you are ready to play, click the Submit button. Submit the completed puzzle to your instructor.

⑪ Lab Exercises

Click the number 11 button. When the Lab Exercises menu appears, click the exercise assigned by your instructor. A new browser window will open. Follow the on-screen instructions to complete the exercise. When finished, click the Exit button. If required, submit your results to your instructor.

⑫ Choosing a Printer

The printer is a key component of any new personal computer that you purchase. Whether you are printing black-and-white reports or producing photo-lab-quality pictures, determining which printer is best for your individual needs requires some research. Printers are available in a range of speeds and capabilities. Click the number 12 button for a tutorial about how to select the printer that is best for your particular requirements.

⑬ In the News

Display device technology continues to advance. Not long ago, computer users would have considered connecting their $1,000 computers to a color television instead of paying outrageous prices for a color monitor. Today, you can purchase a 20-inch monitor that is faster and sharper than that color television for less than $300. Yet, as prices fall, consumers surely will purchase the display devices for HDTV and crystal-clear Internet access. Click the number 13 button and then read a news article about a new or improved output device. What is the device? Who manufactures it? How is the output device better than, or different from, earlier devices? Who do you think is most likely to use the device? Why?

⑭ Chapter Discussion Forum

Select an objective from this chapter on page 299 about which you would like more information. Click the number 14 button and post a short message listing a meaningful message title accompanied by one or more questions concerning the selected objective. In two days, return to the threaded discussion by clicking the number 14 button. Submit to your instructor your original message and at least one response to your message.

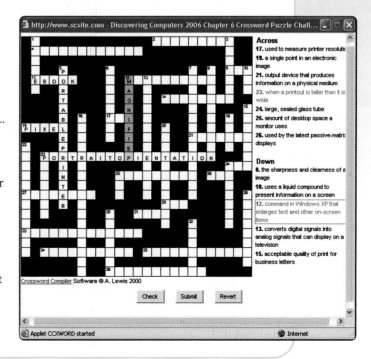

Quizzes and Learning Games

Computer Genius
Crossword Puzzle
DC Track and Field
Practice Test
Quiz Yourself
Wheel of Terms
You're Hired!

Exercises

Case Studies
Chapter Review
Checkpoint
Key Terms
▶ Learn How To
Learn It Online
Web Research

Beyond the Book

Career Corner
Companies
FAQs
High-Tech Talk
Looking Ahead
Making Use of the Web
Trailblazers
Web Links

Features

Chapter Forum
Install Computer
Lab Exercises
Maintain Computer
Tech News
Timeline 2006

 # Learn How To

Use the Learn How To activities to learn fundamental skills when using a computer and accompanying technology. Complete the exercises and submit them to your instructor. Visit scsite.com/dc2006/ch6/howto to obtain more information pertaining to each activity.

LEARN HOW TO 1: Adjust the Sound on a Computer

Every computer today contains a **sound card** and associated hardware and software that allow you to play and record sound. You can adjust the sound by completing the following steps:

1. Click the Start button on the Windows taskbar and then click Control Panel on the Start menu.
2. When the Control Panel window opens, click Sounds, Speech, and Audio Devices and then click Adjust the system volume; or double-click Sounds and Audio Devices. *The Sounds and Audio Devices Properties dialog box is displayed (Figure 6-38).*
3. To adjust the volume for all devices connected to the sound card, drag the Device volume slider left or right to decrease or increase the volume.
4. If you want to mute the sound on the computer, click the Mute check box so it contains a check mark, and then click the OK button or the Apply button.
5. If you want to place the volume icon on the Windows taskbar, click the Place volume icon in the taskbar check box so it contains a check mark, and then click the OK button or the Apply button. You can click the icon on the taskbar to set the volume level or mute the sound.
6. To make sound and other adjustments for each device on the computer, click the Advanced button in the Device volume area. *The Play Control or Recording Control window opens, depending on prior choices for this window (Figure 6-39).*
7. If the Recording Control window is opened, click Options on the window menu bar, click Properties on the Options menu, click the Playback option button, and then click the OK button.
8. In the Play Control window, Play Control volume is the same as the volume adjusted in the Sounds and Audio Devices Properties dialog box. The other columns in the Play Control window refer to devices found on the computer. To select the columns that are displayed, click Options on the menu bar and then click Properties. With Playback selected, place checks in the check boxes for those devices you want to be displayed in the Control window.
9. To adjust volumes, drag the Volume sliders up or down for each device. To adjust the speaker balance, drag the Balance sliders.

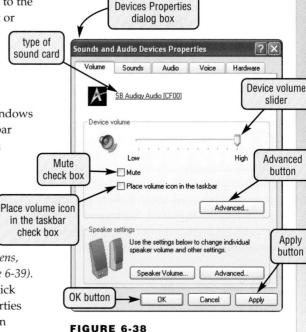

FIGURE 6-38

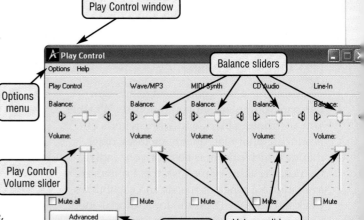

FIGURE 6-39

Learn How To

10. If the Advanced button is not displayed in the Play Control window, click Options on the menu bar and then click Advanced Controls on the Options menu. Click the Advanced button. You can control the Bass and Treble settings by using the sliders in the Tone Controls area of the Advanced Controls for Play Control dialog box.

Exercise

1. Open the Control Panel window and then display the Sounds and Audio Devices Properties dialog box. What kind of sound card is on the computer? Click the Place volume icon in the taskbar check box and then click the Apply button. What change did you notice on the Windows taskbar? Do the same thing again. What change occurred on the Windows taskbar? Click the Advanced button in the Device volume area. Ensure the Play Control window is open. What devices are chosen for control in the Play Control window? How would you change what devices are chosen? Submit your answers to your instructor.

LEARN HOW TO 2: Control Printing on Your Computer

When you print using a computer, you control printing at two different points: first, before the printing actually begins, and second, after the document has been sent to the printer and either is physically printing or is waiting to be printed. To set the parameters for printing and then print the document, complete the following steps:

1. Click File on the menu bar of the program that will be used for printing and then click Print on the File menu. *The Print dialog box is displayed (Figure 6-40). The Print dialog box will vary somewhat depending on the program used.*

2. In the Print dialog box, make the selections for what printer will be used, what pages will be printed, the number of copies to be printed, and any other choices available. For further options, click the Properties button (or, sometimes, the Preferences button) or click the Options button.

3. Click the OK button or the Print button. The document being printed is sent to a **print queue**, which is an area on disk storage from which documents actually are printed.

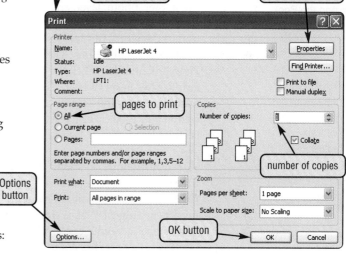

FIGURE 6-40

When you click the Print button to send the document to the print queue, a printer icon [🖨] may appear on the Windows taskbar. To see the print queue and control the actual printing of documents on the printer, complete the following steps:

1. If the printer icon appears on the Windows taskbar, double-click it; otherwise, click the Start button on the Windows taskbar, click Printers and Faxes on the Start menu, and then double-click the printer icon with the check mark. The check mark indicates the default printer. *A window opens with the name of the printer on the title bar. All the documents either printing or waiting to be printed are listed in the window. The Status column indicates whether the document is printing or waiting. In addition, the owner of the file, number of pages, size, date and time submitted, and printer port are listed.*

2. If you click Printer on the menu bar in the printer window, you can set printing preferences from the Printer menu. In addition, you can pause all printing and cancel all printing jobs from the Printer menu.

3. If you select a document in the document list and then click Document on the menu bar, you can cancel the selected document for printing, or you can pause the printing for the selected document. To continue printing for the selected document, click Document on the menu bar and then click Resume on the Document menu.

Exercise

1. Start WordPad from the Accessories submenu. Type `The Print dialog box is displayed by clicking Print on the File menu.`

2. Display the Print dialog box and then click the Preferences button. What choices do you have in the Layout sheet? Close the Printing Preferences dialog box. How do you select the number of copies you want to print? How would you print pages 25–35 of a document? Submit your answers to your instructor.

Quizzes and Learning Games

Computer Genius
Crossword Puzzle
DC Track and Field
Practice Test
Quiz Yourself
Wheel of Terms
You're Hired!

Exercises

Case Studies
Chapter Review
Checkpoint
Key Terms
Learn How To
Learn It Online
Web Research

Beyond the Book

Career Corner
Companies
FAQs
High-Tech Talk
Looking Ahead
Making Use of the Web
Trailblazers
Web Links

Features

Chapter Forum
Install Computer
Lab Exercises
Maintain Computer
Tech News
Timeline 2006

Web Research

Use the Internet-based Web Research exercises to broaden your understanding of the concepts presented in this chapter. Visit scsite.com/dc2006/ch6/research to obtain more information pertaining to each exercise. To discuss any of the Web Research exercises in this chapter with other students, post your thoughts or questions at scsite.com/dc2006/ch6/forum.

① Scavenger Hunt   Use one of the **search engines** listed in Figure 2-10 in Chapter 2 on page 78 or your own favorite search engine to find the answers to the questions below. Copy and paste the Web address from the Web page where you found the answer. Some questions may have more than one answer. If required, submit your answers to your instructor. (1) What company introduced the first laser printer? When? (2) What is the most common type of ink-jet technology? (3) Who developed the liquid crystal display? (4) What is the purpose of backlight on an LCD screen? (5) What is an ambient light sensor on a monitor?

② Search Sleuth   Some search engines use computers to index the World Wide Web automatically, so they generally find more Web sites that human indexers can catalog. One of the most aggressive automatic, or robot, search engines is **AltaVista** (altavista.com), which attempts to catalog the entire World Wide Web. AltaVista and many other search engines have a wildcard matching feature. Assume that you want to search for all information pertaining to printers, including ink-jet, photo, laser, and wireless. In this instance, you could use the wildcard symbol (*) to indicate missing letters. Your search query would be *printer, where the * substitutes for any variation of the word, printer. Visit this Web site and then use your word processing program to answer the following questions. Then, if required, submit your answers to your instructor. (1) Click the Help link and then click the Search link. Scroll down and then read about the features AltaVista emphasizes in its Web search results page. What are these features? (2) Click your browser's Back button or press the BACKSPACE key twice to return to the AltaVista home page. (3) Use the wildcard option and type *printer. (4) Scroll through the results until you reach the AltaVista News section. Read at least two of the news stories and then write a 50-word summary.

③ Journaling   Respond to your readings in this chapter by writing at least one page about your reactions, evaluations, and reflections about using **output devices**. For example, have you printed photos taken with a digital camera? Do you purchase recyclable printer supplies, such as toner or ink-jet cartridges? Where would you dispose of old monitors and printers and used toner? Have you listened to audio books? Should all employers accommodate the needs of physically challenged employees by making computers accessible? You also can write about the new terms you learned by reading this chapter. If required, submit your journal to your instructor.

④ Expanding Your Understanding   If you are using a Tablet PC and your coworker is using a PDA, it is cumbersome to transfer files from one device to the other. Engineers are developing **digital pens** that might ease the file exchange process. Using this special pen, one user can select a file on his computer and then place the pen on the other user's computer to transfer the file. Other digital pens allow users to write or draw and then retrieve all the handwritten information on a computer. Visit a local electronics store or Web site to learn more about digital pens. Compare their features, cost, file transfer process, and warranty. Write a report summarizing your findings, focusing on comparing and contrasting the digital pens. If required, submit your report to your instructor.

⑤ Ethics in Action   **Internet addiction disorder** (IAD) may be affecting some Internet users. People claim to be addicted when they spend up to 10 hours a day online, they occasionally binge for extended Internet sessions, and they suffer withdrawal symptoms when they have not been online for some time. "Netomania" is not a recognized disorder, however, and some researchers believe the Internet problem is just a symptom of other psychiatric disorders, such as manic-depression. View online sites that provide information about IAD, including the Center for Online and Internet Addiction (netaddiction.com). Write a report summarizing your findings and include a table of links to Web sites that provide additional details. If required, submit your report to your instructor.

Case Studies

Use the Case Studies to apply the concepts presented in the chapter to real-world situations. Visit scsite.com/dc2006/ch6/cases to obtain more information pertaining to each exercise. To discuss the Case Studies in this chapter with other students, visit scsite.com/dc2006/ch6/forum and post your thoughts or questions.

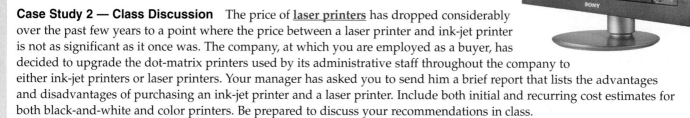

Case Study 1 – Class Discussion   You are a manager of a 25-member telemarketing group. Your company provides desktop computers for each of the telemarketers. The current computers have 15-inch CRT monitors. The telemarketers have been complaining that the monitors are too small. Use the Web and/or print media to investigate the costs associated with upgrading the current monitors to 17-inch or 19-inch **flat-panel display devices**. What are the advantages and disadvantages of flat-panel display devices? What is the best screen size? Why? When you have finished reviewing flat-panel display device characteristics, write a brief report to your supervisor summarizing your recommendations. Include a list of the five factors you think are the most important to consider when purchasing a flat-panel display device. Be prepared to discuss your recommendations in class.

Case Study 2 — Class Discussion   The price of **laser printers** has dropped considerably over the past few years to a point where the price between a laser printer and ink-jet printer is not as significant as it once was. The company, at which you are employed as a buyer, has decided to upgrade the dot-matrix printers used by its administrative staff throughout the company to either ink-jet printers or laser printers. Your manager has asked you to send him a brief report that lists the advantages and disadvantages of purchasing an ink-jet printer and a laser printer. Include both initial and recurring cost estimates for both black-and-white and color printers. Be prepared to discuss your recommendations in class.

Case Study 3 — Research   Printing requirements vary greatly among users. The local insurance agency where you are employed part time is shopping for a **printer**. The owner is aware that you are taking a computer class and has asked you to assist her in making a decision on what printer to buy. Figure 6-12 on page 310 lists several questions that should be considered when choosing a printer. Use what you learned in class to answer the questions posed in Figure 6-12. Answer each question according to what you believe to be your employer's needs. Then, use the Web and/or print media to find at least two printers that fit the requirements. List the name of each printer and note their advantages and disadvantages. Which of the two printers would you buy? Why? Prepare a report and/or PowerPoint presentation and share your findings with your class.

Case Study 4 — Research   While printers produce an image on a page from top to bottom, **plotters** can draw on any part of a page at random, and then move on to any other part. This capability, coupled with their capacity to use large sheets of paper, makes plotters particularly valuable to people who produce maps or blueprints. A local engineering firm that has used hand drawings for the past 50 years has hired you to assist them in purchasing three 42-inch plotters with a maximum print length of 300 feet and at least 1200 × 600 dpi. What is the advantage or disadvantage of using a plotter compared to simply creating a drawing by hand? Use the Web and/or print media to research both the initial and recurring costs of plotters that meet the stated requirements from three different manufacturers. Include in your research how long each plotter takes to produce an image and other noteworthy information. Prepare a report and/or PowerPoint presentation summarizing your findings.

Case Study 5 — Team Challenge   Three accountants at the company you work for want to go off on their own and set up a small accounting office with approximately 20 to 25 employees. They have hired your group as consultants to help with the setup. The goal is to determine the type of output devices you think they will need within the office. Consider the types and number of printers, types and number of display devices, **audio devices**, microphones, LCD projectors, considerations for the physically challenged, and whether fax machines, fax modems, and/or multifunction peripherals are needed. Form a three-member team and assign each team member one or more categories of output devices. Have the team members use the Web and/or print media to research their assignments. Combine your findings in a table listing the advantages and disadvantages of the various devices, your team's recommendations, and a short explanation of why the team selected each device. Share your findings with your class.

Special Feature

Digital Imaging and Video Technology

Everywhere you look, people are capturing moments they want to remember. They take pictures or make movies of their vacations, birthday parties, activities, accomplishments, sporting events, weddings, and more. Because of the popularity of digital cameras and digital video cameras, increasingly more people desire to capture their memories digitally, instead of on film. With digital technology, photographers have the ability to modify and share the digital images and videos they create. When you use special hardware and/or software, you can copy, manipulate, print, and distribute digital images and videos using your personal computer and the Internet. Amateurs can create professional quality results by using more sophisticated hardware and software.

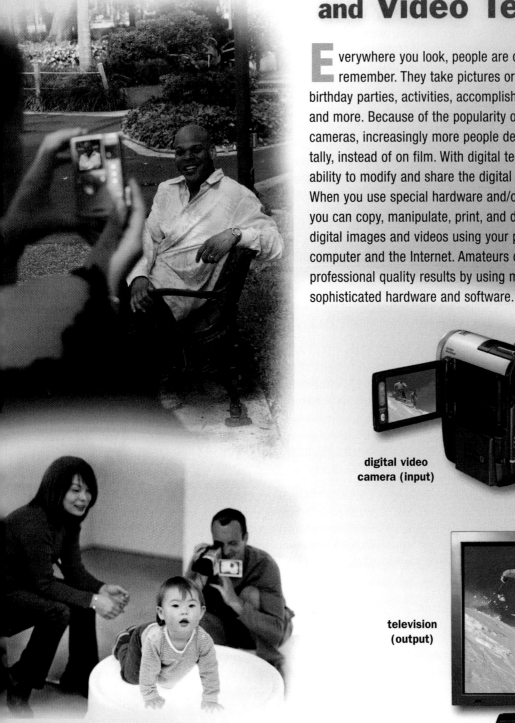

digital camera (input)

digital video
camera (input)

FireWire or USB 2.0

television
(output)

FIGURE 1 The top portion of the figure shows a typical home digital imaging setup, and the lower portion of the figure shows a typical home setup for editing personal video.

Digital photography and recordings deliver significant benefits over film-based photography and movie making. With digital cameras, no developing is needed. Instead, the images reside on storage media such as a hard disk, DVD, or flash memory card. Unlike film, storage media can be reused, which reduces costs, saves time, and provides immediate results. Digital technology allows greater control over the creative process, both while taking pictures and video and in the editing process. You can check results immediately after capturing a picture or video to determine whether it meets your expectations. If you are dissatisfied with a picture or video, you can erase it and recapture it, again and again.

As shown in the top portion of Figure 1, a digital camera functions as an input device when it transmits pictures through a cable to a personal computer via a USB port or FireWire port. Using a digital camera in this way allows you to edit the pictures, save them on storage media, and print them on a photographic-quality printer via a parallel port or USB port.

The lower portion of Figure 1 illustrates how you might use a digital video camera with a personal computer. The process typically is the same for most digital video cameras. You capture the images or video with the video camera. Next, you connect the video camera to your personal computer using a FireWire or USB 2.0 port, or you place the storage media used on the camera in the computer. The video then is copied or downloaded to the computer's hard disk. Then, you can edit the video using video editing software. If desired, you can preview the video during the editing process on a television. Finally, you save the finished result to the desired media, such as a VHS tape or DVD+RW or, perhaps, e-mail the edited video. In this example, a VCR and a DVD player also can be used to input video from a VHS tape or a DVD.

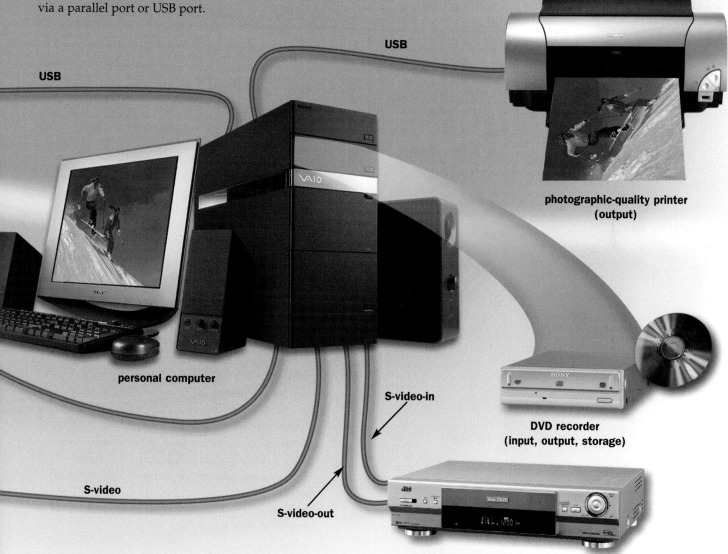

USB

USB

photographic-quality printer (output)

personal computer

S-video-in

DVD recorder (input, output, storage)

S-video

S-video-out

VCR (input, output, storage)

DIGITAL IMAGING TECHNOLOGY

Digital imaging technology involves capturing and manipulating still photographic images in an electronic format. The following sections outline the steps involved in the process of using digital imaging technology.

1 Select a Digital Camera

A **digital camera** is a type of camera that stores photographed images electronically instead of on traditional film. Digital cameras are divided into three categories (Figure 2) based mainly on image resolution, features, and of course, price. The image resolution is measured in pixels (short for picture element). The image quality increases with the number of pixels. The image resolution usually is measured in **megapixels** (million of pixels), often abbreviated as **MP**. Features of digital cameras include red-eye reduction, zoom, autofocus, flash, self-timer, and manual mode for fine-tuning settings. Figure 3 summarizes the three categories of digital cameras.

FIGURE 2 The point-and-shoot digital camera (a) requires no adjustments before shooting. The field digital camera (b) offers improved quality and features that allow you to make manual adjustments before shooting and use a variety of lenses. The studio digital camera (c) offers better color and resolution and greater control over exposure and lenses.

TYPES OF DIGITAL CAMERAS

Type	Resolution Range	Features	Price
Point and shoot	Less than 6 MP	Fully automatic; fits in your pocket; easy to use; ideal for average consumer usage.	Less than $600
Field cameras	Greater than 5 MP	Used by photojournalists; portable but flexible; provides ability to change lenses and use other attachments; great deal of control over exposure and other photo settings.	$800 to $2,000
Studio cameras	Greater than 5 MP	Stationary camera used for professional studio work; flexible; widest range of lenses and settings.	$1,500 and up

FIGURE 3 Digital cameras often are categorized by image resolution, features, and price.

2 Take Pictures

Digital cameras provide you with several options that are set before a picture is taken. Three of the more important options are the resolution, compression, and image file format in which the camera should save the picture. While a camera may allow for a very high resolution for a large print, you may choose to take a picture at a lower resolution if the image does not require great detail or must be a small size. For example, you may want to use the image on a Web page where smaller image file sizes are beneficial.

Compression results in smaller image file sizes. Figure 4 illustrates the image file sizes for varying resolutions and compressions under standard photographic conditions using a 4 megapixel digital camera. Figure 4 also shows the average picture size for a given resolution. The camera may take more time to save an image at lower compression, resulting in a longer delay before the camera is ready to take another picture. A higher compression, however, may result in some loss of image quality. If a camera has a 16 MB flash memory card, you can determine the number of pictures the card can hold by dividing 16 MB by the file size. Flash memory cards are available in sizes from 16 MB to 8 GB.

Most digital cameras also allow you to choose an image file format. Two popular file formats are TIFF and JPEG. The **TIFF** file format saves the image uncompressed. All of the image detail is captured and stored, but the file sizes can be large. The **JPEG** file format is compressed. The resolution of the image may be the same as a TIFF file, but some detail may be lost in the image.

Finally, before you take the photograph, you should choose the type of media on which to store the resulting image file. Some cameras allow for a choice of media to which you can store the image, such as a CompactFlash card or Memory Stick, while others allow for only one type of storage media. One major advantage of a digital camera is that you easily can erase pictures from its media, freeing up space for new pictures.

IMAGE FILE SIZE WITH A FOUR MEGAPIXEL DIGITAL CAMERA

Resolution in Pixels	COMPRESSION			Picture Size in Inches
	Low	Medium	High	
	Resulting Image File Size			
2272 × 1704	2 MB	1.1 MB	556 KB	11 by 17
1600 × 1200	1 MB	558 KB	278 KB	8 by 10
1024 × 768	570 KB	320 KB	170 KB	4 by 6
640 × 480	249 KB	150 KB	84 KB	3 by 5

FIGURE 4   Image file sizes for varying resolutions and compressions under standard photographic conditions using a 4 megapixel digital camera.

3 Transfer and Manage Image Files

The method of transferring images from the camera to the personal computer differs greatly depending on the capabilities of both. Digital cameras use a variety of storage media (Figure 5). If your camera uses a flash memory card such as a CompactFlash, Memory Stick, SmartMedia, or Secure Digital (SD), you can remove the media from the camera and place it in a slot on the personal computer or in a device, such as a card reader, connected to the personal computer. The Microdrive media shown in Figure 5 is a type of CompactFlash media. Your camera or card reader also may connect to the personal computer using a USB, USB 2.0, or FireWire (Figure 6) port. When you insert the memory card or connect the camera, software on the personal computer guides you through the process of transferring the images to the hard disk. Some operating systems and software recognize a memory card or camera as though it is another hard disk on the computer. This feature allows you to access the files, navigate them, and then copy, delete, or rename the files while the media still is in the camera.

After you transfer the files to the hard disk on your personal computer, you should organize the files by sorting them or renaming them so that information, such as the subject, date, time, and purpose, is saved along with the image. Finally, before altering the images digitally or using the images for other purposes, you should back up the images to another location, such as a CD or DVD, so the original image is recoverable.

Microdrive

CompactFlash

Memory Stick

FIGURE 5   Microdrives, CompactFlash, and Memory Sticks are popular storage devices for digital cameras.

FIGURE 6   Using a USB or FireWire connection, you can add a card reader to your personal computer.

④ Edit Images

Image editing software allows you to edit digital images. The following list summarizes the more common image enhancements or alterations:

- Adjust the contrast and brightness; correct lighting problems; or help give the photograph a particular feeling, such as warm or stark.
- Remove red-eye.
- Crop an image to remove unnecessary elements and resize it.
- Rotate the image to change its orientation.
- Add elements to the image, such as descriptive text, a date, a logo, or decorative items; create collages or add missing elements.
- Replace individual colors with a new color.
- Add special effects, such as texture or motion blurring to enhance the image.

Figure 7 shows some of the effects available in Jasc's Paint Shop Pro on the Artistic Effects submenu.

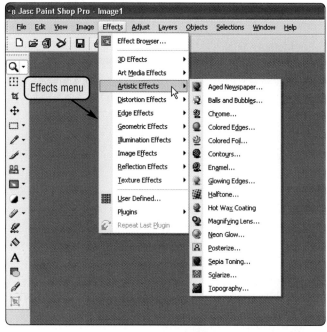

FIGURE 7 The capability of applying effects separates digital photography from film photography.

⑤ Print Images

Once an image is digitally altered, it is ready to be printed. You can print images on a personal color printer or send them to a professional service that specializes in digital photo printing.

When printing the images yourself, make sure that the resolution used to create the image was high enough for the size of the print you want to create. For example, if the camera used a resolution of 640 × 480 pixels, then the ideal print size is a wallet size. If you print such an image at a size of 8-by-10 inches, then the image will appear **pixilated**, or blurry. Use high-quality photo paper for the best results. A photo printer gives the best results when printing digital photography.

Many services print digital images, either over the Internet or through traditional photo developing locations and kiosks (Figure 8), such as those found in drug stores or shopping marts. Some services allow you to e-mail or upload the files to the service, specify the size, quality, and quantity of print; and then receive the finished prints via the postal service. Other services allow you to drop off flash memory cards, CD-ROMs, or floppy disks at a photo shop and later pick up the prints, just as you do with traditional photo developing shops.

FIGURE 8
A Pixel Magic Imaging Photo Ditto kiosk allows you to print digital images in high resolution on photo paper.

6 Distribute Images Electronically

Rather than printing images, you often need to use the images electronically. Depending on the electronic use of the image, the image may require additional processing. If you use the images on a Web site or want to e-mail a photo, you probably want to send a lower-resolution image. Image editing software allows you to lower the resolution of the image, resulting in a smaller file size. You also should use standard file formats when distributing an electronic photo. The JPEG format is viewable using most personal computers or Web browsers.

You can store very high resolution photos on a DVD or a CD. **DVD and CD mastering software** (Figure 9) allows you to create slide show presentations on a recordable DVD or CD that can play in many home DVD players or personal computer DVD drives.

Finally, you should back up and store images that you distribute electronically with the same care as you store your traditional film negatives.

FIGURE 9   Nero PhotoShow Elite and similar software applications allow you to create your own photo slide show on DVD or CD.

DIGITAL VIDEO TECHNOLOGY

Digital video technology allows you to input, edit, manage, publish, and share your videos using a personal computer. With digital video technology, you can transform home videos into Hollywood-style movies by enhancing the videos with scrolling titles and transitions, cutting out or adding scenes, and adding background music and voice-over narration. The following sections outline the steps involved in the process of using digital video technology.

1 Select a Video Camera

Video cameras record in either analog or digital format. **Analog formats** include 8mm, Hi8, VHS, VHS-C, and Super VHS-C. The last three formats use the types of tapes similar to those used in a standard VCR. **Digital formats** include Mini-DV, MICROMV, Digital8, and DVD. Consumer digital video cameras are by far the most popular type among consumers. They fall into three general categories: high-end consumer, consumer, and webcasting and monitoring (Figure 10). Digital video cameras provide more features than analog video cameras, such as a higher level of zoom, better sound, or greater control over color and lighting.

(a) high-end consumer

(b) consumer

(c) webcasting and monitoring

FIGURE 10   The high-end consumer digital video camera (a) can produce professional-grade results. The consumer digital video camera (b) produces amateur-grade results. The webcasting and monitoring digital video camera (c) is appropriate for webcasting and security monitoring.

② Record a Video

Most video cameras provide you with a choice of recording programs, which sometimes are called automatic settings. Each recording program includes a different combination of camera settings, so you can adjust the exposure and other functions to match the recording environment. Usually, several different programs are available, such as point and shoot, point and shoot with manual adjustment, sports, portrait, spotlit scenes, and low light. You also have the ability to select special digital effects, such as fade, wipe, and black and white. If you are shooting outside on a windy day, then you can enable the wind screen to prevent wind noise. If you are shooting home videos, then the point-and-shoot recording program is sufficient.

③ Transfer and Manage Videos

After recording the video, the next step is to transfer the video to your personal computer. Most video cameras connect directly to a USB 2.0 or FireWire port on your personal computer (Figure 11). Transferring video with a digital camera is easy, because the video already is in a digital format that the computer can understand.

An analog camcorder or VCR requires additional hardware to convert the analog signals to a digital format before the video can be manipulated on a personal computer. The additional hardware includes a special video capture card using a standard RCA video cable or an S-video cable (Figure 12). *S-video* cables provide sharper

images and greater overall quality. When you use video capture hardware with an analog video, be sure to close all open programs on your computer because capturing video requires a great deal of processing power.

FIGURE 11 A digital video camera is connected to the personal computer via a FireWire or USB 2.0 port. No additional hardware is needed.

FIGURE 12 An analog camcorder or VCR is connected to the personal computer via an S-video port on a video capture card.

When transferring video, plan to use approximately 15 to 30 gigabytes of hard disk storage space per hour of digital video. A typical video project requires about four times the amount of raw footage as the final product. Therefore, at the high end, a video that lasts an hour may require up to 120 gigabytes of storage for the raw footage, editing process, and final video. This storage requirement can vary depending on the software you use to copy the video from the video camera to the hard disk and the format you select to save the video. For example, Microsoft claims that the latest version of its Windows Movie Maker can save 15 hours of video in 10 gigabytes when creating video for playback on a computer, but saves only 1 hour of video in 10 gigabytes when creating video for playback on a DVD or VCR.

The video transfer requires application software on the personal computer (Figure 13). Windows XP includes the Windows Movie Maker software that allows you to transfer the video from your video camera. Depending on the length of video and the type of connection used, the video may take a long time to download. Make certain that no other programs are running on your personal computer while transferring the video.

When transferring video, the software may allow you to choose a file format and a codec to store the video. A video **file format** holds the video information in a manner specified by a vendor, such as Apple or Microsoft. Three of the more popular file formats are listed in Figure 14.

File formats support codecs to encode the audio and video into the file formats. A particular file format may be able to store audio and video in a number of different codecs. A **codec** specifies how the audio and video is compressed and stored within the file. Figure 15 shows some options available for specifying a file format and codec in a video capture application. The dialog box in Figure 15 allows the user to determine whether the video is smoother in playback or if the video is more crisp, meaning that it includes more detail. The file format and codec you choose often is based on what you plan to do with the movie. For example, if you plan to stream video over the Web using RealNetworks software, the best choice for the file format is the RealMedia format, which uses the RealVideo codec.

After transferring the video to a personal computer, and before manipulating the video, you should store the video files in appropriate folders, named correctly, and backed up. Most video transfer application software helps manage these tasks.

POPULAR VIDEO FILE FORMATS

File Format		File Extensions
Apple QuickTime		.MOV or .QT
Microsoft Windows Media Video		.WMV or .ASF
RealNetworks RealMedia		.RM or .RAM

FIGURE 14 Apple, Microsoft, and RealNetworks offer the more popular video file formats.

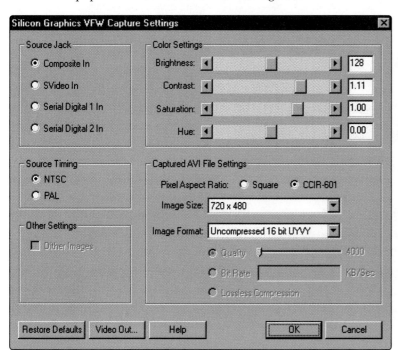

FIGURE 13 Some video editing software allows you to transfer your video from any video source to a hard disk. This dialog box allows the user to set various video parameters for capturing video from a camera or other device.

FIGURE 15 Video editing software applications allow you to specify a combination of file format and codec when saving a video.

4 Edit a Video

Once the video is stored on your hard disk, the next step is to edit, or manipulate, the video. If you used a video capture card to transfer analog video to your computer (Figure 12 on page 348), the files may require extra initial processing. When you use a video capture card, some of the video frames may be lost in the transfer process. Some video editing programs allow you to fix this problem with **frame rate correction** tools.

The first step in the editing process is to split the video into smaller pieces, or *scenes*, that you can manipulate more easily. This process is called *splitting*. Most video software automatically splits the video into scenes, thus sparing you the task. After splitting, you should cut out unwanted scenes or portions of scenes. This process is called *pruning*.

After you create the scenes you want to use in your final production, you edit each individual scene. You can *crop*, or change the size of, scenes. That is, you may want to cut out the top or a side of a scene that is irrelevant. You also can resize the scene. For example, you may be creating a video that will be displayed in a Web browser.

Making a smaller video, such as 320 × 200 pixels instead of 640 × 480 pixels, results in a smaller file that transmits faster over the Internet.

If video has been recorded over a long period, using different cameras or under different lighting conditions, the video may need color correction. *Color correction tools* (Figure 16) analyze your video and match brightness, colors, and other attributes of video clips to ensure a smooth look to the video.

You can add logos, special effects, or titles to scenes. You can place a company logo or personal logo in a video to identify yourself or the company producing the video. Logos often are added on the lower-right corner of a video and remain for the duration of the video. Special effects include warping, changing from color to black and white, morphing, or zoom motion. *Morphing* is a special effect in which one video image is transformed into another image over the course of several frames of video, creating the illusion of metamorphosis. You usually add titles at the beginning and end of a video to give the video context. A training video may have titles throughout the video to label a particular scene, or each scene may begin with a title.

FIGURE 16 Color correction tools in video editing software allow a great deal of control over the mood of your video creation.

The next step in editing a video is to add audio effects, including voice-over narration and background music. Many video editing programs allow you to add additional tracks, or *layers*, of sound to a video in addition to the sound that was recorded on the video camera. You also can add special audio effects.

The final step in editing a video is to combine the scenes into a complete video (Figure 17). This process involves ordering scenes and adding transition effects between scenes (Figure 18). Video editing software allows you to combine scenes and separate each scene with a transition. *Transitions* include fading, wiping, blurry, bursts, ruptures, erosions, and more.

FIGURE 17 In Windows Movie Maker 2, scenes, shown on the top, are combined into a sequence on the bottom of the screen.

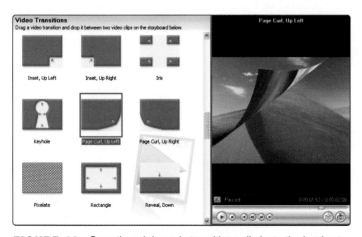

FIGURE 18 Smooth and dynamic transitions eliminate the hard cuts between scenes typically found in raw footage.

5 Distribute the Video

After editing the video, the final step is to distribute it or save it on an appropriate medium. You can save video in a variety of formats. Using special hardware, you can save the video on standard video tape. *A digital-to-analog converter* is necessary to allow your personal computer to transmit video to a VCR. A digital-to-analog converter may be an external device that connects to both the computer and input device, or may be a video capture card inside the computer.

Video also can be stored in digital formats in any of several DVD formats, on CD-R, or on video CD (VCD). *DVD* or *CD creation software*, which often is packaged with video editing software, allows you to create, or *master*, DVDs and CDs. You can add interactivity to your DVDs. For example, you can allow viewers to jump to certain scenes using a menu (Figure 19). A *video CD (VCD)* is a CD format that stores video on a CD-R that can be played in many DVD players.

You also can save your video creation in electronic format for distribution over the Web or via e-mail. Your video editing software must support the file format and codec you want to use. For example, RealNetworks's Helix media delivery system allows you to save media files in the RealVideo file formats.

Professionals use hardware and software that allow them to create a film version of digital video that can be played in movie theaters. This technology is becoming increasingly popular and has been used in such movies as the recent *Lord of the Rings* movies. Some Hollywood directors believe that eventually, all movies will be recorded and edited digitally.

After creating your final video for distribution or your personal video collection, you should backup the final video file. You can save your scenes for inclusion in other video creations or create new masters using different effects, transitions, and ordering of scenes.

FIGURE 19 DVD mastering software allows you to create interactive menus on your DVD.

CHAPTER SEVEN

Storage

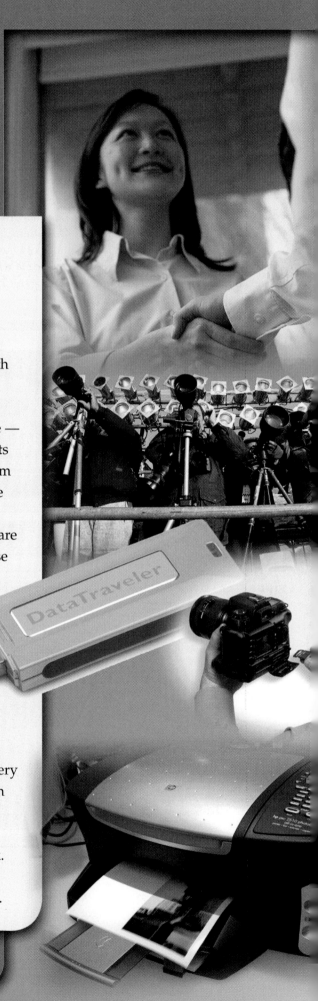

Picture Yourself Working with Mobile Storage Media

At the end of the job interview, the supervisor asks, "When can you start?" You are thrilled to get this job with the local newspaper. The flexible hours are a perfect arrangement with your school schedule. As an added bonus, the job will give you experience toward your major — computer technology.

You will be working with the photojournalists in the office — more precisely, with their mobile media. The photojournalists take many pictures while on various assignments. All of them use digital cameras. Your job is to print pictures taken by the photojournalists. Because the photojournalists each use different makes and models of cameras, the digital pictures are stored on a variety of mobile media. Some of the cameras use flash memory cards such as CompactFlash cards, xD Picture cards, and Memory Sticks. One photojournalist transfers his pictures to a USB flash drive, from which you print the images. Some copy their pictures on a CD, and another gives you a Zip disk containing all her pictures.

After you receive the media, you insert it in the appropriate card reader, card slot, drive, or port. You then begin the process of storing the images on a hard disk and finally printing the images. The office has a very liberal personal use policy that allows you to print your own digital pictures during off-the-clock time — as long as you supply the paper. When you are away from the office, however, you print personal pictures using an in-store kiosk.

To learn about these various types of mobile media, read Chapter 7 and discover many other types of storage devices.

OBJECTIVES

After completing this chapter, you will be able to:

1. Differentiate between storage devices and storage media

2. Describe the characteristics of magnetic disks

3. Differentiate between floppy disks and Zip disks

4. Describe the characteristics of a hard disk

5. Describe the characteristics of optical discs

6. Differentiate among CD-ROMs, recordable CDs, rewritable CDs, DVD-ROMs, recordable DVDs, and rewritable DVDs

7. Identify the uses of tape

8. Discuss PC Cards and the various types of miniature mobile storage media

9. Identify uses of microfilm and microfiche

CONTENTS

STORAGE

MAGNETIC DISKS

    Floppy Disks

    Zip Disks

    Hard Disks

OPTICAL DISCS

    Care of Optical Discs

    Types of Optical Discs

    CD-ROMs

    CD-Rs and CD-RWs

    DVD-ROMs

    Recordable and Rewritable DVDs

TAPE

PC CARDS

MINIATURE MOBILE STORAGE MEDIA

    Flash Memory Cards

    USB Flash Drives

    Smart Cards

MICROFILM AND MICROFICHE

ENTERPRISE STORAGE

PUTTING IT ALL TOGETHER

CHAPTER SUMMARY

HIGH-TECH TALK

    Disk Formatting and File Systems

COMPANIES ON THE CUTTING EDGE

    Maxtor

    SanDisk Corporation

TECHNOLOGY TRAILBLAZERS

    Al Shugart

    Mark Dean

STORAGE

Storage holds data, instructions, and information for future use. Every computer uses storage to hold system software and application software. To start up, a computer locates an operating system (system software) in storage and loads it into memory. When a user issues a command to start application software, such as a word processing program or a Web browser, the operating system locates the program in storage and loads it into memory.

In addition to programs, users store a variety of data and information on mainframe computers, servers, desktop computers, notebook computers, Tablet PCs, handheld computers, PDAs, and smart phones. For example, all types of users store digital photographs; appointments, schedules, and contact/address information; and correspondence, such as letters and e-mail messages. Other items stored by specific types of users include the following:

- The home user might also store budgets, bank statements, a household inventory, records of stock purchases, tax data, homework assignments, recipes, music, and videos.
- The small office/home office user also often stores faxes, business reports, financial records, tax data, travel records, customer orders, payroll records, inventory records, and Web pages.

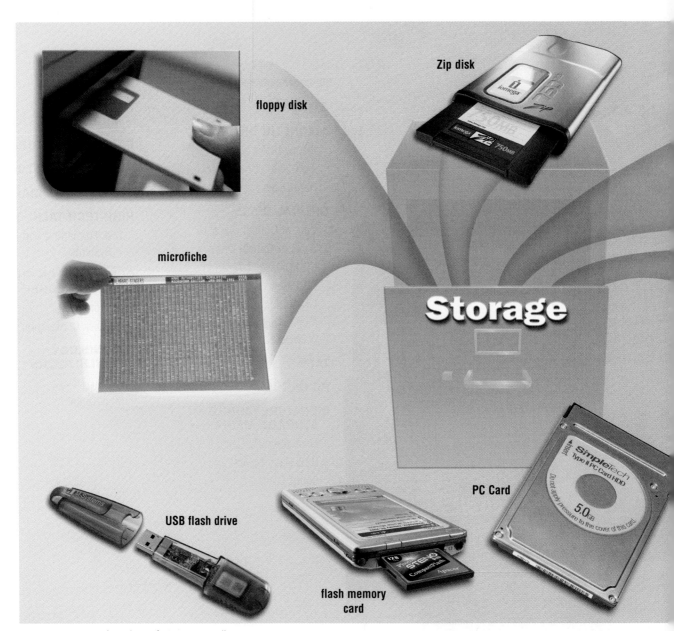

floppy disk

Zip disk

microfiche

Storage

USB flash drive

flash memory card

PC Card

FIGURE 7-1 A variety of storage media.

- The mobile user usually also stores faxes, presentations, travel records, homework assignments, and quotations.
- The power user also stores diagrams, drawings, blueprints, designs, marketing literature, corporate newsletters, product catalogs, videos, audio recordings, multimedia presentations, and Web pages.
- The large business user also accesses many stored items such as tax data, inventory records, presentations, contracts, marketing literature, and Web pages. The large business user accesses hundreds or thousands of employee, customer, and vendor records, including data and information about orders, invoices, payments, and payroll.

Storage requirements among these users vary greatly. Home users, small office/home office users, and mobile users typically have much smaller storage requirements than the large business user or power user. For example, a home user may need 80 billion bytes of storage, while large businesses may require 50 trillion bytes of storage.

A **storage medium** (media is the plural), also called *secondary storage*, is the physical material on which a computer keeps data, instructions, and information. Examples of storage media are floppy disks, Zip disks, hard disks, CDs and DVDs, tape, PC Cards, flash memory cards, USB flash drives, and microfiche (Figure 7-1). Memory, by contrast, typically consists of one or more chips on the motherboard or some other circuit board in the computer.

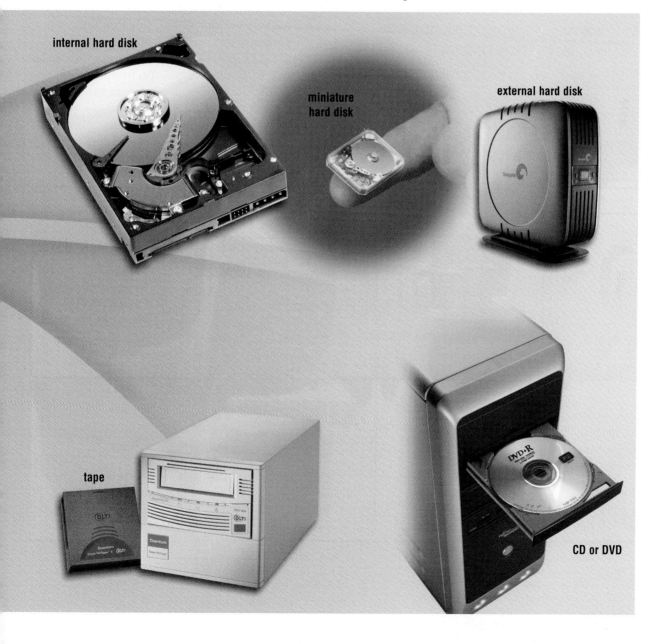

internal hard disk

miniature hard disk

external hard disk

tape

CD or DVD

Capacity is the number of bytes (characters) a storage medium can hold. Figure 7-2 identifies the terms manufacturers use to define the capacity of storage media. For example, a typical floppy disk can store up to 1.44 MB of data (approximately 1.4 million bytes) and a typical hard disk has 80 GB (approximately 80 billion bytes) of storage capacity.

Items on a storage medium remain intact even when power is removed from the computer. Thus, a storage medium is nonvolatile. Most memory, by contrast, holds data and instructions temporarily and thus is volatile. Figure 7-3 illustrates the concept of volatility. For an analogy, think of a filing cabinet that holds file folders as a storage medium, and the top of your desk as memory. When you want to work with a file, you remove it from the filing cabinet (storage medium) and place it on your desk (memory). When you are finished with the file, you remove it from your desk (memory) and return it to the filing cabinet (storage medium).

A **storage device** is the computer hardware that records and/or retrieves items to and from storage media. **Writing** is the process of transferring data, instructions, and information from memory to a storage medium. **Reading** is the process of transferring these items from a storage medium into memory. When storage devices write data on storage media, they are creating output. Similarly, when storage devices read from storage media, they function as a source of input. Nevertheless, they are categorized as storage devices, not as input or output devices.

STORAGE TERMS

Storage Term	Approximate Number of Bytes	Exact Number of Bytes
Kilobyte (KB)	1 thousand	2^{10} or 1,024
Megabyte (MB)	1 million	2^{20} or 1,048,576
Gigabyte (GB)	1 billion	2^{30} or 1,073,741,824
Terabyte (TB)	1 trillion	2^{40} or 1,099,511,627,776
Petabyte (PB)	1 quadrillion	2^{50} or 1,125,899,906,842,624
Exabyte (EB)	1 quintillion	2^{60} or 1,152,921,504,606,846,976
Zettabyte (ZB)	1 sextillion	2^{70} or 1,180,591,620,717,411,303,424
Yottabyte (YB)	1 septillion	2^{80} or 1,208,925,819,614,629,174,706,176

FIGURE 7-2   The capacity of a storage medium is measured by the amount of bytes it can hold.

AN ILLUSTRATION OF VOLATILITY

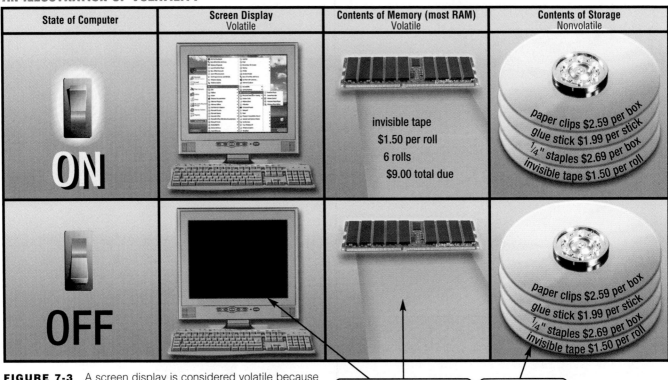

State of Computer	Screen Display Volatile	Contents of Memory (most RAM) Volatile	Contents of Storage Nonvolatile
ON		invisible tape $1.50 per roll 6 rolls $9.00 total due	paper clips $2.59 per box glue stick $1.99 per stick 1/4" staples $2.69 per box invisible tape $1.50 per roll
OFF			paper clips $2.59 per box glue stick $1.99 per stick 1/4" staples $2.69 per box invisible tape $1.50 per roll

screen displays and contents of most RAM (memory) erased when power is off

contents of storage retained when power is off

FIGURE 7-3   A screen display is considered volatile because its contents disappear when power is removed. Likewise, most RAM chips are volatile. That is, their contents are erased when power is removed from the computer. Storage, by contrast, is nonvolatile. Its contents remain when power is off.

The speed of storage devices and memory is defined by access time. **Access time** measures (1) the amount of time it takes a storage device to locate an item on a storage medium or (2) the time required to deliver an item from memory to the processor. The access time of storage devices is slow, compared with the access time of memory. Memory (chips) accesses items in billionths of a second (nanoseconds). Storage devices, by contrast, access items in thousandths of a second (milliseconds).

Instead of, or in addition to access time, some manufacturers state a storage device's transfer rate because it affects access time. *Transfer rate* is the speed with which data, instructions, and information transfer to and from a device. Transfer rates for disks are stated in *KBps* (kilobytes per second) and *MBps* (megabytes per second).

Numerous types of storage media and storage devices exist to meet a variety of users' needs. Figure 7-4 shows how different types of storage media and memory compare in terms of transfer rates and uses. This chapter discusses these and other storage media.

	Stores...
Memory (most RAM)	Items waiting to be interpreted and executed by the processor
Hard Disk	Operating system, application software, user data and information, including pictures, music, and videos
Flash Memory Cards and USB Flash Drives	Digital pictures or files to be transported
CDs and DVDs	Software, backups, movies, music
Tape	Backups
Floppy Disk	Small files to be transported

(Memory spans: Memory; Storage spans: Hard Disk, Flash Memory, CDs and DVDs, Tape, Floppy Disk)

faster transfer rates ↑ ... slower transfer rates ↓

FIGURE 7-4 A comparison of different types of storage media and memory in terms of relative speed and uses. Memory is faster than storage but is expensive and not practical for all storage requirements. Storage is less expensive but is slower than memory.

MAGNETIC DISKS

Magnetic disks use magnetic particles to store items such as data, instructions, and information on a disk's surface. Depending on how the magnetic particles are aligned, they represent either a 0 bit or a 1 bit. Recall from Chapter 4 that a bit (binary digit) is the smallest unit of data a computer can process. Thus, the alignment of the magnetic particles represents the data.

Before any data can be read from or written on a magnetic disk, the disk must be formatted. **Formatting** is the process of dividing the disk into tracks and sectors (Figure 7-5), so the operating system can store and locate data and information on the disk. A *track* is a narrow recording band that forms a full circle on the surface of the disk. The disk's storage locations consist of pie-shaped sections, which break the tracks into small arcs called *sectors*. On a magnetic disk, a sector typically stores up to 512 bytes of data.

For reading and writing purposes, sectors are grouped into clusters. A *cluster* is the smallest unit of disk space that stores data and information. Each cluster, also called an *allocation unit*, consists of two to eight sectors (the number varies depending on the operating system). Even if a file consists of only a few bytes, it uses an entire cluster. Each cluster holds data from only one file. One file, however, can span many clusters.

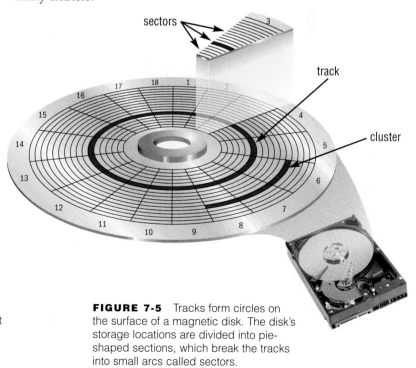

FIGURE 7-5 Tracks form circles on the surface of a magnetic disk. The disk's storage locations are divided into pie-shaped sections, which break the tracks into small arcs called sectors.

Sometimes, a sector has a flaw and cannot store data. When you format a disk, the operating system marks these bad sectors as unusable. For a technical discussion about formatting, read the High-Tech Talk article on page 382.

Three types of magnetic disks are floppy disks, Zip disks, and hard disks. Some of these disks are portable; others are not. With respect to a storage medium, the term *portable* means you can remove the medium from one computer and carry it to another computer. The following sections discuss specific types of magnetic disks.

Floppy Disks

A **floppy disk**, also called a *diskette*, is a portable, inexpensive storage medium that consists of a thin, circular, flexible plastic Mylar film with a magnetic coating enclosed in a square-shaped plastic shell. Although the exterior of current floppy disks is not bendable, users refer to this storage medium as a floppy disk because of the flexible film inside the rigid plastic 3.5-inch outer cover.

A standard floppy disk can store up to 500 double-spaced pages of text, several digital photographs, or a small audio file. Floppy disks are not as widely used as they were 15 years ago because of their low storage capacity. They are used, however, for specific applications. For example, some users work with floppy disks to transport small files to and from nonnetworked personal computers, such as from school or work to home.

A **floppy disk drive** is a device that reads from and writes on a floppy disk. A user inserts a floppy disk in and removes it from a floppy disk drive. Desktop personal computers and notebook computers may have a floppy disk drive installed inside the system unit (Figure 7-6a). Some computers use an *external floppy disk drive*, in which the drive is a separate device with a cable that plugs in a port on the system unit (Figure 7-6b). These external drives are attached to the computer only when the user needs to access items on a floppy disk.

If a personal computer has one floppy disk drive, it is named drive A. To read from or write on a floppy disk, a floppy disk drive must support that floppy disk's density. *Density* is the number of bits in an area on a storage medium. A disk with a higher density has more bits in an area and thus has a larger storage capacity. Most standard floppy disks today are high density (*HD*).

The average time it takes a current floppy disk drive to locate an item on a disk (access time) is 84 milliseconds, or approximately 1/12 of a second. The transfer rates range from 250 to 500 KBps.

You can read from and write on a floppy disk any number of times. To protect a floppy

FIGURE 7-6a (floppy disk drive installed inside a desktop computer)

FIGURE 7-6b (external floppy disk drive attached to computer with a cable)

FIGURE 7-6 Two types of floppy disk drives.

disk from accidentally being erased, the plastic outer shell on the disk contains a write-protect notch in its corner. A **write-protect notch** is a small opening that has a tab you slide to cover or expose the notch (Figure 7-7). If the write-protect notch is open, the drive cannot write on the floppy disk. If the write-protect notch is covered, or closed, the drive can write on the floppy disk. A floppy disk drive can read from a floppy disk whether the write-protect notch is open or closed. On the opposite corner, some floppy disks have a second opening without a small tab. This opening identifies the disk as a high-density floppy disk.

As mentioned earlier, a floppy disk is a type of magnetic media that stores data in tracks and sectors. A typical floppy disk stores data on both sides of the disk, has 80 tracks on each side of the recording surface, and has 18 sectors per track. To compute a disk's storage capacity, you multiply the number of sides on the disk, the number of tracks on the disk, the number of sectors per track, and the number of bytes in a sector. For example, the following is the formula for a high-density 3.5-inch floppy disk: 2 (sides) $\times$ 80 (tracks) $\times$ 18 (sectors per track) $\times$ 512 (bytes per sector) = 1,474,560 bytes (Figure 7-8). Disks often store system files in some tracks, which means the available capacity on a disk may be less than the total possible capacity.

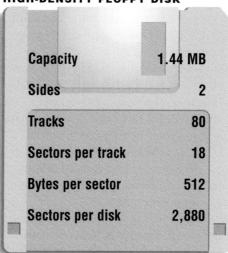

CHARACTERISTICS OF A 3.5-INCH HIGH-DENSITY FLOPPY DISK

Capacity	1.44 MB
Sides	2
Tracks	80
Sectors per track	18
Bytes per sector	512
Sectors per disk	2,880

FIGURE 7-8 Most of today's personal computers use high-density disks.

Zip Disks

A **Zip disk** is a type of portable magnetic media that can store from 100 MB to 750 MB of data. The larger capacity Zip disks hold about 500 times more than a standard floppy disk. These large capacities make it easy to transport many files or large items such as graphics, audio, or video files. Another popular use of Zip disks is to back up important data and information. A **backup** is a duplicate of a file, program, or disk that you can use in case the original is lost, damaged, or destroyed. Chapter 8 discusses backup utilities.

Zip disks are slightly larger than and about twice as thick as a 3.5-inch floppy disk. A **Zip drive** is a high-capacity disk drive developed by Iomega Corporation that reads from and writes on a Zip disk (Figure 7-9). These drives cannot read standard 3.5-inch floppy disks.

Many users prefer to purchase an external Zip drive, which connects to a USB port or FireWire port on the system unit. The external Zip drive is convenient for users with multiple computers, because it allows them to move the drive from computer to computer as needed. As an alternative, some users prefer to order a computer with a built-in Zip drive.

WEB LINK 7-1

Floppy Disks
For more information, visit scsite.com/dc2006/ch7/weblink and then click Floppy Disks.

WEB LINK 7-2

Zip Disks
For more information, visit scsite.com/dc2006/ch7/weblink and then click Zip Disks.

write-protected

not write-protected

hole on this side means disk is high density

notch open means you cannot write on the disk

notch closed means you can write on the disk

FIGURE 7-7 To protect data from being erased accidentally, floppy disks have a write-protect notch. By sliding a small tab, you either can cover or expose the notch.

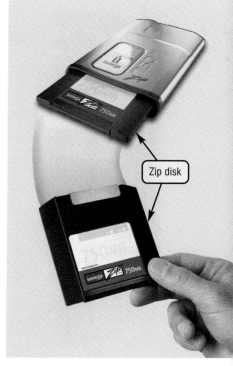

Zip disk

FIGURE 7-9 An external Zip drive and Zip disk.

Hard Disks

A **hard disk**, also called a *hard disk drive*, is a storage device that contains one or more inflexible, circular platters that magnetically store data, instructions, and information. Home users store documents, spreadsheets, presentations, databases, e-mail messages, Web pages, digital photographs, music, videos, and software on hard disks. Businesses use hard disks to store correspondence, reports, financial records, e-mail messages, customer orders and invoices, payroll records, inventory records, presentations, contracts, marketing literature, schedules, and Web sites.

The system unit on most desktop and notebook computers contains at least one hard disk. The entire device is enclosed in an airtight, sealed case to protect it from contamination. A hard disk that is mounted inside the system unit sometimes is called a *fixed disk* because it is not portable (Figure 7-10). Portable hard disks are discussed later in this chapter.

Current personal computer hard disks have storage capacities from 40 to 300 GB and more (read Looking Ahead 7-1 for a look at the next generation of hard disk storage capacities).

Hard disks are read/write storage media. That is, you can read from and write on a hard disk any number of times. If the computer contains only one hard disk, the operating system designates it as drive C. Additional hard disks are assigned the next available drive letter.

FAQ 7-1

Have personal computer hard disk capacities grown much since their inception?

Yes, hard disk capacities have grown phenomenally over the past several years, as shown in the chart below. This trend is expected to continue at a rate of 60 percent annually. For more information, visit scsite.com/dc2006/ch7/faq and then click Hard Disk Capacities.

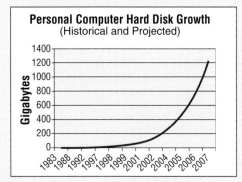

Personal Computer Hard Disk Growth
(Historical and Projected)

LOOKING AHEAD 7-1

Heat Increases Disk Capacity

Things are heating up in the data storage industry. Engineers at IBM Research are testing the use of heat to record data inexpensively on magnetic media, such as hard disks.

Within the next ten years, the researchers predict that this new technique will allow storage of more than one terabit per square inch; today's magnetic media can store approximately 60 gigabits per square inch. With this capacity, a hard disk drive that can store seven terabits will be commonplace.

IBM calls this new storage system *Millipede*. It uses heated tips mounted on the ends of cantilevers, in a fashion similar to the way the stylus on an old phonograph sat on the grooves of vinyl records. For more information, visit scsite.com/dc2006/ch7/looking and then click Heated Storage.

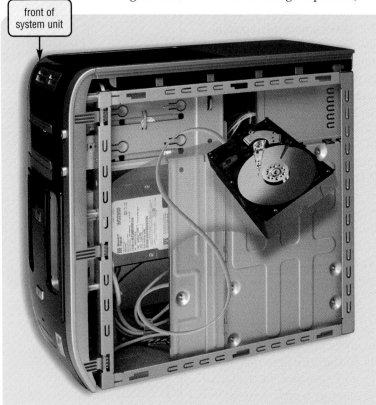

FIGURE 7-10 The hard disk in a desktop personal computer is enclosed inside an airtight, sealed case inside the system unit.

CHARACTERISTICS OF A HARD DISK

Characteristics of a hard disk include its capacity, platters, read/write heads, cylinders, sectors and tracks, revolutions per minute, transfer rate, and access time. Figure 7-11 shows characteristics of a sample 120 GB hard disk. The following paragraphs discuss each of these characteristics.

The capacity of a hard disk is determined from the number of platters it contains, together with composition of the magnetic coating on the platters. A *platter* is made of aluminum, glass, or ceramic and is coated with an alloy material that allows items to be recorded magnetically

on its surface. The coating usually is three millionths of an inch thick.

On desktop computers, platters most often have a *form factor*, or size, of approximately 3.5 inches in diameter; on notebook computers and mobile devices, the form factor is 2.5 inches or less. A typical hard disk has multiple platters stacked on top of one another. Each platter has two read/write heads, one for each side. The hard disk has arms that move the read/write heads to the proper location on the platter (Figure 7-12). A *read/write head* is the mechanism that reads items and writes items in the drive as it barely touches the disk's recording surface.

SAMPLE HARD DISK CHARACTERISTICS

Advertised capacity	120 GB
Platters	3
Read/write heads	6
Cylinders	16,383
Bytes per sector	512
Sectors per track	63
Sectors per drive	234,441,648
Revolutions per minute	7,200
Transfer rate	133 MB per second
Access time	8.9 ms

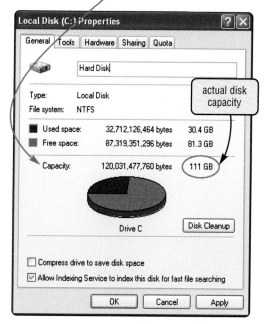

FIGURE 7-11 Characteristics of a sample 120 GB hard disk. The actual disk's capacity sometimes is different from the advertised capacity because of bad sectors on the disk.

FIGURE 7-12 HOW A HARD DISK WORKS

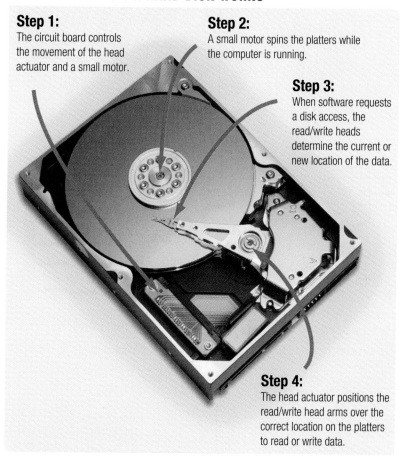

Step 1:
The circuit board controls the movement of the head actuator and a small motor.

Step 2:
A small motor spins the platters while the computer is running.

Step 3:
When software requests a disk access, the read/write heads determine the current or new location of the data.

Step 4:
The head actuator positions the read/write head arms over the correct location on the platters to read or write data.

The location of the read/write heads often is referred to by its cylinder. A *cylinder* is the vertical section of a track that passes through all platters (Figure 7-13). A single movement of the read/write head arms accesses all the platters in a cylinder. If a hard disk has two platters (four sides), each with 1,000 tracks, then it will have 1,000 cylinders with each cylinder consisting of 4 tracks (2 tracks for each platter).

While the computer is running, the platters in the hard disk rotate at a high rate of speed. This spinning, which usually is 5,400 to 15,000 *revolutions per minute* (*rpm*), allows nearly instant access to all tracks and sectors on the platters. The platters typically continue to spin until power is removed from the computer. (On many computers, the hard disk stops spinning after a specified time to save power.) The spinning motion creates a cushion of air between the platter and its read/write head. This cushion ensures that the read/write head floats above the platter instead of making direct contact with the platter surface. The distance between the read/write head and the platter is about two millionths of one inch.

As shown in Figure 7-14, this close clearance leaves no room for any type of contamination. Dirt, hair, dust, smoke, and other particles could cause the hard disk to have a head crash. A *head crash* occurs when a read/write head touches the surface of a platter, usually resulting in a loss of data or sometimes loss of the entire drive. Although current internal hard disks are built to withstand shocks and are sealed tightly to keep out contaminants, head crashes do occasionally still occur. Thus, it is crucial that you back up your hard disk regularly. Chapter 8 discusses backup techniques.

Depending on the type of hard disk, transfer rates range from 15 MBps to 320 MBps. Access time for today's hard disks ranges from approximately 3 to 12 ms (milliseconds). The average hard disk access time is at least seven times faster than the average floppy disk drive.

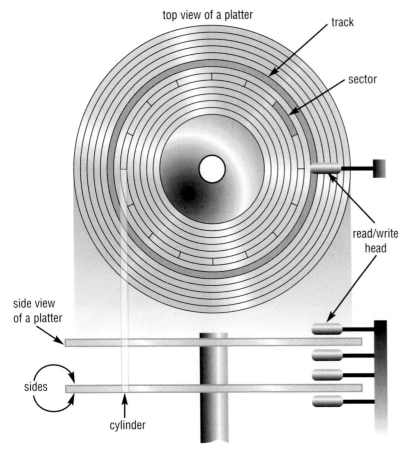

FIGURE 7-13 A cylinder is the vertical section of track through all platters on a hard disk.

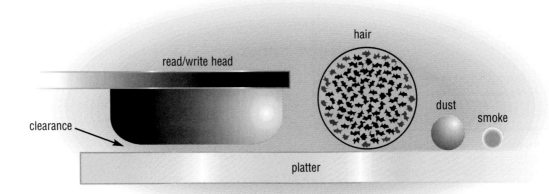

FIGURE 7-14 The clearance between a disk read/write head and the platter is about two millionths of an inch. A smoke particle, dust particle, human hair, or other contaminant could render the drive unusable.

Hard disks improve their access time by using disk caching. *Disk cache* (pronounced cash), sometimes called a buffer, consists of a memory chip(s) on a hard disk that stores frequently accessed items such as data, instructions, and information (Figure 7-15). Disk cache and memory cache work in a similar fashion. When a processor requests data, instructions, or information from the hard disk, the hard disk first checks its disk cache — before moving any mechanical parts to access the platters. If the requested item is in disk cache, the hard disk sends it to the processor. If the hard disk does not find the requested item in the disk cache, then the processor must wait for the hard disk to locate and transfer the item from the disk to the processor. Hard disks today contain between 2 MB and 16 MB of disk cache. The greater the disk cache, the faster the hard disk.

FIGURE 7-15 HOW DISK CACHE WORKS

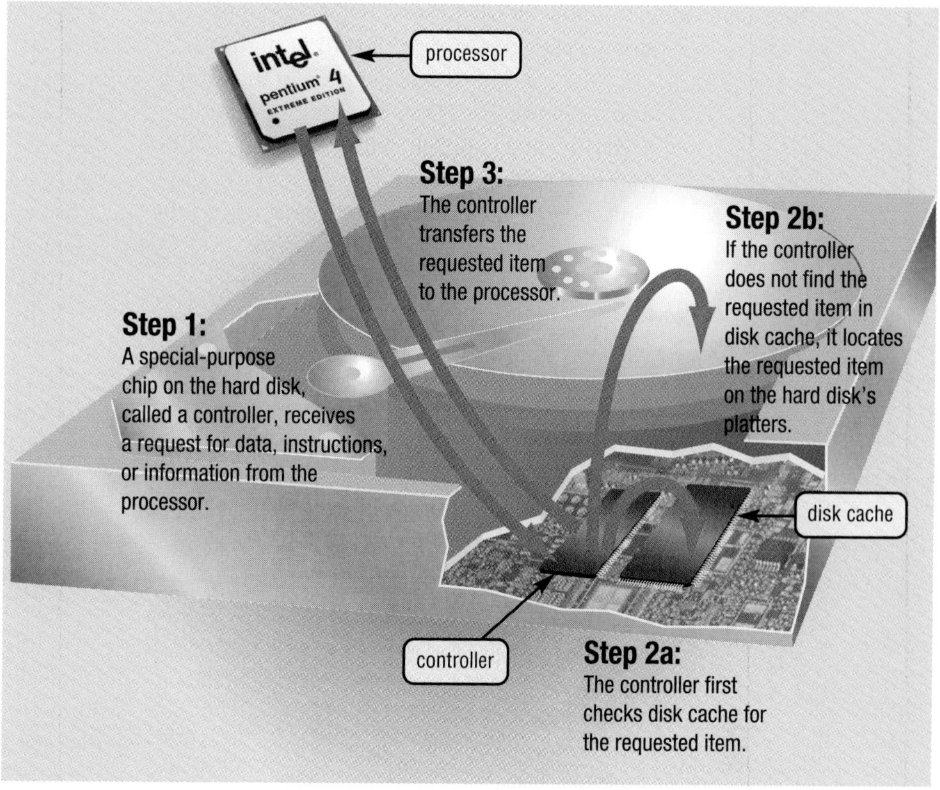

Step 1:
A special-purpose chip on the hard disk, called a controller, receives a request for data, instructions, or information from the processor.

Step 2a:
The controller first checks disk cache for the requested item.

Step 2b:
If the controller does not find the requested item in disk cache, it locates the requested item on the hard disk's platters.

Step 3:
The controller transfers the requested item to the processor.

processor

controller

disk cache

FAQ 7-2

How do manufacturers specify hard disk reliability?

Hardware manufacturers often specify a device's service life (expected useful life) and *MTBF* (mean time between failures), which is the total number of hours all devices were observed operating divided by the total number of failures that occurred. Although MTBF can be as high as 1.4 million hours for hard disks, many people rely on the service life estimate instead. For more information, visit scsite.com/dc2006/ch7/faq and then click MTBF.

MINIATURE HARD DISKS Many mobile devices and consumer electronics include miniature hard disks, which provide users with greater storage capacities than flash memory. These tiny hard disks, some of which have form factors of less than 1 inch (Figure 7-16), are found in devices such as music players, digital cameras, smart phones, and PDAs. Miniature hard disks have storage capacities that range from 2 GB to 100 GB.

FIGURE 7-16 This hard disk has a form factor of 0.85 inch and storage capacities up to 4 GB.

PORTABLE HARD DISKS Portable hard disks either are external or removable and have storage capacities up to 250 GB or higher.

An **external hard disk**, shown in the top picture in Figure 7-17, is a separate free-standing hard disk that connects with a cable to a USB port or FireWire port on the system unit. As with the internal hard disk, the entire hard disk is enclosed in an airtight, sealed case.

A **removable hard disk** is a hard disk that you insert and remove from either a dock or a drive. Sometimes the dock or drive is built in the system unit. Others are external devices that connect with a cable to a USB port or FireWire port on the system unit. Removable hard disks that insert in a dock are self-contained units, similar to external hard disks. Removable hard disks that insert in a

drive, shown in the bottom picture in Figure 7-17, operate in a manner similar to a floppy disk drive, reading from and writing on the removable hard disk.

External hard disks and removable hard disks offer the following advantages over internal hard disks (fixed disks):

- Transport a large number of files
- Back up important files or an entire internal hard disk
- Easily store large audio and video files
- Secure your data; for example, at the end of a work session, remove the hard disk and lock it up, leaving no data in the computer
- Add storage space to a notebook computer or Tablet PC
- Add storage space to a desktop computer without having to open the system unit
- Share a drive with multiple computers

As the prices of portable hard disks drop, increasingly more users will purchase one to supplement a home or office internal hard disk. Keep in mind, though, that external or removable hard disks transfer data at slower rates than internal hard disks.

HARD DISK CONTROLLERS A *disk controller* consists of a special-purpose chip and electronic circuits that control the transfer of data, instructions, and information from a disk to and from the system bus and other components in the computer. That is, it controls the interface between the hard disk and the system bus. A disk controller for a hard disk, called the hard disk controller, may be part of a hard disk or the motherboard, or it may be a separate adapter card inside in the system unit.

In their personal computer advertisements, vendors usually state the type of hard disk interface supported by the hard disk controller. Thus, you should understand the types of available hard disk interfaces. In addition to USB and FireWire (external hard disk interfaces), three other types of hard disk interfaces for internal use in personal computers are SATA, EIDE, and SCSI.

- *SATA (Serial Advanced Technology Attachment)*, the newest type of hard disk interface, uses serial signals to transfer data, instructions, and information. The primary advantage of SATA interfaces is their cables are thinner, longer, more flexible, and less susceptible to interference than cables used by hard disks

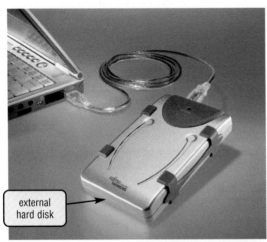

external hard disk

one type of removable hard disk

FIGURE 7-17 Examples of portable hard disks.

WEB LINK 7-3

Hard Disks

For more information, visit scsite.com/ dc2006/ch7/weblink and then click Hard Disks.

that use parallel signals. SATA interfaces have data transfer rates of up to 300 MBps. In addition to hard disks, SATA interfaces support connections to CD and DVD drives.

- *EIDE* (*Enhanced Integrated Drive Electronics*) is a hard disk interface that uses parallel signals to transfer data, instructions, and information. EIDE interfaces can support up to four hard disks at 137 GB per disk. These interfaces have data transfer rates up to 100 MBps. EIDE interfaces also provide connections for CD and DVD drives and tape drives. Some manufacturers market their EIDE interfaces as Fast ATA or Ultra ATA.
- *SCSI* interfaces, which also use parallel signals, can support up to eight or fifteen peripheral devices. Supported devices include hard disks, CD and DVD drives, tape drives, printers, scanners, network cards, and much more. Recall from Chapter 4 that SCSI is an acronym for Small Computer System Interface. Some computers have a built-in SCSI interface, while others use an adapter card to add a SCSI interface. SCSI interfaces provide up to 320 MBps data transfer rates.

FAQ 7-3

What are the transfer rates of USB and FireWire?

USB 2.0, also called *Hi-Speed USB*, has transfer rates up to 480 *Mbps* (megabits per second). FireWire has transfer rates up to 800 Mbps. For more information, visit scsite.com/dc2006/ch7/faq and then click USB and FireWire.

MAINTAINING DATA STORED ON A HARD DISK Most manufacturers guarantee their hard disks to last approximately three to five years. Many last much longer with proper care. To prevent the loss of items stored on a hard disk, you regularly should perform preventive maintenance such as defragmenting or scanning the disk for errors. Chapter 8 discusses these and other utilities in depth.

ONLINE STORAGE Some users choose online storage instead of storing data locally on a hard disk. **Online storage** is a service on the Web that provides hard disk storage to computer users,

usually for a minimal monthly fee (Figure 7-18). Fee arrangements for use of these Internet hard disks vary. For example, one online storage service charges $10 per month for 5 GB of storage. Many offer free trial periods.

Users subscribe to an online storage service for a variety of reasons:

- To access files on the Internet hard disk from any computer or device that has Internet access
- To store large audio, video, and graphics files on an Internet hard disk instantaneously, instead of spending time downloading to a local hard disk
- To allow others to access files on their Internet hard disk so others can listen to an audio file, watch a video clip, or view a picture — instead of e-mailing the file to them
- To view time-critical data and images immediately while away from the main office or location; for example, doctors can view x-ray images from another hospital, home, or office, or while on vacation
- To store offsite backups of data (Chapter 8 presents this and other backup strategies)

Once users subscribe to the online storage service, they can save on the Internet hard disk in the same manner they save on their local hard disk or any other drive.

WEB LINK 7-4

Online Storage
For more information, visit scsite.com/dc2006/ch7/weblink and then click Online Storage.

FIGURE 7-18 An example of one Web site advertising its online storage service.

Test your knowledge of pages 354 through 365 in Quiz Yourself 7-1.

QUIZ YOURSELF 7-1

Instructions: Find the true statement below. Then, rewrite the remaining false statements so they are true.

1. Floppy disks are a type of optical disc.

2. Hard disks contain one or more inflexible, circular platters that magnetically store data, instructions, and information.

3. SATA is a hard disk interface that uses parallel signals to transfer data, instructions, and information.

4. Storage media is the computer hardware that records and/or retrieves items to and from a storage device.

5. Three types of manual disks are floppy disks, Zip disks, and hard disks.

6. Users can move an internal Zip drive from computer to computer as needed by connecting the drive to a USB port or FireWire port on the system unit.

Quiz Yourself Online: To further check your knowledge of storage devices and storage media, magnetic disks, floppy disks, Zip disks, and hard disks, visit scsite.com/dc2006/ch7/quiz and then click Objectives 1 – 4.

OPTICAL DISCS

An *optical disc* is a type of storage media that consists of a flat, round, portable disc made of metal, plastic, and lacquer that is written and read by a laser. (Recall from Chapter 1 that the term disk is used for magnetic media, and disc is used for optical media.) Optical discs used in personal computers are 4.75 inches in diameter and less than one-twentieth of an inch thick. Smaller computers and devices, however, use *mini discs* that have a diameter of 3 inches or less.

Optical discs primarily store software, data, digital photographs, movies, and music. Some optical disc formats are read only, meaning users cannot write (save) on the media. Others are read/write, which allows users to save on the disc just as they save on a hard disk.

Nearly every personal computer today has some type of optical disc drive installed in a drive bay. On these drives, you push a button to slide out a tray, insert the disc, and then push the same button to close the tray (Figure 7-19). Other convenient features on most of these drives include a volume control button and a headphone port (or jack) so you can use headphones to listen to audio without disturbing others nearby.

With some discs, you can read and/or write on one side only. Manufacturers usually place a silk-screened label on the top layer of these single-sided discs. You insert a single-sided disc in the drive with the label side up. Other discs are double-sided. Simply remove the disc from the drive, flip it over, and reinsert it in the drive

Push the button to slide out the tray.

Insert the disc, label side up.

Push the same button to close the tray.

FIGURE 7-19 On optical disc drives, you push a button to slide out a tray, insert the disc, and then push the same button to close the tray.

to use the other side of the disc. Double-sided discs often have no label; instead each side of the disc is identified with small writing around the center of the disc.

The drive designation of an optical disc drive usually follows alphabetically after that of all the hard disks and portable disks. For example, if the computer has one hard disk (drive C), a Zip disk drive (drive D), and an external hard disk (drive E), then the first optical disc drive is drive F. A second optical disc drive would be drive G.

Optical discs store items by using microscopic pits (indentations) and lands (flat areas) that are in the middle layer of the disc (Figure 7-20). A high-powered laser light creates the pits. A lower-powered laser light reads items from the disc by reflecting light through the bottom of the disc, which usually is either solid gold or silver in color. The reflected light is converted into a series of bits the computer can process. A land causes light to reflect, which is read as binary digit 1. Pits absorb the light; this absence of light is read as binary digit 0.

Optical discs commonly store items in a single track that spirals from the center of the disc to the edge of the disc. As with a hard disk, this single track is divided into evenly sized sectors on which items are stored (Figure 7-21).

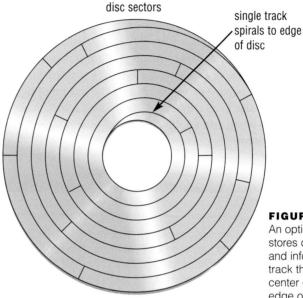

disc sectors

single track spirals to edge of disc

FIGURE 7-21
An optical disc typically stores data, instructions, and information in a single track that spirals from the center of the disc to the edge of a disc.

FIGURE 7-20   HOW A LASER READS DATA ON AN OPTICAL DISC

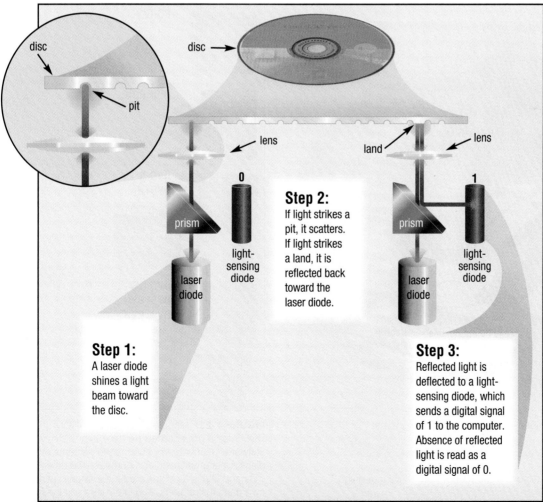

disc

disc

pit

lens

land

lens

0

1

prism

prism

light-sensing diode

light-sensing diode

laser diode

laser diode

Step 2:
If light strikes a pit, it scatters. If light strikes a land, it is reflected back toward the laser diode.

Step 1:
A laser diode shines a light beam toward the disc.

Step 3:
Reflected light is deflected to a light-sensing diode, which sends a digital signal of 1 to the computer. Absence of reflected light is read as a digital signal of 0.

Care of Optical Discs

Manufacturers claim that a properly cared for high-quality optical disc will last 5 years but could last up to 100 years. Figure 7-22 offers some guidelines for the proper care of optical discs. Never bend a disc; it may break. Do not expose discs to extreme temperatures or humidity. The ideal temperature range for disc storage is 50 to 70 degrees Fahrenheit. Stacking discs, touching the underside of discs, or exposing them to any type of contaminant may scratch a disc. Place an optical disc in its protective case, called a *jewel box*, when you are finished using it and store in an upright (vertical) position.

FAQ 7-4

Can I clean a disc?

Yes, you can remove dust, dirt, smudges, and fingerprints from the surface of an optical disc. Moisten a soft cloth with warm water or rubbing alcohol and then wipe the disc in straight lines from the center outward. You also can repair scratches on the surface with a specialized disc repair kit. For more information, visit scsite.com/dc2006/ch7/faq and then click Cleaning and Repairing Discs.

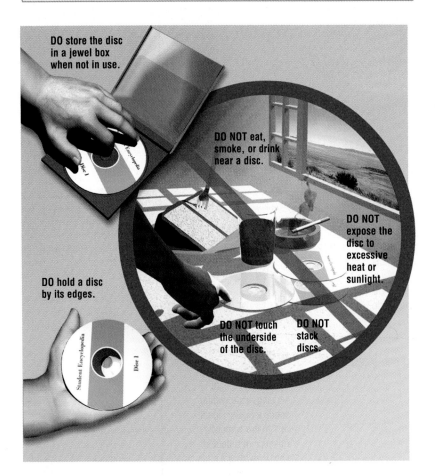

DO store the disc in a jewel box when not in use.

DO NOT eat, smoke, or drink near a disc.

DO NOT expose the disc to excessive heat or sunlight.

DO hold a disc by its edges.

DO NOT touch the underside of the disc.

DO NOT stack discs.

FIGURE 7-22 Some guidelines for the proper care of optical discs.

Types of Optical Discs

Many different formats of optical discs exist today. Two general categories are CDs and DVDs, with DVDs having a much greater storage capacity than CDs. Specific formats include CD-ROM, CD-R, CD-RW, DVD-ROM, DVD-R, DVD+R, DVD-RW, DVD+RW, and DVD+RAM. Figure 7-23 identifies each of these optical disc formats and specifies whether a user can read from the disc, write to the disc, and/or erase the disc. The following sections describe characteristics unique to each of these disc formats.

OPTICAL DISC FORMATS

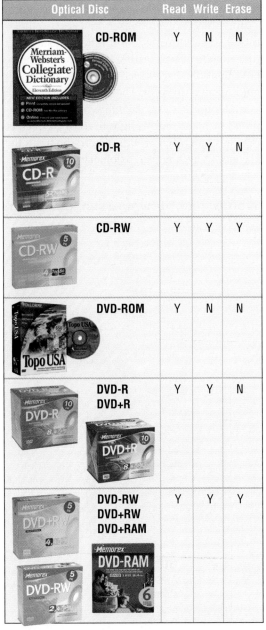

Optical Disc	Read	Write	Erase
CD-ROM	Y	N	N
CD-R	Y	Y	N
CD-RW	Y	Y	Y
DVD-ROM	Y	N	N
DVD-R DVD+R	Y	Y	N
DVD-RW DVD+RW DVD+RAM	Y	Y	Y

FIGURE 7-23 Manufacturers sell CD-ROM and DVD-ROM media prerecorded (written) with audio, video, and software. Users cannot change the contents of these discs. Users, however, can purchase the other formats of CDs and DVDs as blank media and record (write) their own data, instructions, and information on these discs.

CD-ROMs

A **CD-ROM** (pronounced SEE-DEE-rom), or *compact disc read-only memory*, is a type of optical disc that users can read but not write (record) or erase — hence, the name read-only. Manufacturers write the contents of standard CD-ROMs. A standard CD-ROM is called a *single-session disc* because manufacturers write all items on the disc at one time. Software manufacturers often distribute their programs using CD-ROMs (Figure 7-24).

A typical CD-ROM holds from 650 MB to 1 GB of data, instructions, and information. This is equivalent to about 450 high-density 3.5-inch floppy disks.

To read a CD-ROM, insert the disc in a **CD-ROM drive** or a CD-ROM player. Because audio CDs and CD-ROMs use the same laser technology, you may be able to use a CD-ROM drive to listen to an audio CD while working on the computer. Some music companies, however, configure their CDs so the music will not play on a computer. They do this to protect themselves from customers illegally copying and sharing the music. Read At Issue 7-1 for a related discussion.

The speed of a CD-ROM drive determines how fast it installs programs and accesses the disc. Original CD-ROM drives were single-speed drives with transfer rates of 150 KBps (kilobytes per second). Manufacturers measure all optical disc drives relative to this original CD-ROM drive. They use an X to denote the original transfer rate of 150 KBps. For example, a 48X CD-ROM drive has a data transfer rate of 7,200 (48 × 150) KBps, or 7.2 MBps.

Current CD-ROM drives have transfer rates, or speeds, ranging from 48X to 75X or faster. The higher the number, the faster the CD-ROM drive. Faster CD-ROM drives are more expensive than slower drives.

WEB LINK 7-5

CD-ROMs
For more information, visit scsite.com/dc2006/ch7/weblink and then click CD-ROMs.

AT ISSUE 7-1

Does Music Sharing Harm CD Sales?

With over a billion songs illegally available on file sharing networks, such as Kazaa, the music industry claims that sharing music is harming CD sales, which results in less money in the artists' pockets. A recent study by researchers at Harvard University and the University of North Carolina showed that the availability and sharing of recent CD releases did not have an effect on the sales of the CDs. The researchers found that those who obtained the music from the Internet were often the least likely to purchase the CDs in the first place. While record companies have seen a modest decline in sales since the advent of music sharing, they have released significantly fewer titles, and some claim that the quality of music has declined. Also, CD sales may have been exceptionally high in the 1990s as people replaced older media, such as cassette tapes and vinyl albums, with the newer CD format. While clearly in violation of the music publishers' copyright, does music sharing harm CD sales? Why? Is it possible that music sharing actually results in higher sales for record companies in some cases? Why or why not? What are some possible strategies the music industry can adopt in response to the music sharing phenomenon?

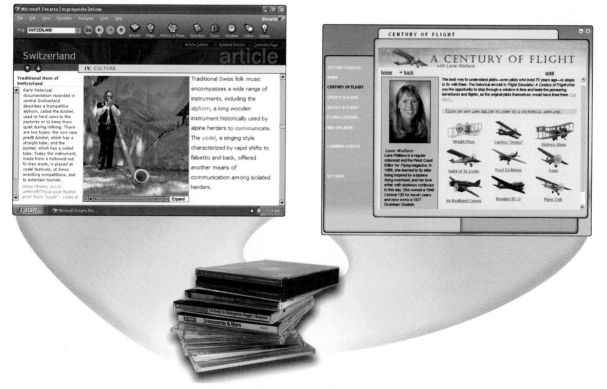

FIGURE 7-24 Encyclopedias, games, simulations, and many other programs are distributed on CD-ROM.

PICTURE CDs A Kodak **Picture CD** is a single-session CD-ROM that stores digital versions of a single roll of film using a jpg file format. Many film developers offer Picture CD service for consumers when they drop off film to be developed. That is, in addition to printed photographs and negatives, you also receive a Picture CD containing the film's pictures. The resolution of images stored on a Picture CD usually is 1024 × 1536 pixels. The additional cost for a Picture CD is about $10 per roll of film.

Most optical disc drives can read a Picture CD. Using photo editing software and photographs on the Picture CD, you can remove red eye, crop the photograph, enhance colors, trim away edges, adjust the lighting, and edit just about any aspect of a photograph. In addition, a Picture CD allows you to print copies of the photographs on glossy paper with an ink-jet printer. If you do not have a printer to print the images, many stores have kiosks at which you can print pictures from a Picture CD (Figure 7-25).

WEB LINK 7-6

Picture CDs

For more information, visit scsite.com/ dc2006/ch7/weblink and then click Picture CDs.

FAQ 7-5

How do I share my digital pictures with others?

You can send them as e-mail attachments, copy them to online storage, or post them to a personal Web page or a photo community. At a *photo community*, users can create online photo albums and share their digital photographs on the Web. Some photo communities provide free, unlimited storage space; others charge a nominal fee. For more information, visit scsite.com/dc2006/ch7/faq and then click Photo Communities.

FIGURE 7-25 HOW A PICTURE CD WORKS

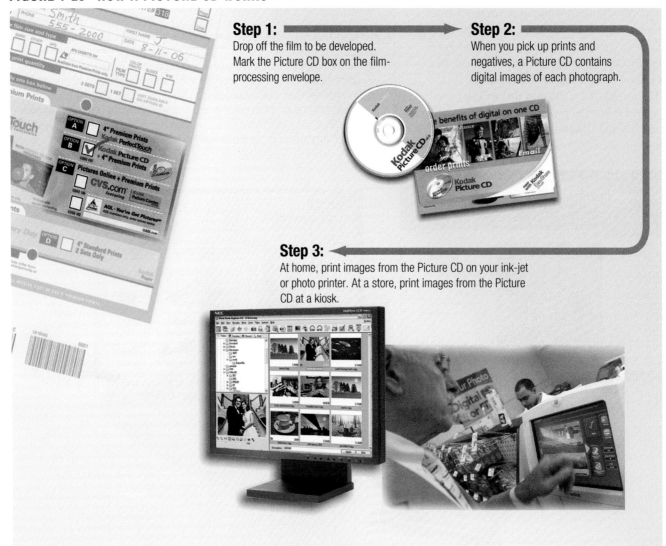

Step 1:
Drop off the film to be developed. Mark the Picture CD box on the film-processing envelope.

Step 2:
When you pick up prints and negatives, a Picture CD contains digital images of each photograph.

Step 3:
At home, print images from the Picture CD on your ink-jet or photo printer. At a store, print images from the Picture CD at a kiosk.

CD-Rs and CD-RWs

A **CD-R** (*compact disc-recordable*) is a multisession optical disc on which users can write, but not erase, their own items such as text, graphics, and audio. *Multisession* means you can write on part of the disc at one time and another part at a later time. Each part of a CD-R, however, can be written on only one time, and the disc's contents cannot be erased.

Writing on the CD-R requires a *CD recorder* or a **CD-R drive**. A CD-R drive usually can read both audio CDs and standard CD-ROMs. These drives read at speeds of 48X or more and write at speeds of 40X or more. Manufacturers often list the write speed first, for example, as 40/48.

A **CD-RW** (*compact disc-rewritable*) is an erasable multisession disc you can write on multiple times. CD-RW overcomes the major disadvantage of CD-R because it allows users to write and rewrite data, instructions, and information on the CD-RW disc multiple times — instead of just once. Reliability of the disc tends to drop, however, with each successive rewrite.

To write on a CD-RW disc, you must have CD-RW software and a **CD-RW drive**. These drives have write speeds of 52X or more, rewrite speeds of 24X or more, and read speeds of 52X or more. Manufacturers state the speeds in this order; that is, write speed, rewrite speed, and read speed is stated as 52/24/52. Most CD-RW drives can read audio CDs, CD-ROMs, CD-Rs, and CD-RWs.

Many personal computers today include a CD-RW drive as a standard feature so users can burn their own discs. The process of writing on an optical disc is called *burning*. Some operating systems, such as Windows XP, include the capability of burning discs.

Using a CD-RW disc, users easily back up large files from a hard disk. Another popular use of CD-RW and CD-R discs is to create audio CDs. For example, users can record their own music and save it on a CD, purchase and download MP3 songs from the Web, or rearrange tracks on a purchased music CD. The process of copying an individual song from a purchased audio CD and converting it to a digital format is called *ripping*. Read At Issue 7-2 for a related discussion.

WEB LINK 7-7

CD-Rs and CD-RWs
For more information, visit scsite.com/ dc2006/ch7/weblink and then click CD-Rs and CD-RWs.

FAQ 7-6

Is it legal to copy songs to a CD?

It is legal to copy songs from an audio CD that you obtained legally, if you use the copied music for your own personal use. If you share the copy with a friend, however, you are violating copyright law. It is legal to download copyrighted music if the song's copyright holder has granted permission for users to download and play the song. In most cases, you pay a fee for the song. For more information, visit scsite.com/dc2006/ch7/faq and then click Copying Music.

AT ISSUE 7-2

Is It Ethical to Copy CDs or DVDs?

A musician's recent release quickly became the second most-played CD in computer CD drives — before the CD even appeared on store shelves. CD-R and DVD-R technology makes copying music and movies easy and affordable. People use CD-R and DVD-R technology to copy CDs and DVDs they have purchased, borrowed, or pirated on the Internet. At some campuses, students use college servers to create music Web sites, download copyrighted music, and then record and distribute unauthorized copies. The recording industry claims this practice is unfair to the industry and, in essence, steals from the recording artists. Others, however, insist that bootlegged music actually is a marketing vehicle, influencing listeners who pay to attend concerts eventually to purchase the CD. The music industry has gone as far as placing technology on CDs that makes them impossible or very difficult to copy. Opponents to this practice say that these measures infringe on the CD owner's right to fair use, such as making personal backup copies, which courts have upheld as exceptions to copyright laws. Is it ethical to download and copy portions of a music CD, or an entire music CD, from the Internet? Why? If you purchase a CD, is it ethical to make copies for yourself? For a friend? Why? Should recording or movie companies be able to use formatting techniques to keep people from copying CDs or DVDs? What practices should be allowed within the doctrine of fair use?

DVD-ROMs

A **DVD-ROM** (*digital versatile disc-read-only memory* or *digital video disc-read-only memory*) is an extremely high-capacity optical disc on which users can read but not write or erase. Manufacturers write the contents of DVD-ROMs and distribute them to consumers. DVD-ROMs store movies, music, music videos, huge databases, and complex software (Figure 7-26).

The storage capacity of a DVD-ROM is more than enough to hold a telephone book containing every resident in the United States. Not only is the storage capacity of a DVD-ROM greater than that of a CD, a DVD-ROM's quality also far surpasses that of CDs because images are stored at higher resolution.

To read a DVD-ROM, you must have a **DVD-ROM drive** or DVD player. Most DVD-ROM drives also can read audio CDs, CD-ROMs, CD-Rs, and CD-RWs. DVD-ROM drives can read DVDs at speeds of 16X or more and CDs at speeds of 52X or more.

Although the size and shape of a CD-ROM and DVD-ROM are similar, a DVD-ROM stores data, instructions, and information in a slightly different manner and thus achieves a higher storage capacity. Widely used DVD-ROMs are capable of storing 4.7 GB to 17 GB, depending on the storage techniques used (Figure 7-27). The first storage technique involves making the disc denser by packing the pits closer together. The second involves using two layers of pits. For this technique to work, the lower layer of pits is semitransparent so the laser can read through it to the upper layer. This technique doubles the capacity of the disc. Finally, some DVD-ROMs are double-sided. A newer, quite expensive type of DVD, called a *Blu-Ray disc*, currently has storage capacities of 27 GB, with expectations of exceeding 50 GB in the future. Read Looking Ahead 7-2 for a look at a future application of Blu-Ray technology.

FIGURE 7-26   A DVD-ROM is an extremely high-capacity optical disc.

FAQ 7-7

What is a DVD/CD-RW drive?

It is a combination drive that reads DVD and CD media; it also writes to CD-RW media. This drive allows you to watch a DVD or burn a CD. For more information, visit scsite.com/dc2006/ch7/faq and then click DVD/CD-RW Drives.

DVD-ROM STORAGE CAPACITIES

Sides	Layers	Storage Capacity
1	1	4.7 GB
1	2	8.5 GB
2	1	9.4 GB
2	2	17 GB

FIGURE 7-27   Storage capacities of DVD-ROMs.

LOOKING AHEAD 7-2

Paper Discs Offer Increased Capacity

The next generation high-capacity optical storage media will be composed of 51 percent paper and will hold as much as 50 GB of data. These discs will store more than 13 hours of video, which is more than five times the 8.5 GB capacity of current DVD discs. This recording capacity will become increasingly important as consumers purchase more high-definition television products and desire to record and view movies, photos, and other digital content on these devices.

The products are expected to cost no more than a currently priced DVD disc when produced in mass quantities and will be based on Blu-Ray disc technology. Destroying unwanted or sensitive data will be easy: just cut the disc with scissors. For more information, visit scsite.com/dc2006/ch7/looking and then click Paper Discs.

Recordable and Rewritable DVDs

Many types of recordable and rewritable DVD formats are available. *DVD-R* and *DVD+R* are competing DVD-recordable formats, each with up to 4.7 GB storage capacity. Both allow users to write on the disc once and read (play) it many times. In concept, DVD-R and DVD+R are similar to CD-R.

Instead of recordable DVDs, however, most users work with rewritable DVDs because these discs can be written on multiple times and also erased. Three competing rewritable DVD formats exist, each with storage capacities up to 4.7 GB per side: **DVD-RW**, **DVD+RW**, and **DVD+RAM**. These rewritable DVDs are similar in concept to CD-RW. With DVD-RW and DVD+RW discs, a user can erase and write (record) more than 1,000 times. To write on these discs, you must have a DVD-RW drive, a DVD+RW drive, or a DVD recorder. DVD-RW and DVD+RW drives have rewrite speeds of 12X or more, and read speeds of 40X or more. The drives usually can read DVD-ROM, DVD-R, DVD+R, and all CD media, and they can write on DVD-RW or DVD+RW, DVD-R, CD-R, and CD-RW media.

DVD+RAM (DVD+random access memory) allows users to erase and record on a DVD+RAM disc more than 100,000 times. These discs can be read by DVD+RAM drives and some DVD-ROM drives and players.

As the cost of DVD technologies becomes more reasonable, many industry professionals expect that DVD eventually will replace all CD media.

FAQ 7-8

Do any digital video cameras record movies on DVD?

Yes. Video cameras that store at least 120 minutes of recording on mini-DVD media are available. Once recorded, users can view the DVD media in a standard computer DVD drive or a DVD player. Many video cameras include the capability of editing the video right in the camera. For more information, visit scsite.com/dc2006/ch7/faq and then click DVD Video Recorders.

WEB LINK 7-8

DVDs
For more information, visit scsite.com/dc2006/ch7/weblink and then click DVDs.

Test your knowledge of pages 366 through 373 in Quiz Yourself 7-2.

QUIZ YOURSELF 7-2

Instructions: Find the true statement below. Then, rewrite the remaining false statements so they are true.

1. A CD-RW is a type of optical disc on which users can read but not write (record) or erase.

2. A DVD-RAM is a single-session disc that stores digital versions of a single roll of film using a jpg file format.

3. DVDs have the same storage capacities as CDs.

4. Optical discs are written and read by mirrors.

5. Single session means you can write on part of the disc at one time and another part at a later time.

6. Three competing rewritable DVD formats are DVD-RW, DVD+RW, and DVD+RAM.

Quiz Yourself Online: To further check your knowledge of optical discs and various optical disc formats, visit scsite.com/dc2006/ch7/quiz and then click Objectives 5 – 6.

TAPE

One of the first storage media used with mainframe computers was tape. **Tape** is a magnetically coated ribbon of plastic capable of storing large amounts of data and information at a low cost. Tape no longer is used as a primary method of storage. Instead, business and home users utilize tape most often for long-term storage and backup.

Comparable to a tape recorder, a **tape drive** reads and writes data and information on a tape. Although older computers used reel-to-reel tape drives, today's tape drives use tape cartridges. A *tape cartridge* is a small, rectangular, plastic housing for tape (Figure 7-28). Tape cartridges that contain quarter-inch-wide tape are slightly larger than audiocassette tapes. Business and home users sometimes back up personal computer hard disks to tape. Transfer rates of tape drives range from 1.25 MBps to 6 MBps.

Some personal computers have external tape units. Others have the tape drive built into the system unit. On larger computers, tape cartridges are mounted in a separate cabinet called a *tape library*.

Tape storage requires *sequential access*, which refers to reading or writing data consecutively. As with a music tape, you must forward or rewind the tape to a specific point to access a specific piece of data. For example, to access item W requires passing through points A through V sequentially.

Floppy disks, Zip disks, hard disks, CDs, and DVDs all use direct access. *Direct access*, also called *random access*, means that the device can locate a particular data item or file immediately, without having to move consecutively through items stored in front of the desired data item or file. When writing or reading specific data, direct access is much faster than sequential access.

WEB LINK 7-9

Tape

For more information, visit scsite.com/dc2006/ch7/weblink and then click Tape.

FIGURE 7-28 A tape drive and a tape cartridge.

PC CARDs

As discussed in Chapter 4, a **PC Card** is a thin, credit-card-sized device that fits into a PC Card slot. Different types and sizes of PC Cards add storage, additional memory, fax/modem, networking, sound, and other capabilities to a desktop or notebook computer. PC Cards commonly are used in notebook computers (Figure 7-29).

Originally, PC Cards were called PCMCIA cards. Three kinds of PC Cards are available: Type I, Type II, and Type III (Figure 7-30). The only difference in size among the three types is their thickness. Some digital cameras use a Type II or Type III PC Card to store photographs. PC Cards that house a hard disk have storage capacities up to 5 GB. The advantage of a PC Card for storage is portability. You easily can transport large amounts of data, instructions, and information from one computer to another using a Type II or Type III PC Card.

FIGURE 7-29 A PC Card in a notebook computer.

PC CARDS

Category	Thickness	Use
Type I	3.3 mm	RAM, SRAM, flash memory
Type II	5.0 mm	Modem, LAN, SCSI, sound, TV tuner, hard disk, or other storage
Type III	10.5 mm	Rotating storage such as a hard disk

FIGURE 7-30 Various uses of PC Cards.

MINIATURE MOBILE STORAGE MEDIA

Miniature mobile storage media allow mobile users easily to transport digital images, music, or documents to and from computers and other devices (Figure 7-31). Many desktop computers, notebook computers, Tablet PCs, PDAs, smart phones, digital cameras, and music players have built-in slots or ports to read from and write on miniature mobile storage media. For computers or devices without built-in slots, users insert the media in separate peripherals such as a card reader/writer, which typically plugs in a USB port, or a device such as a *digital photo viewer*, which connects to a television port for on-screen picture viewing. The following sections discuss the widely used miniature storage media: flash memory cards, USB flash drives, and smart cards.

FIGURE 7-31 Many types of computers and devices use miniature mobile storage media.

Flash Memory Cards

Previously, this chapter discussed miniature hard disks (magnetic media) and mini discs (optical media). Flash memory cards, by contrast, are a type of *solid-state media*, which means they consist entirely of electronic components and contain no moving parts. Common types of flash memory cards include *CompactFlash* (*CF*), *SmartMedia*, *Secure Digital* (*SD*), *xD Picture Card*, and *Memory Stick*. The table in Figure 7-32 compares storage capacities and uses of these media.

Depending on the device, manufacturers claim miniature mobile storage media can last from 10 to 100 years. Transfer rates range from about 1 MBps to 10 MBps or more, depending on the device. Flash memory cards are quite expensive compared to other storage media.

For example, the cost of a 2 GB CompactFlash card is three times that of a 120 GB hard disk.

To view, edit, or print images and information stored on miniature mobile storage media, you transfer the contents to your desktop computer or other device such as a digital photo viewer. Some printers have slots to read PC Cards and flash memory cards. If your computer or printer does not have a built-in slot, you can purchase a *card reader/writer*, which is a device that reads and writes data, instructions, and information stored on PC Cards or flash memory cards. Card reader/writers usually connect to the USB port, FireWire port, or parallel port on the system unit. The type of card you have will determine the type of card reader/writer needed. Figure 7-33 shows how one type of flash memory card works with a card reader/writer.

WEB LINK 7-10

Flash Memory Cards

For more information, visit scsite.com/ dc2006/ch7/weblink and then click Flash Memory Cards.

VARIOUS FLASH MEMORY CARDS

Media Name	Storage Capacity	Use
CompactFlash 	32 MB to 4 GB	Digital cameras, PDAs, smart phones, photo printers, music players, notebook computers, desktop computers
SmartMedia 	32 MB to 128 MB	Digital cameras, PDAs, smart phones, photo printers, music players
Secure Digital 	64 MB to 1 GB	Digital cameras, digital video cameras, PDAs, smart phones, photo printers, music players
xD Picture Card 	64 MB to 512 MB	Digital cameras, photo printers
Memory Stick 	256 MB to 2 GB	Digital cameras, digital video cameras, PDAs, photo printers, smart phones, notebook computers

FIGURE 7-32 A variety of flash memory cards.

FIGURE 7-33 HOW ONE TYPE OF FLASH MEMORY CARD WORKS

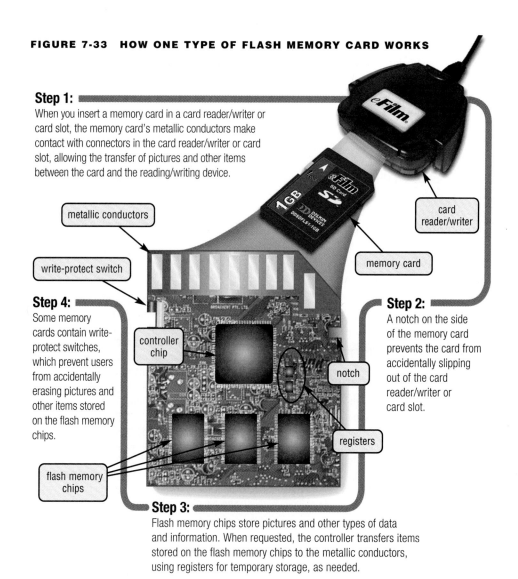

Step 1:
When you insert a memory card in a card reader/writer or card slot, the memory card's metallic conductors make contact with connectors in the card reader/writer or card slot, allowing the transfer of pictures and other items between the card and the reading/writing device.

metallic conductors

write-protect switch

Step 4:
Some memory cards contain write-protect switches, which prevent users from accidentally erasing pictures and other items stored on the flash memory chips.

controller chip

flash memory chips

card reader/writer

memory card

notch

registers

Step 2:
A notch on the side of the memory card prevents the card from accidentally slipping out of the card reader/writer or card slot.

Step 3:
Flash memory chips store pictures and other types of data and information. When requested, the controller transfers items stored on the flash memory chips to the metallic conductors, using registers for temporary storage, as needed.

USB Flash Drives

A **USB flash drive**, sometimes called a *pen drive*, is a flash memory storage device that plugs in a USB port on a computer or mobile device (Figure 7-34). USB flash drives are convenient for mobile users because they are small and lightweight enough to be transported on a keychain or in a pocket. Current USB flash drives have data transfer rates of about 12 MBps and storage capacities up to 4 GB.

Experts predict that USB flash drives will become the mobile user's primary portable storage device, eventually making the floppy disk obsolete because they have much greater storage capacities and are much more convenient to carry.

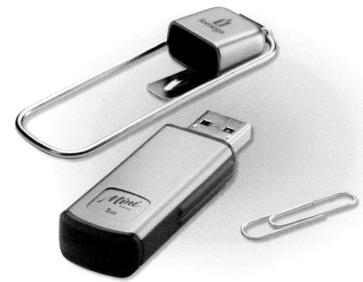

FIGURE 7-34 A USB flash drive.

Smart Cards

A **smart card**, which is similar in size to a credit card or ATM card, stores data on a thin microprocessor embedded in the card. Smart cards contain a processor and have input, process, output, and storage capabilities. When you insert the smart card in a specialized card reader, the information on the smart card is read and, if necessary, updated (Figure 7-35).

Uses of smart cards include storing medical records, vaccination data, and other health-care and identification information; tracking information such as customer purchases or employee attendance; storing a prepaid amount of money; and authenticating users such as for Internet purchases. Read At Issue 7-3 for a related discussion.

FAQ 7-9

Are some credit cards smart cards?

Yes. More than 60 million people around the world have a smart Visa card, which contains a microchip filled with their personal information. Credit card smart cards offer the consumer the convenience of using the card to make purchases in stores and online. For more information, visit scsite.com/dc2006/ch7/faq and then click Credit Card Smart Cards.

AT ISSUE 7-3

Should the World Become a Cashless Society?

Do you toss your loose change in a jar with the hopes of making a special purchase with the savings someday? Futurists predict that this practice may one day go the way of making purchases with silver and gold. Some forecasters say that the world is moving toward a cashless society. One form of payment that could end the need for cash is the smart card, which can store a dollar amount on a thin microprocessor and update the amount whenever a transaction is made. Advocates claim that smart cards would eliminate muggings and robberies, make it difficult to purchase illegal goods, and reduce taxes by identifying tax cheats. Smart cards already are common in Europe, but many Americans cite privacy concerns as reasons to avoid them. In a recent survey, most Americans said that they would not use a smart card even if privacy was guaranteed. A cash purchase usually is anonymous. Yet, a smart card purchase preserves a record of the transaction that could become available to other merchants, advertisers, government agencies, or hackers. Considering the advantages and disadvantages, should the world become a cashless society? Why or why not? Would you be comfortable using a smart card instead of cash? Why?

WEB LINK 7-11

Smart Cards

For more information, visit scsite.com/ dc2006/ch7/weblink and then click Smart Cards.

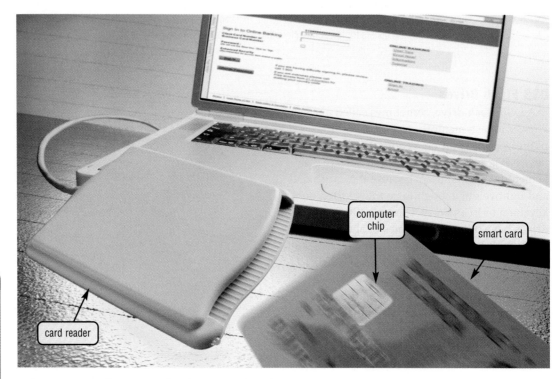

FIGURE 7-35 A smart card and smart card reader.

MICROFILM AND MICROFICHE

Microfilm and microfiche store microscopic images of documents on roll or sheet film. **Microfilm** is a 100- to 215-foot roll of film. **Microfiche** is a small sheet of film, usually about 4 inches by 6 inches. A *computer output microfilm recorder* is the device that records the images on the film. The stored images are so small that you can read them only with a microfilm or microfiche reader (Figure 7-36).

Applications of microfilm and microfiche are widespread. Libraries use these media to store back issues of newspapers, magazines, and genealogy records. Large organizations use microfilm and microfiche to archive inactive files. Banks use them to store transactions and canceled checks. The U.S. Army uses them to store personnel records.

The use of microfilm and microfiche provides a number of advantages. They greatly reduce the amount of paper firms must handle. They are inexpensive and have the longest life of any storage media (Figure 7-37).

ENTERPRISE STORAGE

A large business, commonly referred to as an enterprise, has hundreds or thousands of employees in offices across the country or around the world. Enterprises use computers and computer networks to manage and store huge volumes of data and information about customers, suppliers, and employees.

To meet their large-scale needs, enterprises use special hardware geared for heavy use, maximum availability, and maximum efficiency. One or more servers on the network have the sole purpose of providing storage to connected users. For high-speed storage access, entire networks are dedicated exclusively to connecting devices that provide storage to other servers. In an enterprise, some storage systems can provide more than 185 terabytes (trillion bytes) of storage capacity. CD-ROM servers and DVD-ROM servers hold hundreds of CD-ROMs or DVD-ROMs.

An enterprise's storage needs usually grow daily. Thus, the storage solutions an enterprise chooses must be able to store its data and information requirements today and tomorrow. Read At Issue 7-4 for a related discussion.

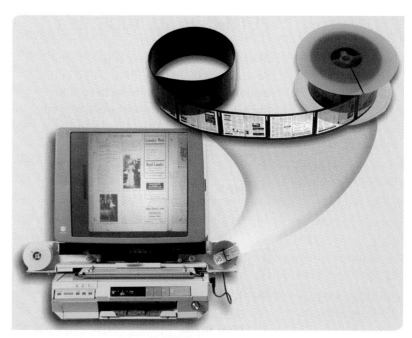

FIGURE 7-36 Images on microfilm can be read only with a microfilm reader.

MEDIA LIFE EXPECTANCIES (when using high-quality media)

Media Type	Guaranteed Life Expectancy	Potential Life Expectancy
Magnetic disks	3 to 5 years	20 to 30 years
Optical discs	5 to 10 years	50 to 100 years
Microfilm	100 years	500 years

FIGURE 7-37 Microfilm is the medium with the longest life.

 AT ISSUE 7-4

Who Is Looking at Your Medical Records?

A medical transcriber based in Pakistan and hired by a U.S. medical center threatened to post private medical records to the Internet if she was not paid more. With the widespread use of computers and an explosion in data storage capacity around the world, private information, such as medical records, requires increased diligence by companies, governments, and individuals to maintain this privacy. Updates to the Health Insurance Portability and Accountability Act (HIPAA) effective in 2003 set rigorous standards for medical record privacy. The law, however, still leaves much of your medical information at risk. The law does not cover financial records, education records, or employment records — each of which may contain medical information about you. Your medical information also may be examined by insurance companies, government agencies, the Medical Information Bureau (MIB), employers, and the courts. You also inadvertently may pass on medical information to direct marketers when you participate in informal health screenings or surveys. Some people have found that discussing medical conditions via Internet chat rooms or newsgroups has resulted in unwanted attention, and they later regret the disclosures. You can limit the amount of information available about you by discussing confidentiality with your medical providers and by requesting additional restrictions when you sign waivers to release your medical records, such as when applying for a job or applying for insurance. Should more limits be placed on what other people can do with your medical information? Why or why not? What are the advantages of increased access to medical records? What are the disadvantages?

PUTTING IT ALL TOGETHER

Many factors influence the type of storage devices you should use: the amount of data, instructions, and information to be stored; the hardware and software in use; and the desired cost. The table in Figure 7-38 outlines several suggested storage devices for various types of computer users.

CATEGORIES OF USERS

User	Typical Storage Devices
HOME 	• 80 GB hard disk • Online storage • CD or DVD drive • Card reader/writer • USB flash drive and/or 3.5-inch floppy disk drive
SMALL OFFICE/ HOME OFFICE	• 750 MB Zip drive • 120 GB hard disk • Online storage • CD or DVD drive • External hard disk for backup • USB flash drive and/or 3.5-inch floppy disk drive
MOBILE 	• 80 GB hard disk • Online storage • CD or DVD drive • Card reader/writer • Portable hard disk for backup • USB flash drive, and/or 2 GB PC Card hard disk, and/or 3.5-inch floppy disk drive
POWER 	• CD or DVD drive • 300 GB hard disk • Online storage • Portable hard disk for backup • USB flash drive and/or 3.5-inch floppy disk drive

LARGE BUSINESS 	• Desktop Computer
	  - 160 GB hard disk
	  - CD or DVD drive
	  - Smart card reader
	  - Tape drive
	  - USB flash drive and/or 3.5-inch floppy disk drive
	• Server or Mainframe
	  - Network storage server
	  - 40 TB hard disk system
	  - CD-ROM or DVD-ROM server
	  - Microfilm or microfiche

FIGURE 7-38 Recommended storage devices for various users.

Test your knowledge of pages 374 through 380 in Quiz Yourself 7-3.

QUIZ YOURSELF 7-3

Instructions: Find the true statement below. Then, rewrite the remaining false statements so they are true.

1. A smart card stores data on a thin magnetic stripe embedded in the card.

2. A USB flash drive is a flash memory storage device that plugs in a parallel port on a computer or mobile device.

3. Flash memory cards are a type of magnetic media, which means they consist entirely of electronic components and contain no moving parts.

4. Microfilm and microfiche have the shortest life of any storage media.

5. Tape storage requires direct access, which refers to reading or writing data consecutively.

6. The only difference in size among Type I, Type II, and Type III PC Cards is their thickness.

Quiz Yourself Online: To further check your knowledge of tape, PC Cards, miniature mobile storage media, and microfilm and microfiche, visit scsite.com/dc2006/ch7/quiz and then click Objectives 7 – 9.

CHAPTER SUMMARY

Storage holds data, instructions, and information, which includes pictures, music, and videos, for future use. Users depend on storage devices to provide access to their storage media for years and decades to come. Read At Issue 7-5 for a discussion about the future of storage.

This chapter identified and discussed various storage media and storage devices. Storage media covered included floppy disks, Zip disks, internal hard disks, portable hard disks, CD-ROMs, recordable CDs, rewritable CDs, DVD-ROMs, recordable DVDs, rewritable DVDs, tape, PC Cards, flash memory cards, USB flash drives, smart cards, and microfilm and microfiche.

AT ISSUE 7-5

Will Digital Data Last Forever?

Up to 75 percent of today's data was born digital and never existed on paper. Historical data from hundreds or thousands of years ago still exists because it was written down. Although written documents can be read hundreds of years after they are created, rapid changes in computer technology can make digital records almost inaccessible in just one decade. For most computer users, hardware changes have made data stored on once-popular 5.25-inch floppy disks, or on the 8-inch floppy disks used in the early '70s, unavailable today. Loss of data on aging CDs and DVDs threatens the stored photo and video memories of countless families. Software changes also take a toll. One computer expert claims that trying to read material written with an obsolete word processing program is like trying to interpret Egyptian hieroglyphics without the Rosetta stone. Pennsylvania State University recently admitted that almost 3,000 student and school files could not be accessed due to lost or outdated software. Is the potential unavailability of digital data a problem? Why or why not? What can be done to keep today's digital information available in the future?

CAREER CORNER

Computer Technician

The demand for computer technicians is growing in every organization and industry. For many, this is the entry point for a career in the computer/information technology field. The responsibilities of a *computer technician*, also called a computer service technician, include a variety of duties. Most companies that employ someone with this title expect the technician to have basic across-the-board knowledge of concepts in the computer electronics field. Some of the tasks are hardware repair and installation; software installation, upgrade, and configuration; and troubleshooting client and/or server problems. Because the computer field is changing rapidly, technicians must work to remain abreast of current technology and become aware of future developments. Computer technicians generally work with a variety of users, which requires expert people skills, especially the ability to work with groups of non-technical users.

Most entry-level computer technicians possess the *A+ certification*. This certification attests that a computer technician has demonstrated knowledge of core hardware and operating system technology including installation, configuration, diagnosing, preventive maintenance and basic networking that meets industry standards and has at least six months of experience in the field. The Electronics Technicians Association also provides a Computer Service Technician (CST) certification program.

Because this is an entry-level position, the pay scale is not as high as other more demanding and skilled positions. Individuals can expect an average annual starting salary of around $28,000 to $42,000. Companies pay more for computer technicians with experience and certification. For more information, visit scsite.com/dc2006/ch7/careers and then click Computer Technician.

High-Tech Talk

DISK FORMATTING AND FILE SYSTEMS

Formatting a disk can be compared to starting a library. Before any books can be put in place, you must install the bookshelves and a catalog system. Similarly, a disk must have a file system set up to make it ready to receive data. This is true of many different storage media — including floppy disks, hard disks, removable hard disks, and CDs and DVDs — all of which must be formatted, to allow a way to organize and find files saved on the disk.

This discussion focuses on the formatting process required to take a hard disk from its newly manufactured state to a fully functional storage medium. Three main steps are involved in the process of formatting a hard disk: (1) low-level (physical) formatting, (2) partitioning, and (3) high-level (logical) formatting.

A hard disk must be formatted physically before it can be formatted logically. The hard disk manufacturer usually performs a hard disk's physical formatting, or *low-level formatting*. A hard drive physically formats a hard disk by writing a pattern of 1s and 0s on the surface of the disk. The 1s and 0s act as small electronic markers, which divide the hard disk platter into its basic physical elements: tracks, sectors, and cylinders.

These elements define the way data is written on and read from the disk physically. As the read/write head moves over the spinning disks, it reads the electronic markers that define the tracks, sectors, and cylinders to determine where it is in relation to the data on the disk's surface.

Once a hard disk has been formatted physically, it can be partitioned. *Partitioning* is the process of dividing the hard disk into regions called partitions. Each partition occupies a group of adjacent cylinders. Partitioning allows you to organize a hard disk into segments and lets you run multiple operating systems on a single computer. You also can keep the entire hard disk as one partition. After a disk partition has been formatted, it is referred to as a *volume*.

After a hard disk has been formatted physically and partitioned, it must be formatted logically. Logical formatting, known as *high-level formatting*, places a file system on the disk. A *file system* allows an operating system, such as Windows XP or Linux, to use the space available on a hard disk to store and retrieve files. The operating system uses the file system to store information about the disk's directory, or folder, structure.

The file system also defines the size of the clusters used to store data on the hard disk. A cluster, or *block*, is made up of two or more sectors on a single track on a hard disk. A cluster is the minimum unit the operating system uses to store information. Even if a file has a size of 1 byte, a cluster as large as 64 KB might be used to store the file on large drives. The number of sectors and tracks and, therefore, the number of clusters that a drive can create on a disk's surface determine the capacity of the disk.

While creating the file system during logical formatting, the drive creates a special table in the disk's first sector, sector 0. This table stores entries that the operating system uses to locate files on a disk. Each entry in the table takes up a certain number of bits, which is why file systems often are referred to as 12-bit, 16-bit, or 32-bit. The content of each entry consists of a whole number, which identifies one or more clusters where the file is stored.

Depending on the operating system used to format the disk, the file system can be one of several types, as shown in the table in Figure 7-39. Whatever file system is used, the file system is the interface between the operating system and drives. For more information, visit scsite.com/dc2006/ch7/tech and then click Disk Formatting.

File System	Description	Key Features
FAT (also called FAT12 and FAT16)	The standard file system for DOS and Windows. Because of its widespread use, FAT also is accessible by most other operating systems.	• FAT12 is used for floppy disk drives and very small hard disks (up to 16 MB) • FAT16 is used for small to moderate-sized hard disk volumes (up to 2 GB)
VFAT (Virtual FAT)	A newer protected-mode version of the FAT file system, introduced with Windows 95.	• Supports long file names up to 255 characters • Faster than FAT because the computer can read files at least 32 bits at a time
FAT32	A 32-bit version of FAT, introduced with Windows 95.	• Same key features as VFAT • Used for medium-sized to very large hard disk volumes (up to 2 terabytes)
NTFS (NT File System)	The 32-bit file system currently used for Windows NT, Windows 2000, and Windows XP.	• 32- or 64-bit entries in file system table • Fully recoverable file system, designed to restore consistency after a system crash • Used for medium-sized to very large hard disk volumes (up to 16 billion GB)

FIGURE 7-39   Comparison of various file systems.

Companies on the Cutting Edge

MAXTOR
INFORMATION STORAGE SUPPLIER

Computer-industry experts predict that 68 million hard disks will be needed for consumer electronic applications by 2007. *Maxtor* is poised to meet the demands of this rapidly growing market with its hard disks manufactured for the digital video recorder/personal video recorder (DVR/PVR) market.

Maxtor is a leading manufacturer of hard disks and storage solutions for desktop computers, high-performance servers, and consumer electronics, including digital video recorders and game consoles. Its wholly owned subsidiary, MMC Technology, manufactures nearly 50 million disks each year.

Maxtor's 250 GB OneTouch external hard disk was honored as the "Product of the Year" by *CRN* magazine and received a World Class Award from *PC World* in 2004. For more information, visit scsite.com/dc2006/ch7/companies and then click Maxtor.

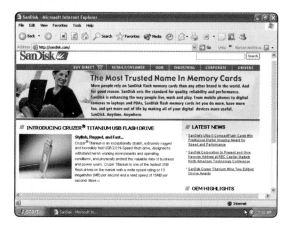

SANDISK CORPORATION
WORLD'S LARGEST FLASH MEMORY CARD SUPPLIER

The next time you buy milk at the grocery store or shampoo at the drug store, you might want to purchase a flash memory card for your digital camera, too. *SanDisk Corporation* products can be found in more than 10,000 retail stores across the United States, including Rite Aid and Kmart.

With retail sales of flash memory cards soaring, SanDisk executives believe consumers buy multiple flash memory cards to store their digital photographs in much the same manner as they formerly stored film negatives in shoe boxes. They also prefer to take a separate flash memory card to digital photo processing centers, which produce high-quality prints.

SanDisk also designs, develops, and manufactures USB flash drives and readers, Memory Sticks, and Wi-Fi cards. For more information, visit scsite.com/dc2006/ch7/companies and then click SanDisk.

Technology Trailblazers

AL SHUGART
STORAGE EXPERT

Al Shugart enjoys fixing broken items and developing new technology. The day after receiving his bachelor's degree in 1951, he went to work at IBM to repair broken machines. IBM then promoted him to supervisor of the product development team that developed the first removable rigid read/write disk drive.

He left IBM in 1969 and went to work as vice president of product development for Memorex. In 1973, he started Shugart Associates, a pioneer in the manufacture of floppy disks. Six years later, he and some associates founded Seagate Technology, Inc., which is a leader in designing and manufacturing storage products.

Today he serves as president, chairman, and CEO of Al Shugart International, a venture capital firm in California. For more information, visit scsite.com/dc2006/ch7/people and then click Al Shugart.

MARK DEAN
IBM INVENTOR

The next generation of IBM's hardware and software might be the work of *Mark Dean*. As vice president of IBM's Almaden Research Center lab in California, Dean is responsible for developing innovative products.

His designs are used in more than 40 million personal computers manufactured each year. He has more than 40 patents or patents pending, including four of the original seven for the architecture of the original personal computer.

Dean joined IBM in 1979 after graduating at the top of his class at the University of Tennessee. Dean earned his Ph.D. degree at Stanford, and he headed a team at IBM that invented the first CMOS microprocessor to operate at 1 gigahertz (1,000 MHz). For more information, visit scsite.com/dc2006/ch7/people and then click Mark Dean.

Quizzes and Learning Games

Computer Genius
Crossword Puzzle
DC Track and Field
Practice Test
Quiz Yourself
Wheel of Terms
You're Hired!

Exercises

Case Studies
► Chapter Review
Checkpoint
Key Terms
Learn How To
Learn It Online
Web Research

Beyond the Book

Career Corner
Companies
FAQs
High-Tech Talk
Looking Ahead
Making Use of the Web
Trailblazers
Web Links

Features

Chapter Forum
Install Computer
Lab Exercises
Maintain Computer
Tech News
Timeline 2006

Chapter Review

The Chapter Review section summarizes the concepts presented in this chapter. To listen to the audio version of this Chapter Review, visit scsite.com/dc2006/ch7/review. To obtain help from other students regarding any subject in this chapter, visit scsite.com/dc2006/ch7/forum and post your thoughts or questions.

① How Are Storage Devices Different from Storage Media? A **storage medium** (media is the plural) is the physical material on which a computer keeps data, instructions, and information, which includes pictures, music, and videos. The number of bytes (characters) a storage medium can hold is its **capacity**. A **storage device** is the computer hardware that records and/or retrieves items to and from storage media. **Writing** is the process of transferring items from memory to a storage medium, and **reading** is the process of transferring these items from a storage medium into memory.

② What Are the Characteristics of Magnetic Disks? *Magnetic disks* use magnetic particles to store data, instructions, and information on a disk's surface. Before any data can be read from or written on a magnetic disk, the disk must be formatted. **Formatting** is the process of dividing the disk into *tracks* and *sectors*. Three types of magnetic disks are floppy disks, Zip disks, and hard disks.

③ What Are the Differences between Floppy Disks and Zip Disks? A **floppy disk** is a portable, inexpensive storage medium that consists of a thin, circular, flexible plastic Mylar film with a magnetic coating enclosed in a square-shaped plastic shell. A standard floppy disk can store up to 500 double-spaced pages of text, several digital photographs, or a small audio file. A **floppy disk drive** is a device that reads from and writes on a floppy disk. A **Zip disk** is a type of portable magnetic media that can store up to 500 times more than a standard floppy disk. These large capacities make it easy to transport many files or large items. Another popular use of Zip disks is to make a **backup**, or duplicate, of a file, program, or disk that you can use in case the original is lost, damaged, or destroyed.

④ What Are the Characteristics of a Hard Disk? A **hard disk**, also called a *hard disk drive*, is a storage device that contains one or more inflexible, circular platters that store data, instructions, and information. A *platter* is made of aluminum, glass, or ceramic and is coated with a material that allows items to be recorded magnetically on its surface. Each platter has two read/write heads, one for each side. The location of a *read/write head* often is referred to by its *cylinder,* which is the vertical section of a track that passes through all platters. While the computer is running, the platters rotate at 5,400 to 15,000 *revolutions per minute (rpm)*, which allows nearly instant access to all tracks and sectors on the platters. The spinning creates a cushion of air between the platters and the read/write heads. A *head crash* occurs when a read/write head touches the surface of a platter, usually resulting in a loss of data.

Visit scsite.com/dc2006/ch7/quiz or click the Quiz Yourself button. Click Objectives 1 – 4.

⑤ What Are the Characteristics of Optical Discs? An *optical disc* is a type of storage media that consists of a flat, round, portable disc made of metal, plastic, and lacquer that is written and read by a laser. Optical discs, which primarily store software, data, digital photographs, movies, and music, contain microscopic pits (indentations) and lands (flat areas) in their middle layer. Optical discs commonly store items in a single track that spirals from the center

Chapter Review

of the disc to its edge. Like a hard disk, the single track is divided into evenly sized sectors. Common optical discs used today are CD-ROM, CD-R, CD-RW, DVD-ROM, DVD-R, DVD+R, DVD-RW, DVD+RW, and DVD+RAM.

(6) How Are CD-ROMs, Recordable CDs, Rewritable CDs, DVD-ROMs, Recordable DVDs, and Rewritable DVDs Different? A **CD-ROM**, or *compact disc read-only memory*, is a type of optical disc that uses laser technology to store items. A typical CD-ROM holds from 650 MB to 1 GB of data, instructions, and information. Users can read the contents of standard CD-ROMs but cannot erase or modify their contents. A **CD-R** (*compact disc-recordable*) is a *multisession* disc on which users can record their own items. Each part of a CD-R can be written on only one time, and the disc's contents cannot be erased. A **CD-RW** (*compact disc-rewritable*) is an erasable disc that can be written on multiple times. A **DVD-ROM** (*digital versatile disc-ROM* or *digital video disc-ROM*) is an extremely high capacity optical disk capable of storing from 4.7 GB to 17 GB. Not only is the storage capacity of a DVD-ROM greater than that of a CD-ROM, a DVD-ROM's quality also far surpasses that of a CD-ROM. **DVD-RW** and **DVD+RW** discs are a recordable version of DVD that allows users to erase and record more than 1,000 times. **DVD+RAM** allows users to erase and record on a DVD+RAM more than 100,000 times.

> connect
> Visit scsite.com/dc2006/ch7/quiz or click the Quiz Yourself button. Click Objectives 5 – 6.

(7) How Is Tape Used? **Tape** is a magnetically coated ribbon of plastic capable of storing large amounts of data and information at a low cost. A **tape drive** reads and writes data and information on tape. Businesses and home users sometimes back up personal computer hard disks on tape.

(8) What Are PC Cards and Other Types of Miniature Mobile Storage Media? A **PC Card** is a thin, credit-card-sized device that fits into a PC Card slot to add storage or other capabilities to a desktop or notebook computer. Many desktop and notebook computers, Tablet PCs, PDAs, smart phones, digital cameras, and music players have built-in slots or ports for miniature mobile storage media. Common types of miniature mobile storage media include flash memory cards, USB flash drives, and smart cards. A **USB flash drive** is a flash memory storage device that plugs in a port on a computer or mobile device. Common flash memory cards include *CompactFlash* (*CF*), *SmartMedia*, *Secure Digital* (*SD*), *xD Picture Card*, and *Memory Stick*. A **smart card**, which is similar in size to a credit or ATM card, stores data on a thin microprocessor embedded in the card.

(9) How Are Microfilm and Microfiche Used? **Microfilm** is a 100- to 215-foot roll of film. **Microfiche** is a small sheet of film, usually about 4 inches by 6 inches. Libraries use microfilm and microfiche to store back issues of newspapers, magazines, and records; large organizations use them to archive inactive files; banks use them to store transactions and canceled checks; and the U.S. Army uses them to store personnel records.

> connect
> Visit scsite.com/dc2006/ch7/quiz or click the Quiz Yourself button. Click Objectives 7 – 9.

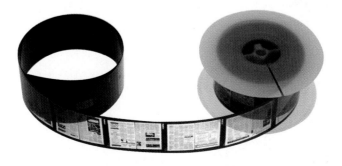

Quizzes and Learning Games

Computer Genius
Crossword Puzzle
DC Track and Field
Practice Test
Quiz Yourself
Wheel of Terms
You're Hired!

Exercises

Case Studies
Chapter Review
Checkpoint
▷ Key Terms
Learn How To
Learn It Online
Web Research

Beyond the Book

Career Corner
Companies
FAQs
High-Tech Talk
Looking Ahead
Making Use of the Web
Trailblazers
Web Links

Features

Chapter Forum
Install Computer
Lab Exercises
Maintain Computer
Tech News
Timeline 2006

Key Terms

You should know the Primary Terms and be familiar with the Secondary Terms. Use the list below to help focus your study. To further enhance your understanding of the Key Terms in this chapter, visit scsite.com/dc2006/ch7/terms. See an example of and a definition for each term, and access current and additional information about the term from the Web.

Primary Terms
(shown in bold-black characters in the chapter)

access time (357)
backup (359)
capacity (356)
CD-R (371)
CD-R drive (371)
CD-ROM (369)
CD-ROM drive (369)
CD-RW (371)
CD-RW drive (371)
DVD+RAM (373)
DVD+RW (373)
DVD-ROM (372)
DVD-ROM drive (372)
DVD-RW (373)
external hard disk (364)
floppy disk (358)
floppy disk drive (358)
formatting (357)
hard disk (360)
microfiche (379)
microfilm (379)
online storage (365)
PC Card (374)
Picture CD (370)
reading (356)

removable hard disk (364)
smart card (378)
storage device (356)
storage medium (355)
tape (374)
tape drive (374)
USB flash drive (377)
write-protect notch (359)
writing (356)
Zip disk (359)
Zip drive (359)

Secondary Terms
(shown in italic characters in the chapter)

allocation unit (357)
Blu-Ray disc (372)
burning (371)
card reader/writer (376)
CD recorder (371)
cluster (357)
compact disc read-only memory (369)
compact disc-recordable (371)
compact disc-rewritable (371)
CompactFlash (CF) (376)
computer output microfilm recorder (379)
cylinder (362)
density (358)
digital photo viewer (375)
digital versatile disc-read-only memory (372)
digital video disc-read-only memory (372)
direct access (374)
disk cache (363)
disk controller (364)
diskette (358)
DVD+R (373)
DVD-R (373)
EIDE (Enhanced Integrated Drive Electronics) (365)
external floppy disk drive (358)

fixed disk (360)
form factor (361)
hard disk drive (360)
head crash (362)
HD (358)
jewel box (368)
KBps (357)
magnetic disks (357)
MBps (357)
Memory Stick (376)
mini discs (366)
multisession (371)
optical disc (366)
pen drive (377)
platter (361)
portable (358)
random access (374)
read/write head (361)
revolutions per minute (rpm) (362)
ripping (371)
SATA (Serial Advanced Technology Attachment) (364)
SCSI (365)
secondary storage (355)
sectors (357)
Secure Digital (SD) (376)
sequential access (374)
single-session disc (369)
SmartMedia (376)
solid-state media (376)
storage (354)
tape cartridge (374)
tape library (374)
track (357)
transfer rate (357)
xD Picture Card (376)

SHELLY CASHMAN SERIES. **387**

Select a chapter: 1 2 3 4 5 6 7 8 9 10 11 12 13 14 15

Checkpoint

Use the Checkpoint exercises to check your knowledge level of the chapter. The Beyond the Book exercises will help broaden your understanding of the concepts presented in this chapter. To complete the Checkpoint exercises interactively, visit scsite.com/dc2006/ch7/check.

 Label the Figure Identify the storage media.

a. CD or DVD
b. external hard disk
c. tape
d. miniature hard disk
e. Zip disk
f. flash memory card
g. USB flash drive

 True/False Mark T for True and F for False. (See page numbers in parentheses.)

_____ 1. Every computer uses storage to hold software, specifically, system software and application software. (354)

_____ 2. A storage medium is the physical material on which a computer keeps data, instructions, and information. (355)

_____ 3. Reading is the process of transferring data, instructions, and information from memory to a storage medium. (356)

_____ 4. A sector is a narrow recording band that forms a full circle on the surface of the disk. (357)

_____ 5. A cluster can hold data from only one file. (357)

_____ 6. A typical hard disk contains only one platter. (361)

_____ 7. An external hard disk is a separate, free-standing hard disk that connects with a cable to a port on the system unit. (364)

_____ 8. SCSI, the newest type of hard disk interface, uses serial signals to transfer data, instructions, and information. (364)

_____ 9. All optical discs are double-sided. (366)

_____ 10. Optical discs commonly store items in a single track. (367)

_____ 11. When writing or reading specific data, direct access is much slower than sequential access. (374)

_____ 12. A smart card sometimes is called a pen drive. (377)

Quizzes and Learning Games

Computer Genius
Crossword Puzzle
DC Track and Field
Practice Test
Quiz Yourself
Wheel of Terms
You're Hired!

Exercises

Case Studies
Chapter Review
▶ Checkpoint
Key Terms
Learn How To
Learn It Online
Web Research

Beyond the Book

Career Corner
Companies
FAQs
High-Tech Talk
Looking Ahead
Making Use of the Web
Trailblazers
Web Links

Features

Chapter Forum
Install Computer
Lab Exercises
Maintain Computer
Tech News
Timeline 2006

Checkpoint

 Multiple Choice Select the best answer. (See page numbers in parentheses.)

1. Examples of storage media include all of the following, except _____. (355)
   a. monitors and printers
   b. floppy disks and hard disks
   c. CDs and DVDs
   d. tape and PC Cards

2. A _____ is a narrow recording band that forms a full circle on the surface of a floppy disk. (357)
   a. track
   b. cluster
   c. shutter
   d. sector

3. On a floppy disk, if the write-protect notch is closed, the floppy disk drive _____. (359)
   a. can write on but cannot read from the floppy disk
   b. can write on and read from the floppy disk
   c. can read from but cannot write on the floppy disk
   d. cannot read from or write on the floppy disk

4. A Zip disk can store from _____ of data. (359)
   a. 10 MB to 75 MB
   b. 100 MB to 750 MB
   c. 10 GB to 75 GB
   d. 100 GB to 750 GB

5. If a computer contains only one hard disk drive, the operating system designates it as drive _____. (360)
   a. A   b. B
   c. C   d. D

6. Portable hard disks offer all of the following advantages over internal hard disks, except _____. (364)
   a. they can transport a large number of files
   b. they can add storage space to a notebook computer
   c. they can be shared with multiple computers
   d. they can transfer data at much faster rates

7. Users store data and information on online storage to _____. (365)
   a. save time by storing large files instantaneously
   b. allow others to access files
   c. store offsite backups of data
   d. all of the above

8. When a laser light reads CDs or DVDs, a land _____. (367)
   a. causes light to reflect, which is read as binary digit 0
   b. causes light to reflect, which is read as binary digit 1
   c. absorbs the light, which is read as binary digit 0
   d. absorbs the light, which is read as binary digit 1

9. All of the following are guidelines for the proper care of optical discs except _____. (368)
   a. do not expose the disc to extreme temperatures
   b. do not stack discs
   c. do not hold a disc by its edges
   d. do not eat, smoke, or drink near a disc

10. The process of writing on an optical disc is called _____. (371)
    a. formatting   b. ripping
    c. burning   d. reading

11. A storage technique that a DVD-ROM uses to achieve a higher storage capacity than a CD-ROM is _____. (372)
    a. making the disc denser by packing the pits closer together
    b. using two layers of pits
    c. using both sides of the disc
    d. all of the above

12. _____ storage requires sequential access. (374)
    a. Hard disk
    b. Tape
    c. Floppy disk
    d. CD

13. Which of the following is not true of flash memory cards? (376)
    a. they are a type of solid-state media
    b. they contain moving parts
    c. they can last 10 to 100 years
    d. they are quite expensive compared to other storage media

14. Microfilm and microfiche _____. (379)
    a. greatly increase the amount of paper firms must handle
    b. are expensive
    c. have the longest life of any storage media
    d. all of the above

Checkpoint

Matching

Match the terms with their definitions. (See page numbers in parentheses.)

_____ 1. transfer rate (357)

_____ 2. cluster (357)

_____ 3. form factor (361)

_____ 4. cylinder (362)

_____ 5. disk cache (363)

_____ 6. disk controller (364)

_____ 7. Picture CD (370)

_____ 8. Blu-Ray disc (372)

_____ 9. tape library (374)

_____ 10. pen drive (377)

a. memory chips that the processor uses to store frequently accessed items

b. speed with which data, instructions, and information move to and from a device

c. flash memory storage device that plugs in a USB port

d. piece of metal on a floppy disk that slides to expose the surface of the disk

e. smallest unit of disk space that stores data and information

f. size of hard disk platters on desktop computers

g. compact disc that stores digital versions of a single roll of film

h. newer, expensive type of DVD with storage capacities of 27 GB

i. vertical section of a track that passes through all platters

j. separate cabinet on which tape cartridges are mounted on larger computers

k. special-purpose chip and electronic circuits that control the transfer of items to and from the system bus

Short Answer

Write a brief answer to each of the following questions.

1. What is access time? _____ Why is the average hard disk access time faster than the average floppy disk access time? _____

2. What is density? _____ What is the purpose of a write-protect notch, and how does it work? _____

3. Why is a hard disk inside the system unit sometimes called a fixed disk? _____ What are the different types of portable hard disks? _____

4. How is a single-session disc different from a multisession disc? _____ How is a CD-R different from a CD-RW? _____

5. What are PC Cards, and why are they used? _____ What is the advantage of a PC Card? _____

Beyond the Book

Read the following book elements, learn more about each using the Web, and then write a brief report.

1. At Issue — Does Music Sharing Harm CD Sales? (369), Is It Ethical to Copy CDs or DVDs? (371), Should the World Become a Cashless Society? (378), Who Is Looking at Your Medical Records? (379), or Will Digital Data Last Forever? (381)

2. Career Corner — Computer Technician (381)

3. Companies on the Cutting Edge — Maxtor or SanDisk Corporation (383)

4. FAQs (360, 363, 365, 368, 370, 371, 372, 373, 378)

5. High-Tech Talk — Disk Formatting and File Systems (382)

6. Looking Ahead — Heat Increases Disk Capacity (360) or Paper Discs Offer Increased Capacity (373)

7. Making Use of the Web — Shopping (123)

8. Picture Yourself Working with Mobile Storage Media (352)

9. Technology Trailblazers — Al Shugart or Mark Dean (383)

10. Web Links (359, 364, 365, 369, 370, 371, 373, 374, 376, 378)

Quizzes and Learning Games

Computer Genius
Crossword Puzzle
DC Track and Field
Practice Test
Quiz Yourself
Wheel of Terms
You're Hired!

Exercises

Case Studies
Chapter Review
Checkpoint
Key Terms
Learn How To
▶ Learn It Online
Web Research

Beyond the Book

Career Corner
Companies
FAQs
High-Tech Talk
Looking Ahead
Making Use of the Web
Trailblazers
Web Links

Features

Chapter Forum
Install Computer
Lab Exercises
Maintain Computer
Tech News
Timeline 2006

Learn It Online

Use the Learn It Online exercises to reinforce your understanding of the chapter concepts. To access the Learn It Online exercises, visit scsite.com/dc2006/ch7/learn.

(1) At the Movies — Repair Your CD Scratches

To view the Repair Your CD Scratches movie, click the number 1 button. Locate your video and click the corresponding High-Speed or Dial-Up link, depending on your Internet connection. Watch the movie and then complete the exercise by answering the questions that follow. Just because your favorite CD has a few scratches is no reason to discard it. A few options are available to help you keep those scratched CDs playing smoothly longer. How does resurfacing work to restore your scratched CDs? What common household product can be used to repair a CD?

(2) At the Movies — Online Data Storage Options

To view the Online Data Storage Options movie, click the number 2 button. Locate your video and click the corresponding High-Speed or Dial-Up link, depending on your Internet connection. Watch the movie and then complete the exercise by answering the question that follows. Online data storage broadens your options for file sharing and frees up space on your personal computer. If you store files online, anyone who knows the password can access them from anywhere in the world. Several free storage systems offer a moderate amount of space; however, if you need more you can sign up and pay for additional storage for as little as $15 a month. What are some of the most important reasons for backing up your files online?

(3) Student Edition Labs — Maintaining a Hard Drive

Click the number 3 button. When the Student Edition Labs menu appears, click *Maintaining a Hard Drive* to begin. A new browser window will open. Follow the on-screen instructions to complete the Lab. When finished, click the Exit button. If required, submit your results to your instructor.

(4) Student Edition Labs — Managing Files and Folders

Click the number 4 button. When the Student Edition Labs menu appears, click *Managing Files and Folders* to begin. A new browser window will open. Follow the on-screen instructions to complete the Lab. When finished, click the Exit button. If required, submit your results to your instructor.

(5) Practice Test

Click the number 5 button. Answer each question. When completed, enter your name and click the Grade Test button to submit the quiz for grading. Make a note of any missed questions. If required, submit your results to your instructor.

(6) Who Wants To Be a Computer Genius²?

Click the number 6 button to find out if you are a computer genius. Directions about how to play the game will be displayed. When you are ready to play, click the Play button. Submit your score to your instructor.

(7) Wheel of Terms

Click the number 7 button to reinforce important terms you learned in this chapter by playing the Shelly Cashman Series version of this popular game. Directions about how to play the game will be displayed. When you are ready to play, click the Play button. Submit your score to your instructor.

Learn It Online

8 DC Track and Field

Click the number 8 button to use what you have learned in this chapter to compete against other students in three track and field events. Directions about how to play the game will be displayed. When you are ready to play, click the start first event button. If required, submit your score to your instructor.

9 You're Hired!

Click the number 9 button to use what you have learned in this chapter to embark on the path to a career in computers. Directions about how to play the game will be displayed. When you are ready to play, click the begin game button. If required, submit your score to your instructor.

10 Crossword Puzzle Challenge

Click the number 10 button. Complete the puzzle to reinforce skills you learned in this chapter. Directions about how to play the game will be displayed. When you are ready to play, click the Submit button. Submit the completed puzzle to your instructor.

11 Lab Exercises

Click the number 11 button. When the Lab Exercises menu appears, click the exercise assigned by your instructor. A new browser window will open. Follow the on-screen instructions to complete the exercise. When finished, click the Exit button. If required, submit your results to your instructor.

12 In the News

Hitachi sells a small disk drive, about the size of a quarter, which is capable of storing up to 4 GB of information, as much as 50 CDs. The drive is used in devices such as PDAs or digital cameras. What other storage devices are on the horizon? Click the number 12 button and read a news article about a new or improved storage device. What is the device? Who manufactures it? How is the storage device better than, or different from, earlier devices? How will the device be used? Why?

13 Chapter Discussion Forum

Select an objective from this chapter on page 353 about which you would like more information. Click the number 13 button and post a short message listing a meaningful message title accompanied by one or more questions concerning the selected objective. In two days, return to the threaded discussion by clicking the number 13 button. Submit to your instructor your original message and at least one response to your message.

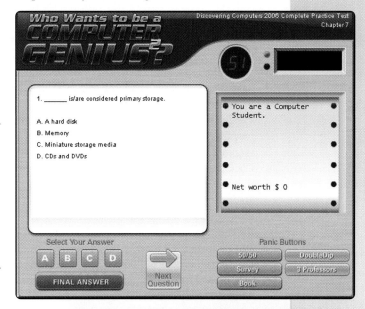

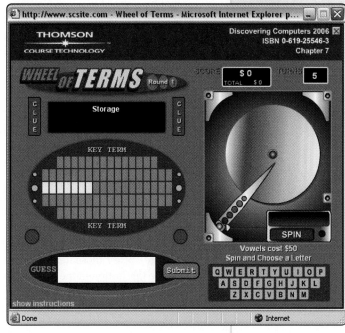

Quizzes and Learning Games

Computer Genius
Crossword Puzzle
DC Track and Field
Practice Test
Quiz Yourself
Wheel of Terms
You're Hired!

Exercises

Case Studies
Chapter Review
Checkpoint
Key Terms
▷ Learn How To
Learn It Online
Web Research

Beyond the Book

Career Corner
Companies
FAQs
High-Tech Talk
Looking Ahead
Making Use of the Web
Trailblazers
Web Links

Features

Chapter Forum
Install Computer
Lab Exercises
Maintain Computer
Tech News
Timeline 2006

 Learn How To

Use the Learn How To activities to learn fundamental skills when using a computer and accompanying technology. Complete the exercises and submit them to your instructor. Visit scsite.com/dc2006/ch7/howto to obtain more information pertaining to each activity.

LEARN HOW TO 1: Maintain a Hard Disk

A computer's hard disk is used for the majority of storage requirements. It is important, therefore, to ensure that each hard disk on a computer is operating at peak efficiency.

Three tasks that maximize disk operations are detecting and repairing disk errors by using the Check Disk utility program; removing unused or unnecessary files and folders by using the Disk Cleanup utility program; and, consolidating files and folders into contiguous storage areas using the Disk Defragmenter utility program.

A. Check Disk

To detect and repair disk errors using the Check Disk utility program, complete the following steps:
1. Click the Start button on the Windows taskbar and then click My Computer on the Start menu.
2. When the My Computer window opens, right-click the hard disk icon for drive C (or any other hard disk you want to select), and then click Properties on the shortcut menu.
3. In the Properties dialog box, if necessary click the Tools tab.
   The Tools sheet contains buttons to start the Check Disk program, the Defragment program, and the Backup program (Figure 7-40).
4. Click the Check Now button. *The Check Disk dialog box is displayed.*
5. To do a complete scan of the disk and correct any errors that are found, place a check mark in the Scan for and attempt recovery for bad sectors check box, and then click the Start button. Four phases of checking the disk will occur. While the checking is in progress, the disk being checked cannot be used for any purpose whatsoever; furthermore, once it has started, the process cannot be stopped.
6. When the four phases are complete (this may take more than one-half hour, depending on the size of the hard disk and how many corrections must occur), a dialog box is displayed with the message, Disk Check Complete. Click the OK button in the dialog box.

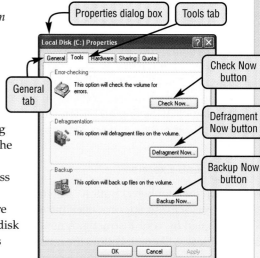

FIGURE 7-40

B. Cleanup Disk

After checking the disk, your next step can be to clean up the disk by removing any programs and data that are not required for the computer. To do so, complete the following steps:
1. Click the General tab (Figure 7-40) in the disk drive Properties dialog box to display the General sheet.
2. Click the Disk Cleanup button in the General sheet.
3. The Disk Cleanup dialog box is displayed and contains a message that indicates the amount of space that can be freed up is being calculated.
4. After the calculation is complete, the Disk Cleanup dialog box specifies the amount of space that can be freed up and the files to delete, some of which are checked automatically (Figure 7-41 on the next page). Select those items from which you wish to delete files.
5. Click the OK button in the Disk Cleanup dialog box.
6. A dialog box asks if you are sure you want to perform these actions. Click the Yes button. The Disk Cleanup dialog box illustrates the progress of the cleanup. When the cleanup is complete, the dialog box closes.

Learn How To

C. Defragment Disk

The next step in disk maintenance is to **defragment** all the files on the disk. When a file is stored on disk, the data in the file sometimes is stored contiguously, and other times is stored in a noncontiguous manner. When a file is stored in a noncontiguous manner, it can take significantly longer to find and retrieve data from the file. Therefore, one of the more useful utilities to speed up disk operations is the defragmentation program, which combines all files so that no files are stored in a noncontiguous manner. To use the defragmentation program, complete the following steps:

1. If necessary, click the Tools tab in the Properties dialog box for the hard disk to be defragmented.
2. Click the Defragment Now button in the Tools sheet. *The Disk Defragmenter window opens (Figure 7-42). This window displays the hard disks on the computer and shows the size and amount of free space for each disk. During defragmentation, the Estimated disk usage before defragmentation area and the Estimated disk usage after defragmentation area display the layout of the data on the disk. If you click the Analyze button, the disk will be analyzed for its data layout but defragmentation will not occur.*
3. Click the Defragment button. The defragmentation process begins. The amount of processing completed is shown on the status bar at the bottom of the window. The defragmentation process can consume more than one hour in some cases. You can pause or stop the operation at any time by clicking the Pause or Stop button in the Disk Defragmenter window.
4. When the process is complete, the Disk Defragmenter dialog box displays the message, Defragmentation is complete for (C:). Click the View Report button to see a complete report about the hard disk.
5. Click the Close button to close the Disk Defragmenter dialog box.

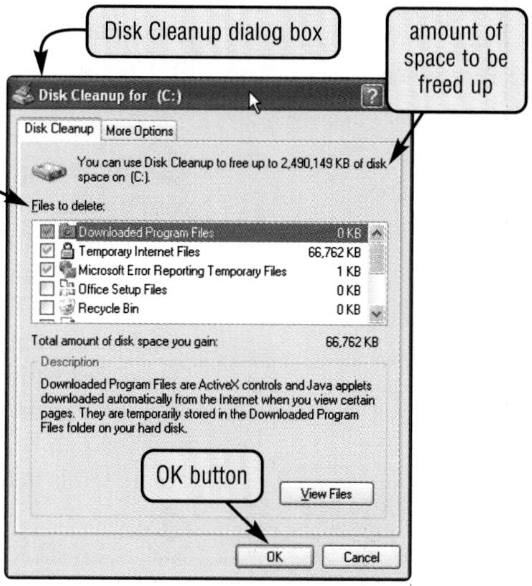

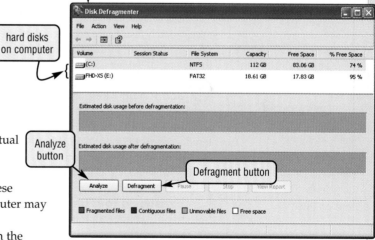

FIGURE 7-41

FIGURE 7-42

Exercise

Caution: The exercises for this chapter that require the actual disk maintenance are optional. If you are performing these exercises on a computer that is not your own, obtain explicit permission to complete these exercises. Keep in mind that these exercises can require significant computer time and the computer may be unusable during this time.

1. Display the Properties dialog box for a hard disk found on the computer. Display the Tools sheet. Click the Check Now button and then place a check mark in the Scan for and attempt recovery for bad sectors check box. Click the Start button. How long did it take to complete the check of the hard disk? Were any errors discovered and corrected? Submit your answers to your instructor.
2. Display the Properties dialog box for a hard disk found on the computer. Display the General sheet. What is the capacity of the hard disk? How much space is used? How much free space is available? Click the Disk Cleanup button. How much space can be freed up if you use the Disk Cleanup program? Click the OK button to clean up the disk. How long did it take to perform the disk cleanup? Submit your answers to your instructor.
3. Display the Properties dialog box for a hard disk found on the computer. Display the Tools sheet. Click the Defragment Now button. In the Disk Defragmenter window, click the Analyze button. Does the hard disk need to be defragmented? Click the View Report button. How many files are stored on the disk? What is the average size of the files stored on the disk? If necessary, click the Defragment button in the Analysis Report window. How long did defragmentation require? Submit your answers to your instructor.

Quizzes and Learning Games

Computer Genius
Crossword Puzzle
DC Track and Field
Practice Test
Quiz Yourself
Wheel of Terms
You're Hired!

Exercises

Case Studies
Chapter Review
Checkpoint
Key Terms
Learn How To
Learn It Online
▶ Web Research

Beyond the Book

Career Corner
Companies
FAQs
High-Tech Talk
Looking Ahead
Making Use of the Web
Trailblazers
Web Links

Features

Chapter Forum
Install Computer
Lab Exercises
Maintain Computer
Tech News
Timeline 2006

Web Research

Use the Internet-based Web Research exercises to broaden your understanding of the concepts presented in this chapter. Visit scsite.com/dc2006/ch7/research to obtain more information pertaining to each exercise. To discuss any of the Web Research exercises in this chapter with other students, post your thoughts or questions at scsite.com/dc2006/ch7/forum.

① Scavenger Hunt   Use one of the search engines listed in Figure 2-10 in Chapter 2 on page 78 or your own favorite search engine to find the answers to the questions that follow. Copy and paste the Web address from the Web page where you found the answer. Some questions may have more than one answer. If required, submit your answers to your instructor. (1) What are the three different laser powers used in a CD-rewritable recorder? How do two of the powers affect the recording layer? During writing, to what temperature does the laser beam selectively heat areas of the recording material? (2) Daniel Bernoulli's principle has many practical applications. Describe two of them, and then explain how Iomega used the principle in its Bernoulli drive. (3) What is the Red Book standard? (4) What is the function of a hard disk's actuator? (5) What is areal density? What unit of measurement is used to describe this density?

② Search Sleuth   Many computer users search the World Wide Web by typing words in the search text box, and often they are overwhelmed when the search engine returns thousands of possible Web sites. You can narrow your search by typing quotation marks around phrases and by adding words that give details about the phrase. Go.com is a Web portal developed by the Walt Disney Internet Group. It features a search engine, the latest ABC news and ESPN sports stories, stock market quotes, weather forecasts, maps, and games. Visit this Web site and then use your word processing program to answer the following questions. Then, if required, submit your answers to your instructor. (1) Click the Search for text box at the top of the page. Type hard disk in the box. How many search results are returned that are not sponsored links? (2) Type "hard disk" in the Search for box. How many search results are returned that are not sponsored links? (3) Scroll down to the bottom of the page and then type "access time" in the text box to search within the "hard disk" results and narrow your results. How many search results are returned that are not sponsored links? (4) Review the Hard Disks section of your textbook for additional words that give details about this device. Perform two more searches with these words. Review your search results and then write a 50-word summary of your findings.

③ Journaling   Respond to your readings in this chapter by writing at least one page about your reactions, evaluations, and reflections about using storage devices. For example, have you used USB flash drives, smart cards, or Zip disks? How do you care for your floppy disks? Have you ever encountered a corrupt floppy disk? What is the storage capacity of your school, office, or home computer's hard disk? Do you clean your CDs and DVDs? You also can write about the new terms you learned by reading this chapter. If required, submit your journal to your instructor.

④ Expanding Your Understanding   Bill Gates, Microsoft's chief software architect, considers holographic storage an impressive new storage system. The holographic process can store more than 100 movie, photo, and music files on one disc holding one terabyte of data. View Web sites to learn more about holographic storage. What factors are driving the rush to develop this system? How are images stored? What companies are researching and developing this technology? Write a report summarizing your findings, focusing on the possible uses of this storage medium and current engineering efforts to commercialize the technology. If required, submit your report to your instructor.

⑤ Ethics in Action   The United States Federal Bureau of Investigation uses a controversial program to monitor and store the e-mail and Internet activity of suspected criminals. Originally called Carnivore, the surveillance program has been renamed DCS1000. The program is designed to track the activities of potential terrorists, spies, drug traffickers, and organized crime ring members. FBI agents must obtain a court order to monitor an individual, but privacy advocates claim the software tracks people not covered under the court order. View online sites that provide information about DCS1000 or Carnivore, including HowStuffWorks (computer.howstuffworks.com/carnivore.htm). Write a report summarizing your findings, and include a table of links to Web sites that provide additional details. If required, submit your report to your instructor.

Case Studies

Use the Case Studies to apply the concepts presented in the chapter to real-world situations. Visit scsite.com/dc2006/ch7/cases to obtain more information pertaining to each exercise. To discuss the Case Studies in this chapter with other students, visit scsite.com/dc2006/ch7/forum and post your thoughts or questions.

CASE STUDY 1 — Class Discussion   The owner of the tractor repair shop where you are employed as a part-time office manager is tired of continually upgrading the company's computer system. After attending a seminar on how small businesses can make use of the Internet, she asked you to look into the feasibility of using <u>online storage</u> (also called an Internet hard disk, rather than purchasing additional storage for the company's computer. Write a brief report outlining the advantages and disadvantages of using online storage. Compare Yahoo! and Google's online storage offerings. Which company offers the best arrangement? Why? Be prepared to discuss your recommendations in class.

CASE STUDY 2 — Class Discussion   PJ Cement Company has hired you as an IT consultant. The company plans to purchase 15 computers for use in the accounting department. The first task assigned to you by the president of the company is to recommend the number and types of <u>CD and DVD drives</u> to include with the computers they plan to purchase. They want to use CDs and/or DVDs to share data and information between employees and to back up critical files. Create a brief memo that includes a table summarizing the advantages and disadvantages of using CD-ROM, recordable CD, rewritable CD, DVD-ROM, recordable DVD, and rewritable DVD. Include in the table both the approximate cost of the drive and the media. Be prepared to discuss your findings in class.

CASE STUDY 3 — Research   An old aphorism claims, "You never can have too much money." Many computer users support a similar maxim, "You never can have too much storage." Your manager at MJ National Bank where you are employed as an analyst, however, is tired of buying more hardware to meet the bank's storage needs. She wants you to investigate alternative ways to improve <u>storage capacity</u>. Use the Web and/or print media to find out more about hard disk partitions and data compression as a means of increasing storage capacity. How do partitions increase the capacity of hard disks? What kind of data compression is most suitable for communications devices? What are the most well known data compression algorithms? How can compression ratios of different algorithms be compared? What are some formats for data compression archives? Prepare a report and/or PowerPoint presentation and share your findings with your class.

CASE STUDY 4 — Research   A major national retail chain, where you are employed as a technology buyer, has grown enormously over the past few years. The growth has required the company to triple its storage capacity each year to keep pace with its expanding business. Your manager, who is up for promotion, wants to impress his boss by expanding the storage capacity by tenfold this year while staying under the budget earmarked for storage improvements. He has asked you to look into the latest cutting-edge <u>storage technologies</u>, such as holographic and heat-assisted storage. Use the Web and/or print media to develop a features/benefits breakdown that compares the latest storage technologies to the more traditional hard disk technology. What do the different technologies entail? Are they available today? If not, when? What are their costs? Prepare a report and/or PowerPoint presentation summarizing your findings.

CASE STUDY 5 — Team Challenge   Your team has been assigned to do IT research for a new local magazine-subscription telemarketing company that is about to open for business. The company's business plan calls for 150 telemarketers to make a minimum of 100 calls a day. If a telemarketer does not meet the minimum number of calls, then he or she is required to finish the calls from home. The company plans to buy used computers for each telemarketer to use at home. The company also has to decide on the type of <u>storage device</u> to provide the telemarketers so that when they have to make calls from home, they have a way to take the necessary data home with them. Senior management has narrowed down their choice to three storage devices — floppy disks, USB flash drives, or Zip drives. Form a three-member team and have each team member choose a different storage device. Using the Web and/or print media, have each team member determine the advantages and disadvantages of their chosen device. Include such features as capacity, access time, durability of media, and cost. As a team, merge your findings into a team report and/or PowerPoint presentation and share your recommendations with your class.

CHAPTER EIGHT

Operating Systems and Utility Programs

Picture Yourself Getting a Virus through E-Mail

With a break between classes, you and some classmates sit outside and enjoy the nice weather. Everyone decides to exchange e-mail addresses and phone numbers, so you can communicate while away from school.

Later that night at home, you notice a classmate has sent you a picture via e-mail. As soon as you open the picture, your computer freezes. You click the mouse button. Nothing happens. You press a key on the keyboard. The computer beeps. You click the mouse again. Still no response. You restart the computer. The Windows XP desktop never appears.

At that moment, your smart phone rings. A panicked friend says his computer stopped working as soon as he opened that picture. Realizing the picture file probably had a virus, you call a technical support hotline. After explaining the situation, the support technician asks you several questions, and you answer: Did you have antivirus software installed on the computer? "No." Were the operating system's firewall settings enabled? "I don't know." Do you have a backup of the computer's hard disk? "No, I haven't learned how to burn CDs to make backups." Can you find the computer's recovery disc? "Yes, it's right here." The bad news is you lost *everything* on your computer and had to reinstall Windows XP — the good news is your computer is functional again. Now, you need to protect your computer from future infections.

Read Chapter 8 to learn about antivirus software, firewall settings, backups, and recovery discs, and discover features of most operating systems and utility programs.

OBJECTIVES

After completing this chapter, you will be able to:

1. Identify the types of system software

2. Summarize the startup process on a personal computer

3. Describe the functions of an operating system

4. Discuss ways that some operating systems help administrators control a network and administer security

5. Explain the purpose of the utilities included with most operating systems

6. Summarize the features of several stand-alone operating systems

7. Identify various network operating systems

8. Identify devices that use several embedded operating systems

9. Explain the purpose of several stand-alone utility programs

CONTENTS

SYSTEM SOFTWARE

OPERATING SYSTEMS

OPERATING SYSTEM FUNCTIONS
Starting a Computer
Providing a User Interface
Managing Programs
Managing Memory
Scheduling Jobs
Configuring Devices
Establishing an Internet Connection
Monitoring Performance
Providing File Management and Other Utilities
Controlling a Network
Administering Security

OPERATING SYSTEM UTILITY PROGRAMS
File Manager
Image Viewer
Personal Firewall
Uninstaller
Disk Scanner
Disk Defragmenter
Diagnostic Utility
Backup Utility
Screen Saver

TYPES OF OPERATING SYSTEMS

STAND-ALONE OPERATING SYSTEMS
DOS
Windows XP
Mac OS X
UNIX
Linux

NETWORK OPERATING SYSTEMS
NetWare
Windows Server 2003
UNIX
Linux
Solaris

EMBEDDED OPERATING SYSTEMS
Windows CE
Windows Mobile
Palm OS
Embedded Linux
Symbian OS

STAND-ALONE UTILITY PROGRAMS
Antivirus Programs
Spyware Removers
Internet Filters
File Compression
File Conversion
CD/DVD Burning
Personal Computer Maintenance

CHAPTER SUMMARY

HIGH-TECH TALK
Windows XP: A Useful Way to Complete a Wide Range of Tasks

COMPANIES ON THE CUTTING EDGE
Red Hat
Symbian

TECHNOLOGY TRAILBLAZERS
Alan Kay
Linus Torvalds

SYSTEM SOFTWARE

When you purchase a personal computer, it usually has system software installed on its hard disk. **System software** consists of the programs that control or maintain the operations of the computer and its devices. System software serves as the interface between the user, the application software, and the computer's hardware.

Two types of system software are operating systems and utility programs. Several types of utility programs are provided with an operating system. Other utility programs are available stand-alone, that is, as programs separate from the operating system. This chapter discusses the operating system and its functions, as well as several types of utility programs for personal computers.

OPERATING SYSTEMS

An **operating system** (**OS**) is a set of programs containing instructions that coordinate all the activities among computer hardware resources. Most operating systems perform similar functions that include starting a computer, providing a user interface, managing programs, managing memory, scheduling jobs, configuring devices, establishing an Internet connection,

start the computer

administer security

operating system

control a network

provide file management and other utilities

FIGURE 8-1   Most operating systems perform the functions illustrated in this figure.

monitoring performance, and providing file management utilities. Some operating systems also allow users to control a network and administer security (Figure 8-1).

In most cases, the operating system is installed and resides on the computer's hard disk. On handheld computers and many mobile devices such as PDAs and smart phones, however, the operating system may reside on a ROM chip.

Different sizes of computers typically use different operating systems. For example, a mainframe computer does not use the same operating system as a personal computer. Even the same types of computers, such as desktop computers, may not use the same operating system. Furthermore, the application software designed for a specific operating system may not run when using another operating system. For example, PCs often use Windows XP, and iMacs use Mac OS X. When purchasing application software, you must ensure that it works with the operating system installed on your computer.

The operating system that a computer uses sometimes is called the *platform*. On purchased application software, the package identifies the required platform (operating system). A *cross-platform* program is one that runs the same on multiple operating systems.

provide a user interface

manage programs

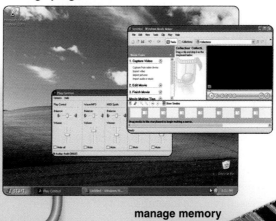

manage memory

monitor performance

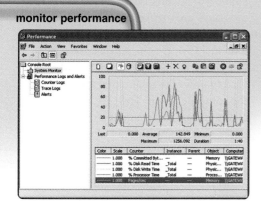

establish an Internet connection

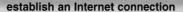

schedule jobs and configure devices

OPERATING SYSTEM FUNCTIONS

Many different operating systems exist, designed for all types of computers. Regardless of the size of the computer, however, most operating systems provide similar functions. The following sections discuss functions common to most operating systems. The operating system handles many of these functions automatically, without requiring any instructions from a user.

Starting a Computer

The process of starting or restarting a computer is called **booting**. When turning on a computer that has been powered off completely, you are performing a **cold boot**. A **warm boot**, by contrast, is the process of using the operating system to restart a computer. A warm boot properly closes any open processes and programs. With Windows XP, you can perform a warm boot by clicking the Start button on the taskbar, clicking Turn Off Computer on the Start menu, and then clicking Restart in the Turn off computer dialog box (Figure 8-2). Some computers have a reset button that when pressed restarts a computer as if it had been powered off. A reset button does not properly close open processes.

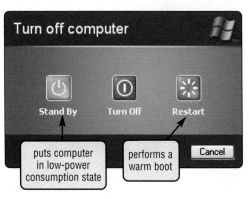

FIGURE 8-2 To reboot a running computer, click the Restart button in the Turn off computer dialog box.

When you install new software, often an on-screen prompt instructs you to restart the computer. In this case, a warm boot is appropriate. If your computer stops responding, try to restart it with a warm boot first. If it does not respond to the warm boot, then try pushing the reset button on the computer, if the computer has a reset button. As a last resort, restart the computer with a cold boot; that is, push the power button.

Each time you boot a computer, the kernel and other frequently used operating system instructions are loaded, or copied, from the hard disk (storage) into the computer's memory (RAM). The *kernel* is the core of an operating system that manages memory and devices, maintains the computer's clock, starts applications, and assigns the computer's resources, such as devices, programs, data, and information. The kernel is *memory resident*, which means it remains in memory while the computer is running. Other parts of the operating system are *nonresident*, that is, these instructions remain on the hard disk until they are needed.

When you boot a computer, a series of messages may be displayed on the screen. The actual information displayed varies depending on the make and type of the computer and the equipment installed. The boot process, however, is similar for large and small computers.

The steps in the following paragraphs explain what occurs during a cold boot on a personal computer using the Windows XP operating system. The steps in Figure 8-3 illustrate and correspond to the steps discussed in the following paragraphs.

Step 1: When you turn on the computer, the power supply sends an electrical signal to the components in the system unit.

Step 2: The charge of electricity causes the processor chip to reset itself and find the ROM chip(s) that contains the BIOS. The **BIOS** (pronounced BYE-ose), which stands for *basic input/output system*, is firmware that contains the computer's startup instructions.

Step 3: The BIOS executes a series of tests to make sure the computer hardware is connected properly and operating correctly. The tests, collectively called the *power-on self test (POST)*, check the various system components including the buses, system clock, adapter cards, RAM chips, mouse, keyboard, and drives. As the POST executes, LEDs (tiny lights) flicker on devices such as the disk drives and keyboard. Several beeps also sound, and messages are displayed on the screen.

Step 4: The POST results are compared with data in a CMOS chip. As discussed in Chapter 4, CMOS is a technology that uses battery power to retain information when the computer is off. The CMOS chip stores configuration information about the computer, such as the amount of memory; type of disk drives, keyboard, and monitor; the current date and time; and other startup information. It also detects any new devices connected to the computer. If any problems are identified, the computer may beep, display error messages, or cease operating — depending on the severity of the problem.

Step 5: If the POST completes successfully, the BIOS searches for specific operating system files called *system files*. The BIOS may look first to see if a disk in the floppy disk drive or a disc in a CD or DVD drive contain the system files. If these drives do not contain media or if the system files are not on media

in the drive, the BIOS looks in drive C (the designation usually given to the first hard disk) for the system files.

Step 6: Once located, the system files load into memory (RAM) from storage (usually the hard disk) and execute. Next, the kernel of the operating system loads into memory. Then, the operating system in memory takes control of the computer.

Step 7: The operating system loads system configuration information. In Windows XP,

WEB LINK 8-1

BIOS
For more information, visit scsite.com/dc2006/ch8/weblink and then click BIOS.

FIGURE 8-3   HOW A PC BOOTS UP

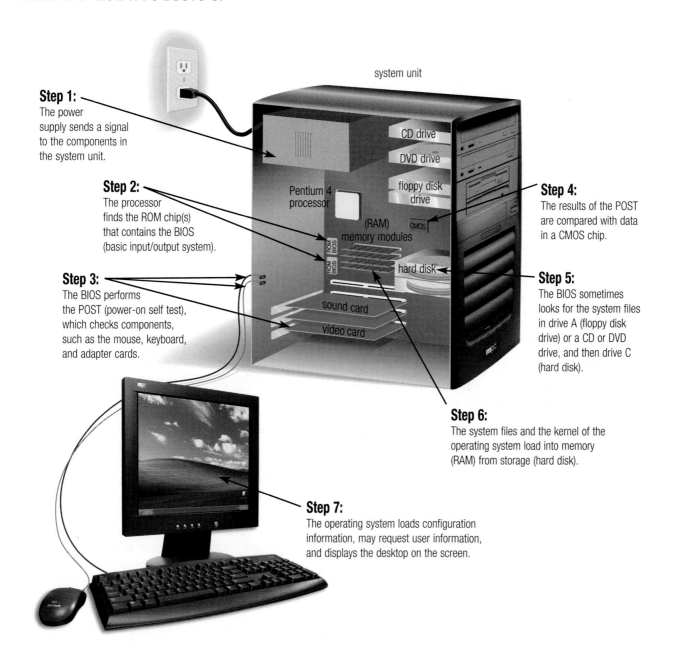

Step 1:
The power supply sends a signal to the components in the system unit.

Step 2:
The processor finds the ROM chip(s) that contains the BIOS (basic input/output system).

Step 3:
The BIOS performs the POST (power-on self test), which checks components, such as the mouse, keyboard, and adapter cards.

Step 4:
The results of the POST are compared with data in a CMOS chip.

Step 5:
The BIOS sometimes looks for the system files in drive A (floppy disk drive) or a CD or DVD drive, and then drive C (hard disk).

Step 6:
The system files and the kernel of the operating system load into memory (RAM) from storage (hard disk).

Step 7:
The operating system loads configuration information, may request user information, and displays the desktop on the screen.

system unit

CD drive
DVD drive
floppy disk drive

Pentium 4 processor

(RAM) memory modules   CMOS

ROM BIOS

hard disk

sound card

video card

the *registry* consists of several files that contain the system configuration information. Windows XP constantly accesses the registry during the computer's operation for information such as installed hardware and software devices and individual user preferences for mouse speed, passwords, and other information.

Necessary operating system files are loaded into memory. On some computers, the operating system verifies that the person attempting to use the computer is a legitimate user. Finally, the Windows XP desktop and icons are displayed on the screen. The operating system executes programs in the *Startup folder*, which contains a list of programs that open automatically when you boot the computer.

RECOVERY DISK A **boot drive** is the drive from which your personal computer boots (starts). In most cases, drive C (the hard disk) is the boot drive. Sometimes a hard disk becomes damaged and the computer cannot boot from the hard disk. In this case, you can boot from a special disk, called a **recovery disk** or a **boot disk**, that contains a few system files that will start the computer. When you purchase a computer, it usually includes a recovery disk in the form of a CD. If you do not have a recovery disk, the operating system usually provides a means to create one.

FAQ 8-1

When I am finished using the computer, can I simply turn it off?

No! You must use the operating system's shut-down procedure so various processes are closed in sequence and items in memory released properly. Depending on the computer, several shut-down options exist. The Turn Off command removes power from the computer. Restart does a warm boot. *Hibernate* saves all documents in memory and then turns off the computer. *Stand By* places the entire computer in a low-power state but does not turn it off. With Hibernate and Stand By, the next time you resume work on the computer, the desktop is restored to exactly how you left it. For more information, visit scsite.com/dc2006/ch8/faq and then click Shut-Down Options.

Providing a User Interface

You interact with software through its user interface. That is, a **user interface** controls how you enter data and instructions and how information is displayed on the screen. Three types of user interfaces are command-line, menu-driven, and graphical. Operating systems often use a combination of these interfaces to define how a user interacts with a computer.

COMMAND-LINE INTERFACE To configure devices, manage system resources, and troubleshoot network connections, network administrators and other advanced users work with a command-line interface. In a *command-line interface*, a user types commands or presses special keys on the keyboard (such as function keys or key combinations) to enter data and instructions (Figure 8-4a). Command-line interfaces often are difficult to use because they require exact spelling, grammar, and punctuation. Minor errors, such as a missing period, generate an error message. Command-line interfaces, however, give a user more control to manage detailed settings. For a technical discussion about a command-line interface, read the High-Tech Talk article on page 430.

When working with a command-line interface, the set of commands entered into the computer is called the *command language*. Programs that contain command language instructions are called *scripts*. Network administrators and Web page programmers often use scripts.

MENU-DRIVEN INTERFACE A *menu-driven interface* provides menus as a means of entering commands (Figure 8-4b). Menu-driven interfaces are easier to learn than command-line interfaces because users do not have to learn the rules of entering commands.

GRAPHICAL USER INTERFACE Most users today work with a graphical user interface. With a *graphical user interface* (*GUI*), you interact with menus and visual images such as buttons and other graphical objects to issue commands. Many current GUI operating systems incorporate features similar to those of a Web browser. The Windows XP screen shown in Figure 8-4c, for example, contains links and navigation buttons such as the Back button and the Forward button.

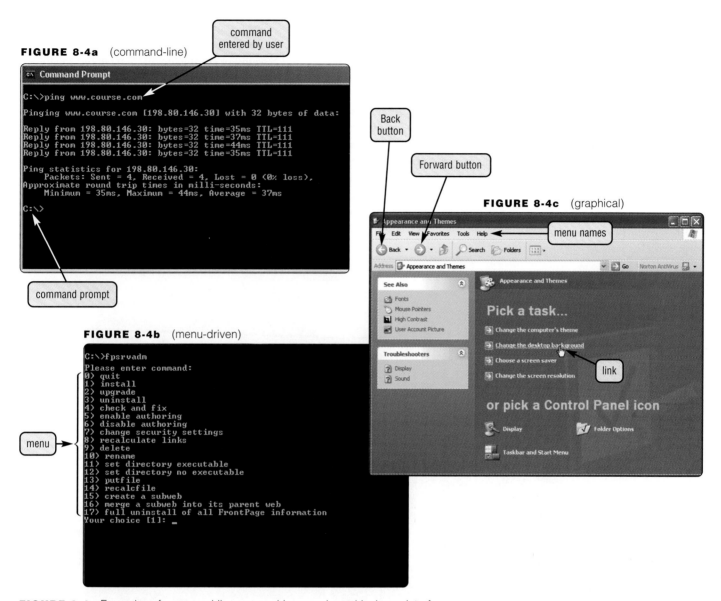

FIGURE 8-4a (command-line)

command entered by user

command prompt

Back button

Forward button

FIGURE 8-4c (graphical)

menu names

link

FIGURE 8-4b (menu-driven)

menu

FIGURE 8-4 Examples of command-line, menu-driven, and graphical user interfaces.

Managing Programs

Some operating systems support a single user and only one running program at a time. Others support thousands of users running multiple programs. How an operating system handles programs directly affects your productivity.

A *single user/single tasking* operating system allows only one user to run one program at a time. For example, if you are working in a graphics program and want to check e-mail messages, you must quit the graphics program before you can run the e-mail program. Early systems were single user/single tasking. Most of today's operating systems are multitasking. PDAs, smart phones, and other small computing

devices, however, often use a single user/single tasking operating system.

A *single user/multitasking* operating system allows a single user to work on two or more programs that reside in memory at the same time. Using the example just cited, if you are working with a single user/multitasking operating system, you do not have to quit the graphics program to run the e-mail program. Both programs can run concurrently. Users today typically run multiple programs concurrently. It is common to have an e-mail program and Web browser open at all times, while working with application programs such as word processing or graphics.

When a computer is running multiple programs concurrently, one program is in the foreground and the others are in the background. The one in the *foreground* is the active program, that is, the one you currently are using. The other programs running but not in use are in the *background*. In Figure 8-5, the PowerPoint program, which is showing a slide show, is in the foreground, and three other programs are running in the background (Paint Shop Pro, Encarta Encyclopedia, and iTunes). For example, iTunes can be playing music while you are modifying the slide show.

The foreground program typically displays on the desktop, and the background programs are partially or completely hidden behind the foreground program. You easily can switch between foreground and background programs. To make a program active (in the foreground) in Windows XP, click its program button on the taskbar. This causes the operating system to place all other programs in the background.

In addition to application programs, an operating system manages other processes. These processes include utilities or routines that provide support to other programs or hardware.

FIGURE 8-5 The foreground program, PowerPoint, is displayed on the desktop. The other programs (Paint Shop Pro, Encarta Encyclopedia, and iTunes) are in the background.

Some are memory resident. Others run as they are required. Figure 8-6 shows a list of all processes running on a Windows XP computer. The list contains the applications programs running, as well as other programs and processes.

Some operating systems use preemptive multitasking to prevent any one process from monopolizing the computer's resources. With *preemptive multitasking*, the operating system interrupts a program that is executing and passes control to another program waiting to be executed. An advantage of preemptive multitasking is the operating system regains control if one program stops operating properly.

A *multiuser* operating system enables two or more users to run programs simultaneously. Networks, midrange servers, mainframes, and supercomputers allow hundreds to thousands of users to connect at the same time, and thus are multiuser.

A *multiprocessing* operating system supports two or more processors running programs at the same time. Multiprocessing involves the coordinated processing of programs by more than one processor. Multiprocessing increases a computer's processing speed.

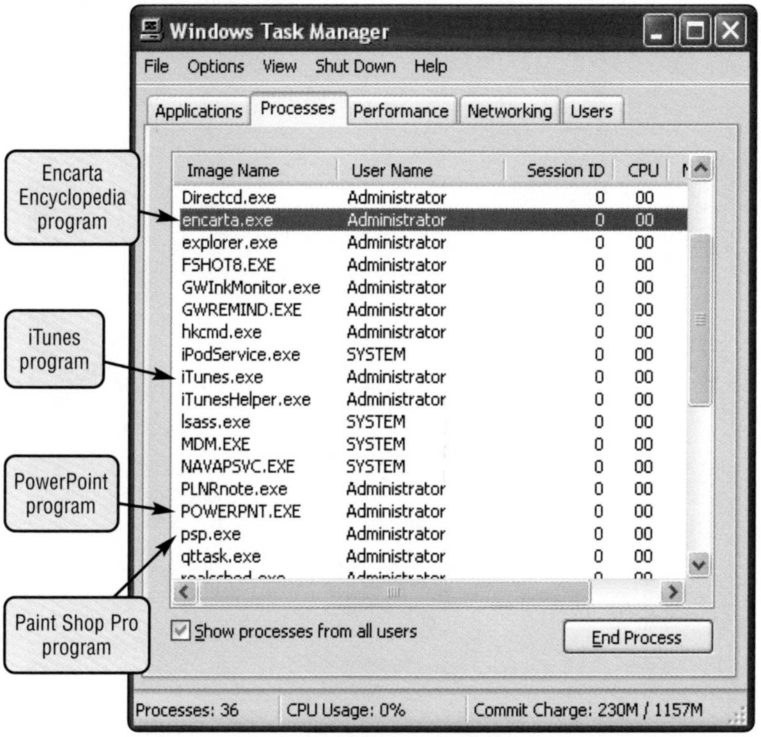

A computer with separate processors also can serve as a fault-tolerant computer. A *fault-tolerant computer* continues to operate when one of its components fails, ensuring that no data is lost. Fault-tolerant computers have duplicate components such as processors, memory, and disk drives. If any one of these components fails, the computer switches to the duplicate component and continues to operate. Airline reservation systems, communications networks, automated teller machines, and other systems that must be operational at all times use fault-tolerant computers.

Managing Memory

The purpose of **memory management** is to optimize the use of random access memory (RAM). As discussed in Chapter 4, RAM consists of one or more chips on the motherboard that hold items such as data and instructions while the processor interprets and executes them. The operating system allocates, or assigns, data and instructions to an area of memory while they are being processed. Then, it carefully monitors the contents of memory. Finally, the operating system releases these items from being monitored in memory when the processor no longer requires them.

If you have multiple programs running simultaneously, it is possible to run out of RAM. For example, assume an operating system requires 128 MB of RAM, an antivirus program — 128 MB of RAM, a Web browser — 32 MB of RAM, a business software suite — 64 MB of RAM, and a photo editing program — 128 MB of RAM. With all these programs running simultaneously, the total RAM required would be 480 MB of RAM (128 + 128 + 32 + 64 + 128). If the computer has only 256 MB of RAM, the operating system may have to use virtual memory to solve the problem.

FIGURE 8-6 An operating system manages multiple programs and processes while you use the computer.

With **virtual memory**, the operating system allocates a portion of a storage medium, usually the hard disk, to function as additional RAM (Figure 8-7). As you interact with a program, part of it may be in physical RAM, while the rest of the program is on the hard disk as virtual memory. Because virtual memory is slower than RAM, users may notice the computer slowing down while it uses virtual memory.

The area of the hard disk used for virtual memory is called a *swap file* because it swaps (exchanges) data, information, and instructions between memory and storage. A *page* is the amount of data and program instructions that can swap at a given time. The technique of swapping items between memory and storage, called *paging*, is a time-consuming process for the computer.

When an operating system spends much of its time paging, instead of executing application software, it is said to be *thrashing*. If application software, such as a Web browser, has stopped responding and the hard disk's LED blinks repeatedly, the operating system probably is thrashing.

FAQ 8-2

How can I stop a computer from thrashing?

Try to quit the program that stopped responding. If the computer does not respond and continues to thrash, do a warm boot. When the computer reboots, check whether the available hard disk space is less than 200 MB. If it is, remove unnecessary files from the hard disk and if possible uninstall seldom used programs. Defragment the hard disk (discussed later in this chapter). If thrashing continues to occur, you may need to install more RAM in the computer. For more information, visit scsite.com/dc2006/ch8/faq and then click Optimizing Memory.

Scheduling Jobs

The operating system determines the order in which jobs are processed. A **job** is an operation the processor manages. Jobs include receiving data from an input device, processing instructions, sending information to an output device, and transferring items from storage to memory and from memory to storage.

FIGURE 8-7 HOW A COMPUTER MIGHT USE VIRTUAL MEMORY

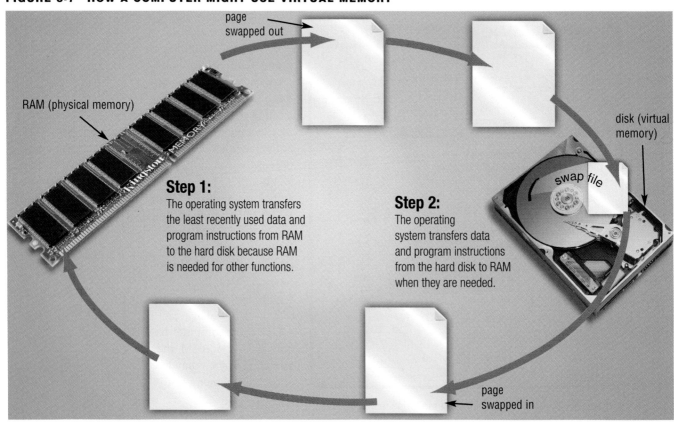

page swapped out

RAM (physical memory)

disk (virtual memory)

swap file

Step 1:
The operating system transfers the least recently used data and program instructions from RAM to the hard disk because RAM is needed for other functions.

Step 2:
The operating system transfers data and program instructions from the hard disk to RAM when they are needed.

page swapped in

A mulituser operating system does not always process jobs on a first-come, first-served basis. Sometimes, one user may have a higher priority than other users. In this case, the operating system adjusts the schedule of jobs.

Sometimes, a device already may be busy processing one job when it receives a second job. This occurs because the processor operates at a much faster rate of speed than peripheral devices. For example, if the processor sends five print jobs to a printer, the printer can print only one document at a time.

While waiting for devices to become idle, the operating system places items in buffers. A **buffer** is a segment of memory or storage in which items are placed while waiting to be transferred from an input device or to an output device.

The operating system commonly uses buffers with print jobs. This process, called **spooling**, sends print jobs to a buffer instead of sending them immediately to the printer. The buffer holds the information waiting to print while the printer prints from the buffer at its own rate of speed. By spooling print jobs to a buffer, the processor can continue interpreting and executing instructions while the printer prints. This allows users to work on the computer for other tasks while a printer is printing. Multiple print jobs line up in a **queue** (pronounced Q)

in the buffer. A program, called a *print spooler*, intercepts print jobs from the operating system and places them in the queue (Figure 8-8).

Configuring Devices

A **driver**, short for *device driver*, is a small program that tells the operating system how to communicate with a specific device. Each device on a computer, such as the mouse, keyboard, monitor, printer, card reader/writer, and scanner, has its own specialized set of commands and thus requires its own specific driver. When you boot a computer, the operating system loads each device's driver. These devices will not function without their correct drivers.

If you attach a new device to a computer, such as a printer or scanner, its driver must be installed before you can use the device. Today, many devices and operating systems support Plug and Play. As discussed in Chapter 4, **Plug and Play** means the operating system automatically configures new devices as you install them. Specifically, it assists you in the device's installation by loading the necessary drivers automatically and checking for conflicts with other devices. With Plug and Play, a user plugs in a device, turns on the computer, and then uses the device without having to configure the system manually.

WEB LINK 8-2

Plug and Play
For more information, visit scsite.com/dc2006/ch8/weblink and then click Plug and Play.

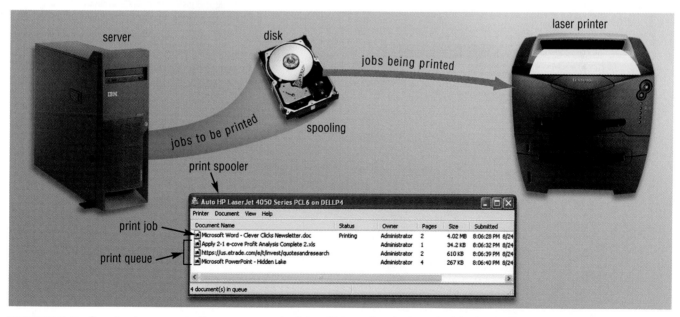

FIGURE 8-8 Spooling increases both processor and printer efficiency by placing print jobs in a buffer on disk before they are printed. This figure illustrates three jobs in the queue with one job printing.

For devices that are not Plug and Play, Windows XP provides a wizard to guide users through the installation steps. Figure 8-9 shows how to install a driver for a printer. You follow the same general steps to install drivers for any type of hardware. For many devices, the computer's operating system may include the necessary drivers. If it does not, you can install the drivers from the CD or disk provided with the purchased device.

When you attach a Plug and Play device to a computer, the operating system determines an

FIGURE 8-9 HOW TO INSTALL DRIVERS FOR NEW HARDWARE IN WINDOWS XP

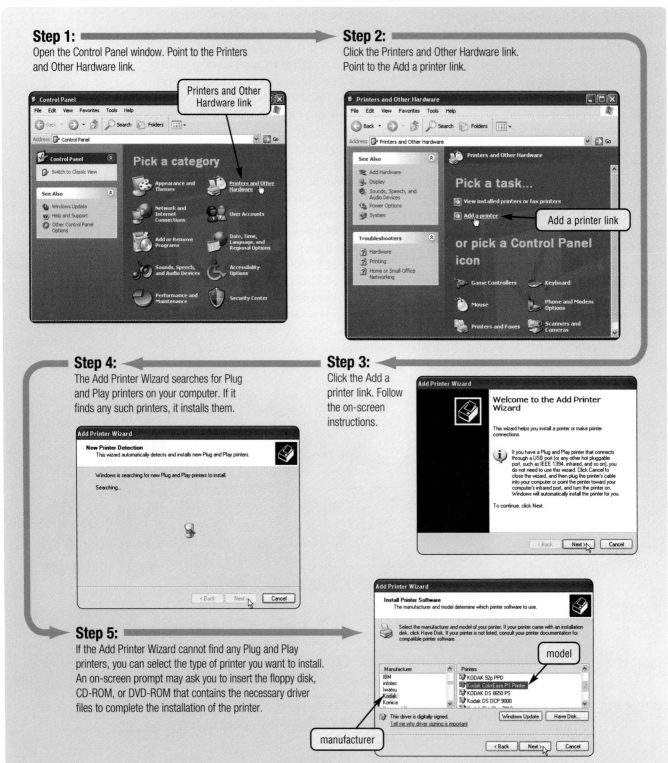

Step 1:
Open the Control Panel window. Point to the Printers and Other Hardware link.

Step 2:
Click the Printers and Other Hardware link. Point to the Add a printer link.

Step 4:
The Add Printer Wizard searches for Plug and Play printers on your computer. If it finds any such printers, it installs them.

Step 3:
Click the Add a printer link. Follow the on-screen instructions.

Step 5:
If the Add Printer Wizard cannot find any Plug and Play printers, you can select the type of printer you want to install. An on-screen prompt may ask you to insert the floppy disk, CD-ROM, or DVD-ROM that contains the necessary driver files to complete the installation of the printer.

appropriate IRQ to use. An *IRQ* (*interrupt request line*) is a communications line between a device and the processor. If the operating system uses an IRQ that already is assigned to another device, an IRQ conflict may occur and the computer may not work properly. If an IRQ conflict occurs, you will have to obtain the correct IRQ for the device. This information typically is located in the installation directions that accompany the device. Most personal computers have 16 IRQs.

FAQ 8-3

What if I do not have the driver for a device?

When reinstalling an operating system, you may have to supply a device's driver. If you do not have the original driver disk, visit the manufacturer's Web site. Most post drivers for download at no cost, or they may suggest a similar driver that will work. If you do not have Internet access, call the manufacturer and request a new disk via the postal service. For more information, visit scsite.com/dc2006/ch8/faq and then click Drivers.

Establishing an Internet Connection

Operating systems typically provide a means to establish Internet connections. For example, Windows XP includes a New Connection Wizard that guides users through the process of setting up a connection between a computer and an Internet service provider (Figure 8-10).

Some operating systems also include a Web browser and an e-mail program, enabling you to begin using the Web and communicate with others as soon as you set up the Internet connection. Some also include a built-in firewall to protect computers from unauthorized intrusions.

Monitoring Performance

Operating systems typically contain a performance monitor. A **performance monitor** is a program that assesses and reports information about various computer resources and devices (Figure 8-11). For example, users can monitor the processor, disks, memory, and network usage. A performance monitor also can check the number of reads and writes to a disk.

The information in performance reports helps users and administrators identify a problem with resources so they can try to resolve any problems. If a computer is running extremely slow, for example, the performance monitor may determine that the computer's memory is being used to its maximum. Thus, you might consider installing additional memory in the computer.

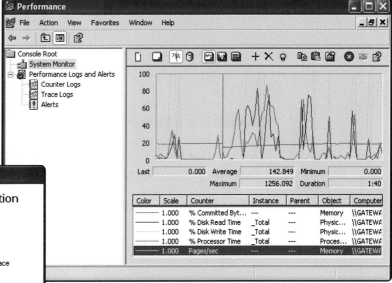

FIGURE 8-11 The System Monitor above is tracking the kernel usage and the amount of unused physical memory.

FIGURE 8-10 To display the New Connection Wizard in Windows XP, click the Start button, point to All Programs, point to Accessories, point to Communications, and then click New Connection Wizard on the Communications submenu.

Providing File Management and Other Utilities

Operating systems often provide users with the capability of managing files, viewing images, securing a computer from unauthorized access, uninstalling programs, scanning disks, defragmenting disks, diagnosing problems, backing up files and disks, and setting up screen savers. A later section in the chapter discusses these utilities in depth. Read At Issue 8-1 for a related discussion.

AT ISSUE 8-1

Who Is Responsible for Operating System Security?

A few years ago, the Sasser worm infected almost one million computers in the stretch of a weekend. Surprisingly, most computer users already had the necessary means to stop this worm before it even got started. The Windows XP operating system comes equipped with built-in firewall protection, but, by default, the feature was turned off. Microsoft later released a service pack, or update, for the operating system in which the feature was turned on by default. Most operating system manufacturers allow users automatically to download and install up-to-date security patches. It is up to the users to make use of this service properly and make certain that their operating system software is up-to-date. Sometimes, as was the case with the Sasser worm, the updates come too late. Often, users are not technically savvy enough to keep up with the security updates or to configure a network connection with a firewall properly. Who should be responsible for operating system security? Why? Should operating system manufacturers be required to send security updates to computer users? Why or why not? Should users be required to take responsibility for worms and viruses that they spread to others due to lax security? Why or why not?

Controlling a Network

Some operating systems are network operating systems. A **network operating system**, or *network OS*, is an operating system that organizes and coordinates how multiple users access and share resources on a network. Resources include hardware, software, data, and information. For example, a network OS allows multiple users to share a printer, Internet access, files, and programs.

Some operating systems have network features built into them. In other cases, the network OS is a set of programs separate from the operating system on the client computers that access the network. When not connected to the network, the client computers use their own operating

system. When connected to the network, the network OS may assume some of the operating system functions.

The *network administrator*, the person overseeing network operations, uses the network OS to add and remove users, computers, and other devices to and from the network. The network administrator also uses the network operating system to install software and administer network security.

Administering Security

The network administrator uses the network OS to establish permissions to resources. These permissions define who can access certain resources and when they can access those resources.

For each user, the network administrator establishes a user account, which enables a user to access, or **log on** to, a computer or a network. Each user account typically consists of a user name and password (Figure 8-12). A **user name**, or **user ID**, is a unique combination of characters, such as letters of the alphabet or numbers, that identifies one specific user. Many users select a combination of their first and last names as their user name. A user named Henry West might choose H West as his user name.

A **password** is a private combination of characters associated with the user name that allows access to certain computer resources. Some operating systems allow the network

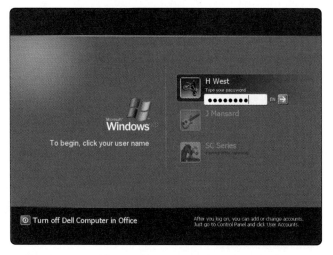

FIGURE 8-12   Most multiuser operating systems allow each user to log on, which is the process of entering a user name and a password into the computer.

administrator to assign passwords to files and commands, restricting access to only authorized users.

To prevent unauthorized users from accessing computer resources, keep your password confidential. While entering your password, most computers hide the actual password characters by displaying some other characters, such as asterisks (*) or dots. After entering a user name and password, the operating system compares the user's entry with a list of authorized user names and passwords. If the entry matches the user name and password kept on file, the operating system grants the user access. If the entry does not match, the operating system denies access to the user.

The operating system records successful and unsuccessful logon attempts in a file. This allows the network administrator to review who is using or attempting to use the computer. Network administrators also use these files to monitor computer usage.

To protect sensitive data and information further as it travels over the network, a network operating system may encrypt it. *Encryption* is the process of encoding data and information into an unreadable form. Network administrators can set up a network to encrypt data as it travels over the network to prevent unauthorized users from reading the data. When an authorized user attempts to read the data, it automatically is decrypted, or converted back into a readable form.

Test your knowledge of pages 398 through 411 in Quiz Yourself 8-1.

QUIZ YOURSELF 8-1

Instructions: Find the true statement below. Then, rewrite the remaining false statements so they are true.

1. A buffer is a small program that tells the operating system how to communicate with a specific device.
2. A cold boot is the process of using the operating system to restart a computer.
3. A password is a public combination of characters associated with the user name that allows access to certain computer resources.
4. Firmware that contains the computer's startup instructions is called the kernel.
5. The program you currently are using is in the background, and the other programs running but not in use are in the foreground.
6. Two types of system software are operating systems and application programs.
7. With virtual memory, the operating system allocates a portion of a storage medium, usually the hard disk, to function as additional RAM.

Quiz Yourself Online: To further check your knowledge of system software and features common to most operating systems, visit scsite.com/dc2006/ch8/quiz and then click Objectives 1 – 4.

OPERATING SYSTEM UTILITY PROGRAMS

A **utility program**, also called a **utility**, is a type of system software that allows a user to perform maintenance-type tasks, usually related to managing a computer, its devices, or its programs. Most operating systems include several built-in utility programs (Figure 8-13). Users often buy stand-alone utilities, however, because they offer improvements over those included with the operating system.

FAQ 8-4

What are the guidelines for selecting a good password?

Choose a password that no one could guess. Do not use any part of your first or last name, your spouse's or child's name, telephone number, street address, license plate number, Social Security number, and so on. Be sure your password is at least six characters long, mixed with letters and numbers. For more information, visit scsite.com/dc2006/ch8/faq and then click Passwords.

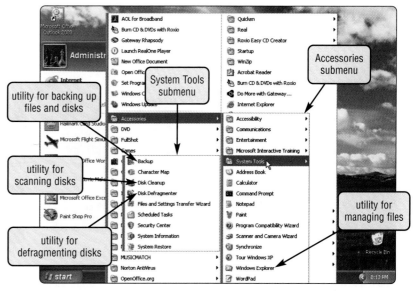

FIGURE 8-13 Many utilities available in Windows XP are accessible through the Accessories and System Tools submenus.

Utility programs included with most operating systems provide the following functions: managing files, viewing images, securing a computer from unauthorized access, uninstalling programs, scanning disks, defragmenting disks, diagnosing problems, backing up files and disks, and setting up screen savers. The following sections briefly discuss each of these utilities.

File Manager

A **file manager** is a utility that performs functions related to file and disk management. Windows XP includes a file manager called *Windows Explorer*. Some of the file and disk management functions that a file manager performs are formatting and copying disks; displaying a list of files on a storage medium (Figure 8-14); checking the amount of used or free space on a storage medium; organizing, copying, renaming, deleting, moving, and sorting files; and creating shortcuts. A **shortcut** is an icon on the desktop that provides a user with immediate access to a program or file.

Formatting is the process of preparing a disk for reading and writing. Most floppy and hard disk manufacturers preformat their disks. If you must format a floppy disk or other media, you can do so using the file manager. For a technical discussion about formatting, read the High-Tech Talk article on page 382 in Chapter 7.

Image Viewer

An **image viewer** is a utility that allows users to display, copy, and print the contents of a graphics file. With an image viewer, users can see images without having to open them in a paint or image editing program. Windows XP includes an image viewer called *Windows Picture and Fax Viewer* (Figure 8-15). To display a file in this image viewer, simply double-click the thumbnail of the image in the file manager. For example, double-clicking a thumbnail in Windows Explorer (Figure 8-14) displays the image in a Windows Picture and Fax Viewer window.

FIGURE 8-15 Windows Picture and Fax Viewer allows users to see the contents of a graphics file.

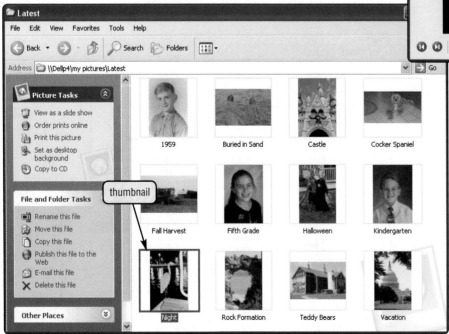

FIGURE 8-14 With Windows Explorer, which is the file manager included with Windows XP, users can display a list of graphics files on a disk. In this case, thumbnails of the files are displayed.

Personal Firewall

A **personal firewall** is a utility that detects and protects a personal computer from unauthorized intrusions. Personal firewalls constantly monitor all transmissions to and from a computer.

When connected to the Internet, your computer is vulnerable to attacks from a hacker. A *hacker* is someone who tries to access a computer or network illegally. Users with broadband Internet connections, such as through DSL and Internet cable television service, are even more susceptible than those with dial-up access because the Internet connection is always on.

The latest update to Windows XP automatically enables the built-in personal firewall upon installation. This firewall, called Windows Firewall, is easy to access and configure (Figure 8-16). If your operating system does not include a personal firewall or you want additional protection, you can purchase a stand-alone personal firewall utility or a hardware firewall, which is a device such as a router that has a built-in firewall.

Uninstaller

An **uninstaller** is a utility that removes a program, as well as any associated entries in the system files. In Windows XP, the uninstaller is available through the Add/Remove Programs command in the Control Panel.

When you install a program, the operating system records the information it uses to run the software in the system files. The uninstaller deletes files and folders from the hard disk, as well as removes program entries from the system files.

FAQ 8-5

Should I use the file manager to delete a program?

No! If you remove software from a computer by deleting the files and folders associated with the program without running the uninstaller, the system file entries are not updated. This may cause the operating system to display error messages when you start the computer. If the program has an uninstaller, always use it to remove software. For more information, visit scsite.com/dc2006/ch8/faq and then click Uninstalling Programs.

WEB LINK 8-3

Personal Firewalls

For more information, visit scsite.com/dc2006/ch8/weblink and then click Personal Firewalls.

FIGURE 8-16   Through the Security Center in the Control Panel of Windows XP, users can configure Windows Firewall, which is a personal firewall utility built into the latest upgrade of Windows XP.

Disk Scanner

A **disk scanner** is a utility that (1) detects and corrects both physical and logical problems on a hard disk and (2) searches for and removes unnecessary files. A physical disk problem is a problem with the media such as a scratch on the surface of the disk. A logical disk problem is a problem with the data, such as a corrupt file. Windows XP includes two disk scanner utilities. One detects problems and the other searches for and removes unnecessary files such as temporary files (Figure 8-17).

FIGURE 8-17   Disk Cleanup searches for and removes unnecessary files.

Disk Defragmenter

A **disk defragmenter** is a utility that reorganizes the files and unused space on a computer's hard disk so the operating system accesses data more quickly and programs run faster. When an operating system stores data on a disk, it places the data in the first available sector on the disk. It attempts to place data in sectors that are contiguous (next to each other), but this is not always possible. When the contents of a file are scattered across two or more noncontiguous sectors, the file is *fragmented*.

Fragmentation slows down disk access and thus the performance of the entire computer. **Defragmenting** the disk, or reorganizing it so the files are stored in contiguous sectors, solves this problem (Figure 8-18). Windows XP includes a disk defragmenter available on the System Tools submenu.

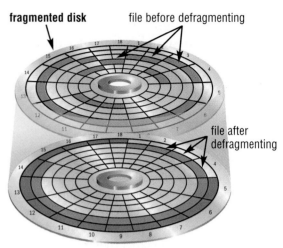

FIGURE 8-18   A fragmented disk has many files stored in noncontiguous sectors. Defragmenting reorganizes the files so they are located in contiguous sectors, which speeds access time.

Diagnostic Utility

A **diagnostic utility** compiles technical information about your computer's hardware and certain system software programs and then prepares a report outlining any identified problems. For example, Windows XP includes the diagnostic utility, *Dr. Watson*, which diagnoses problems as well as suggests courses of action (Figure 8-19). Information in the report assists technical support staff in remedying any problems.

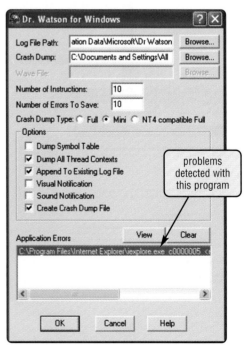

FIGURE 8-19   Dr. Watson is a diagnostic utility included with Windows.

Backup Utility

A **backup utility** allows users to copy, or *back up*, selected files or an entire hard disk to another storage medium. During the backup process, the backup utility monitors progress and alerts you if it needs additional discs or tapes. Many backup programs *compress*, or shrink the size of, files during the backup process. By compressing the files, the backup program requires less storage space for the backup files than for the original files.

Because they are compressed, you usually cannot use backup files in their backed up form. In the event you need to use a backup file, a **restore program** reverses the process and returns backed up files to their original form. Backup utilities include restore programs.

You should back up files and disks regularly in the event your originals are lost, damaged, or destroyed. Windows XP includes a backup utility (Figure 8-20). Instead of backing up to a local disk storage device, some users opt to use online storage to back up their files. As described in Chapter 7, online storage is a service on the Web that provides hard disk storage to computer users, usually for a minimal monthly fee.

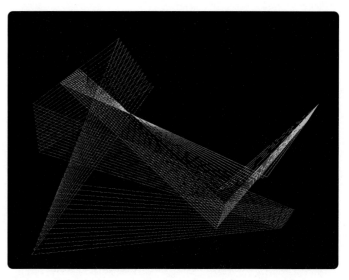

FIGURE 8-21 A Windows XP screen saver.

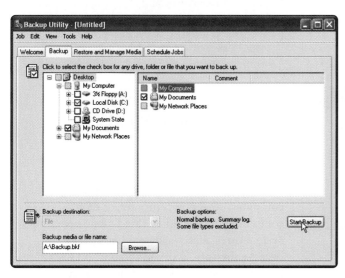

FIGURE 8-20 A backup utility allows users to copy files or an entire hard disk to another storage medium.

Screen Saver

A **screen saver** is a utility that causes a display device's screen to show a moving image or blank screen if no keyboard or mouse activity occurs for a specified time (Figure 8-21). When you press a key on the keyboard or move the mouse, the screen saver disappears and the screen returns to the previous state.

Screen savers originally were developed to prevent a problem called *ghosting*, in which images could be permanently etched on a monitor's screen. Although ghosting is not as severe of a problem with today's displays, manufacturers continue to recommend that users install screen savers for this reason. Screen savers also are popular for security, business, and entertainment purposes. To secure a computer, users configure their screen saver to require a password to deactivate. In addition to those included with the operating system, many screen savers are available in stores and on the Web for free or a minimal fee.

WEB LINK 8-4

Screen Savers
For more information, visit scsite.com/dc2006/ch8/weblink and then click Screen Savers.

TYPES OF OPERATING SYSTEMS

Many of the first operating systems were device dependent and proprietary. A *device-dependent* program is one that runs only on a specific type or make of computer. *Proprietary software* is privately owned and limited to a specific vendor or computer model. Some operating systems still are device dependent. The trend today, however, is toward *device-independent* operating systems that run on computers provided by a variety of manufacturers. The advantage of device-independent operating systems is you can retain existing application software and data files even if you change computer models or vendors.

When you purchase a new computer, it typically has an operating system preinstalled. As new versions of the operating system are released, users upgrade their existing computers to incorporate features of the new version. An upgrade usually costs less than purchasing the entire operating system.

Some software manufacturers, such as Microsoft and IBM, release free downloadable updates to their software, often called a *service pack*. Users also can order service packs on CD for a minimal shipping fee. Service packs provide enhancements to the original software and fix bugs (errors) in the software. Read At Issue 8-2 for a related discussion.

New versions of an operating system usually are downward compatible. That is, they recognize and work with application software written for an earlier version of the operating system (or platform). The application software, by contrast, is said to be upward compatible, meaning it will run on new versions of the operating system.

The three basic categories of operating systems that exist today are stand-alone, network, and embedded. The table in Figure 8-22 lists specific names of operating systems in each category. The following pages discuss the operating systems listed in the table.

AT ISSUE 8-2

Should Software Manufacturers Be Liable for Defective Software?

Several years ago in Panama, 28 patients receiving radiation treatment were given massive overdoses of radiation due to a software bug. Over the next several years, five of these patients died due to radiation poisoning and others were considered to be at risk of developing further complications. In another mishap, bugs in retail tax return preparation software caused erroneous tax calculations on individuals' tax returns. It is estimated that defective software costs U.S. businesses approximately $60 billion annually. In a software license, software manufacturers usually include a disclaimer that limits the manufacturer's liability in the event that software malfunctions. Due to the increase in viruses, worms, and well-publicized software failures, such as the one that caused the power blackout in much of the northeastern U.S. a few years ago, many people are calling for the government to force software manufacturers to assume more liability. Software manufacturers claim that more liability — and consequently more cost — will result in less software and fewer features. Should the government enact more rules regarding software quality and liability? Why or why not? Who should be held accountable, if anyone, when faulty software causes injury or financial loss? Why? Will the free market eventually force makers of bug-ridden software to go out of business?

CATEGORIES OF OPERATING SYSTEMS

Category	Operating System Name
Stand-alone	• DOS • Early Windows versions (Windows 3.x, Windows 95, Windows NT Workstation, Windows 98, Windows 2000 Professional, Windows Millennium Edition) • Windows XP • Mac OS X • UNIX • Linux
Network	• NetWare • Early Windows Server versions (Windows NT Server, Windows 2000 Server) • Windows Server 2003 • UNIX • Linux • Solaris
Embedded	• Windows CE • Windows Mobile • Palm OS • Embedded Linux • Symbian OS

FIGURE 8-22 Examples of stand-alone, network, and embedded operating systems. Some stand-alone operating systems include the capability of configuring small home or office networks.

STAND-ALONE OPERATING SYSTEMS

A **stand-alone operating system** is a complete operating system that works on a desktop computer, notebook computer, or mobile computing device. Some stand-alone operating systems are called *client operating systems* because they also work in conjunction with a network operating system. Client operating systems can operate with or without a network. Other stand-alone operating systems include networking capabilities, allowing the home and small business user to set up a small network.

Examples of stand-alone operating systems are DOS, Windows XP, Mac OS X, UNIX, and Linux. The following paragraphs briefly discuss these operating systems.

DOS

The term **DOS** (*Disk Operating System*) refers to several single user operating systems developed in the early 1980s by Microsoft for personal computers. The two more widely used versions of DOS were PC-DOS and MS-DOS. The functionality of these two operating systems was essentially the same.

DOS used a command-line interface when Microsoft first developed it. Later versions included both command-line and menu-driven user interfaces. At its peak, DOS was a widely used operating system, with an estimated 70 million computers running it. DOS hardly is used today because it does not offer a graphical user interface and it cannot take full advantage of modern 32-bit personal computer processors.

Windows XP

In the mid-1980s, Microsoft developed its first version of Windows, which provided a graphical user interface (GUI). Since then, Microsoft continually has updated its Windows operating system, incorporating innovative features and functions with each subsequent version (Figure 8-23). **Windows XP** is Microsoft's fastest, most reliable Windows operating system yet, providing quicker startup, better performance, and a simplified visual look.

FAQ 8-6

How many people use Windows?

According to Microsoft, the number of Windows PCs will grow to more than one billion by 2010. Studies by industry analysts estimate that 96 percent of desktop computers worldwide currently use Windows. For more information, visit scsite.com/dc2006/ch8/faq and then click Windows Users.

HIGHLIGHTS OF STAND-ALONE WINDOWS VERSIONS

Windows Version	Year Released	Highlights
Windows 3.x	1990	• Provided a GUI • An operating environment only — worked in combination with DOS
Windows NT 3.1	1993	• Client OS that connected to a Windows NT Advanced Server • Interface similar to Windows 3.x
Windows 95	1995	• True multitasking operating system • Improved GUI • Included support for networking, Plug and Play technology, longer file names, and e-mail
Windows NT Workstation 4.0	1996	• Client OS that connected to a Windows NT Server • Interface similar to Windows 95 • Network integration
Windows 98	1998	• Upgrade to Windows 95 • More integrated with the Internet; included *Internet Explorer* (a Web browser) • Faster system startup and shutdown, better file management, support for multimedia technologies (e.g., DVDs), and USB connectivity
Windows Millennium Edition	2000	• Upgrade to Windows 98 • Designed for the home user who wanted music playing, video editing, and networking capabilities
Windows 2000 Professional	2000	• Upgrade to Windows NT Workstation 4.0 • Complete multitasking client OS designed for business personal computers • Certified device drivers, faster performance, adaptive Start menu, image viewer, enhanced for mobile users
Windows XP	2001	• Upgrade to Windows Millennium Edition called Windows XP Home Edition • Upgrade to Windows 2000 Professional called Windows XP Professional • Windows XP Tablet PC Edition designed for Tablet PC users • Windows XP Media Center Edition designed for PCs used for home entertainment • Windows XP 64-bit Edition designed for workstations with an Itanium 2 processor • Improved interface and increased performance in all editions
Windows XP SP2 (Service Pack 2)	2004	• Enhancement to Windows XP that offers more built-in security technologies • Improved firewall utility • Automatic blocking of Internet pop-up advertisements

FIGURE 8-23 Microsoft released many versions of Windows before Windows XP.

Windows XP is available in five editions: Home Edition, Professional (Figure 8-24), Media Center Edition, Tablet PC Edition, and 64-bit Edition. The table in Figure 8-25 highlights features in all editions of Windows XP; the following page identifies the differences. Read Looking Ahead 8-1 for a look at the next generation of the Windows operating system.

FIGURE 8-24 Windows XP, with its simplified look, is the fastest and most reliable Windows operating system to date.

LOOKING AHEAD 8-1

The Future of Windows

Searching for computer files can be a frustrating experience. Microsoft, however, plans to simplify the process with an eventual add-on to its next version of the Windows operating system, currently code-named *Longhorn*.

With this search feature, called *WinFS* (Windows Future Storage), users will be able to locate e-mail messages, documents, and multimedia images, no matter what their format, on a stand-alone computer and on a network.

Longhorn is being developed as a consumer-friendly product with a completely object-oriented interface. When this major update to Windows XP is released in 2006 or later, it will recognize users and tailor the systems for their specific needs. It also will feature new security technology called Palladium, an antivirus program, and recordable DVD capabilities. For more information, visit scsite.com/dc2006/ch8/looking and then click Longhorn.

WINDOWS XP FEATURES

Appearance and Performance
- New look and feel to the user interface
- Increased reliability and security
- Increased performance to run programs faster
- Redesigned Start menu and Control Panel
- Minimized clutter on the taskbar with multiple open windows organized into groups
- Crisper display of images on LCD screens with ClearType

Administration
- Improved interface for creating multiple user accounts and switching among accounts
- Enhanced system recovery from failure with System Restore, without causing loss of data
- Easy-to-install home or small office network
- Windows Firewall to protect a home or small office network from hackers
- Improved wireless network support
- Improved battery-life management for notebook computers

Help and Support
- Comprehensive Help and Support system
- Remote Assistance that allows another person (with your permission) to control your computer remotely to demonstrate a process or solve a problem

Communications and the Web
- New version of Windows Messenger to send instant messages; communicate in real time using text, graphics, video, and voice to other online users; and a whiteboard available for use in video conferences
- New version of Internet Explorer with improved look
- Remote Desktop to access data and applications on your desktop computer while away from the computer using another Windows-based computer with a network or Internet connection
- Publish, store, and share text, graphics, photographs, and other items on the Web

Digital Media
- New version of Windows Media Player to listen to more than 3,000 Internet radio stations, play MP3 and Microsoft's WMA music format, copy music and data onto blank CDs, and watch DVD movies
- New version of Movie Maker
- Transfer images from a digital camera or scanner to your computer

FIGURE 8-25 Some features of Windows XP.

WINDOWS XP HOME EDITION *Windows XP Home Edition* is an upgrade to Windows Millennium Edition. In addition to providing the capabilities of Windows Millennium Edition, Windows XP Home Edition offers features and functionality that allow users to perform the following tasks:

- Acquire, organize, and share digital pictures
- Download, store, and playback high-quality music through Windows Media Player
- Create, edit, and share videos with Windows Movie Maker
- Easily network and share multiple home computers
- Use built-in instant messaging and video conferencing with Windows Messenger
- Recover from problems with easy-to-use tools

WINDOWS XP PROFESSIONAL *Windows XP Professional* is an upgrade to Windows 2000 Professional. In addition to providing the capabilities of Windows 2000 Professional, Windows XP Professional includes all the capabilities of Windows XP Home Edition and offers the following features and functionality:

- Greater data security through encryption of files and folders
- Remote access to a computer, its data, and its files from any other computer anywhere
- Simpler administration of groups of users or computers
- Multiple language user interface
- Support for secured wireless network access

WINDOWS XP MEDIA CENTER EDITION *Windows XP Media Center Edition* includes all the features of Windows XP Professional and is designed for Media Center PCs. A *Media Center PC* is a home entertainment personal computer that includes a mid- to high-end processor, large-capacity hard disk, CD and DVD drives, a remote control, and advanced graphics and audio capabilities. These computers often use a television as their display device. Windows XP Media Center Edition offers the following media features:

- Access to digital entertainment including live and recorded television programs, movies, music, radio, and photographs via a remote control device (Figure 8-26)
- Up-to-date online television program guide
- Parental control for television programs
- Capability to record television programs while away from the computer
- On-screen telephone call notification alert
- Download, play, copy, and listen to music
- Listen to Internet and FM radio stations

FIGURE 8-26 With Windows XP Media Center Edition, users access recorded videos, pictures, music, television programs, radio stations, or movies via a remote control device.

FAQ 8-7

How do I connect a television to a Media Center PC?
Plug one end of a cable in the TV out port on the Media Center PC and the other end of the cable in the input port on the television. Many users have two display devices for a Media Center PC: a monitor for computing purposes and a television for entertainment. For more information, visit scsite.com/dc2006/ch8/faq and then click Media Center PC.

WINDOWS XP TABLET PC EDITION *Windows XP Tablet PC Edition* includes all the features of Windows XP Professional and provides the following additional features that are designed to make users more productive while working on their Tablet PCs:

- Write on screen or issue instructions to the Tablet PC using a digital pen
- Save documents in handwritten form or convert them to typewritten text for use in other application software
- Add handwritten notes to documents created in other application software
- Enter text and instructions by speaking into the Tablet PC

WINDOWS XP 64-BIT EDITION *Windows XP 64-bit Edition* is designed for workstations that use an Itanium 2 processor and offers the following features and functionality:

- Supports up to 16 GB of RAM and 16 TB of virtual memory
- Supports multiprocessing
- Integrates 64-bit and 32-bit applications

WEB LINK 8-5

Windows XP

For more information, visit scsite.com/dc2006/ch8/weblink and then click Windows XP.

Mac OS X

Since it was released in 1984 with Macintosh computers, Apple's **Macintosh operating system** has set the standard for operating system ease of use and has been the model for most of the new GUIs developed for non-Macintosh systems. The latest version, **Mac OS X**, is a multitasking operating system available only for computers manufactured by Apple (Figure 8-27).

Mac OS X includes features from previous versions of the Macintosh operating system such as large photo-quality icons, built-in networking support, e-mail, online shopping, enhanced speech recognition, CD burning, and enhanced multimedia capabilities. In addition, Mac OS X includes these features:

- Built-in AOL-compatible instant messenger
- 3-D video conferencing
- Voice chats
- Filter to eliminate junk e-mail messages
- Contact lists synchronized with PDA or Bluetooth-enabled smart phone
- Web search without a browser
- Latest version of QuickTime to listen to music and view videos on the Internet
- Easy networking of computers and devices
- Conversion of handwritten text to typewritten text
- Windows network connection and shared Windows documents

WEB LINK 8-6

Mac OS X

For more information, visit scsite.com/dc2006/ch8/weblink and then click Mac OS X.

UNIX

UNIX (pronounced YOU-nix) is a multitasking operating system developed in the early 1970s by scientists at Bell Laboratories. Bell Labs (a subsidiary of AT&T) was prohibited from actively promoting UNIX in the commercial marketplace because of federal regulations. Bell Labs instead licensed UNIX for a low fee to numerous colleges and universities, where UNIX obtained a wide following. UNIX was implemented on many different types of computers. After deregulation of the telephone companies in the 1980s, UNIX was licensed to many hardware and software companies.

Several versions of this operating system exist, each slightly different. When programmers move application software from one UNIX version to another, they sometimes have to rewrite some of the programs. Although some versions of UNIX have a command-line interface, most versions of UNIX offer a graphical user interface (Figure 8-28).

Today, a version of UNIX is available for most computers of all sizes. Power users often work with UNIX because of its flexibility and power. Manufacturers such as Sun and IBM sell personal computers and workstations with a UNIX operating system.

WEB LINK 8-7

UNIX

For more information, visit scsite.com/dc2006/ch8/weblink and then click UNIX.

FIGURE 8-27 Mac OS X is the operating system used with Apple Macintosh computers.

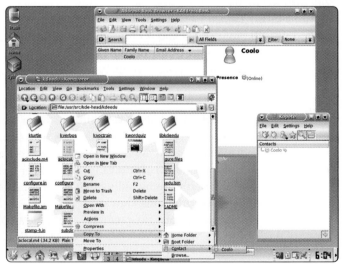

FIGURE 8-28 Some versions of UNIX have a graphical user interface.

Linux

Linux is one of the faster growing operating systems. **Linux** (pronounced LINN-uks) is a popular, multitasking UNIX-type operating system. In addition to the basic operating system, Linux also includes many free programming languages and utility programs.

Linux is not proprietary software like the operating systems discussed thus far. Instead, Linux is *open source software*, which means its code is provided for use, modification, and redistribution. It has no restrictions from the copyright holder regarding modification of the software's internal instructions and redistribution of the software. Many programmers have donated time to modify and redistribute Linux to make it the best possible version of UNIX. Promoters of open source software state two main advantages: users who modify the software share their improvements with others, and customers can personalize the software to meet their needs. Read At Issue 8-3 for a related discussion.

Some versions of Linux are command-line. Others are GUI. The two most popular GUIs available for Linux are GNOME and KDE. Some companies such as Red Hat market software applications that run on their own version of Linux (Figure 8-29). Many application programs, utilities, and plug-ins have Linux versions, including OpenOffice.org, StarOffice, Mozilla, Netscape, Yahoo! Messenger, RealPlayer, QuickTime, and Acrobat Reader.

Users obtain Linux in a variety of ways. Some download it free from the Web. Others purchase it from vendors such as Red Hat or IBM, who bundle their own software with the operating system. Linux CD-ROMs are included in many Linux books and also are available for purchase from vendors. Some retailers such as Dell will preinstall Linux on a new computer's hard disk on request. Read Looking Ahead 8-2 for a look at the next generation of Linux.

AT ISSUE 8-3

Closed Source vs. Open Source Software

Linux is a fast-growing, innovative operating system. One of the features that make it different from other operating systems is that Linux is open source and its source code, along with any changes, remains public. Since its introduction in 1991, Linux has been altered, adapted, and improved by hundreds of programmers. Unlike Linux, most operating systems are proprietary, and their program code often is a zealously guarded secret. At one large software developer, an employee reported that application programmers had little opportunity to contribute to operating system programs because they had no access to the operating system program source code. Supporters of open source maintain that source code should be open to the public so that it can be scrutinized, corrected, and enhanced. In light of concerns about security and fears of possible virus problems, however, some people are not sure open source software is a good idea. Besides, they argue, programmers should be able to control, and profit from, the operating systems they create. On the other hand, open source software can be scrutinized for errors by a much larger group of people and changes can be made immediately. Is open source software a good idea? Why or why not? Can the concerns about open source software be addressed? How? What are the advantages and disadvantages of open versus closed source software? Does open source software lead to better software?

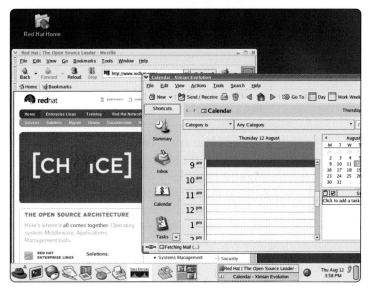

FIGURE 8-29 Red Hat provides a version of Linux called Red Hat Linux.

LOOKING AHEAD 8-2

The Future of Linux

The Linux operating system has been altered and enhanced since Linus Torvalds wrote the initial source code in 1991. With hundreds of programmers donating their time to make Linux the best possible version of UNIX, the software literally has changed on a daily basis.

As these developers work to improve Linux, their efforts are helping to shape the software's future. Experts predict the operating system may change by establishing a consistent desktop environment that is easy for all computer users to use. They also believe that hardware manufacturers will promote Linux-approved systems that maximize the software's features. Others forecast that a few major distributors will issue the software, in contrast to the hundreds of independent distributors that now exist. For more information, visit scsite.com/dc2006/ch8/looking and then click Linux Future.

Test your knowledge of pages 411 through 421 in Quiz Yourself 8-2.

QUIZ YOURSELF 8-2

Instructions: Find the true statement below. Then, rewrite the remaining false statements so they are true.

1. A file manager is a utility that detects and protects a personal computer from unauthorized intrusions.
2. Fragmenting a disk is the process of reorganizing it so the files are stored in contiguous sectors.
3. Linux is available in five editions: Home Edition, Professional, Media Center Edition, Tablet PC Edition, and 64-bit Edition.
4. Mac OS X is a multitasking operating system available only for computers manufactured by Apple.
5. Windows XP is a UNIX-type operating system that is open source software.
6. You should uninstall files and disks regularly in the event your originals are lost, damaged, or destroyed.

Quiz Yourself Online: To further check your knowledge of utilities included with most operating systems and stand-alone operating systems, visit scsite.com/dc2006/ch8/quiz and then click Objectives 5 – 6.

NETWORK OPERATING SYSTEMS

As discussed earlier in this chapter, a network operating system is an operating system that is designed specifically to support a network. A network operating system typically resides on a server. The client computers on the network rely on the server(s) for resources. Many of the client operating systems discussed in the previous section work in conjunction with a network operating system.

Some of the stand-alone operating systems discussed in the previous section include networking capability; however, network operating systems are designed specifically to support all sizes of networks, including medium to large-sized businesses and Web servers. Examples of network operating systems include NetWare, Windows Server 2003, UNIX, Linux, and Solaris.

NetWare

Novell's *NetWare* is a network operating system designed for client/server networks. NetWare has a server portion that resides on the network server and a client portion that resides on each client computer connected to the network. NetWare supports open source software and runs on all types of computers from mainframes to personal computers.

The server portion of NetWare allows users to share hardware devices attached to the server (such as a printer), as well as e-mail, databases, or any other files and software

stored on the server. The client portion of NetWare communicates with the server. Client computers also can have their own stand-alone operating system such as Windows XP, Mac OS X, or a Linux-based client.

Windows Server 2003

Windows Server 2003 is an upgrade to Windows 2000 Server, which was an upgrade to Windows NT Server. Windows Server 2003, which includes features of previous server versions, offers the following capabilities:
- Web site management and hosting
- Delivery and management of multimedia across intranets and the Internet
- Document storage in Web folders
- Central information repository about network users and resources with *Active Directory*
- Client support using Windows XP and earlier versions of Windows, Mac OS X, UNIX, and Linux

To meet the needs of all sizes of businesses, the **Windows Server 2003 family** includes five products:
- *Windows Small Business Server 2003* designed for businesses with fewer than 75 users and limited networking expertise
- *Windows Server 2003, Standard Edition* for the typical small- to medium-sized business network
- *Windows Server 2003, Enterprise Edition* for medium- to large-sized businesses, including those with e-commerce operations; available in 64-bit version

WEB LINK 8-8

NetWare
For more information, visit scsite.com/dc2006/ch8/weblink and then click NetWare.

- *Windows Server 2003, Datacenter Edition* for businesses with huge volumes of transactions and large-scale databases; available in 64-bit version
- *Windows Server 2003, Web Edition* for Web server and Web hosting businesses

Windows Server 2003 is part of Windows Server System. In addition to Windows Server 2003, *Windows Server System* provides developers with dynamic development tools that allow businesses and customers to connect and communicate easily via the Internet. Through Windows Server System, programmers have the ability to use *Web services*, which are Web applications created with any programming language or any operating system to communicate and share data seamlessly.

UNIX

In addition to being a stand-alone operating system, UNIX also is a network operating system. That is, UNIX is capable of handling a high volume of transactions in a multiuser environment and working with multiple processors using multiprocessing. For this reason, some computer professionals call UNIX a *multipurpose operating system* because it is both a stand-alone and network operating system. Many Web servers use UNIX as their operating system.

Linux

Some network servers use Linux as their operating system. Thus, Linux also is a multipurpose operating system. With Linux, a network administrator can configure the network, administer security, run a Web server, and process e-mail. Clients on the network can run Linux, UNIX, or Windows. Versions of Linux include both the Netscape and Mozilla Web browsers.

FAQ 8-8

How widespread is Linux usage?

Forecasters predict that Linux will command one-third of the server market by 2008. Desktop personal computers, however, have a much lower Linux usage — only one percent worldwide. For more information, visit scsite.com/dc2006/ch8/faq and then click Linux Users.

Solaris

Solaris, a version of UNIX developed by Sun Microsystems, is a network operating system designed specifically for e-commerce applications. Solaris manages high-traffic accounts and incorporates security necessary for Web transactions. Client computers often use a desktop program, such as GNOME desktop, that communicates with the Solaris operating system.

EMBEDDED OPERATING SYSTEMS

The operating system on most PDAs and small devices, called an **embedded operating system**, resides on a ROM chip. Popular embedded operating systems today include Windows CE, Windows Mobile, Palm OS, Embedded Linux, and Symbian OS. The following sections discuss these operating systems.

Windows CE

Windows CE is a scaled-down Windows operating system designed for use on communications, entertainment, and computing devices with limited functionality. For example, set-top boxes, which enable you to access the Internet on a television, often use Windows CE. A widely used communications application of Windows CE is Internet telephony (Figure 8-30).

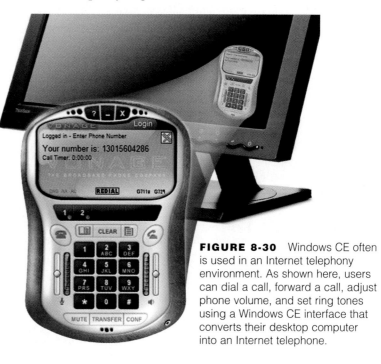

FIGURE 8-30 Windows CE often is used in an Internet telephony environment. As shown here, users can dial a call, forward a call, adjust phone volume, and set ring tones using a Windows CE interface that converts their desktop computer into an Internet telephone.

Windows CE is a GUI that supports color, sound, multitasking, multimedia, e-mail, Internet access, and Web browsing. A built-in file viewer allows users to view files created in popular applications such as Word, Excel, and PowerPoint.

Devices equipped with Windows CE can communicate wirelessly with computers and other devices using Bluetooth or other wireless technologies, as long as the device is equipped with the necessary communications hardware.

Windows Mobile

Windows Mobile enhances Windows CE to include functionality, applications, and a user interface designed for a specific type of PDA, called a **Pocket PC**, and smart phones (Figure 8-31). With this operating system and a Pocket PC or smart phone, users have access to all the basic PIM (personal information manager) functions such as contact lists, schedules, tasks, calendars, and notes. Information on the PDA or smart phone easily synchronizes with a personal computer or prints on a printer using a cable or a wireless technology.

Windows Mobile, which has a Windows XP look, also provides numerous additional features that allow users to check e-mail, browse the Web, listen to music, watch a video, send and receive instant messages, record a voice message, manage finances, or read an e-book. Many applications, such as Word, Excel, Outlook, and Internet Explorer, have scaled-down versions that run with Windows Mobile.

Some devices with Windows Mobile also support handwriting and voice input. With the Pocket PC Phone Edition devices, users can make telephone calls and send text messages using the PDA.

Palm OS

A competing operating system to Windows Mobile is *Palm OS*, which runs on PDAs and smart phones (Figure 8-32). With Palm OS devices, users manage schedules and contacts, telephone messages, project notes, reminders, task and address lists, and important dates and appointments. Information on the PDA or smart phone easily synchronizes with a personal computer or prints on a printer using a cable or a wireless technology. Palm users also can exchange information with other Palm users wirelessly through IrDA technology.

Palm OS includes handwriting recognition software, called Graffiti. Many Palm OS devices allow users to connect wirelessly to the Internet; browse the Web; and send and receive e-mail messages and instant messages. The latest version of Palm OS includes improved security for data transmission, allows for biometric identification, and supports the use of smart cards.

WEB LINK 8-9

Windows Mobile

For more information, visit scsite.com/dc2006/ch8/weblink and then click Windows Mobile.

WEB LINK 8-10

Palm OS

For more information, visit scsite.com/dc2006/ch8/weblink and then click Palm OS.

FIGURE 8-31 Windows Mobile runs on Pocket PCs and many smart phones.

FIGURE 8-32 Palm OS runs on PDAs and smart phones.

Embedded Linux

Embedded Linux is a scaled-down Linux operating system designed for PDAs, smart phones, smart watches, set-top boxes, Internet telephones, and many other types of devices and computers requiring an embedded operating system (Figure 8-33). PDAs and smart phones with embedded Linux offer calendar and address book and other PIM functions, touch screens, and handwriting recognition. Many also allow you to connect to the Internet, take pictures, play videos, listen to music, and send e-mail and instant messages. Devices that use embedded Linux synchronize with desktop computers using a variety of technologies including Bluetooth.

FIGURE 8-33
A PDA that uses embedded Linux.

Symbian OS

Symbian OS is an open source multitasking operating system designed for smart phones (Figure 8-34). In addition to making telephone calls, users of Symbian OS can maintain contact lists; save appointments; browse the Web; and send and receive text and picture messages, e-mail messages, and faxes using a smart phone. Users enter data by pressing keys on the keypad or keyboard, touching the screen, writing on the screen with a stylus, or speaking into the smart phone. Symbian OS allows users to communicate wirelessly using a variety of technologies including Bluetooth and IrDA.

FIGURE 8-34 This smart phone uses the Symbian OS.

STAND-ALONE UTILITY PROGRAMS

Although operating systems typically include some built-in utilities, many stand-alone utility programs are available for purchase. For example, you can purchase personal firewall, backup utilities, and screen savers. These stand-alone utilities typically offer improvements over those features built into the operating system or provide features not included in an operating system.

Other functions provided by stand-alone utilities include protecting against viruses, removing spyware, filtering Internet content, compressing files, converting files, burning CDs and DVDs, and maintaining a personal computer. The following sections discuss each of these utilities.

Antivirus Programs

The term, computer **virus**, describes a potentially damaging computer program that affects, or infects, a computer negatively by altering the way the computer works without the user's knowledge or permission. More specifically, a computer virus is a segment of program code from some outside source that implants itself in a computer. Once the virus is in a computer, it can spread throughout and may damage your files and operating system.

Currently, more than 81,000 known virus programs exist with an estimated 6 new virus programs discovered each day. Computer viruses do not generate by chance. The programmer of a virus, known as a *virus author*, intentionally writes a virus program. Some virus authors find writing viruses a challenge. Others write virus programs to cause destruction. Writing a virus program usually requires significant programming skills.

Some viruses are harmless pranks that simply freeze a computer temporarily or display sounds or messages. The Music Bug virus, for example, instructs the computer to play a few chords of music. Other viruses destroy or corrupt data stored on the hard disk of the infected computer. If you notice any unusual changes in your computer's performance, it may be infected with a virus. Figure 8-35 outlines some common symptoms of virus infection.

SIGNS OF VIRUS INFECTION

- An unusual message or image is displayed on the computer screen
- An unusual sound or music plays randomly
- The available memory is less than what should be available
- A program or file suddenly is missing
- An unknown program or file mysteriously appears
- The size of a file changes without explanation
- A file becomes corrupted
- A program or file does not work properly
- System properties change

FIGURE 8-35 Viruses attack computers in a variety of ways. This list indicates some of the more common signs of virus infection.

Viruses are just one type of malicious-logic program. A *malicious-logic program* is a program that acts without a user's knowledge and deliberately alters the computer's operations. In addition to viruses, other malicious-logic programs are worms and Trojan horses.

A **worm**, such as Sasser or CodeRed, copies itself repeatedly, for example, in memory or over a network, using up system resources and possibly shutting the system down. A **Trojan horse** (named after the Greek myth) hides within or looks like a legitimate program such as a screen saver. A certain condition or action usually triggers the Trojan horse. Unlike a virus or worm, a Trojan horse does not replicate itself to other computers. For a more technical discussion about computer viruses, read the High-Tech Talk article in Chapter 3 on page 168.

To protect a computer from virus attacks, users should install an antivirus program and update it frequently. An **antivirus program** protects a computer against viruses by identifying and removing any computer viruses found in memory, on storage media, or on incoming files (Figure 8-36). Most antivirus programs also protect against worms and Trojan horses. When you purchase a new computer, it often includes antivirus software.

The two more popular antivirus programs are McAfee VirusScan and Norton AntiVirus. As an alternative to purchasing these products on CD, both McAfee and Norton offer Web-based

WEB LINK 8-11

Spyware Removers

For more information, visit scsite.com/ dc2006/ch8/weblink and then click Spyware Removers.

antivirus programs. That is, during your paid subscription period, the program continuously protects the computer against viruses.

FAQ 8-9

What steps should I take to prevent virus infections on my computer?

Set up the antivirus software to scan on a regular basis. Update your virus definitions regularly. Never open an e-mail attachment unless you are expecting the attachment and it is from a trusted source. If you use Windows, install the latest updates. Set macro security in programs such as word processing and spreadsheet so you can enable or disable macros. Back up files regularly. For more information, visit scsite.com/dc2006/ch8/faq and then click Preventing Virus Infections.

Spyware Removers

Spyware is a program placed on a computer without the user's knowledge that secretly collects information about the user, often related to Web browsing habits. Spyware often enters a computer as a result of a user installing a new program. The spyware program communicates information it collects to some outside source while you are online.

A **spyware remover** is a program that detects and deletes spyware. Most spyware removers cost less than $50; some are available on the Web at no cost.

Internet Filters

Filters are programs that remove or block certain items from being displayed. Three widely used Internet filters are anti-spam programs, Web filters, and pop-up blockers.

ANTI-SPAM PROGRAMS *Spam* is an unsolicited e-mail message or newsgroup posting sent to many recipients or newsgroups at once. Spam is Internet junk mail. The content of spam ranges from selling a product or service, to promoting a business opportunity, to advertising offensive material. An **anti-spam program** is a filtering program that attempts to remove spam before it reaches your inbox. If your e-mail program does not include an anti-spam program, many anti-spam programs are available at no cost on the Web.

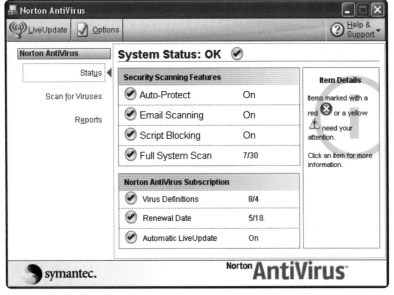

FIGURE 8-36 An antivirus program scans memory, disks, and incoming e-mail messages and attachments for viruses and attempts to remove any viruses it finds.

FAQ 8-10

Should anti-spam programs be installed on home computers?

Yes. With more than 65 percent of all e-mail categorized as spam, home and business users could lose valuable time sifting through messages related to the variety of subjects shown in the chart below. For more information, visit scsite.com/dc2006/ch8/faq and then click Anti-Spam Programs.

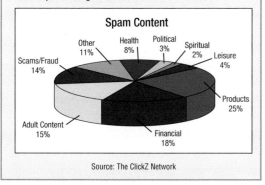

Spam Content

Other 11%
Health 8%
Political 3%
Spiritual 2%
Leisure 4%
Scams/Fraud 14%
Products 25%
Adult Content 15%
Financial 18%

Source: The ClickZ Network

WEB FILTERS   Web filtering software is a program that restricts access to certain material on the Web. Some restrict access to specific Web sites; others filter sites that use certain words or phrases. Many businesses use Web filtering software to limit employee's Web access. Some schools, libraries, and parents use this software to restrict access to minors.

POP-UP BLOCKERS   A *pop-up ad* is an Internet advertisement that appears in a new window in the foreground of a Web page displayed in your browser. A **pop-up blocker** is a filtering program that stops pop-up ads from displaying on Web pages. If your operating system does not block pop-up ads, many pop-up blockers can be downloaded from the Web at no cost.

File Compression

A **file compression utility** shrinks the size of a file(s). A compressed file takes up less storage space than the original file (Figure 8-37). Compressing files frees up room on the storage media and improves system performance. Attaching a compressed file to an e-mail message, for example, reduces the time needed for file transmission. Uploading and downloading compressed files to and from the Internet reduces the file transmission time.

Compressed files, sometimes called **zipped files**, usually have a .zip extension. When you receive or download a compressed file, you must uncompress it. To **uncompress**, or *unzip*, a file, you restore it to its original form. Some operating systems such as Windows XP include uncompress capabilities. To compress a file, however, you need a stand-alone file compression utility. Two popular stand-alone file compression utilities are PKZIP and WinZip.

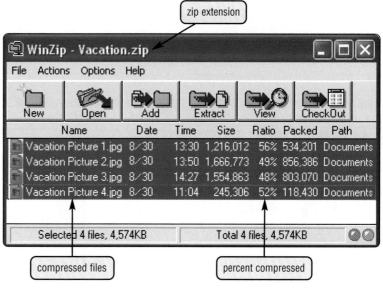

zip extension

compressed files

percent compressed

FIGURE 8-37   This file (Vacation) contains four compressed files. Without being compressed, these files consume 4,574 KB. Compressing them reduced the amount of storage by about 50 percent.

File Conversion

A *file conversion utility* transforms the contents of a file or data from one format to another. When a business develops a new information system, often the data in the current system is not in the correct format for the new system. Thus, part of the system development process is to convert data — instead of having users reenter all the existing data in the new system. On a smaller scale, when home users purchase new software, they may need to convert files so the files will be displayed properly in the new software.

CD/DVD Burning

CD/DVD burning software writes text, graphics, audio, and video files on a recordable or rewritable CD or DVD. This software enables the home user easily to back up contents of their hard disk on a CD/DVD and make duplicates of uncopyrighted music or movies. CD/DVD burning software usually also includes photo editing, audio editing, and video editing capabilities (Figure 8-38).

When you buy a recordable or rewritable CD or DVD, it typically includes CD/DVD burning software. You also can buy CD/DVD burning software for a cost of less than $100.

Personal Computer Maintenance

Operating systems typically include a diagnostic utility that diagnoses computer problems but does not repair them. A **personal computer maintenance utility** identifies and fixes operating system problems, detects and repairs disk problems, and includes the capability of improving a computer's performance. Additionally, some personal computer maintenance utilities continuously monitor a computer while you use it to identify and repair problems before they occur. Norton SystemWorks is a popular personal computer maintenance utility designed for Windows operating systems (Figure 8-39).

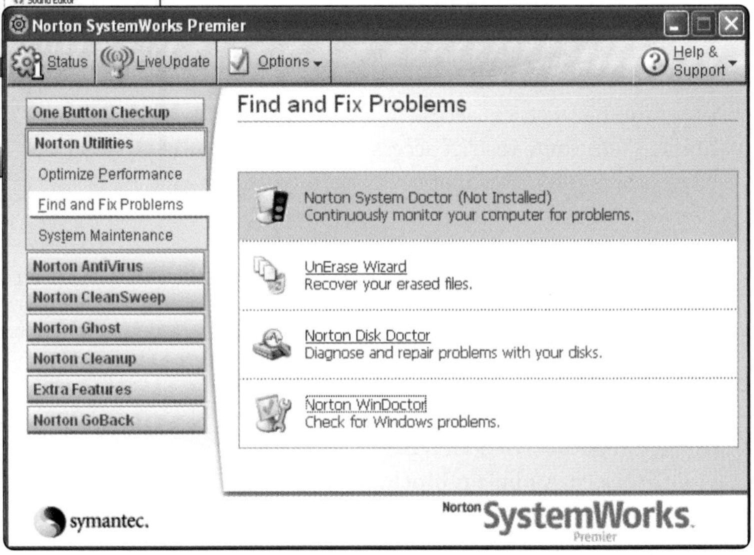

FIGURE 8-38 Using CD/DVD burning software, you can copy text, graphics, audio, and video files on CD or DVD, provided you have the correct type of CD/DVD drive and media.

FIGURE 8-39 A popular maintenance program for Windows users.

Test your knowledge of pages 422 through 428 in Quiz Yourself 8-3.

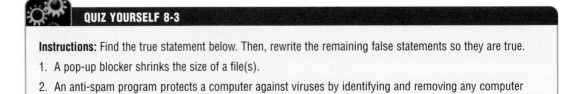

QUIZ YOURSELF 8-3

Instructions: Find the true statement below. Then, rewrite the remaining false statements so they are true.

1. A pop-up blocker shrinks the size of a file(s).

2. An anti-spam program protects a computer against viruses by identifying and removing any computer viruses found in memory, on storage media, or on incoming files.

3. Examples of network operating systems include NetWare, Windows Server 2003, UNIX, Linux, and Solaris.

4. Pocket PCs use Palm OS as their operating system.

5. Web filtering software writes text, graphics, audio, and video files to a recordable or rewritable CD or DVD.

Quiz Yourself Online: To further check your knowledge of network operating systems, embedded operating systems, and stand-alone utility programs, visit scsite.com/dc2006/ch8/quiz and then click Objectives 7 – 9.

CHAPTER SUMMARY

This chapter defined an operating system and then discussed the functions common to most operating systems. Next, it introduced several utility programs commonly found in operating systems (read At Issue 8-4 for a related discussion). The chapter discussed a variety of stand-alone operating systems, network operating systems, and embedded operating systems. Finally, the chapter described several stand-alone utility programs.

AT ISSUE 8-4

What Should Be in an Operating System?

Microsoft includes a Web browser, movie making software, a word processing program, plug-ins, a personal firewall, and other programs, utilities, and features with its Windows operating system. Apple bundles QuickTime, CD burning software, and other programs, utilities, and features into Mac OS X. Manufacturers say that combining additional features and programs with their operating systems is a convenience for consumers and sometimes integral to the operating systems' performance. Microsoft's built-in personal firewall, for example, helps protect computers from malicious attacks. Yet, because other developers create programs and features similar to those included with operating systems, some consumer advocates argue that bundling applications is unfair and leads to monopolies. Microsoft's bundling of its Web browser with its Windows operating system was the proximate cause of an antitrust action against the software giant. Critics also insist that bundling applications with an operating system forces consumers to pay for programs they may never use. Is bundling applications with an operating system fair, or is it a monopolistic practice? Why? Who should decide what an operating system should include? Why? Should computer manufacturers be allowed to choose which bundled applications are installed on computers that they ship to customers? Why or why not?

CAREER CORNER

Systems Programmer

System software is a key component in any computer. A *systems programmer* evaluates, installs, and maintains system software and provides technical support to the programming staff.

Systems programmers work with the programs that control computers, such as operating systems, network operating systems, and database systems. They identify current and future processing needs and then recommend the software and hardware necessary to meet those needs. In addition to selecting and installing system software, systems programmers must be able to adapt system software to the requirements of an organization, provide regular maintenance, measure system performance, determine the impact of new or updated software on the system, design and implement special software, and provide documentation. Because they are familiar with the entire system, systems programmers often help application programmers to diagnose technical problems.

Systems programmers must be acquainted thoroughly with a variety of operating systems. They must be able to think logically, pay attention to detail, work with abstract concepts, and devise solutions to complex problems. Systems programmers often work in teams and interact with programmers and nontechnical users, so communications skills are important.

Most systems programmers have a four-year B.S. degree in Computer Science or Information Technology. Depending on responsibilities and experience, salaries range from $53,000 to more than $100,000. For more information, visit scsite.com/dc2006/ch8/careers and then click Systems Programmer.

High-Tech Talk

WINDOWS XP: A USEFUL WAY TO COMPLETE A WIDE RANGE OF TASKS

When Microsoft developed the Windows XP operating system, it gave it a fresh, new graphical user interface. You still, however, can complete many important tasks using the command-line interface. Microsoft's first operating system, MS-DOS, was based entirely on a command-line interface. Today, Windows XP supports many of the original MS-DOS commands — and many new commands that help you complete tasks.

With Windows XP, you enter commands via a command shell. A *command shell* is a program with a nongraphical, command-line interface that provides an environment to run text-based application software and utility programs. The Windows XP command shell is called *Command Prompt*; the file name for the Command Prompt application is cmd.exe.

To open the Command Prompt window, click the Start button and point to All Programs, point to Accessories on the All Programs submenu, and then click Command Prompt on the Accessories submenu. Clicking Run on the Start menu and then typing cmd in the Run dialog box also opens the Command Prompt window. To execute a command, type one command per line and then press the ENTER key. Many commands allow you to enter one or more *options*, or *arguments*, which are additions to a command that change or refine the command in a specified manner. To close the Command Prompt window, type exit and then press the ENTER key or click the Close button in the Command Prompt window.

The Command Prompt window allows you to complete a wide range of tasks, including troubleshooting network connections. The *ping command*, for example, allows you to test TCP/IP connectivity for network and Internet connections (Figure 8-4a on page 403). When you enter the ping command with an IP address, your computer sends a special packet called ICMP Echo to that address. If everything is working, a reply comes back; if not, the ping times out. You also can use *TRACERT* (*traceroute*), a command-line utility that traces a data packet's path to its destination. When you enter tracert scsite.com, for example, the tracert utility traces the path from your computer to the Shelly Cashman Web server (Figure 8-40). The tracert command sends information to each device (called a hop) three times. The traceroute program sends the information three times to give you some idea of the variance in transit times. The time it takes for the device to respond each time is displayed. When you access a Web site, your request usually will pass through several routers before you connect to the destination server. For example, the tracert command for scsite.com passed through 15 other routers before connecting to the destination server (www.scsite.com).

You also can use the Windows XP Command Prompt to help manage your computer. When you enter the *systeminfo command*, Command Prompt queries your computer for basic system information, including operating system configuration and hardware properties, such as RAM and disk space. If you enter the *tasklist command*, the Command Prompt window returns a list of processes running on a computer, with each process identified by a process ID (PID). You can terminate any process by entering the *taskkill command* and the PID as the argument. Network administrators can use this command to fix problems on networked computers by closing applications.

The Windows XP Command Prompt also supports commands used to manage the files and file system on your hard disk. The *chkdsk command* checks for and corrects errors on the disk. You also can defragment your hard disk by entering the *defrag command*, with an argument specifying the drive to defragment (for example, defrag c:). When you are done working, you can use the *shutdown command* to shut down or restart your local or a remote computer.

In most cases, the command-line tools perform functions similar to the GUI application. The Disk Defragmenter utility and the defrag command, for example, provide similar functionality. In others, the command-line tools provide additional functionality. For instance, the *diskpart command* starts the command-line version of the DiskPart utility and gives you access to advanced features not available in the GUI version.

The commands discussed here are just some of the wide range of commands supported by Windows XP. For more information, visit scsite.com/dc2006/ch8/tech and then click Windows XP Command Prompt.

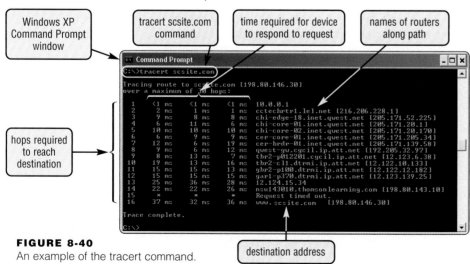

FIGURE 8-40
An example of the tracert command.

Windows XP Command Prompt window

tracert scsite.com command

time required for device to respond to request

names of routers along path

hops required to reach destination

destination address

Companies on the Cutting Edge

RED HAT
SHARING OPEN SOURCE SOFTWARE

When you were young, you were taught to share. University professors share their research with colleagues throughout the world; and *Red Hat* shares software code, or instructions, with computer users.

Red Hat is the largest supplier of open source software, which allows buyers to view, modify, and perhaps improve, the software. The company delivers the software improvements to customers through the Red Hat Network, the company's Internet service.

Bob Young and Marc Ewing founded Red Hat in 1994 and started distributing a version of the Red Hat Linux operating system complete with documentation and support. Today, Linux is Red Hat's most well-known product. In addition, its open source Apache Web server commands 67 percent of the market, according to E-Soft, a consulting firm that tracks online services. For more information, visit scsite.com/dc2006/ch8/companies and then click Red Hat.

SYMBIAN
HANDHELD COMPUTING DEVICES MANUFACTURER

The next time you send a text message using your smart phone, you may be using an operating system developed by *Symbian*. This British company's operating system is the global industry standard and is licensed to leading cellular telephone manufacturers, including Ericsson, Matsushita (Panasonic), Motorola, Nokia, and Psion, which account for more than 80 percent of annual worldwide mobile phone sales.

In 1994, former CEO Colly Myers began experimenting with his programming expertise with the goal of developing a full operating system for a handset rivaling that found on a mainframe computer. Four years later, he convinced Ericsson, Motorola, and Nokia to invest in his product.

The Symbian open standards allow manufacturers to customize services and user interfaces, including graphics, e-mail, and touch screens. For more information, visit scsite.com/dc2006/ch8/companies and then click Symbian.

Technology Trailblazers

ALAN KAY
COMPUTER PIONEER

Chances are that every time you use your computer you use one of *Alan Kay*'s ideas. More than 35 years ago — long before the personal computer became ubiquitous — he was developing a notebook computer complete with a flat screen, wireless network, and storage. More than 20 years ago, he engineered a graphical user interface, object-oriented languages, and personal computer networks.

Kay did much of his early work at the U.S. Defense Department's Advance Research Project Agency (DARPA) and Xerox's Palo Alto Research Center (PARC). Today he is a senior fellow at HP Labs and a computer science professor at UCLA. In 2004, he won three major awards for his breakthrough inventions that have enhanced society scientifically, culturally, and spiritually. For more information, visit scsite.com/dc2006/ch8/people and then click Alan Kay.

LINUS TORVALDS
LINUX CREATOR

When *Linus Torvalds* developed a new operating system in 1991, he announced his project in an Internet newsgroup, made the source code available, and asked for suggestions. Computer users responded by reviewing the system and offering enhancements. Three years later, Torvalds released a much-enhanced version of open source operating system he called Linux.

Torvalds decided to create the innovative operating system when he was a 21-year-old computer science student in Finland. Today, Linux is estimated to be running on at least 10 percent of computers and is Microsoft's main competitor. Torvalds leads the development of Linux as a fellow at OSDL (Open Source Development Labs), a not-for-profit consortium of companies dedicated to developing and promoting the operating system. For more information, visit scsite.com/dc2006/ch8/people and then click Linus Torvalds.

Quizzes and Learning Games

Computer Genius
Crossword Puzzle
DC Track and Field
Practice Test
Quiz Yourself
Wheel of Terms
You're Hired!

Exercises

Case Studies
▶ Chapter Review
Checkpoint
Key Terms
Learn How To
Learn It Online
Web Research

Beyond the Book

Career Corner
Companies
FAQs
High-Tech Talk
Looking Ahead
Making Use of the Web
Trailblazers
Web Links

Features

Chapter Forum
Install Computer
Lab Exercises
Maintain Computer
Tech News
Timeline 2006

Chapter Review

The Chapter Review section summarizes the concepts presented in this chapter. To listen to the audio version of this Chapter Review, visit scsite.com/dc2006/ch8/review. To obtain help from other students regarding any subject in this chapter, visit scsite.com/dc2006/ch8/forum and post your thoughts or questions.

① What Are the Types of System Software? **System software** consists of the programs that control or maintain the operations of a computer and its devices. Two types of system software are operating systems and utility programs. An **operating system (OS)** contains instructions that coordinate all the activities among computer hardware resources. A **utility program** performs maintenance-type tasks, usually related to managing a computer, its devices, or its programs.

② What Is the Startup Process on a Personal Computer? **Booting** is the process of starting or restarting a computer. When a user turns on a computer, the power supply sends a signal to the system unit. The processor chip finds the ROM chip(s) that contains the **BIOS**, which is firmware with the computer's startup instructions. The BIOS performs the *power-on self test* (*POST*) to check system components and compares the results with data in a CMOS chip. If the POST completes successfully, the BIOS searches for the *system files* and the *kernel* of the operating system, which manages memory and devices, and loads them into memory from storage. Finally, the operating system loads configuration information, requests any necessary user information, and displays the desktop on the screen.

③ What Are the Functions of an Operating System? The operating system provides a user interface, manages programs, manages memory, schedules jobs, configures devices, establishes an Internet connection, and monitors performance. The **user interface** controls how data and instructions are entered and how information is displayed. Three types of user interfaces are a *command-line interface*, a *menu-driven interface*, and a *graphical user interface* (*GUI*). Managing programs refers to how many users, and how many programs, an operating system can support at one time. An operating system can be *single user/single tasking*, *single user/multitasking*, *multiuser*, or *multiprocessing*. **Memory management** optimizes the use of random access memory (RAM). If memory is insufficient, the operating system may use **virtual memory**, which allocates a portion of a storage medium to function as additional RAM. Scheduling jobs determines the order in which jobs are processed. A **job** is an operation the processor manages. Configuring devices involves loading each device's driver when a user boots the computer. A **driver** is a program that tells the operating system how to communicate with a specific device. Establishing an Internet connection sets up a connection between a computer and an Internet service provider. A **performance monitor** is an operating system program that assesses and reports information about computer resources and devices.

④ How Can Operating Systems Help Administrators Control a Network and Manage Security? A **network operating system**, or *network OS*, is an operating system that organizes and coordinates how multiple users access and share network resources. A *network administrator* uses the network OS to add and remove users, computers, and other devices to and from the network. A network administrator also uses the network OS to administer network security. For each user, the network administrator establishes a user account that enables the user to **log on**, or access, the network by supplying the correct **user name** and **password**.

connect Visit scsite.com/dc2006/ch8/quiz or click the Quiz Yourself button. Click Objectives 1 – 4.

⑤ What Is the Purpose of the Utilities Included with Most Operating Systems? Most operating systems include several built-in utility programs. A **file manager** performs functions related to file and disk management. An **image viewer** displays, copies, and prints the contents of a graphics file. A **personal firewall** detects and protects a computer from unauthorized intrusions. An **uninstaller** removes a program and any associated entries in the system files. A **disk scanner** detects and corrects problems on a disk and searches for and removes unnecessary files. A **disk defragmenter** reorganizes the files and unused space on a computer's hard disk. A

Chapter Review

diagnostic utility compiles and reports technical information about a computer's hardware and certain system software programs. A **backup utility** is used to copy, or *back up*, selected files or an entire hard disk. A **screen saver** displays a moving image or blank screen if no keyboard or mouse activity occurs for a specified time.

(6) **What Are Features of Several Stand-Alone Operating Systems?**   A **stand-alone operating system** is a complete operating system that works on a desktop computer, notebook computer, or mobile computing device. Stand-alone operating systems include DOS, Windows XP, Mac OS X, UNIX, and Linux. **DOS** (*Disk Operating System*) refers to several single user, command-line operating systems developed for personal computers. **Windows XP** is Microsoft's fastest, most reliable Windows operating system, providing better performance and a simplified look. **Mac OS X** is a multitasking operating system available only for Apple computers. **UNIX** is a multitasking operating system developed at Bell Laboratories. **Linux** is a popular, multitasking UNIX-type operating system that is *open source software*, which means its code is available to the public.

Visit scsite.com/dc2006/ch8/quiz or click the Quiz Yourself button. Click Objectives 5 – 6.

(7) **What Are Various Network Operating Systems?**   Network operating systems include NetWare, Windows Server 2003, UNIX, Linux, and Solaris. Novell's *NetWare* is a network OS designed for client/server networks. **Windows Server 2003** is an upgrade to Windows 2000 Server and includes features of previous server versions. Linux, like UNIX, is a *multipurpose operating system* because it is both a stand-alone and network operating system. *Solaris*, a version of UNIX developed by Sun Microsystems, is a network OS designed for e-commerce applications.

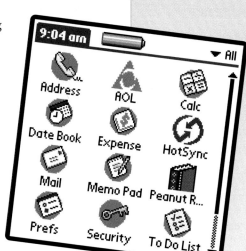

(8) **What Devices Use Embedded Operating Systems?**   Most PDAs and small devices have an **embedded operating system** that resides on a ROM chip. Popular embedded operating systems include Windows CE, Windows Mobile, Palm OS, embedded Linux, and Symbian OS. **Windows CE** is a scaled-down Windows operating system designed for use on communications, entertainment, and computing devices with limited functionality. **Windows Mobile** enhances Windows CE and provides a user interface designed for a specific type of PDA, called the **Pocket PC**. *Palm OS* is an operating system used on PDAs and smart phones. *Embedded Linux* is a scaled-down operating system for PDAs, smart phones and watches, and other devices with embedded operating systems. *Symbian OS* is an open source multitasking operating system designed for smart phones.

(9) **What Is the Purpose of Several Stand-Alone Utility Programs?**   Stand-alone utility programs offer improvements over features built into the operating system or provide features not included in the operating system. An **antivirus program** protects computers against a **virus**, or potentially damaging computer program, by identifying and removing any computer viruses. A

spyware remover detects and deletes *spyware*. Internet filter programs can include an **anti-spam** program, **Web filtering software**, and a **pop-up blocker**. A **file compression utility** shrinks the size of a file so that it takes up less storage space. A *file conversion utility* transforms the contents of a file from one format to another. **CD/DVD burning software** writes to a recordable or rewritable CD or DVD. A **personal computer maintenance utility** identifies and repairs operating system problems or disk problems, and improves a computer's performance.

Visit scsite.com/dc2006/ch8/quiz or click the Quiz Yourself button. Click Objectives 7 – 9.

Quizzes and
Learning Games

Computer Genius
Crossword Puzzle
DC Track and Field
Practice Test
Quiz Yourself
Wheel of Terms
You're Hired!

Exercises

Case Studies
Chapter Review
Checkpoint
▶ Key Terms
Learn How To
Learn It Online
Web Research

Beyond the Book

Career Corner
Companies
FAQs
High-Tech Talk
Looking Ahead
Making Use of
the Web
Trailblazers
Web Links

Features

Chapter Forum
Install Computer
Lab Exercises
Maintain Computer
Tech News
Timeline 2006

Key Terms

You should know the Primary Terms and be familiar with the Secondary Terms. Use the list below to help focus your study. To further enhance your understanding of the Key Terms in this chapter, visit scsite.com/dc2006/ch8/terms. See an example of and a definition for each term, and access current and additional information about the term from the Web.

Primary Terms

(shown in bold-black characters in the chapter)

anti-spam program (426)
antivirus program (426)
backup utility (415)
BIOS (400)
boot disk (402)
boot drive (402)
booting (400)
buffer (407)
CD/DVD burning software (428)
cold boot (400)
defragmenting (414)
diagnostic utility (414)
disk defragmenter (414)
disk scanner (414)
DOS (417)
driver (407)
embedded operating system (423)
file compression utility (427)
file manager (412)
formatting (412)
image viewer (412)
job (406)
Linux (421)
log on (410)
Mac OS X (420)
Macintosh operating system (420)
memory management (405)
network operating system (410)
operating system (OS) (398)
password (410)
performance monitor (409)
personal computer maintenance utility (428)
personal firewall (413)
Plug and Play (407)
Pocket PC (424)
pop-up blocker (427)
queue (407)
recovery disk (402)
restore program (415)
screen saver (415)
shortcut (412)
spooling (407)
spyware remover (426)
stand-alone operating system (416)
system software (398)
Trojan horse (426)
uncompress (427)
uninstaller (413)
UNIX (420)
user ID (410)
user interface (402)
user name (410)
utility (411)
utility program (411)
virtual memory (406)
virus (425)
warm boot (400)
Web filtering software (427)
Windows Mobile (424)
Windows Server 2003 (422)
Windows Server 2003 family (422)
Windows CE (423)
Windows XP (417)
worm (426)
zipped files (427)

Secondary Terms

(shown in italic characters in the chapter)

Active Directory (422)
back up (415)
background (404)
basic input/output system (400)
client operating systems (416)
command language (402)
command-line interface (402)
compress (415)
cross-platform (399)
device driver (407)
device-dependent (415)
device-independent (415)
Disk Operating System (417)
Dr. Watson (414)
embedded Linux (425)
encryption (411)
fault-tolerant computer (405)
file conversion utility (427)
foreground (404)
fragmented (414)
ghosting (415)
graphical user interface (GUI) (402)
hacker (413)
IRQ (interrupt request line) (409)
kernel (400)
malicious-logic program (426)
Media Center PC (419)
memory resident (400)
menu-driven interface (402)
multiprocessing (405)
multipurpose operating system (423)
multiuser (405)
NetWare (422)
network administrator (410)
network OS (410)
nonresident (400)
open source software (421)
page (406)
paging (406)
Palm OS (424)
platform (399)
pop-up ad (427)
power-on self test (POST) (400)
preemptive multitasking (405)
print spooler (407)
proprietary software (415)
registry (402)
scripts (402)
service pack (416)
single user/multitasking (403)
single user/single tasking (403)
Solaris (423)
spam (426)
spyware (426)
Startup folder (402)
swap file (406)
Symbian OS (425)
system files (401)
thrashing (406)
unzip (427)
virus author (425)
Web services (423)
Windows Explorer (412)
Windows Picture and Fax Viewer (412)
Windows Server 2003, Datacenter Edition (423)
Windows Server 2003, Enterprise Edition (422)
Windows Server 2003, Standard Edition (422)
Windows Server 2003, Web Edition (423)
Windows Server System (423)
Windows Small Business Server 2003 (422)
Windows XP 64-bit Edition (419)
Windows XP Home Edition (419)
Windows XP Media Center Edition (419)
Windows XP Professional (419)
Windows XP Tablet PC Edition (419)

Checkpoint

Use the Checkpoint exercises to check your knowledge level of the chapter. The Beyond the Book exercises will help broaden your understanding of the concepts presented in this chapter. To complete the Checkpoint exercises interactively, visit scsite.com/dc2006/ch8/check.

Label the Figure

Identify the various elements of virtual memory.

a. disk (virtual memory)
b. page swapped in
c. swap file
d. page swapped out
e. RAM (physical memory)

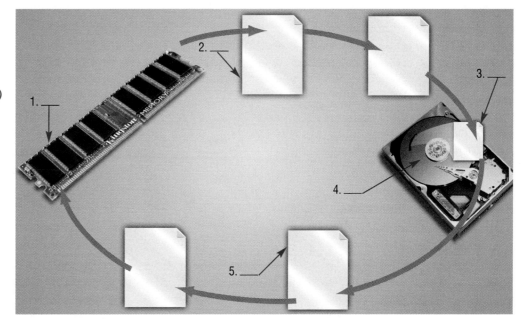

True/False

Mark T for True and F for False. (See page numbers in parentheses.)

_____ 1. All sizes of computers typically use the same operating system. (399)

_____ 2. Booting is the process of starting or restarting a computer. (400)

_____ 3. A user interface controls how you enter data and instructions and how information is displayed on the screen. (402)

_____ 4. By spooling print jobs to a buffer, a processor can continue interpreting and executing instructions while the printer prints, which allows users to work on the computer for other tasks. (407)

_____ 5. A utility program is a program that assesses and reports information about various computer resources and devices. (409)

_____ 6. A disk scanner is a utility that reorganizes the files and unused space on a computer's hard disk so the operating system accesses data more quickly and programs run faster. (414)

_____ 7. Some stand-alone operating systems are called client operating systems because they also work in conjunction with a network operating system. (416)

_____ 8. Some versions of Linux are command-line, and others are GUI. (421)

_____ 9. Most antivirus programs do not protect against worms or Trojan horses. (426)

_____ 10. A spyware remover is a utility program that detects and protects a personal computer from unauthorized intrusions. (426)

Quizzes and Learning Games

Computer Genius
Crossword Puzzle
DC Track and Field
Practice Test
Quiz Yourself
Wheel of Terms
You're Hired!

Exercises

Case Studies
Chapter Review
Checkpoint
Key Terms
Learn How To
Learn It Online
Web Research

Beyond the Book

Career Corner
Companies
FAQs
High-Tech Talk
Looking Ahead
Making Use of the Web
Trailblazers
Web Links

Features

Chapter Forum
Install Computer
Lab Exercises
Maintain Computer
Tech News
Timeline 2006

Checkpoint

 Multiple Choice   Select the best answer. (See page numbers in parentheses.)

1. The _____ chip, which uses battery power, stores configuration information about the computer. (400)
   a. BIOS   b. POST
   c. CMOS   d. RAM

2. In Windows XP, the _____ consists of several files that contain the system configuration information. (401)
   a. shortcut   b. page
   c. registry   d. swap file

3. Many current _____ operating systems incorporate features similar to those of a Web browser, such as links and navigation buttons. (402)
   a. command-line interface
   b. menu-driven interface
   c. graphical user interface
   d. all of the above

4. When an operating system spends much of its time paging, instead of executing application software, it is said to be _____. (406)
   a. booting
   b. thrashing
   c. spooling
   d. formatting

5. Encryption is the process of _____. (411)
   a. encoding data and information into an unreadable form
   b. recording successful and unsuccessful logon attempts in a file
   c. establishing a user account that allows a user to log on to a network
   d. entering a user name and password

6. Defragmenting reorganizes the files on a disk so they are located in _____ access time. (414)
   a. noncontiguous sectors, which slows
   b. noncontiguous sectors, which speeds
   c. contiguous sectors, which slows
   d. contiguous sectors, which speeds

7. Windows XP includes the _____, Dr. Watson, which detects problems as well as suggests courses of action. (414)
   a. file manager
   b. backup utility
   c. image viewer
   d. diagnostic utility

8. _____ used a command-line interface when Microsoft first developed it, although later versions included menu-driven user interfaces. (417)
   a. Windows XP
   b. DOS
   c. Mac OS X
   d. UNIX

9. Apple's _____ has set the standard for operating system ease of use and has been the model for most of the new GUIs. (420)
   a. UNIX operating system
   b. Macintosh operating system
   c. Windows XP operating system
   d. Linux operating system

10. In addition to being a stand-alone operating system, _____ also is a network operating system. (423)
    a. DOS   b. UNIX
    c. NetWare   d. Windows XP

11. _____, developed by Sun Microsystems, manages high-traffic accounts and incorporates security necessary for Web transactions. (423)
    a. Solaris
    b. Linux
    c. Windows Server 2003
    d. Netware

12. _____ is an open source multitasking operating system designed for smart phones. (425)
    a. Solaris
    b. Linux
    c. Symbian OS
    d. Palm OS

13. A _____ is a malicious-logic program that does not replicate itself to other computers. (426)
    a. virus   b. Trojan horse
    c. worm   d. all of the above

14. Web filtering software _____. (427)
    a. shrinks the size of a file
    b. enters a computer without a user's knowledge and secretly collects information about the user
    c. restricts access to certain material on the Web
    d. all of the above

Checkpoint

Matching

Match the terms with their definitions. (See page numbers in parentheses.)

_____ 1. kernel (400)

_____ 2. fault-tolerant computer (405)

_____ 3. page (406)

_____ 4. buffer (407)

_____ 5. IRQ (409)

_____ 6. user name (410)

_____ 7. shortcut (412)

_____ 8. restore program (415)

_____ 9. proprietary software (415)

_____ 10. uncompress (427)

a. communications line between a device and the processor

b. program that tells the operating system how to communicate with a device

c. continues to operate when one of its components fails

d. unique combination of characters that identifies one specific user

e. reverses the backup process and restores backed up files

f. core of an operating system that manages memory and devices, maintains system clock, starts applications, and other tasks

g. restore a zipped file to its original form

h. with virtual memory, the amount of data and program instructions that can be swapped at a given time

i. icon on the desktop that provides immediate access to a program or file

j. privately owned and limited to a specific vendor or computer model

k. segment of memory or storage in which items are placed while waiting to be transferred

l. contains a list of programs that open when a computer boots up

Short Answer

Write a brief answer to each of the following questions.

1. How is a cold boot different from a warm boot? _____ How is a memory-resident part of an operating system different from a nonresident part of an operating system? _____

2. What is a user interface? _____ How are a command-line interface, a menu-driven interface, and a graphical user interface different? _____

3. How is a single user/single tasking operating system different from a single user/multitasking operating system? _____ What is preemptive multitasking? _____

4. What is the difference between device-dependent and device-independent software? _____ What is proprietary software? _____

5. What is a malicious-logic program? _____ How is a worm different from a Trojan horse? _____

Beyond the Book

Read the following book elements, learn more about each using the Web, and then write a brief report.

1. At Issue — Who Is Responsible for Operating System Security? (410), Should Software Manufacturers Be Liable for Defective Software? (416), Closed Source vs. Open Source Software (421), or What Should Be in an Operating System? (429)

2. Career Corner — Systems Programmer (429)

3. Companies on the Cutting Edge – Red Hat or Symbian (431)

4. FAQs (402, 406, 409, 411, 413, 417, 419, 423, 426, 427)

5. High-Tech Talk — Windows XP: A Useful Way to Complete a Wide Range of Tasks (430)

6. Looking Ahead — The Future of Windows (418) or The Future of Linux (421)

7. Making Use of the Web — Weather, Sports, and News (124)

8. Picture Yourself Getting a Virus through E-Mail (396)

9. Technology Trailblazers — Alan Kay or Linus Torvalds (431)

10. Web Links (401, 407, 413, 415, 419, 420, 422, 424, 426)

Quizzes and Learning Games

Computer Genius
Crossword Puzzle
DC Track and Field
Practice Test
Quiz Yourself
Wheel of Terms
You're Hired!

Exercises

Case Studies
Chapter Review
Checkpoint
Key Terms
Learn How To
Learn It Online
Web Research

Beyond the Book

Career Corner
Companies
FAQs
High-Tech Talk
Looking Ahead
Making Use of the Web
Trailblazers
Web Links

Features

Chapter Forum
Install Computer
Lab Exercises
Maintain Computer
Tech News
Timeline 2006

Learn It Online

Use the Learn It Online exercises to reinforce your understanding of the chapter concepts. To access the Learn It Online exercises, visit scsite.com/dc2006/ch8/learn.

1 At the Movies — Windows XP Media Center Edition

To view the Windows XP Media Center Edition movie, click the number 1 button. Locate your video and click the corresponding High-Speed or Dial-Up link, depending on your Internet connection. Watch the movie and then complete the exercise by answering the questions that follow. Windows XP Media Center Edition 2004 is software that easily can enable advanced multimedia interactivity on your computer. With one touch of the remote control, you can activate your music, photographs, videos, radio shows, or television programs. Why is the Windows XP Media Center prone to viruses? How can you make sure your computer is protected from viruses?

2 At the Movies — Beam DVDs From Room to Room

To view the Beam DVDs From Room to Room movie, click the number 2 button. Locate your video and click the corresponding High-Speed or Dial-Up link, depending on your Internet connection. Watch the movie and then complete the exercise by answering the question that follows. With a moderately priced audio/video sender and receiver system you easily could hook up a small camera and monitor in any room in the house. What are the pros and cons of using video monitoring in your home?

3 Student Edition Labs — Installing and Uninstalling Software

Click the number 3 button. When the Student Edition Labs menu appears, click *Installing and Uninstalling Software* to begin. A new browser window will open. Follow the on-screen instructions to complete the Lab. When finished, click the Exit button. If required, submit your results to your instructor.

4 Practice Test

Click the number 4 button. Answer each question. When completed, enter your name and click the Grade Test button to submit the quiz for grading. Make a note of any missed questions. If required, submit your results to your instructor.

5 Who Wants To Be a Computer Genius²?

Click the number 5 button to find out if you are a computer genius. Directions about how to play the game will be displayed. When you are ready to play, click the Play button. Submit your score to your instructor.

6 Wheel of Terms

Click the number 6 button to reinforce important terms you learned in this chapter by playing the Shelly Cashman Series version of this popular game. Directions about how to play the game will be displayed. When you are ready to play, click the Play button. Submit your score to your instructor.

7 DC Track and Field

Click the number 7 button to use what you have learned in this chapter to compete against other students in three track and field events. Directions about how to play the game will be displayed. When you are ready to play, click the start first event button. If required, submit your score to your instructor.

Learn It Online

(8) You're Hired!

Click the number 8 button to use what you have learned in this chapter to embark on the path to a career in computers. Directions about how to play the game will be displayed. When you are ready to play, click the begin game button. If required, submit your score to your instructor.

(9) Crossword Puzzle Challenge

Click the number 9 button. Complete the puzzle to reinforce skills you learned in this chapter. Directions about how to play the game will be displayed. When you are ready to play, click the Submit button. Submit the completed puzzle to your instructor.

(10) Lab Exercises

Click the number 10 button. When the Lab Exercises menu appears, click the exercise assigned by your instructor. A new browser window will open. Follow the on-screen instructions to complete the exercise. When finished, click the Exit button. If required, submit your results to your instructor.

(11) In the News

When Windows XP was introduced in October 2001, hundreds queued up at computer outlets. It is unclear, however, whether the anticipation was caused by the new operating system or by the promotions many dealers offered. Click the number 11 button and read a news article about the impact, quality, or promotion of an operating system. What operating system was it? What was done to sell the operating system? Is the operating system recommended? Why or why not?

(12) Chapter Discussion Forum

Select an objective from this chapter on page 397 about which you would like more information. Click the number 12 button and post a short message listing a meaningful message title accompanied by one or more questions concerning the selected objective. In two days, return to the threaded discussion by clicking the number 12 button. Submit to your instructor your original message and at least one response to your message.

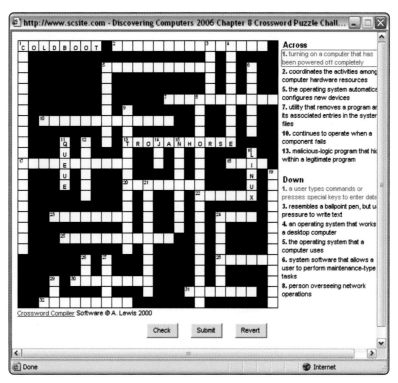

http://www.scsite.com - Discovering Computers 2006 Chapter 8 Crossword Puzzle Chall...

Across
1. turning on a computer that has been powered off completely
2. coordinates the activities among computer hardware resources
5. the operating system automatically configures new devices
7. utility that removes a program and its associated entries in the system files
10. continues to operate when a component fails
13. malicious-logic program that hides within a legitimate program

Down
1. a user types commands or presses special keys to enter data
3. resembles a ballpoint pen, but uses pressure to write text
4. an operating system that works on a desktop computer
5. the operating system that a computer uses
6. system software that allows a user to perform maintenance-type tasks
8. person overseeing network operations

Crossword Compiler Software © A. Lewis 2000

Check   Submit   Revert

Done   Internet

Quizzes and
Learning Games

Computer Genius
Crossword Puzzle
DC Track and Field
Practice Test
Quiz Yourself
Wheel of Terms
You're Hired!

Exercises

Case Studies
Chapter Review
Checkpoint
Key Terms
▶ Learn How To
Learn It Online
Web Research

Beyond the Book

Career Corner
Companies
FAQs
High-Tech Talk
Looking Ahead
Making Use of
the Web
Trailblazers
Web Links

Features

Chapter Forum
Install Computer
Lab Exercises
Maintain Computer
Tech News
Timeline 2006

Learn How To

Use the Learn How To activities to learn fundamental skills when using a computer and accompanying technology. Complete the exercises and submit them to your instructor. Visit scsite.com/dc2006/ch8/howto to obtain more information pertaining to each activity.

LEARN HOW TO 1: Install a Computer

Once you have purchased a computer, you must install it for use. Based on years of experience, a set of guidelines for installing and using your computer has been developed. To examine these guidelines, complete the following steps:
1. Start the browser on your computer.
2. Type the Web address `scsite.com/dc2006` in the Address box and then press the ENTER key.
3. Click the Chapter 8 link in the top navigation bar.
4. Click **Install Computer** in the left sidebar below the heading, Features.
5. Read the material presented about how to install a computer.

Exercise

1. Using your Web search skills, research the latest recommendations with respect to proper ergonomics for using a computer. What information did you find that you did not know before? What changes would you make to your current computer setup that might make you more productive? Submit your answers to your instructor.
2. Many people report illnesses or injuries from using computers. Perform research in a library or on the Web to discover the five most common ailments associated with using a computer. Determine the actions people can take to minimize or eliminate these ailments. Submit a report to your instructor describing your findings.
3. Your computer lab at school contains multiple computers for student use. Using the knowledge you have obtained from this Learn How To activity, evaluate the computer installation in your school lab. In a report to your instructor, specify those items you think can be improved in the lab.

LEARN HOW TO 2: Maintain a Computer

While computers are amazingly resilient and reliable, you still should perform certain activities to ensure they maintain peak performance. To learn about these activities, complete the following steps:
1. Start the browser on your computer.
2. Type the Web address `scsite.com/dc2006` in the Address box and then press the ENTER key.
3. Click the Chapter 8 link in the top navigation bar.
4. Click **Maintain Computer** in the left sidebar below the heading, Features.
5. Read the material presented about how to maintain a computer.

Exercise

1. On either your computer or the computer on which you are working, perform a hardware and software inventory of at least five hardware devices and five application programs on the computer. List the vendor, product, vendor Web address, vendor e-mail address, and vendor support telephone number. Submit your inventory to your instructor.
2. Record the serial number of the computer on which you are working. Then, record the serial number for seven different application programs on the computer. Submit this information to your instructor.

Learn How To

LEARN HOW TO 3: Keep Windows XP Up-to-Date

Keeping Windows XP up-to-date is a critical part of keeping your computer in good working order. The updates made available by Microsoft for no charge over the Internet will keep errors from occurring on your computer and will ensure that all security safeguards are in place. To update Windows, complete the following steps:

1. Click the Start button on the Windows taskbar, point to All Programs, and then click Windows Update on the All Programs submenu (Figure 8-41). *A browser window will open and display the Windows Update page.*
2. Click the Express Install (Recommended) link. Your computer will be examined and then a list of recommended updates for your computer will be shown.
3. If necessary, select those updates you wish to install and then click the Install button. Be aware that some updates might take 20 minutes or more to download and install, based primarily on your Internet access speed.
4. Often, after installation of updates, you must restart your computer to allow those updates to take effect. Be sure to save any open files before restarting your computer.

FIGURE 8-41

You also can schedule automatic updates for your computer. To do so, complete the following steps:

1. Click the Start button on the Windows taskbar and then click Control Panel on the Start menu.
2. In the Control Panel window, ensure that Category view is displayed, and then click Performance and Maintenance.
3. In the Performance and Maintenance window, click System.
4. In the System Properties dialog box, click the Automatic Updates tab. *The Automatic Updates sheet is displayed in the System Properties dialog box (Figure 8-42).*
5. Select the option you want to use for Windows updates. Microsoft, together with all security and operating system experts, strongly recommends you select Automatic so updates will be installed on your computer automatically. Notice that if you select Automatic, you also should select a time when your computer will be on and be connected to the Internet. A secondary choice is to download the suggested updates and then choose when you want to install them.
6. When you have made your selection, click the OK button in the System Properties dialog box.

Updating Windows on your computer is vital to maintain security and operational integrity.

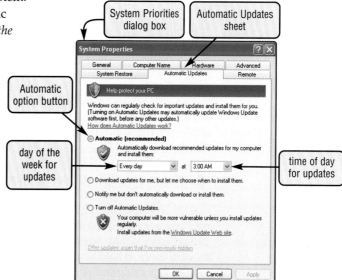

FIGURE 8-42

Exercise

1. Open the Windows Update window in your browser. Make a list of the recommended updates to Windows XP on the computer you are using. Add to the list the Custom Install updates that are available. If you are using your own computer, install the updates of your choice on your computer. Submit the list of updates to your instructor.
2. Optional: If you are not using your own computer, do not complete this exercise. Display the Automatic Updates sheet in the System Properties dialog box. Select the level of automatic updates you want to use. Write a report justifying your choice of automatic updates and then submit the report to your instructor.

Quizzes and Learning Games

Computer Genius
Crossword Puzzle
DC Track and Field
Practice Test
Quiz Yourself
Wheel of Terms
You're Hired!

Exercises

Case Studies
Chapter Review
Checkpoint
Key Terms
Learn How To
Learn It Online
Web Research

Beyond the Book

Career Corner
Companies
FAQs
High-Tech Talk
Looking Ahead
Making Use of the Web
Trailblazers
Web Links

Features

Chapter Forum
Install Computer
Lab Exercises
Maintain Computer
Tech News
Timeline 2006

Web Research

Use the Internet-based Web Research exercises to broaden your understanding of the concepts presented in this chapter. Visit scsite.com/dc2006/ch8/research to obtain more information pertaining to each exercise. To discuss any of the Web Research exercises in this chapter with other students, post your thoughts or questions at scsite.com/dc2006/ch8/forum.

① Scavenger Hunt Use one of the search engines listed in Figure 2-10 in Chapter 2 on page 78 or your own favorite search engine to find the answers to the questions that follow. Copy and paste the Web address from the Web page where you found the answer. Some questions may have more than one answer. If required, submit your answers to your instructor. (1) What are the three file systems for disk partitions on a computer running the Windows XP operating system? Which of the three does Microsoft recommend using? Why? (2) If you use Microsoft Office on a computer running Windows XP, can you use the same software on a computer running the UNIX or Linux operating system? Why or why not? (3) What did Gary Kildall develop in 1974 while working for Intel? What is the basis of the lawsuit Caldera Inc. filed against Microsoft in 1996?

② Search Sleuth A search engine using a concept-based search system seeks Web sites containing a search term along with related concepts. For example, if you search for "operating systems," this type of search engine also returns links to books, professional organizations, and other operating system-related topics. Many researchers consider Excite (excite.com) the best concept-based search engine. Visit this Web site and then use your word processing program to answer the following questions. Then, if required, submit your answers to your instructor. (1) Click the Member Info link at the bottom of the page. What are the benefits of free membership? (2) Click the Web search text box and type "utility programs" in the box. How many search results are returned that are not sponsored links? (3) Click the View By Search Engine option button near the top of the page. What are three search engines Excite used to return results? Which search engine returned the most links? (4) Click two of the unsponsored links that discuss backing up and recovering files. Review these articles and then write a 50-word summary of your findings.

③ Journaling Respond to your readings in this chapter by writing at least one page about your reactions, evaluations, and reflections about using stand-alone utility programs. For example, does your computer have an antivirus program? If so, how often do you check for new virus definition updates? Has a virus ever infected one of your files or your computer? Do you have a backup of your hard disk? Do you have a recovery disk? Do you have a personal firewall? You also can write about the new terms you learned by reading this chapter. If required, submit your journal to your instructor.

④ Expanding Your Understanding Instant messaging (IM) is moving into the workplace. According to America Online, 59 percent of Internet users use IM, and 27 percent of these people use IM at work. Computer industry analysts predict this method of electronic communication will overtake e-mail during the next few years. With IM's popularity comes spim, a junk message. Yahoo! reports that 2 percent of the instant messages sent over its network are spim. View Web sites to learn more about IM's popularity and spim. What programs allow you to filter instant messages? Write a report summarizing your findings, focusing on the possible uses of this method of communication in the workplace. If required, submit your report to your instructor.

⑤ Ethics in Action Several automobile insurers, including Progressive Casualty Insurance Company, are promising drivers insurance premium discounts if they install a data recorder in their cars to track their driving and then exercise good driving behavior. Progressive customers voluntarily taking part in this TripSense program upload the data from their monitors monthly and hope to decrease their insurance bills by a maximum of 25 percent. Privacy experts predict more insurance companies will offer this monitoring system and that it eventually will become mandatory. These critics fear that negative data will be used against poor drivers and possibly be subpoenaed in litigation. View online sites that provide information about vehicle monitoring devices. Write a report summarizing your findings and include a table of links to Web sites that provide additional details. If required, submit your report to your instructor.

Case Studies

Use the Case Studies to apply the concepts presented in the chapter to real-world situations. Visit scsite.com/dc2006/ch8/cases to obtain more information pertaining to each exercise. To discuss the Case Studies in this chapter with other students, visit scsite.com/dc2006/ch8/forum and post your thoughts or questions.

CASE STUDY 1 — Class Discussion   Many students at the local college have been using the college's computers to download music from the Internet. You have been asked to serve on a student committee to draft a policy addressing this questionable use of the college's computers. Is it the college's responsibility to block music downloads? Why or why not? How would the college prevent students from **downloading music**? What is the difference between taping a song heard on the radio and downloading music from the Internet? Should violators be expelled, fined, required to attend a seminar on the ethical use of computers, or given a verbal warning? What recommendations would you give to the committee regarding the downloading of music? Draft a memo addressed to all students regarding this matter. Be prepared to discuss your recommendations in class.

CASE STUDY 2 — Class Discussion   It is legal to **copy songs from a CD**, provided it was purchased legally. A principal at a local high school, however, has learned that students have been copying popular tracks from purchased music CDs to other CDs using the school's computer and then selling the CDs for $1.00 each. As the dean of students, what action would you take against the students copying the CDs? What action would you take against students buying the illegal copies? Write a brief report, and be prepared to discuss your recommendations in class.

CASE STUDY 3 — Research   Your neighbor is buying a new computer both for personal use and to run her floral business, which she operates out of her home. She is undecided on the Windows operating system to purchase with her new computer. **Windows XP** Professional Edition is intended for business and power users. Windows XP Home Edition is designed for home computing. She has asked you to help her decide if she should buy one or the other. Use the Web and/or print media to develop a report that lists the differences. Which Windows XP Professional Edition features are not available in Windows XP Home Edition? Submit your report or use PowerPoint to create a presentation and share your findings with your class.

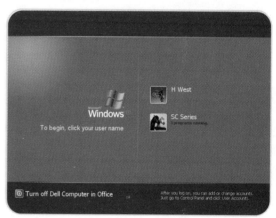

CASE STUDY 4 — Research   Many programs are available for users of personal computers. The owner of the pet store, Friendly Pets, where you work part time is interested in purchasing an **antivirus program**. Because you are taking a computer class, she has asked you to help her choose the best program. Choose at least two competing manufacturers of antivirus programs. Use the Web and/or print media and compare the programs. For each program, answer the following questions: What is the program's function? What are the system requirements? How easy is the program to use? Does it include a firewall? Does it protect against spam and spyware? How do you obtain updates to the program? How much does the program cost? In your opinion, is the program worth the price? Why or why not? Which one would you buy? Why? Write a brief report or use PowerPoint to create a presentation and share your findings with your class.

CASE STUDY 5 — Team Challenge   Your team members are employed as analysts at Soap-n-Suds, an international manufacturer of laundry soaps. The company currently uses an early version of the Windows operating system on its 5,000 desktop computers. Next year, the company plans to upgrade the operating system and, if necessary, its desktop computers. The vice-president of information technology has asked your team to compare the latest desktop versions of the Windows operating system, the **Mac operating system**, and the Linux operating system. Assign each member of your team an operating system. Have each member use the Web and/or print media to develop a feature/benefit report. What is the initial cost of the operating system per computer? What are the memory and storage requirements? Will the operating system require the company to purchase new computers? Are training costs involved? Which one is best at avoiding viruses, spam, and spyware? Which operating system is easier to use? Why? Can Microsoft Office run under the operating system? As a team, merge your findings into a team report and/or PowerPoint presentation and share your findings with your class.

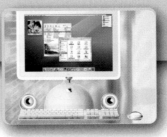

Special Feature

Buyer's Guide 2006:
How to Purchase a Personal Computer

(a) desktop computer

At some point, perhaps while you are taking this course, you may decide to buy a personal computer. The decision is an important one and will require an investment of both time and money. Like many buyers, you may have little computer experience and find yourself unsure of how to proceed. You can get started by talking to your friends, coworkers, and instructors about their computers. What type of computers did they buy? Why? For what purposes do they use their computers? You also should answer the following four questions to help narrow your choices to a specific computer type, before reading this Buyer's Guide.

(b) mobile computer (notebook computer or Tablet PC)

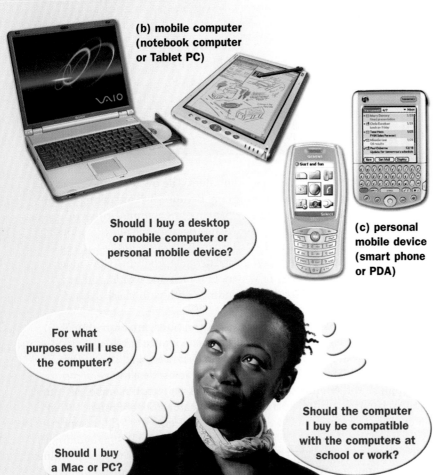

Should I buy a desktop or mobile computer or personal mobile device?

(c) personal mobile device (smart phone or PDA)

For what purposes will I use the computer?

Should the computer I buy be compatible with the computers at school or work?

Should I buy a Mac or PC?

1 **Do you want a desktop computer, mobile computer, or personal mobile device?** A desktop computer (Figure 1a) is designed as a stationary device that sits on or below a desk or table in a location such as a home, office, or dormitory room. A desktop computer must be plugged into an electrical outlet to operate. A mobile computer, such as a notebook computer or Tablet PC (Figure 1b), is smaller than a desktop computer, more portable, and has a battery that allows you to operate it for a period without an electrical outlet. A personal mobile device (Figure 1c) runs on a battery for a longer period of time than a notebook computer or Tablet PC and can fit in your pocket.

Desktop computers are a good option if you work mostly in one place and have plenty of space in your work area. Desktop computers generally give you more performance for your money.

Increasingly, more desktop computer users are buying mobile computers to take advantage of their portability to work in the library, at school, while traveling, and at home. The past disadvantages of mobile computers, such as lower processor speeds, poor-quality monitors, weight, short battery life, and significantly higher prices, have all but disappeared when compared with desktop computers.

FIGURE 1

If you are thinking of using a mobile computer to take notes in class or in business meetings, then consider a Tablet PC with handwriting and drawing capabilities. Typically, note-taking involves writing text notes and drawing charts, schematics, and other illustrations. By allowing you to write and draw directly on the screen with a digital pen, a Tablet PC eliminates the distracting sound of the notebook keyboard tapping and allows you to capture drawings. Some notebook computers can convert to Tablet PCs.

A personal mobile device, such as a smart phone or a PDA, is ideal if you require a pocket-sized computing device as you move from place to place. Personal mobile devices provide personal organizer functions, such as a calendar, appointment book, address book, and many other applications. The small size of the processor, screen, and keyboard, however, limit a personal mobile device's capabilities when compared with a desktop or notebook computer or a Tablet PC. For this reason, most people who purchase personal mobile devices also have a desktop or notebook computer to handle heavy-duty applications.

Drawbacks of mobile computers and personal mobile devices are that they tend to have a shorter useful lifetime than desktop computers and lack the high-end capabilities. Their portability makes them susceptible to vibrations, heat or cold, and accidental drops, which can cause components such as hard disks or display devices to fail. Also, because of their size and portability, they are easy to lose and are the prime targets of thieves.

② **For what purposes will you use the computer?** Having a general idea of the purposes for which you want to use your computer will help you decide on the type of computer to buy. At this point in your research, it is not necessary to know the exact application software titles or version numbers you might want to use. Knowing that you plan to use the computer primarily to create word processing, spreadsheet, database, and presentation documents, however, will point you in the direction of a desktop or notebook computer. If you want the portability of a smart phone or PDA, but you need more computing power, then a Tablet PC may be the best alternative. You also must consider that some application software runs only on a Mac, while others run only on a PC with the Windows operating system. Still other software may run only on a PC running the UNIX or Linux operating system.

③ **Should the computer be compatible with the computers at school or work?** If you plan to bring work home, telecommute, or take distance education courses, then you should purchase a computer that is compatible with those at school or work.

Compatibility is primarily a software issue. If your computer runs the same operating system version, such as Microsoft Windows XP, and the same application software, such as Microsoft Office, then your computer will be able to read documents created at school or work and vice versa. Incompatible hardware can become an issue if you plan to connect directly to a school or office network using a cable or wireless technology. You usually can obtain the minimum system requirements from the Information Technology department at your school or workplace.

④ **Should the computer be a Mac or PC?** If you ask a friend, coworker, or instructor, which is better — a Mac or a PC — you may be surprised by the strong opinion expressed in the response. No other topic in the computer industry causes more heated debate. The Mac has strengths, especially in the areas of graphics, movies, photos, and music. The PC, however, has become the industry standard with 95 percent of the market share. Figure 2 compares features of the Mac and PC in several different areas. Overall, the Mac and PC have more similarities than differences, and you should consider cost, compatibility, and other factors when choosing whether to purchase a Mac or PC.

Area	Comparison
Cost and availability	A Mac is priced slightly higher than a PC. Mac peripherals also are more expensive. The PC offers more available models from a wide range of vendors. You can custom build, upgrade, and expand a PC for less money than a Mac.
Exterior design	The Mac has a more distinct and stylish appearance than most PCs.
Free software	Although free software for the Mac is available on the Internet, significantly more free software applications are available for the PC.
Market share	The PC dominates the personal computer market. While the Mac sells well in education, publishing, Web design, graphics, and music, the PC is the overwhelming favorite of businesses.
Operating system	Users claim that Mac OS X provides a better all-around user experience than Microsoft Windows XP. Both the Mac and PC supports other operating systems, such as Linux and UNIX.
Program control	Both have simple and intuitive graphical user interfaces. The Mac relies more on the mouse and less on keyboard shortcuts than the PC. The mouse on the Mac has one button, whereas the mouse on a PC has a minimum of two buttons.
Software availability	The basic application software most users require, such as Microsoft Office, is available for both the Mac and PC. More specialized software, however, often is available only for PCs. Many programs are released for PCs long before they are released for Macs.
Speed	The PC provides faster processors than the Mac.
Viruses	Dramatically fewer viruses attack Macs. Mac viruses also generally are less infectious than PC viruses.

FIGURE 2 Comparison of Mac and PC features.

After evaluating the answers to these four questions, you should have a general idea of how you plan to use your computer and the type of computer you want to buy. Once you have decided on the type of computer you want, you can follow the guidelines presented in this Buyer's Guide to help you purchase a specific computer, along with software, peripherals, and other accessories.

Many of the desktop computer guidelines presented also apply to the purchase of a notebook computer, Tablet PC, and personal mobile device. Later in this Buyer's Guide, sections on purchasing a notebook computer or Tablet PC address additional considerations specific to those computer types.

This Buyer's Guide concentrates on recommendations for purchasing a desktop computer or mobile computer. For recommendations on purchasing a personal mobile device, see page 296 in the Personal Mobile Devices feature that follows Chapter 5.

Type of Computer	Web Site	Web Address
PC	CNET Shopper	shopper.cnet.com
	PC World Magazine	pcworld.com
	BYTE Magazine	byte.com
	PC Magazine	zdnet.com/reviews
	Yahoo! Computers	computers.yahoo.com
	MSN Shopping	eshop.msn.com
	Dave's Guide to Buying a Home Computer	css.msu.edu/PC-Guide
Mac	Macworld Magazine	macworld.com
	Apple	apple.com
	Switch to Mac Campaign	apple.com/switch

For an updated list of hardware and software reviews and their Web site addresses, visit scsite.com/dc2006/ch8/buyers.

FIGURE 3 Hardware and software reviews.

HOW TO PURCHASE A DESKTOP COMPUTER

Once you have decided that a desktop computer is most suited to your computing needs, the next step is to determine specific software, hardware, peripheral devices, and services to purchase, as well as where to buy the computer.

1 **Determine the specific software you want to use on your computer.** Before deciding to purchase software, be sure it contains the features necessary for the tasks you want to perform. Rely on the computer users in whom you have confidence to help you decide on the software to use. The minimum requirements of the software you select may determine the operating system (Microsoft Windows XP, Linux, UNIX, Mac OS X) you need. If you have decided to use a particular operating system that does not support software you want to use, you may be able to purchase similar software from other manufacturers.

Many Web sites and trade magazines, such as those listed in Figure 3, provide reviews of software products. These Web sites frequently have articles that rate computers and software on cost, performance, and support.

Your hardware requirements depend on the minimum requirements of the software you will run on your computer. Some software requires more memory and disk space than others, as well as additional input, output, and storage devices. For example, suppose you want to run software that can copy one CD's or DVD's contents directly to another CD or DVD, without first copying the data to your hard disk. To support that, you should consider a desktop computer or a high-end notebook computer, because the computer will need two CD or DVD drives: one that reads from a CD or DVD, and one that reads from and writes on a CD or DVD. If you plan to run software that allows your computer to work as an entertainment system, then you will need a CD or DVD drive, quality speakers, and an upgraded sound card.

2 **Look for bundled software.** When you purchase a computer, it may come bundled with software. Some sellers even let you choose which software you want. Remember, however, that bundled software has value only if you would have purchased the software even if it had not come with the computer. At the very least, you probably will want word processing software and a browser to access the Internet. If you need additional applications, such as a spreadsheet, a database, or presentation graphics, consider purchasing Microsoft Works, Microsoft Office, OpenOffice.org, or Sun StarOffice, which include several programs at a reduced price.

3 **Avoid buying the least powerful computer available.** Once you know the application software you want to use, you then can consider the following important criteria about the computer's components: (1) processor speed, (2) size and types of memory (RAM) and storage, (3) types of input/output devices, (4) types of ports and adapter cards, and (5) types of communications devices. The information in Figures 4 and 5 can help you determine what system components are best for you. Figure 4 outlines considerations for specific hardware components. Figure 5 (on page 449) provides a Base Components worksheet that lists PC recommendations for each category of user discussed in this book: Home User,

Small Office/Home Office User, Mobile User, Power User, and Large Business User. In the worksheet, the Home User category is divided into two groups: Application Home User and Game Home User. The Mobile User recommendations list criteria for a notebook computer, but do not include the PDA or Tablet PC options.

Computer technology changes rapidly, meaning a computer that seems powerful enough today may not serve your computing needs in a few years. In fact, studies show that many users regret not buying a more powerful computer. To avoid this, plan to buy a computer that will last you for two to three years. You can help delay obsolescence by purchasing the fastest processor, the most memory, and the largest hard disk you can afford. If you must buy a less powerful computer, be sure you can upgrade it with additional memory, components, and peripheral devices as your computer requirements grow.

CD/DVD Drives: Most computers come with a 32X to 48X speed CD-ROM drive that can read CDs. If you plan to write music, audio files, and documents on a CD, then you should consider upgrading to a CD-RW. An even better alternative is to upgrade to a DVD+RW combination drive. It allows you to read DVDs and CDs and to write data on (burn) a DVD or CD. A DVD has a capacity of at least 4.7 GB versus the 650 MB capacity of a CD.

Card Reader/Writer: A card reader/writer is useful for transferring data directly to and from a removable flash memory card, such as the ones used in your camera or music player. Make sure the card reader/writer can read from and write on the flash memory cards that you use.

Digital Camera: Consider an inexpensive point-and-shoot digital camera. They are small enough to carry around, usually operate automatically in terms of lighting and focus, and contain storage cards for storing photographs. A 2- to 4-megapixel camera with an 8 MB or 16 MB storage card is fine for creating images for use on the Web or to send via e-mail.

Digital Video Capture Device: A digital video capture device allows you to connect your computer to a camcorder or VCR and record, edit, manage, and then write video back on a VCR tape, a CD, or a DVD. The digital video capture device can be an external device or an adapter card. To create quality video (true 30 frames per second, full-sized TV), the digital video capture device should have a USB 2.0 or FireWire port. You will find that a standard USB port is too slow to maintain video quality. You also will need sufficient storage: an hour of data on a VCR tape takes up about 5 GB of disk storage.

Floppy Disk Drive: If you plan to use a floppy disk drive, then make sure the computer you purchase has a standard 3.5", 1.44 MB floppy disk drive. A floppy disk drive is useful for backing up and transferring files.

Hard Disk: It is recommended that you buy a computer with 40 to 60 GB if your primary interests are browsing the Web and using e-mail and Office suite-type applications; 60 to 80 GB if you also want to edit digital photographs; 80 to 100 GB if you plan to edit digital video or manipulate large audio files even occasionally; and 100 to 160 GB if you will edit digital video, movies, or photography often; store audio files and music; or consider yourself to be a power user.

Joystick/Wheel: If you use your computer to play games, then you will want to purchase a joystick or a wheel. These devices, especially the more expensive ones, provide for realistic game play with force feedback, programmable buttons, and specialized levers and wheels.

Keyboard: The keyboard is one of the more important devices used to communicate with the computer. For this reason, make sure the keyboard you purchase has 101 to 105 keys, is comfortable and easy to use, and has a USB connection. A wireless keyboard should be considered, especially if you have a small desk area.

Microphone: If you plan to record audio or use speech recognition to enter text and commands, then purchase a close-talk headset with gain adjustment support.

Modem: Most computers come with a modem so that you can use your telephone line to dial out and access the Internet. Some modems also have fax capabilities. Your modem should be rated at 56 Kbps.

Monitor: The monitor is where you will view documents, read e-mail messages, and view pictures. A minimum of a 17" screen is recommended, but if you are planning to use your computer for graphic design or game playing, then you may want to purchase a 19" or 21" monitor. The LCD flat panel monitor should be considered, especially if space is an issue.

FIGURE 4 Hardware guidelines.

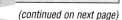

(continued on next page)

(continued from previous page)

Mouse: As you work with your computer, you use the mouse constantly. For this reason, spend a few extra dollars, if necessary, and purchase a mouse with an optical sensor and USB connection. The optical sensor replaces the need for a mouse ball, which means you do not need a mouse pad. For a PC, make sure your mouse has a wheel, which acts as a third button in addition to the top two buttons on the left and right. An ergonomic design is also important because your hand is on the mouse most of the time when you are using your computer. A wireless mouse should be considered to eliminate the cord and allow you to work at short distances from your computer.

Network Card: If you plan to connect to a network or use broadband (cable or DSL) to connect to the Internet, then you will need to purchase a network card. Broadband connections require a 10/100 PCI Ethernet network card.

Printer: Your two basic printer choices are ink-jet and laser. Color ink-jet printers cost on average between $50 and $300. Laser printers cost from $200 to $2,000. In general, the cheaper the printer, the lower the resolution and speed, and the more often you are required to change the ink cartridge or toner. Laser printers print faster and with a higher quality than an ink-jet, and their toner on average costs less. If you want color, then go with a high-end ink-jet printer to ensure quality of print. Duty cycle (the number of pages you expect to print each month) also should be a determining factor. If your duty cycle is on the low end — hundreds of pages per month — then stay with a high-end ink-jet printer, rather than purchasing a laser printer. If you plan to print photographs taken with a digital camera, then you should purchase a photo printer. A photo printer is a dye-sublimation printer or an ink-jet printer with higher resolution and features that allow you to print quality photographs.

Processor: For a PC, a 2.8 GHz Intel or AMD processor is more than enough processor power for application home and small office/home office users. Game home, large business, and power users should upgrade to faster processors.

RAM: RAM plays a vital role in the speed of your computer. Make sure the computer you purchase has at least 512 MB of RAM. If you have extra money to invest in your computer, then consider increasing the RAM to 1 GB or more. The extra money for RAM will be well spent.

Scanner: The most popular scanner purchased with a computer today is the flatbed scanner. When evaluating a flatbed scanner, check the color depth and resolution. Do not buy anything less than a color depth of 48 bits and a resolution of 1200 x 2400 dpi. The higher the color depth, the more accurate the color. A higher resolution picks up the more subtle gradations of color.

Sound Card: Most sound cards today support the Sound Blaster and General MIDI standards and should be capable of recording and playing digital audio. If you plan to turn your computer into an entertainment system or are a game home user, then you will want to spend the extra money and upgrade from the standard sound card.

Speakers: Once you have a good sound card, quality speakers and a separate subwoofer that amplifies the bass frequencies of the speakers can turn your computer into a premium stereo system.

PC Video Camera: A PC video camera is a small camera used to capture and display live video (in some cases with sound), primarily on a Web page. You also can capture, edit, and share video and still photos. The camera sits on your monitor or desk. Recommended minimum specifications include 640 x 480 resolution, a video with a rate of 30 frames per second, and a USB 2.0 or FireWire connection.

USB Flash Drive: If you work on different computers and need access to the same data and information, then this portable miniature mobile storage device is ideal. USB flash drive capacity varies from 16 MB to 4 GB.

Video Graphics Card: Most standard video cards satisfy the monitor display needs of application home and small office users. If you are a game home user or a graphic designer, you will want to upgrade to a higher quality video card. The higher refresh rates will further enhance the display of games, graphics, and movies.

Wireless LAN Access Point: A Wireless LAN Access Point allows you to network several computers, so they can share files and access the Internet through a single cable modem or DSL connection. Each device that you connect requires a wireless card. A Wireless LAN Access Point can offer a range of operations up to several hundred feet, so be sure the device has a high-powered antenna.

Zip Drive: Consider purchasing a Zip drive to back up important files. The Zip drive, which has a capacity of up to 750 MB, is sufficient for most users. An alternative to purchasing a backup drive is to purchase a CD-RW or DVD+RW and burn backups of key files on a CD or DVD.

BASE COMPONENTS

	Application Home User	Game Home User	Small Office/Home Office User	Mobile User	Large Business User	Power User
HARDWARE						
Processor	Pentium 4 at 2.8 GHz	Pentium 4 at 3.0 GHz	Pentium 4 at 3.0 GHz	Pentium 4M at 2.4 GHz	Pentium 4 at 3.4 GHz	Multiple Itanium at 1.6 GHz
RAM	512 MB	1 GB	512 MB	512 MB	1 GB	2 GB
Cache	256 KB L2	512 KB L2	512 KB L2	512 KB L2	512 KB L2	2 MB L3
Hard Disk	80 GB	120 GB	120 GB	60 GB	160 GB	300 GB
Monitor/LCD Flat Panel	17" or 19"	21"	19" or 21"	15.7" Wide Display	19" or 21"	23"
Video Graphics Card	256 MB	512 MB	256 MB	32 MB	128 MB	256 MB
CD/DVD Bay 1	48x CD-ROM	48x CD-RW Drive	48x CD-ROM	24X CD-RW/DVD	48x CD-RW Drive	16x DVD-ROM
CD/DVD Bay 2	8x DVD+RW	12x DVD+RW	8x DVD+RW	4x DVD+RW	12x DVD+RW	8x DVD+RW
Floppy Disk Drive	3.5"	3.5"	3.5"	3.5"	3.5"	3.5"
Printer	Color Ink-Jet	Color Ink-Jet	18 ppm Laser	Portable Ink-Jet	50 ppm Laser	10 ppm Laser
PC Video Camera	Yes	Yes	Yes	Yes	Yes	Yes
Fax/Modem	Yes	Yes	Yes	Yes	Yes	Yes
Microphone	Close-Talk Headset with Gain Adjustment	Close-Talk Headset with Gain Adjustment	Close-Talk Headset with Gain Adjustment	Close-Talk Headset with Gain Adjustment	Close-Talk Headset with Gain Adjustment	Close-Talk Headset with Gain Adjustment
Speakers	Stereo	Full-Dolby Surround	Stereo	Stereo	Stereo	Full-Dolby Surround
Pointing Device	IntelliMouse or Optical Mouse	Laser Mouse and Joystick	IntelliMouse or Optical Mouse	Touchpad or Pointing Stick and Laser Mouse	IntelliMouse or Optical Mouse	IntelliMouse or Laser Mouse and Joystick
Keyboard	Yes	Yes	Yes	Built-In	Yes	Yes
Backup Disk/Tape Drive	250 MB Zip®	External or Removable Hard Disk	External or Removable Hard Disk	External or Removable Hard Disk	Tape Drive	External or Removable Hard Disk
USB Flash Drive	128 MB	256 MB	256 MB	256 MB	4 GB	2 GB
Sound Card	Sound Blaster Compatible	Sound Blaster Audigy 2	Sound Blaster Compatible	Built-In	Sound Blaster Compatible	Sound Blaster Audigy 2
Network Card	Yes	Yes	Yes	Yes	Yes	Yes
TV-Out Connector	Yes	Yes	Yes	Yes	Yes	Yes
USB Port	6	8	6	2	8	8
FireWire Port	2	2	2	1	2	2
SOFTWARE						
Operating System	Windows XP Home Edition with Service Pack 2	Windows XP Home Edition with Service Pack 2	Windows XP Professional with Service Pack 2	Windows XP Professional with Service Pack 2	Windows XP Professional with Service Pack 2	Windows XP Professional with Service Pack 2
Application Suite	Office 2003 Standard Edition	Office 2003 Standard Edition	Office 2003 Small Business Edition	Office2003 Small Business Edition	Office 2003 Professional	Office 2003 Professional
Antivirus	Yes, 12-Mo. Subscription	Yes, 12-Mo. Subscription	Yes, 12-Mo. Subscription	Yes, 12-Mo. Subscription	Yes, 12-Mo. Subscription	Yes, 12-Mo. Subscription
Internet Access	Cable, DSL, or Dial-up	Cable or DSL	Cable, DSL, or Dial-up	Wireless or Dial-up	LAN/WAN (T1/T3)	Cable or DSL
OTHER						
Surge Protector	Yes	Yes	Yes	Portable	Yes	Yes
Warranty	3-Year Limited, 1-Year Next Business Day On-Site Service	3-Year Limited, 1-Year Next Business Day On-Site Service	3-year On-Site Service	3-Year Limited, 1-Year Next Business Day On-Site Service	3-year On-Site Service	3-year On-Site Service
Other		Wheel	Postage Printer	Docking Station Carrying Case Fingerprint Scanner Portable Data Projector		Graphics Tablet Plotter or Large-Format Printer

Optional Components for All Categories	
802.11g Wireless Card	Graphics Tablet
Bluetooth Enabled	iPod Music Player
Biometric Input Device	IrDa Port
Card Reader/Writer	Mouse Pad/Wrist Rest
Digital Camera	Multifunction Peripheral
Digital Video Capture	Photo Printer
Digital Video Camera	Portable Data Projector
Dual-Monitor Support with Second Monitor	Scanner
Ergonomic Keyboard	TV/FM Tuner
External Hard Disk	Uninterruptible Power Supply

FIGURE 5 Base desktop and mobile computer components and optional components. A copy of the Base Components worksheet is on the Data Disk. To obtain a copy of the Data Disk, see the inside cover of this book for instructions.

4 **Consider upgrades to the mouse, keyboard, monitor, printer, microphone, and speakers.** You use these peripheral devices to interact with your computer, so you should make sure they are up to your standards. Review the peripheral devices listed in Figure 4 on pages 447 and 448 and then visit both local computer dealers and large retail stores to test the computers on display. Ask the salesperson what input and output devices would be best for you and whether you should upgrade beyond what comes standard. Consider purchasing a wireless keyboard and wireless mouse to eliminate bothersome wires on your desktop. A few extra dollars spent on these components when you initially purchase a computer can extend its usefulness by years.

5 **Determine whether you want to use telephone lines or broadband (cable or DSL) to access the Internet.** If your computer has a modem, then you can access the Internet using a standard telephone line. Ordinarily, you call a local or toll-free 800 number to connect to an ISP (see Guideline 6 on the next page). Using a dial-up Internet connection is relatively inexpensive but slow.

DSL and cable connections provide much faster Internet connections, which are ideal if you want faster file download speeds for software, digital photos, and music. As you would expect, they also are more expensive. DSL, which is available through local telephone companies, also may require that you subscribe to an ISP. Cable is available through your local cable television provider and some online service providers (OSPs). If you get cable, then you would not use a separate Internet service provider or online service provider.

6 **If you are using a dial-up or wireless connection to connect to the Internet, then select an ISP or OSP.** You can access the Internet via telephone lines in one of two ways: an ISP or an OSP. Both provide Internet access for a monthly fee that ranges from $6 to $25. Local ISPs offer Internet access to users in a limited geographic region, through local telephone numbers. National ISPs provide access for users nationwide (including mobile users), through local and toll-free telephone numbers and cable. Because of their size, national ISPs generally offer more services and have a larger technical support staff than local ISPs. OSPs furnish Internet access as well as members-only features for users nationwide. Figure 6 lists several national ISPs and OSPs. Before you choose an ISP or OSP, compare such features as the number of access hours, monthly fees, available services (e-mail, Web page hosting, chat), and reliability.

Company	Service	Web Address
America Online	OSP	aol.com
AT&T Worldnet	ISP	www.att.net
Comcast	OSP	comcast.net
CompuServe	OSP	compuserve.com
EarthLink	ISP	earthlink.net
Juno	OSP	juno.com
NetZero	OSP	netzero.com
MSN	OSP	msn.com
SBC Prodigy	ISP/OSP	prodigy.net

For an updated list of national ISPs and OSPs and their Web site addresses, visit scsite.com/dc2006/ch8/buyers.

FIGURE 6 National ISPs and OSPs.

7 **Use a worksheet to compare computers, services, and other considerations.** You can use a separate sheet of paper to take notes on each vendor's computer and then summarize the information on a worksheet, such as the one shown in Figure 7. You can use Figure 7 to compare prices for either a PC or a Mac. Most companies advertise a price for a base computer that includes components housed in the system unit (processor, RAM, sound card, video card), disk drives (floppy disk, hard disk, CD-ROM, CD-RW, DVD-ROM, and DVD+RW), a keyboard, mouse, monitor, printer, speakers, and modem. Be aware, however, that some advertisements list prices for computers with only some of these components. Monitors and printers, for example, often are not included in a base computer's price. Depending on how you plan to use the computer, you may want to invest in additional or more powerful components. When you are comparing the prices of computers, make sure you are comparing identical or similar configurations.

PC or Mac Cost Comparison Worksheet

Dealers list prices for computers with most of these components (instead of listing individual component costs). Some dealers do not supply a monitor. Some dealers offer significant discounts, but you must subscribe to an Internet service for a specified period to receive the discounted price. To compare computers, enter overall system price at top and enter a 0 (zero) for components included in the system cost. For any additional components not covered in the system price, enter the cost in the appropriate cells.

Items to Purchase	Desired System (PC)	Desired System (Mac)	Local Dealer #1	Local Dealer #2	Online Dealer #1	Online Dealer #2	Comments
OVERALL SYSTEM							
Overall System Price	< $1,500	< $1,500					
HARDWARE							
Processor	Pentium 4 at 2.8 GHz	PowerPC G4 at 800 MHz					
RAM	512 MB	512 MB					
Cache	256 KB L2	256 KB L2					
Hard Disk	80 GB	80 GB					
Monitor/LCD Flat Panel	17"	17"					
Video Graphics Card	128 MB	128 MB					
Floppy Disk Drive	3.5 Inch	NA					
USB Flash Drive	128 MB	128 MB					
CD/DVD Bay 1	48x CD-ROM	4x DVD+RW					
CD/DVD Bay 2	8x DVD+RW	NA					
Speakers	Stereo	Stereo					
Sound Card	Sound Blaster Compatible	Sound Blaster Compatible					
USB Ports	6	6					
FireWire Port	2	2					
Network Card	Yes	Yes					
Fax/Modem	56 Kbps	56 Kbps					
Keyboard	Standard	Apple Pro Keyboard					
Pointing Device	IntelliMouse	IntelliMouse or Apple Pro Mouse					
Microphone	Close-Talk Headset with Gain Adjustment	Close-Talk Headset with Gain Adjustment					
Printer	Color Ink-Jet	Color Ink-Jet					
Backup	250 MB Zip	250 MB Zip					
SOFTWARE							
Operating System	Windows XP Home Edition	Mac OS X					
Application Software	Office 2003 Small Business Edition	Office 2004 for Mac					
Antivirus	Yes - 12 Mo. Subscription	Yes - 12 Mo. Subscription					
OTHER							
Card Reader							
Digital Camera	4-Megapixel	4-Megapixel					
Internet Connection	1-Year Subscription	1-Year Subscription					
Joystick	Yes	Yes					
PC Video Camera	With Microphone	With Microphone					
Scanner							
Surge Protector							
Warranty	3-Year On-Site Service	3-Year On-Site Service					
Wireless Card	Internal	Internal					
Wireless LAN Access Point	LinkSys	Apple AirPort					
Total Cost			$ -	$ -	$ -	$ -	

FIGURE 7 A worksheet is an effective tool for summarizing and comparing components and prices of different computer vendors. A copy of the PC or Mac Cost Comparison Worksheet is on the Data Disk. To obtain a copy of the Data Disk, see the inside cover of this book for instructions.

8 **If you are buying a new computer, you have several purchasing options: buying from your school bookstore, a local computer dealer, a local large retail store, or ordering by mail via telephone or the Web.** Each purchasing option has certain advantages. Many college bookstores, for example, sign exclusive pricing agreements with computer manufacturers and, thus, can offer student discounts. Local dealers and local large retail stores, however, more easily can provide hands-on support. Mail-order companies that sell computers by telephone or online via the Web (Figure 8) often provide the lowest prices, but extend less personal service. Some major mail-order companies, however, have started to provide next-business-day, on-site services. A credit card usually is required to buy from a mail-order company. Figure 9 lists some of the more popular mail-order companies and their Web site addresses.

9 **If you are buying a used computer, stay with name brands such as Dell, Gateway, Hewlett-Packard, and Apple.** Although brand-name equipment can cost more, most brand-name computers have longer, more comprehensive warranties, are better supported, and have more authorized centers for repair services. As with new computers, you can purchase a used computer from local computer dealers, local large retail stores, or mail

order via the telephone or the Web. Classified ads and used computer sellers offer additional outlets for purchasing used computers. Figure 10 lists several major used computer brokers and their Web site addresses.

10 **If you have a computer and are upgrading to a new one, then consider selling or trading in the old one.** If you are a replacement buyer, your older computer still may have value. If you cannot sell the computer through the classified ads, via a Web site, or to a friend, then ask if the computer dealer will buy your old computer. An increasing number of companies are taking trade-ins, but do not expect too much money for your old computer. Other companies offer free disposal of your old PC.

11 **Be aware of hidden costs.** Before purchasing, be sure to consider any additional costs associated with buying a computer, such as an additional telephone line, a cable or DSL modem, an uninterruptible power supply (UPS), computer furniture, a USB flash drive, paper, and computer training classes you may want to take. Depending on where you buy your computer, the seller may be willing to include some or all of these in the computer purchase price.

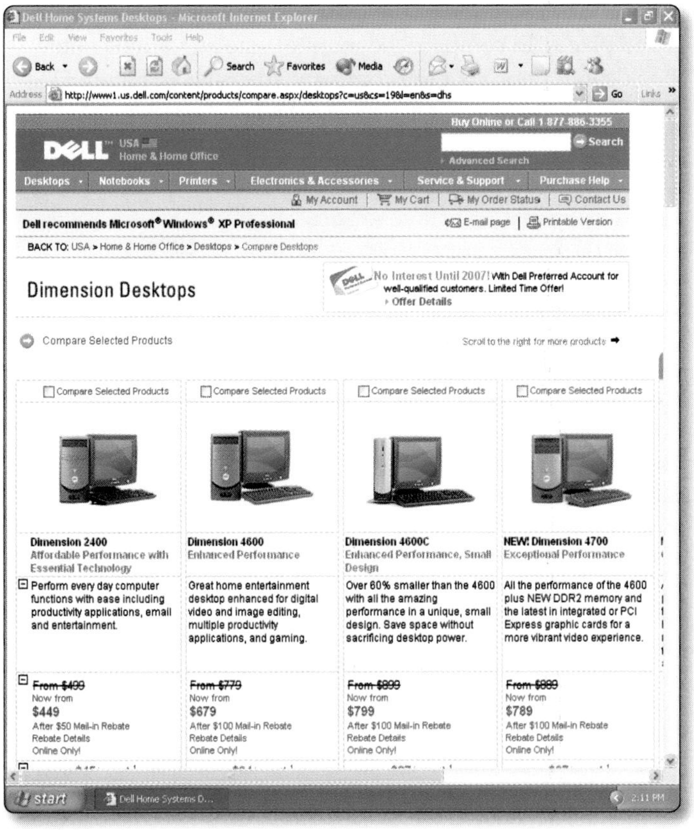

FIGURE 8 Mail-order companies, such as Dell, sell computers online.

Type of Computer	Company	Web Address
PC	CNET Shopper	shopper.cnet.com
	Hewlett-Packard	hp.com
	CompUSA	compusa.com
	Dartek	dartek.com
	Dell	dell.com
	Gateway	gateway.com
Macintosh	Apple Computer	store.apple.com
	ClubMac	clubmac.com
	MacConnection	macconnection.com
	PC & MacExchange	macx.com

For an updated list of new mail-order computer companies and their Web site addresses, visit scsite.com/dc2006/ch8/buyers.

FIGURE 9 Computer mail-order companies.

Company	Web Address
Amazon.com	amazon.com
Off-Lease Computers	off-leasecomputers.com
American Computer Exchange	www.amcoex.com
U.S. Computer Exchange	usce.org
eBay	ebay.com

For an updated list of used computer mail-order companies and their Web site addresses, visit scsite.com/dc2006/ch8/buyers.

FIGURE 10 Used computer mail-order companies.

12 **Consider more than just price.** The lowest-cost computer may not be the best long-term buy. Consider such intangibles as the vendor's time in business, the vendor's regard for quality, and the vendor's reputation for support. If you need to upgrade your computer often, you may want to consider a leasing arrangement, in which you pay monthly lease fees, but can upgrade or add on to your computer as your equipment needs change. No matter what type of buyer you are, insist on a 30-day, no-questions-asked return policy on your computer.

13 **Avoid restocking fees.** Some companies charge a restocking fee of 10 to 20 percent as part of their money-back return policy. In some cases, no restocking fee for hardware is applied, but it is applied for software. Ask about the existence and terms of any restocking policies before you buy.

14 **Use a credit card to purchase your new computer.** Many credit cards offer purchase protection and extended warranty benefits that cover you in case of loss of or damage to purchased goods. Paying by credit card also gives you time to install and use the computer before you have to pay for it. Finally, if you are dissatisfied with the computer and are unable to reach an agreement with the seller, paying by credit card gives you certain rights regarding withholding payment until the dispute is resolved. Check your credit card terms for specific details.

15 **Consider purchasing an extended warranty or service plan.** If you use your computer for business or require fast resolution to major computer problems, consider purchasing an extended warranty or a service plan through a local dealer or third-party company. Most extended warranties cover the repair and replacement of computer components beyond the standard warranty. Most service plans ensure that your technical support calls receive priority response from technicians. You also can purchase an on-site service plan that states that a technician will come to your home, work, or school within 24 hours. If your computer includes a warranty and service agreement for a year or less, think about extending the service for two or three years when you buy the computer.

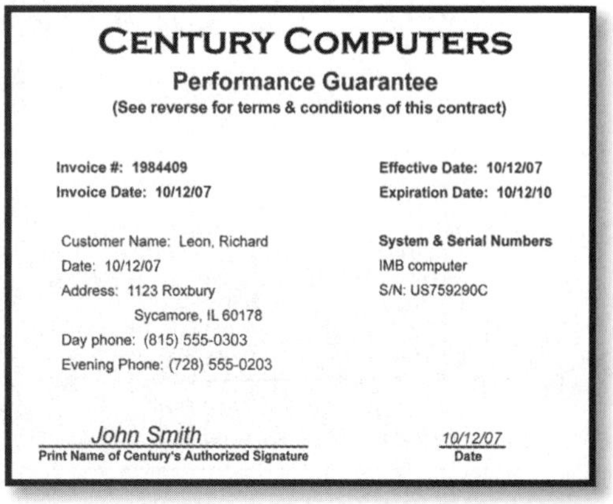

HOW TO PURCHASE A NOTEBOOK COMPUTER

I f you need computing capability when you travel or to use in lecture or meetings, you may find a notebook computer to be an appropriate choice. The guidelines mentioned in the previous section also apply to the purchase of a notebook computer. The following are additional considerations unique to notebook computers.

1 **Purchase a notebook computer with a sufficiently large active-matrix screen.** Active-matrix screens display high-quality color that is viewable from all angles. Less expensive, passive-matrix screens sometimes are difficult to see in low-light conditions and cannot be viewed from an angle. Notebook computers typically come with a 12.1-inch, 13.3-inch, 14.1-inch, or 15.7-inch display. For most users, a 14.1-inch display is satisfactory. If you intend to use your notebook computer as a desktop computer replacement, however, you may opt for a 15.7-inch display. Notebook computers with these larger displays weigh seven to ten pounds, however, so if you travel a lot and portability is essential, you might want a lighter computer with a smaller display. The lightest notebook computers, which weigh less than 3 pounds, are equipped with a 12.1-inch display. Regardless of size, the resolution of the display should be at least 1024 x 768 pixels. To compare the monitor size on various notebook computers, visit the company Web sites in Figure 11.

Type of Notebook	Company	Web Address
PC	Acer	global.acer.com
	Dell	dell.com
	Fujitsu	fujitsu.com
	Gateway	gateway.com
	Hewlett-Packard	hp.com
	IBM	ibm.com
	NEC	nec.com
	Sony	sony.com
	Toshiba	toshiba.com
Mac	Apple	apple.com

For an updated list of companies and their Web site addresses, visit scsite.com/dc2006/ch8/buyers.

FIGURE 11 Companies that sell notebook computers.

CENTURY COMPUTERS
Performance Guarantee
(See reverse for terms & conditions of this contract)

Invoice #: 1984409   Effective Date: 10/12/07
Invoice Date: 10/12/07   Expiration Date: 10/12/10

Customer Name: Leon, Richard   System & Serial Numbers
Date: 10/12/07   IMB computer
Address: 1123 Roxbury   S/N: US759290C
      Sycamore, IL 60178
Day phone: (815) 555-0303
Evening Phone: (728) 555-0203

John Smith   *10/12/07*
Print Name of Century's Authorized Signature   Date

2 **Experiment with different keyboards and pointing devices.** Notebook computer keyboards are far less standardized than those for desktop computers. Some notebook computers, for example, have wide wrist rests, while others have none. Notebook computers also use a range of pointing devices, including pointing sticks, touchpads, and trackballs. Before you purchase a notebook computer, try various types of keyboard and pointing devices to determine which is easiest for you to use. Regardless of the pointing device you select, you also may want to purchase a regular mouse to use when you are working at a desk or other large surface.

3 **Make sure the notebook computer you purchase has a CD and/or DVD drive.** Loading and installing software, especially large Office suites, is much faster if done from a CD-ROM, CD-RW, DVD-ROM, or DVD+RW. Today, most notebook computers come with an internal or external CD-ROM drive. Some notebook computers even come with a CD-ROM drive and a CD-RW drive or a DVD-ROM drive and a CD-RW or DVD+RW drive. Although DVD drives are slightly more expensive, they allow you to play CDs and DVD movies using your notebook computer and a headset.

4 **If necessary, upgrade the processor, memory, and disk storage at the time of purchase.** As with a desktop computer, upgrading your notebook computer's memory and disk storage usually is less expensive at the time of initial purchase. Some disk storage is custom designed for notebook computer manufacturers, meaning an upgrade might not be available in the future. If you are purchasing a lightweight notebook computer, then it should include at least a 2.4 GHz processor, 512 MB RAM, and 80 GB of storage.

5 **The availability of built-in ports on a notebook computer is important.** A notebook computer does not have a lot of room to add adapter cards. If you know the purpose for which you plan to use your notebook computer, then you can determine the ports you will need. Most notebooks come with common ports, such as a mouse port, IrDA port, serial port, parallel port, video port, and USB port. If you plan to connect your notebook computer to a TV, however, then you will need a PCtoTV port. If you want to connect to networks at school or in various offices, make sure the notebook computer you purchase has a built-in network card. If your notebook computer does not come with a built-in network wireless card, then you will have to purchase an external network card that slides into an expansion slot in your notebook computer, as well as a network cable. If you expect to connect an iPod portable digital music player to your notebook computer, then you will need a FireWire port.

6 **If you plan to use your notebook computer for note-taking at school or in meetings, consider a notebook computer that converts to a Tablet PC.** Some computer manufacturers have developed convertible notebook computers that allow the screen to rotate 180 degrees on a central hinge and then fold down to cover the keyboard and become a Tablet PC (Figure 12). You then can use a stylus to enter text or drawings into the computer by writing on the screen.

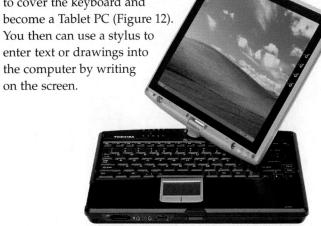

FIGURE 12 The Toshiba Protégé M200 notebook computer converts to a Tablet PC.

7 **Consider purchasing a notebook computer with a built-in wireless card to connect to your home network.** Many users today are setting up wireless home networks. With a wireless home network, the desktop computer functions as the server, and your notebook computer can access the desktop computer from any location in the house to share files and hardware, such as a printer, and browse the Web. If your notebook computer does not come with a built-in wireless card, you can purchase an external one that slides into your notebook computer. Most home wireless networks allow connections from distances of 150 to 800 feet.

8 **If you are going to use your notebook computer for long periods without access to an electrical outlet, purchase a second battery.** The trend among notebook computer users today is power and size over battery life, and notebook computer manufacturers have picked up on this. Many notebook computer users today are willing to give up longer battery life for a larger screen, faster processor, and more storage. In addition, some manufacturers typically sell the notebook with the lowest capacity battery. For this reason, you need to be careful in choosing a notebook computer if you plan to use it without access to electrical outlets for long periods, such as an airplane flight. You also might want to purchase a second battery as a backup. If you anticipate running your notebook computer on batteries frequently, choose a computer that uses lithium-ion batteries, which last longer than nickel cadmium or nickel hydride batteries.

9 **Purchase a well-padded and well-designed carrying case.** An amply padded carrying case will protect your notebook computer from the bumps it will receive while traveling. A well-designed carrying case will have room for accessories such as spare floppy disks, CDs and DVDs, a user manual, pens, and paperwork (Figure 13).

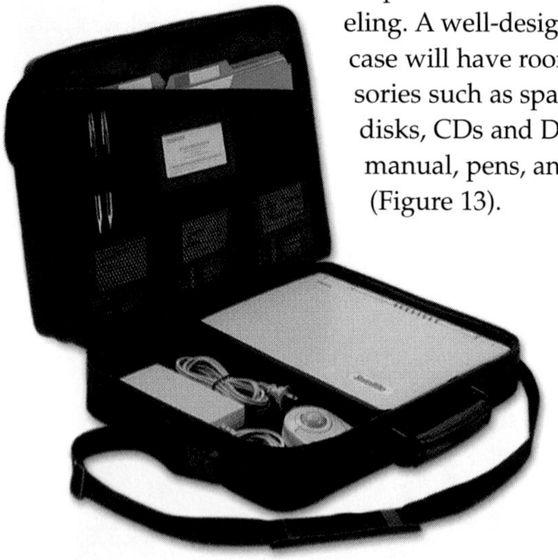

FIGURE 13
A well-designed notebook computer carrying case.

10 **If you travel overseas, obtain a set of electrical and telephone adapters.** Different countries use different outlets for electrical and telephone connections. Several manufacturers sell sets of adapters that will work in most countries.

11 **If you plan to connect your notebook computer to a video projector, make sure the notebook computer is compatible with the video projector.** You should check, for example, to be sure that your notebook computer will allow you to display an image on the computer screen and projection device at the same time (Figure 14). Also, ensure that your notebook computer has the ports required to connect to the video projector.

12 **For improved security, consider a fingerprint scanner.** More than a quarter of a million notebook computers are stolen or lost each year. If you have critical information stored on your notebook computer, then consider purchasing one with a fingerprint scanner (Figure 15) to protect the data if your computer is stolen or lost. Fingerprint security offers a level of protection that extends well beyond the standard password protection.

FIGURE 15 Fingerprint scanner technology offers greater security than passwords.

FIGURE 14
A notebook computer connected to a video projector projects the image displayed on the screen.

HOW TO PURCHASE A TABLET PC

The Tablet PC (Figure 16) combines the mobility features of a traditional notebook computer with the simplicity of pencil and paper, because you can create and save Office-type documents by writing and drawing directly on the screen with a digital pen. Tablet PCs use the Windows XP Tablet PC Edition operating system, which expands on Windows XP Professional by including digital pen and speech capabilities. A notebook computer and a Tablet PC have many similarities. For this reason, if you are considering purchasing a Tablet PC, review the guidelines for purchasing a notebook computer, as well as the guidelines below.

FIGURE 16
The lightweight Tablet PC, with its handwriting capabilities, is the latest addition to the family of mobile computers.

1 **Make sure the Tablet PC fits your mobile computing needs.** The Tablet PC is not for every mobile user. If you find yourself in need of a computer in class or you are spending more time in meetings than in your office, then the Tablet PC may be the answer. Before you invest money in a Tablet PC, however, determine the programs you plan to use on it. You should not buy a Tablet PC simply because it is a new and interesting type of computer. For additional information on the Tablet PC, visit the Web sites listed in Figure 17. You may have to use the search capabilities on the home page of the companies listed to locate information about the Tablet PC.

Company	Web Address
Fujitsu	fujitsu.com
Hewlett-Packard	hp.com
Microsoft	microsoft.com/windowsxp/tabletpc
ViewSonic	viewsonic.com
For an updated list of companies and their Web site addresses, visit scsite.com/dc2006/ch8/buyers.	

FIGURE 17 Companies involved with Tablet PCs and their Web sites.

2 **Decide whether you want a convertible or pure Tablet PC.** Convertible Tablet PCs have an attached keyboard and look like a notebook computer. You rotate the screen and lay it flat against the computer for note-taking. The pure Tablet PCs are slim and lightweight, weighing less than four pounds. They have the capability of easily docking at a desktop to gain access to a large monitor, keyboard, and mouse. If you spend a lot of time attending lectures or meetings, then the pure Tablet PC is ideal. Acceptable specifications for a Tablet PC are shown in Figure 18.

TABLET PC SPECIFICATIONS

Dimensions	12" × 9" × 1.2"
Weight	Less than 4 Pounds
Processor	Pentium III processor-M at 1.33 GHz
RAM	512 MB
Hard Disk	40 GB
Display	12.1" XGA TFT
Digitizer	Electromagnetic Digitizer
Battery	4-Cell (3-Hour)
USB	2
FireWire	1
Docking Station	Grab and Go with CD-ROM, Keyboard, and Mouse
Bluetooth Port	Yes
Wireless	802.11b/g Card
Network Card	10/100 Ethernet
Modem	56 Kbps
Speakers	Internal
Microphone	Internal
Operating System	Windows XP Tablet PC Edition
Application Software	Office Small Business Edition
Antivirus Software	Yes – 12 Month Subscription
Warranty	1-Year Limited Warranty Parts and Labor

FIGURE 18 Tablet PC specifications.

3 **Be sure the weight and dimensions are conducive to portability.** The weight and dimensions of the Tablet PC are important because you carry it around like a notepad. The Tablet PC you buy should weigh four pounds or less. Its dimensions should be approximately 12 inches by 9 inches by 1.2 inches.

Port availability, battery life, and durability are even more important with a Tablet PC than they are with a notebook computer. Make sure the Tablet PC you purchase has the ports required for the applications you plan to run. As with any mobile computer, battery life is important especially if you plan to use your Tablet PC for long periods without access to an electrical outlet. A Tablet PC must be durable because if you use it the way it was designed to be used, then you will be handling it much like you handle a pad of paper.

 Experiment with different models of the Tablet PC to find the digital pen that works best for you. The key to making use of the Tablet PC is to be comfortable with its handwriting capabilities and on-screen keyboard. Not only is the digital pen used to write on the screen (Figure 19), you also use it to make gestures to complete tasks, in a manner similar to the way you use a mouse. Figure 20 compares the standard point-and-click of a mouse with the gestures made with a digital pen. Other gestures with the digital pen replicate some of the commonly used keys on a keyboard.

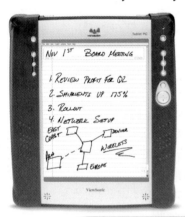

FIGURE 19 A Tablet PC lets you handwrite notes and draw on the screen using a digital pen.

Mouse	Digital Pen
Point	Point
Click	Tap
Double-click	Double-tap
Right-click	Tap and hold
Click and drag	Drag

FIGURE 20 Standard point-and-click of a mouse compared with the gestures made with a digital pen.

 Check out the comfort level of handwriting in different positions. You should be able to handwrite on a Tablet PC with your hand resting on the screen. You also should be able to handwrite holding the Tablet PC in one hand, as well as with it sitting in your lap.

 Make sure the LCD display device has a resolution high enough to take advantage of Microsoft's ClearType technologies. Tablet PCs use a digitizer under a standard 10.4-inch motion-sensitive LCD display to make the digital ink on the screen look like real ink on paper. To ensure you get the maximum benefits from the new ClearType technology, make sure the LCD display has a resolution of 800×600 in landscape mode and a 600×800 in portrait mode.

 Test the built-in Tablet PC microphone and speakers. With many application software packages recognizing human speech, such as Microsoft Office, it is important that the Tablet PC's built-in microphone operates at an acceptable level. If the microphone is not to your liking, you may want to purchase a close-talk headset with your Tablet PC. Increasingly more users are sending information as audio files, rather than relying solely on text. For this reason, you also should check the speakers on the Tablet PC to make sure they meet your standards.

 Consider a Tablet PC with a built-in PC video camera. A PC video camera adds streaming video and still photography capabilities to your Tablet PC, while still allowing you to take notes in lectures or meetings.

 Review the docking capabilities of the Tablet PC. The Microsoft Windows XP Tablet PC Edition operating system supports a grab-and-go form of docking, so you can pick up and take a docked Tablet PC with you, just as you would pick up a notepad on your way to a meeting (Figure 21).

FIGURE 21 A Tablet PC docked to create a desktop computer with the Tablet PC as the monitor.

 Wireless access to the Internet and your e-mail is essential with a Tablet PC. Make sure the Tablet PC has wireless networking, so you can access the Internet and your e-mail anytime and anywhere. Your Tablet PC also should include standard network connections, such as dial-up and Ethernet connections.

Review available accessories to purchase with your Tablet PC. Tablet PC accessories include docking stations, mouse units, keyboards, security cables, additional memory and storage, protective handgrips, screen protectors, and various types of digital pens.

APPENDIX A

*Coding Schemes
and Number Systems*

CODING SCHEMES

As discussed in Chapter 4, a computer uses a coding scheme to represent characters. This section of the appendix presents the ASCII, EBCDIC, and Unicode coding schemes and discusses parity.

ASCII and EBCDIC

Two popular coding schemes that represent characters in a computer are ASCII and EBCDIC. The **American Standard Code for Information Interchange**, or ASCII (pronounced ASK-ee), coding scheme is the most widely used coding scheme to represent data. Many personal computers and midrange servers use ASCII. The **Extended Binary Coded Decimal Interchange Code**, or EBCDIC (pronounced EB-see-dik), coding scheme is used primarily on mainframe computers and high-end servers. As shown in Figure A-1, the combination of bits (0s and 1s) is unique for each character in the ASCII and EBCDIC coding schemes.

When a computer uses the ASCII or EBCDIC coding scheme, it stores each represented character in one byte of memory. Other binary formats exist, however, that the computer sometimes uses to represent numeric data. For example, a computer may store, or pack, two numeric characters in one byte of memory. The computer uses these binary formats to increase storage and processing efficiency.

Unicode

The 256 characters and symbols that are represented by ASCII and EBCDIC codes are sufficient for English and western European languages but are not large enough for Asian and other languages that use different alphabets. Further compounding the problem is that many of these languages use symbols, called **ideograms**, to represent multiple words and ideas. One solution to this situation is Unicode. **Unicode** is a 16-bit coding scheme that has the capacity of representing all the world's current languages, as well as classic and historical languages, in more than 65,000 characters and symbols.

ASCII	SYMBOL	EBCDIC
00110000	0	11110000
00110001	1	11110001
00110010	2	11110010
00110011	3	11110011
00110100	4	11110100
00110101	5	11110101
00110110	6	11110110
00110111	7	11110111
00111000	8	11111000
00111001	9	11111001
01000001	A	11000001
01000010	B	11000010
01000011	C	11000011
01000100	D	11000100
01000101	E	11000101
01000110	F	11000110
01000111	G	11000111
01001000	H	11001000
01001001	I	11001001
01001010	J	11010001
01001011	K	11010010
01001100	L	11010011
01001101	M	11010100
01001110	N	11010101
01001111	O	11010110
01010000	P	11010111
01010001	Q	11011000
01010010	R	11011001
01010011	S	11100010
01010100	T	11100011
01010101	U	11100100
01010110	V	11100101
01010111	W	11100110
01011000	X	11100111
01011001	Y	11101000
01011010	Z	11101001
00100001	!	01011010
00100010	"	01111111
00100011	#	01111011
00100100	$	01011011
00100101	%	01101100
00100110	&	01010000
00101000	(	01001101
00101001	)	01011101
00101010	*	01011100
00101011	+	01001110

FIGURE A-1

A Unicode code for a symbol, as shown in Figure A-2, is obtained by appending the symbol's corresponding digit in the left-most column to the end of the symbol's corresponding three-digit code in the column heading. For

	003	004	005	006	007
0	0 0030	@ 0040	P 0050	` 0060	p 0070
1	1 0031	A 0041	Q 0051	a 0061	q 0071
2	2 0032	B 0042	R 0052	b 0062	r 0072
3	3 0033	C 0043	S 0053	c 0063	s 0073
4	4 0034	D 0044	T 0054	d 0064	t 0074
5	5 0035	E 0045	U 0055	e 0065	u 0075
6	6 0036	F 0046	V 0056	f 0066	v 0076
7	7 0037	G 0047	W 0057	g 0067	w 0077
8	8 0038	H 0048	X 0058	h 0068	x 0078
9	9 0039	I 0049	Y 0059	i 0069	y 0079
A	: 003A	J 004A	Z 005A	j 006A	z 007A
B	; 003B	K 004B	[005B	k 006B	{ 007B
C	< 003C	L 004C	\ 005C	l 006C	| 007C
D	= 003D	M 004D	] 005D	m 006D	} 007D
E	> 003E	N 004E	^ 005E	n 006E	~ 007E
F	? 003F	O 004F	_ 005F	o 006F	DEL 007F

FIGURE A-2

example, the Unicode for the capital letter C is 0043. In Unicode, 30,000 codes are reserved for future use, such as ancient languages, and 6,000 codes are reserved for private use. Existing ASCII coded data is fully compatible with Unicode because the first 256 codes are the same. Unicode is implemented in several operating systems, including Windows XP, Mac OS X, and Linux. Unicode-enabled programming languages and software include Java, XML, Microsoft Office, and Oracle. Some experts believe that Unicode eventually will replace all other coding schemes.

Parity

Regardless of the coding scheme used to represent characters in memory, it is important that the computer store characters accurately. For each byte of memory, most computers have at least one extra bit, called a **parity bit**, that the computer uses for error checking. A parity bit can detect if one of the bits in a byte has been changed inadvertently. While such errors are extremely rare (most computers never have a parity error during their lifetime), they can occur because of voltage fluctuations, static electricity, or a memory failure.

Computers are either odd- or even-parity machines. In computers with odd-parity, the total number of on bits in the byte (including the parity bit) must be an odd number (Figure A-3). In computers with even parity, the total number of on bits must be an even number. The computer checks parity each time it uses a memory location. When the computer moves data from one location to another in memory, it compares the parity bits of both the sending and receiving locations to see if they are the same. If the computer detects a difference or if the wrong number of bits is on (e.g., an odd number in a computer with even parity), an error message is displayed. Many computers use multiple parity bits that enable them to detect and correct a single-bit error and detect multiple-bit errors.

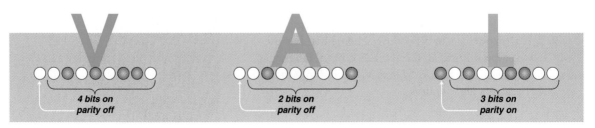

FIGURE A-3

NUMBER SYSTEMS

This section of the appendix describes the number systems used with computers. Technical computer personnel require a thorough knowledge of this subject, but most users need only a general understanding of number systems and how they relate to computers.

The binary (base 2) number system is used to represent the electronic status of the bits in memory. It also is used for other purposes such as addressing the memory locations. Another number system commonly used with computers is **hexadecimal** (base 16). The computer uses the hexadecimal number system to communicate with a programmer when a problem with a program exists, because it would be difficult for the programmer to understand the 0s and 1s of binary code. Figure A-4 shows how the decimal values 0 through 15 are represented in binary and hexadecimal number systems.

The mathematical principles that apply to the binary and hexadecimal number systems are the same as those that apply to the decimal number system. To help you better understand these principles, this section starts with the familiar decimal system, then progresses to the binary and hexadecimal number systems.

The Decimal Number System

The decimal number system is a base 10 number system (deci means ten). The base of a number system indicates how many symbols it uses. The decimal number system uses 10 symbols: 0 through 9. Each of the symbols in the number system has a value associated with it. For example, 3 represents a quantity of three and 5 represents a quantity of five.

The decimal number system also is a positional number system. This means that in a number such as 143, each position in the number has a value associated with it. When you look at the decimal number 143, the 3 is in the ones, or units, position and represents three ones (3×1); the 4 is in the tens position and represents four tens (4×10); and the 1 is in the hundreds position and represents one hundred (1×100). The number 143 is the sum of the values in each position of the number ($100 + 40 + 3 = 143$). The chart in Figure A-5 shows how you can calculate the positional values (hundreds, tens, and units) for a number system. Starting on the right and working to the left, the base of the number system, in this case 10, is raised to consecutive powers (10^0, 10^1, 10^2). These calculations are a mathematical way of determining the place values in a number system.

When you use number systems other than decimal, the same principles apply. The base of the number system indicates the number of symbols that it uses, and each position in a number system has a value associated with it. By raising the base of the number system to consecutive powers beginning with zero, you can calculate the positional value.

DECIMAL	BINARY	HEXADECIMAL
0	0000	0
1	0001	1
2	0010	2
3	0011	3
4	0100	4
5	0101	5
6	0110	6
7	0111	7
8	1000	8
9	1001	9
10	1010	A
11	1011	B
12	1100	C
13	1101	D
14	1110	E
15	1111	F

FIGURE A-4

power of 10	10^2	10^1	10^0	1	4	3	=	
positional value	100	10	1	(1×10^2) +	(4×10^1) +	(3×10^0)	=	
				(1×100) +	(4×10) +	(3×1)	=	
number	1	4	3	100 +	40 +	3	=	143

FIGURE A-5

The Binary Number System

As previously discussed, binary is a base 2 number system (bi means two), and the symbols it uses are 0 and 1. Just as each position in a decimal number has a place value associated with it, so does each position in a binary number. In binary, the place values, moving from right to left, are successive powers of two (2^0, 2^1, 2^2, 2^3 or 1, 2, 4, 8). To construct a binary number, place ones in the positions where the corresponding values add up to the quantity you want to represent and place zeros in the other positions. For example, in a four-digit binary number, the binary place values are (from right to left) 1, 2, 4, and 8. The binary number 1001 has ones in the positions for the values 1 and 8 and zeros in the positions for 2 and 4. Therefore, as shown in Figure A-6, the quantity represented by binary 1001 is 9 (8 + 0 + 0 + 1).

The Hexadecimal Number System

The hexadecimal number system uses 16 symbols to represent values (hex means six). These include the symbols 0 through 9 and A through F (Figure A-4 on the previous page). The mathematical principles previously discussed also apply to hexadecimal (Figure A-7).

The primary reasons the hexadecimal number system is used with computers are (1) it can represent binary values in a more compact and readable form, and (2) the conversion between the binary and the hexadecimal number systems is very efficient.

An eight-digit binary number (a byte) can be represented by a two-digit hexadecimal number. For example, in the ASCII code, the character M is represented as 01001101. This value can be represented in the hexadecimal number system as 4D. One way to convert this binary number (4D) to a hexadecimal number is to divide the binary number (from right to left) into groups of four digits, calculate the value of each group, and then change any two-digit values (10 through 15) to the symbols A through F that are used in the hexadecimal number system (Figure A-8).

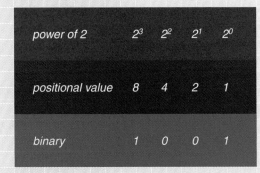

power of 2	2^3	2^2	2^1	2^0		**1**	**0**	**0**	**1**	**=**	
						(1×2^3) +	(0×2^2) +	(0×2^1) +	(1×2^0) =		
positional value	8	4	2	1		(1×8) +	(0×4) +	(0×2) +	(1×1) =		
binary	1	0	0	1		**8** +	**0** +	**0** +	**1** =	**9**	

FIGURE A-6

power of 16	16^1	16^0		**A**	**5**	**=**	
				(10×16^1) +	(5×16^0)	=	
positional value	16	1		(10×16) +	(5×1)	=	
hexadecimal	A	5		**160** +	**5**	**=**	**165**

FIGURE A-7

	positional value	8421	8421
	binary	0100	1101
	decimal	4	13
	hexadecimal	4	D

FIGURE A-8

APPENDIX B

Quiz Yourself Answers

Following are possible answers to the Quiz Yourself boxes throughout the book.

Quiz Yourself 1-1

1. A computer is ~~a motorized~~an electronic device that processes ~~output~~input into ~~input~~output.
2. A storage device records (~~reads~~writes) and/or retrieves (~~writes~~reads) items to and from storage media.
3. An ~~output~~input device is any hardware component that allows you to enter data and instructions into a computer.
4. True Statement
5. Computers have the ~~dis~~advantages of fast speeds, ~~high~~low failure rates, producing consistent results, storing ~~small~~enormous amounts of data, and communicating with others.
6. Three commonly used ~~input~~output devices are a printer, a monitor, and speakers.

Quiz Yourself 1-2

1. A ~~resource~~network is a collection of computers and devices connected together via communications devices and transmission media.
2. True Statement
3. Popular ~~system~~application software includes Web browsers, word processing software, spreadsheet software, database software, and presentation graphics software.
4. The ~~Internet~~Web is one of the more popular services on the ~~Web~~Internet.
5. Two types of ~~application~~system software are the operating system and utility programs.

Quiz Yourself 1-3

1. A ~~desktop computer~~notebook computer (or laptop computer) is a portable, personal computer designed to fit on your lap.
2. True Statement
3. Each ~~large business~~home user spends time on the computer for different reasons that include budgeting and personal financial management, Web access, communications, and entertainment.
4. A ~~home~~power user requires the capabilities of a workstation or other powerful computer.

5. ~~Mainframes~~Supercomputers are the fastest, most powerful computers — and the most expensive.
6. The elements of an information system are hardware, ~~e-mail~~software, data, people, and ~~the Internet~~procedures.
7. With ~~embedded computers~~online banking, users access account balances, pay bills, and copy monthly transactions from the bank's computer right into their personal computers.

Quiz Yourself 2-1

1. True Statement
2. ~~A WISP~~An IP address (or Internet Protocol address) is a number that uniquely identifies each computer or device connected to the Internet.
3. ~~An IP address~~A domain name, such as www.google.com, is the text version of ~~a domain name~~an IP address.
4. Dial-up access takes place when the modem in your computer uses ~~the cable television network~~a standard telephone line to connect to the Internet.
5. The World Wide Web Consortium (W3C) oversees research and ~~owns~~sets standards and guidelines for many areas of the Internet.

Quiz Yourself 2-2

1. True Statement
2. A ~~Web browser~~subject directory classifies Web pages in an organized set of categories, such as sports or shopping, and related subcategories.
3. Audio and video files are ~~downloaded~~compressed to reduce their file sizes.
4. Popular ~~portals~~players include iTunes, RealOne Player, and Windows Media Player.
5. The more widely used ~~search engines~~Web browsers for personal computers are Internet Explorer, Netscape, Mozilla, Opera, and Safari.
6. To develop a Web page, you do not have to be a computer programmer.
7. To improve your Web searches, use ~~general~~specific nouns and put the ~~least~~most important terms first in the search text.

Quiz Yourself 2-3

1. True Statement
2. An e-mail address is a combination of a user name and ~~an e-mail program~~a domain name that identifies a user so he or she can receive Internet e-mail.
3. ~~Business~~Consumer-to-consumer e-commerce occurs when one consumer sells directly to another, such as in an online auction.
4. FTP is an Internet standard that permits file ~~reading~~ uploading and ~~writing~~ downloading with other computers on the Internet.
5. ~~Spam~~Internet telephony uses the Internet (instead of the public switched telephone network) to connect a calling party to one or more called parties.
6. Netiquette is the code of ~~un~~acceptable behaviors while on the Internet.
7. On a newsgroup, a ~~subscription~~ thread (or threaded discussion) consists of the original article and all subsequent related replies.

Quiz Yourself 3-1

1. True Statement
2. ~~Public domain~~Packaged software is mass produced, copyrighted retail software that meets the needs of a wide variety of users, not just a single user or company.
3. To use ~~system~~ application software, your computer must be running ~~application~~ system software.
4. When an application is started, the program's instructions load from ~~memory~~ a storage medium into ~~a storage medium~~ memory.

Quiz Yourself 3-2

1. ~~Audio~~ Video editing software typically includes ~~video~~ audio editing capabilities.
2. ~~Enterprise computing~~Image editing software provides the capabilities of paint software and also includes the ability to modify existing images.
3. Millions of people use ~~spreadsheet~~ word processing software every day to develop documents such as letters, memos, reports, fax cover sheets, mailing labels, newsletters, and Web pages.
4. Professional ~~accounting~~ DTP (or desktop publishing) software is ideal for the production of high-quality color documents such as textbooks, corporate newsletters, marketing literature, product catalogs, and annual reports.

5. ~~Spreadsheet~~ Presentation graphics software is application software that allows users to create visual aids for presentations to communicate ideas, messages, and other information to a group.
6. Two of the more widely used ~~CAD programs~~software suites are Microsoft Office and Sun StarOffice.
7. True Statement

Quiz Yourself 3-3

1. An ~~anti-spam~~antivirus program protects a computer against viruses by identifying and removing any computer viruses found in memory, on storage media, or in incoming files.
2. ~~Computer~~Web-based training is a type of ~~Web~~computer-based training that uses Internet technology and consists of application software on the Web.
3. True Statement
4. ~~Legal~~Personal finance software is a simplified accounting program that helps home users and small office/home office users balance their checkbooks, pay bills, track investments, and evaluate financial plans.
5. ~~Personal DTP~~Photo editing software is a popular type of image editing software that allows users to edit digital photographs.

Quiz Yourself 4-1

1. True Statement
2. Four basic operations in a machine cycle are: (1) ~~comparing~~fetching, (2) decoding, (3) executing, and, if necessary, (4) ~~pipelining~~storing.
3. Processors contain a ~~motherboard~~ control unit and an arithmetic logic unit (ALU).
4. The ~~central processing unit~~motherboard, sometimes called a system board, is the main circuit board of the system unit.
5. The leading processor chip manufacturers for personal computers are ~~Microsoft~~Intel, AMD, IBM, Motorola, and Transmeta.
6. The pace of the system clock, called the clock speed, is measured by the number of ticks per ~~minute~~second.
7. The system unit is a case that contains ~~mechanical~~ electronic components of the computer used to process data.

Quiz Yourself 4-2

1. True Statement
2. A gigabyte (GB) equals approximately 1 ~~trillion~~ billion bytes.
3. Memory cache helps speed the processes of the computer because it stores ~~seldom~~ frequently used instructions and data.
4. Most computers are ~~analog~~ digital, which means they recognize only two discrete states: on and off.
5. Most RAM ~~retains~~ loses its contents when the power is removed from the computer.
6. Read-only memory (ROM) refers to memory chips storing ~~temporary~~ permanent data and instructions.

Quiz Yourself 4-3

1. A ~~bus~~ port is the point at which a peripheral attaches to a system unit so the peripheral can send data to or receive information from the computer.
2. An ~~AC adapter~~ expansion slot is a socket on the motherboard that can hold an adapter card.
3. Near the power supply is a ~~heater~~ fan that keeps components of the system unit ~~warm~~ cool.
4. ~~Serial~~ USB ports can connect up to 127 different peripherals together with a single connector type.
5. The higher the bus clock speed, the ~~slower~~ faster the transmission of data.
6. True Statement

Quiz Yourself 5-1

1. A keyboard is an ~~output~~ input device that contains keys users press to enter data in a computer.
2. A ~~light pen~~ graphics tablet is a flat, rectangular, electronic plastic board.
3. A ~~trackball~~ touch pad is a small, flat, rectangular pointing device commonly found on notebook computers.
4. True Statement
5. Operations you can perform with a ~~wheel~~ mouse include point, click, right-click, double-click, triple-click, drag, right-drag, rotate wheel, press wheel button, and tilt wheel.
6. ~~PDAs~~ Tablet PCs use a pressure-sensitive digital pen, and ~~Tablet PCs~~ PDAs use a stylus.

Quiz Yourself 5-2

1. True Statement
2. DV cameras record video as ~~analog~~ digital signals.
3. ~~Instant messaging~~ Voice recognition (or speech recognition) is the computer's capability of distinguishing spoken words.
4. Many smart phones today have a built-in or attachable camera so users easily can send ~~text~~ picture messages.
5. The ~~lower~~ higher the resolution of a digital camera, the better the image quality, but the more expensive the camera.

Quiz Yourself 5-3

1. A fingerprint scanner captures curves and indentations of a ~~signature~~ fingerprint.
2. After swiping a credit card through ~~an MICR~~ a magstripe (or magnetic stripe card) reader, a POS terminal connects to a system that authenticates the purchase.
3. ATMs ask you to enter a password, called a ~~biometric identifier~~ PIN (or personal identification number), which verifies that you are the holder of the bankcard.
4. Four types of ~~source documents~~ scanners are flatbed, pen, sheet-fed, and drum.
5. Retail and grocery stores use the ~~POSTNET~~ UPC (Universal Product Code) bar code.
6. RFID is a technology that uses ~~laser~~ radio signals to communicate with a tag placed in an object, an animal, or a person.
7. True Statement

Quiz Yourself 6-1

1. A ~~lower~~ higher resolution uses a greater number of pixels and thus provides a smoother image.
2. An output device is any type of ~~software~~ hardware component that conveys information to one or more people.
3. Documents often include ~~text~~ graphics to enhance their visual appeal and convey information.
4. ~~LCD~~ CRT monitors have a larger footprint than ~~CRT~~ LCD monitors.
5. Types of ~~CRTs~~ flat-panel displays include LCD monitors, LCD screens, plasma monitors, and many HDTVs.
6. True Statement

Quiz Yourself 6-2

1. A ~~laser~~thermal printer generates images by pushing electrically heated pins against heat-sensitive paper.
2. A ~~photo~~laser printer creates images using a laser beam and powdered ink, called toner.
3. An ink-jet printer is a type of impact printer that forms characters and graphics by spraying tiny drops of liquid ~~nitrogen~~ink onto a piece of paper.
4. Printed information is called ~~soft~~hard copy.
5. Two commonly used types of impact printers are ~~ink-jet~~dot-matrix printers and line printers.
6. True Statement

Quiz Yourself 6-3

1. A digital light processing (DLP) projector uses tiny ~~lightbulbs~~mirrors to reflect light.
2. True Statement
3. Many personal computer users add surround sound ~~printer systems~~speakers to their computers to generate a higher-quality sound.
4. Multifunction peripherals require ~~more~~less space than having a separate printer, scanner, copy machine, and fax machine.
5. Some joysticks and wheels include ~~real-time action~~force feedback, which is a technology that sends resistance to the device in response to actions of the user.

Quiz Yourself 7-1

1. Floppy disks are a type of ~~optical disc~~magnetic disk.
2. True Statement
3. SATA is a hard disk interface that uses ~~parallel~~serial signals to transfer data, instructions, and information.
4. ~~Storage media~~A storage device is the computer hardware that records and/or retrieves items to and from ~~a storage device~~media.
5. Three types of ~~manual~~magnetic disks are floppy disks, Zip disks, and hard disks.
6. Users can move an ~~internal~~external Zip drive from computer to computer as needed by connecting the drive to a USB port or FireWire port on the system unit.

Quiz Yourself 7-2

1. A ~~CD-RW~~CD-ROM is a type of optical disc on which users can read but not write (record) or erase.
2. A ~~DVD-RAM~~Picture CD is a single-session disc that stores digital versions of a single roll of film using a jpg file format.
3. DVDs have the ~~same~~much greater storage capacities ~~as~~than CDs.
4. Optical discs are written and read by ~~mirrors~~a laser.
5. ~~Single-session~~Multisession means you can write on part of the disc at one time and another part at a later time.
6. True Statement

Quiz Yourself 7-3

1. A smart card stores data on a thin ~~magnetic stripe~~microprocessor embedded in the card.
2. A USB flash drive is a flash memory storage device that plugs in a ~~parallel~~USB port on a computer or mobile device.
3. Flash memory cards are a type of ~~magnetic~~solid-state media, which means they consist entirely of electronic components and contain no moving parts.
4. Microfilm and microfiche have the ~~shortest~~longest life of any storage media.
5. Tape storage requires ~~direct~~sequential access, which refers to reading or writing data consecutively.
6. True Statement

Quiz Yourself 8-1

1. A ~~buffer~~driver is a small program that tells the operating system how to communicate with a specific device.
2. A ~~cold~~warm boot is the process of using the operating system to restart a computer.
3. A password is a ~~public~~private combination of characters associated with the user name that allows access to certain computer resources.
4. Firmware that contains the computer's startup instructions is called the ~~kernel~~BIOS.
5. The program you currently are using is in the ~~background~~foreground, and the other programs running but not in use are in the ~~foreground~~background.
6. Two types of system software are operating systems and ~~application~~utility programs.
7. True Statement

Quiz Yourself 8-2

1. A ~~file manager~~firewall is a utility that detects and protects a personal computer from unauthorized intrusions.
2. ~~Fragmenting~~ Defragmenting a disk is the process of reorganizing it so the files are stored in contiguous sectors.
3. ~~Linux~~ Windows XP is available in five editions: Home Edition, Professional, Media Center Edition, Tablet PC Edition, and 64-bit Edition.
4. True Statement
5. ~~Windows XP~~Linux is a UNIX-type operating system that is open source software.
6. You should ~~uninstall~~ back up files and disks regularly in the event your originals are lost, damaged, or destroyed.

Quiz Yourself 8-3

1. A ~~pop-up blocker~~file compression utility shrinks the size of a file(s).
2. An ~~anti-spam~~antivirus program protects a computer against viruses by identifying and removing any computer viruses found in memory, on storage media, or on incoming files.
3. True Statement
4. Pocket PCs use ~~Palm OS~~Windows Mobile as their operating system.
5. ~~Web filtering~~CD/DVD burning software writes text, graphics, audio, and video files to a recordable or rewritable CD or DVD.

APPENDIX C
Computer Acronyms

Acronym	Description	Page
AA	Audible Audio	87
AAC	Advanced Audio Coding	87
AC adapter	alternating current adapter	213
ADA	Americans with Disabilities Act	266
ADC	analog-to-digital converter	38
AGP	Accelerated Graphics Port	212
AIFF	Audio Interchange File Format	87
ALU	arithmetic logic unit	188
AMD	Advanced Micro Devices	219
AOL	America Online	72, 82
ARPA	Advanced Research Projects Agency	69
ARPANET	Advanced Research Projects Agency network	69
ASCII	American Standard Code for Information Interchange	195
ASF	Advanced Streaming (or Systems) Format	87
ASP	application service provider	164
ATC	advanced transfer cache	201
ATM	automated teller machine	262
B2B	business-to-business	92
B2C	business-to-consumer	92
BIOS	basic input/output system	400
Bit	binary digit	195
BMP	bit map	85
BTW	by the way	100
C2C	consumer-to-consumer	92
CAD	computer-aided design	327
CAD software	computer-aided design software	150, 151
CAI	computer-aided instruction	160
CAM	computer-aided manufacturing	36
CBT	computer-based training	160
CCD	charge-coupled device	251
CD	compact disc	8, 9, 17, 27, 89, 357
CD drive	compact disc drive	27
CD/DVD burner	compact disc/digital versatile disc burner	162
CD recorder	compact disc recorder	371
CD-R	compact disc-recordable	371
CD-R drive	compact disc-recordable drive	371
CD-ROM	compact disc read-only memory	369-70
CD-ROM drive	compact disc read-only memory drive	369
CD-RW	compact disc-rewritable	371
CD-RW drive	compact disc-rewritable drive	371
CF	CompactFlash	376
CMOS	complementary metal-oxide semiconductor	203
CMOS battery	complementary metal-oxide semiconductor battery	203

Acronym	Description	Page
CMOS chip	complementary metal-oxide semiconductor chip	400
COBOL	COmmon Business-Oriented Language	53
COM port	communications port	207
CPU	central processing unit	8, 187
CRT	cathode-ray tube	307
CRT monitor	cathode-ray tube monitor	307-8
CST	Computer Service Technician	381
DAC	digital-to-analog converter	38
DDR SDRAM	double data rate synchronous dynamic random access memory	199
DHCP	Dynamic Host Configuration Protocol	102
DIMM	dual inline memory module	199
DL	distance learning	166
DLP projector	digital light processing projector	324
DNS	domain name system	74
DNS server	domain name system server	74, 102
DOS	Disk Operating System	417
Dpi	dots per inch	252, 313
DRAM	dynamic random access memory	199
DSL	Digital Subscriber Line	70, 449
DSP	digital signal processor	38
DTP	desktop publishing	152
DTP software	desktop publishing software	152
DTV	digital television	306
DV camera	digital video camera	253
DVD	digital versatile disc or digital video disc	8, 17, 59, 89, 357
DVD/CD-RW	digital video disc/compact disc-rewritable drive	368, 372
DVD drive	digital versatile disc or digital video disc drive	9, 27, 212
DVD recorder	digital versatile disc or digital video disc recorder	373
DVD+R	digital versatile disc or digital video disc recordable	373
DVD-R	digital versatile disc or digital video disc recordable	373
DVD+RAM	digital versatile disc or digital video disc + random access memory	373
DVD-ROM	digital versatile disc or digital video disc read-only memory	9, 372
DVD-ROM drive	digital versatile disc or digital video disc read-only memory drive	372
DVD+RW	digital versatile disc or digital video disc + rewritable	373
DVD-RW	digital versatile disc or digital video disc + rewritable	373
DVD+RW drive	digital versatile disc or digital video disc + rewritable drive	373
DVD-RW drive	digital versatile disc or digital video disc + rewritable drive	373

Acronym	Description	Page
DVI	Digital Video Interface	305
DVI port	Digital Video Interface port	305
Dynamic IP address	dynamic Internet Protocol address	102
EB	exabyte	356
EBCDIC	Extended Binary Coded Decimal Interchange Code	195
E-book	electronic book	61, 303
E-commerce	electronic commerce	28, 30, 60, 61, 91-92
EEPROM	electrically erasable programmable read-only memory	202
E-file	electronic filing	157
EIDE	Enhanced Integrated Drive Electronics	365
E-mail	electronic mail	12, 31, 69, 92-95, 101, 161
E-mail address	electronic mail address	94
E-mail program	electronic mail program	93, 161
EMR	electromagnetic radiation	308
ENIAC	Electronic Numerical Integrator and Computer	52
Enterprise ASP	enterprise application service provider	164
FAQ	frequently asked questions	6, 100
Fax	facsimile	322-23
Fax machine	facsimile machine	322-23
Fax modem	facsimile modem	322, 323
Fortran	FORmula TRANslator	53
FTP	File Transfer Protocol	68, 96, 134, 161
FTP server	File Transfer Protocol server	96
FWIW	for what it's worth	100
FYI	for your information	100
GB	gigabyte	197, 356
GHz	gigahertz	189
GIF	Graphics Interchange Format	85
GIGO	garbage in, garbage out	10
GPU	graphics processing unit	305
GUI	graphical user interface	15, 137, 402, 420, 421
HD	high density	358
HDTV	high-definition television	306-7
HIPAA	Health Insurance Portability and Accountability Act	379
Hi-Speed USB	high speed universal serial bus	365
HP	Hewlett-Packard	329
http	Hypertext Transfer Protocol	76, 477
Hz	hertz	189
IBM	International Business Machines	53, 54, 55, 138
IBM processor	International Business Machines processor	190
IC	integrated circuit	186
ICANN	Internet Corporation for Assigned Names and Numbers	74
IEEE 1394 port	Institute of Electrical and Electronics Engineers 1394 port	209

Acronym	Description	Page
IM	instant messaging	98
IMHO	in my humble opinion	100
Interactive TV	interactive television	307
IP address	Internet Protocol address	73, 102
IPng	Internet Protocol Next Generation	102
IPv6	Internet Protocol version 6	102
IrDA	Infrared Data Association	210
IrDA port	Infrared Data Association port	210
IRQ	interrupt request	409
IS	information system	25
ISP	Internet service provider	72
IT	information technology	25
IT department	information technology department	30
JPEG	Joint Photographic Experts Group	85, 345
JPEG 2000	Joint Photographic Experts Group 2000	324
K	kilobyte	197
KB	kilobyte	197
KBps	kilobytes per second	357, 369
L1 cache	Level 1 cache	201
L2 cache	Level 2 cache	201
L3 cache	Level 3 cache	201
LAN	local area network	55
LCD	liquid crystal display	304
LCD monitor	liquid crystal display monitor	302-7, 325
LCD projector	liquid crystal display projector	324
Local/regional ASP	local/regional application service provider	164
Mac OS	Macintosh Operating System	19
Mac OS X	Macintosh Operating System X	39, 135, 195, 420
MB	megabyte	197, 356
MBps	megabytes per second	357, 365
Mbps	megabits per second	365
M-commerce	mobile commerce	91
MHz	megahertz	203
MIB	Medical Information Bureau	379
MICR	magnetic-ink character recognition	260
MICR reader	magnetic-ink character recognition reader	260
MIDI	Musical Instrument Digital Interface	209, 246
MIDI port	Musical Instrument Digital Interface port	209
Mini-DVD media	mini-digital video disc media	373
MIPS	millions of instructions per second	190
Modem	modulate/demodulate	9
MP	million pixels	252
MP3	Moving Pictures Experts Group Audio Layer 3 (MPEG-3)	86, 87, 89, 202
MPEG	Moving Pictures Experts Group	88
MPEG-4	Moving Pictures Experts Group 4	88
MRAM	magnetoresistive random access memory	199
μs	microsecond	203
ms	millisecond	203

Acronym	Description	Page
MS-DOS	Microsoft Disk Operating System	417, 430
MSN	Microsoft Network, The	72, 82
MSN Hotmail	Microsoft Network Hotmail	94
MT/ST	Magentic Tape/Selectric Typewriter	54
MTBF	mean time between failures	363
National ISP	national Internet service provider	72
Netiquette	Internet etiquette	100
Network OS	network operating system	410, 422-23
NLQ	near letter quality	318
ns	nanosecond	203
NSF	National Science Foundation	70
OCR	optical character recognition	257
OCR devices	optical character recognition devices	257
OCR software	optical character recognition software	256
OLE	object linking and embedding	57
OLED	organic light emitting diode	304
OMR	optical mark recognition	257
OS	operating system	15-16, 398-425
OSP	online service provider	72
Palm OS	Palm operating system	283, 424
PB	petabyte	356
PC	personal computer	19-20, 445
PC Card	personal computer card	205, 374
PC camera	personal computer camera	253
PC Card bus	personal computer card bus	212
PC Card slot	personal computer card slot	205
PC video camera	personal computer video camera	7, 27, 253, 448
PC-compatible	personal computer compatible	19
PC-DOS	personal computer Disk Operating System	417
PCI bus	Peripheral Component Interconnect bus	212
PCL	Printer Control Language	316
PCMCIA	Personal Computer Memory Card International Association	205
PCMCIA cards	Personal Computer Memory Card International Association cards	205, 374
PC-to-TV port	personal computer-to-television port	453
PDA	personal digital assistant	22, 31, 265, 282, 325
PDF	Portable Document Format	89
PDL	page description language	316
Personal DTP software	personal desktop publishing software	158
Picture CD	picture compact disc	370
PIM	personal information manager	148
PIN	personal identification number	262
Pixel	picture element	252, 304
PNG format	Portable Network Graphics format	85
POP	point of presence	72
POP	Post Office Protocol	95
POP3	Post Office Protocol 3	95

Acronym	Description	Page
POS	point of sale	261
POS terminal	point of sale terminal	261
POST	power-on self test	400
ppi	pixels (picture elements) per inch	252
PROM chip	programmable read-only memory chip	202
ps	picosecond	203
Pure Tablet PCs	Pure Tablet personal computers	455
QT	QuickTime	87
RA	RealAudio	87
RAM	random access memory	197, 198-200
RAM chips	random access memory chips	400
Rambus DRAM	Rambus dynamic random access memory	199
RDRAM	Rambus dynamic random access memory	199
Regional ISP	regional Internet service provider	72
RFID	radio frequency identification	197, 259
RFID reader	radio frequency identification reader	197, 259
RFID tags	radio frequency identification tags	64, 259
RIAA	Recording Industry Association of America	63, 153
RIMM	Rambus inline memory module	199
ROM	read-only memory	201-2
ROM chips	read-only memory chips	400
Rpm	revolutions per minute	362
SATA	Serial Advanced Technology Attachment	364-65
SCSI	small computer system interface	210
SCSI interface	small computer system interface controller	365
SCSI port	small computer system interface port	210
SD	Secure Digital	376
SDRAM	synchronous dynamic random access memory	199, 203
SIMM	single inline memory module	199
SMTP	simple mail transfer protocol	94
SOHO	small office/home office	28
Specialist ASP	specialist application service provider	164
SRAM	static random access memory	199
Static IP addresses	static Internet Protocol addresses	102
Super XGA	Super Extended Graphics Array	305
SVGA	super video graphics array	305
SXGA	Super Extended Graphics Array	305
Symbian OS	Symbian operating system	283, 425
Synchronous DRAM	synchronous dynamic random access memory	199
TB	terabyte	197, 356
TFT display	thin-film transistor display	304
TIFF	Tagged Image File Format	85, 345
TRACERT	traceroute	430
TTFN	ta ta for now	100
TYVM	thank you very much	100

Acronym	Description	Page
UGA	Ultra Extended Graphics Array	305
Ultra XGA	Ultra Extended Graphics Array	305
UNIVAC I	UNIVersal Automatic Computer	52
UPC	Universal Product Code	258
UPS	uninterruptible power supply	451
URL	Uniform Resource Locator	76
USB	universal serial bus	207, 212
USB 2.0	universal serial bus 2.0	208, 365
USB flash drive	universal serial bus flash drive	8, 64, 205, 355, 357, 377, 448
USB hub	universal serial bus hub	208
USB port	universal serial bus port	206, 208, 214
USB transfer rate	universal serial bus transfer rate	365
User ID	user identification	410
VCD	video CD	351
Vertical market ASP	vertical market application service provider	164
Voice over IP	voice over Internet Protocol	99

Acronym	Description	Page
Volume business ASP	volume business application service provider	164
VR	virtual reality	88
VR world	virtual reality world	88
W3C	World Wide Web Consortium	70, 327
WAV	Windows waveform	87
WBT	Web-based training	166
Wireless LAN Access Point	wireless local area network Access Point	448
WISP	wireless Internet service provider	72
WMA	Windows Media Audio	87, 89, 202
WWW	World Wide Web	75, 103
WYSIWYG	what you see is what you get	137
XGA	Extended Graphics Array	305
YB	yottabyte	356
ZB	zettabyte	356

INDEX

3-D interface, 137
3-D search engines, 81

A9.com, 78
A+: Hardware certification that tests entry-level knowledge of personal computer setup, configuration, maintenance, troubleshooting; basic networking skills; and system software. **381**
AA, 87. *See also* Audible Audio
AAC, 87. *See also* Advanced Audio Coding
AC adapter: External power supply, used by some external peripherals, that converts AC power into DC power that the peripheral requires. **213**
Accelerated Graphics Port (AGP): Expansion bus designed by Intel to improve the speed with which 3-D graphics and video transmit. **212**
Access provider: Business that provides individuals and companies access to the Internet free or for a fee. **71–72**
Access time: Measurement of the amount of time it takes the process to read data, instructions, and information from memory. **203, 357**
floppy disk drive, 358
hard disk, 362
Accounting software: Software that helps companies record and report their financial transactions. **149**
Accurate information: Information that is error free. 25
Active Directory: Windows Server 2003 central repository about network users and resources. **422**
Active-matrix display: LCD monitor or screen technology that uses a separate transistor to apply charges to each liquid crystal cell and thus displays high-quality color that is viewable from all angles. Also called TFT (thin-film transistor) display. **304.** *See also* **TFT (thin-film transistor) display**
ADA, 266. *See also* **Americans with Disabilities Act**

Adapter card: Circuit board that enhances functions of a component of a system unit and/or provides connections to peripherals. 186, **204.** *See also* **Expansion card**
ADC, 38. *See also* **Analog-to-digital converter**
Address
e-mail, 94
Internet protocol, 73, 102
mailing lists, 97
Web, 76, 77, 78
Address (memory): Unique number that identifies the location of a byte in memory. **196**
Address (memory cell), 218
Address book (e-mail): List of names and e-mail addresses, created and stored by a user. **94**
Address book (personal mobile device), 285
Address bus: The part of a bus that transfers information about where data should reside in memory. **211**
Adobe Acrobat Reader, 152, 303
Adobe PDF format, 152
Adobe Systems, 169,
Advanced Audio Coding (AAC), 87
Advanced Micro Devices (AMD), 190, 191, 219
Advanced Research Projects Agency (ARPA): Agency of the U.S. Department of Defense that built an early computer network called ARPANET. **69–70**
Advanced transfer cache (ATC) : L2 cache built directly on the processor chip. **201**
Advocacy Web site, 84
AGP, 212. *See also* **Accelerated Graphics Port**
AIFF, 87. *See also* Audio Interchange File Format
All-in-one devices: Output device that looks like a copy machine but provides the functionality of a printer, scanner, copy machine, and perhaps a fax machine. See also multifunction peripheral. **323.** *See also* **Multifunction peripheral**
Allocation unit: Smallest unit of disk space that stores data and information. Also called a cluster. **357.** *See also* **Block; Cluster**
AlltheWeb, 78
Alta Vista, 78, 82

ALU, 188. *See also* **Arithmetic logic unit**
AMD, 219. *See also* Advanced Micro Devices
America Online (AOL), 72, 82
American Standard Code for Information Interchange (ASCII): The most widely used coding system to represent data. **195**
Americans with Disabilities Act (ADA): Federal law that requires any company with 15 or more employees to make reasonable attempts to accommodate the needs of physically challenged workers. **266**
Analog: Continuous (wave form) signals. **38, 194**
Analog format, 347
Analog sound, playing, 328
Analog-to-digital converter (ADC), 38, 251, 328
Andreessen, Marc, 58
Animated GIF: Animation technique that combines several GIF images in a single GIF file. **86**
Animation: Appearance of motion created by displaying a series of still images in sequence. **86**
multimedia and, 86
Anonymous FTP: Feature of many FTP sites whereby anyone can transfer some, if not all, available files. **96**
Anti-spam program: Program that attempts to remove spam before it reaches a user's inbox. **162,** 426, 427
Antivirus program: Program that protects a computer against viruses by identifying and removing any computer viruses found in memory, on storage media, or on incoming files. **162, 425, 426**
AOL, 72, 82. *See also* **America Online**
AOL Search, 78
AOMI, 78
Apple Computer, 19, 39, 56, 59, 329
history of, 55
Macintosh processor, 190, 192, 420, 429
QuickTime, 429
operating system, 135, 420. *See also* Mac OS X
Application service provider (ASP): Third-party organization that manages and distributes software and services on the Web. **164**

Application software: Program designed to make users more productive and/or assist them with personal tasks. **16, 134–67**
  bundling with operating system, 429
  business software, 134, **138**-50
  communications, 161
  educational use, 160
  graphics and, 150–54
  home use, 155–60
  learning aids, 164–65
  memory and, 196, 199–200
  multimedia and, 150–54
  note taking, 147
  PDA, 148
  personal use, 155–60
  purchasing desktop computer and, 446
  RAM and, 198–99
  support tools, 164–65
  system software and, 135
  uninstalling, 412, 413
  on Web, 163–64
  Web browser as, 75
Appointment calendar, in personal information manager, 148
Arguments, 430. *See also* **Options**
Arithmetic logic unit (ALU): Component of a processor that performs arithmetic, comparison, and other operations. **188**
Arithmetic operations: Basic calculations such as addition, subtraction, multiplication, and division. **188**
ARPA, 69. *See also* **Advanced Research Projects Agency**
ARPANET: Network developed by the Pentagon's Advanced Research Projects Agency (ARPA) that linked scientific and academic researchers across the United States. 54, 69–70
Arrow keys, on keyboard, 237
Articles: Messages previously entered in a newsgroup. **96**
Array, 218
Arts and literature, Web site and, 131
ASCII: The most widely used coding system to represent data. **195.** *See also* **American Standard Code for Information Interchange**
ASF, 87. *See also* Advanced Streaming for Systems
Ask Jeeves, 78
ASP, 164. *See* **Application service provider**
AT&T WorldNet, 72
Atanasoff, John, 52
Atanasoff-Berry Computer (ABC), 52

ATC, 201. *See also* advanced transfer cache.
Attacks
  Internet, 558–64
  network, 558–64
ATM (banking), 262. *See also* **Automated teller machine**
Attachment, e-mailing document as, 142
Audible Audio (AA), 87
Audio: Music, speech, or any other sound. **86–87**
  MIDI port and, 209
  multimedia and, 86
  streaming, 86
  on Web page, 75
Audio books, 321
Audio CD, 27
  copying from, 371
  using CD-ROM drive to listen to, 369
Audio editing software: Application software that allows a user to modify audio clips and produce studio-quality soundtracks. **153**
Audio input: Process of entering any sound, such as speech, music, and sound effects, into the computer. 234, **246**
Audio Interchange File Format (AIFF), 87
Audio output device: Component of a computer that produces music, speech, or other sounds, such as beeps. 301, **320–22**
Audio resolution, 328
Automated teller machine (ATM): Special-purpose terminal, connected to a host computer through a network that functions as a self-service banking machine. **262**
AutoSave feature, 142

B2B, 92. *See also* **Business-to-business (B2B) e-commerce**
B2C, 92. *See also* **Business-to-consumer (B2C) e-commerce**
Back up: To make a copy of a file. **415**
Background: Programs that are running, but not in use. **404**
Backup: Duplicate or copy of a file, program, or disk that can be used if the original is lost, damaged, or destroyed. **359**
  CD-RW used for, 371
  enterprise storage system and, 379
  Internet, 365
Backup utility: Utility program that allows users to copy, or back up, selected files or an entire hard disk to another storage medium, which can be used if the original is lost, damaged, or destroyed. **415**

Backward compatible, 208
Ballmer, Steve, 803
Band printer: Line printer that prints fully formed characters when hammers strike a horizontal, rotating band that contains shapes of numbers, letters of the alphabet, and other characters. **319**
Bandwidth: The amount of data, instructions, and information that can travel over a communications channel. **71**
Banking
  e-commerce used for, 91
  MICR used by, 260
  online. *See* **Online banking**
  voice verification used in, 263
Bar chart: Chart that displays bars of various lengths to show the relationship of data. **144.** *See also* **Column chart**
Bar code: Identification code consisting of vertical lines and spaces of different widths that represent a manufacturer and an item. **258, 261**
Bar code reader: Optical reader that uses laser beams to read bar codes by using light patterns that pass through the bar code lines. Also called a barcode scanner. **258,** 261. *See also* **Bar code scanner**
Bar code scanner, 258. *See* **Bar code reader**
Bardeen, John, 52
BASIC: Beginners All-purpose Symbolic Instruction Code, developed by John Kemeny and Thomas Kurtz as a simple, interactive problem-solving language. **54.** *See also* **Beginner's All-purpose Symbolic Instruction Code**
Basic input/output system, 400. *See* **BIOS**
Battery
  CMOS and, 203
  notebook computers, 189, 453
  real-time clock, 189
Bay: Opening inside the system unit in which additional equipment can be installed. 186, **212**
Bell Laboratories, 420
Berners-Lee, Tim, 57, 103
Berry, Clifford, 52
Binary digit: The smallest unit of data a computer can process. Also known as a bit. **195**
Binary system: Number system used by computers that has just two unique digits, 0 and 1, called bits. 38, **195**
Biometric authentication, 268

Biometric device: Device that translates a personal characteristic into a digital code that is compared with a digital code stored in a computer. **262**

Biometric identifier: Physiological or behavioral characteristic, such as fingerprints, hand geometry, facial features, voice, signatures, and eye patterns. **262**

Biometrics: Technology of authenticating a person's identity by verifying a personal characteristic. **262–64**
popularity of, 264

BIOS: Basic input/output system; firmware that contains the computer's startup instructions. **400**

Bit: The smallest unit of data a computer can process. Bit is short for binary digit. **195**
bus width and, 211
stored by video card, 308
stored in pixel, 252
word size, 211

Bit depth: The number of bits a video card uses to store information about each pixel. Also called color depth. **306**, 308. *See also* **Color depth**

Blackberry, 283

Block, 382. *See also* **Allocation unit; Cluster**

Blog: Web site that uses a regularly updated journal format to reflect the interests, opinions, and personalities of the author and sometimes site visitors. Blog is short for Web log. **84**

Bluetooth: Network standard, specifically a protocol, that defines how two Bluetooth devices use short-range radio waves to transmit data. **210**, 312
Blatand, Harald, 312
keyboard and, 238

Bluetooth printing: Type of printing process that uses radio waves to transmit output to a printer. **311**

Blu-Ray disc: Newer, expensive type of DVD with storage capacities of 27 GB, and expectations of exceeding 50 GB in the future. **372**, 373

BMP, 85

Boot disk: Special disk that contains a few system files capable of starting a computer, which is used when the computer cannot boot from its hard disk. **402.** *See also* **Recovery disk**

Boot drive: Drive from which a personal computer boots (starts). **402**

Boot sector virus, 168

Booting: Process of starting or restarting a computer. **400–2**
cold, 400
warm, 400, 406

Braille printer: Type of printer that prints information on paper in Braille for use by visually impaired users. **326**

BrainGate, 137

Brain implants, for paralyzed users, 266

Brattain, Walter, 52

Bricklin, Dan, 169

Broadband: Type of media that transmits multiple signals simultaneously. **70, 72**
hackers and, 413

Browser: Application software that allows users to access and view Web pages. Also called a Web browser. **75**
micro-, 76

Buffer: Segment of memory or storage in which items are placed while waiting to be transferred from an input device or to an output device. **407**

Bundled software, 446

Burning: Process of writing on an optical disc. **371**

Bus (computer): Electrical channel that transfers electronic bits internally within the circuitry of a computer, allowing the devices both inside and attached to the system unit to communicate with each other. **211–12**

BIOS testing, 400

Bus width: The size of a bus, which determines the number of bits that a computer can transmit at one time. **211**

Business
See also **E-commerce; Enterprise computing**

Business networks, 11

Business software: Application software that assists people in becoming more effective and efficient while performing their daily business activities. 134, **138**–50
personal mobile device and, 286–87

Business/marketing Web site, 82

Business-to-business (B2B) e-commerce: E-commerce that takes place between businesses. **92**

Business-to-consumer (B2C) e-commerce: The sale of goods and services to the general public. **92**

Button: Graphical element that is activated to cause a specific action to take place. **136**

Buying personal computers, 200

Buyer's guide, 444–56

Byte: Eight bits that are grouped together as a unit. A byte provides enough different combinations of 0s and 1s to represent 256 individual characters. **195**, 196, 197

C2C, 92. *See* **Consumer-to-consumer (C2C) e-commerce**

Cable modem: Digital modem that sends and receives digital data over the cable television (CATV) network. Also called a broadband modem. **70**
purchasing desktop computer and, 449

Cable television (CATV)

Cache: Area of memory that stores the contents of frequently used data or instructions. **201**

Cache controller, 363

CAD software, 150, 151. *See also* **Computer-aided design (CAD) software**

CAI (computer-aided instruction), 160. *See also* **Computer-based training**

CAM, 36. *See* **Computer-aided manufacturing**

Camera
digital. *See* **Digital camera**
digital video (DV), 253
PC video. *See* **PC video camera**
personal mobile device and, 284
video, 253–54
Web, 254

Candela: Standard unit of luminous intensity. **304**

Capacitor, 218

Capacity: The number of bytes (characters) a storage medium can hold. **356**
CD-ROM, 369
DVD+RW, 373
DVD-ROM, 372
external hard disk, 364
floppy disk, 358
hard disk, 360
miniature mobile storage media, 376
PC Card, 374
removable hard disk, 364
Zip disk, 359

Car computers
cyber cars, 163

Car kit, for personal mobile device, 284

Card reader, 260

Card reader/writer: Device that reads and writes data, instructions, and information stored on PC Cards or flash memory cards and transmits that data to a computer or printer through a connection to a port. **376**
purchasing desktop computer and, 447
Career
as computer engineer, 217
as computer technician, 381
as data entry clerk, 267
as graphic designer/illustrator, 327
as Help Desk specialist and, 167
as personal computer salesperson, 37
searching for, 130
as systems programmer, 429
as Web developer, 101
Case, used for personal mobile device, 284
Cathode-ray tube (CRT): Large, sealed glass tube whose front, the screen, is coated with dots of red, green, and blue phosphor material. **307.** *See also* **CRT**
CATV, 482. *See also* Cable television
CBT. *See* **Computer-based training**
CCD, 251. *See also* **Charge-coupled device**
CD. *See* Compact disc
CD creation software: Software packaged with video editing software that allows a user to create CDs. **351**
CD drive, 27
CD recorder: Device that can read both audio CDs and standard CD-ROM. **371.** *See also* **CD-R drive**
CD/DVD burner: Utility program that writes text, graphics, audio, and video files to a recordable or rewritable CD or DVD. **162**
CD/DVD burning software: Stand-alone utility program that writes text, graphics, audio, and video files to a recordable or rewritable CD or DVD. **428**
CD-R: Multisession optical disc on which users can write, but not erase, their own items such as text, graphics, and audio. **371.** *See also* **Compact disc-recordable**
CD-R drive: Device that can read both audio CDs and standard CD-ROM. **371.** *See also* **CD recorder**

CD-ROM: Type of optical disc that uses laser technology to store data, instructions, and information that users can read but not write on or erase. **369–70.** *See also* **Compact disc read-only memory**
CD-ROM drive: Drive that can read CD-ROM discs and sometimes audio CDs. **369**
CD-RW drive: Drive that can read audio CDs, standard CD-ROMs, CD-Rs, CD-RWs, and can write on, or record, CD-RWs. **371**
Celeron: Intel processor used by less-expensive basic PCs. **190,** 191
Cell: Intersection of a column and a row in a worksheet. **143**
Cellular telephone
flash memory and, 202, 205
sending text messages using, 248
smart. *See* Smart phones
Central processing unit (CPU): Electronic component on a computer's motherboard that interprets and carries out the basic instructions that operate the computer. Also called a processor. 8, **187**
comparison of, 190–91
components of, 187–90
installation and upgrades, 190–91
machine cycle and, 188–89
multiple, 194
purchasing, 192
RAM and, 198
registers, 189
role of, 185
system clock and, 189–90
CF, 376. *See also* **CompactFlash (CF)**
Chair, health issues and, 452
Charge-coupled device (CCD): Digital camera chip that generates an analog symbol that represents an image. **251**
Charger, used for personal mobile device, 284
Charting: Spreadsheet software feature that depicts data in a graphical form. **144**
Chassis: Case of the system unit made of metal or plastic that protects the internal electronic components from damage. **184**
Chat: Real-time typed conversation that takes place on a computer. **98**
Chat client: Program that allows a user to connect to a chat server to participate in a chat session. **98**
Chat client software, 161

Chat room: Location on an Internet server that permits users to chat with each other. **98**
software, 161
Checks, MICR characters on, 260
Children, Internet access for, 427
Chip: Small piece of semiconducting material, usually silicon, on which integrated circuits are etched. **186**
EEPROM, 202
implanted in brain, 266
memory, 196–203
packaging, 186
PROM, 202
RAM. *See* RAM
ROM. *See* Read-only memory
Chkdsk command: Command that checks for and corrects errors on the specified hard disk. **430**
Chu, James, 329
Clark, Jim, 58
Cleaning the computer, 216
Cleaning the disc, 368
ClearType: Technology developed by Microsoft to improve the quality of reading material on LCD screens, such as e-books. **456**
Click: To move the mouse pointer to a button or link on the computer screen, and then to press and release the left mouse button. **77, 136**
Client: Computer on a network that requests resources from the server. **11**
Client operating systems: Complete operating system that works on a desktop computer, notebook computer, or mobile computing device and that also works in conjunction with a network operating system. **416.** *See also* **Stand-alone operating system**
Client/server network: Network in which one or more computers act as a server, and the other computers on the network request services from the server.
operating system for, 422
Clip art: Collection of drawings, diagrams, maps, and photographs that a user can insert in documents. **138–39**
presentation graphics software, 146
public-domain, 139
Clip art/image gallery: Collection of clip art and photographs that often is included in application software. **159**

Clipboard: Temporary storage location for document content that is used in cutting and pasting or copying and pasting operations. **141**

Clock
kernel maintaining, 400
real-time. *See* **Real-time clock**
system. *See* **System clock**

Clock cycle: One tick of the system clock. **189**

Clock speed: Pace of the system clock, measured by the number of ticks per second. **189**
bus, 212
needs, 192

Clothing and computers, 267

Cluster: Smallest unit of disk space that stores data and information. Also called an allocation unit. **357, 382.** *See also* **Allocation unit; Block**

CMOS, 203. *See also* **Complementary metal-oxide semiconductor**

CMOS battery. *See* Complementary metal-oxide semiconductor battery

CMOS chip, POST results compared with data in, 400

COBOL: COmmon Business-Oriented Language. Programming language designed for business applications, which evolved out of a joint effort between the United States government, businesses, and major universities in the early 1960s. 53. *See also* **COmmon Business-Oriented Language**

Codec, 349

Coding schemes, 195

Cold boot: Process of turning on a computer that has been powered off completely. **400**

Color, 302
depth of, 306
ink-jet printers, 312
laser printers, 315
mobile printers, 317
LCD monitors, 304
LCD screens, 304
video card and, 308, 306

Color correction tools: Tools used to analyze video to create a smooth look. **350**

Color depth: The number of bits a video card uses to store information about each pixel. Also called bit depth. **306.** *See also* **Bit depth**

Color library: Standard set of colors used by designers and printers to ensure that colors will print exactly as specified. **152**

Colossus, 52

Column: Term used by users of relational databases for field. 145

Column chart: Chart that displays bars of various lengths to show the relationship of data. **144.** *See also* **Bar chart**

COM port: Serial port on the system unit. Com port is short for communications port. **207**

Command: Instruction on a menu that causes a program to perform a specific action. **137, 235**
function keys for, 237

Command language: The set of commands entered into a computer with a command-line interface. **402**

Command Prompt, 430

Command shell, 430

Command-line interface: Type of user interface in which a user types commands or presses special keys on the keyboard (such as function keys or key combinations) to enter data and instructions. **402,** 417, 420, 421, 430

Communications: Process in which two or more computers or devices transfer data, instructions, and information.
network. *See* **Network**
software, 161

Communications device: Any type of hardware capable of transmitting data, instructions, and information between a sending device and a receiving device. **9**
purchasing desktop computer and, 446

Compact disc (CD), 8, 9, 17, 27
audio. *See* Audio CD
booting from, 402
burning, 371
direct access and, 374
music sharing, 369
USB 2.0 ports and, 208

Compact disc (CD) drive
bays and, 212

Compact disc read-only memory: Type of optical disc that uses laser technology to store data, instructions, and information that users can read but not write on or erase. **369.** *See also* **CD-ROM**

Compact disc-recordable: Multisession optical disc on which users can write, but not erase, their own items such as text, graphics, and audio. **371.** *See also* **CD-R**

Compact disc-rewritable: Erasable multisession optical disc on which users can write data, instructions, and information multiple times. **371.** *See also* **CD-RW**

CompactFlash (CF): Type of miniature mobile storage medium that is a flash memory card capable of storing between 32 MB and 4 GB of data. **376**

Comparison operations: Operations that involve comparing one data item with another to determine whether the first item is greater than, equal to, or less than the other item. **188**

Compaq, 56

Complementary metal-oxide semiconductor (CMOS): Technology used by some RAM chips, flash memory chips, and other types of memory chips that provides high speeds and consumes little power by using battery power to retain information even when the power to a computer is off. **203**

Complementary metal-oxide semiconductor (CMOS) battery, 203

Compress: To shrink the size of a file. **415**

Compression, 344

Computer: Electronic device, operating under the control of instructions stored in its own memory, that can accept data, process the data according to specified rules, produce results, and store the results for future use. **6**
ability to think, 187
applications in society, 32–37
buyer's guide, 444–56
categories of, 18–24
cleaning of, 216
clothing, 267
components of, 7–9
DNA, 215
examples of usage, 26–31
fastest, 190
fault-tolerant, 405
optimum performance and, 414
personal. *See* **Personal computer**
power of, 10
purchasing, 444–54
refurbishment of, 193
starting. *See* **Booting**
timeline, history of, 52–65
waste of, 193

Computer engineer, 217

Computer fan, 213

Computer games, violence in, 16

Computer literacy: The knowledge and understanding of computers and their uses. **5**

Computer output microfilm recorder: Device that records images on microfilm and microfiche. **379**

Computer service technician, 381

Computer service technician (CST), 381

Computer technician: Employee who installs, maintains, and repairs hardware; installs, upgrades, and configures software; and troubleshoots hardware problems. 381

Computer-aided design (CAD) software: Sophisticated type of application software that assists a professional user in creating engineering, architectural, and scientific designs. **150**, 151

graphic designer/illustrator using, 327

Computer-aided instruction (CAI). *See* **Computer-based training**

Computer-based training (CBT): Type of education in which students learn by using and completing exercises with instructional software. Also called computer-aided training. **160**

Configuration information flash memory and, 202 loaded by operating system, 401 stored in CMOS chip, 400 Windows XP, 430

Connecting to Internet, 70–71

Connector: Device that joins a cable to a peripheral. 186, **206**, 208 setting up computer and, 454

Consistency, and computers, 10

Consumer devices flash memory cards and, 205 processors in, 190

Consumer-to-consumer (C2C) e-commerce: E-commerce that occurs when one consumer sells directly to another, such as in an online auction. **92**

Continuous speech: Flowing conversation tone recognized by most of today's voice recognition software. **246**

Continuous-form paper: Type of paper, used by most dot-matrix printers, which consists of thousands of pages connected together end to end. **319**

Contracts, legal software and, 157

Control unit: Component of a processor that directs and coordinates most of the operations in the computer. **187**

Controller
cache, 363
disk, 364–65
EIDE, 365
SATA, 364–65
SCSI, 365

Convergence, Trend of offering similar functions that make it increasingly difficult to differentiate between two similar mobile devices. 22

Convertible Tablet PCs: Tablet PCs with an attached keyboard that look like notebook computers. **455**

Copying
items in document, 141

Copyright: Exclusive rights given to authors and artists to duplicate, publish, and sell their materials.
audio CDs and, 371
music and video and, 153

Copyrighted software, 86
freeware, 135
packaged, 134
shareware, 135

Cordless keyboard: Battery-powered keyboard that transmits data using wireless technology, such as radio waves or infrared light waves. **238**, 269. *See also* **wireless keyboard**.

Cordless mouse: Battery-powered device that transmits data using wireless technology, such as radio waves or infrared light waves. **239**, 269

Corporate/government software and personal mobile devices, 288–89

Corrupt files, 414

Costs, for Internet access, 71

CPU, 8, 187. *See also* **Central processing unit**

Create: To enter text or numbers, insert graphical images, and perform other tasks with a document using an input device such as a keyboard, mouse, microphone, or digital pen. **141**

Credit cards
POS terminals processing, 262
purchasing computers using, 451, 452

Crop, 350

Cross-platform: Program that runs the same on multiple operating systems. **399**

CRT, 307. *See* **Cathode-ray tube (CRT)**

CRT monitor: Type of desktop monitor that contains a cathode-ray tube. **307–8**
flat screen, 308
quality of, 308
video cards and, 308

CST. *See* Computer service technician

Cursor (application program): Symbol on a computer screen, usually a blinking vertical bar, that indicates where the next character a user types will display. **237**. *See also* **Insertion point**

Cursor (graphics tablet): Pointing device on a graphics tablet that looks similar to a mouse pointer, except it has windows and cross hairs. **244**

Custom software: Software that performs functions specific to a business or industry, developed by a user or at a user's request. **135**

Cylinder: The vertical section of a hard disk track that passes through all platters. **362**

DAC, 38. *See also* **Digital-to-analog converter**

Daisy chain: Method of attaching multiple peripherals in which the first USB device connects to the USB port on the computer, the second USB device connects to the first USB device, the third USB device connects to the second USB device, and so on. **208**, 210

Data: Collection of unprocessed items, which can include text, numbers, images, audio, and video. **6, 234**
accuracy of, 10, 25
backup. *See* **Backup**
encryption of, 411
input of. *See* **Input; Input device**
organized in database, 145
organized in worksheet, 142–44
output of. *See also* **Output device**
representation in computer, 194–96
sharing, 10
storage of. *See* **Storage; Storage medium**
traveling on Internet, 72

Date book, (personal mobile device): 285

Data bus: Part of a bus that transfers actual data. **211**

Data collection device: Device that obtains data directly at the location where the transaction or event takes place. **261**

Data entry clerk, 267

Data flow diagram: Systems analysis and design tool that graphically shows the flow of data in a system. **32–33**

Data projector: Output device that takes the text and images displaying on a computer screen and projects them on a larger screen so an audience can see the image clearly. **323–24, 454**

Database: Collection of data organized in a manner that allows access retrieval, and use of that data. **145**
largest, 145

Database software: Application software used to create, access, and manage a database; add, change, and delete data in the database; sort and retrieve data from the database; and create forms and reports using the data in the database. See also database management system (DBMS). **145.** *See also* **Database management system (DBMS)**

Day, real-time clock and, 189

DDR SDRAM, 199. *See also* **Double Data Rate SDRAM**

Dean, Mark, 383

Decoding: Processor operation that translates a program instruction into signals the computer can execute. **188**

Defrag command: Command that defragments the specified hard disk. **430**

Defragmenting: Reorganizing a disk so the files are stored in contiguous sectors, thus speeding up disk access and the performance of the entire computer. 365, 406, **414,** 430, 456

Deleting programs, 413

Dell, Michael, 39

Dell, 39

Demodulate/demodulation: To convert an analog signal into a digital signal. **38**

Density: Number of bits in an area on a storage medium. **358**

Desktop: On-screen work area that has a graphical user interface. **136**

Desktop computer: Computer designed so the system unit, input devices, output devices, and any other devices fit entirely on or under a desk or table. **20**
display devices, 302, 307
floppy disk drive in, 358
hard disk in, 360, 361
keyboards, 236, 237, 238

LCD monitor, 302–6
motherboard, 186
purchasing, 444, 446–52
small office/home office (SOHO), 28
system unit, 184, 185
as workstation, 20
See also **Personal computer**

Desktop publishing (DTP), 152

Desktop publishing (DTP) software: Application software used by professional designers to create sophisticated documents that can contain text, graphics, and many colors. **152**

Device driver: Small program that tells an operating system how to communicate with a specific device. **407,** 409. *See also* **Driver**

Device-dependent: Program that runs only on a specific type or make of computer. **415**

Device-independent: Operating systems that run on computers provided by a variety of manufacturers. **415**

Devices
detecting new, 400–1
kernel managing, 400

DHCP, 102. *See also* **Dynamic Host Configuration Protocol**

Diagnostic utility: Utility program that compiles technical information about a computer's hardware and certain system software programs and then prepares a report outlining any identified problems. **414**

Diagrams, clip art, 139

Dialog box: Special window that provides information, presents available options, or requests a response. **137**

Dial-up access: Method of connecting to the Internet using a modem in a computer and a standard telephone line. **70**

Digital: Representation of data using only two discrete states: on (1) and off (0). **38,** 194

Digital camera: Camera that stores its photographed images digitally, instead of on traditional film. 7, **250-52, 344**
attaching to PDA, 248
flash memory cards and, 205
PC Cards, 374
in PDA, 248
printer and, 315
professional photographers and, 251
purchasing desktop computer and, 447
quality, 252
storage media, 9, 374, 375, 376

transferring pictures into computer from, 7, 158
types of, 251

Digital cinema, 324
projectors and, 324

Digital data, duration of, 381

Digital format, 347

Digital image
converting paper documents into, 256
quality of, 252
storing, 370
See also **Digital camera**

Digital imaging technology, 344–47

Digital light processing (DLP) projector: Projector that uses tiny mirrors to reflect light, which produces crisp, bright, colorful images that remain in focus and can be seen clearly, even in a well-lit room. **324**

Digital movies, 324

Digital music players
flash memory cards and, 205
purchasing notebook computer and, 453

Digital pen: Input device that allows users to write or draw on the screen by pressing the pen and issue instructions to a Tablet PC by tapping on the screen. **21, 243,** 456. *See also* **Stylus**

Digital photo printer: Thermal printer that uses heat to transfer colored dye to specially coated paper. **317.** *See also* **Dye-sublimation printer**

Digital photo viewer: Device that connects to a television port for on-screen picture viewing. **375**

Digital signal processor (DSP), 38, 328

Digital sound, recording, 328

Digital Subscriber Line: Type of digital technology that provides high-speed Internet connections using regular copper telephone lines. Commonly called DSL. **70.** *See also* **DSL**

Digital technology, 324
Digital cinema, 324
JPG 2000, 324

Digital television (DTV): Television that receives digital television signals and produces a higher-quality picture. **306.** *See also* **DTV**

Digital versatile disc-ROM: Extremely high capacity optical disc on which users can read, but not write or erase, that is capable of storing 4.7 GB to 17 GB of data. See also digital versatile disc-ROM; digital video disc-ROM, digital video disc read-only memory. **372.** *See also* **Digital video disc-ROM; DVD-ROM**

Digital video (DV) camera: Video camera that records video as digital signals instead of as analog signals. **253**
recording on DVD and, 373
storage media for, 376

Digital video capture device, purchasing desktop computer and, 447

Digital video disc-ROM: Extremely high capacity optical disc on which users can read, but not write or erase, that is capable of storing 4.7 GB to 17 GB of data. See also digital versatile disc-ROM; digital video disc-ROM; digital versatile disc read-only memory. **372.** *See also* **Digital versatile disc-ROM; DVD-ROM**

Digital Video Interface (DVI), 305

Digital video technology: Technology used to input, edit, manage, publish, and share videos using a personal computer. **347–51**

Digital-to-analog converter (DAC): Computer component that converts digital data into an analog voltage for output. **38, 328, 351**

Digitizer: Large-scale application term for a graphics tablet. **244.** *See also* **Graphics tablet**

Dijsktra, Edsger, 54

DIMM (dual inline memory module): Type of memory module that has pins on opposite sides of the circuit board that do not connect, thereby forming two sets of contacts. DIMM typically hold SDRAM chips. **199**

Direct access: Type of data access in which the storage device can locate a particular data item or file immediately, without having to move consecutively through items stored in front of the desired data item or file. **374.** *See also* **Random access**

Discrete speech: Voice pattern required by some voice recognition software in which the speaker speaks slowly and separates each word with a short pause. **246**

Disk cache: Memory chips on a hard disk that store frequently accessed items such as data, instructions, and information. Also called a buffer. **363**

Disk controller: Special-purpose chip and electronic circuits that control the transfer of data, instructions, and information between a disk and the system bus and other components in a computer. **364–65**

Disk defragmenter: Utility that reorganizes the files and unused space on a computer's hard disk so the operating system accesses data more quickly and programs run faster. **414, 430, 456**

Disk Operating System: Any one of several single user operating systems that were developed in the early 1980s by Microsoft for personal computers. See also DOS. **417.** *See also* **DOS**

Disk scanner: Utility that (1) detects and corrects both physical and logical problems on a hard disk and (2) searches for and removes unnecessary files. **414**

Diskette: Portable, inexpensive storage medium that consists of a thin, circular, flexible plastic Mylar film with a magnetic coating, enclosed in a square shaped plastic shell. **358.** *See also* **Floppy disk**

Diskpart command, 430

Display: Output device that visually conveys text, graphics, and video information electronically, for a temporary period. **302** *See also* **Display**

Display device: Output device that visually conveys text, graphics, and video information. **302**
CRT monitors, 307–8
ergonomics and, 589
flat-panel display, 302–6
video cards and, 305
viewed content, 308

Distance learning (DL): Delivery of education at one location while the learning takes place at other locations. **166**

DL. *See* **Distance learning**

DLP projector. *See* Digital light processing projector

DNA computer, 215

DNS, 74. *See also* **Domain name system**

DNS server: Internet server that usually is associated with an Internet access provider. **74, 102**

Docking station: External device that attaches to a mobile computer or device and contains a power connection and provides connections to peripherals. **249**
digital camera, 251
Tablet PC, 249, 456

Documents
desktop publishing, 152
scanning, 255–56, 256
source, 255
word processing, 138–40

Domain name: Text version of an IP address. **73,** 76

Domain name system (DNS): Method that the Internet uses to store domain names and their corresponding IP addresses. **74**

DOS: Any one of several single user operating systems that were developed in the early 1980s by Microsoft for personal computers. See also Disk Operating System. **417.** *See also* **Disk Operating System**

Dot pitch: The distance in millimeters between pixels on a display device. Also called pixel pitch. **304,** 308. *See also* **Pixel pitch**

Dot-com: Term sometimes used to describe organizations with a top-level domain of com. 60, **73**

Dot-matrix printer: Type of impact printer that produces printed images when tiny wire pins on a print head mechanism strike an inked ribbon. **319**

Dots per inch: Printer resolution measurement of the number of dots a printer can print. **252, 313.** *See also* **Dpi**

Dotted decimal number, 102

Dotted quad, 102

Double Data Rate SDRAM (DDR SDRAM): Type of RAM that is even faster than SDRAM because it transfers data twice for each clock cycle, instead of just once. **199**
access time, 203

Download (camera): Process of transferring a copy of images from a digital camera to a computer's hard disk. **251**

Downloading: Process of a computer receiving information, such as a Web page, from a server on the Internet. **76**

Downward compatible, 416

Dpi (dots per inch), 252, 313

Dr. Watson: Diagnostic utility included with Windows XP. **414**

DRAM, 199. *See also* **Dynamic RAM**

Drawings, clip art, 139

Drive
BIOS testing, 400
CD-ROM. *See* **CD-ROM drive**
DVD. *See* DVD drive
floppy. *See* **Floppy disk drive**
hard. *See* **Hard disk drive**

Drive bays: Rectangular openings inside the system unit that typically hold disk drives. 186, **212**
hard disk mounted in, 360

Driver: Small program that tells an operating system how to communicate with a specific device. **407–9**
operating system and, 407–9
See also **Device driver**

DSL: Type of digital technology that provides high-speed Internet connections using regular copper telephone lines. 70, 449

DSP, 38. *See also* **Digital signal processor**

DTP. *See* Desktop publishing

DTP software. *See* **Desktop publishing (DTP) software**

DTV: Digital television; television that receives digital television signals and produces a higher-quality picture. **306.** *See also* **Digital television**

Dual inline memory module, 199. *See also* **DIMM**

Dual-core processor: A chip that has two separate processors, which ensure higher levels of performance with lower levels of power consumption. **190**

Dubinsky, Donna, 329

Dumb terminal: Terminal that cannot function as an independent device because it has no processing power. **261**

DV camera, 253. *See also* **Digital video (DV) camera**

DVD (digital versatile disc or digital video disc), 8, 17, 59, 89, 357
direct access and, 374

DVD and CD mastering software, 347

DVD creation software, 351

DVD drive, 9, 27
bays and, 212

DVD recorder: Device that can write to, or record, DVD+RW discs. **373.** *See also* **DVD+RW drive**

DVD/CD-RW, 368, **372**

DVD-R (DVD-recordable): DVD-recordable format with up to 4.7 GB capacity that allows users to write on the disc once and read it many times. **373**

DVD+R (DVD-recordable): DVD-recordable format with up to 4.7 GB capacity that allows users to write on the disc once and read it many times. **373**

DVD+RAM (DVD+random access memory): Type of optical disc that can be erased and written on, or recorded on, more than 100,000 times. DVD+RAM discs can be read by DVD+RAM drives and some DVD-ROM drives and players. **373**

DVD-recordable, 373. *See also* **DVD-R**

DVD-rewritable, 373. *See also* **DVD+RW**

DVD-ROM: Extremely high capacity optical disc on which users can read, but not write or erase, that is capable of storing 4.7 GB to 17 GB of data. 9, **372.** *See also* **Digital versatile disc-ROM; Digital video disc-ROM**

DVD-ROM drive: Device that can read a DVD-ROM. Most DVD-ROM drives also can read audio CDs, CD-ROMs, CD-Rs, and CD-RWs. **372**

DVD+RW: Rewritable DVD format with capacities up to 4.7 GB per side that can be erased and written on, or recorded on, more than 1,000 times. **373.** *See also* **DVD-rewritable**

DVD-RW: Rewritable DVD format with capacities up to 4.7 GB per side that can be erased and written on, or recorded on, more than 1,000 times. **373.** *See also* **DVD-rewritable**

DVD+RW drive, **373.** *See also* DVD writer

DVD-RW drive, **373.** *See also* DVD writer

DVD writer, 62

DVI (Digital Video Interface), 305. *See also* Digital Video Interface (DVI)

DVI port: Digital Video Interface; video card port that enables digital signals to transmit directly to an LCD monitor. **305**

Dvorak keyboard, 237

Dye-sublimation printer: Thermal printer that uses heat to transfer color dye to specially coated paper, creating images of photographic quality. **17.** *See also* **Digital photo printer**

Dynamic Host Configuration Protocol (DHCP), 102

Dynamic IP address, 102

Dynamic RAM (DRAM): Type of RAM chip that must be re-energized constantly or lose its contents. **199**

Dynamic Web page: A Web page that allows visitors to customize some or all of the viewed content. **75**

EarthLink, 72

EB. *See* Exabyte

Ebay, 103

EBCDIC, 195. *See also* **Extended Binary Coded Decimal Interchange**

E-book, 61, **303**
See also **Electronic book**

Eckert, J. Presper, 52

E-commerce: Short for electronic commerce, a business transaction conducted over the Web. **28,** 30, 60, **91–92**
types of, 91–92

Edit: To make changes to the existing content of a document. **141**

Editing
audio, 153
digital images, 251
document, 141
images, 152, 158
photographs, 159
scanned file, 256
video, 153

Education
computers used in, 32
online, 82
Web site, 125

Educational software: Application software that teaches a particular skill. **160**
personal mobile devices and, 293

Educational use, application software for, 160

Educational Web site, 82

EEPROM (electrically erasable programmable read-only memory): Variation of a PROM chip that allows a programmer to erase microcode with an electric signal. **202**

E-filing, 157

EIDE (Enhanced Integrated Drive Electronics): Interface that uses parallel signals to transfer data, instructions, and information and can support up to four hard disks at 137 GB per disk. **365**

Electrical adapters, purchasing notebook computer and, 454

Electrically erasable programmable read-only memory, 202. *See also* **EEPROM**

Electromagnetic radiation (EMR): Magnetic field that travels at the speed of light. CRT monitors produce a small amount of electromagnetic radiation. **308, 452**

Electronic book, 61, 303. *See also* **E-book**

Electronic commerce, 91. *See* **E-commerce**

Electronic mail, 92. *See* **E-mail**

Electronic Numerical Integrator And Computer (ENIAC), 52

Electronic storefront: Online business a customer visits that contains product descriptions, graphics, and a shopping cart. **92**

E-mail: Short for electronic mail, the transmission of messages and files via a computer network. 12, 31, 69, **92**–95, 101

companies monitoring, 161

monitoring, 237

sending digital images via, 251, 252, 253

users and, 31

viruses spread through, 95, 426

E-mail address: Combination of a user name and a domain name that identifies a user so he or she can receive Internet e-mail. **94**

E-mail program: Software used to create, send, receive, forward, store, print, and delete e-mail messages. **93,** 161

Embedded computer: Special-purpose computer that functions as a component in a larger product. 19, **24**

Embedded Linux: Scaled-down Linux operating system designed for PDAs, smart phones, smart watches, set-top boxes, and many other types of devices and computers requiring an embedded operating system. 283, **425**

Embedded operating system: The operating system that resides on a ROM chip inside most PDAs and small devices. **423**–25

Emoticons: Symbols used on the Internet to express emotion. **100**

text messaging using, 248

Employee monitoring: The use of computers to observe, record, and review an employee's use of a computer, including communications such as e-mail messages, keyboard activity (used to measure productivity), and Web sites visited. 161, 237

EMR, 308. *See also* **Electromagnetic radiation**

Encryption: Process of converting readable data into unreadable characters to prevent unauthorized access. **411**

Energy, conserving, 307

ENERGY STAR program: Program, developed by the U.S. Department of Energy and the U.S. Environmental Protection Agency, that encourages manufacturers of computer components to create energy-efficient devices requiring little power when they are not in use. **307**

Engelbart, Douglas, 269

Enhanced Integrated Drive Electronics, 365. *See also* **EIDE**

Enhanced keyboard: Keyboard that has twelve function keys along the top; two Control (CTRL) keys and two Alternate (ALT) keys along the bottom; and a set of keys and additional keys between the typing area and the numeric keypad. **236**

Enhanced resolution: Digital camera resolution calculated by a special formula that adds pixels between those generated by optical resolution. **252**

ENIAC, 52. *See* Electronic Numerical Integrator And Computer

Enrollment template, 268

Enterprise ASP: Application service provider that customizes and delivers high-end business applications, such as finance and database. **164**

Enterprise computing: The use of computers in networks, such as LANs and WANs, or a series of interconnected networks that encompass a variety of different operating systems, protocols, and network architectures. **30**

software applications, 150

Enterprise computing software, 150

Entertainment software: Application software, such as interactive games, videos, and other programs designed to support a hobby or provide amusement and enjoyment. **160**

personal mobile device and, 294

Entertainment Web site, 84, 117

Environment, and computers, 193

Environmental Web site, 127

Ergonomic keyboard: Keyboard whose design reduces the chance of wrist or hand injuries. **238**

Ergonomics: The science of incorporating comfort, efficiency, and safety into the design of the workplace. **238**

Errors

on hard disk, 365

Ethernet: Network standard that specifies no central computer or device on the network should control when data can be transmitted.

development of, 55

Ethical issues,

copying CDs, 371

Exabyte (EB), 356

Excite, 78, 82

Execute: Process of a computer carrying out the instructions in a program. **17,** 234–5

Executing: Processor operation that carries out commands; part of the machine cycle. **188**

Expansion bus: Bus that allows the processor to communicate with peripherals. **212**

Expansion card: Circuit board that enhances functions of a component of a system unit and/or provides connections to peripherals. See also adapter card. **204.** *See also* **Adapter card**

Expansion slot: Socket on a motherboard that can hold an adapter card. **204**

Extended Binary Coded Decimal Interchange (EBCDIC): Coding scheme used primarily on mainframe computers and high-end servers. **195**

eXtended Graphics Array, 305. *See* **XGA.**

External drive bay: Drive bay that allows access to a drive from outside the system unit. **212**

External floppy disk drive: Type of floppy disk drive that is a separate device with a cable that plugs in a port on the system unit. **358**

External hard disk: Separate freestanding hard disk that connects with a cable to a USB port or FireWire port on the system unit. **364**

Eyes
computer effect on, 302, 307, 308

Face recognition system: Biometric device that captures a live face image and compares it with a stored image to determine if the person is a legitimate user. **263**

Facsimile machine, 322. *See also* Fax machine

Fan, computer, 213

Fanning, Shawn, 60

FAQ (frequently asked questions): List that helps a user find answers to commonly asked questions. **6, 100**

Fast ATA, 365

Fast infrared port: A high-speed IrDA port. **210**

Fault-tolerant computer: Computer that has duplicate components so it can continue top operate when one of its main components fail. **405**

Fax: Document sent or received via a fax machine. 322–23
sending digital images, 251

Fax machine: Output device that codes and encodes documents so they can be transmitted over telephone lines. **322–23.** *See also* **Facsimile machine**

Fax modem: Modem used to send (and sometimes receive) electronic documents as faxes. **322, 323**

Female connectors: Connectors that have matching holes to accept the pins on a male connector. **206**

Fetching: Processor operation that obtains a program instruction or data item from memory. **188**

Field: A combination of one or more related characters or bytes, a field is the smallest unit of data a user accesses. **145**

Field camera: Portable digital camera with many lenses and other attachments. **251**

File: Named collection of stored data, instructions, or information. **85, 137**
backup of, 359, 362, 415, 425, 426

compressing, 415, 427
conversion, 427
corrupt, 414
fragmented, 414
graphics, 85
multimedia, 85
restoring, 415
system, 401, 402
uncompressing, 427
zipped, 427

File compression utility: Utility program that shrinks the size of a file(s), so the file takes up less storage space than the original file. **162, 427**

File conversion utility: Program that transforms a file from one format to another, eliminating the need to reenter data in a new program. **162, 427**

File format, 349

File management, operating system and, 410, 412, 430

File manager: Utility that performs functions related to file and disk management. **412**

File name: Unique combination of letters of the alphabet, numbers, or other characters that identifies a file. **137**

File system, 382

File Transfer Protocol: Internet standard that permits file uploading and downloading with other computers on the Internet. 68, 96. *See also* **FTP**

File virus, 168

Filters: Audio editing software feature designed to enhance audio quality. **153**

Finance, computers used in, 32–33

Financial planning, with personal finance software, 156

Financial transactions
accounting software tracking, 149
personal finance software and, 156

Financial Web site, 119

Fingerprint scanner: Biometric device that captures curves and indentations of a fingerprint and compares them with those of a stored image. **262-63, 454**

Fiorina, Carly, 39

FireWire bus: Expansion bus that eliminates the need to install cards in expansion slots. **212**

FireWire port: Port that can connect multiple types of devices that require faster data transmission speeds. **209**
downloading from digital camera using, 251
purchasing notebook computer and, 453

FireWire transfer rate, 365

Firmware: ROM chips that contain permanently written data, instructions, or information, recorded on the chips when they were manufactured. **202, 400**

Fixed disk: Name sometimes given to the hard disk mounted inside a system unit. **360**

Fixed wireless: High-speed Internet connection that uses an antenna on a house or business to communicate with a tower location via radio signals. **70.** *See also* **Microwaves**

Flame wars: Exchanges of flames using the Internet. **100**

Flames: Abusive or insulting messages sent using the Internet. **100**

Flash memory: Type of nonvolatile memory that can be erased electronically and rewritten. **202**

Flash memory card: Removable flash memory device that allows users to transfer data and information from mobile devices to their desktop computers. **202, 205**
digital cameras using, 250
types of, 376

Flat display, 308

Flat screen CRT monitors, 307, 308

Flatbed scanner: Type of light-sensing input device that scans a document and creates a file of the document in memory instead of a paper copy. **256**

Flat-panel display: Display device with a shallow depth and flat screen that typically uses LCD or gas plasma technology. **302–6**

Flat-panel monitor: Desktop monitor that uses a liquid crystal display instead of a cathode-ray tube to produce images on a screen, resulting in a sharp, flicker-free display. Also called LCD monitor. **64, 302–6**
quality of, 304
video card and, 305

Flexible screens, 304

Floppy disk: Portable, inexpensive storage medium that consists of a thin, circular, flexible plastic Mylar film with a magnetic coating, enclosed in a square shaped plastic shell. *See also* diskette. **8, 358–59**
digital cameras using, 251

direct access and, 374
formatting, 412
protecting, 453
See also **Diskette**
Floppy disk drive: Device that reads from and writes on a floppy disk. **358**
bays and, 212
purchasing desktop computer and, 447
Folder, Startup, 402
Font: Name assigned to a specific design of characters. **141**
Font size: Size of the characters in a particular font. **141**
Font style: Font design, such as bold, italic, and underline, that can add emphasis to a font. **141**
Footer: Text that appears at the bottom of each page of a document. **140**
Footprint: Amount of desk space a display device occupies. **302**
Force feedback: Technology that sends resistance to a joystick or wheel in response to actions of the user. **324**
Foreground: Program with which the user currently is interacting. **404**
Form: Window on the screen that provides areas for entering or changing data in a database. Also called data entry form. **145**. *See also* **Data entry form**
Form factor: Term that refers to the size of platters in a hard disk. **282, 361**
Format: To change a document's appearance. **141–42**
Formatting: Process of dividing a disk into tracks and sectors so the operating system can store and locate data and information on the disk. **357, 382, 412**
Formula: Expression used to perform calculations on the data in a worksheet and display the resulting value in a cell. **143**
Fortran: FORmula TRANslator, one of the first high-level programming languages used for scientific applications. **53**
Fragmented: State of a file whose contents are scattered across two or more noncontiguous sectors of a disk. **414**
Frame rate correction, 350
FRED, 612. *See also* Forensic Recovery of Digital Evidence
Freeware: Copyrighted software provided at no cost to a user by an individual or a company that retains all rights to the software. **135**

Frequently asked questions. *See* **FAQ**
FTP (File Transfer Protocol): Internet standard that permits file uploading and downloading with other computers on the Internet. 68, 96, 134, 161
software, 161
FTP server: Computer that allows users to upload and/or download files using FTP.@INs:**96**
Function: Predefined worksheet formula that performs common calculations. **143**
Function keys: Special keys programmed to issue commands to a computer. **236-37**

Games,
interactive, 160
pointing devices for, 242
Garbage in, garbage out (GIGO): Computing phrase that points out the accuracy of a computer's output depends on the accuracy of the input. **10**. *See also* **GIGO**
Gates, Bill, 39, 55
GB, 197, 356. *See also* **Gigabyte**
Gender changer: Device that joins two connectors that are both female or both male. **206**
Gesture recognition: Computer's capability of detecting human motion. 137, **266**
Ghosting: The permanent etching of images on a monitor's screen. **415**
GHz, 189. *See also* **Gigahertz**
GIF: Graphics format that uses compression techniques to reduce file sizes. **85**
animated, 86
Gigablast, 78
Gigabyte (GB): Approximately 1 billion bytes. **197**
Gigahertz (GHz): One billion ticks of the system clock per second. **189**
GIGO: Computing phrase that points out the accuracy of a computer's output depends on the accuracy of the input. See also garbage in, garbage out. **10**. *See also* **Garbage in, garbage out (GIGO)**
GNOME, 423
GO.com, 82
Google, 78, 81, **103**
Government
computers used in, 33
Internet structure and, 69, 70
personal mobile device and, 288
Web sites, 122

GPS receiver: Handheld, mountable, or embedded device that contains an antenna, or radio receiver, and a processor.
personal mobile device and, 284
GPU. *See* Graphics processing unit
Graphic: Digital representation of nontext information such as a drawing, chart, or photograph. **85**. *See also* **Graphical image**
Graphic designer/illustrator: Employee who creates visual impressions of products and advertisements in the fields of graphics, theater, and fashion. **327**
Graphic illustrator. *See* **Graphic designer/illustrator**
Graphical image: Digital representation of nontext information such as a drawing, chart, or photograph. **85**. *See also* **Graphic**
Graphical user interface (GUI): Type of user interface that allows a user to interact with software using text, graphics, and visual images, such as icons. **15, 137, 402, 420, 421**
pointer and, 239
Graphics, 85–86
AGP bus, 212
application software and, 150–54
business software and, 150–54
downloading Web page without, 76
importing into slide, 146
monitor resolution and, 308
multimedia and, 85–86
output, 300, 308
processors and, 192
on Web page, 75
See also **Clip art**
Graphics card: Adapter card that converts computer output into a video signal that travels through a cable to the monitor, which displays an image on the screen. **204, 308**. *See also* **Video card**
Graphics file, viewing, 412
Graphics processing unit (GPU): Chip that controls the manipulation and display of graphics on a display device. **305**
Graphics tablet: Flat, rectangular, electronic, plastic board that is used to create drawings and sketches. **244**
GUI. *See* **Graphical user interface**

Hacker: Someone who accesses a computer or network illegally. **413**
passwords and, 411
Hand geometry system: Biometric device that measures the shape and size of a person's hand and compares these measurements to stored measurements. **263**
Handheld computer: Computer small enough to fit in one hand. **21,** 22. *See also* **handtop computer**
data collection using, 261
keyboards, 238
operating systems for, 399, 424–25
See also **Mobile computer; Mobile device**
Handhelds, 22
Handspring, 62, 329
Handtop computer: Computer small enough to fit in one hand. **21.** *See also* **handheld computer**
Handwriting recognition, 243, 247, 248
PDAs and, 424
Handwriting recognition software: Software that translates handwritten letters and symbols into characters that a computer or device can process. **243,** 247–48
Hard copy: Printed information that exists physically and is a more permanent form of output than that presented on a display device (soft copy). Also called a printout. **310.** *See also* **Printout**
Hard disk: Type of storage device that contains one or more inflexible, circular platters that store data, instructions, and information. Also called a hard disk drive. 8, **360–65.** *See also* **Hard disk drive**
amount of space on, 405
backing up, 415
booting and, 400, 402
bus connection for, 212
characteristics of, 361–63
checking for errors on, 430
controller, 364–65
defragmenting, 414, 430
direct access and, 374
downloading from digital camera to, 251
external, 364
formatting and copying, 412
maintaining data stored on, 365
miniature, 363, 376
operating system on, 399
portable, 364
problems on, 414

purchasing desktop computer and, 447
purchasing notebook computer and, 453
removable, 364
used for virtual memory, 405–6
Hard disk drive: Type of storage device that contains one or more inflexible, circular platters that store data, instructions, and information. Also called a hard disk. **360.** *See also* **Hard disk**
Hard drive, Internet. *See* **Internet hard drive**
Hardware: Electric, electronic, and mechanical components contained in a computer. **7–9**
BIOS testing, 400
diagnostic utility, 414
drivers, 407–9
information system and, 25
input device. *See* **Input device**
operating system coordinating, 398
output device. *See* **Output device**
performance monitoring, 409
Plug and Play, 205, 208
purchasing notebook computer and, 453
storage. *See* **Storage; Storage medium**
system unit. *See* **System unit**
Hardware theft: The act of stealing computer equipment. 69–70
Hawkins, Jeff, 329
Hayes, first modem and, 56
HD: High density. **358**
HDTV: High definition television; the most advanced form of digital television, working with digital broadcast signals, transmitting digital sound, supporting wide screens, and providing resolutions up to 1920 x 1080 pixels. **306–7.** *See also* **High-definition television**
Head crash: Type of hard disk failure that occurs when a read/write head touches the surface of a platter. **362**
Header: Text that appears at the top of each page of a document. **140**
Head-mounted pointer: Pointer that is placed on a user's head and can be used by a physically challenged person. **266**
Headphone port, on optical disc drives, 366
Headset: Pointer that is placed on a user's head and can be used by a physically challenged person. **321**
personal mobile device and, 284

sound card and, 204
Health care, computers used in, 34
Health information, storing on smart cards, 379
Health issues,
CRT monitors, 307, 308
eyestrain, 307, 308, 302
keyboards, 238
mouse, 240
radiation, 308
Health Insurance Portability and Accountability Act (HIPAA), 379
Health Web sites, 128
Hearing impaired users, output devices for, 326
Heat pipe: Small cooling device used to cool processors in notebook computers. **193**
Heat sink: Small ceramic or metal component with fins on its surface that absorbs and ventilates heat produced by electrical components. **193**
video card with, 305–6
Help
application software and, 164
Online. *See* **Online Help**
Web-based, 164
Help desk specialist: Employee who answers hardware, software, or networking questions in person, over the telephone, and/or in a chat room. 167
Hertz (Hz): One clock cycle per second. **189**
Hewlett-Packard (HP), 39, 56, 329
Hibernate, 402
High-definition television: The most advanced form of digital television, working with digital broadcast signals, transmitting digital sound, supporting wide screens, and providing resolutions up to 1920 x 1080 pixels. **306-7.** *See also* **HDTV**
High-level formatting, 382
HIPAA. *See* Health Insurance Portability and Accountability Act
Hi-speed USB, 365 *See also* **USB 2.0**
History, timeline of, 52–65
Hits: Web page names displayed by a search engine that contain the search text specified by a user. **80–81**
Hoff, Ted, 55
Home design/landscaping software: Application software that assists users with the design, remodeling, or improvement of a home, deck, or landscape. **160**

Home network: Network consisting of multiple devices and computers connected together in a home. 11

Home page: First page that a Web site displays. **76**
changing, 76

Home user: User who spends time on a computer at home. **26-27, 31**
application software for, 155–60
digital cameras, 250, 251
input devices, 265
output devices, 310, 312, 315, 325
printers, 310, 315
processor selection, 192, 215
RAM needs, 200
storage and, 354, 380
Web cams, 254

Hopper, Grace, 53

Host: Any computer that provides services and connections to other computers on a network. **69**
for dumb terminals, 261

Hot plugging: The ability to insert and remove a device while the computer is running. **205,** 208

HotBot, 78

Hot spot: Wireless network that provides Internet connections to mobile computers and other devices. 71

HotBot, 82

HP. *See* Hewlett-Packard

HR. *See* Human Resources

http: A set of rules that defines how pages transfer on the Internet. **76.** *See also* **Hypertext Transfer Protocol**

Hyperlink: Built-in connection to another related Web page or part of a Web page. **77.** *See also* **Link**

Hypertext Transfer Protocol: A set of rules that defines how pages transfer on the Internet. **76.** *See also* **http**

Hyper-Threading (HT) Technology: Technology used in Intel's latest processor chips, which improves processing power and time by allowing the processor chip to mimic the power of two processors. **190**

Hz. *See* Hertz

IBM (International Business Machines), 53, 54, 55, 138
Millipede storage device, 360

IBM-compatible PCs, MS-DOS used by, 417

IBM processor: Processor developed by IBM that has a design different from the Intel-style processor. 190

IC. *See* Integrated circuit

ICANN, 74. *See also* **Internet Corporation for Assigned Names and Numbers**

Icon: Miniature image displayed on a computer screen that represents a program, an instruction, a document, or some other object. **15, 136**

IEEE 1394 port: Port that can connect multiple types of devices that require faster data transmission speeds. **209.** *See also* **FireWire port**

Illustration software: Application software that allows users to draw pictures, shapes, and other graphical images with various onscreen tools. See also paint software. **152.** *See also* **Paint software**

IM: Instant messaging. **98.** *See also* **Instant messaging**

iMac, 59

Image editing software: Application software that provides the capabilities of paint software and also includes the capability to enhance and modify existing images and pictures. **152, 346**
personal, 158
professional, 152

Image processing: Business practice that consists of capturing, storing, analyzing, displaying, printing, and manipulating images with scanners. **256**

Image processing system: Storing and indexing electronic documents to provide access to exact reproductions of the original documents. **256**

Image viewer: Storing and indexing electronic documents to provide access to exact reproductions of the original documents. **412**

Images
as links, 77
personal DTP software, 158
See also Graphics; **Video**

Impact printer: Type of printer that forms characters and graphics on a piece of paper by striking a mechanism against an inked ribbon that physically contacts the paper. **318**-19

Import: To bring graphics into a document. **146**

Index, of electronic documents, 256

Information: Processed data that conveys meaning and is useful to people. **6**
accuracy of, 10, 25
downloading, 76

memory processing, 196, 199, 201
RAM and, 199
reading. *See* **Reading**
ROM and, 201–2
searching for on the Web, 78–81
sharing, 10
storage of. *See* **Storage; Storage medium**
writing. *See* **Writing**

Information processing cycle: Series of input, process, output, and storage activities performed by a computer. **6**

Information system (IS): Collection of hardware, software, data, people, and procedures that work together to produce quality information. **25**

Information technology

Information technology (IT) department: Department in most medium and large businesses responsible for keeping computers and networks running smoothly. 25, **30**

Informational Web site, 82

Infrared (IR): Wireless transmission medium that sends signals using infrared light waves.
cordless keyboards using, 238
See also **IrDA**

Infrared Data Association, 210. *See also* **IrDA**

Infrared printing: Printing that uses infrared light waves to transmit output to a printer. **311**

Ink-jet printer: Type of nonimpact printer that forms characters and graphics by spraying tiny drops of liquid ink on a piece of paper. **312**–14
refilling cartridges, 314

Input: Any data and instructions entered into the memory of a computer. **234**–69
accuracy of, 10, 25
audio, 246
biometric, 262–64
device. *See also* **Input device**
digital cameras, 250–52
storage devices as source of, 356
terminals, 261–62
video, 253–54
voice, 245–46, 248

Input device: Any hardware component that allows users to enter data and instructions into a computer. **7, 236**–69
biometric, 262–64
keyboard, 236–38, 261, 266, 269
mobile computers and devices, 243, 244, 247–49

pointing. *See also* **Pointing device**
purchasing desktop computer and, 446
scanners, 255–61
sound card connected to, 328
video, 253–54
voice, 245–46
Insertion point: Symbol on a computer screen, usually a blinking vertical bar, that indicates where the next character a user types will be displayed. **237.** *See also* **cursor**
Installing (software): Process of setting up software to work with the computer, printer, and other hardware components. **7,** 400
Instant messaging (IM): Real-time Internet communications service that notifies a user when one or more people are online and then allows the user to exchange messages or files or join a private chat room with those people. 12, **98**
live images added to, 253
software for, 98, 161
Instant messenger: Software used by people to participate in instant messaging. **98,** 161
Instructions: Steps that tell the computer how to perform a particular task. **6, 234**
cache and, 201
input of, 234–35
memory processing, 196, 201, 405
operating system allocating to memory, 405
reading. *See* **Reading**
ROM and, 201–2
storage of. *See* **Storage; Storage medium**
writing. *See* **Writing**
Integrated circuit (IC): Electronic component that contains many microscopic pathways capable of carrying electrical current. . **186**
invention of, 53
Intel, 59, 61, 64, 219
Accelerated Graphics Port, 212
Centrino mobile technology, 219
processors, 190, 191, 192, 219
Intel-compatible processors: Processors that have an internal design similar to that of Intel processors, perform the same functions as Intel processors, and can be as powerful, but often are less expensive. **190,** 192
Interactive applications, creating using multimedia authoring software, 154

Interactive TV: A two-way communications technology in which users interact with television programming. **307**
Interface, disk controller as, 364
Intermediate server, 288
Internal drive bay: Drive bay that is concealed entirely within the system unit. **212**
Internal sources: Source of data obtained from inside an enterprise, which might include sales order, inventory records, or financial data from accounting and financial analyses. **28**
Internet: Worldwide collection of networks that connects millions of businesses, government agencies, educational institutions, and individuals. Also called the Net. 11, **12**–14, **68**–105
broadcasting images over, 253, 254
chat rooms on, 98
control of, 70
data traveling on, 72
e-mail using, 92–95
history of, 69–70
how it works, 70–74
instant messaging on, 161
mailing lists and, 97–98
Netiquette and, 100
newsgroups on, 96–97
sales tax, 92
search engines, 78
telephone calls over, 99–100, 253
video conference using, 254
World Wide Web and. *See* **World Wide Web**
Internet access, 68, 70–74
car, 163
purchasing desktop computer and, 448, 449–50
Tablet PCs, 456
Internet access provider. *See* **Access provider**
Internet attacks, 358–64
Internet backbone: Major carriers of network traffic on the Internet. **72**
Internet connection, 70–71
Internet Corporation for Assigned Names and Numbers (ICANN): Group that assigns and controls top-level domains. **74**
browsers for, 76
portal for, 82
Internet etiquette, 100. *See also* **Netiquette**
Internet Explorer. *See* **Microsoft Internet Explorer**
Internet filters, 426–27
anti-spam program, 426
pop-up blocker, 427
Web filters, 427

Internet hard drive, 365. *See also* Online storage
Internet postage: Digital postage technology that allows users with an authorized postage account to print postage stamps on a postage printer. **318**
Internet Protocol address: A number that uniquely identifies each computer or device connected to the Internet. **73.** *See also* **IP address**
Internet service provider. *See* **ISP**
Internet telephony: Technology that allows users to speak to other users over the Internet using their desktop computer, mobile computer, or mobile device. Also called Voice over IP.@INs:**99**-100, **322.** *See also* **Voice over IP (VoIP)**
Internet wearables, 321. *See also* Wearable Web devices
Internet2, 70
Internet-enabled: Technology that allows mobile devices to connect to the Internet wirelessly. **21**–22, 29
Interrupt request line (IRQ): Communications line between a device and the processor. See also IRQ. **409**
Investing
online. *See* **Online investing**
e-commerce for, 91
IP address: A number that uniquely identifies each computer or device connected to the Internet. **73,** 102. *See also* **Internet Protocol address**
IPng (IP Next Generation), 102
iPod music player, purchasing notebook computer and, 453
IPv6, 102
IrDA (Infrared Data Association): Network standard used to transmit data wirelessly via infrared (IR) light waves. **210**
IrDA port: Port that uses infrared light waves to transmit signals between a wireless device and a computer. **210**
IrisNet, 254
Iris recognition system: Biometric device that uses iris recognition technology to read patterns in the iris of the eye. **264**
IRQ: Interrupt request line; communications line between a device and the processor. **409.** *See also* **Interrupt request**
ISP (Internet service provider): Regional or national Internet access provider. **72**
subscribing to, 449–50

IT. *See* Information technology

IT department: Group of employees who work together as a team to meet the information requirements of their organization and are responsible for keeping all the computer operations and networks running smoothly. 30. *See* **Information technology (IT) department**

Itanium: Intel processor used by workstations and low-end servers. **190**, 191

Jack: Term sometimes used to identify an audio or video port. **206**

Java: Object-oriented programming language developed by Sun Microsystems. 58

Jewel box: Protective case that is used to store CDs and DVDs when not in use. **368**

Job: Operation that the processor manages. **406**

Jobs, Steve, 39, 55, 329

Jobs
    outsourcing, 10

Joystick: Pointing device used for games or flight and driving simulations that is a vertical lever mounted on a base. **242**
    force feedback and, 324
    purchasing desktop computer and, 447

JPEG: Format that compresses graphics to reduce their file size. **85**, **345**
    Picture CD using, 370

JPEG 2000, 324

K, 197. *See also* **Kilobyte**

Kay, Alan, 431

Kazaa, 369

KB, 197. *See also* **Kilobyte**

KBps: Kilobytes per second. **357**, **369**

Kemeny, John, 54

Kernel: The core of an operating system that manages memory and devices, maintains the computer's clock, starts applications, and assigns the computer's resources. **400**, 401

Keyboard: Input device that contains keys users press to enter data and instructions into a computer. 7, **236–38**
    BIOS testing, 400
    connections, 238
    ergonomics, 238
    fingerprint scanner on, 263
    health issues, 238
    keyguard for, 266
    on-screen, 247, 266
    personal mobile device and, 284
    portable, 248

purchasing desktop computer and, 447, 449
    purchasing notebook computer and, 453
    terminal, 261

Keyboard monitoring software, 237

Keyguard: Metal or plastic plate placed over the keyboard that allows users to rest their hands on the keyboard without accidentally pressing any keys. **266**

Keywords: Words or phrases entered in a search engine's text box to find information on a Web page. 80–81

Kilby, Jack, 53, 219

Kilobyte (KB or K): Exactly 1,024 bytes. **197**

Kiosk: Freestanding computer, usually with a touch screen, used by some businesses in public locations. **30**, 242

Kodak, Picture CD and, 370

Komiyama, Hideki, 269

L1 cache: A type of memory cache that is built directly into the processor chip, with a capacity of 8 KB to 16 KB. **201**

L2 cache: A type of memory cache that is slightly slower than L1 cache, but has a much larger capacity, ranging from 64 KB to 16 MB. **201**

L3 cache: Cache on the motherboard that is separate from the processor. **201**

Label: Text entered in a worksheet cell that identifies the worksheet data and helps organize the worksheet. **143**

Label printer: Small printer that prints on adhesive-type material that can be placed on items such as envelopes, packages, floppy disks, CDs, DVDs, audio cassettes, photographs, file folders, and toys. **318**

LAN, 55. *See also* **Local area network**

Landscape orientation: A printout that is wider than it is tall with information printed across the widest part of the paper. **310**

Landscaping software. *See* **Home design/landscaping software**

Laptop computer. *See* **Notebook computer**

Large business user: Computer user working for a business that has hundreds or thousands of employees in offices across a region, the country, or the world. 26, **30**, 31
    input devices, 265

operating systems for, 422
    output devices, 310, 315, 325
    printers, 310, 315
    processor selection and, 215
    storage and, 355, 380

Large-format printer: Printer that creates photo-realistic quality color prints, used mainly by graphic artists. **318**

Laser printer: Type of high-speed, high-quality nonimpact printer that creates images using a laser beam and powdered ink called toner. **315–16**

Layers, 351

LCD, 304. *See also* **Liquid crystal display**

LCD monitor: Desktop monitor that uses a liquid crystal display instead of a cathode-ray tube to produce images on a screen, resulting in a sharp, flicker-free display. Also called flat-panel monitor **302–7**, 325
    quality of, 304
    on mobile computers and devices, 303
    See also **Flat-panel monitor**

LCD projector: Projector that uses liquid crystal display technology that attaches directly to a computer and uses its own light source to display the information shown on the computer screen. **324**

Learning
    computer-based training and, 160
    computers used in, 32
    distance, 166
    educational software for, 160
    online, 82

Left-handed mouse users, 240

Legal issues
    copyright. *See* **Copyright**

Legal software: Application software that assists in the preparation of legal documents and provides legal information to individuals, families, and small businesses. **157**

Light pen: Handheld input device that can detect the presence of light. **242**

Line chart: Chart that shows a trend during a period of time, as indicated by a rising or falling line. **144**

Line printer: Type of high-speed impact printer that prints an entire line at a time. **319**

Link: Built-in connection to another related Web page or part of a Web page. Short for hyperlink. **77**

animation, 86
search engine and, 79, 80
Linux: Popular, multitasking UNIX-type operating system. 58, 60, 64, 195, **421**, 423, 431, 431
future of, 421
Liquid cooling technology: A continuous flow of fluid(s), such as water and glycol, that transfers the heated fluid away from the processor, cools the liquid, then returns the cooled fluid to the processor. **193**
Liquid crystal display (LCD): Type of display that uses a liquid compound to present information on a display device. **304**
for Tablet PCs, 456
LISTSERVs: Mailing list named after a popular mailing list program. **97**, 98
Lithium-ion batteries, 453
Load: Process of a computer copying a program from storage to memory. **17**, 135, 137
Local/regional ASP: Application service provider that offers a variety of software applications to a specific geographic region **164**
Log on: To access a computer or network as a user. **410**
Logic bomb, 168
Logitech, 269
Longhorn, 418
LookSmart, 78, 82
Lotus 1–2–3, 56
Lotus Development Corporation, 56
Low-level formatting, 382
Lycos, 78, 82

Mac OS, 19
Mac OS X: Multitasking operating system that is the latest version of the Macintosh operating system. 39, 135, 195, **420**
Machine cycle: The four basic operations (fetching, decoding, executing, and storing) performed by a processor. **188**–89
Macintosh, purchasing, 445–46
Macintosh operating system: Operating system for Apple's Macintosh computer. 19, 135, **420**
Macro (application program): Series of statements that instructs an application how to complete a task. **140**
Macro virus, 168
security and, 426
Magazines
online, 35

Magnetic disks: Storage medium that uses magnetic particles to store items such as data, instructions, and information on a disk's surface. **357**–65
floppy disk, 358–59
hard disk, 360–65
types of, 358
Zip disk, 356
Magnetic stripe card reader: Reading device that reads the magnetic stripe on the back of credit, entertainment, bank, and other similar cards. **260.** *See also* **magstrip reader**
POS terminal, 260
Magnetic Tape/Selectric Typewriter (MT/ST), 54
Magnetic-ink character recognition, 260. *See* **MICR**
Magnetoresistive RAM (MRAM): Newer type of RAM that stores data using magnetic charges instead of electrical charges. **199**
Magstrip reader: Reading device that reads the magnetic stripe on the back of credit, entertainment, bank, and other similar cards. **260.** *See also* **Magnetic stripe card reader**
Mailing list: Group of e-mail names and addresses given a single name. **97**–98
Main memory: Type of memory that can be read from and written to by the processor and other devices. Programs and data are loaded into RAM from storage devices such as a hard disk and remain in RAM as long as the computer has continuous power. **198.** *See also* **RAM**
Mainframe: Large, expensive, powerful computer that can handle hundreds or thousands of connected users simultaneously, storing tremendous amounts of data, instructions, and information. 19, **23**
printers and, 310
processors for, 187
Male connectors: Connectors that have one or more exposed pins. **206**
Malicious-logic programs: Program that acts without a user's knowledge and deliberately alters the computer's operations. **168, 426**
Manufacturers
processors, 190–91
ROM chips, 202
Maps
clip art, 139

Margins: The portion of a page outside the main body of text, including the top, the bottom, and both sides of the paper. **139**
Marketing
CD-ROMs, 369
Master, 351
Match template, 268
Mauchley, John, 52
Maxtor, 383
MB, 197, 356. *See also* **Megabyte**
MBps: Megabytes per second. **357, 365**
Mbps. *See* Megabits per second
McAfee VirusScan, 426
M-commerce (mobile commerce): E-commerce that takes place using mobile devices. **91**
Mean time between failures (MTBF), 363
Mechanical mouse: Mouse that has a rubber or metal ball on its underside. **239**
Media card, printing photos using, 315
Media Center PC: Home entertainment personal computer that often uses a television as its display device and includes a mid- to high-end processor, large capacity hard disk, CD and DVD drives, a remote control, and advanced graphics and audio capabilities. **419**
connecting a television, 419
Medical Information Bureau (MIB), medical records from, 379
Medical software and personal mobile devices, 290
Meeting
using video conference, 254
Megabits per second (Mbps), 365
Megabyte (MB): Approximately 1 million bytes. **197**
Megapixels, 344. *See also* **MP**
Megahertz (MHz), access time stated in, 203
Memory: Electronic components in a computer that store instructions waiting to be executed and data needed by those instructions. **8, 196**–203
access times, 203, 357
address, 196
address bus, 211
application software in, 135
buffer, 407
cache, 201
CMOS, 203
creating document and, 142
disk cache and, 363
flash, 202
laser printers, 316
nonvolatile, 197, 201–2
operating system files loaded into, 135, 401

operating system managing, 405–6
program input into, 235
program loading into, 17, 135
purchasing desktop computer and, 446
purchasing notebook computer and, 453
RAM. *See* **RAM**
read-only. *See* **Read-only memory**
role of, 185
ROM. *See* **Read-only memory**
video cards, 306
virtual, 405–6
volatile, 197, 198–99
Memory cache: Cache that helps speed the processes of a computer by storing frequently used instructions and data. **201**
Memory cards, 8, 9
personal mobile device and, 284
Memory cell, 218
Memory controller, 218
Memory management: Operating system activity that optimizes the use of random access memory (RAM). **05–6**
Memory module: Small circuit board that houses RAM chips and is held in a memory slot on the motherboard. **199**
Memory resident: Remaining in memory while a computer is running. **400,** 404
Memory slots: Slots on the motherboard that hold memory modules. **199**
Memory Stick: Type of miniature mobile storage medium that is a flash memory card capable of storing between 256 MB and 2 GB of data. **376**
digital cameras using, 250
Menu: Item on the computer screen that contains a list of commands from which a user can make selections. **137,** 237
sub-, 137
Menu-driven interface: Type of user interface that provides menus as means of entering commands. **402,** 417
Message board: Popular Web-based type of discussion group that does not require a newsreader. **97,** 161
Messaging
instant. *See* **Instant messaging**
Metcalfe, Robert M., 55
MHz. *See* Megahertz
MIB. *See* Medical Information Bureau

MICR (magnetic-ink character recognition): Technology that reads text printed with magnetized ink. **260.** *See also* **Magnetic-ink character recognition**
MICR reader: Reading device that converts MICR characters into a form that a computer can process. **260**
Microbrowser: Special type of browser designed for the small screens and limited computing power of Internet-enabled mobile devices. **76**
Microcode: Instructions programmers use to program a PROM chip. **202**
Microfiche: A small sheet of film, usually about 4 inches by 6 inches in size, on which microscopic images of documents are stored. **379**
Microfilm: A roll of film, usually 100 to 215 feet long, on which microscopic images of documents are stored. **379**
Microphone, 7, 322
input using, 245, 246
purchasing desktop computer and, 447, 449
purchasing Tablet PC and, 456
sound card and, 204
video conference using, 254
Microprocessor: Term used by some computer and chip manufacturers to refer to a processor chip for a personal computer. **187.** *See also* **Processor**
development of, 55
Microsecond (µs), 203
Microsoft, 39, 55, 56, 57, 58, 59, 60, 61, 62, 63, 65, **169**
application software, 148
ClearType technologies, 456
legal issues, 60, 62
MS-DOS, 417
operating system, 15, 135, 195. *See also* **Windows XP**
Microsoft Internet Explorer: Web browser included with the Windows operating system, starting with Windows 98. 59, 75, **417**
Microsoft Network, The (MSN), 72, 82
Microsoft Office, 60, 148
elements of, 148
Microsoft Office OneNote 2003, 138
Microsoft Office System, 148
Microsoft Outlook, 93
Microsoft Reader, 303
Microsoft Word, 138, 141

MIDI: Short for Musical Instrument Digital Interface. **209, 246.** *See also* **Musical Instrument Digital Interface**
MIDI port: Special type of serial port that connects the system unit to a musical instrument, such as an electronic keyboard. **209**
Midrange server: Server that is more powerful and larger than a workstation computer, typically supporting several hundred and sometimes up to a few thousand connected computers at the same time. 19, **23**
Millisecond (ms), 203
Millions of instructions per second, 190. *See also* **MIPS**
Millipede, 360
Miniature mobile storage media, 375–78
Mini disc, digital cameras using, 250
Mini discs: Optical disc with a size of three inches or less used by smaller computers and devices. **366**
Mini-DVD media, 373
Minutiae, 268
MIPS (millions of instructions per second): Measurement of a system clock's speed. **190**
MITS, Inc., 55
Mobile commerce. *See* **M-commerce**
Mobile computer: Personal computer that a user can carry from place to place. 19, **20**
Mobile device: Computing device small enough for a user to hold in his or her hand. 19, **20,** 21–22
data collection using, 261
display device, 303
flash memory and, 202, 205
input devices, 243, 244, 247–49
LCD screens, 302
miniature hard disk, 363
personal, 282–97
printer, 317
storage media for, 355, 375–78, 380
system unit, 185
touch screens, 243
viruses and, 250
Web access and, 72
Mobile printer: Small, lightweight, battery-powered printer used by a mobile user to print from a notebook computer, Tablet PC, PDA, or smart phone while traveling. **317**

Mobile users: Users who work on a computer while away from a main office or school. 26, **29**, 31
e-commerce and, 91
input devices, 265
Internet access by, 70–71
mobile printers, 317
output devices, 303, 317, 325
processor selection, 215, 219
storage and, 355, 375–78, 380
system unit, 213–15
Mobile Web blogs, 84. *See also* moblogs.
Moblogs, 84. *See also* Mobile Web blogs.
Modem: Communications device that converts a computer's digital signals to analog signals. Also called a dial-up modem. 9
bus connection, 212
cable, 70
fax, 322, 323
Internet access using, 70
port, 207
purchasing desktop computer and, 447
wireless, 72
Moderated newsgroup: A newsgroup with a moderator who decides if an article is relevant to the discussion. **97**
Moderator: Person who reviews content of a newsgroup article and then posts it, if appropriate. **97**
Modulate/modulation: To change into an analog signal. **38**
Money
counterfeiting, 315
Monitor: Display device that is packaged as a separate peripheral. 8, **302–8**
CRT. *See* **CRT monitor**
flat-panel, 302–6
largest, 306
purchasing desktop computer and, 447, 449
purchasing notebook computer and, 452
Mono, 328
Monochrome: Display device capability in which information appears in one color on a different color background. **302**
Moore, Gordon, 193, 219
Moore's Law, 193, 219
Morphing, 350
Motherboard: Main circuit board of the system unit, which has some electronic components attached to it and others built into it. 8, 185, **186**. *See also* **System board**
memory slots on, 199

Motorola processor: Processor used in Apple computer that have a design different from the Intel-style processor. **190**, 191, 192
Mouse: Pointing device that fits comfortably under the palm of a user's hand. 7, **239**–40
BIOS testing, 400
connections, 239
creator of, 269
left-handed users, 240
manufacturer, 269
purchasing desktop computer and, 448, 449
repetitive strain injuries and, 238
types, 239
using, 136, 240
Mouse gestures: Capability that allows users to perform certain operations by holding a mouse button while moving the mouse in a particular pattern. **240**
Mouse pad: Rectangular rubber or foam pad that provides traction for a mechanical mouse. **239**
Mouse pointer: Small symbol displayed on a computer screen whose location and shape changes as a user moves a mouse. **239**
Movies, digital, 324
Moving Pictures Experts Group (MPEG): Group that defines a popular video compression standard. **88**
Mozilla, 65, 75
MP: One million pixels. **252**
MP3: Format that reduces an audio file to about one-tenth of its original size, while preserving much of the original quality of the sound. **86**, 87, 89, 202
MP3 players
flash memory and, 202
USB 2.0 ports and, 208
See also Digital music players
MPEG, 88. *See also* **Moving Pictures Experts Group**
MPEG-4: Current version of a popular video compression standard. **88**
MPR II standard: Set of standards that defines acceptable levels of electromagnetic radiator for a monitor. **308**
MRAM, 199. *See also* **Magnetoresistive RAM**
μs. *See* Microsecond
ms. *See* Millisecond
MSBlast worm, 63
MS-DOS, 417, 430
MSN. *See* Microsoft Network, The
MSN Hotmail, 94
MSN Search, 78

MTBF. *See* Mean time between failures
MT/ST. *See* Magnetic Tape/Selectric Tape Typewriter
Multifunction peripheral: Output device that looks like a copy machine but provides the functionality of a printer, scanner, copy machine, and perhaps a fax machine. **323**. *See also* **All-in-one device**
Multimedia: Any application that combines text, graphics, audio, and video. **29**, **85–89**
application software and, 150–54
processors and, 192
RAM needs, 200
Multimedia authoring software: Software that allows users to combine text, graphics, audio, video, and animation in an interactive application and that often is used for computer-based training and Web-based presentations. **154**
Multimedia software and personal mobile devices, 294
Multiprocessing: In reference to operating systems, supports two or more processors running programs at the same time. **405**
Multipurpose operating system: Operating system that is both a stand-alone operating system and a network operating system. **423**
Multisession disc: Optical disc that can be written on more than once, allowing users to save additional data on the disc at a later time. **371**
Multitasking, preemptive, 405
Multitasking operating system, 403, 420, 421, 424
Multiuser: In reference to operating systems, enables two or more users to run programs simultaneously. **405**, 407
Music, 86
downloading, 86–87
illegal sharing, 369
input, 246
MIDI port and, 209
on DVD, 373
See also **Audio; MIDI; MP3**
Music players, storage media for, 375, 376
Musical Instrument Digital Interface (MIDI): Electronic music industry's standard that defines how devices represent sounds electronically. **209**, 246

Name
file. *See* File name
Names
mailing lists, 97
user, 94
Nanosecond (ns): One billionth of a second. **203**
Napster, 60
NAS, 742–43. *See also* **Network attached storage (NAS)**
National Academy of Sciences, 241
OSHA, 241
National ISP: Internet service provider that provides Internet access in cities and towns nationwide. **72**
National Science Foundation (NSF), 70
Native resolution: The specific resolution for which an LCD is geared. **304**
Near letter quality (NLQ): Printer output that is slightly less clear than what is acceptable for business letters. See also NLQ. **318**
Net: Worldwide collection of networks that links millions of businesses, government agencies, educational institutions, and individuals. **68.** *See also* **Internet**
Netiquette: Short for Internet etiquette, the code of acceptable behaviors users should follow while on the Internet. **100**
Netscape Communications Corporation, 58, 75, 82
Netscape Navigator, 58
Netscape Search, 78
NetWare: Network operating system designed by Novell for client/server networks. **422**
Network: Collection of computers and devices connected together via communications devices and transmission media, allowing computers to share resources. **11–14**
attacks, 358–64
business, 11
home, 11
host, 69
Internet. *See* **Internet**
purchasing notebook computer and, 453
security, 410–11
troubleshooting connections, 430
Network administrator: Employee who installs, configures, and maintains LANs, WANs, intranets, and Internet systems; identifies and resolves connectivity issues. 410
security and, 410–11

Network card: Adapter card, PC Card, or flash card that enables the computer or device to access a network. Also called a network interface card (NIC). **204**
purchasing desktop computer and, 448
purchasing notebook computer and, 453
Network operating system (network OS): Operating system that organizes and coordinates how multiple users access and share resources on a network. **410,** 422–23
Neural network: System that attempts to imitate the behavior of the human body. **34**
News server: Computer that stores and distributes newsgroup messages. **96**
News Web site, 82, 124
Newsgroup: Online area in which users have written discussions about a particular subject. **96–97,** 161
Newspapers, online, 35
Newsreaders: Program necessary for participating in a newsgroup. **96,** 161
Nit: Unit of visible light intensity that is equal to one candela per square meter. **304**
NLQ: Printer output that is slightly less clear than what is acceptable for business letters. **318.** *See also* **Near letter quality**
Nonimpact printer: Type of printer that forms characters and graphics on a piece of paper without actually striking the paper. **312–18**
Nonresident: Instructions that remain on a hard disk until they are needed. **400**
Nonvolatile memory: Type of memory that does not lose its contents when a computer's power is turned off. **197,** 201–2
Norton AntiVirus, 426
Norton SystemWorks, 428
Note taking software: Application software that enables users to enter typed text, handwritten comments, drawings, or sketches anywhere on a page. 134, 138, **147**
Notebook computer: Portable, personal computer designed to fit on a user's lap. **20,** 29. *See also* **laptop computer**
converting to Tablet PC, 453
display device, 303
face recognition system, 263

floppy disk drive in, 358
hard disk in, 360
keyboards, 236, 238
PC Cards, 374
pointing stick, 242
power supply, 190
printing from, 317
processors, 190, 219
purchasing, 444, 452–54
sales force using, 724
storage media, 358, 374, 375, 376
system unit, 185
touch screens, 243
touchpads, 241
wireless modems in, 72
Notepad, in personal information manager, 148
NS: One billionth of a second. **203.** *See also* **Nanosecond**
NSF. *See* National Science Foundation
NSFnet: The National Science Foundation's network of five supercomputers. **70**
Number systems, coding systems and, 195
Numbers
input of, 234
used in worksheets, 143
Numeric keypad, 236, 237

Object linking and embedding (OLE), 57
OCR, 257. *See also* **Optical character recognition**
OCR devices: Optical character recognition devices that include small optical scanners for reading characters and sophisticated software to analyze what is read. **257**
OCR (optical character recognition) software: Software that enables scanners to read and convert text documents into electronic files. **256**
OLE. *See* Object linking and embedding
OLED, 304. *See also* **Organic LED**
OMR, 257. *See also* **Optical mark recognition**
On demand computing: Technology that allows companies to use the processing power sitting idle in a network located somewhere else in the world. Also called utility computing. **63.** *See also* **Utility computing**
Onboard navigation system, 36
Online: Describes the state of a computer when it is connected to a network. **11**

Online auction: E-commerce method that allows consumers to bid on an item being sold by someone else. **92, 121**

Online banking: Online connection to a bank's computer to access account balances, pay bills, and copy monthly transactions to a user's computer. **32, 156**

Online Help: Electronic equivalent of a user manual that usually is integrated in a program. **164–65**

Online investing: Use of a computer to buy and sell stocks and bonds online, without using a broker. **33**

Online learning, 82

Online print service, for photographs, 159

Online service provider (OSP): Company that provides Internet access as well as many members-only features. **72**

subscribing to, 449–50

Online shopping, 123

Online storage: Service on the Web that provides hard disk storage to computer users, usually for a minimal monthly fee. **365, 415.** *See also* **Internet hard drive**

On-screen keyboard: Type of keyboard, sometimes used by physically challenged users, in which a graphic of a standard keyboard is displayed on the user's screen. 247, **266**

Open Directory Project, 78

Open source software: Software provided for use, modification, and redistribution. 60, **135, 421,** 425, 431

Opening Adobe PDF files, 152

Opera, 75

Operating system (OS): Set of programs that coordinates all the activities among computer hardware devices. **15–16, 398–425**

application software and, 135, 399

booting and, 400–2

bundling applications, 429

client, 416

device configuration, 407–9

device-dependent, 415

device-independent, 415

embedded, 423–25

file management, 410, 412, 430

functions of, 398–99, 400–11

handheld computers, 399, 424–25

Internet connection and, 409

job scheduling, 406–7

managing programs, 403–5

memory and, 196, 197

multiprocessing, 405

multipurpose, 423

multitasking, 403, 420, 421, 424

multiuser, 405

network, 410, 422–23

PDAs, 424

performance monitoring, 410

personal firewall and, 413, 564

purchasing desktop computer and, 446

RAM and, 198

security and, 410–11

stand-alone, 416–21

types of, 19, 415–21

user interface and, 402

utility programs, 398, 411–15

See also **Platform**

Optical, 17

Optical character recognition (OCR): Optical reader technology that involves reading typewritten, computer-printed, or hand-printed characters from ordinary documents and translating the images to a form that a computer can process. **257**

faxes and, 323

Optical character recognition software, 256. *See also* **OCR (optical character recognition) software**

Optical discs: Type of storage medium that consists of a flat, round, portable disc made of metal, plastic, and lacquer that is written on and read by a laser. 17, **366–73**

care of, 368

characteristics of, 366–67

cleaning, 368

paper disks, 373

types of, 368

Optical mark recognition (OMR): Optical reader technology that reads hand-drawn marks such as small circles or rectangles. **257**

Optical mouse: Mouse that uses devices, such as optical sensors or lasers, that emit and sense light to detect the mouse's movement. **239**

Optical reader: Device that uses a light source to read characters, marks, and codes and then converts them into digital data that a computer can process. **257**

Optical resolution: The actual photographed resolution at which a digital camera can capture a digital image. **252**

Optical scanner: Light-sensing input device that reads printed text and graphics and

then translates the results into a form the computer can process. **255.** *See also* **Scanner**

Optical storage medium. *See* CD (compact disc); DVD (digital versatile disc or digital video disc)

Options, 430. *See also* **Arguments**

OQO handheld computer, 65

Organic LED (OLED): TFT technology that uses organic molecules that produce an even brighter, easier-to-read display than standard TFT displays. Also called OLED. **304**

flexible screens and, 304

OS, 398. *See also* **Operating system (OS)**

Outlook Express, 93

Output: Data that has been processed into a useful form. **300–29**

input accuracy and, 10

types of, 300–1

voice, 321–22

See also **Output device**

Output device: Any hardware component that conveys information to one or more people. **8, 301**

audio, 320–22

data projector, 323–24, 454

display. *See also* **Display device**

fax machine, 322

force feedback joysticks and wheels, 324

headsets, 321

multifunction peripheral, 323

physically challenged users, 326–27

printers, 310–19

purchasing desktop computer and, 446

speakers, 320–21

Overature, 78

Packaged software: Mass-produced, copyrighted, prewritten software available for purchase. **134**

Page: Amount of data and program instructions that can swap at a given time. **406**

Page description language (PDL): Software that tells a printer how to lay out the contents of a printed page. **316**

Page layout: Process of arranging text and graphics in a document on a page-by-page basis. **152**

Page printer. *See* **Laser printer**

Paging: Technique of swapping items between memory and storage. **406**

Paint program, starting, 136

Paint software: Application software that allows users to draw pictures, shapes, and other graphical images with various onscreen tools. See also illustration software. **152.** *See also* **Illustration software**
personal, 158
professional, 152
starting, 136
Palm, 329
palmOne, 269, 329
PalmPilot, 58, 329
Palm OS: Scaled-down operating system that works on Palm-powered devices. 283, **424**
Paper
discs, 373
ink-jet printer, 312–13
laser printer, 315
photo printing, 314, 315
Parallel port: Type of interface that connects devices to the system unit by transferring more than one bit at a time. 206, **208**
Parallel processing: Processing method that uses multiple processors simultaneously to execute a program in order to speed processing times. **194**
Partitioning, 382
Passive-matrix display: LCD monitor or screen technology that uses fewer transistors, requires less power, and is less expensive than an active-matrix display. **304**
Password: Private combination of characters associated with a user name that allows access to certain computer resources. **410**
guidelines, 411
malicious-logic program stealing, 168
Pasting: Process of transferring an item from a clipboard to a specific location in a document. **141**
Payload: Destructive event or prank a malicious-logic program is intended to deliver. **168**
PB. *See* Petabyte
PC. *See* Personal computer
PC camera, 253, 373. *See also* **PC video camera**
PC Card: Thin, credit-card-sized device that adds memory, storage, sound, fax/modem, network, and other capabilities to mobile computers. **205, 374**
PC Card bus: Expansion bus for a PC Card. **212**

PC Card slot: Special type of expansion slot in notebook and other mobile computers that can hold a PC Card. **205**
PC video camera: Type of digital video camera that enables a home or small business user to capture video and still images, send e-mail messages with video attachments, add live images to instant messages, broadcast live images over the Internet, and make video telephone calls. 7, 27, **253**, 373
privacy and, 254
purchasing desktop computer and, 448
purchasing Tablet PC and, 456
PC-compatible: Any personal computer based on the original IBM personal computer design. **19**
PC-DOS, 417
PCI bus (Peripheral Component Interconnect bus): High-speed expansion bus that connects higher speed devices. **212**
PCL (Printer Control Language): Standard printer language that supports the fonts and layout used in standard office documents. **316**
PCMCIA, 205. *See also* **Personal Computer Memory Card International Association**
PCMCIA cards: Now called PC Cards. **205**, 374. *See also* **PC Card**
PC-to-TV port, 453
PDA: One of the more popular lightweight mobile devices in use today, providing personal organizer functions such as a calendar, appointment book, address book, calculator, and notepad. **22**, 265, **282**, 325. *See also* **Personal digital assistant**
business software, 148
camera in, 250
data collection using, 261
display devices, 303
flash memory cards, 205
industry-specific applications, 22
input, 243, 247–48
operating system, 399, 424–25
Palm devices, 329
palmOne, 269, 329
PalmPilot, 329
printing from, 317
scanner, 248
screens, 303
software for, 134, 148
storage media for, 375, 376
stylus, 243, 247

system unit, 185
touch screens, 243
users and, 31
voice input, 248
Web access, 72
PDF. *See* Portable Document Format
PDL, 316. *See also* **Page description language**
Pearson VUE, 795
Pen drive: Flash memory device that plugs in a USB port on a computer or portable device. **377.** *See also* **USB flash drive**
Pen input: Input device used by mobile users to write, draw, and tap on a flat surface to enter input. **243**
Pentium: Family of Intel processors used by most high-performance PCs. 57, 61, 62, **190**, 191
Pentium M: Intel processor used in notebook computers and Tablet PCs. **190**, 191
Performance monitor (operating system): Operating system program that assesses and reports information about various computer resources and devices. **409**
Peripheral: Device that connects to a system unit and is controlled by the processor in the computer. **204**
Peripheral Component Interconnect bus, 212. *See also* **PCI bus**
Personal computer (PC): Computer that can perform all of its input, processing, output, and storage activities by itself and contains a processor, memory, one or more input and output devices, and storage devices. **19–20**
buying, 200
cache, 201
desktop. *See* **Desktop computer**
notebook. *See* **Notebook computer**
price of, 200
processor, 187
purchasing, 200, 445–46
transferring information between PDA and, 148
transferring pictures from digital camera into, 158
Personal computer maintenance utility: Utility program that identifies and fixes operating system problems, detects and repairs disk problems, and includes the capability of improving a computer's performance. **162, 428**

Personal Computer Memory Card International Association (PCMCIA): Association that developed standards for PC cards to help ensure the interchangeability of the cards among mobile computers. **205**

Personal computer salesperson, 37

Personal digital assistant: One of the more popular lightweight mobile devices in use today, providing personal organizer functions. **22.** *See also* **PDA**

Personal DTP (desktop publishing) software: Application software that helps home and small office/home office users create newsletters, brochures, advertisements, postcards, greeting cards, letterhead, business cards, banners, calendars, logos, and Web pages. **158**

Personal finance software: Simplified accounting program that helps home users or small office/home office users manage finances. **156**

Personal firewall utility: Program that detects and protects a personal computer and its data from unauthorized intrusions. **413**

Personal identification number (PIN), ATM: Password that can be used with a bankcard at an ATM, which verifies the user is the holder of the bankcard. **262**

Personal information manager (PIM): Application software that includes features to help users organize personal information. **148**

Personal mobile devices, 282–97
accessories for, 284
installing software on, 295
operating systems and, 283
purchasing, 296–97
software for, 285–94

Personal paint/image editing software: Application software that provides an easy-to-use interface, usually with more simplified capabilities that allows users to draw pictures, shapes, and other images. **158**

Personal use, software for, 155–60

Personal Web site, 84

Petabyte (PB), 356

Phishing: Scam in which a perpetrator sends an official looking e-mail that attempts to obtain your personal and financial information. 65

Photo community: Web site that allows users to create an online photo album and store their electronic photographs. **14,** 159, 251, 256, **370**

Photo editing software: Popular type of image editing software that allows users to edit digital photographs and create electronic photo albums. **159,** 251, 370

Photo printer: Type of nonimpact color printer that produces photo-lab-quality pictures. **314–15**
paper for, 315
storage media for, 376

Photographs, 85
altering, 153
clip art, 139
editing, 153, 159
online print service for, 159
personal DTP software, 158
Picture CDs and, 370

Physically challenged users
input devices for, 266
output devices for, 326–27

Picosecond (ps), 203

Picture CD: Single-session CD-ROM that stores digital versions of a single roll of film using a jpg file format. **370**

Picture messaging: Service that allows users to send graphics, pictures, video clips, and sound files, as well as short text messages to another smart phone, PDA, or computer. **249.** *See also* **MMS (multimedia message service)**

Pictures
scanning, 256

Pie chart: Chart that is displayed in the shape of a round pie cut into slices to show the relationship of parts to a whole. **144**

PIM. *See* **Personal information manager**

PIN, 262. *See* **Personal identification number (PIN)**

Ping command, 430

Pipelining: Concept in which the processor begins fetching a second instruction before it completes the machine cycle for the first instruction. **189**

Pixar, 329

Pixel: The smallest element in an electronic image. Short for picture element. **252, 304**
CRT monitor, 307, 308
digital camera and, 252

distance between, 308
scanners and, 256

Pixel pitch: The distance in millimeters between pixels on a display device. Also called dot pitch. **304,** 308. *See also* **Dot pitch**

Pixels per inch (ppi): Number of pixels in one inch of screen display. **252**

Pixilated, 346

PKZIP, 427

Plagiarism, Internet, 141

Plasma monitor: Display device that uses gas plasma technology, which sandwiches a layer of gas between two glass plates. **306**

Platform: Set of programs containing instructions that coordinate all the activities among computer hardware resources. **399**

Platter: Component of a hard disk that is made of aluminum, glass, or ceramic and is coated with an alloy material that allows items to be recorded magnetically on its surface. **361–62**

Player: Software used by a person to listen to an audio file on a computer. **86**

Plotters: Sophisticated printers that produce high-quality drawings such as blueprints, maps, and circuit diagrams using a row of charged wires (called styli) to draw an electrostatic pattern on specially coated paper and then fuse toner to the pattern. **318**

Plug and Play: Technology that gives a computer the capability to configure adapter cards and other peripherals automatically as a user installs them. **205,** 208, **407–8**

Plug-in: Program that extends the capability of a browser; often used to enhance multimedia. **89**

PNG format: Graphics format that improves upon the GIF format. **85**

Pocket PC: Type of PDA. **424**

Point: Measure of font size, equal to about 1/72 of an inch in height. **141**

Point of presence (POP): Access point on the Internet to which a user connects when using dial-up access. **72**

Point of sale (POS): Location in a retail or grocery store where a consumer pays for goods or services. **261**

Point-and-shoot camera: Affordable and lightweight camera that provides acceptable quality photographic images for home or small office users. 251–52

Pointer: Small symbol displayed on a computer screen whose location and shape changes as a user moves a pointing device. **136, 239**
head-mounted, 266

Pointing device: Input device that allows a user to control a pointer on the screen. **239–44**
cursor, 244
digital pen, 243–44, 249
joystick, 242
light pen, 242
mouse, 239–40
physically challenged users, 266
pointing stick, 242
purchasing notebook computer and, 453
stylus, 243, 247
touch screen, 243
touchpad, 241
trackball, 241
wheel, 242

Pointing stick: Pressure-sensitive pointing device shaped like a pencil eraser that is positioned between keys on a keyboard and moved by pushing the pointing stick with a finger. **242**

Polymorphic virus, 168

POP, 95. *See also* **Post Office Protocol**

POP (Internet service provider), 72. *See also* **Point of presence**

POP3: Latest version of Post Office Protocol. **95**

Pop-up ad: Internet advertisement that appears in a new window in the foreground of a Web page displayed in the user's browser. **427**

Pop-up blocker: Filtering program that stops pop-up ads from displaying on Web pages. **162, 427**

Port: Point at which a peripheral attaches to a system unit so it can send data to or receive information from the computer. 186, **206–10**
Bluetooth, 210
COM, 207
FireWire, 209
IrDA, 210
parallel, 206, 208
purchasing desktop computer and, 446
purchasing notebook computer and, 453

SCSI, 210
serial, 206, 207

Portable (storage medium): The capability of a storage medium to be removed from one computer and carried to another computer. **358**

Portable computer. *See* **Notebook computer**

Portable Document Format (PDF), 89

Portable hard disks, 364

Portable keyboard: Full-size keyboard conveniently used with a PDA or other mobile device. **248**

Portal: Web site that offers a variety of Internet serves from a single, convenient location. **82**

Portrait orientation: A printout that is taller than it is wide, with information printed across the shorter width of the paper. **310**

POS, 261. *See also* **Point of sale**

POS terminal: Terminal used by retail stores to record purchases, process credit or debit cards, and update inventory. **261**
magnetic stripe card readers and, 260

POST, 400. *See also* **Power-on self test**

Post: Add articles to a newsgroup. **96**

Post Office Protocol (POP): Communications protocol used by some incoming mail servers. **95**

Postage printer: Special type of label printer that has a built-in digital scale and prints postage stamps. **318**

PostScript: Standard printer language used by professionals in the desktop publishing and graphics arts fields, designed for complex documents with intense graphics and colors. **316**

Power
flat-panel monitor use of, 304
Power button, restarting computer using, 400
Power Macintosh, processor in, 190, 192

Power supply: Component of the system unit that converts wall outlet AC power to the DC power that is used by a computer. 186, **213**
CMOS, 203
notebook computers, 190
RAM and, 198

Power user: User who requires the capabilities of a workstation or other powerful computer, typically working with multimedia applications and using industry-specific software. 26, **29**, 31
input devices for, 265
operating system for, 420
output devices, , 325
processor selection, 192, 215
RAM needs, 200
storage and, 355, 380
UNIX and, 420

Power-on self test (POST): Series of tests that is executed by the BIOS to make sure the computer hardware is connected properly and operating correctly. **400**

PowerPC G4, 192
PowerPC G5, 192

Ppi, 252. *See also* **Pixels per inch**

Preemptive multitasking: Process in which the operating system interrupts a program that is executing and passes control to another program waiting to be executed. **405**

Presentation graphics software: Application software that allows a user to create visual aids for presentations to communicate ideas, messages, and other information to a group. 16, **146**

Presentations
developing using presentation graphics software, 16, 146
multimedia, 154

Price
of personal computers, 200
scanned items and, 258

Primary storage. *See also* **RAM**

Print: Placing the copy of a document on paper or some other medium. **142**

Print spooler: Program that intercepts print jobs from the operating system and places them in a queue. **407**

Printer: Output device that produces text and graphics on a physical medium such as paper or transparency film. 8, **310**-19
connections, 311
dot-matrix, 319
impact, 318–19
ink-jet, 312–14
label, 318
large-format, 318
laser, 315–16
line, 319
mobile, 317
nonimpact, 312–18
parallel ports, 208

photo, 314–15
postage, 318
purchasing desktop computer and, 448, 449
ROM chips in, 201
storage media for, 376
thermal, 317
wireless, 318
Printer Control Language, 316. *See also* **PCL**
Printing
digital images, 250, 251
hardware, 8
pictures from Picture CD, 370
process of, 142
screen display and, 137
spooling and, 407
Printout: Printed information that exists physically and is a more permanent form of output than that presented on a display device (soft copy). Also called hard copy. **310.** *See also* **Hard copy**
Privacy
employee monitoring and, 161, 237
smart cards, 378
video cameras and, 254, 373
Process ID, 430
Processing
multi-, 405
Processor: Electronic component on a computer's motherboard that interprets and carries out the basic instructions that operate the computer. Also called CPU or central processing unit. See also central processing unit (CPU). **8, 187.** *See also* **Central processing unit (CPU); Microprocessor**
cache controller and, 363
purchasing desktop computer and, 446, 448
purchasing notebook computer and, 453
video card, 306
Product activation: Process that attempts to prevent software piracy by requiring users to provide a software product's 25-character identification number in order to receive an installation identification number. **135**
Professional photographers and digital cameras, 251
Program: Series of instructions that tells a computer what to do and how to do it. Also called software. **15, 234–35**
background, 404
backup of, 359
foreground, 404
input of, 234–35
kernel managing, 400

Programmable read-only memory chip, 202. *See also* **PROM (programmable read-only memory) chip**
Programmer: Person who writes and modifies computer programs. Also called a developer. **18**
input by, 234–35
PROM chip and, 202
Project management software (system developers): Software that assists in planning, scheduling, and controlling development projects. **24**
Project management software (users): Application software that allows a user to plan, schedule, track, and analyze the events, resources, and costs of a project. **149**
Projector, data, 323, 454
PROM (programmable read-only memory) chip: Blank ROM chip on which a programmer can write permanently. **202**
Proprietary software: Software that is privately owned and limited to a specific vendor or computer model. **415.** *See also* **Application software; Software**
Protocol, Internet address, 73, 76
Pruning, 350
Ps. *See* Picosecond
Public-domain clip art, 139
Public-domain software: Free software that has been donated for public use and has no copyright restrictions. **135**
Publish: Process of creating a Web page and making it available on the Internet for others to see. **14**
Publishing, computers used in, 35
Pull: Request information from a Web server. **76**
Purchasing processors, 192
Pure Tablet PCs, 455
Push: Process of a Web server sending content to a computer at regular intervals, such as current sport scores or weather reports. **76**

QT. *See* QuickTime audio, video, or 3-D animation
Query: Request for specific data from a database. **145**
Queue: Lineup of multiple print jobs within a buffer. **407**
QuickTime (QT) audio, video, or 3-D animation, 87

QWERTY keyboard: The most widely used type of keyboard, so named because the first letters on the top alphabetic line spell QWERTY. **237**

RA. *See* RealAudio sound file
Radiation, display devices and, 308
Radio frequency identification (RFID), 197, 259. *See also* **RFID**
RAM (random access memory): Type of memory that can be read from and written to by the processor and other devices. Programs and data are loaded into RAM from storage devices such as a hard disk and remain in RAM as long as the computer has continuous power. 197, **198–200.** *See also* **Main memory**
access times, 203
adding, 200
booting computer and, 400
operating system managing, 405–6
operations of, 218
purchasing desktop computer and, 446, 448
system files loaded into, 401
types of, 199
video card and, 306
RAM chips, BIOS testing, 400
Rambus DRAM (RDRAM): Type of DRAM that is much faster than SDRAM because it uses pipelining techniques. **199**
Rambus inline memory module, 199. *See also* **RIMM**
Random access: Type of data access in which the storage device can locate a particular data item or file immediately, without having to move consecutively through items stored in front of the desired data item or file. See also direct access. **374.** *See also* **Direct access**
Random access memory (RAM): Type of memory that can be read from and written to by the processor and other devices. Programs and data are loaded into RAM from storage devices such as a hard disk and remain in RAM as long as the computer has continuous power. **198–202.** *See also* **RAM**
RDRAM, 199
access time, 203
See also **Rambus DRAM**

Reading: Process of transferring data, instructions, and information from a storage medium into memory. **356**
CD-R, 371
CD-ROM, 369
CD-RW, 371
direct access and, 374
floppy disk, 358–59
hard disk, 360
Read-only memory (ROM): Type of nonvolatile memory that is used to store permanent data and instructions. **201–2**
access times, 203
Read/write head: Mechanism in a disk drive that reads items or writes items as it barely touches the disk's recording surface. **361**
hard disk, 361–62
Real time: Describes users and the people with whom they are conversing being online at the same time. **8**
RealAudio (RA) sound file, 87
RealOne Player, 86
Real-time clock, 189, 202
Recalculation, in spreadsheets, 144
Record: Group of related fields in a database. **145**
Recording Industry Association of America (RIAA), 63, 153
Recovery disk (boot): Special disk that contains a few system files capable of restarting a computer, which is used when the computer cannot boot from its hard disk. **402, 456.** *See also* **Boot disk**
Recycling
toner cartridges, 316
Red Hat, 431
Reference software: Application software that provides valuable and thorough information for all individuals. **160**
Refresh operation, 218
Refresh rate: The number of times per second a monitor redraws an image on the screen. Also called scan rate. **308.** *See also* **Scan rate**
CRT monitor, 308
Regional ISP: Internet service provider that usually provides Internet access to a specific geographic area. **72**
Registers: Small, high-speed storage locations in a process that temporarily hold data and instructions. **189**
Registrar, 74
Registry: Several files that contain the system configuration information. **402**

Regulation, Internet and, 70
Reliability of computers, 10
Removable hard disk: Hard disk that can be inserted and removed from either a dock or drive. **364.** *See also* miniature hard disks, 363
USB 2.0 ports and, 208
Repetitive strain injury (RSI): Injury or disorder of the muscles, nerves, tendons, ligaments, and joints. 238, 241, 452. *See also* **Musculoskeletal disorder (MSD)**
government standards and, 241
Replace: Word processing feature, used in conjunction with the search feature, that allows a user to substitute existing characters or words in a document with new ones. **139**
Research
Web site, 129
Reset button, restarting computer using, 400
Resolution: The number of horizontal and vertical pixels in a display device. **252, 304**
CRT monitor, 307–8
DVD-ROM, 372
enhanced, 252
ink-jet printers, 313
LCD displays, 304
optical, 252
scanners, 256
Resources: Hardware, software, data, and information shared using a network. **11**
Resources, Web site and, 120
Response time: The time in milliseconds (ms) that it takes to turn a pixel on or off. **304**
Restarting a computer, 400
Restore program: Program that reverses the backup process and returns backed up files to their original form. **415**
Revolutions per minute (rpm): The number of times per minute that a hard disk platter rotates. **362**
RFID (radio frequency identification): Short for radio frequency identification; standard, specifically a protocol, that defines how a network uses radio signals to communicate with a tag placed in or attached to an object, an animal, or a person. **197, 259.** *See* **Radio frequency identification**
RFID reader: Reading device that reads information on an RFID tag via radio waves. 197, **259**
RFID tags, 64, 259

RIAA. *See* Recording Industry Association of America
Right mouse button, 136
RIMM (Rambus inline memory module): Type of memory module that houses RDRAM chips. **199**
Ripping: Process of copying an individual song from a purchased audio CD and converting it to a digital format. **371**
Robots, 32, 36
ROM, 201–2. *See also* **Read-only memory**
ROM chips, containing BIOS, 400
Routing slip, collaboration and, 467
Row (database): Term used by users of relational databases for record. 145
Row (spreadsheet), 143
Rpm, 362. *See also* **Revolutions per minute (rpm)**
Run: Process of using software. **17**

Safari, 75
Sales tax, Internet, 92
Sampling, 328
Sampling rate, 328
SanDisk Corporation, 383
Sans serif font: Font that does not have the short decorative lines at the upper and lower ends of the characters. **141**
Sasser worm, 410
SATA: Newest type of hard disk interface that uses serial signals to transfer data, instructions, and information and has transfer rates of up to 300 MBps. **364–65.** *See also* **Serial Advanced Technology Attachment**
Satellite companies
Internet structure and, 70
Satellite modem: Internet connection that communicates with a satellite dish to provide high-speed Internet connections via satellite. **70**
Satellite speakers: Speakers positioned around one or two center speakers and positioned so sound emits from all directions. **320**
Save: To transfer a document from a computer's memory to a storage medium. **142**
Scan rate: The number of times per second a monitor redraws an image on the screen. Also called refresh rate. **308.** *See also* **Refresh rate**

Scanner: Light-sending input device that reads printed text and graphics and then translates the results into a form the computer can process. 7, **255–56.** *See also* **optical scanner**
bar code, 258
face, 263
fingerprint, 262–63
flatbed, 256
improving quality of documents, 256
optical, 255–57
purchasing desktop computer and, 448
Scanner fraud, 258
Scanning hard disk, for errors, 365
Scenes, 350
School
connecting to Internet through, 71
networks in, 11
Science, computers used in, 34
Science Web site, 136
Scientific software and personal mobile devices, 290–91
Screen, 302
Screen resolution, 252
Screen saver: Utility program that causes a display device's screen to show a moving image or blank screen if no mouse activity occurs for a specified time. **415**
Scripts: Programs that contain command language instructions. **402**
Scrolling: Process of moving different portions of a document on the computer's screen into view. **139**
SCSI: Small computer system interface. **210.** *See also* **Small computer system interface**
SCSI interface, 365
SCSI port: Special high-speed parallel port to which peripherals, such as disk drives and printers, can be attached. **210**
SD, 376. *See also* **Secure Digital**
SDRAM, 199
access time, 203
See also **Synchronous DRAM**
Search: Word processing feature that allows a user to locate all occurrences of a certain character, word, or phrase. **139**
Search engine: Program that finds Web sites and Web pages. **78–81,** 82, 129
3-D, 81
popular search sites and, 129
using, 129
Search sites, popular, 129

Search text: Word or phrase entered in a search engine's text box to find information on a Web page. **80–81.** *See also* **Keywords**
Search tools, 129
Secondary storage, 355. *See* **Storage medium**
Sectors: The small arcs into which tracks on a disk are divided. **357**
floppy disk, 359
optical discs, 367
storing data and, 414
Secure Digital (SD): Type of miniature mobile storage medium that is a flash memory card capable of storing between 16 MB and 1 GB of data. **376**
Security
biometric devices and, 262–64
enterprise storage system and, 379
operating system and, 410–11
passwords and, 410
screen savers for, 415
Sense amplifier, 218
Sequential access: Type of data access in which the storage device reads or writes data consecutively. **374**
Serial Advanced Technology Attachment: Newest type of hard disk interface that uses serial signals to transfer data, instructions, and information and has transfer rates of up to 300 MBps. **364.** *See* **SATA**
Serial port: Type of interface that connects a device to the system unit by transmitting data one bit at a time. 206, **207**
Serif font: Font that has short decorative lines at the upper and lower edges of the characters. **141**
Server: Computer that controls access to the hardware, software, and other resources on a network and provides a centralized storage area for programs, data, and information. **11.** *See also* **Host computer**
cache, 201
DNS, 74, 102
FTP, 96
midrange, 23
network operating system on, 422
news, 96
processors, 190
Web, 76
Service pack: Free downloadable updates to software released by the software manufacturer. **416**

Service plan, purchasing computer and, 452
Shareware: Copyrighted software that is distributed at no cost for a trial period. **135**
Sharing
copyrighted music, 153
copyrighted videos, 153
resources, 10
Shockly, William, 52
Shopping
e-commerce used for, 92
Shopping cart: Element of an electronic storefront that allows a customer to collect purchases. **92**
Shortcut: Icon on the desktop that provides a user with immediate access to a program or file. **412**
Shugart, Al, 54, 55, 383
Shutdown command, 430
Shuttle-matrix printer: High-speed line printer that functions like a dot-matrix printer. **319**
Signature verification system: Biometric device that recognizes the shape of a person's handwritten signature and measures the pressure exerted and the motion used to write the signature. **263**
SIMM (single inline memory module): Type of memory module that has pins on opposite sides of the circuit board that connect together to form a single set of contacts. SIMMs typically hold SDRAM chips. **199**
Simple mail transfer protocol (SMTP). 94. *See* **SMTP**
Single inline memory module, 199. *See also* **SIMM**
Single user/multitasking: In reference to an operating system, allowing a single user to work on two or more programs that reside in memory at the same time. **403**
Single user/single tasking: In reference to an operating system allowing only one user to run one program at a time. **403**
Single-session disc: Disc on which manufacturers write all items at one time. **369**
Picture CD, 370
Slide show: Display of a presentation on a large monitor or a projection screen. **146**
Slide sorter view: Slide show presentation in which all slides are viewed as thumbnail versions, similar to how 35mm slides look on a photographer's light table. **146**

Small computer system interface: Type of high-speed parallel interface used to attach peripheral devices to a computer. **210.** *See also* **SCSI**

Small office/home office (SOHO): Describes any company with fewer than 50 employees, as well as the self-employed who work from home. 26, **28**, 31

input devices for, 265

output devices, 325

processor selection, 215

storage and, 354, 380

Smart card: Card, similar in size to a credit card or ATM card, that stores data on a thin microprocessor embedded in the card. **378**

Smart card (biometric): Card that stores personal biometric data on a thin microprocessor embedded in the card. **264**

Smart dust, 259

Smart Media: Type of miniature mobile storage medium that is a flash memory card capable of storing between 32 MB and 128 MB of data. **376**

Smart pagers, 282

Smart phone: Internet-enabled telephone that usually also provides PDA capabilities. **22,** 65, 247, 248, 249, **282**

camera in, 250

home user, 27

moblogs, 84

mobile users, 29

operating system for, 424

screen on, 303

storage media, 375, 376

system unit, 185

using while driving, 249

wireless Internet service provider and, 72

Smart shoes, 214

Smart tags, 140

Smart terminal: Terminal that has a processor, which gives it the capability of performing some functions independent of the host computer. **261**

Smart watch: Internet-enabled watch. **22**

SMTP (simple mail transfer protocol): Communications protocol used by some outgoing mail servers. **94**

SoBig virus, 63

Society

computer applications in, 32–37

Soft copy: Temporary output presented on a display device. **302**

Software: Series of instructions that tells a computer what to do and how to do it. Also called a program. **15**–18

bundled, 446

compatibility, 445

custom, 135

defective, 416

development of, 18

installing new, 400

integrated, 156

open source, 421, 425, 431

packaged, 134

purchasing desktop computer and, 445

system, 15–16

trial versions of, 154

Software manufacturers, liability, 416

Software suite: Collection of individual programs sold as a single package. Business software suites typically include word processing, spreadsheet, e-mail, and presentation graphics software. **148,** 156, 446

SOHO, 28. *See also* **Small office/home office**

Solaris: A version of UNIX developed by Sun Microsystems that is a network operating system designed specifically for e-commerce applications. **423**

Solid-state media: Term used to refer to components that consist entirely of electronic components and contain no moving parts. **376**

Son, Masayoshi, 169

Sony, 269

Sound, 86, 246. *See also* **Audio; Microphone; Music; Sound card;** Speakers

Sound card: Adapter card that enhances the sound generating capabilities of a personal computer by allowing sound to be input through a microphone and output through external speakers or headset. 186, **204**

audio input and, 246

bus connection, 212

MIDI standard, 209

operation of, 328

purchasing desktop computer and, 448

Source document: Document that contains the original form of data to be processed. **255**

Spam: Unsolicited e-mail message or newsgroups posting sent to many recipients or newsgroups at once. 65, **100,** 426

Speaker-dependent software: Software that makes a profile of a user's voice, which requires the user to train the computer to recognize his or her voice. **246,** 263

Speaker-independent software: Software that has a built-in set of word patterns so that a user need not train the computer to recognize his or her voice. **246**

Speakers: Audio output devices that generate sound. 8, **320**

Specialist ASP: Application service provider that delivers applications to meet a specific business need, such as human resources or project management. **164**

Special-purpose terminal, 261–62

Speech, 86

continuous, 246

discrete, 246

Speech recognition: Computer's capability of distinguishing spoken words. Also called voice recognition. **140, 245.** *See also* **Voice recognition**

Speed

access times, 203

bus, 212

bus width, 211

cache, 201

of computers, 10

processor, 190–91

RAM, 199–200

of storage devices and memory, 357, 362

system clock influence on, 189

word size, 211

Spelling checker: Feature in some application software that reviews the spelling of individual words, sections of a document, or the entire document. **139**

Spider: Program used to build and maintain lists of words found on Web sites. **81**

Spim: Spam sent through an instant messaging service. 65

Spit: Spam sent via Internet telephony. 65

Splitting, 350

Spoiler: Message that reveals a solution to a game or ending to a movie or program. **100**

Spooling: Operating system process that sends print jobs to a buffer instead of sending them immediately to the printer. The buffer then holds the information waiting to print while the printer prints from the buffer at its own rate of speed. **407**

Sports, Web site and, 124
Spreadsheet software:
Application software that allows a user to organize data in rows and columns and to perform calculations on the data. 16, **142–44**
Spyware: Program placed on a computer without the user's knowledge that secretly collects information about the user. 65, **426**
Spyware remover Program that detects and deletes spyware on a user's computer. **162, 426**
SRAM, 199. *See also* **Static RAM**
Stand By, 402
Stand-alone operating system:
Complete operating system that works on a desktop computer, notebook computer, or mobile computing device and that also works in conjunction with a network operating system. See also client operating system. **416–21.** *See also* **Client operating system**
Stand-alone utility programs, 162, 411, **425–28**
Start button (Windows XP), starting application using, 137
Starting
application software, 136–137
computer, 202
See also **Booting**
Startup folder: Contains a list of programs that open automatically when you boot a computer. **402**
Startup information, stored in CMOS chip, 400
Startup instructions, flash memory holding, 202
Static IP addresses, 102
Static RAM (SRAM): Type of RAM that is faster and more reliable than any variation of DRAM. **199**
Static Web page: A fixed Web page where visitors all see the same content. **75**
Stealth virus, 168
Stereo, 328
Storage: Location in which data, instructions, and information are held for future use. 197, **354–83**
back up and, 415
buffer, 407
Clipboard used for, 141
compressed files, 415
digital cameras using, 250
file manager functions, 412, 413
files and, 85
paper discs, 373
registers, 189
saving document and, 142

swapping data between memory and, 406
terms, 356
Storage device: Hardware used to record (write and/or read) items to and from storage media. **8–9, 356**
size of, 197
Storage media: The physical material on which a computer keeps data, instructions, and information. **8–9, 355**
access times, 357
capacity, 356
CD, 369–71
CD-R, 371
CD-ROM, 369–70
CD-RW, 371
DVD, 373–74
DVD+RW, 373
DVD-ROM, 372
floppy disk, 358–59
formatting and, 357, 382
hard disk, 360–65
Internet hard drive, 365
microfiche, 379
microfilm, 379
miniature mobile, 375–78
optical discs, 366–73
PC Card, 374
Picture CD, 370
smart card, 378
tape, 374
transfer rates, 357
USB flash drive, 8
viruses and, 426
Zip disk, 359
Stored program concept:
Concept of using memory to store both data and programs. **196**
Storing: Processor operation that writes a result to memory. **188.** *See also* **Storage**
Streaming: Process of transferring data in a continuous and even flow. **86**
Streaming audio: Transfer of audio data in a continuous and even flow. **86**
Streaming cam: Type of Web cam that has the illusion of moving images because it sends a continual stream of still images. **254**
Streaming video: Transfer of video data in a continuous and even flow. **88**
Striping: RAID storage technique that splits data, instructions, and information across multiple disks in the array. **741**
Studio camera: Stationary camera used for professional studio work. **251**

Stylus: Small metal or plastic device that looks like a ballpoint pen, but uses pressure instead of ink to write, draw, or make selections. **21, 243,** 247, 450. *See also* **Digital pen**
Subject directory: Search tool that classifies Web pages in an organized set of categories and subcategories. **78–79, 82,** 129
popular search sites and, 129
using, 129
Submenu: Menu that is displayed when a user points to a command on a previous menu. **137**
Subscribe (mailing list): Process of a user adding his or her e-mail name and address to a mailing list. **97**
Subscribe (newsgroup): Process of saving a newsgroup location in a newsreader for easy future access. **97**
Subwoofer: Speaker component that boosts low bass sounds. **320**
Sun, 56, 423
Sun StarOffice, 148
Super video graphics array, 305. *See also* **SVGA**
Super XGA, 305. *See* **SXGA.**
Supercomputer: Fastest, most powerful, and most expensive computer, capable of processing more than 100 trillion instructions in a single second. 19, **23**
processors for, 187
Superscalar: Term describing processors that can execute more than one instruction per clock cycle. **189**
Support tools, for application software, 164–65
Surfing the Web: Activity of using links to explore the Web. **77**
SVGA (super video graphics array): Super Video Graphics Array; video standard with a resolution of 800 x 600. **305**
S-video, 348
S-video port: Video card port that allows users to connect external devices such as a television, DVD player, or video recorder to the computer. **305**
Swap file: Area of the hard disk used for virtual memory. **406**
SXGA: Super XGA; video standard with a resolution of 1280 x 1024. **305.** *See also* **Super XGA.**
Sybase, 541, 673, 783, 800
Symbian, 431

Symbian OS: An open source multitasking operating system designed for smart phones and allows users to perform a variety of functions in addition to making telephone calls. 283, **425**

Synchronization software, 286

Synchronous DRAM (SDRAM): Type of RAM that is much faster than DRAM because it is synchronized to the system clock. **199,** 203

SyncML, 286

Synthesizer: Peripheral or chip that creates sound from digital instructions. **209**

System board: Name sometimes used for the motherboard. **186.** *See also* **Motherboard**

System bus: Bus that is part of the motherboard and connects the processor to main memory. **212**

System clock: Small quartz crystal circuit that is used by the processor to control the timing of all computer operations. **189–90**

BIOS testing, 400

System files, 401, 402

uninstalling programs and, 413

System on a chip: New type of processor that integrates the functions of a processor, memory, and a video card on a single chip. **190**

System software: Programs that control or maintain the operations of a computer and its devices. **15–16, 135,** 398–428

memory and, 197

role of, 135

storage of, 354

System unit: Case that contains the electronic components of a computer that are used to process data. **8, 184–219**

adapter cards, 204–5

bays, 212

buses, 211–12

cleaning, 216

connectors, 206–10

data representation and, 194–96

expansion slots, 204

hard disk in, 360

memory and, 196–203, 218

mobile computers and devices, 213–15

motherboard, 186

ports, 206–10

power supply, 213

processor. *See* **Processor**

Systeminfo command, 430

Systems programmer: Person who evaluates, installs, and maintains system software and provides technical support to the programming staff. 429

Tablet PC: Special type of notebook computer that resembles a letter-sized slate, which allows a user to write on the screen using a digital pen. **21,** 185, 214, **249–50**

Centrino, 219

convertible, 249

purchasing, 444–45, 455–56

slate, 249

Tape: Magnetically coated ribbon of plastic capable of storing large amounts of data and information at a low cost. **374**

Tape cartridge: Small, rectangular, plastic housing for tape. **374**

Tape drive: Device used to read and write data and information on tape. **374**

bays and, 212

Tape library: Separate cabinet for larger computers in which tape cartridges are mounted. **374**

Taskkill command, 430

Tasklist command, 430

Tax preparation software: Application software that is used to guide individuals, families, or small businesses through the process of filing federal taxes. **157**

Taxes, e-commerce and, 92

TB, 197, 356. *See also* **Terabyte**

Telecommuting: Work arrangement in which employees work away from a company's standard workplace and often communicate with the office through the computer. **30,** 59

Telematics: Wireless communications capabilities used in automobiles, including navigation systems and Internet access. **24**

Telemedicine: Form of long-distance health care where health-care professionals in separate locations conduct live conferences on the computer. **34**

Telephone

calls on PDA, 248

cellular. *See* **Cellular telephone**

smart. *See* **Smart phone**

Telephone adapters, purchasing notebook computer and, 454

Telephone companies, Internet structure and, 70

Telephone line

connecting to Internet through, 70, 71

Television

cable. *See* Cable television

connecting computer to, 453

digital, 306–7

digital camera connected to, 250, 251–52

high-definition. *See also* **HDTV**

interactive, 307

interfacing computer with, 453

Template: Document that contains the formatting necessary for a specific document type. **140, 165**

Teoma, 78

Terabyte (TB): Approximately one trillion bytes. **197**

Terminal: Device that consists of a keyboard, a monitor, a video card, and memory, which often all are housed in a single unit. 23, **261–62**

Text

editing in word processing document, 141

input, 234, 256

links, 77

optical character recognition and, 256, 257

output, 300

search, 80–81

Web page, 75, 85

worksheet, 143

Text messaging: Service that allows users to send and receive short text messages on a smart phone or PDA. **248.** *See also* **SMS (short message service)**

TFT (thin-film transistor) display: Thin-film transistor; LCD monitor or screen technology that uses a separate transistor to apply charges to each liquid crystal cell and thus displays high-quality color that is viewable from all angles. **304.** *See also* **Active-matrix display**

The Microsoft Network. *See* Microsoft Network, The

Theft

hardware. *See* **Hardware theft**

Thermal printer: Type of non-impact printer that generates images by pushing electrically heated pins against heat-sensitive paper. **317**

Thermal wax-transfer printer: Thermal printer that generates images by using heat to melt colored wax onto heat-sensitive paper. **317**

Thin-film transistor (TFT) display: LCD monitor or screen technology that uses a separate transistor to apply charges to each liquid crystal cell and thus displays high-quality color that is viewable from all angles. **304.** *See also* **Active-matrix display; TFT display**

Thrashing: The state of an operating system that spends much of its time paging, instead of executing application software. **406**

Thread: Group of newsgroup articles consisting of the original article and all subsequent related replies. **97.** *See also* **Threaded discussion**

Threaded discussion: Group of newsgroup articles consisting of the original article and all subsequent related replies. **97.** *See also* **Thread**

Thumbnail: Small version of a larger graphic. **86**
image viewer and, 412

TIFF, 85, **345**

Time, real-time clock and, 189

Time bomb, 168

Timeline, computer history, 52–65

Title bar: Horizontal space, located at the top of a window, that contains the window's name. **137**

Toggle key: Key that switches between two states each time a user presses the key. **237**

Toner: Type of powdered ink that is used by some laser printers and copy machines to produce output. **316**

Top-level domain: Identifies the type of organization associated with the domain. **73**

Topology. *See* **Network topology**

Torvalds, Linus, 58, 421, 431

Touch screen: Touch-sensitive display device with which users interact by touching areas of the screen. **243**

Touchpad: Small, flat, rectangular pointing device that is sensitive to pressure and motion. **241**

Tower: Tall and narrow system unit that can sit on the floor vertically if desktop space is limited. **20**

Traceroute, 430. *See also* **TRACERT (traceroute)**

TRACERT (traceroute), 430. *See also* **Traceroute**

Track: Narrow recording band that forms a full circle on the surface of a disk. 357

floppy disk, 359
hard disk, 361
optical discs, 367

Trackball: Stationary pointing device with a ball on its top or side. **241**

Traffic: Communications activity on the Internet. **70**

Training
computer-based. *See* **Computer-based training**
distance learning, 166
Web-based, 166

Transfer rate: The speed at which data, instructions, and information transfer to and from a device. **357**
CD-ROM drives, 369
EIDE controller, 365
FireWire, 365
floppy disk, 358
hard disk, 362
miniature mobile storage media, 376
SCSI interface, 365
tape drive, 374
USB, 365

Transistor: Element of an integrated circuit that can act as an electronic switch that opens or closes the circuit for electrical charges. **186,** 218
invention of, 52
LCD and, 304
number of, 190

Transitions, 351

Transmission speed, 70

Travel software and personal mobile devices, 292

Travel, computers used in, 36

Travel Web sites, 119

Treo, 329

Trial versions, 154

Trojan horse: Malicious-logic program named after the Greek myth that hides within or looks like a legitimate program. **168,** 426

Turing, Alan, 52

Turnaround document: Document that a user returns to the company that has created and sent it. **257**

UGA: Ultra XGA; video standard with a resolution of 1600 x 1200. **305.** *See also* **Ultra XGA.**

Ultra XGA, 305. *See* **UGA**

Uncompress: To restore a compressed, or zipped, file to its original form. **427.** *See also* **Unzip**

Unicode: 16-bit coding scheme that has the capability of representing more than 65,000 characters and symbols. **195**

Uniform Resource Locator: Unique address for a Web page. **76.** *See also* **URL; Web address**

Uninstaller: Utility program that removes a program, as well as any associated entries in the system files. **413**

Uninstalling programs, 412, 413

UNIVAC I (Universal Automatic Computer), 52

Universal Product Code (UPC), 258. *See also* **UPC**

Universal serial bus: Bus that eliminates the need to install cards in expansion slots. 212

Universal serial bus port: Port that can connect up to 127 different peripherals with a single connector type. **208.** *See also* **USB port**

UNIX: Multitasking operating system that now is available for most computers of all sizes. **420,** 423

Unsubscribe: Process of a user removing his or her e-mail name and address from a mailing list. **97**

Unzip: To restore a compressed, or zipped, file to its original form. **427.** *See also* **Uncompress**

UPC (Universal Product Code): Bar code used by retail and grocery stores. **258**

Upgrade, 416

Uploading: Process of transferring documents, graphics, and other objects from a computer to a server on the Internet. **96**
compressed files, 427

UPS, 451. *See* **Uninterruptible power supply (UPS)**

Upward compatible, 416

URL (Uniform Resource Locator): Unique address for a Web page. Also called a Web address. **76**

U.S. Robotics, 58

USB (universal serial bus), 207, 212

USB 2.0: Latest version of USB, which is a more advanced and faster type of USB. **208, 365** *See* **Hi-Speed USB**

USB flash drive: Flash memory storage device that plugs in a USB port on a computer or portable device. 8, 64, **205,** 355, 357, **377,** 448. *See also* **Pen drive**

USB hub: Device that plugs in a USB port on the system unit and contains multiple USB ports in which cables from USB devices can be plugged. **208**

USB port: Port that can connect up to 127 different peripherals with a single connector type. 206, **208**, 214

downloading from digital camera using, 251

keyboards with, 237

USB transfer rate, 365

Usenet: Entire collection of Internet newsgroups. **96**

User: Anyone who communicates with a computer or utilizes the information it generates. **9**

User ID: Unique combination of characters, such as letters of the alphabet or numbers, that identifies one specific user. Also called user name. **410.** *See also* **User name**

User interface: The portion of software that defines how a user interacts with a computer, including how the user enters data and instructions and how information is displayed on the screen. 15, **402**

command-line, 402, 417, 420, 421, 430

graphical. *See* **Graphical user interface (GUI)**

menu-driven, 402, 417

next generation, 137

User name: Unique combination of characters, such as letters of the alphabet and/or numbers, that identifies a specific user. **94, 410.** *See also* **User ID**

User response: An instruction a user issues by replying to a question displayed by a program. **235**

Users

authenticating using biometric devices, 262–64

commands issued by, 235

home, 26–27, 31

information system and, 25

Large business, 30, 31

mobile, 29, 31

names, 94

number on Internet, 68

physically challenged. *See* Physically challenged users

small office/home office, 28, 31

types of, 26–31

Utility: Type of system software that allows a user to perform maintenance-type tasks, usually related to managing a computer, its devices, or its programs. **411.** *See also* **Utility program**

Utility program: Type of system software that allows a user to perform maintenance-type tasks usually related to managing a computer, its devices, or its programs. **16,** 398,

411–15. *See also* **Utility**

anti-spam, 162

antivirus, 162, 425–26

backup, 415

CD/DVD burner, 162

diagnostic, 414

disk defragmenter, 414

disk scanner, 414

file compression, 162, 427

file conversion, 162, 427

file manager, 412

image viewer, 412

Internet filters, 426–27

operating system, 398, 411–15

personal computer maintenance, 162, 428

personal firewall, 413

pop-up blocker, 162

screen saver, 415

spyware remover, 162, 426

stand-alone, 162, 411, 425–28

uninstaller, 413

Web filter, 162

See also **Utility**

Value: Number contained in a worksheet cell that can be used in a calculation. **143**

VCD, 351. *See also* **video CD**

Vendors

purchasing computers from, 451, 452

See also Manufacturers

Vertical market ASP: Application service provider that provides applications for a particular industry, such as construction, health care, or retail. **164**

Video: Full-motion images that are played back at various speeds. **88**

AGP bus, 212

entertainment software and, 160

multimedia and, 88

processors and, 192

storing on DVD, 372

on Web page, 75

Video camera. *See* PC video camera

Video cameras, in society, 373

Video capture card: Adapter card that converts an analog video signal to a digital signal that a computer can process. **253**

Video card: Adapter card that converts computer output to a video signal that travels through a cable to a monitor, which displays an image on the screen. 186, **204, 308.** *See also* **Graphics card**

analog to digital conversion by, 38

bus connection, 212

cost, 306

LCD monitors and, 305

memory, 306

processor, 306

purchasing desktop computer and, 448

standards and, 306

terminal and, 261

See also **Graphics card**

Video CD (VCD), 351

Video conference: Meeting between two or more geographically separated people who use a network or the Internet to transmit audio and video data. **254**

Popularity of, 254

Video editing software: Application software that allows a user to modify a segment of video, called a clip. **153**

Video input: Process of capturing full-motion images and storing them on a computer's storage medium. 234, **253–54**

Video memory, video card and, 306

Video output, 301, 308

connecting notebook computer to, 454

Video telephone call: Telephone call made using a PC video camera that allows both parties to see each other as they communicate over the Internet. 27, **253**

Viewable size: Diagonal measurement of the actual viewing area provided by the screen in a CRT monitor. **307**

Viewsonic, 329

Violence, computer games and, 16

Virtual memory: A portion of a storage medium, usually the hard disk, that the operating system allocates to function as additional RAM. 405, **406**

Virtual reality (VR): Computers used to simulate a real or imagined environment that appears as a three dimensional (3-D) space. **88**

multimedia and, 88

Virus: Potentially damaging computer program that affects, or infects, a computer negatively by altering the way the computer works without a user's knowledge or permission. **95, 162, 425**

cost of attack, 162

first, 55

mobile computers and devices with, 250

prevention, 426

protection from, 426

Virus author: Programmer who intentionally writes a virus program. **425**

VisiCalc, 55

Visual Studio 2005: Latest suite of program development tools from Microsoft that assists programmers in building programs for Windows, Windows Mobile, or operating systems that support Microsoft's .NET architecture. 65

Visually impaired users, output devices for, 326

Voice input: Process of entering data by speaking into a microphone. **245–46**

PDAs, 248

Voice output: Audio output that occurs when a user hears a person's voice or when a computer talks to the user through the speakers on the computer. **321–22**

Voice over IP (VoIP): Technology that allows users to speak to other users over the internet using their desktop computer, mobile computer, or mobile device. See also Internet telephony. **99.** *See also* **Internet telephony**

Voice recognition: Computer's capability of distinguishing spoken words. Also called speech recognition. **140, 245–46**

RAM needed for, 200

See also **Speech recognition**

Voice verification system: Biometric device that compares a person's live speech with his or her stored voice pattern to determine if the person is a legitimate user. **263**

VoIP, 99. *See also* **Voice over IP (VoIP)**

Volatile memory: Type of memory that loses its contents when a computer's power is turned off. **197,** 198–99

Volume, 382

Volume business ASP: Application service provider that supplies prepackaged applications, such as accounting, to businesses. **164**

Volume control, for optical disc drives, 366

Von Neumann, John, 52

VR. *See* Virtual reality

VR world: 3-D Web site that contains infinite space and depth created with special VR software. **88**

W3C, 70, 327. *See also* **World Wide Web Consortium**

Warm boot: Process of using the operating system to restart a computer. **400,** 406

Warranty, purchasing computer and, 452

WAV. *See* Windows waveform

WBT, 166. *See also* **Web-based training**

Weather, Web site and, 124

Wearable computer, 267

Wearable Web devices, 321. *See also* Internet wearables

Web: Worldwide collection of electronic documents called Web pages, the Web is one of the more popular services on the Internet. Also called the World Wide Web. **12,** 14, 68, **75–91**

addresses, 76

application service providers and, 164

application software on, 163–64

browsing. *See* **Web browser**

creator of, 103

e-commerce on, 91–92

freeware on, 135

multimedia on, 85–89

navigating, 77

public-domain software on, 135

publishing Web pages on. *See* Web publishing

searching for information on, 78–81

shareware on, 135

surfing, 77

text-based documents and, 300

types of Web sites, 82–84

See also **Internet**

Web address: Unique address for a Web page. Also called a URL (Uniform Resource Locator). **76**

Web application: Application software that exists on a Web site. **163,** 423

Web browser: Application software that allows users to access and view Web pages. Also called a browser. **75**

home page, 76

online service provider, 72

software, 161

Web cam: Video camera that displays its output on a Web page. **28, 254**

Web clippings, 288

Web community: Web site that joins a specific group of people with similar interests or relationships. **82**

Web developer, 101

Web filter: Program that restricts access to specified Web sites. **162, 427**

Web filtering software: Program that restricts access to certain material on the Web. **427**

Web log: Web site that uses a regularly updated journal format to reflect the interests, opinions, and personalities of the author and sometimes site visitors. **84.** *See also* **Blog**

Web page: Electronic document on the Web, which can contain text, graphics, audio, and video and often has built-in connections to other documents, graphics, Web pages, or Web sites. **12, 75**

browsing, 75–76

downloading, 76

multimedia on, 85

navigating, 77

searching for, 78–79

Web page authoring, 90

Web page authoring software: Software used to create Web pages that include graphical images, video, audio, animation, and other special effects with interactive content. 90, **154**

Web publishing: Development and maintenance of Web pages. 71, 89–**90**

Web server: Computer that delivers requested Web pages to a computer. **75**

Web services: Set of software technologies that allows businesses to create products and B2B (business-to-business) interactions over the Internet. **423**

Web site: Collection of related Web pages and associated items, such as documents and pictures, stored on a Web server. 12, 30, **75**

analyzing and designing, 90

arts and literature, 131

auctions, 121

careers, 130

creating, 89–90

directories, 78

education, 125

entertainment, 117

environment, 127

evaluating, 84

finance, 118

government, 122

graphics and, 301

guide to, 116–31

health, 128

home page, 76

Internet hard drive and, 365

news, 124

planning, 90

posting photographs on, 251

posting scanned object to, 256

research, 129

resources, 121

restricted access to, 427
science, 126
shopping, 123
sports, 124
travel, 118
types of, 82–84, 116–31
weather, 124
Web-based Help: Help located on Web sites that provides updates and comprehensive resources to respond to technical issues about software. **164**
Web-based training (WBT): Computer-based training that uses Internet technology and consists of application software on the Web. **166**
Webcrawler, 78
What-if analysis: Spreadsheet software feature that allows a user to change certain values in a spreadsheet to reveal the effects of those changes. **144**
Wheel: Steering-wheel-type input device that is used to simulate driving a vehicle. **242**
force feedback, 324
Wheel mouse, 240
White House, Web site and, 57
Whitman, Meg, 103
Whiteboard: Video conference feature in which another window on the screen displays notes and drawings simultaneously on all participants' screens. **54**
Wi-Fi (wireless fidelity), hot spot, 71
Winchester hard drive, 55
Window: Rectangular area of a computer screen that displays data or information. **137**
Windows CE: Scaled-down Windows operating system designed for use on communications, entertainment, and computing devices with limited functionality. **423–24**
Windows, number of users, 417
Windows operating system, 15, 19
Windows 2000 Professional, 419
Windows 2000 Server, 422
Windows Explorer: A file manager that is included with Windows XP. **412**
Windows Future Storage (WinFS), 418
Windows Media Audio (WMA), 87, 89, 202
Windows Media Player, 86
Windows Millennium Edition, 419

Windows Mobile: Embedded operating system that enhances Windows CE to add functionality, applications, and a user interface for Pocket PCs and smart phones. **424**
for Pocket PC, 283
for Pocket PC Phone Edition, 283
for Smartphone, 283
Windows NT Server, 422
Windows Picture and Fax Viewer: An image viewer that is included with Windows XP. **412**
Windows Small Business Server 2003, 422
Windows Server 2003: Network operating system designed by Microsoft that offers a wide variety of features, including Web site management and hosting, delivery and management of multimedia across intranets and the Internet, document storage in Web folders, central information repository about network users and resources, and client support using various versions of Windows, Mac OS X, UNIX, and Linux. **422**
Windows Server 2003, Datacenter Edition: Network operating system designed for use by businesses with huge volumes of transactions and large-scale databases. **423**
Windows Server 2003, Enterprise Edition: Network operating system designed for use by medium- to large-sized businesses, including those with e-commerce operations. **422**
Windows Server 2003 family: Collection of network operating system products, including Windows Small Business Server 2003; Windows Server 2003, Standard Edition; Windows Server 2003, Enterprise Edition; Windows Server 2003, Datacenter Edition; and Windows Server 2003, Web Edition. **422–23**
Windows Server 2003, Standard Edition: Network operating system designed for the use of typical small- to medium-sized business network. **422**
Windows Server 2003, Web Edition: Network operating system designed for Web server and Web hosting businesses. **423**

Windows Server System: Network operating system that includes Windows Server 2003 and additional development tools that allow businesses and customers to connect and communicate easily via the Internet. **423**
Windows Small Business Server 2003: Network operating system designed for businesses with fewer than 75 users and limited networking expertise. **422**
Windows waveform (WAV), 87
Windows XP: The latest version of the Windows operating system, which is Microsoft's fastest, most reliable Windows operating system. 15, 65, 195, **417–19**
Command Prompt, 430
date and time and, 203
desktop, 136
diagnostic utility, 414
disk defragmenter, 414
features of, 418
file manager, 412
Internet connection, 409
personal firewall and, 413
role of, 135
system configuration information, 401–2
uninstaller, 413
Windows XP 64-bit Edition: Version of windows XP designed for workstations that use an Itanium 2 processor. **419**
Windows XP Home Edition: Version of the Windows XP operating system that allows users to organize and share digital pictures, download and listen to music, create and edit videos, network home computers, and communicate with instant messaging. **419**
Windows XP Media Center Edition: Version of the Windows XP operating system that includes all the features of Windows XP Professional and is designed for Media Center PCs. 65, **419**
Windows XP Professional: Version of the Windows XP operating system that includes all the capabilities of Windows XP Home Edition and also offers greater data security, remote access to a computer, simpler administration of groups of users, multiple language user interface, and support for a wireless network. **419**

Windows XP Tablet PC Edition: Version of the Windows XP operating system that includes all the features of Windows XP Professional and provides additional features to make users more productive while they are working on Tablet PCs. **419,** 456

WinZip, 427

Wireless communication, 63

Wireless data collection, 261

Wireless data transmission, 261

Wireless Internet access, 72, 456

Wireless Internet service provider (WISP): Type of Internet service provider that provides wireless Internet access to computers with wireless modems or access devices or to Internet-enabled mobile computers or devices. **72**

Wireless keyboard: Battery-powered keyboard that transmits data using wireless technology, such as radio waves or infrared light waves. **238.** *See also* **Cordless keyboard**

Wireless LAN Access Point, 448

Wireless mobile devices, 288

Wireless mouse: Battery-powered device that transmits data using wireless technology, such as radio waves or infrared light waves. **239.** *See also* **cordless mouse.**

Wireless network
home, 453
purchasing notebook computer and, 453

Wireless pens, 243–44

Wireless port, 210

Wireless portal: Portal designed for Internet-enabled mobile devices. **82**

Wireless printing, 318

WISP, 72. *See also* **Wireless Internet service provider (WISP)**

Wizard: Automated assistant that helps a user complete a task by asking questions and then automatically performing actions based on the responses. **165**

WLAN, 471. *See* **Wireless LAN (WLAN)**

WMA. *See* Windows Media Audio

Word processing software: One of the more widely used types of application software; allows a user to create and manipulate documents containing mostly text and sometimes graphics. 16, **138–40.** *See also* **Word processor**
developing document using, 141–42
as part of integrated software, 156
See also **Word processor**

Word processor: One of the more widely used types of application software; allows a user to create and manipulate documents containing mostly text and sometimes graphics. **138.** *See also* **Word processing software**

Word size: Number of bits a computer can interpret and execute at a given time. **211**

Wordwrap: Feature of word processing software that allows users to type words in a paragraph continually without pressing the ENTER key at the end of each line. **139**

Worksheet: Rows and columns used to organize data in a spreadsheet. **142–44**

Workstation, 10, 20

World Wide Web (WWW): Worldwide collection of electronic documents. **75,** 103. *See also* **Web**
invention of, 57

World Wide Web Consortium (W3C): Consortium of more than 350 organizations from around the world that oversees research and sets standards and guidelines for many areas of the Internet. 57, **70**
accessibility guidelines and, 327

Worm: Malicious-logic program that copies itself repeatedly, using up system resources and possibly shutting down the system. **168,** 410, **426**
Sasser, 410

Wozniak, Steve, 39, 55

Write-protect notch: Small opening on a floppy disk that has a tab a user can slide to cover or expose the notch. **359**

Writing: Process of transferring data, instructions, and information from memory to a storage medium. **356**
CD-R, 371
CD-ROMs, 369
CD-RW, 371
direct access and, 374
DVD+RW, 373
floppy disk, 358–59
hard disk, 360

WWW: Worldwide collection of electronic documents. Also called the Web or World Wide Web. **75,** 103. *See also* **World Wide Web**

WYSIWYG (what you see is what you get), 137

Xeon: Intel processor used by workstations and low-end servers. **190,** 191

xD Picture Card: Type of miniature mobile storage media that is a flash memory card capable of storing between 64 MB and 512 MB of data. **376**

XGA: EXtended Graphics Array; video standard with a resolution of 1024 x 768. **305.** *See also* **eXtented Graphics Array)**

Y2K bug, 60

Yahoo!, 78, 82, 94, **103**

YB. *See* **Yottabyte**

Yottabyte (YB), 356

ZB. *See* **Zettabyte**

Zettabyte (ZB), 356

Zip disk: Type of portable magnetic storage media that can store from 100 MB to 750 MB of data. 8, **359**
direct access and, 374

Zip drive: High-capacity disk drive developed by Iomega Corporation that reads from and writes on a Zip disk. 8, **359**
bay and, 212
purchasing desktop computer and, 448

Zipped files: Type of compressed files that usually have a .zip extension. **427**

PHOTO CREDITS

Chapter 1: PY1-01, study hall, ©Bill Aron/PhotoEdit Inc.; PY1-02, laptop user, © Jose Luis Pelaez, Inc./CORBIS; PY1-03, computer store, ©Spencer Grant/PhotoEdit Inc.; PY1-04, people in coffee shop, ©Gary Conner/PhotoEdit Inc.; PY1-05, Camera, Courtesy of Sony Electronics Inc.; PY1-06, wireless bluetooth card, Courtesy of 3Com Corporation; PY1-07, USB flash drive, Courtesy of SimpleTech, Inc.; PY1-08, instructor, Photodisc Collection/Getty Images; Figure 1-01a, Person using PDA, © Thierry Dosogne/Getty Images Figure 1-01b, Person using notebook computer, © Roy Morsch/CORBIS; Figure 1-01c, Person using desktop computer, © Jose Luis Pelaez, Inc./CORBIS; Figure 1-01d, Person using Tablet PC, Courtesy of Motion Computing, Inc.; Figure 1-01e, Person using smartphone, Siemens AG Press Picture; Figure 1-02, payroll check, © C Squared Studios/Getty Images; Figure 1-03a, Computer with CD drive, DVD drive, Zip® drive, and floppy drive, keyboard, flat panel monitor, mouse, speakers, Courtesy of Acer America Corp.; Figure 1-03b, PC video camera (input device), Courtesy of Logitech, Inc.; Figure 1-03c, Microphone, Courtesy of Logitech, Inc.; Figure 1-03d, Open flatbed scanner, Courtesy of Umax Systems GmbH; Figure 1-03e, External card reader, Courtesy of Sandisk Corporation; Figure 1-03f, USB flash drive, Courtesy of Sandisk Corporation; Figure 1-03g, External cable modem, Courtesy of Linksys, a Division of Cisco Systems Inc.; Figure 1-03h, digital camera, Courtesy of Umax Systems GmbH; Figure 1-03i, Ink-jet printer, Courtesy of Epson America, Inc.; Figure 1-04, Hard disk, Courtesy of Seagate Technology; Figure 1-05, DVD disc in the DVD tray, ©Rachel Epstein/Photo Edit; Looking Ahead 1-1, Implant and/or robotics (Bionics), © AP/WIDE WORLD PHOTOS; Figure 1-06a,b,c, desktop computers, Courtesy of Sony Electronics Inc.; Figure 1-07a, desktop computer, Courtesy of Acer America Corp.; Figure 1-07b, desktop computer, Courtesy of Sony Electronics Inc.; Figure 1-07c, desktop computer, © Gateway, Inc.; Figure 1-07d, desktop computer, Courtesy of Acer America Corp.; Figure 1-07e, smartphone, Courtesy of Nokia; Figure 1-07f, PDA, Courtesy of Sony Electronics Inc.; Figure 1-11, person standing in the software aisle at a computer store, ©Bonnie Kamin/Photo Edit; Figure 1-12, notebook computers, Courtesy of Acer America Corp.; Figure 1-15, IBM ThinkCentre Computer, Courtesy of IBM Corporation; Figure 1-16, Latest iMac with 20" monitor, Courtesy of Apple Computer, Inc.; Figure 1-17, Notebook computer, Courtesy of Sony Electronics Inc.; Figure 1-18, Tablet PC, Courtesy of Motion Computing, Inc.; Figure 1-19, WORLD'S SMALLEST AND LIGHTEST WINDOWS XP PC, VAIO TYPE U, © ISSEI KATO/Reuters/Corbis; Figure 1-20a, PDA with keyboard, Courtesy of palmOne, Inc. palmOne, Zire, Tungsten, Treo, logos, stylizations and design marks associated with all the preceding, and trade dress associated with palmOne, Inc.'s products, are among the trademarks or registered trademarks owned by or exclusively licensed to palmOne, Inc.; Figure 1-20b, PDA without keyboard, Courtesy of Sony Electronics Inc.; Figure 1-20c, stylus, Courtesy of Belkin Corporation; Figure 1-21, Smartphone in a person's hand (close-up), Courtesy of Nokia; Figure 1-22, Smart watch, Courtesy of Fossil, Inc. ; Figure 1-23, Midrange server, Copyright 2005 Sun Microsystems, Inc. All Rights Reserved. Used by permission.; Figure 1-24, Mainframe computer, Courtesy of IBM Corporation; Figure 1-25, Earth Simulator computer, COPYRIGHT: JAMSTEC/ESC; Figure 1-26a, car with an onboard navigation system, Toyota photo; Figure 1-26b, Deplyed airbag, © Patti McConville/Imagestate; Figure 1-26c, on-board navigation system, Toyota photo; Figure 1-26d, Gas pedal/brake pedal in car, Toyota photo; Figure 1-26e, Wheel in motion, © DiMaggio/Kalish/CORBIS; Figure 1-26f, Cruise control on a steering wheel, Toyota photo; Figure 1-27, Step 3, Midrange server, Courtesy of Fujitsu Siemens Computers; Figure 1-27, Step 4, Corporate Printer System, Courtesy of IBM Corporation; Figure 1-28, Home user, © Jose Luis Pelaez, Inc./CORBIS; Figure 1-29, couple looking at digital camera, Courtesy of Sony Electronics Inc.; Figure 1-30, home office/small business user, © Britt Erlanson/Getty Images; Figure 1-31a, Mobile user with a notebook computer, © Andersen-Ross/Brand X Pictures; Figure 1-31b, Mobile user with PDA, © David Pollack/CORBIS; Figure 1-31c, tablet PC user, Courtesy of Motion Computing, Inc; Figure 1-31d, Mobile user with smart phone, © Edward Bock/CORBIS; Figure 1-32, Power user, © Richard T. Nowitz/CORBIS; Figure 1-33, Many users in large business, © Comstock Images; Figure 1-34, Customer using a kiosk, Courtesy of IBM Corporation; Figure 1-35a, telecommuter working at home, © Jose Luis Pelaez, Inc./CORBIS; Figure 1-35b, home office, © Britt Erlanson/Getty Images; Figure 1-35c, laptop user, © Andersen-Ross/Brand X Pictures; Figure 1-35d, Power user, © Richard T. Nowitz/CORBIS; Figure 1-35e, users in a large office, © Comstock Images; Looking Ahead 1-2, QRIO robot, Courtesy of Sony Electronics Inc.; Figure 1-36, red-head girl using laptop at school, © David Roth/Getty Images; Figure 1-38, Police officer in police car that has a notebook computer and shows officer using a PDA, Courtesy of IBM Corporation; Figure 1-39, medical professional and computer, © Peter Beck/CORBIS; Figure 1-40a, How a Camera Pill Works — hand holding camera pill, © AP/WIDE WORLD PHOTOS; Figure 1-40c, How a Camera Pill Works — Doctor looking at x-rays in front of a computer, © Gabe Palmer/CORBIS; Figure 1-42, person using notebook computer, © EPA/Ulrich Perrey/Landov; Figure 1-43, Robot in a CAM (computer aided manufacturing) environment, © Charles O'Rear/CORBIS; Career Corner, Personal computer salesperson, © Jana Birchum/Getty Images; Technology Trailblazer 1, Bill Gates, © Justin Sullivan/Getty Images; Technology Trailblazer 2, Carly Fiorina, © Justin Sullivan/Getty Images; **Special Feature: Timeline** 1937, COLLAGE: Clifford Berry, Courtesy of Iowa State University; 1937, Atanasoff-Berry-Computer (ABC), Courtesy of Iowa State University; 1937, Dr. John V. Atanasoff, Courtesy of Iowa State University; 1943, Alan Turing, Photo courtesy of Computer History Museum; 1943, Colossus computer, Photo courtesy of Computer History Museum; 1945, Dr. John von Neumann, Courtesy of the Archives of the Institute for Advanced Study; 1945, Dr. Von Neumann with computer, Courtesy of the Archives of the Institute for Advanced Study; 1946, The ENIAC (Electronic Numerical Integrator And Computer) created by Dr. John W. Mauchly and J. Presper Eckert, Jr., From the Collections of the University of Pennsylvania Archives; 1947, transfer resistence device (transistor), © IBM Corporate Archives; 1947, close-up of transistor with pencil, © IBM Corporate Archives; 1951, Univac I (UNIVersal Automatic Computer), Courtesy Unisys Corporation; 1952, Dr. Grace Hopper, Courtesy of Hagley Museum and Library; 1953, IBM model 650 (hands holding magnifying glass), © IBM Corporate Archives; 1957, Fortran (FORmula TRANslation) is introduced by John Backus, © IBM Corporate Archives; 1957, IBM 305 RAMAC system uses magnetic disk for external storage, © IBM Corporate Archives; 1957, close-up of magnetic disks for storage, Courtesy of the Department of the Navy; 1958, Jack Kilby, Courtesy of Texas Instruments; 1958, integrated circuit, Courtesy of Texas Instruments; 1959, IBM 1602 CADET, © IBM Corporate Archives; 1960, Dr. Grace Hopper invents COBOL, Courtesy of Hagley Museum and Library; 1964, computer chip on finger, © IBM Corporate Archives; 1964, TYPEWRITER, © IBM Corporate Archives; 1964, IBM System/360, © IBM Corporate Archives; 1965, Dr. John Kenney of Dartmouth, Courtesy of Dartmouth College; 1965, Digital Equipment Corp. (DEC) introduces the first mini-computer the PDP-8, Courtesy of Digital Equipment Corporation; 1970, LSI chip (large-scale integration), © IBM Corporate Archives; 1971, Dr. Ted Hoff, Courtesy of Intel Corporation; 1971, Intel 4004 - microprogrammable computer chip, Courtesy of Intel Corporation; 1975, Bob Metcalfe (develops Ethernet), Courtesy of InfoWorld; 1975, Altair - one of the first microcoputers., Photo courtesy of Computer History Museum; 1976, Image of first Apple Computer, Courtesy of Apple Computer, Inc.; 1976, Steve Wozniak and Steve Jobs, © Bettmann/CORBIS; 1979, Bob Frankston and Dan Bricklin, writers of VisiCalc, Photo courtesy of Computer History Museum; 1980, Alan Shugart introduces Winchester hard drive, © IBM Corporate Archives; 1980, Bill Gates, Courtesy of Microsoft Corporation; 1981, IBM PC is introduced, © IBM Corporate Archives; 1982, Hayes 300 bps smart modem, Courtesy of Zoom Telephonics, Inc. ; 1983, Box shot of Lotus 1-2-3, © IBM Corporate Archives; 1983, Cover of mag. Announces computer as "Machine of the Year", © Time Life Pictures/Getty Images; 1984, Hewlett-Packard introduces laser-jet printer, Courtesy of Hewlett-Packard Company; 1984, Macintosh computer introduced, Courtesy of Apple Computer, Inc.; 1989, Intel 486 transistor microprocessor, Courtesy of Intel Corporation; 1989, Tim Berners-Lee, © 1997-1998 W3C (MIT, INRIA, Keio); 1992, Screen shot of Windows 3.1, Courtesy of Microsoft Corporation; 1993, Intel Pentium processor chip, Courtesy of Intel Corporation; 1993, photo of the White House, © Costa Cruise Lines/Getty Images; 1994, Screen shot of Netscape Navigator 1.0, Courtesy of Netscape Communications Corporation; 1995, box shot of Windows 95, Box shot reprinted with permission from Microsoft Corporation; 1995, Java logo, Copyright 2005 Sun Microsystems, Inc. All Rights Reserved. Used by permission; 1996, box shot Microsoft Windows NT 4.0 Server, Box shot reprinted with permission from Microsoft Corporation; 1996, PalmPilot, Courtesy of palmOne, Inc. palmOne, Zire, Tungsten, Treo, logos, stylizations and design marks associated with all the preceding, and trade dress associated with palmOne, Inc.'s products, are among the trademarks or registered trademarks owned by or exclusively licensed to palmOne, Inc.; 1997, Intel Pentium II, Courtesy of Intel Corporation; 1997, Teminator CD, Motion Picture & Television Archives; 1997, DVD player, Courtesy of Denon Electronics; 1998, Box shot Windows 98, Box shot reprinted with permission from Microsoft Corporation; 1998, telecommuting, © Andersen Ross/Getty Images; 1998, Apple introduces iMac, Courtesy of Apple Computer, Inc.; 1999, box shot, Microsoft Office 2000, Box shot reprinted with permission from Microsoft Corporation; 2000, Microsoft Windows Me, Box shot reprinted with permission from Microsoft Corporation; 2000, Micrsoft's Windows 2000 Professional, Box shot reprinted with permission from Microsoft Corporation; 2000, telemedicine, © B Busco/Getty Images; 2001, Intel Pentium 4 chip, Courtesy of Intel Corporation; 2001, box shot, Box shot reprinted with permission from Microsoft Corporation; 2001, e-book, Courtesy of RCA/Thomson Consumer Electronics; 2002, Open DVD drive, © Scott Goodwin Photography; 2002, digital video camera, Courtesy of Sharp Electronics; 2002, web cam, Courtesy of Intel Corporation; 2002, Tablet PC, Courtesy of ViewSonic® Corporation; 2002, Handspring TREO, Courtesy of Handspring, Inc.; 2002, Pentium 4 with .13 micron processor, Courtesy of Intel Corporation; 2002, judge with gavel, © Getty Images; 2003, PC with open cd TRAY, Courtesy of Sony Electronics Inc.; 2003, Palm VIIx, Courtesy of palmOne, Inc. palmOne, Zire, Tungsten, Treo, logos, stylizations and design marks associated with all the preceding, and trade dress associated with palmOne, Inc.'s products, are among the trademarks or registered trademarks owned by or exclusively licensed to palmOne, Inc.; 2003, man with notebook computer, ©LWA-JDC/CORBIS; 2003, girl with notebook computer, © Royalty-Free/CORBIS; 2003, child with a PDA, © Jim Cummins/CORBIS; 2003, Man using desktop computer, © Ed Bock/CORBIS; 2003, woman watching plasma tv, © Koichi Kamoshida/Getty Images; 2003, Computer with bugs, © Jeff Nishinaka/Getty Images; 2003, downloading graphic, © Nick Koudis/Getty Images; 2003, Recording Industry Association of America (RIAA), © REUTERS/Mannie Garcia; 2003, box shot, Box shot reprinted with permission from Microsoft Corporation; 2004, lcd monitor, Courtesy of Sony Electronics Inc.; 2004, crt monitor, Courtesy of ViewSonic® Corporation. All rights reserved.; 2004, USB flash drive #1, © Transcend Information Inc. All rights reserved.; 2004, USB flash drive #2, Courtesy of Sandisk Corporation; 2004, RFID tags, Siemens press picture; 2004, front view photo of iMacG5, Courtesy of Apple Computer, Inc.; 2005, FireFox logo, Courtesy of The Mozilla Foundation; 2005, OQO handheld computer, Courtesy of OQO, Inc.; 2005, smart phone, Courtesy of palmOne, Inc. palmOne, Zire, Tungsten, Treo, logos, stylizations and design marks associated with all the preceeding, and trade dress associated with palmOne, Inc.'s products, are among the trademarks or registered trademarks owned by or exclusively licensed to palmOne, Inc.; **Chapter 2:** PY2-1, movie theater, © Ryan McVay/Getty Images; Py2-2, movie theater 2, © Tom Brakefield/Imagestate; PY2-3, PC video camera, Courtesy of Logitech, Inc.; PY2-4, friends sending video message, © Image Source/Imagestate; PY2-5, smartphone, Siemens press picture; PY2-6, smarphone user, © Wilfried Krecichwost/Getty Images; PY2-7, smartphone screen, Courtesy of AT&T Wireless; PY2-8, popcorn, © Ross Durant/FoodPix; Figure 2-01f, instant messaging screen shot, Courtesy of Microsoft Corporation; Looking Ahead 2-1, Internet2 logo, Courtesy of Internet2; Figure 2-02a, Hand holding an internet-enabled smartphone, Siemens press picture; Figure 2-02b, mMode wireless screen for smartphone from AT&T, Courtesy of AT&T Wireless; Figure 2-02c, Woman using desktop computer, © Paul C. Chauncey/CORBIS; Figure 2-02d, Mother and daughter using desktop computer, ©LWA-Dann Tardif/CORBIS; Figure 2-02e, Man using desktop computer, ©LWA-Dann Tardif/CORBIS; Figure 2-02f, Woman using desktop computer, © Paul C. Chauncey/CORBIS; Figure 2-02f, Couple using desktop computer, © Rob Lewine/CORBIS; Figure 2-03 Step 2, cable modem, Courtesy of Motorola, Inc.; Figure 2-03 Step 3, cable modem termination system (CMTS), Courtesy of Terayon Communication Systems, Inc.; Figure 2-03 Step 4, Headquarters of a cable Internet provider, © Stephen Chernin/Getty Images; Figure 2-03 Step 6, Web server, Courtesy of Fujitsu Siemens Computers; Figure 2-07a2, internet-enabled PDA, Courtesy of Sony Electronics Inc.; Figure 2-07b1, Internet-enabled smart phone with Internet screen, Courtesy of AT&T Wireless; Looking Ahead 2-2, 3-D search engine screen, Courtesy of The Princeton Shape Retrieval and Analysis Group, Department of Computer Science, Princeton University; Figure 2-20 Step 2, router, Copyright 2005 Sun Microsystems, Inc. All Rights Reserved. Used by permission.; Figure 2-20 Step 3, desktop PC, Courtesy of Sony Electronics Inc.; Figure 2-24 Step 1, Male thinking, © Yang Liu/CORBIS; Figure 2-24 Step 2, close-up of Male writing, © Romilly Lockyer/Getty Images; Figure 2-24 Step 3, posed headshot of Male, © Yang Liu/CORBIS; Figure 2-25, person holding a credit card and sitting at a computer, © Roy Morsch/CORBIS; Figure 2-27, Woman using notebook computer, © Getty Images; Figure 2-28 Step 1 and 4, desktop computer, Courtesy of Acer America Corp.; Figure 2-28 Step 2, web server, Copyright 2005 Sun Microsystems, Inc. All Rights Reserved. Used by permission.; Figure 2-28 Step 3, Internet router, Courtesy of Juniper Networks, Inc. ; Figure 2-31, talking male (instant messaging), © Dex Images, Inc./CORBIS; Figure 2-32, desktop PC, Courtesy of Acer America Corp.; Figure 2-32, desktop PC, Courtesy of Sony Electronics Inc.; Figure 2-32, desktop PC, © Gateway, Inc.; Figure 2-33a, server, Courtesy of Acer America Corp.; Figure 2-33b, desktop PC, © Gateway, Inc.; Figure 2-34a, DSL modem, Courtesy of D-Link Systems; Figure 2-34b, Phone adapter for Internet telephony service, Courtesy of Vonage; Figure 2-34c, desktop PC, Courtesy of IBM Corporation; Career Corner, Web developer, © Manchan/Getty Images; Technology Trailblazer 1, Tim Berners-Lee, © EPA/Landov; Technology Trailblazer 2, Meg Whitman (CEO of Ebay), © LAURENT FIEVET/AFP/Getty Images; Chapter Review, smart phone, Siemens press picture; Chapter Review, man using cell phone, © Betsie Van der Meer/Getty Images; **Special Feature: Making Use of the Web:** Opener, woman using laptop, © PhotoDisc Collection/Getty Images; Opener, video conference, © Manchan/Getty Images; Opener, students using laptop, © 2005 Masterfile Corporation; Opener, contractor using laptop, © David Oliver/Getty Images; Opener, girls using digital camera, © Via Productions/Brand X Pictures; **Chapter 3:** PY3-01, tablet PC, Courtesy of Agilix Labs Inc.; PY3-02, flight simulator screen from cockpit, Courtesy of Microsoft Game Studios; PY3-03, Microsoft Word 2003 box shot, Word 2003 Box shot(s) reprinted with permission from Microsoft Corporation; PY3-04, Quicken Log-in screen (personal finance software), Courtesy of Intuit Inc. ; PY3-05a, ViewSonic PDA, Courtesy of Microsoft Corporation; PY3-05b, PDA calendar screen, Courtesy of Microsoft Corporation; PY3-06, AOL you've got mail sign, Copyright ©David Young-Wolff/Photo Edit — All rights reserved.; PY3-07, Professor teaching biology class, © Jose Luis Pelaez, Inc./CORBIS; PY3-08, Man using laptop computer in kitchen, Copyright ©Don Smetzer/Photo Edit — All rights reserved.; Figure 3-02a, woman using computer, © Getty Images; Figure 3-02b, laser printer, Courtesy of Xerox Corporation; Figure 3-14, note taking software, Courtesy of Agilix Labs, Inc.; Figure 3-15, current model PDA connected to a desktop computer, Courtesy of Sendo; Figure 3-16, Project Management Software, Courtesy of Microsoft Corporation; Figure 3-17, Accounting Software, Peachtree screen shot courtesy of Best Software SB, Inc.; Figure 3-19, CAD software, Courtesy of Autodesk, Inc.; Figure 3-20, Desktop publishing software (DTP), Courtesy of Adobe; Figure 3-21, Image editing software, Screen shot(s) are © Copyright 2003 Corel Corporation, reprinted by permission.; Figure 3-22, Video editing software, Courtesy of Ulead Systems, Inc.; Figure 3-23, Multimedia authoring software, Courtesy of SumTotal Systems, Inc.; Figure 3-24, Web page authoring software, Courtesy of Macromedia, Inc.; Figure 3-26, person sitting at computer, © Yellow Dog Productions/Getty Images; Figure 3-27, Legal software, © 2003 Riverdeep Interactive Learning Limited, and its licensors.; Figure 3-28, Tax preparation software, Courtesy of Intuit Inc.; Figure 3-30a, output from paint/image editing programs, Courtesy of Jasc Software, Inc.; Figure 3-31, photo editing software, Courtesy of Ulead Systems, Inc.; Figure 3-32, Clip art/image gallery software, © 2003 Riverdeep Interactive Learning Limited, and its licensors.; Figure 3-33, Microsoft's Movie Maker, Courtesy of Microsoft Corporation; Figure 3-34, Home design/landscaping software, © 2003 Riverdeep Interactive Learning Limited, and its licensors.; Figure 3-36, Entertainment software, Courtesy of Microsoft Game Studios; Figure 3-41,

Computer trade Bookstore, © Gary Herrington Photography; Looking Ahead 3-2, Computerized car, © RAINER SCHIMM/ dpa/Landov; Career Corner, Help Desk Specialist (female), © Royalty-Free/CORBIS; Technology Trailblazer 1, Dan Bricklin, © Louis Fabian Bachrach/Daniel Bricklin; Technology Trailblazer 2, Masayoshi Son, © Tom Wagner/Corbis; Chapter Review, box shots, Box shot reprinted with permission from Microsoft® Corporation; **Chapter 4:** PY4-01, Female speaking on phone, © Thinkstock; PY4-02, Male speaking on phone, © Jim McGuire/Indexstock; PY4-03, neighborhood, © Getty Images; PY4-04, can of compressed air, Courtesy of ACL Staticide, Inc., www.aclstaticide.com; PY4-05, antistatic wristband, Courtesy of MARTEK Electronics, www.Martekelec@nc.rr.com; PY4-06, memory module, Courtesy of SimpleTech, Inc.; PY4-07, adapter card, Courtesy of Matrox Graphics Inc.; PY4-08, desktop PC, Courtesy of Acer America Corp.; Figure 4-01a, media center PC, © Gateway, Inc.; Figure 4-01b, 20-inc iMac, Courtesy of Apple Computer, Inc.; Figure 4-01c, laptop, Toshiba America Information Systems, Inc.; Figure 4-01d, Tablet PC - slate style, Courtesy of Microsoft Corporation; Figure 4-01f, PDA, Toshiba America Information Systems, Inc.; Figure 4-01f, smartphone, Courtesy of palmOne, Inc. palmOne, Zire, Tungsten, Treo, logos, stylizations and design marks associated with all the preceding, and trade dress associated with palmOne, Inc.'s products, are among the trademarks or registered trademarks owned by or exclusively licensed to palmOne, Inc.; Figure 4-02a, system unit opened, © Gary Herrinton Photography; Figure 4-02b, Pentium 4 processor, Courtesy of Intel Corporation; Figure 4-02c, memory chips on a module, Courtesy of SMART Modular Technologies, Inc.© 2002; Figure 4-02d, sound card, Courtesy of Creative Labs, Inc. Copyright © 2003 Creative Technology Ltd. (SOUND BLASTER AUDIGY 2S). All rights reserved.; Figure 4-02e, video card (graphics card), Courtesy of Matrox Graphics Inc.; Figure 4-03, motherboard, © Gary Herrington Photography; Figure 4-05, student working on a computer, © Image Source/Imagestate; Looking Ahead 4-1, U.S. Plans World's Fastest Computer, © Denis Scott/CORBIS; Figure 4-08a1, Intel Itanium 2 processor, Courtesy of Intel Corporation; Figure 4-08a2, Intel® Xeon™ Processor MP for Multi-Processor Servers, Courtesy of Intel Corporation; Figure 4-08a3, Opteron processor, Courtesy of Advanced Micro Devices, Inc.; Figure 4-08a4, Athlon MP processor, Courtesy of Advanced Micro Devices, Inc.; Figure 4-08b1, Intel Pentium4 Extreme Edition processor (for power users), Courtesy of Intel Corporation; Figure 4-08b2, Athlon 64 FX (for power users), Courtesy of Advanced Micro Devices, Inc.; Figure 4-08c1, Intel Celeron Processor At 1.7 GHz (for home users), Courtesy of Intel Corporation; Figure 4-08c2, Sempron processor (for desktop computers, home users), Courtesy of Advanced Micro Devices, Inc.; Figure 4-08d1, Mobile Intel® Pentium® 4 Processor-M (for mobile computers), Courtesy of Intel Corporation; Figure 4-08d2, Efficeon™ TM8600 processor (for mobile computers), Courtesy of Transmeta Corporation; Figure 4-08d3, Sempron Mobile Processor, Courtesy of Advanced Micro Devices, Inc.; Figure 4-09, heatsink on motherboard, © Gary Herrington Photography; Figure 4-14a, keyboard, Courtesy of Logitech; Figure 4-14b, open system unit, © Gary Herrington Photography; Figure 4-14c, monitor, Courtesy of ViewSonic Corporation; Figure 4-15, seats in a concert hall/auditorium, © Jeremy Walker/Getty Images; Figure 4-17a, hard-disk, Courtesy of Seagate Technology; Figure 4-17b, memory module of RAM, Courtesy of Kingston Technology Company, Inc. ; Figure 4-17c, flat-screen monitor, Courtesy of ViewSonic® Corporation; Figure 4-18a, hands installing a memory module in a memory slot on a motherboard, © Gary Herrington Photography; Figure 4-18b, DIMM memory module, Courtesy of Kingston Technology Company, Inc.; Figure 4-21a, 256 MB flash memory MP3 player, MPIO FY200 (www.mpio.com); Figure 4-21b, inside of mp3 player from above, MPIO FY200 (www.mpio.com); Figure 4-23a, person blinking - eye open, © Royalty-Free/CORBIS; Figure 4-23b, person blinking - eye closed, © Royalty-Free/CORBIS; Figure 4-25, adapter card being inserted on motherboard, © Gary Herrington Photography; Figure 4-26, PC card sticking out of laptop computer, © Gary Herrington Photography; Figure 4-27, flash memory devices, Courtesy of Kingston Technology Company, Inc. ; Figure 4-28, the backside and front side ports on a media center PC, © 2004 Tim Gilman; Figure 4-33a, communicating with a computer with an IrDA port, Courtesy of Acer America Corp.; Figure 4-33b, smartphone w/IrDA port, Courtesy of Nokia; Figure 4-34, Bluetooth communications, Courtesy of Sony Ericsson Mobile Communications AB. All rights reserved.; Figure 4-35a, Pentium 4 chip, Courtesy of Intel Corporation; Figure 4-35b, memory module, Courtesy of Kingston Technology Company, Inc.; Figure 4-36, system unit, Courtesy of Fujitsu Siemens Computers; Figure 4-37a, Notebook computer, © Gary Herrington Photography; Figure 4-37b, PDA with flash card, Courtesy of ASUSTeK Computer Inc.; Figure 4-37c, Smartphone with flash memory card, Courtesy of Sendo; Figure 4-38, ports on laptop computer, Courtesy of Fujitsu Siemens Computers; Figure 4-39, ports on a convertible tablet PC (left-side view), Courtesy of Acer America Corp.; Looking Ahead 4-2, DNA Computer Works to Fight Cancer, Courtesy of Shlomit Davidzon, Graphics department, Weizmann Institute of Science.; Figure 4-40a, home user, © Jose Luis Pelaez, Inc./CORBIS; Figure 4-40b, home office, © Britt Erlanson/Getty Images; Figure 4-40c, laptop user, © Andersen-Ross/Brand X Pictures; Figure 4-40d, Power user, © Richard T. Nowitz/CORBIS; Figure 4-40e, users in a large office, © Comstock Images; Figure 4-41a, lint-free computer wipes, Courtesy of Fellowes, Inc.; Figure 4-41b, rubbing alcohol, Courtesy of First-Aid-Product.com, a division of American CPR; Figure 4-41c, mini computer vacuum, Courtesy of Belkin Corporation; Figure 4-41d, mini computer screwdriver, Courtesy of Fellowes, Inc.; Figure 4-41e, cleaning inside of system unit, © Gary Herrington Photography; FAQ 4-08, bluetooth table, Source: In-Stat/MDR; Career Corner, Computer Engineer, © Stephen Derr/Getty Images; Technology Trailblazer 1, Jack Kilby, © CORBIS SYGMA; Technology Trailblazer 2, Gordon Moore, © Andy Rain/Bloomberg News/Landov; **Chapter 5:** PY5-01, young woman teaching mother the computer, © Larry Dale Gordon/Getty Images; PY5-02, hands using wireless mouse/keyboard, © Tom Merton/ Getty Images; PY5-03, scissors cutting telephone, © Richard Schneider/Getty Images; PY5-04, CompUSA store, Copyright © Bonnie Kamin/Photo Edit — All rights reserved.; PY5-05, pen, Courtesy of Nokia; PY5-06, Nokia lifeblog smartphone, Courtesy of Nokia; PY5-07, screen-shot for symbian-based smartphone, Courtesy of UIQ Technology; PY5-08, digital cameras on store shelf, Copyright ©Tony Freeman/Photo Edit — All rights reserved.; Figure 5-01a, hands typing on keyboard, © Gary Buss/Getty Images; Figure 5-01b, hand holding mouse, © Premium Stock/Imagestate; Figure 5-01c, wheel, Courtesy of Logitech; Figure 5-01c, joystick, Courtesy of Logitech; Figure 5-01d, hand using touchscreen kiosk, Courtesy of 3M Touch Systems; Figure 5-01e1, hand using digital pen on tablet PC, Courtesy of Agilix Labs Inc.; Figure 5-01e2, hand using stylus on smartphone, Courtesy of Sony Ericsson Mobile Communications AB. All rights reserved.; Figure 5-01e3, person using digital pen on graphics tablet, © Andersen-Ross/Getty Images; Figure 5-01f, person talking to microphone headset in front of monitor, © Comstock Images; Figure 5-01g, photo editing software, Courtesy of Adobe; Figure 5-01g, digital camera, Courtesy of Umax Systems GmbH; Figure 5-01g, lcd monitor, Courtesy of Sony Electronics Inc.; Figure 5-01h, smartphone with picture on screen, Courtesy of Sony Ericsson Mobile Communications AB. All rights reserved.; Figure 5-01i, person using PC video camera, © Jose Luis Pelaez, Inc./CORBIS; Figure 5-01j, document in scanner, Courtesy of Epson America, Inc.; Figure 5-01k1, Optical marks and characters, © Michelle Joyce/Index Stock Imagery; Figure 5-01k2, OCR characters, Copyright ©Bill Aron/Photo Edit — All rights reserved.; Figure 5-01l1, grocery store scanner, Copyright ©NOVASTOCK/Photo Edit — All rights reserved.; Figure 5-01l2, handheld scanner, © Royalty-Free/CORBIS; Figure 5-01m, RFID reader, Courtesy of Gilbarco Veeder-Root Inc.; Figure 5-01n, MICR characters on a check, Copyright ©Myrleen Ferguson Cate/Photo Edit — All rights reserved.; Figure 5-01o, data collection device, Courtesy of Symbol Technologies; Figure 5-01p1, hand inserting card into ATM, © Thinkstock; Figure 5-01p2, hand swiping credit card in reader, © James Leynse/CORBIS; Figure 5-01q, finger in fingerprint scanner, © Stephen Chernin/Getty Images; Figure 5-01r, eyeball in iris scanner (biometric input), © William Thomas Cain/Getty Images; Figure 5-02, internet keyboard, Courtesy of Logitech; Figure 5-04a, COLLAGE: bluetooth keyboard, Courtesy of Microsoft Corporation; Figure 5-04b, COLLAGE: Bluetooth receiver, Courtesy of Belkin Corporation; Figure 5-04c, COLLAGE: cable plugged in a USB port on system unit, © Gary Herrington Photography; Figure 5-06a, optical mouse, Courtesy of Microsoft Corporation; Figure 5-06b, laser cordless mouse, Courtesy of Logitech; Figure 5-08, hand using trackball, © Comstock Images; Figure 5-09a, finger using touchpad, © Comstock Images; Figure 5-10a, finger using touchstick/pointing stick, Courtesy of IBM Corporation; Figure 5-10b, finger using touchstick, © Getty Images; Figure 5-11a, wheel, Courtesy of Logitech; Figure 5-11b, joystick, Courtesy of Logitech; Figure 5-12, person using light pen, © Royalty-Free/CORBIS; Figure 5-13, touchscreen voting machine, © REUTERS/Jim Ruymen/Landov; Figure 5-14, person touching screen on a smart phone with stylus, Courtesy of Sony Ericsson Mobile Communications AB. All rights reserved; Figure 5-15, tablet PC's use pressure sensitive pen, Courtesy of Wacom Technology Corp.; Figure 5-16a, person using a graphics tablet with a pen, Courtesy of Wacom Technology Corp.; Figure 5-16b, person using a cursor on a digitizer, © Comstock Images; Figure 5-17, digital pens have built-in digital cameras, Courtesy of Logitech; Figure 5-18, person talking into headset and looking at computer, © Comstock Images; Figure 5-19, person using a musical instrument to record music into a computer, © Gerard Fritz/Imagestate; Figure 5-20a, PDA with a color screen and attachments, Courtesy of ViewSonic® Corporation; Figure 5-20b, stylus, Courtesy of ViewSonic® Corporation; Figure 5-20c, pen/stylus combination, Courtesy of Belkin Corporation; Figure 5-20d, PDA digital camera, Courtesy of LifeView, Inc.; Figure 5-20e, pen input, Courtesy of Seiko Instruments USA Inc.; Figure 5-20f, PDA scanner, Courtesy of Socket Communications, Inc.; Figure 5-20g, desktop computer, Courtesy of IBM Corporation; Figure 5-20gh, screen-shot from Handmark, Courtesy of Handmark, Inc.; Figure 5-20h, PDA connected, Courtesy of ViewSonic® Corporation; Figure 5-21, portable keyboard opening up, Courtesy of Think Outside Inc.; Figure 5-22, smartphone, © Edward Bock/CORBIS; Figure 5-23, tablet PC, Courtesy of Motion Computing, Inc.; Figure 5-24, person using a digital camera, © Steven Puetzer/Masterfile; Figure 5-25a, digital camera, front and back, Courtesy of Sony Electronics Inc.; Figure 5-25, memory stick, Courtesy of Sony Electronics Inc.; Figure 5-26, girl with microphone, © Getty Images; Figure 5-27, transferring video to desktop or laptop computer, Courtesy of Sony Electronics Inc.; Figure 5-28, home user using PC video camera to communicate, Copyright ©David Young-Wolff/Photo Edit — All rights reserved.; Figure 5-29, business people having a video conference, © Steve Chenn/ CORBIS; Figure 5-30a, flatbed scanner, Courtesy of Umax Systems GmbH; Figure 5-30b, Pen scanner, Courtesy of C Technologies AB; figure 5-30c, sheet-fed scanner, Courtesy of Visioneer, Inc.; Figure 5-30d, Drum Scanner, Howtek HiResolve 8000 Drum Scanner, image courtesy of Howtek, Inc.; Figure 5-31a, flatbed scanner, Courtesy of Umax Systems GmbH; Figure 5-31b, desktop computer, Courtes of Acer America Corp.; Figure 5-33, ocr characters on a bill, Copyright ©Bill Aron/Photo Edit — All rights reserved; Figure 5-34a, barcode scanner, grocery, Copyright ©David Young-Wolff/Photo Edit — All rights reserved.; Figure 5-34b, barcode scanner book, Copyright ©Colin Young-Wolff/Photo Edit — All rights reserved.; Figure 5-35, uPC code on product close-up, Copyright ©Susan Van Etten/Photo Edit — All rights reserved.; Figure 5-36, RFID tag, Courtesy of Tibbett & Britten Group; Looking Ahead 5-1, Smart Dust Monitors the Environmen, B.A. Warneke, M.D. Scott, B.S. Leibowitz, L. Zhou, C.L. Bellew, J.A. Chediak, J.M. Kahn, B.E. Boser, K.S.J. Pister, "An Autonomous 16mm3 Solar-Powered Node for Distributed Wireless Sensor Networks," IEEE International Conference on Sensors 2002, Orlando, FL, June 12-14, 2002."; Figure 5-37, magnetic stripe on credit card, Copyright ©Spencer Grant/Photo Edit; Figure 5-39, handheld computer, which includes a bar code reader, Courtesy of Symbol Technologies; Figure 5-40, self serve grocery store checkout, Copyright ©Dennis MacDonald/Photo Edit — All rights reserved.; Figure 5-41, person using ATM, © Steve Dunwell/Index Stock Imagery; Figure 5-42, fingerprint scanner, © William Thomas Cain/Getty Images; Figure 5-43, hand geometry system, Courtesy of Recognition Systems, Inc.; Figure 5-44, IRIS recognition system, © BORIS ROESSLER/dpa/Landov; Figure 5-45a, smart card reader, Courtesy of Athena Smartcard Solutions - www.athena-scs.com; Figure 5-45b, smart card that shows microprocessor, Courtesy of Athena Smartcard Solutions - www.athena-scs.com; Figure 5-46a, home user, © Jose Luis Pelaez, Inc./CORBIS; Figure 5-46b, home office, © Britt Erlanson/ Getty Images; Figure 5-46c, laptop user, © Andersen-Ross/Brand X Pictures; Figure 5-46d, Power user, © Richard T. Nowitz/ CORBIS; Figure 5-46e, users in a large office, © Comstock Images; Figure 5-47, Keyguard, Courtesy of Keytools Ltd.; Figure 5-49, head-mounted pointer (Receiver/camera on desktop PC), Courtesy of NaturalPoint, Inc.; Looking Ahead 5-2, Wearable Computers, © Webb Chappell; Career Corner, Data entry clerk, © Romilly Lockyer/Getty Images; Technology Trailblazer, Hideki Komiyama, © Steven Henry/Getty Images; Technology Trailblazer, Douglas Engelbart, © AP/WIDE WORLD PHOTOS; EOC, woman using laptop, © D Betty/PhotoLink/Getty Images; **Special Feature: Personal Mobile Devices:** Intro 1, woman using PDA, © Juan Silva/Getty Images; Intro 2, two PDA users, Courtesy of Sendo; Figure 01a, physician using Palm device, © Wayne Eardley/ Masterfile; Figure 01b, person using Windows Pocket PC Phone Edition, © Digital Vision; Figure 01c, Salesperson using smartphone, Courtesy of Sendo; Figure 01d, Executiveusing Blackberry., Courtesy of Research In Motion (RIM); Figure 02a, Personal mobile device operating systems, Courtesy of Nokia; Figure 02b, Personal mobile device operating systems, Courtesy of Research In Motion (RIM); Figure 03a, Accesories for Personal Mobile Devices — Bluetooth headset, © THOMAS SCHULZE/ DPA/Landov; Figure 03b, Accesories for Personal Mobile Devices — WiFi Card, Courtesy of SanDisk Corporation; Figure 03b, screen-shot for PDA device, Courtesy of Microsoft Corporation; Figure 03c, Accesories for Personal Mobile Devices — GPS device for PDA, Courtesy of Garmin Ltd.; Figure 03d, Accesories for Personal Mobile Devices — keyboard, Courtesy of Belkin Corporation; Figure 03e, Accesories for Personal Mobile Devices — car charger for PDA, Courtesy of Belkin Corporation; Figure 04a, built-in personal mobile devices software, Courtesy of palmOne, Inc. palmOne, Zire, Tungsten, Treo, logos, stylizations and design marks associated with all the preceding, and trade dress associated with palmOne, Inc.'s products, are among the trademarks or registered trademarks owned by or exclusively licensed to palmOne, Inc.; Figure 06, businessperson using mobile device, © P. Scholey/Masterfile; Figure 07a, person using PDA that looks wireless with antenna, © Rick Gomez/Masterfile; Figure 07b, communications software for personal mobile devices - SnapperMail, Courtesy of Snapperfish Ltd. SnapperMail, Snapperfish, FingerNav, StylusNav and their respective logos are trademarks of Snapperfish Ltd.; Figure 08a, policeman using PDA, Courtesy of Symbol Technologies; Figure 08b, army personnel using PDA's in Kuwait, 2004, © STAN HONDA/AFP/Getty Images; Figure 09, doctor using PDA, © Masterfile; Figure 10a, farmer using PDA, © David Frazier/The Image Works; Figure 10a, doctor using PDA with scanner, Courtesy of Symbol Technologies; Figure 11a, man using PDA for travel, © Digital Vision; Figure 12a, student using PDA, © AP/WIDE WORLD PHOTOS; Figure 12b, librarian holding PDA with book title on screen, © AP/WIDE WORLD PHOTOS; Figure 12c, educational software for personal mobile devices, Courtesy of Handmark Inc.; Figure 14, entertainment software for personal mobile devices, Courtesy of Handmark Inc.; Figure 16a, Panasonic X700 smartphone from Symbian, Courtesy of Symbian Ltd.; Figure 16b, Danger HipTop "2hands_sidekick" image, Courtesy of Danger, Inc.; Figure 16c, smart phone, Courtesy of Microsoft® Corporation; **Chapter 6:** PY6-01, friends having dinner, ©Mary Kate Denny/PhotoEdit Inc.; PY6-02, bank online, © Royalty-Free/CORBIS; PY6-03, woman's hands printing, © AP/WIDE WORLD PHOTOS; PY6-04, notebook computer and package, © AP/WIDE WORLD PHOTOS; PY6-05, calendar stock for photo printer, Courtesy of Xerox Corporation; PY6-06, LCD monitor, Courtesy of Sony Electronics Inc.; PY6-07, photo printer paper, Courtes of Epson America Inc.; PY6-08, labels for photo printer, Courtesy of Xerox Corporation; PY6-09, card stock for photo printer, Courtesy of Sony Electronics Inc.; Figure 6-1a1, PDA with text on screen, Courtesy of Toshiba America Information Systems, Inc.; Figure 6-1a2, screen shot, Courtesy of Handmark, Inc.; Figure 6-1a3, Laser printer, Courtesy of TallyGenicom; Figure 6-1a4, LCD monitor, Courtesy of BenQ America Corp.; Figure 6-1b1, Tablet PC, Courtesy of Motion Computing; Figure 6-01b1, screen-shot for tablet PC, Courtesy of Microsoft Corporation; Figure 6-1b2, Photo printer, Courtesy of Epson America, Inc.; Figure 6-1b3, PDA, Courtesy of Microsoft Corporation; Figure 6-1b3, screen for PDA, Courtesy of Handmark, Inc.; Figure 6-1c1, Speakers, Courtesy of Logitech; Figure 6-1c2, smartphone with earphones, Courtesy of Sony Ericsson; Figure 6-01d1, CRT monitor, Courtesy of ViewSonic® Corporation; Figure 6-1d2, smart phone, Courtesy of Sony Ericsson Mobile Communications AB. All rights reserved.; Figure 6-02, LCD monitor, Courtesy of NEC-Mitsubishi Electronics Display of America Inc.; Figure 6-03, multiple LCD monitors, Courtesy of ViewSonic® Corporation; Figure 6-04a, notebook, Courtesy of Acer America Corp.; Figure 6-04b, TabletPC, Courtesy of Acer America Corp.; Figure 6-04c, PDA with color screen, Courtesy of Sony Electronics Inc.; Figure 6-04d, smart phone with color screen, Siemens press picture; Figure 6-06, video card, "FireGL™ V5100 is[are] used under license and is [are] a registered trademark[s] or trademark[s] of ATI Technologies Inc. in the United States and other countries."; Looking Ahead 6-1, pliable organic light-emitting diodes "OLED", Courtesy of Universal Display Corp.; Figure 6-07, gas plasma monitor, Courtesy of

BenQ America Corp.; Figure 6-08, HDTV monitor, © Gene Blevins/LA Daily News/Corbis; Figure 6-09, CRT monitor, Courtesy of NEC-Mitsubishi Electronics Display of America Inc.; Figure 6-13a1, USB plug, © David Muir/Masterfile; Figure 6-13a2, parallel plug, © Royalty-Free/CORBIS; Figure 6-13a3, printer connected to computer with a cable, © Chuck Savage/CORBIS; Figure 6-13b1, printer printing via Bluetooth, Courtesy of Nokia; Figure 6-13b2, printer printing via infrared, © OSHIKAZU TSUNO/AFP/Getty Images; Figure 6-13c, printer connected to a network, ©David Young-Wolff/Photo Edit Inc.; Figure 6-13d, printer printing from camera via a cable, Courtesy of Sony Electronics Inc.; Figure 6-13e, camera in docking station printer, Courtesy of Eastman Kodak Company; Figure 6-13f, printer printing from media card, Courtesy of Epson America, Inc.; Figure 6-13g, digital camera that has a compact flash card slot, QV3000EX camera photo courtesy of Casio Inc.; Figure 6-14a, ink-jet printer with various output, Courtesy of Epson America, Inc.; Figure 6-16, printer with top open, © Gary Herrington Photography; Figure 6-17a, printer that just prints 4 x 6, Courtesy of Epson America, Inc.; Figure 6-17b, printer that prints up to 8x10, Courtesy of Epson America, Inc.; Figure 6-17c, printer that prints up to 13 x 19, Courtesy of Epson America, Inc.; Figure 6-18a, black/white laser printer, Courtesy of Xerox Corporation; Figure 6-18b, color laser printer, Courtesy of Xerox Corporation; Figure 6-20a, dye sublimation printer for professionals, Courtesy of Mitsubishi Digital Electronics America, Inc.; Figure 6-20a2, output for professional dye sub printer, © Mel Yates/Getty Images; Figure 6-20a2, output for professional dye sub printer, © Mel Yates/Getty Images; Figure 6-20b, dye sublimation printer for home, Courtesy of Sony Electronics Inc.; Figure 6-21, mobile printer, Courtesy of Canon USA Inc.; Figure 6-22, label printer, Courtesy of Seiko Instruments USA Inc.; Figure 6-23, large format printer, Courtesy of MacDermid ColorSpan, Inc.; Figure 6-24, dot matrix printer, Courtesy of Oki Data Amercas, Inc.; Figure 6-25, line printer, Courtesy of Printronix, Inc.; Figure 6-26, PC with 5:1 stereo speakers and a woofer, Courtesy of Mind Computer Products; Figure 6-27, people wearing headsets at computer, ©Jeff Greenberg/PhotoEdit Inc.; figure 6-29, person using fax machine, © John A Rizzo/Getty Images; Figure 6-30a, laptop, Courtesy of MPC Computers, LLC.; Figure 6-30b, PC card fax modem, Courtesy of U.S. Robotics Corporation; Figure 6-30c, fax machine, ©Spencer Grant/Photo Edit Inc.; Figure 6-30d, PC, Courtesy of MPC Computers, LLC.; Figure 6-31, multifunction peripheral — fax, copier, printer, scanner, Courtesy of Xerox Corporation; Figure 6-32, data projector, Courtesy of InFocus® Corporation; Looking Ahead 6-2, Digital Cinema Just the Right Picture, © Nick Koudis/Getty Images; Figure 6-33a, Forcefeed joystick, Courtesy of Logitech; Figure 6-33b, Forcefeedback wheel, Courtesy of Microsoft Corporation; Figure 6-34a, home user, © Jose Luis Pelaez, Inc./CORBIS; Figure 6-34b, home office, © Britt Erlanson/Getty Images; Figure 6-34c, laptop user, © Andersen-Ross/Brand X Pictures; Figure 6-34d, Power user, © Richard T. Nowitz/CORBIS; Figure 6-34e, users in a large office, © Comstock Images; Figure 6-36A, braille printer, Courtesy of Enabling Technologies; Figure 6-36b, close-up of finger reading braille, © Don Farrall/Getty Images; Figure 6-37, Intel pentium 4, Courtesy of Intel Corporation; Career Corner, graphic designer, © Robert Llewellyn/Imagestate; Technology Trailblazer 1, Steve Jobs, © Fujifotos/The Image Works; Technology Trailblazer 2, Donna Dubinsky, © AP/WIDE WORLD PHOTOS; **Special Feature: Digital Imaging and Video Technology:** Intro 1, family at beach, © Comstock Images; Intro 2, graduation, © Comstock Images; Intro 3, Asian girls getting picture taken, © Tim Pannell/CORBIS; Figure 01a, Digital camera, Courtesy of Nikon USA; Figure 01b, Digital video camera, Courtesy of Sony Electronics Inc.; Figure 01c, Television, Courtesy of BenQ America Corp.; Figure 01d, Personal computer, Courtesy of Sony Electronics Inc.; Figure 01e, Photographic-quality printer, Courtesy of Canon USA Inc.; Figure 01f, DVD recorder, Courtesy of Sony Electronics Inc.; Figure01f2, DVD, © Spike Mafford/Getty Images; Figure 01g, VCR, Courtesy of JVC Company of America; Figure 01h, action shot, © Getty Images; Figure 01i, Person using digital camera, © Tim Kiusalaas/Masterfile; Figure 01j, Person using digital video camera, © J. Fisher/Zefa/Masterfile; Figure 02a, Point and shoot camera, Courtesy of Sony Electronics Inc.; Figure 02b, field digital camera, Courtesy of Canon U.S.A, Inc.; Figure 02c, studio digital camera, Courtesy of Canon U.S.A, Inc.; Figure 05a, microdrive, Courtesy of Hitachi Global Storage Technologies; Figure 05b, Compact Flash, Courtesy of Lexar Media, Inc.; Figure 05c, memory stick 1 GB, Courtesy of Sony Electronics Inc.; Figure 06, FireWire Compact Flash Card Reader, Courtesy of SanDisk Corporation; Figure 08, photo kiosk, Courtesy of Pixel Magic Imaging™, Inc.; Figure 09, photo slide show software, Courtesy of Ulead Systems, Inc.; Figure 10a, high-end consumer digital video camera, Courtesy of Sony Electronics Inc.; figure 10b, consumer digital video camera, Courtesy of Sony Electronics Inc.; Figure 10c, webcasting and monitoring digital video camera, Courtesy of Logitech; Figure 11a, PC, Courtesy of Sony Electronics Inc.; Figure 11b, screen photos, © Royalty-Free/CORBIS ; Figure 11c, Digital video camera, Courtesy of Sony Electronics Inc.; Figure 12a, S-VCR, Courtesy of JVC Company of America; Figure 12b, video capture card (PCi card), Courtesy of Pinnacle Systems, Inc.; Figure 12c, analog camera, Courtesy of Matsushita Electric Corporation of America; Figure 12d, screen image, © Chase Jarvis/Getty Images; Figure 12e, PC, Courtesy of Sony Electronics Inc.; Figure 15, DivX codec, Courtesy of DivXNetworks, Inc.; Figure 16, Color correction for video editing (screen), Screenshot reprinted by permission from Apple Computer, Inc.; Figure 17, video editing "sequencing" screen-shot — Windows Movie Maker, Courtesy of Microsoft Corporation; Figure 18a, Video editing "transitions", Courtesy of Microsoft Corporation; Figure 19, screen-shot, Courtesy of Pinnacle Systems, Inc.; **Chapter 7:** PY7-01, job interview, © Noel Hendrickson/Masterfile; PY7-02, photojournalists, © Photodisc Collection; PY7-03, mini storage media, Courtesy of SanDisk Corporation; PY7-04, card reader, Courtesy of Delkin Devices, Inc.; PY7-05, compact flash, Courtesy of Lexar Media, Inc.; PY7-06, Sandisk 2GB, Courtesy of SanDisk Corporation; PY7-07, keychain USB, Courtesy of Kingston Technology Company, Inc.; PY7-08, photo station in store, Courtesy of Sony Electronics Inc.; PY7-09, print photos on HP printer, © RICK MAIMAN/Bloomberg News/Landov; PY7-10, newspaper printing, Copyright ©NOVASTOCK/Photo Edit — All rights reserved.; Figure 7-1a, Inserting a floppy disk, © Masterfile; Figure 7-1b, Zip disk sticking out of drive, Photo Courtesy of Iomega Corporation. Copyright © 2003 Iomega Corporation. All Rights Reserved. Zip is a registered trademark in the United States and/or other countries. Iomega, the stylized "i" logo and product images are property of Iomega Corporation in the United States and/or other countries.; Figure 7-1c, SATA (serial ATA) hard disk, Courtesy of Western Digital; Figure 7-01d, miniature hard disk, Courtesy of Toshiba America Information Systems, Inc.; Figure 7-1e, external hard drive, Courtesy of Seagate Technology; Figure 7-1f, CD-ROM/DVD-ROM, Courtesy of Fujitsu Siemens Computers; Figure 7-1g, tape cassette and tape drive, Courtesy of Quantum Corp.; Figure 7-1h, PC card product shot, Courtesy of SimpleTech, Inc.; Figure 7-1i, media card in PDA, Courtesy of ASUSTEK Computer, Inc.; Figure 7-1j, USB flash drive, Courtesy of M-Systems Flash Disk Pioneers Ltd.; Figure 7-1k, microfiche, Copyright ©Bill Aron/Photo Edit — All rights reserved.; Figure 7-05, internal hard disk, Courtesy of Western Digital; Figure 7-06a, person inserting floppy disk into PC, Courtesy of Quantum Corp.; Figure 7-06b, external floppy disk drive, Photo Courtesy of Iomega Corporation. Copyright © 2003 Iomega Corporation. All Rights Reserved. Zip is a registered trademark in the United States and/or other countries. Iomega, the stylized "i" logo and product images are property of Iomega Corporation in the United States and/or other countries.; Figure 7-09a, Iomega 750 MB Zip disk and drive, Photo Courtesy of Iomega Corporation. Copyright © 2003 Iomega Corporation. All Rights Reserved. Zip is a registered trademark in the United States and/or other countries. Iomega, the stylized "i" logo and product images are property of Iomega Corporation in the United States and/or other countries.; Figure 7-10a, system unit opened with SATA hard disk, © 2004 Tim Gilman; Figure 7-10b, SATA hard disk, Courtesy of Western Digital; Looking Ahead 7-1, Heat Increases Disk Capacity, Courtesy of IBM Corporation; Figure 7-12, SATA hard disk, Courtesy of Maxtor Corporation. © 2004 Maxtor Corporation. All rights reserved.; Figure 7-15a, processor chip, Coutesy of Intel Corporation; Figure 7-16, Mini hard disk, Courtesy of Toshiba America Information Systems, Inc.; Figure 7-17a, external hard disk drive plugged into a computer, Courtesy of Fujitsu Siemens Computers; Figure 7-17b, removable hard disk drive, Photo Courtesy of Iomega Corporation. Copyright © 2003 Iomega Corporation. All Rights Reserved. Zip is a registered trademark in the United States and/or other countries. Iomega, the stylized "i" logo and product images are property of Iomega Corporation in the United States and/or other countries.; Figure 7-23a, Dictionary CD-ROM, Courtesy of Merriam-Webster; Figure 7-23b, CD-R (box shot), Courtesy of Memorex Products, Inc.; Figure 7-23c, CD-RW box shot, Courtesy of Memorex

Products, Inc.; Figure 7-23d1, TopoUSA DVD-ROM, © 2004 DeLorme (www.delorme.com) Topo USA®; Figure 7-23d2, DVD-ROM (disk), © 2004 DeLorme (www.delorme.com) Topo USA®; Figure 7-23e1, DVD-R (box shot), Courtesy of Memorex Products, Inc.; Figure 7-23e2, DVD+R (box shot), Courtesy of Memorex Products, Inc.; Figure 7-23f1, DVD-RW (box shot), Courtesy of Memorex Products, Inc.; Figure 7-23f2, DVD+RW (box shot), Courtesy of Memorex Products, Inc.; Figure 7-23f3, DVD-RAM (box shot), Courtesy of Memorex Products, Inc.; Figure 7-24c, stack of CD Roms, © Gary Herrington Photography; Figure 7-25a, photo processing envelope with Photo CD check box, Courtesy of AR Photo Research; Figure 7-25b, picture CD with envelope of processed pictures, Courtesy of AR Photo Research; Figure 7-25c, Kodak picture kiosk, © Steven Brahms/Bloomberg News/Landov; Figure 7-25d1, flat panel monitor with photo editing software, Courtesy of NEC Solutions (America), Inc.; Figure 7-25d2, photo editing software, Courtesy of Ulead Systems, Inc.; Figure 7-25d, photo editing software, © Steven Brahms/Bloomberg News/Landov; Figure 7-26a, TopoUSA screen shot for LCD monitor, © 2004 DeLorme (www.delorme.com) Topo USA®; Figure 7-26b, TopoUSA DVD software disc, © 2004 DeLorme (www.delorme.com) Topo USA®; Looking Ahead 7-2, Paper Disks Offer Increased Capacity, © YOSHIKAZU TSUNO/AFP/Getty Images); Figure 7-28, tape cartridge and tape drive, Courtesy of Sony Electronics Inc.; Figure 7-29a, PC card sticking out of laptop computer, Courtesy of Toshiba America Information Systems, Inc.; Figure 7-31a, USB flash drive in desktop computer, Courtesy of Fujitsu Siemens Computers; Figure 7-31b, card reader in notebook computer, Courtesy of SanDisk Corporation; Figure 7-31c, miniature storage media sticking out of PDA, Courtesy of Sandisk Corporation; Figure 7-31c2, miniature storage media sticking out of PDA, Courtesy of palmOne, Inc. palmOne, Zire, Tungsten, Treo, logos, stylizations and design marks associated with all the preceeding, and trade dress assocated with palmOne, Inc.'s products, are among the trademarks or registered trademarks owned by or exclusively licensed to palmOne, Inc.; Figure 7-31d, smartcard for access control, Siemens press picture; Figure 7-31e1, digital photo viewer with a card sticking out, Courtesy of Delkin Devices, Inc.; Figure 7-31e2, TV, Courtesy of JVC Company of America; Figure 7-32a, CompactFlash 4.0 Sandisk, Courtesy of Sandisk Corporation; Figure 7-32b, SmartMedia 32MB to 128MB, Courtesy of Sandisk Corporation; Figure 7-32c, SecureDigital card 64MB to 1 GB, Courtesy of Sandisk Corporation; Figure 7-32d, 1G xD-Picture Card 64 MB to 512 MB, Courtesy of Lexar Media, Inc.; Figure 7-32e, memory stick 256MB to 2GB, Courtesy of Sandisk Corporation; Figure 7-33, SD card reader, Courtesy of Delkin Devices, Inc.; Figure 7-33b, SD card 1GB, Courtesy of Delkin Devices, Inc.; Figure 7-34, USB flash drive, Photo courtesy of Iomega Corporation. Copyright © 2003 Iomega Corporation. All Rights Reserved. Zip is a registered trademark in the United States and/or other countries. Iomega, the stylized "i" logo and product images are property of Iomega Corporation in the United States and/or other countries; Figure 7-35, smart card in use, © Jean-Yves Bruel/Masterfile; Figure 7-36a, microfilm in microfilm reader, Copyright ©Bill Aron/Photo Edit — All rights reserved.; Figure 7-36b, microfilm in roll, Copyright ©Bill Aron/Photo Edit — All rights reserved.; Figure 7-38a, home user, © Jose Luis Pelaez, Inc./CORBIS; Figure 7-38b, home office, © Britt Erlanson/Getty Images; Figure 7-38c, laptop user, © Andersen-Ross/Brand X Pictures; Figure 7-38d, Power user, © Richard T. Nowitz/CORBIS; Figure 7-38e, users in a large office, © Comstock Images; Career Corner, Computer Technician, © Noel Hendrickson/Masterfile; Technology Trailblazer 1, Al Shugart, Courtesy of Al Shugart International; Technology Trailblazer 2, Mark Dean, Courtesy of IBM Research; **Chapter 8:** PY8-01, college students talking outside, © Mark Scott/Getty Images; PY8-02, new mail message screen, © VCL/Spencer Rowell/Getty Images; PY8-03, distraught female looking at computer, © Paul Thomas/Getty Images; PY8-04, female hand holding a phone, © Masterfile Royalty-free; PY8-05, distraught male on phone, Lawrence Lawry/PhotoDisc/Getty Images; PY8-07, Norton Internet Security boxshot, Courtesy of Symantec; PY8-08, Windows XP boxshot, Courtesy of Microsoft Coporation; PY8-09, technical support center, Manchan/PHotoDisc/Getty Images; PY8-10, Windows XP installation screen, Courtesy of Microsoft Coporation; PY8-11, Windows splash screen, Courtesy of Microsoft Coporation; Figure 8-01a, hand switching on computer, © Gary Herrington Photography; Figure 8-01b, memory module, Courtesy of Kingston Technology; Figure 8-01c, laser printer, Courtesy of Lexmark; Figure 8-01d, CPU, monitor, keyboard,speakers, Courtesy of Acer; Figure 8-01e, system unit, Courtesy of Acer; Figure 8-03, monitor, keyboard and mouse, Courtesy of Motion Computing; Figure 8-07a, memory module, Courtesy of Kingston Technology; Figure 8-07b, hard disk, Courtesy of Seagate Technology; Figure 8-08a, server, Courtesy of IBM Corporation; Figure 8-08b, hard disk, Courtesy of Seagate Technology; Figure 8-08c, laser printer, Courtesy of Lexmark; Looking Ahead 8-1, longhorn, © PhotoDisc Collection/Getty Images; Figure 8-26, Media Center PC, © Getty Images; Figure 8-26b, Windows XPscreenshot, Courtesy of Microsoft Coporation; Figure 8-27, Mac OSX screenshot, Screenshot reprinted by permission from Apple Computer, Inc.; Figure 8-28, UNIX screenshot, Courtesy of the K Destop Environment; Figure 8-29, RedHat Linux screenshot, Courtesy of RedHat; Looking Ahead 8-2, Linux Penguin, Courtesy of The Gimp, lewing@isc.tamu.edu; Figure 8-30, Vonage softphone, Courtesy of Vonage; Figure 8-31a, Pocket PC using Windows Mobile, Courtesy of Fujitsu Siemens; Figure 8-31b, smart phone using Windows Mobile, Courtesy of Microsoft Coporation; Figure 8-32a, Palm powered PDA, Courtesy of palmOne, Inc. palmOne, Zire, Tungsten, Treo, logos, stylizations and design marks associated with all the preceding, and trade dress associated with palmOne, Inc.'s products, are among the trademarks or registered trademarks owned by or exclusively licensed to palmOne, Inc.; Figure 8-32b, Palm powered smartphone, Courtesy of Kyocera; Figure 8-33, Sharp Zaurus, Courtesy of Sharp Electronics; Figure 8-34, Symbian Operating system smartphone, Courtesy of Symbian; Figure 8-38, Roxio Easy Media Creator 7, Courtesy of Roxio; Figure 8-39, Norton System Works, Courtesy of Symantec; Career Corner, systems programmer, © MTPA Stock/Masterfile; Technology Trailblazer, Alan Kay, © AP/Wide World Photos; Technology Trailblazer, Linus Torvalds, © Kim Kulish/CORBIS; **Special Feature: Buyer's Guide:**, Intro 1, desktop computer, Courtesy of Acer America Corp.; Intro 2, iMac, Courtesy of Apple Computer, Inc.; 8SF, Intro 3, notebook, Courtesy of Acer America Corp.; Intro 4, background art, © Jason Reed/Photodisc/Getty Images; Figure 01a, desktop computer, Courtesy of IBM Corporation; Figure 8-01b1, mobile computer, Courtesy of Sony Electronics, Inc.; Figure 01b2, notebook computer/tablet PC, Courtesy of Motion Computing; Figure 01c1, personal mobile device, Courtesy of palmOne, Inc. palmOne, Zire, Tungsten, Treo, logos, stylizations and design marks associated with all the preceding, and trade dress associated with palmOne, Inc.'s products, are among the trademarks or registered trademarks owned by or exclusively licensed to palmOne, Inc.; Figure 01c2, smartphone or PDA, Siemens press picture; Figure 01d, African-American female, Digital Vision/Getty Images; Figure 04a, CD/DVD drives, Courtesy of JVC; Figure 04b, Card Reader/Writer, Courtesy of Sandisk; Figure 04c, Digital Camera, Courtesy of UMAX; Figure 04d, Digital Video Capture Device, Courtesy of Pinnacle Systems, Inc.; Figure 04f, Hard Disk, Courtesy of Seagate; Figure 04g, Joystick/Wheel, Courtesy of Logitech; Figure 04h, Keyboard, Courtesy of Microsoft; Figure 04j, Modem, Courtesy of US Robotics; Figure 04k, Monitor, Courtesy of ViewSonic Corporation; Figure 04l, Mouse, Courtesy of Microsoft; Figure 04m, Network Card, Courtesy of 3Com Corporation; Figure 04n, Printer, Courtesy of EPSON America, Inc.; Figure 04o, Processer, Courtesy of Intel Corporation; Figure 04p, RAM, Courtesy of Kingston Technology; Figure 04q, Scanner, Courtesy of UMAX; Figure 04s, Speakers, Courtesy of Logitech; Figure 04t, PC Video Camera, Courtesy of Logitech; Figure 04u, USB Flash Drive, Courtesy of Sandisk; Figure 04v, Video Graphics Card, Courtesy of 3Com Corporation; Figure 04x, Zip Drive, Photo Courtesy of Iomega Corporation. Copyright © 2003 Iomega Corporation. All Rights Reserved. Zip is a registered trademark in the United States and/or other countries. Iomega, the stylized "i" logo and product images are property of Iomega Corporation in the United States and/or other countries; Figure 12, notebook computer converts to a Tablet PC, Courtesy of Toshiba America Information Systems, Inc.;, Figure 13, notebook computer carrying case, Courtesy of Toshiba America Information Systems, Inc.; Figure 14, a notebook computer connected to a video projector, Britt Erlanson/Getty Images; Figure 16, Tablet PC with handwriting, Thomas Barwick/PhotoDisc Collection/Getty Images; Figure 19, Tablet PC with handwriting, Courtesy of ViewSonic Corporation; Figure 21, A Tablet PC docked, Courtesy of Fujitsu Siemens Computers